DATE DUE

THE
AMY
VANDERBILT
COMPLETE
BOOK OF
ETIQUETTE

THE
AMY
VANDERBILT
COMPLETE
BOOK OF
ETIQUETTE

ENTIRELY REWRITTEN
AND UPDATED BY

NANCY TUCKERMAN
AND
NANCY DUNNAN

Illustrations by Jackie Aber

DOUBLEDAY

NEW YORK   LONDON   TORONTO   SYDNEY   AUCKLAND

PUBLISHED BY DOUBLEDAY
a division of Bantam Doubleday Dell Publishing Group, Inc.
1540 Broadway, New York, New York 10036

DOUBLEDAY and the portrayal of an anchor with a dolphin are
trademarks of Doubleday, a division of Bantam Doubleday Dell
Publishing Group, Inc.

Library of Congress Cataloging-in-Publication Data
Tuckerman, Nancy, 1928–
    The Amy Vanderbilt complete book of etiquette / entirely
rewritten and updated by Nancy Tuckerman and
Nancy Dunnan. — 1st ed.
        p.   cm.
    1. Etiquette—United States.   I. Dunnan, Nancy.
II. Vanderbilt, Amy, Etiquette.   III. Title.
BJ1853.T83   1995   93-44452
                                    CIP
395—dc20

ISBN 0-385-41342-4

Printed in the United States of America

February 1995

FIRST EDITION

1   3   5   7   9   10   8   6   4   2

Once again this book is dedicated
to the memory of
the late Amy Vanderbilt,
whose taste and style
are reflected in this revised edition.

CONTENTS

ACKNOWLEDGMENTS   IX

INTRODUCTION   XI

CHAPTER 1   YOUR PRIVATE LIFE   1

Introduction / Family Life / The Newborn Baby / The Younger Child / The Child in the Family / The Child in Society / The Teenager / Preserving Family Ties / Couples / The Single Life / Personal Appearance / Men and Women Interacting / Behavior in Public Places / Car Etiquette / Taxi Etiquette / Helping People With Special Needs / Today's Club Life / Money—the Human Aspect / The Art of Tipping / Working With a Real Estate Broker / Working With an Interior Designer / Health-Related Matters / The Official Side of Life / Gift Giving

CHAPTER 2   ENTERTAINING WITH EASE   138

Introduction / The Formal Seated Dinner With a Staff / The Informal Seated Dinner With a Maid / The Informal Seated Dinner Without a Maid / The Formal Seated Lunch With a Staff / The Informal Seated Lunch With or Without a Maid / Table Settings / Working With a Caterer / Menus / Wines / Buffet Lunches and Dinners / Brunches / Teas / Cocktail Parties / Receptions / Balls and Dances / Benefits / Surprise Parties / Costume Parties / Game Parties / Instruction Groups / Cookouts / Picnics / Pool Parties / Coffees / Potluck Suppers / The Bring-Your-Own Party / Open House / Housewarmings / Farewell Parties / The Houseguest

CHAPTER 3   WEDDINGS   246

Introduction / Engagement / Wedding Plans / Wedding Attire for Women / Wedding Attire for Men / Putting Together the Invitation List / Invitations / Bridal Registry / The Wedding Consultant / The Hotel or Club Banquet Manager / The Caterer / The Food / The Cake / The Liquor / The Floral Designer / Music for the Wedding / The Photographer / Transportation / Reserving

Hotel/Motel Rooms for Out-of-Town Guests / The Honeymoon / Presents / Wedding Announcements / Newspaper Announcement of Wedding / Married Woman and Her Surname / Postponing a Wedding / Canceling a Wedding / The Role of the Guest / The Role of the Wedding Attendants / Pre-Wedding Parties / Who Accompanies the Bride Up the Aisle? / The Pre-Rehearsal Briefing / The Double Wedding / The Military Wedding / The Rehearsal / The Rehearsal Dinner / The Wedding Ceremony / The Wedding Reception / Getting Married Again / Reaffirmation of Marriage Vows

CHAPTER 4   OTHER CEREMONIAL OCCASIONS   **411**

Introduction / Christenings / Brith Milah / Baby Showers / First Communion / Confirmation / Bar and Bat Mitzvah / Sweet Sixteen Parties / Graduation / Debuts / Birthdays / Wedding Anniversaries / Funerals

CHAPTER 5   YOUR PROFESSIONAL LIFE   **459**

Introduction / Getting a Job / Leaving a Job / Issues for the Employer to Consider / Volunteerism / Life in the Office / Dressing for Work / Oral Communication in Business / Business Stationery, Cards, Invitations / Written Communication in Business / Business Entertaining / Meetings and Conventions / Business Travel / Business Gift Giving / International Business Etiquette

CHAPTER 6   TRAVEL   **543**

Introduction / Planning Your Trip / Traveling Alone or With Others / By Air / By Ship / By Car / By Train / By Bus / Hotels and Motels / Country Inns, Most Particularly Bed and Breakfasts / Tipping

CHAPTER 7   SPORTS AND EXERCISE   **590**

Introduction / Golf / Tennis / Other Racquet Sports / Boating / Swimming / Skiing / Ice Skating / Jogging and Walking / Hiking / Cycling / Horseback Riding and Fox Hunting / Gyms and Health Clubs / Croquet / Bowling

CHAPTER 8   THE ART OF COMMUNICATING   **631**

Introduction / Stationery / Calling Cards / Invitations / Use of Names and Titles / Signing Your Name / Addressing Envelopes / Letter Writing / Other Forms of Communication / Introductions / Étiquette in Conversation / Telephone Manners / Toasts / Public Speaking / Television and Radio Appearances / Heraldic Devices (Crests) / Correct Forms of Address

INDEX   **759**

ACKNOWLEDGMENTS

In great part, the scope and authoritativeness of the book can be attributed to the efforts of many professionals, colleagues, and friends, who willingly commented and gave advice on innumerable issues, all of which have added to the authenticity of the many topics covered. While space prevents listing all those who gave generously of their time and knowledge, we would like to express appreciation to Ann Patron, Smythson of Bond Street; Steven L. Feinberg, Crane & Co., Inc.; John Loring, Tiffany & Company; Matthew Flood, Dempsey & Carroll Company; Rex Scouten, The White House; Anne Liu, The Social List of Washington, D.C.; Barbara D. Tober, BRIDE'S; Andrea Feld, BRIDE'S; Vera Wang, Vera Wang Bridal House; Sean Driscoll, Glorious Food, Inc.; Jay Jolly, Glorious Food, Inc.; Gary Boyd Roberts, New England Historic Genealogical Society; Roberta Maneker, Christie's; Jeanne Trudeau, Trudeau Photography Studio; Jeff Moravec, Hazelden; Ellen Archer, Ann Arensberg, Amy Baron, Lazinka Benton, Winifred Brown, Alan Campbell, Charlotte Cohen, Joseph F. Dash, Paul Gunther, Theresa Kidd, Christine A. Kinser, Mary Kirby, Sherri Steinfeld Maxman, Scott Moyers, Lee Nasso, Jay J. Pack, Leigh Palmer, Phoebe Phillips, Frances Stave, Herbert Teison, Bruce Tracy, Pauline K. Webel, Judith Weinstein. And a very special word of thanks to Hope A. Whipple for her significant role in the preparation of the entertaining and wedding chapters.

Furthermore, we are thankful to many members of the clergy whose judicious counseling helped with the religious aspects of the book: weddings, funerals, other religious observances, and forms of address for the clergy. They are Reverend Michael Crimmins, St. Malachy's Church, New York City; Rabbi Irwin H. Fishbein, Rabbinic Center for Research and Counseling, Westfield, New Jersey; Nancy Hadley-Jaffe, New York

Quarterly Meeting of the Religious Society of Friends, New York City; His Grace Bishop Isaiah, Greek Orthodox Archdiocese of North and South America, New York City; Rabbi David C. Kogen, Jewish Theological Seminary, New York City; Father Robert Larkin, Archdiocese of New York, New York City; Reverend Peter Larom, Grace Church, White Plains, New York; Maura Magennis, St. James' Church, New York City; Reverend Dr. Aaron Manderbach, retired, Salisbury, Connecticut; Reverend Mitzi Noble, Trinity Episcopal Church, Lime Rock, Connecticut; David M. Robertson, Christian Science Committee on Publication for New York, New York City; Rabbi Robert Rubin, Temple Mekor Chayim, Linden, New Jersey; F. Michael Watson, The Church of Jesus Christ of Latter-day Saints, Salt Lake City, Utah. Also, thanks to the Most Reverend Agostino Cacciavillan of the Apostolic Nunciature, Washington, D.C., for his counseling on *An Audience With the Pope* and our gratitude to Ruth Rosenberg for her discerning comments and advice on Jewish religious customs and practices.

Our deepest thanks to Nancy Nicholas, Amy Vanderbilt editor, whose far-reaching knowledge in an astonishing variety of subjects, as well as her imagination and attention to detail, proved invaluable in the writing of the book. We are also grateful to John Duff, the initial editor, who laid the groundwork for the revision, and to Kitty Benedict for the editorial and authorial expertise she brought to the project. Equal appreciation to Lesley Logan and Lesley Seymour for their contribution to the chapter on family life and to Rob Robertson and Renée Zuckerbrot for their editorial assistance. In addition, we are grateful to Doubleday's copy chief, Harold Grabau; to Kathryn Tebbel for the fine job she did copy editing the manuscript and to Estelle Laurence for reading the proofs; and to Marcy Ross, researcher; Jackie Aher, illustrator; Marysarah Quinn, art director; Beverley Gallegos, book designer; Julie Duquet, jacket designer. Not least, thanks to Stephen Rubin, President and Publisher of Doubleday, who saw the need for this updated and expanded edition.

INTRODUCTION

To many people, the word "etiquette" implies white gloves, finger bowls, children curtsying, and other genteel manners that once were the hallmark of proper behavior. But few people know the actual etymology of this rather daunting word that describes a system of conventional rules that regulate social behavior. The word literally means a "ticket" or "card," and refers to the ancient custom of a monarch setting forth ceremonial rules and regulations to be observed by members of his court. As far back as Anglo-Saxon times, consideration for others, as well as observance of a monarch's rules, was a part of etiquette, as demonstrated in the epic poem *Beowulf*, written around A.D. 700, when Queen Wealtheow, "mindful of etiquette," offered the goblet first to the king, then to the courtiers, and finally to herself. And through the centuries the observance of such consideration has remained unquestioned.

While elaborate court rituals have gone the way of other archaic customs, "mindful etiquette" remains constant. Conversely, the world around us never remains constant. Since 1978, when the last edition of this book was published, we have seen new technologies surface that call for modifications in our social customs. For instance, technology has given us the fax machine, voice mail, and cellular phones. Women now play a more prominent role in our work force; thermography frequently replaces engraving; and smoking is not allowed in most public places. Even the basic structure of our family life is very different. Divorce is no longer the exception; the single parent is not unusual; the unmarried couple living together is commonplace; Ms. is a title firmly rooted in our language; and more women than ever are keeping their surnames after marriage.

As would be expected, the more conventional aspects of etiquette that are so much a part of our daily life—being considerate of others, teaching children table manners, letter writing, gift giving, being a guest at a wedding, getting along with coworkers—are covered with equal importance, as are occasions that center around formal dinner parties and dances, anniversaries, bar mitzvahs, and other time-honored rituals. On these more formal occasions when we want to put our best foot forward, an understanding of traditional etiquette is practical as well as reassuring. There's a certain satisfaction that comes with putting our best foot forward. Just as we admire the lawyer who knows how to win a case, the speaker who knows how to hold the audience's attention, the corporate president who knows how to chair a meeting, so too are we admired when we make our guests feel at ease, plan the perfect wedding, or give a loving eulogy.

While the intention of this book is to help you communicate well with others and to feel confident in social situations, bear in mind that it is not the end of the world if you use the wrong fork, stumble over an introduction, or stand up when you are the one being toasted. Still, you'll feel a lot more relaxed if you are familiar with the code of behavior for any given occasion; well primed in this respect, you will find yourself concentrating on others rather than yourself, and—not the least—you'll be better able to enjoy yourself. As Amy Vanderbilt wrote in the introduction to the original 1952 edition: "I believe that knowledge of the rules of living in our society makes us more comfortable . . . [although] some of the rudest and most objectionable people I have ever known have been technically the most "correct." . . . Some of the warmest, most lovable, have had little more than an innate feeling of what is right toward others. But, at the same time, they have had the intelligence to inform themselves, as necessary, on the rules of social intercourse as related to their own experiences. Only a great fool or a great genius is likely to flout all social grace with impunity, and neither one, doing so, makes the most comfortable companion."

Few people will read this book from cover to cover, nor are they expected to. However, like any reference book, there is a place for an etiquette book in every home library and on every office bookshelf. Even the most sophisticated man or woman cannot hope to remember every single aspect of etiquette that applies to even one possible social, or for that matter business, situation. Most of us remember only those details that have or had a relevance to our own way of living. This book addresses as fully and as simply as possible all the major questions of etiquette. It is here for you to turn to when the need arises.

CHAPTER I
YOUR PRIVATE LIFE

INTRODUCTION

Certain formal occasions in our lives remain rooted in tradition. When we have an audience with the Pope, visit the White House, or salute the flag, we follow longstanding customs that require specific codes of conduct. Observing these customs helps us feel at ease in situations of an official nature, knowing what is expected and how to behave.

Where change has entered into our personal lives most obviously is in our social customs. Contemporary living includes dual-city marriages, unmarried women having children, gay couples adopting, as well as terms like "latchkey" child. Needless to say, the rules for behavior in these situations were not imposed by social leaders but rather were created by people whose circumstances made them feel confined by certain conventions and so were motivated to extend the bounds of accepted social behavior. Although not everyone may sanction today's social options, they are discussed here because they aren't going away and must be addressed.

FAMILY LIFE

LIVING HARMONIOUSLY AS A FAMILY

The family can be a great joy, a loving refuge from a difficult world. But it can also be the source of great stress. The tone of a household is determined by the people who run it; in a traditional one, that means the mother and the father. Today it may also mean a single parent, occasionally a gay couple, or two adults of either sex who simply opt to live together. Luckily for us, we have been raised in a society in which democratic principles filter down to the private level. Most heads of American households operate not as dictatorial autocrats but more as chairpersons who help guide the family toward order, stability, and harmony. You and your spouse can create a home that is pleasant to live in and a joy for friends to visit by keeping three things in mind: Maintain

1

your mutual respect. Keep communication lines open. And never, ever, lose your sense of humor.

SOME RULES TO LIVE BY

If each of us lived in a protective glass bubble, never encroached on anyone else's living space, and never interacted with another soul, there would be no need for manners. We could simply do as we pleased, go about our business, and it wouldn't matter to anyone else. But since *Homo sapiens* is gregarious and likes to establish and live in communities, and even in more intimate settings such as houses or apartments, rules of conduct are imperative. The starting point for all rules is the need to treat others with as much kindness and courtesy as you would like them to treat you with.

That means keeping your more self-centered instincts in check. The best way to do this, especially in a family with school-age children, is to establish some guidelines for living together. In the case of a large family, where lots of cooperation is required just to get everyone out the door each morning, it can make sense to periodically hold a kind of town hall meeting at the dinner table. There, members can hash out rules about keeping the bathrooms and bedrooms neat, telephone use, television viewing, guest policies, the sharing of common living space. Rules can be revised weekly or monthly. Such organized rap sessions can defuse daily squabbles because family members know their grievances will have a chance to be aired. A scheduled meeting also gives the aggrieved parties time to come up with constructive solutions to their problems, instead of simply voicing continual—and annoying—complaints.

Parental unity plays a major factor in keeping a household harmonious. Parents who are obviously divided on such basic subjects as permissiveness, religion, work, money, education, exercise, will send conflicting messages to their children. Some children, sensing the discord, may even try to intensify the friction by playing parents off against each other to their advantage. Whenever possible, it's best to settle divisive issues behind closed doors. Children want and need consistency.

Another potential point of friction is the extended family. Almost everyone comes to a marriage with some other family ties—and it's wise to decide policy on future in-laws well before the wedding. Remember, in each culture, in-laws have different expectations. If, say, a woman marries a man who was born in some faraway European city, his parents and distant cousins may see nothing wrong with their making impromptu visits of a few weeks at a time when they feel like it. On the other hand, even the most pleasant in-laws who live close should be sensitive about making unannounced visits. When grandchildren arrive or a parent-in-law is widowed, the entire extended family structure may need to be reevaluated, particularly if you decide to make one or more of your in-laws a permanent resident in your home.

SHARING HOUSEHOLD DUTIES

In order to keep any group—be it a business or a commune—functioning, there has to be an explicit division of labor. And in close living quarters organization is the key. A clean, tidy environment means things are put away where each family member can find them, and that there is a sense of mutual respect. A family should establish a standard of neatness to which its particular household conforms. This does not mean being rigid: there is nothing more boring or annoying than living with a neatnik who picks up a dust ball between his fingers and asks, "Is this yours?" or one who forbids an activity that is fun but messy—such as finger painting—in the house. Children, especially, should not feel that they live in a "don't touch" museum where they can't play freely.

At the same time, this doesn't mean you have to live in the aftermath of a cyclone. From the time a child is eighteen months old, it's important to establish rules about cleaning up. Many toddlers can be taught to take out two or three toys at a time then put them away before taking out others. And all toys—except in a playroom set aside for ongoing projects—should be returned to the toy chest or shelves before dinner. Older children and adults should be expected to rinse dishes as they use them throughout the day and place them in the dishwasher or the draining rack. Bathrooms should be left neat, with towels hung to dry in their proper places. Clean clothing should be put away, dirty ones tossed in the laundry basket.

Unless you have household help, the regular chores to be divided among family members include:

- Taking out the garbage
- Bed making and sheet changing
- Laundry
- Vacuuming
- Dusting
- Sweeping
- Floor washing
- Bathroom and kitchen detail
- Grocery shopping
- Meal preparation and cleanup
- Yard work

Because today the woman of the house may also be putting in an eight-hour day at the office, household chores should no longer be considered women's work. Even a stay-at-home mother—who, by the way, works a twenty-four-hour shift with no vacations or sick days—should parcel out some chores. Make a chart of everyone's duties, then reward jobs well done with stickers or stars, and rotate assignments on a monthly basis. This acts as a hedge against conflict and keeps workers from getting bored. Both boys and girls should learn that folding the laundry or taking out the garbage is not a genetically programmed task.

Even in families with lots of domestic help, children should be taught to pick up after themselves. Self-sufficiency teaches children to be responsible, have self-respect, and be thoughtful of those who live with them. As to whether they should be compensated for routine tasks, many psychologists believe that paying children to perform basic chores around the house—even if it's just a few cents—is not a good idea because it undercuts the idea of expected participation. You are not doing your child or society at large a favor by spoiling him to the point where he comes to expect everyone to wait on him.

MEALS

These days our lives are packed with work, activities, entertainment. And each family member is pulled in twenty different directions—by demands to be with friends, to get to Little League, to finish homework. For many families, the only time they ever have a chance really to communicate is over an evening meal. Therefore most families with children over the age of four try to have as many evening meals together as they can manage. Eating together is an enjoyable experience provided good table manners are observed and everyone makes an effort to communicate. Establish an expected style of behavior at the table to ensure that dinnertime is family time at its best.

Some families have instituted a round-robin forum at mealtime. Each member of the family, from the littlest to the biggest, gets a few minutes of everyone's attention to tell about his or her day, or to say anything he wishes. This gives shy or young or inarticulate family members an opportunity to be heard, which they might not have otherwise.

It is also important to remember that it is at the family dinner table that children learn (or don't learn!) the table manners that will stay with them throughout their lives. Even at casual family gatherings rudimentary manners should be observed. Children who learn table manners early on will instinctively act polite and natural in even the most formal situations. A child should:

- Wash his hands before sitting down.
- Come to the table well groomed and neatly dressed.
- Leave toys, books, and pets behind.
- Upon sitting down, place the napkin in his lap.
- Sit up straight and not slouch.
- Ask politely for dishes to be passed; never reach across the table.

- Wait until everyone is seated and served before starting to eat. If grace is said, wait to eat until it is completed. (Children should not giggle during grace and should take turns saying it.)
- Use flatware from the outside in.
- Except in households with a European influence, keep elbows off the table. (Many French, for example, accept elbows as part of the dining experience.)
- Never chew with his mouth open.
- Never talk with a mouth full of food.
- Use utensils quietly without banging them on the table or plate. The knife should be placed softly on the edge of the plate when not in use.
- Slice butter from the butter dish and place it on his butter plate or other plate. The butter knife should remain with the butter dish.
- Never wave or throw utensils.
- Keep his knife out of his mouth.
- Never play with his food.
- Never grab food from other people's plates.
- Ask politely for seconds if he wants them.
- Ask to be excused from the table.
- Clear his plate from the table and take it into the kitchen. (Young children, of course, are exempt.)
- If there is domestic help, learn to say thank you after being served.

Today it is acceptable to handle a knife and fork in either the American or the European manner. The American method of holding the fork in the left hand while cutting and switching it to the right to eat can be clumsy and difficult for children to master. The European method of not switching the fork, but eating what's on it with your left hand, in many ways is more practical. The same holds true for placing utensils on the plate once you've finished. The American method requires that both fork and knife be balanced on the right side of the plate (where they can often slide off); the European method leaves knife and fork (arched downward) crossed over one another more securely on the center of the plate.

Children should be taught from the earliest ages to respect the dinner hour. When guests are present, infants and toddlers may be brought to the table for an after-dinner snack, but they should be fed their actual meal at an earlier hour. If children become restless, they should be put to bed.

Most important of all, do not place young children in dining situations they are incapable of handling. It is asking for trouble to expect a five-year-old to sit through a dinner beginning at 8 P.M. If you're planning a late evening meal, your best form of table manners is to call a babysitter.

SAYING GRACE Many families throughout the country observe the custom of saying grace. Among religious Jews, prayers are said before and after the meal—especially on Friday night. In Christian homes, grace is said before the meal, with those present standing behind their chairs or sitting at the table, heads slightly bowed, hands resting on their laps. Some families say grace on special occasions only, like Thanksgiving, Christmas, and Easter, often joining hands in a symbolic gesture of brotherliness.

In families where grace is a household ritual, the host or hostess should tell this to any guests as they move into the dining room. That way some unsuspecting friend won't pick up his napkin or start a conversation before the prayer is said. When a clergyman is present, he is asked to say grace, often after everyone is seated. But, in the case of a friend, he should be asked in advance if he would like to say grace, giving him the opportunity to decline if he prefers not to.

YOU AND YOUR NEIGHBORS

Neighbors are somewhat like in-laws: either great fun to be with or irritating. Here are a few tips to help you be the kind of person a neighbor is happy to live next to:

- Avoid making excessive noise, particularly at night. Try to think of your neighbors when you are playing music, vacuuming, doing home repairs, exercising, honking your horn, or having loud arguments.
- Try to prevent your dog from barking.
- End parties at a reasonable hour. And don't embarrass neighbors by talking about a party to which they were not invited.
- Even in an apartment house, give your neighbor privacy. Don't drop in unexpectedly and don't inquire about his comings and goings.
- If you borrow a tool, book, frying pan, or even a cup of sugar, return it immediately, and with appreciation.
- If you, your child, or your pet breaks anything, replace it right away.
- Be generous about sharing your lawn mower, or jumper cables, or whatever else your neighbor might need to borrow.
- Keep your yard or any common living areas as neat and attractive as possible.
- Teach your children to address your neighbors politely.
- Wipe your feet before you enter a neighbor's house and teach your children to do the same.
- Keep feet off furniture.

- Don't light up a cigarette or cigar in someone else's house without asking permission.
- Offer to watch your neighbors' house or apartment (perhaps water plants or feed animals) when they go on vacation.
- In a supermarket, tell someone who has significantly fewer items than you to go ahead of you.
- Welcome new neighbors by dropping them a note introducing yourself and offering to help them in any way you can.

If you have the misfortune to live near someone who is inconsiderate of others, you may encounter some problems. Neighbors who don't respond to a polite knock at their door to ask them to turn down the stereo at three in the morning can be dealt with by the appropriate officials: the coop board, the landlord, or even the police. Large cities even have government agencies to handle noise disputes either formally or informally. However, any intervention on your part will not endear you to your neighbors. For that reason, sometimes it's easier to listen to the occasional dog barking in the middle of the night than to begin a feud.

To establish good feelings with your neighbors, consider having an annual open house, perhaps on a Sunday or at holiday time. Everyone will enjoy getting together and sharing a few refreshments.

THE NEWBORN BABY

EXPECTING A BABY

Awaiting the birth of a child is an extraordinary and unique experience, especially for the first-time mother-to-be. Thinking about what to call the baby, having a friend give a shower, dreaming of the perfect nursery, buying baby clothes, anticipating the event itself, are what makes this glorious time in life so special.

While it may be tempting to tell family and friends you are pregnant shortly after the fact's confirmed, it makes sense to hold off until the second trimester when there's less risk of miscarrying. When you do plan to spread the good news, be sure it's your parents and your husband's parents who are the first to hear.

NAMING THE BABY

To borrow from T. S. Eliot, the naming of babies, as with cats, can be a very difficult thing. Names are given because of family tradition, a desire to honor a relative or a close friend, or simply because the name has always appealed to you. However, you must give careful thought to the naming of your child as he will have to carry the name you choose all his life. If you have no particular name in mind, there are many books on naming a baby you can refer to. Some offer purely American names, others are distinctly ethnic. You might also consider looking for a name in a favorite novel or in the Bible.

In the Jewish faith the practice is to name the firstborn child after a deceased parent or relative. Rarely is a Jewish child named after a living relative, although he may be given a living relative's name as a middle name. Catholic children are usually given the name of a saint for at least one of their names.

If you want to name your child after his father, Thomas Edward Sears, he would be Thomas Edward Sears, Jr. If the father is already junior, the baby is Thomas Sears III. If the child is not given his father's middle name, he is Thomas Dennis Sears. A child named after an uncle or a grandfather has "II" after his name.

Before making a firm decision on a name for your child, think about what nickname might be derived from it and whether or not you would like it. Once a child starts going to school, he's often given a nickname by other children, and there's not much a parent can do about it. Also, certain names seem to generate rather unfortunate nicknames. For instance, Sophia may become Soapy; Fatima, Fatty; Prudence, Prude. (A boy named McCauley who grew up in a homogeneous Connecticut community said, "I've spent my entire life wishing I'd been called Skip or Chip.")

Also be on the alert for names that create awkward monograms, as in the case of Dorothy Ogden Graves or Albert Stinch Strong. And don't give your child a name that seems amusing to you at the time. For example, a family named Hough (pronounced "hoe") called their daughter Ida and she was stuck with this unfortunate name the rest of her life.

If your last name is multisyllabic or complicated to pronounce, a short, simple first name often sounds well and is easy to remember. On the other hand, if your last name is Smith or Jones, giving your child a common name such as John or Mary can cause an indentity problem later in life.

Many names are given to both boys and girls, but with different spellings. For instance, Frances is the female spelling, while Francis is the male; other unisex names distinguished by their spelling are Marian/Marion and Lesley/Leslie. Most name books will indicate the gender-appropriate spelling, although in some cases both spellings have become acceptable for either a boy or a girl. Popular names of today that are used for boys and girls include Lindsay, Kim, Lee, Brett, Ashley, and Jesse. If you decide to give your daughter a name that could also be a boy's name, it makes sense to give her a clearly feminine middle name.

A family name is always a good choice, provided it is not too unusual, and it's possible to make an appropriate nickname out of it. For example, a child may be given his or her mother's maiden name as a first or middle name. A child named for a family member often feels a strong sense of his or her identity.

BIRTH ANNOUNCEMENTS

While proper etiquette does not require the sending of birth announcements, most couples like to spread the happy news of a new family member. Cards are usually sent out as soon as the mother and baby are back home, but certainly no more than a month or so later. By that time the networking system will already have broadcast the news.

The traditional birth announcement has the names of the parents engraved or printed on a calling card with the name of the child and date of birth on a smaller calling card that's attached to the larger one by a pink or blue ribbon.

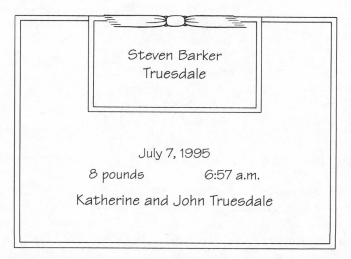

Steven Barker
Truesdale

July 7, 1995

8 pounds   6:57 a.m.

Katherine and John Truesdale

This is one of the most popular styles of birth announcement.
Traditionally, the ribbon is pink or white for a girl, blue for a boy.

Mailgrams are also popular as birth announcements. However, you do not have to go the expensive route. Most stationery stores carry a wide variety of imaginative fill-in announcement cards to choose from. Or you can make your own birth announcement by copying your child's footprint from the hospital birth certificate onto colored paper and printing the vital statistics above it or inside the card. Another idea is to send out wallet-sized photographs of your baby enclosed in a personal letter.

A typical announcement might read: "Edith and David Strong are happy to announce the birth of their daughter, Emma Mary, on the 27th day of December, 1995, 7 lbs. 3 oz., 21 ins."

If the parents use different last names, the announcement reads: "Edith Unger and David Strong are happy to announce the birth of their daughter, Emma Mary Strong." Even in today's liberated society, it's still customary for a child to take the father's last name.

If a couple happens to divorce before the birth of their child, they might decide to send out separate birth announcements, he to his relatives and friends, she to hers. A single woman uses only her name on the birth announcement, although she may choose to include the name of the father, if he agrees. In the case of a lesbian couple, both women are credited on the announcement, even though one woman actually gave birth.

It is customary to send out announcements when a child is adopted, no matter what age that child may be when he comes to live with his new family. The announcement might take these forms:

> Mr. and Mrs. Allen Ingalls Fisher
> announce the arrival of their son
> John David Fisher
> on January 2, 1995
> born November 30, 1994

> Joanne and Allen Fisher
> take pleasure in announcing that
> John David Fisher
> has joined their family

When a gay couple adopt a child, both names appear on an announcement.

It is best not to send out adoption announcements until you have the baby in your arms, as there are often delays and disappointments, especially when the adoption involves bringing a child from a foreign country. It can be informative to include the child's country of origin on an announcement, for example: ". . . announce the adoption of Ling Ng, who has come from Vietnam to join our family."

VISITING THE NEW MOTHER

Since most women stay in the hospital only a day or two after having a baby, it's best to wait until mother and child have been home a few days before going to see them. Never just drop by. Always call first to find out when would be a convenient time to pay a visit. A new mother has all she can handle when she first arrives home, between taking care of the baby and trying to regain her strength. And remember that new mothers (even if it's their second or third time around) can be emotionally stressed out, so keep your visit short and the conversation upbeat and positive.

BRINGING A PRESENT

Even if you received a birth announcement, it does not necessarily mean you have to send a baby present, although close family members and godparents usually give the baby a gift. Often the best present a friend can give the baby is something for the parents. Filling the refrigerator with various foods the day the mother and baby return home is always a good present. Another good idea is having a meal delivered to the family from a local restaurant.

Gifts for the baby might include clothing (hats, booties, play suits, dresses, sweaters, etc.), a baby book, or a photograph album. If the mother had a baby shower, you can assume she has all the practical items she needs, so you might opt for something decorative for the baby's room, such as a nursery light or a picture for the nursery wall.

When you go to see the baby, be sensitive to any siblings she may have. Bring a present for an older brother. He may easily feel a bit left out with everyone oohing and ahing over his sister. Or you might want to give him a more personal gift—your time. Take him to the zoo or to the park, or out for an ice cream soda. Also having the older child out of the house means the mother and baby will have some time together to bond.

BREAST FEEDING IN PUBLIC

Now that medical science has pretty much confirmed the notion that breast feeding is healthier than bottle feeding (it passes along various antibodies that formula cannot), the issue of where and how to breast-feed in public arises. Despite Americans' propensity for selling everything from beer to bicycles with sex, we are still, at heart, a puritanical society. Therefore, the sight of a bare breast, even one performing its natural function, may make many people uneasy. Though a nursing mother will not view her breast as anything other than a convenient way to feed her baby, it is best to be circumspect about nursing in front of others.

While a variety of breast-feeding books are available in bookstores to provide you with ideas for breast feeding discreetly, common sense dictates most of them. If you don't want to express your milk at home and carry it with you in a bottle so you can feed in public, find a secluded spot and toss a billowy scarf over your chest and the baby's head. You might even want to buy a few blouses with slits behind the pockets which were designed just for this purpose. In a restaurant that caters to children, you can always go to the ladies' room to breast-feed. Owners of children's stores are particularly sympathetic when it comes to breast feeding and may allow you a few minutes in a private area, such as an office. If you are visiting friends, ask your hostess if anyone will be made uncomfortable by your breast feeding in front of them. If so, ask if you can go into some other room when it's time to nurse.

BIRTH DEFECTS

If a friend gives birth to a child with a defect, let her take the initiative in bringing up the subject with you. Unless you have gone through the same difficulties your reaction is of no possible interest or use to parents in sorting out their feelings. They will love their child no matter what problems he or she has, and it is your responsibility as a friend to extend that same unconditional love and approval to the baby. If the parent brings up the defect, listen with sympathy and tact. When you first see the child, admire his positive features, of which there are certain to be many.

WHEN A BABY DIES

A baby who is stillborn or who dies within a few days of birth brings unimaginable grief to the parents. There is simply no way you can sympathize or console the bereaved parents because the event is too terrible and personal. There are no compensatory words. Phrases of comfort such as "At least he didn't have to suffer" or "There will be others" are insensitive. It's better to acknowledge how dreadfully unfair such a loss is in a note saying "I am so sad to hear that your baby died," or you may want to send flowers with a note as a gesture of sympathy.

THE YOUNGER CHILD

THE CHILD AT HOME

A child's first reference point is his home, and the way in which you run it will have an enormous influence on how he views the outside world. A home that is safe, orderly, comfortable, and loving will provide a child with a secure launching pad for the necessary forays into the unknown, and it will always be a kind, welcoming refuge to which he may retreat. A home is much more than a place for you and your spouse when you're done with work: it is the center of the familial universe.

It has been well documented that children thrive on routine. Regularly scheduled meals, chores, bath times, and bedtimes give children a sense of order and a feeling of mastery over their small but sometimes overwhelmingly chaotic lives. Habit makes them feel confident and secure because they know just what to expect. They will adhere to almost any schedule you develop. Though such schedules can seem boring or old-fashioned to parents who, before children, enjoyed more flexible, spontaneous lives, it is well worth the effort.

THE BEDROOM

A child's room, it may be said, is his retreat from the world around him, somewhat of a sanctuary where he feels safe and secure. Not every child has a room of his own, but even the child who sleeps with a sibling should have a certain area of the room that's considered his territory.

It is never too early to train your child to be neat and to respect his possessions. He should, for example, be responsible for putting his toys away at the end of the day. In this respect, a toy chest makes an excellent repository to store things in. While an uncovered chest works best with young children, it looks less tidy than one with a lid. Make sure, however, that the lid is childproofed, light enough to lift, and not one that could accidentally hurt your child if it hits him on the head. In addition, wicker baskets or plastic containers are perfect for storing books, small dolls, tiny cars, and other toys. Once a year you should go through all your child's toys and games and give away to a charity or hospital those he has outgrown or no longer plays with. Include your child in this activity. It will help teach him the art of giving.

Aside from places to store toys, a child's room should have a desk or table for writing and drawing, a drawer or shelf large enough to place papers and books in or on, proper lighting, and a bulletin board for showing off his artwork.

CLOTHES

Children develop personal likes and dislikes for particular clothes at an early age, sometimes as young as three. Their specific reason for not liking an article of clothing may be that it itches, clings, or is too bulky. Or it may be an aversion to a certain color. Parents must realize that their child, in order to feel secure, needs to conform to the dress code of his peers. Nothing is more embarrassing to a child than being out of step with his friends—and the wrong clothes can be just the cause of that.

You can help your child learn to dress himself by taping on each drawer of his bureau pictures of what the drawer contains. That way, he will know just where to find his underwear, socks, sweaters, etc. If each picture has the name of the article written on it, in time he will learn to recognize those words. You will find that your child gets dressed for school a lot quicker in the morning if it's decided the night before what he will wear and the clothes are placed on a chair, ready to be put on.

For a special occasion, like a wedding or bar mitzvah, your child should wear a suit (or dress) that *you* feel is appropriate. If he objects, explain to him that what he wears on a daily basis is his choice, but when it comes to events of a more formal nature he must wear what you consider is appropriate attire.

HAND-ME-DOWNS Clothes—as well as toys, furniture, and sports equipment—that are passed down from sibling to sibling or from friend to friend are a great way to help circumvent the all-American economic sinkhole called planned obsolescence. Because children grow so quickly and are often out of shoes and shirts within a season, most hand-me-downs are still in mint or nearly mint condition. You can find them through relatives, friends, consignment or thrift shops, garage or church sales. And you can afford to be choosy (though surely you can overlook your taste to accommodate a winter coat or party dress that is free or costs a mere fraction of the original price). Clothes worn frequently and close to the body such as pajamas, underwear, or socks, are better bought new for hygiene reasons.

Because clothing is so linked to ego and identity even in the early years, it is best to recognize that some children may feel ashamed or slighted if they have to wear nothing but hand-me-downs. You can help make the garment more hers by having the child pick out special patches and sewing them on or by dyeing the item her favorite color. And when possible include younger children when you buy something new—even if it is just a pair of inexpensive socks. If a child asks why she can't have all new clothing, rather than making it a financial consideration, point out that some things are nicer when old. Show her vintage items in the house, or tell her a story about a favorite item of clothing you inherited from a beloved aunt or uncle. You could also show her how some fabrics become softer and more comfortable over time.

If you plan to hand on any clothing or baby equipment, give only those things in good condition. And make sure you have washed or wiped them down.

Be careful you do not hand down to the next sibling anything still of great importance to the older child. Even if you think (or know) he has outgrown his crib quilt, it is wise to ask him first if it can be passed along. Having him present his sister with the crib quilt—with much ceremony—will ease the tension and make him feel a part of the decision-making process.

New mothers should not be embarrassed about using secondhand baby equipment. Most items—from the original Moses basket in which you carry the infant out of the hospital, to Snuglis and high chairs—are in and out of an infant's life within a matter of months. It is foolish to waste one's money on a new Sassy Seat or playpen if such an item is available secondhand. Many equipment manufacturers, in fact, expect things like baby swings to be handed down and will replace missing safety bars, etc., free of charge. A piece of equipment you should not pass down is a car seat that is not in perfect working condition. No one should be using it because it is no longer safe.

CLOTHING AND PEER PRESSURE At some stage in young lives, children want to dress like "the others," whoever those others may be. While you may not like the specific taste of the group your child wishes to belong to, you should recognize the psychological importance of feeling appropriately dressed. Clothes, of course, are an easy way for children to differentiate those who are "in" from those who are "out," and this is particularly true among girls. Children can be quite cruel to those who do not conform. While you may be able to explain to older children the benefits of being a nonconformist (though they probably won't believe you until after college), young children will miss the message entirely. Unless the look they want is completely abhorrent or wildly impractical—such as wearing an unzipped jacket and T-shirt in the dead of winter, halter tops or too short a skirt—you may need to go along. However, in certain situations do not hesitate to say no—children need guidelines and limits.

TELEVISION

Television can be said to be both the bane and boon of modern existence. You cannot keep children from watching it. Nor do you necessarily want to. However, television can become a problem when children watch it excessively, either because it is considered a convenient babysitter or because their parents do not exercise enough control over what programs are appropriate for them to watch. In the latter case, new federal labeling regulations make it easier for parents to decide which programs are suitable. And now, of course, there are remote controls with parental restriction buttons to prevent a child from changing the channel, as well as new television set control keys.

THE CHILD IN THE FAMILY

As more and more women enter the work force full-time, more and more families face a difficult problem: What to do with young children while both parents are at work. Fortunately, there are many options—day care, nanny care, home care, mom care—and parents have to decide which option makes the most sense for them. They have to decide which fits with the family budget and which fits with their aims and goals for raising a child. In most households today, a mother who stays at home full-time is simply not a financially feasible option.

NANNIES

If you found your nanny, au pair, or nurse through an agency, the questions about how to pay will be worked out by the agency. Most have rules and regulations about how and when their client should be paid and many collect finders' fees up front to pay for their services.

A nanny works anywhere from forty to fifty hours a week with two weeks' paid vacation a year (your nanny is expected to take her vacation when you take yours). If you want to give her more time off, that's your decision.

How you pay your nanny, if the agency does not regulate it, is up to you. Easiest for you, and for accounting purposes, is payment by personal check. However, if you decide to pay in cash, you will want to have some kind of initialed receipt from your nanny. You can do this by keeping a logbook or by using an ATM (Automatic Teller Machine) receipt showing your withdrawal to be the exact amount of her salary. You must by law withhold social security tax from her paycheck. This tax is matched by an equal amount of social security that you pay for her; both must be reported to the IRS on a quarterly basis. If you choose to, you may withhold and pay all her taxes. Total wages reported must include any bonuses or overtime expenses she has earned.

In addition to the social security tax, you will probably be asked to pay worker's compensation, disability tax, and unemployment insurance tax. If you do not have an accountant to advise you on these matters, you can call the IRS hotline for information (800-829-3676).

Because the amount you pay your nanny depends on the number of children she cares for and the number of hours she works, nannies' salaries vary. You'll find that nannies love to compare their wages, so don't try to undercut whatever the going rate is. If you do, you may find yourself nanny-less.

Your nanny will need a certain amount of petty cash every week or month for incidental expenses like carfare or taking the children to the movies. At the end of the month she should give you a detailed accounting of her expenses incurred, along with receipts.

To avoid any misunderstandings later on, before hiring a nanny explain what her responsibilities will be (many are expected to take on household chores, shop, do some cooking), how much vacation she will have, etc.

Ideally, a nanny is given a raise every year, the amount depending on what the going rate is. At Christmas (or other appropriate holiday), you should give her a bonus; if she's been with you six months, one week's salary would be appropriate. A nanny who has been with you less than six months usually receives a portion thereof, or instead she may be given a small present such as a scarf or a box of stationery.

"Sponsoring" an illegal nanny—i.e., guaranteeing to give her employment while she goes about filing papers for a green card—can be a long, difficult, and costly process. Though many a family has done it for a very special nanny, it is a commitment of time, energy, and money that should not be taken on lightly. Before entering into any sponsorship agreement with a nanny it is best to talk with an immigration lawyer.

BABYSITTERS

The best way to find a babysitter is through word of mouth or by asking a friend or someone at your church, synagogue, or your child's school. Rates for babysitting vary according to the city or town you live in, the age and experience of the sitter, and the number of children to be taken care of. When you first talk to a potential sitter, ask what her hourly rate is and what you will have to pay her if she spends a night or a weekend at your house, also whether carfare is included in her rate. Some couples find that hiring a babysitter on a monthly basis, and paying her whether or not she works, means they get out of the house on a more regular basis.

DIVORCE

With more than fifty percent of all marriages currently ending in divorce, the yours-mine-and-ours type of household is becoming increasingly commonplace. One little boy even asked his parents when they were going to divorce, because his friends—all products of broken marriages—thought his family was "weird."

As might be expected, with divorce comes the necessity for interpersonal communication. Because the fact is, divorced parents, no matter how estranged, who want the best for their children must continue to communicate about them. This can be especially difficult if the divorce was acrimonious and if one parent is required to support the other financially. In addition, parents with school-age children will have to work out the logistics of who plans to attend teacher conferences, ballet recitals, sports events. Because children come away from any divorce with enough hurt and pain to last a lifetime (even if they don't show it on the surface) it is vital that divorced parents do their utmost to maintain civility between them. This means never denigrating your spouse in front of your child, no matter how negative your feelings may be. Almost every child idealizes his parents and secretly hopes for a reconciliation.

Maligning your spouse to your child by listing his transgressions or faults may backfire. Your child may suddenly resent you for dashing his illusions and may openly rebel and side against you. Left alone in an untainted atmosphere, he will come to his own conclusions, some of which may match your own.

Other negative points to remember are:

- Don't use your child as a go-between to relay hurtful messages or orders such as "Mom says your child support check is a month late!" It will do more harm to the child's ego than to the spouse's.
- Don't use your child to spy on a spouse. If you want to know if he's bought a new Mercedes-Benz, find out for yourself.
- Don't use your child as a pawn in a game of one-upmanship and don't argue in front of him about visitation dates. If you do, he may end up feeling that he's a burden and that neither of you really wants him.
- Don't make your child choose with whom he wants to spend vacations and holidays. Work it out with your spouse and present the idea to the child as something you've agreed to. (Teenagers, of

course, may want and be ready to make their own decisions.) And don't make a scene when a holiday arrives and your child has to leave you. Say you hope he has a good time and that you'll be waiting for him when he returns.

Because divorce is between you and your spouse and not between your spouse and your child, you should do everything possible to ease the transition. Make sure you have informed relatives and friends of your state of affairs so that your child is spared interrogations and embarrassment. Tell him that he has every right not to answer questions about the divorce. But if he chooses to he may talk as openly as he likes to you, his close friends, or relatives. If your child appears unduly upset by the divorce, a short note to his teacher explaining the situation is often beneficial. You should ask the teacher to look out for signs that your child is unhappy or troubled in any way and, if this is the case, to alert you.

If you are involved in a divorce, think twice about taking back your former name. It can make your child feel even more uneasy or alienated if it appears that all his familial ties are being severed. And make an extra effort to see that he keeps up with members of his father's (or mother's) family, no matter how difficult it may be for you. After all, his relatives will always be his relatives and they can lend much-needed support. Also do what you can to maintain your child's daily schedule, the same mealtimes, play times, bedtime. In the midst of emotional upheaval, this will give him a sense of comfort and continuity.

STEPFAMILIES

When one or both divorced parents remarry, the child must readjust his relationships. If it is your spouse who remarries but your child spends most of the time with you, help him get used to his new role by speaking well of the new members of his family—no matter how difficult it may be for you. If your child divides his time between both parents, you can ease the transition by making sure that when he stays with his father (or mother) he always has the clothing he needs, the toys he likes best, his favorite blanket and pillow. This may even mean buying two of every item so that he is not carting possessions back and forth. Surrounding him with familiar objects will reduce the strangeness of the situation.

Stepbrothers and -sisters can be extremely helpful to your child in adapting to his new life. They too have been through a divorce and remarriage and been forced to live with people they don't really know. In some cases, the children band together to support one another over the rough spots. But it is also true that resentment, jealousy, and rivalry may get in the way. For that reason, the parent who has remarried must help his own child to adjust by being scrupulously fair to all the children. If you are the parent who has remarried, when conflicts arise, do your best to see that the children work out their own compromises. Avoid being placed in an "us against them" antagonistic position. Try to celebrate your stepchildren's birthdays as wholeheartedly as those of your own children; give them equally suitable presents at holidays. If you can, be as emotionally available for your stepchildren as for your own. An exception to the fairness doctrine is discipline. Under no circumstances should you try to discipline someone else's child. Leave that to his real parents.

But don't let your relationship with your own children lapse. In the beginning especially, it may be useful to set aside one night a week to be together. That way, there will be a semblance of continuity from your former life. A quick trip together to a restaurant or to a movie, a time to talk in private, will reassure children that, while they now have to share you with others, you still have very special feelings for each other. This, too, gives the children of the other family time to spend alone with their parent.

One of the major problems with divorce is that, if one partner (most often the woman) doesn't remarry, she is likely to find herself with less income. It is particularly difficult if her child is living with her on a tight budget and at the same time is exposed to stepbrothers and/or -sisters living in the lap of luxury. When such inequities exist, the best solution is an increase in child support. If this is not possible, the mother will have to explain it to her child.

FAMILY THERAPY

For truly distressed families, family therapy—even when it involves children—can be helpful. Under the guidance of a trained professional, a family can air their differences and learn effective methods of solving emotional problems. A good therapist can identify and point out any underlying dynamics that are causing friction but may not be obvious on the surface. Ultimately, however, it's the family that must pull together to try to resolve their differences and to learn to live together harmoniously.

THE ADOPTED CHILD

More and more women have been delaying childbirth until they are well into their thirties and early forties. Some women, aware that such pregnancies are high risk both for the mother-to-be and the baby, decide to adopt instead. As a result, there has been a rise in the number of adoptions. For this and other reasons, adoption is no longer the secret it once was. In addition, because many of the children Americans adopt come from other countries, or races other than the parents', and bring with them obviously different skin colorings and looks, children are increasingly being told about the reality of their situation. If you are interested in the subject of adoption, there are many books in libraries and bookstores to turn to.

Until you know a family who have adopted a child well, or until one of the parents or children brings it up, it is best not to initiate a conversation on the subject of adoption. Some parents may be self-conscious about the fact—feeling that adoption somehow means they have failed in their quests to be parents. Others may be more than willing to talk. But let them take the lead. Never refer to an adopted child as "your adopted child." These children are simply sons and daughters like anyone else.

If you do get into a conversation about adoption with a friend or acquaintance who has adopted a child, do not refer to the child's "real mother" or "real father." It is insensitive to the people who are doing the "real" parenting. The proper expression when referring to the parents who provided the genetic material is to call them the "birth" or "natural" parents.

The best thing you can say to a prospective adopting parent is exactly what you'd say to someone pregnant with a child: "Oh, I'm so happy for you. You must be terribly excited." Do not use phrases like "second best" or "now that you've finally given up" which suggest adoption is somehow a lesser way to have a child. For some couples it is their only option and they should be supported for their efforts.

Young children, even those who have not been adopted, often show an interest in the subject and may even hear it discussed on shows like "Sesame Street" and "Mr. Rogers'." If your child asks you to explain adoption you can say that it is the result of a mother simply not being able to take care of her baby, because she was too young or hadn't enough money to buy food and clothes. But because she loved the baby so much she gave it to another mother and father who would love it just as much and take good care of it the way she wished she could. Make it clear that an adopted child is as integral a part of a family as a natural child.

If your adopted child wants to know the circumstances of his birth, you must tell him forthrightly. Your adoption agency will no doubt have briefed you on the best way to do this but it should be an ongoing discussion. Do not spring it on him when he is fifteen. Young children can use the word "adopted" and be comfortable with it as early as age three. Each year their comprehension grows. To aid in the inevitable explaining, you might want to keep a scrapbook of mementos, a diary that records the adoption process, to turn over to your child. Included may be pictures of your child's arrival, of your first hugs together, of his birthday parties. These remembrances will help fortify his identity within the family. If your child comes from another country, you might even want to keep pictures and notes about where he lived before.

SINGLE-PARENT FAMILIES

A single parent will most likely have a harder time raising a child than a parent who has a partner. Four hands are better than two and two incomes are always better than one. Nevertheless, the number of single-parent households is on the rise—not only because of the divorce rate but because an increasing percentage of successful, well-adjusted females are deciding that, instead of waiting till eternity for Mr. Right, they'd rather go the family route alone.

The key to being a successful single parent is to develop a compatible "family" of friends. This includes everyone from the neighbor across the hall who can listen to the baby monitor while you run out to buy some milk to your best friend—either male or female—whose shoulder you can cry on. From time to time, family members should also be called upon and asked to help out. A cousin who loves baseball can teach your son or daughter how to pitch and catch; your best friend can take your child on a museum trip.

Children of single-parent families are asked to participate in parental decisions and chores to a greater extent than children in a two-parent home. But they should not be overwhelmed with responsibilities, particularly those of an emotional nature. Little boys who are asked to "take care of their mothers" at age five or little girls who are asked to "look after Daddy" too early can sacrifice their childhood to a parent's needs. When these children become adults they are often angry and resentful because their own dependency needs were never met.

If you have a friend who is a single parent, you can help out by offering to babysit, to take the children out to dinner, or to have them over to play. What single parents feel the lack of most is time to themselves.

ALTERNATIVE FAMILIES

With the breakdown of the traditional family comes the rise of the alternative family. This means not just the stepfamily, which is now common, but couples of the same sex living together with children. Instead of referring to one of the partners as "husband" or "wife," you use the word "companion." The politically correct term for children of such liaisons is simply "child."

It's up to a gay couple to decide what names they want their child to call them. For instance, in the case of a lesbian couple, one may be Mom and the other Susan, or a name derived from Susan just for the child to use, like Susu.

Outsiders should be kind and respectful of nontraditional families, and especially sensitive about the children raised within them. There are enough difficult social pressures without new ones being added.

HOW A CHILD ADDRESSES ADULTS

A young child should be raised with the knowledge that he should address adults with some degree of formality unless requested to do otherwise. Therefore, friends of his parents are Mr. Smith, Mrs. Davidoff. In a similar manner, teachers, professors, instructors, etc., should be addressed with Mr., Mrs., Miss, Ms. in front of their names. However, a child should feel free to call adults who have asked him to by their first names. If an adult doesn't suggest a child call her by her first name, she probably does not want him to.

WHEN A PARENT DATES AGAIN

When a mother or father begins dating after a divorce or the death of a spouse, or as a single parent, it can be a great moment of hope and happiness for both the parent and the child. Life again is full of promise and excitement; a renewed family life once again seems possible. This is especially true of the parent who begins dating someone the child likes very much. Yet dating can also be a sticky issue. Not only is it difficult for children to view their parents as sexually and romantically available, but dating can bring up or exacerbate unresolved fears about abandonment left over from the divorce, death, or separation. For that reason it is sometimes best, especially with a very young child, simply to say that you're going out for lunch or dinner without further explanation. There is no need to expose a child to fears and emotions she is unable to understand unless it's absolutely necessary.

Only when and if you have a steady, serious man (or woman) in your life should you introduce him to your child. This is to preserve not only the feelings of the suitor but also those of your child who is likely to be threatened by or hopeful of (or both) a match. For that same reason, it is not a good idea to have a date spend the night. Not only are you setting up a double standard that your child will no doubt toss back at you in his teenage years, but you are invading his world by asking him to share the breakfast table with someone he does not know. Home should be the place where he feels safe and secure. Until a steady relationship has formed, a single parent should consider a rather old-fashioned courting dance for the sake of the child.

Widowed parents have an even more difficult task. They must try to go on with their lives and at the same time keep the memory of the deceased spouse alive for the children's sake. This can impinge on any romantic relationship. What you must do is strike a balance. If you are happily dating, you will be a better parent, something your children will respond to positively.

Because single-parent families are often a very close, cohesive unit (by necessity), romantic matchmaking by outsiders may not be received by the children with enthusiasm. If you have engineered a date for a friend, do not discuss it in front of her children.

THE CHILD IN SOCIETY

Parents need to leave home and socialize now and then, and they will often want to take their child with them, not only because it's more convenient but because babies enjoy a change of scene as well. The youngest babies—who don't yet crawl or walk, and who still eat a before-bed meal—are the most transportable and can easily be put to sleep in a sling or on a friend's bed. More mobile babies may be equally easy to take on the social circuit but will require special sleeping arrangements (such as a crib or stroller) and can be quite a handful for parents to watch.

No matter how desperately you want to see friends, do not assume that your host will be thrilled to see your child when you arrive. Always ask if you can bring your baby along to a friend's house and explain that if the child gets inconsolably fussy, you will take him home.

When you do take your child with you, be ultrasensitive toward your hosts. Take toys to entertain the baby and ask where you should change him. And, if he starts wailing with no sign he is going to let up, take him into another room or even outside, weather permitting. (You should do the same in a restaurant or movie house or church; calm the baby down out of earshot of other people.)

If you are having a mother with an infant over to your house, be aware of their needs. Offer to heat bottles and find a comfortable, safe place for the baby and mother to sit (especially if she's nursing). Make sure the temperature of the room is neither too hot nor too cold. Before handling the baby, be sure to wash your hands. Also respect the apprehension of a new mother. If you ask to hold the baby and the mother looks stricken, withdraw the request quickly and change the subject.

SMALL CHILDREN

Children are great observers, and by the time a child starts walking he has already watched and learned from his parents' behaviors. There is little point in anyone trying to teach a toddler manners if he doesn't have a polite, considerate parent in his life after whom to model himself.

A toddler can be as difficult as he can be charming. He is insatiably curious, highly emotional, and has a very low frustration threshold. He is a lot of fun but not for people unaccustomed to his demands and moods. And toddler temperament grows in stages. One week he can be joyously building a tunnel of blocks with a friend, the next week fighting tearfully over every attempt to share. Evaluate your toddler's development and mood at each stage and assess what's best. Sometimes the only solution is for mother and child to stay home and not socialize for a day or two.

And remember that a young child, especially one under the age of three, needs a childproof environment. Otherwise everything within his reach—from an antique vase to a pile of change—will end up in his hands and mouth. Friends who pride themselves on priceless table-top treasures are not the people to take your one- or two-year-old to visit. Invite them to your house instead or hire a babysitter and go alone.

If you invite friends with small children to your house, make sure that any dangerous or valuable articles (including toys made with small easy-to-swallow pieces) are put away. It's nice to have a few creative toys or even blunt kitchen equipment (a steel bowl, a whisk) on hand for them to play with. If the parents are inclined to let their children run wild, you might want to suggest that you all go out for a walk together.

THE IMPORTANCE OF GOOD MANNERS

Good manners are as important to a child's education as reading, writing, and arithmetic. If your child has become accustomed to hearing the words "please" and "thank you" since infancy, he will be more apt to use these words when he starts to talk. By the age of two and a half a child should be asked to say the "magic" words, "please" and "thank you," whenever he wants or is given something. By three or four, he should be able to understand the concepts of courtesy well enough to know what it means to share, show respect for others, to apologize. By the time he is four or five, parents should no longer have to remind him to say "please" and "thank you" or to shake hands. These should be automatic reactions.

Here are a few basic manners a child should be taught:

- to say hello
- to say "please," "thank you," "excuse me," and "I'm sorry"
- to shake hands
- to show respect for older people
- to respect parents' and other people's privacy
- to speak when spoken to
- to not interrupt the conversations of grown-ups
- to be quiet in public places
- to not touch or play with other people's possessions unless invited to
- to get along with siblings or other children

Remember, the table manners you teach should be age-appropriate. It is useless to try to explain to a two-year-old that he should keep his mouth closed when he chews or his elbows off the table. Not only may he lack the physical coordination with which to comply, but he certainly won't understand why he should. If you wait until he is between the ages of four and six, when a child is ready to understand and perform good manners, you will make this training much more pleasant and successful.

Love and respect are the best and most effective tools you can use for teaching manners; fear and intimidation never work over the long run. Children have a fragile dignity and it can be easily crushed by humiliation. If you wish your child to adhere to the basic law of manners, i.e., showing consideration for others, *you* must first show *him* consideration.

If you must discipline your child, don't do it in front of others. Take him to another room. This spares your friends and the child considerable embarrassment and also helps your child recognize the gravity of the situation.

It is always important however to reemphasize a rule the moment it is broken. You are not doing anyone a favor by ignoring poor behavior. Parents who work all day and see their children only at dinnertime may be reluctant to ruin the brief time they are together with discipline. But such a laissez-faire attitude will reap only short-term gains. While dinner may be less stressful if you don't remind your child not to chew with his mouth open, he will be the loser in the long run. Children who have truly good table manners have them only because they were prodded when little.

APPROPRIATE USE OF WORDS

Every parent has a story about the first time his child mimicked the curse word that accidentally spilled out of the parent's mouth in a moment of anger or frustration. What seems so surprising is that, until that moment, the parent hadn't realized the child was actually listening to every word he said. But indeed he was! Parents who use chronic bad language in front of a child will find the words repeated back to them, to a nanny, friend, or teacher, under the most inappropriate and embarrassing circumstances. If your child has picked up curse words that he enjoys saying, don't overreact. Instead explain that they are words that adults sometimes use and are not for children.

Bear in mind that children not only repeat our language, phrases, and accents but also pick up the tone in which we speak to each other. Many parents have been shocked to hear their children yelling at their dolls or bossing around friends. Your child learns to communicate by imitating the way in which you communicate—with friends, family, and strangers—in both language and tone.

CHILDREN IN ADULT SETTINGS

If you are giving a party, your child, depending on his age, can participate by helping to put the house in order beforehand or by taking coats or passing hors d'oeuvres at the party. If your child is relatively young, you may want to have a favorite babysitter on hand or have a friend of your child's over to keep him occupied.

If you are taking a young child (up to the age of five) to a late night party where he'll be put to bed, don't expect him to go to sleep right away. A new environment and lots of noise and excitement will conspire against any schedule; just let everyone sleep late the next morning.

CHILDREN IN RESTAURANTS The average child finds it difficult to sit still for the duration of a restaurant meal. For that reason, a young child should not be taken to a restaurant that does not cater to children. Even at a restaurant that welcomes children, a child should never be allowed to lie on the floor, hide beneath the table, or run around. Running, in particular, is not only annoying to other diners but is a danger to waiters and waitresses carrying hot food and breakable tableware. If your child becomes sufficiently restless to disturb other diners, you have no alternative but to leave the restaurant.

Many restaurants welcome children and are prepared to serve them with a special menu. They may also offer high chairs, paper, crayons, hats, or games to distract them. Such a restaurant is a good place for a child to show off the table manners she's learned at home.

CHILDREN'S PARTIES

The rule of thumb when you are planning a child's birthday party at your house is to invite as many guests as the celebrant has years—plus one. That means inviting three children to your two-year-old's party, and six to your five-year-old's. But be aware that certain schools, especially private ones with classes as small as eleven children, require that, if more than half of the class have been invited to a birthday party, the remaining children must be invited too. This is to keep the children who have not been selected from feeling slighted and left out.

A child of four and five may want to have input into his party. Discuss with him the theme he wants—a Halloween party in October; a swimming party in the summer; or perhaps a "Little Mermaid," "Cinderella," "Peter Pan," or "Ninja Turtle" party, with decorations and games revolving around those characters. Discuss the kind of food you plan to serve and the kind of cake he likes best. Some children can be very particular, and since it is technically "his" day an attempt should be made to satisfy at least the most reasonable of his desires.

When you are planning a party for your child, it is important that you decide how much time should be allotted to games and how much to eating. The entire affair should not last more than two hours. If you wish, you can have a party planner supply the entertainment—such as a visit by Barney or Mother Goose. Or you can organize the entertainment yourself by having the children decorate T-shirts with puffy paint, or make masks out of cardboard, or create Christmas ornaments out of Styrofoam balls. Old-fashioned games like Pin the Tail on the Donkey, Duck, Duck, Goose, or Musical Chairs are always fun, but be careful about planning competitive games with children under six: they tend to get easily upset when, for instance in Musical Chairs, they are "out."

You may or may not want to include present-opening time in the party schedule. If you do, there's always the chance that very young children will be confused as to the actual ownership of the presents. There may be fights over who opens and plays with the toys, which can spoil the party. Assess the temperament of your young guests and decide for yourself. If you wish, give guests goody bags or small toys and games (go easy on candy) as they leave. But do not feel these are necessary, even if other parents give them. Many parents feel tyrannized into keeping up with the "goody bag" status quo (and the "toys" put in them can get quite expensive). Really what children need to learn is that a birthday is a special day for the child who is celebrating. Each child does not need to walk away from every social engagement with a material object in his hand. Nor should he expect to.

Plan your party at an hour when children are less likely to be tired. A good time is midafternoon, when they are rested from their naps. Have a light snack planned. This helps keep the party festive and gives them something nutritional before they eat the cake. Children get jazzed up on sugar, so keep it to a minimum.

Parents who care about their home will quickly come to the conclusion that birthday parties given for any child over the age of four belong in an outside location. Look into taking the group to an age-appropriate movie, a family fun center, or a fast-food restaurant. But make sure the entertainment is age-appropriate. Bowling alleys are well equipped for children's parties as are the new indoor playgrounds and many museums. To make it easier and more affordable, consider a joint party with the child of a friend of yours and hiring someone to plan the event. For a fixed price per child, you can leave the entertainment and cleaning up to someone else. Sometimes you don't even have to provide the cake. More and more parents are finding this is the most practical way to go.

Around age seven slumber parties become an option. Picnics, baseball games, swimming parties are all possibilities for the older, active child. Let him help with the details. It's good practice and he'll be pleased to have played a part in the planning of the occasion.

Although it's not strictly necessary to send thank-you notes for your child's birthday presents if he has thanked the gift giver in person, this is a perfect opportunity to teach him about the writing of thank-you letters. Sit down with your child and go over the names of those who attended the party and what they gave. Let your child help with the notes by drawing on the stationery or, if he's old enough, by writing them himself.

The child who is a guest should be taught to wish his friend "Happy birthday" and to thank the parents giving the party.

THE CHILD AT SCHOOL

With the number of dual-career families on the rise, and our increasing interest in the benefits of early education, children are starting nursery school (or an instructive day-care situation) at younger and younger ages. Today it is not unusual for a child to enter preschool at age three. However, no matter what the age is, the first day of school can be trying for both parent and child. The challenge for any parent is to prepare the child for his new experience, to make it as stress-free and as rewarding as possible. To help a child in this respect, many schools have adopted a kind of adjustment week. In some schools, the process may begin with a home visit from the teacher so that the child can see that he is liked and welcomed by the family. A parent (or caregiver) then joins the child in the classroom the first day, taking gradually longer and longer "coffee breaks" outside the classroom as the days go on. Eventually the child can be left at school on his own. Most schools have very open policies regarding parental involvement, and many, in fact, welcome it.

A good preschool will keep you informed about your child's progress by means of reports or conferences. Teachers may be able to alert you to learning problems, or social or physical difficulties that might go unnoticed at home. But don't be afraid to call up or to ask questions.

The main purpose of day care or nursery school is to get your child accustomed to an "institutional" setting and help him learn to get along with others. As a fringe benefit, your child may also become a better listener, a more generous sharer, a more responsible toy owner.

Depending on where you live, day care may be a less or equally expensive alternative to a full-time babysitter. And many children thrive in such group settings. Others, however, may need the security and nurturing of a one-on-one relationship; only you can decide what is best for your child. It is not necessarily true that a child who has been in nursery school since the age of two will perform better in kindergarten and beyond, but the added social and learning skills will definitely come in handy. Many schools won't accept a child for kindergarten who has not been to nursery school.

SCHOOL AND THE WORKING PARENT If a parent works, having a child in kindergarten can create logistical problems. In most communities, kindergarten offers only a half-day schedule and grammar school usually begins at 8 A.M. and ends around 3 P.M. So you're left with the question: what do I do with my child until six o'clock when I can pick him up? In response to such problems, many schools have instituted inexpensive after-school on-site programs in art, sports, science. High demand usually means they fill up quickly, so it's wise to sign up early. Or a child just beginning an afternoon kindergarten session might attend nursery school in the morning; a teacher might even deliver the child to the kindergarten for you. Your alternative is to hire a part-time babysitter or share one who will retrieve and care for the child after school is over.

A grammar school parent has most likely never been exposed to school-related activities such as the Parent-Teacher Association (PTA), field trips, teacher conferences, homework, scouts, after-school clubs, carpooling, and all the rest. This means scheduling your work and social life more carefully and thoughtfully in order to be as available and involved as possible. These are very important years in your child's life. Although the needs may be different, they are just as important as the needs of an infant.

THE PARENT-TEACHER PARTNERSHIP Because of the amount of time a child spends in school—eventually more than with his parents at home—a child's teachers can become the most important persons in his life. His teachers will have a profound impact upon his personality as well as his education. If you're lucky, his first teachers will be people he admires and finds easy to love and respect. If this is the case, you may feel it is sufficient to limit your relationship with the teachers to regularly scheduled conferences and quick hellos at drop-off time.

If you find your child has developed a crush on his teacher—which often happens—you may want to help him express his warm feelings by allowing him to choose a small gift for her at holiday time, or help him write a note of thanks at the end of the year. You may even want to invite the teacher over for lunch one day. You should never feel threatened if your child develops such a crush. Teachers are often children's first "transitional objects," the first people outside the family unit to whom they may transfer their love for the real parent. Transitional objects help children make the adjustment from a safe, cozy family environment into the possibly threatening unknown.

If your child appears to be having trouble in school, however, or difficulties with a certain classmate, you may want to call the teacher and arrange for a special interview. If you believe your child's problem is with a particular teacher, go directly to the principal. As in any other relationship, personal chemistry can play a part. Some teachers are unable to hit it off with certain children; the key is to rectify the situation before the year progresses. If the personality conflict remains strong and seems to be interfering with his development, you may want to switch your child into another class. (Exhaust all other options first; it can be difficult for a child to adjust to a new class in the middle of the year.) If the bad chemistry seems to be only between you and the teacher, try not to transmit your dissatisfaction to your child. Subtle antagonism between a parent and teacher will probably not influence the child.

CARPOOLS Anywhere but in large cities carpools are the most sensible, if not the only, solution to carting around a population of highly active children. As soon as your child enters school or becomes involved with after-school programs, call or get together with other parents and draw up a carpooling schedule. One parent or caregiver may take the kids to school, another may pick them up. Or the carpool may rotate on a weekly or monthly schedule of full-time duty. Just make sure the schedule you come up with is one you can *all* live with. One parent should perform as group leader and be put in charge of scheduling, schedule changes, and communicating alternative plans if one child is sick or it's a snow day.

She should also make sure the group has a backup plan if the scheduled driver or her child suddenly becomes ill. She might even want to draw up a semester-long calendar with each participant's phone number and name written in on their appointed carpool days.

In any group there will inevitably be some parents who cannot—or will not—participate equally in a carpool. Offer them the opportunity to find a replacement for themselves or to pay another parent to take their turn. Try not to penalize the child for the shortcomings of his parents. Of course, if the problem becomes too burdensome, you may have no alternative but to drop the child from the carpool.

LATCHKEY CHILDREN

The sad truth of the dual-career couple or single-parent family is that they often have no choice but to let their child come home after school to an empty house. If your child is one of the millions of latchkey children in this country, it is extremely important that you set down rules for him to follow when school is let out each day, and that he realizes these rules must be adhered to.

Have a predictable schedule. Each morning before your child leaves for school, check to be certain he has his house key with him. When he gets home, he should call you (or your spouse) immediately. Take time to chat with him about his day and what he plans to do now that he's home. While unsupervised television is generally not recommended for a young child, in this situation you may want to make an exception. This is also a good time for your child to get some homework done. After that he can have the after-school snack you leave for him. And, provided he has your permission, he may make calls to friends or family members.

Be sure your child knows the telephone numbers of neighbors whom he can call if a problem arises and he is unable to reach you. These numbers should also be posted, along with a list of emergency telephone numbers (doctor, police and fire departments), where he can easily read them.

The most important rule is that your child should not leave the house without your permission or open the door to strangers. If you live in an apartment building, he should be told never to buzz in people he is not expecting. If he answers the telephone and it's a stranger asking if he's alone, he should know to say he is not alone—that his mother is resting or taking a bath, and cannot come to the telephone—whatever excuse you want to give him.

It is not advisable for your child to have a friend over when there is no one around to supervise their activities. What's more, friends' parents will probably not want their child in a house unattended by adults. And if anything should go wrong in your absence, you could be held responsible.

DEALING WITH STRANGERS

Many schools have educational programs that teach young children how to react when a stranger, or someone they recognize but do not know well, approaches them. Even so, it is every parent's responsibility to discuss this subject, explaining to his child that if she is ever asked to accompany a stranger she must refuse, and immediately report the encounter to her parent or teacher. While no parent wants to scare his child unnecessarily, this issue is too important to be ignored. And if presented in a calm, nonthreatening manner, it's most likely the child will accept what's told to her without becoming upset.

EXTRACURRICULAR ACTIVITIES AND THE OVERSCHEDULED CHILD

We've all heard about the "overscheduled child," the three-, four-, or five-year-old whose calendar rivals that of a C.E.O., whose line-up of nursery school, play dates, French lessons, art school, gymnastics, computer training, and ballet would give pause to an energetic twenty-year-old. Despite the fact that experts say children learn through unstructured play, many high-achieving parents think that pushing extracurricular classes will give their child a head start. That misapprehension is often compounded by the belief that, if one activity is good, five are better. However, early childhood should not be a time of anxiety, of rushing to be at a scheduled class after school, of performance anxiety. Geniuses are not taught, they happen, and no amount of piano study is going to transform tone-deaf Johnny into Mozart.

You may want to expose your child to various cultural, artistic, and social situations, but it is not profitable to do so until he is ready. A two-and-a-half-year-old simply doesn't have the concentration or coordination to enjoy ballet lessons. Also, let him choose the activity he prefers, and don't overdo it. One lesson a week is fine unless the child is clamoring for more.

If your child wants to take ballet lessons at the age of five because she loves the costumes, and you agree to this, tell her she can have a certain number of lessons to see if she enjoys them. It can be very frustrating to spend time, money, and effort only to hear a child say, after just a few weeks, "I don't like ballet."

Of course, it happens that a child thinks he will love horseback riding but finds he loathes the teacher, is scared of the horse, or cannot master the appropriate skills. A parent can usually tell the difference between a child wanting out because he feels lazy and one who is frightened or uncomfortable. You can help your child get over obstacles he faces by making him stick to an instrument, craft, or practice; but you can also help him emotionally by recognizing his distress. That may mean having him drop the lessons and perhaps resuming them in a year or so if he desires.

SOCIAL DANCING

Children of nine or so often join a social dancing class in which they are taught ballroom dancing as well as other forms of dance. Dancing class is a wonderful opportunity for a child to learn how to behave in a formal setting: how to dress neatly, how to make polite conversation, how to observe the amenities of party-going with a group of peers. Dancing class can also be a great confidence-booster for a child. Knowing what to expect will make her first formal dance or prom a lot less scary. Although a tomboy or macho child may balk at the idea of dancing school, he or she may eventually come to enjoy the experience, particularly if friends are present.

Although most dancing classes no longer require white gloves, you still need to make sure your child arrives clean, neat, and nicely dressed. A boy should wear a jacket and tie; a girl should wear a dress or skirt and party shoes.

CHILDREN AND MONEY

Most of our attitudes about money are formed in early childhood. As a parent, you play an important role in developing your child's ability to manage his money when he grows up. A parent is as responsible for a child's financial education as he is for his moral one. Though some parents are quite good at teaching their children about finances, others fail to help them set realistic goals. And too many parents ignore the subject altogether—because they feel it is too complicated for a child to grasp.

A well-informed child enters the world at eighteen knowing how to balance a checkbook, how to live on a budget, how to delay gratification, how to discriminate between necessities and luxuries, and how to avoid being a dupe and falling for every product sold on television. Children who understand money understand the way of the world.

The sooner you start teaching your child about money, the better. Here are a few money pointers related to your child's age group:

AGES 3 TO 5

Talk about money. Take your child with you to the bank, to the supermarket, the clothing store, the gas station. Explain that you earn money at work to pay for food, clothing, and gas. Because children learn by doing, now and then give your child a small amount of money and let him choose among items to buy. Occasionally give your child pennies or nickels to deposit into a piggy bank.

AGES 6 TO 7

Start an allowance of, say, fifty cents or a dollar. Give it every week at the same time. Don't withhold his allowance as punishment. Instead, discuss what it can be used for.

AGES 8 TO 10

Give annual raises in the allowance. Pick the same date every year, such as the beginning of school or your child's birthday, to increase both the amount of allowance and his household responsibilities. Create ways in which your child can earn extra money. Open a savings account for him and discuss what the savings might be used for.

AGES 11 TO 14

Teach goals. Include your child in some family budget discussions. Talk about long-term goals, such as college or a new car. Encourage him to earn money by doing jobs for people outside the family. At age thirteen or fourteen, or at least during high school, he should open a checking account. Give your child an incentive to save by offering to match his deposits in the bank.

AGES 15 TO 18

Teach independence. Encourage your child to take a part-time or Saturday job. Include him in discussions about college tuition. If you give your child use of a credit card, make it clear what it is to be used for and what items you will pay for. Also explain that he must pay for any other charges on his card or it will be taken away. College students should be required to contribute something toward their education, whether it is spending money or money for transportation or books. The amount will depend upon a family's financial situation. It is a truism that we all appreciate something we have earned much more than something handed to us.

ALLOWANCE Around the age of six an allowance becomes an excellent way to teach a child the value of money and to encourage her sense of responsibility. The size of the allowance should vary with the child's age, your financial situation, and the necessities it is supposed to cover. Discuss the purpose of the allowance with your child. If you expect her to save part of it for buying clothes, gifts, books, or toys, say so. But at least a portion of it must go toward purely discretionary items such as ice cream cones, movies, etc. That way, your child gets to make decisions about how her money can be allocated.

Because receiving her allowance is an important event in a child's life, it should always be given on the same day each week. Raise the amount once a year and increase what expenses it should cover. Your goal: by the time your child graduates from high school she will know how to budget for all her own needs and understand how much her lifestyle costs.

Though an allowance should never be compensation for expected chores, parents who pay children for *extra* work can still help instill a healthy work ethic. Whether it's mowing the lawn or helping the child's grandmother shop for groceries, payment for jobs well done brings pride.

The last thing you want, however, is a child who behaves like a private contractor—charging for every increment of work done—so integrate jobs you pay for with a good number of those you expect her to perform gratis.

As your child gets older you can discuss the family budget with her in a nonthreatening way. Let her know there are limits and that as a family you must make choices—to buy a new car, go on a vacation, or pay for college courses. By high school, your child should be encouraged to be putting something away for college. You can expand on her efforts by matching her savings, perhaps dollar for dollar. When she wants an expensive item like a stereo, insist that she pay for half of it. The contribution will make her appreciate the item much more than she would if you bought it for her.

According to experts, it is dangerous and self-defeating to pay a child for grades. Someone who's given ten dollars for every "A" confuses learning with earning. And in the real world, in fact often, intellectual endeavors are not always rewarded with high salaries. Children must learn to love learning for learning's sake. A thoughtful parent will keep the two concepts separate.

If you bribe a teenager to drop a group of friends or stop seeing a boyfriend, or offer a car in exchange for growing out a Mohawk hairdo, you create another sticky situation. Although your teen may comply because she wants money more than that wretched boyfriend, she will probably find someone not that different later on. This is because her underlying needs will not have been altered. Keep money and love separate.

SAVINGS ACCOUNTS A savings account for a school-age child can be an invaluable learning tool. He gets to see arithmetic in action, is exposed to the concept of accrued interest, and learns more about responsibility and independence. In order to open the account in his name, however, you will need to get him a social security number. Under the social security "enumeration at birth" program, many hospitals can, at a parent's request, forward birth certificate information to the government. The social security office will then automatically assign the child a number and mail the parent a confirmation card. Otherwise, you'll have to fill out a bank application with proof of birth to come. Many banks require that the account be opened jointly with a parent or guardian.

When your child starts saving at a bank, explain to him that the bank is paying interest for the use of his money. And show him that money can be withdrawn, that it is not owned by the bank.

As a child gets older he can open a checking account and even learn about investing. Although a minor is prohibited by law from purchasing stocks, his parents can buy them for him under the Uniform Gift to

Minors Act. A few shares in a company he knows (Apple, Coca-Cola, Reebok) will give him an investment he can keep up with. Explain that he owns a very small part of the company but is technically entitled to attend its annual meeting. Watch the stock price with him in the newspaper. If the company is headquartered nearby, take him to the annual meeting or on a tour of its facilities.

SCHOOL MONEY If your child needs money each day for lunch or other school-related expenses, you may decide, if he is old enough, to give him the full weekly amount each Monday. (Younger children should be given the money daily so as to reduce the temptation to spend it all at once.) Talk with him about his weekly expenses. Then allow him the freedom to stick to a budget or make mistakes. If he spends it all by Wednesday, avoid giving him extra money. He may be in tears but you must not lead him to believe there is always more money available—especially when he doesn't hold to his budget.

CREDIT CARDS Charge cards for teenagers have become a controversial matter these days as more and more banks and stores attempt to lure the young into establishing credit. For some very responsible teens, a credit card is an ideal way to learn about charging. For others it is the beginning of a spiral into terrible debt. "Buy now, pay later" can get way out of hand if the child is not careful. Before you let your child use your credit card or establish one of his own, set up firm guidelines. What is the card to be used for? Who will pay for the items charged? How much can be charged? Is permission to use it required each time?

You may want your teenager to select (and perhaps even pay for) some of his clothes. If so, give him a charge card or let him use yours. At the same time teach him how to use it wisely. You may want your college-bound child to have a card for transportation or emergencies only. Make certain he understands that. If he misuses the card by charging something he's not supposed to, discuss the infraction with him and have him pay for the charge. If it happens a second time you should take the card away—at least until he has learned his lesson. Until your child is economically self-sufficient, use of any credit card should be under your supervision. Keep in mind too that a child with unlimited credit may be tempted to use it to show off or buy friendships—neither of which you want to foster.

GIVING MONEY AS A GIFT You may wish to give a child money as a christening, birthday, bar mitzvah, or graduation present. You can give either cash or a check. (Older people often find shopping for young people difficult and that a present of money is an ideal solution.) If you decide to give cash, use crisp new bills. Place them in an envelope with a personal note or in a greeting card. If you use a card, take time to add a handwritten note. To make the gift more personal, place the money or check inside a book or give it with some other small present.

Your child needs to be taught to say "thank you" for presents of any kind, including cash. Sometimes a child comes to expect money on his birthday from an uncle or grandmother. It is important to explain to him that these presents are not automatic and should not be taken for granted. He should always write a thank-you note for each present. If he is very young, you will have to help him do so.

If the amount of money your child receives from a grandparent or other relative is sufficiently large that he cannot (and should not) be given it directly, talk it over with the giver and deposit the money in the child's bank account or open one for him. Make it clear to your child that the gift is still his and will be put to good use later on. If you put it into a savings account, you can show him the savings book with his name on it or the bank statements and let him see how the interest earned is helping his account grow in size.

DIVORCE AND MONEY ISSUES   One of the saddest and most difficult occurrences a child can face is the divorce of his parents. It has many ramifications, including financial ones. Sometimes after a divorce the relationship of the father to the child is reduced to a monthly support check. Other divorced parents remain friendly and communicate well, especially where their children are concerned. Regardless of your family's circumstances, it's best not to discuss the financial arrangements you've made in front of your child unless you can truthfully say, "You needn't worry about how we'll get along. Dad/Mom is taking good care of us." A child of divorce has enough to deal with emotionally without feeling that he is also a financial burden.

If support checks are late or skipped entirely, it is important not to talk to your child about it. If he overhears such problems, he may become worried that there will not be enough money to live on. He may interpret the situation as somehow being his fault, or he may equate the missed support checks with a withdrawal of love. Newly single mothers face the most difficulty in this area, especially if they are economically dependent upon their ex-husbands. If that is your situation, you may wish to explain to your child that you are now on a different budget and that you must be more careful how you spend your money. Try to say this in a calm, nonthreatening way, without transmitting anger or fear and without criticizing the child's father.

It is not uncommon for children of divorce to play one parent against the other in money matters. By saying, "Mom never gives me enough lunch money," a child may get Dad to hand over a little extra cash. The best approach is for the ex-spouses to communicate about allowances, spending money, gifts of money, and extras. If this is not possible, then each of you must try to reason with your child.

MONEY AND THE BLENDED FAMILY When parents remarry, the family's financial situation often changes. There may be more money, in which case there's no (or less) financial difficulty. Or there may be less, in which case you will have to explain to your child that life will be different, but not less fun or less enjoyable. Sometimes a child must live with step- or half sisters and brothers or at least see them at various family occasions. These children may have more money to spend than he does. While a child may initially be resentful of this fact, you can help mitigate his resentment and jealousy by explaining that you love him and your love is not tied to money. This is a good time to discuss the fact that throughout his life he will meet people who have more money than he does and people who have less—and that neither makes a better human being.

WHEN A PARENT LOSES A JOB One of the greatest shocks for anyone is to lose a job. It is especially frightening and confusing for a child when his parent is out of work. Children seem to have an innate ability to sense lies and cover-ups, so if you aren't honest about it, your child will imagine the worst. Tell him the simple facts and explain that you are looking for new work. It is also important to explain that the situation is temporary, although you do not know exactly when you will be working again.

Every child will react differently. It is possible, for example, that your child's confidence in you as all-powerful may be shaken or that he may in some way blame himself for the family tension unless the real reason for your distress is explained. That is why honesty on your part is essential.

This can also be an opportunity to demonstrate to him the important fact that adversity can be overcome. If your child is apprehensive, do not ignore his feelings. Instead, reassure him that his concern is natural. How much you tell your child depends on his age and adaptability. Obviously you can be more open with a teenager than with a five- or six-year-old.

THE TEENAGER

NOT A CHILD, NOT AN ADULT

Adolescence can be a trying, often confusing period between childhood and adulthood. When a child reaches adolescence even the most stable family can be thrown into turmoil. The basic problem: parents still think of their son as a child while he thinks of himself as an adult. What parents know (and the child hasn't enough experience to recognize) is that he is not yet ready to claim the rights and privileges of the adult world because he does not wholly understand the accompanying responsibilities. As a result, the teenage years, from thirteen to nineteen, present their own unique problems of etiquette. But the good part about having teenagers in the house is their energy, the new things you learn about, and the emergence of a friend from someone who was once just your dependent.

Because of the inherent power struggles, the teenage years are, obviously, not the ideal time to bring up the subject of good manners with your child. Even teens carefully raised to be courteous and to have consideration for others will show stunning lapses in normal, acceptable behavior. But if you've laid a good foundation, and your child knows the basics—good table manners, how to write thank-you notes, how to show respect and empathy for others—you can hope not to lose too much ground.

COMMUNICATION AT HOME

Your home doesn't have to become a battleground, although it could come to feel like one once your child enters adolescence. Although your teenager's emotional storms will surely challenge your patience and good nature and, at times, may even exhaust your reserves of love and understanding, with respect and consideration most families can enjoy these exciting years. And, in fact, parents are often amazed at what a teenager can teach them. Here are some rules of thumb for parents to remember:

- Listen to your child; pay attention to what he says;
- Keep an open mind to new concepts he suggests; perhaps the entire family will become vegetarians along with him;
- Never laugh at his predicaments or mock them in any way;
- Don't take his dark moods personally; enjoy the energetic and enthusiastic side of him;
- Maintain a family code of acceptable behavior, no matter how much he may fight it;
- Be alert to signs of severe unhappiness on his part or wide mood swings;
- Seek professional help if appropriate. But beware. Even the most well-intentioned parent can mistakenly pack his teenager off to a psychiatrist, school counselor, social worker, or self-help group and believe the problem has been resolved, when in reality the child wants to communicate with the parent.

You can open up the lines of communication by initiating a conversation/discussion, or indirectly by way of a card or letter left on his bed, a tape or video created for him to watch. You might even want to give him a book on a relevant topic and say that you'd like to discuss it after you both have read the book.

If direct attempts to communicate go nowhere, gently suggest to your child that he may wish to talk to a third, uninvolved person in private. Or you may want to consider family therapy in which all family members get to state their grievances on neutral territory. Remember, problems that are ignored only fester.

Your teen may go through a strange phase in which he actually seems to be embarrassed by the mere fact that he has parents. He may indulge in fantasies of having been adopted or of running away. Nothing you do is right in his eyes: your job, your way of dressing, your conversations, your friends. He may not want to be seen with you in public or have his friends meet you. He is certain that you will humiliate him in some obscure way just by being yourself. Do not take this behavior personally. Do not defend yourself or exacerbate the problem by intruding on his social engagements. It is a phase that, luckily, passes quickly. His basic love for and need for you will ultimately win out.

THE NEED FOR PRIVACY

It can be difficult for a parent to accept his teenager's right to privacy. After all, many parents only discover that their teenager is up to no good—smoking, using drugs, running with a bad crowd—by accidentally stumbling upon the evidence while putting away the child's laundry or unpacking his book bag. But there is no justification for spying, snooping, entering a child's room without knocking, or listening in on a telephone conversation. Whatever trouble your child is in will no doubt be compounded by the moral outrage he will feel upon learning that you have violated his right to privacy while exercising your right to know. Remember, she is no longer a baby. An attentive, intelligent parent should be able to determine in other ways if there is something amiss with his teenager.

Because most teenagers are by nature secretive and noncommunicative, they need a place in the house to call their own—a room where they can go to be alone, to think, write, draw, dream, without fear of interruption.

THE TEENAGER'S BEDROOM

The teenager is not known for being a neat housekeeper and it may take all your willpower not to interfere in how your child keeps her bedroom, although it's not unreasonable to rule against food being kept in the room. But you can teach her the consequences of her behavior: If she doesn't wish to keep her room neat, she will have to live with her own mess. Unless your teen's way of life is threatening the common areas of the house, you must try not to nag her about it. Many parents just grit their teeth and keep the teenager's bedroom door shut. The posters, the music, the clothes strewn about, must be borne with equanimity and the knowledge that most children outgrow adolescent sloppiness. And sometimes an attempt at rebellious decorating can yield pleasant surprises in the form of interesting fabrics or attractive objects she's acquired.

THE BATHROOM

There is an interesting change that occurs during adolescence, a point at which even the most oblivious young person suddenly discovers the bathroom shower and mirror. This change usually coincides with when they discover the opposite sex and realize that grooming is everything. Which is all fine and dandy except that many teens tend to monopolize the family bathroom. "Proper" primping and grooming may require several showers a day, with accompanying towel and clothing changes. Every available surface may become a way station for cosmetics, hair sprays, hair dryers, and shaving equipment. Getting an entire family in and out of the bathroom during a work-week morning may be a feat of management in itself. But isn't this preferable to grunge?

If you have a number of bathrooms, try to give your teenager one of her own. If she must share a bathroom with other people, she should be given a set amount of time to use it for her own purposes. What's left undone she'll have to take care of in her own room. You might even want to consider buying her a special dressing table or makeup mirror for her bedroom. If the bathroom lacks cabinet space, boys should be required to keep grooming equipment on their dresser top.

THE FAMILY TELEPHONE AND CAR

Two other potential areas of conflict are the family car and the family telephone. Both are vital links to a teenager's social world, so most children will go along with whatever guidelines you establish in order to maintain these privileges.

Teenagers are well known for tying up the telephone for hours on end as they talk over the minutiae of their lives with their friends. One way to deal with the situation is to set aside a certain time of the day when your teenager can have the telephone just for her own use; after homework has been done, for example. Or think about having Call Waiting installed. That way, you can be assured your friends will get through whenever they call. Of course, the best solution of all is to give your teenager her own telephone with her own private number. If you decide to do that, you may want her to pay her own telephone bills from her allowance or money earned from jobs.

The family car can be a bit more problematic. It may not be easy for some parents to watch a newly licensed sixteen-year-old drive off in the car they worked so hard to buy and that is so essential to the family. And of course it's not just the car they worry about, but their child's life. What's inevitable, however, is that all parents must learn to let go of their child eventually and driving is one of the great steps toward adulthood. One of the best ways to make the transition and to show your support is to give your child a driver's license party. Invite friends over for pizza and soft drinks and then have the family's newest driver give everyone a ride around the block.

Before letting your teenager behind the wheel, you need to have a discussion about rules in the car, the most important of which is the strict observance of traffic laws. This includes an absolute ban on speeding, reckless driving, picking up hitchhikers, letting friends drive, or driving while under the influence of drugs or alcohol. You might also want to make it clear to your child that if she is ever in a situation with the car in which it seems even vaguely inappropriate to drive—say, after a beer party when she might have had just a little too much to drink—that she either calls you to come pick her up in another car, or gets a ride home with a friend and retrieves the car later. Auto accidents are still the number-one killers among teenagers.

Together you can work out a schedule for use of the car that suits everyone. Perhaps she can combine errands or shopping for you with the stops she needs to make, or perhaps she can pick you up or drop you off at your destination. You may even want her to pay for part of the insurance and/or make sure that she replaces any gas she uses. If you lay out the rules in the beginning you won't find yourself getting into a car with an empty gas tank, strewn with Burger King wrappers. If she doesn't abide by the rules, suspend her driving privileges.

HELPING WITH SIBLINGS

Teenagers can be a great help with younger children in the family. Younger siblings not only worship their older brothers and sisters but will often obey them more readily than they will their parents. Teenagers can take siblings to the movies, help get them dressed, bathed, into bed, even help them with their homework. But don't abuse this relationship. Any teenager will inevitably resent being regarded as a live-in, unpaid babysitter, and that resentment can sour his feelings toward you and his siblings. If your teenager spends a good deal of time caring for brothers and/or sisters, consider some sort of compensation. It doesn't have to be monetary. For the favors he does for you, you can do some favors for him.

STYLE OF DRESS

There is a kind of herd mentality that overcomes most teenagers, and, because they are struggling for independence at the same time, it creates an interesting dilemma. "Be yourself but don't be too different from us" is the message they seem to be hearing. For that reason, being in sync with the general teenager zeitgeist becomes of utmost importance and means that there is no end to the wacky things a teen will do to his body, hair, and clothes to conform. Many parents will find that battles over appearance only intensify when pressure is applied. Most will simply have to grin and bear it, take plenty of pictures, and hope that when their daughter is twenty-five she'll look back at those pictures and wonder why she wore bizarre outfits and jewelry.

Let her give her way a try but if you can't bear the result, you can always try a little leverage. If you pay for your daughter's clothing, you can veto the choices she makes. You may refuse to buy her a black leather cat suit not only because of how it looks but because it's horrendously expensive. But that doesn't stop her from saving up and buying it with her own money. Then all you can influence is where she wears it. You may request that it not be worn to her cousin's christening, to your friend's wedding, or to her grandmother's office open-house. At certain points you can even appeal to her sense of consideration: "Please, just for me, would you wear that nice outfit I bought you? It would make me so happy" is one way to put it. But realize that putting her looks or dress down or threatening to make her dress a certain way probably will make her even more resistant.

And, because teenagers are so independent and spend so many hours on their own, you cannot realistically prevent them from dressing any way they want. How many of us had a friend who left her house in a prim dress only to change into a wild outfit she had stuffed in her book bag? Parents who are excessively strict may end up teaching their teenager nothing about decency and everything about deceit. What she wears, after all, is much less important than what she's like—and that's mostly up to you.

Luckily, some schools have dress codes so that teenagers who make extreme sartorial statements will be sent home to change—which can be beneficial if you need some outside leverage in coaxing moderation.

Jewelry given to a teenager should be age-appropriate—and certainly not expensive. A sixteenth birthday is not the time to pass down an expensive heirloom or to begin letting your child borrow your good jewelry. If she loses or breaks it she's not in a position to fix or replace it. If you are going to a special family party and you want your daughter, whose taste runs to embarrassing extremes, to look more conservative, you should tell her how you feel and hope she'll follow your suggestion.

BRACES, PIERCED EARS, AND OTHER TRENDS Adolescents can become quite sensitive about their appearance, so it can be traumatic when they have to wear orthodontic braces. (Though braces are usually installed at around age ten or eleven, they are often worn for a few years.) Never, never make light of your child's anguish over braces, glasses, weight, or pimples; you may know that she will blossom into a swan, but your knowledge won't help the feelings of an insecure teenager. Sympathize with her.

Hair, because it is so obvious, easy, and cheap to manipulate and color, has always been a front-line symbol of teenage rebellion. The sixties had long greasy hippie hair, the seventies purple Mohawks, the eighties razor cuts, the nineties dreadlocks. And one can fairly predict that most teenagers will continue to use hairstyles as a quick way to identify someone who's "in" or "out." The best part of an outrageous teenage haircut (at least from the teenagers' point of view), however, is its unparalleled ability to drive parents crazy. Shocked, furious reactions from adults only make it that much more attractive.

The way to keep hair from being an issue in your family is to realize its irrelevance in light of the greater teenage issues of unwanted pregnancy, AIDS, and deaths from drunk driving. And it will always grow out. Try to ignore the hairstyle and concentrate on the person wearing it. If nothing else, it makes for a few laughs over photographs in the future.

Pierced ears are very common these days, not only among girls but among boys. One fad is to have multiple holes in each ear; some even have their noses pierced. Tattoos have also risen in favor. Reason is your best defense. Point out that many potential employers or college interviewers may look upon these fashion trends as frivolous or unkempt. Or that being tattooed hurts and it is even more painful if she decides she no longer is in love with "John" and wants the name removed. You might even try explaining how fads of your own youth became an embarrassment in later years.

If you are adamant about keeping your child from conforming, you may want to try laying down the law. Tell her that she is forbidden to go along with her crowd in any kind of bodily "mutilation." Explain that tattoos and piercing are painful and you'd like to know what she hopes to accomplish by them. Talk to her about her friends who have had these things done: perhaps you can help her come to the conclusion that these practices are foolish. Tell her that she is free to do whatever she wishes when she gets out on her own but that as long as she lives in your house she must abide by your rules. Explain that if she comes home with a nose ring or ten earrings in her ears you will expect her to take them out. If she comes home with a tattoo you will take her to a plastic surgeon to have it removed and she will be expected to pay for the removal out of her allowance.

But be aware that such a stance gives the opposite message from "You are in sole charge of your own body." Which is more important for a young person to believe?

One family found that reason was the best solution when their son came home one evening with an earring in his ear. During dinner, they asked him to tell why he had pierced his ear. He said he simply didn't know. They then discussed the drawbacks of doing things without forethought, without reason. It was a thoughtful conversation, yet at times one full of laughter. About a month or so later, the boy gave his mother his earring in a box. When he received his college degree, she gift-wrapped the box and gave it back to him. They still laugh about it.

PHYSICAL CHANGES

Before your daughter starts menstruating (anytime between the ages of eleven and sixteen), be sure to have a conversation with her about it and have the necessary supplies on hand. She will probably have learned what changes to expect in health class, but she may need to ask you questions she felt uncomfortable bringing up in class. No matter how sophisticated your child is, she may have some concerns about all the changes her body is undergoing. Give her lots of extra love and attention and don't let anyone tease her. Some girls find growing breasts and menstruating an upsetting reminder that they are leaving their comfortable childhood behind. Adolescence can be difficult, not only physically but mentally.

If your daughter is a late bloomer and shows no signs of breasts and hips when other girls do, offer to take her to a lingerie store and buy a "training" bra and some nice bikini panties. For many teenagers, nothing is more humiliating than having to change for gym class in front of a group of full-figured girls while still wearing an undershirt and Carter's Spanky pants.

Teenage boys like to start shaving around sixteen, even younger, whether they need to or not. Buy your son his own razor and shaving cream and resist making jokes about how grown up he's become. Teenagers are very sensitive to real or imagined teasing. What you might find cute or endearing may not seem funny to them.

DATING AND SEXUALITY

Many teenagers start to date seriously around age fifteen or sixteen. (In communities where dating starts as young as twelve or thirteen, it is usually just for fun and to act grown up.) As a child grows older, the concept of "going steady," dating one person exclusively or declaring her love for that person, comes into play. At that point young people may exchange rings or bracelets as a symbol of their commitment to one another; and they may have or contemplate having sex. You have probably talked to your child about sex before this time; if not, do so now. If you find a direct conversation very difficult, give your child one of the many good books or videos about teenage sexuality. They are available from any bookstore or library.

While many schools provide excellent sex education courses, others have programs that are woefully lacking. And some offer no sex education at all. In any case, for largely political reasons, most sex education programs are forced to concentrate on the physical and biological aspects of sex alone. They are prohibited from discussing the emotional, social, and ethical issues. As a result, many teens must learn a great deal about dating and sex from watching those around them—and that includes you. Be sure to take your child's questions very seriously—no matter how silly they may sound—and be available to talk. Remember, too, that she is old enough to learn from what you do and not just from what you say. If you behave one way sexually and preach the opposite to your child, she will surely see—and perhaps even point out to you—the contradictions.

SAFER SEX Truly safe sex, other than total abstinence, doesn't exist. There is only safer sex—and that means always using a latex condom (the HIV virus may be able to penetrate the natural skin condoms). Sexual etiquette has gone beyond just knowing how to be considerate of others or how to ward off unwelcome advances without hurting a date's feelings. Today's sexual etiquette is to protect life.

TEACHING CHILDREN AND TEENAGERS Sexual etiquette education begins by teaching children about their genitals and about the importance of reporting to their parents or teachers anyone who tries to touch them in areas of their bodies that are private. It also means telling them not to worry about hurting the feelings of a person who abuses them this way or to feel guilty about tattling. Sexual etiquette means parents must give children, and especially emerging teens, as soon as they request it, privacy in the bathroom or when undressing. And it means being an "askable" parent, one who is available to answer questions, even ones you might find awkward or embarrassing. If sexual etiquette is handled well in the family, if parents show respect for their children's sexuality, by the time a child is a teenager, he or she should not feel the need to prove sexual identity or virility. By then, respect for one's body and for the bodies and wishes and demands of others will be completely natural.

Because the teenage years are usually the ones during which sexuality becomes an important issue, they are also the white-water years for sexual etiquette. Today, both boys and girls need to know more than the biological mechanics that are taught in most sex education classes (and which they probably know anyway by then). They need to know how to deflect an advance, how to negotiate the use of a condom, what to do if they change their minds mid-encounter. They must learn that it's all right for males and females to carry condoms, that both girls and boys must learn to respect a partner's wishes. The onus is not just on boys to magically divine what a female is thinking: girls are responsible for expressing their feelings clearly. And it's important for teenagers to be aware of the fact that nearly fifty percent of all reported rape victims are adolescents and sixty percent of all reported rapes are committed by an assailant known to the victim.

A teen council of The Center for Population Options has drawn up a list of sensible do's and don'ts for their peers. Almost all the rules indicate how much sexual etiquette has changed and how sexual etiquette can be used to protect your life. Although intended for teens, they come in handy for adults as well.

- Before going on a date find out your destination and how you are getting there and back home.
- Plan to go to places where there are other people around.
- Make sure, when you go on a date, that a brother, sister, parent, or friend knows where you are going.
- Know how to get home on your own in case it is necessary, and have enough money with you.
- Suggest a group date, if it would make you feel more comfortable.
- Don't use drugs or alcohol, which can alter your judgment or behavior.
- Don't have sex just because you feel obligated.
- Don't interpret a no as a yes.
- Date rape does happen. If it happens to you, tell somebody or call a hot line.

SCHOOL LIFE

By the time your child is a teenager you will no longer be the one making decisions about his courses or extracurricular activities at school. Your role now is to offer support, insight, and assistance whenever he needs guidance.

For a child who plans to go to college, high school can be a time of unrelenting pressure as he strives to make good grades, pass anxiety-provoking tests, and navigate nail-biting interviews. And in addition to all those academic pressures comes a new pressure of a whole different sort: the social pressure to date.

Be supportive of your teenager, refrain from nagging about college applications and interviews. That way, he will have a better chance of getting through this stage of life successfully and happily. When your high schooler is studying for those all-important exams, let others in the house know he is not to be disturbed; in this way you can let him know that you appreciate the seriousness of his work and that you will do anything you can to help him do well. If you want to become involved in his college selection, you can help by researching colleges, sending for catalogs, and filing applications. You can even go so far as to listen to or help edit his essays. But the essays must be written by him. If he cannot accomplish the application process by himself, he will certainly not be able to keep up once in college. And remember, if your child doesn't want your help, don't push.

When the time comes to interview at colleges far from home you may want to make it a family trip, remaining sensitive to the needs of the teenager, who may be anxious about the whole ordeal. Give him a private hotel room, budget permitting, and enjoy this time together—it may be one of the last little outings you will take as a family before he leaves home. It can be an exciting experience and one in which all of you will learn about a new place, a new school. Of course, if your child wants to visit nearby colleges on his own, there's no reason for him not to. Sometimes students prefer to visit schools with an aunt, uncle, or close adult friend.

PAID WORK

At fourteen a child is legally eligible to get working papers, which can be applied for at your local high school. Working papers will allow him to be employed in most fields, although he is still not old enough to work in restaurants that serve liquor.

Some boys and girls will find babysitting for younger siblings or children in the neighborhood a great way to make money. Others, however, will prefer delivering papers, mowing lawns, or tutoring. By the time your child is sixteen or seventeen he should be ready to get his first "real" job.

Some parents expect a teenager to get a job after school and on weekends to help pay for college or to contribute to the family living expenses. Other parents prefer that their child concentrate on his schoolwork and try to get by on his allowance. While it may be true that an after-school job can add stress to a teenager's life, it is also true that it is a giant step toward adulthood and independence. Gainful employment can give a teen the kind of self-confidence and sense of self-respect that is not taught in a classroom.

If you have a family business, you may want to hire your teenager in some capacity. Make it official, with a regular salary and performance evaluations. Try to keep the on-the-job relationship as professional as possible.

Of course, if money is not a prerequisite, your child may want to volunteer his services to a community project or some other worthy cause.

Some psychologists believe that in order to be a true learning experience—a genuine experiment in independence and self-sufficiency—the job a teenager takes must be one he decides upon himself. What you can do is help him focus by talking to him about what kind of work he wants to do. Help him decide on a field, give him insight into what to expect at interviews and on the job. You may also prepare him for the possibility that the job may not work out or that the added pressures may affect his schoolwork. Let him know that it's perfectly permissible to leave a job provided he gives reasonable notice.

Once your child has a job the question of what he will do with his money arises. Some parents believe that his earnings are his to spend in whatever way he chooses. Others use his income as a means of teaching him about budgeting and expenses. And yet others want him to save the money for college. Some parents have found that matching their child's savings provides good incentive. It all depends on your family's beliefs, financial status, the desires of your teenager, and how grown up he is.

SOCIAL LIFE

The social life of a teenager is probably the most important part of her existence. Who are her friends? Which clique does she fit into? Which parties is she invited to? Or, more important, which is she not invited to? Whom does she date? (See "Dating and Sexuality" earlier in "The Teenager" section.) These are matters of teenage life and death. Though your daughter's peers may have more sway over her than you, the values you taught her early in life should carry her safely through these necessary experiments in freedom.

FRIENDS Teenagers can be so contrary that, if you voice disapproval of any of your daughter's friends, you often succeed only in cementing the friendship. Though it may be difficult to see your child spending time with people who you believe will threaten her good values, your best course of action is not to attack but to counterattack. That means stepping up your own influence. Increase the amount of time you spend with your teenager: take her out to dinner, talk to her about your life, your job, your own teenage years. Make a real effort to communicate and forge a new relationship with her, one that recognizes her emerging maturity. You will probably find you enjoy her undivided attention as much as she will yours. Many responsible teenagers temporarily fall in with an odd or negative crowd. It's something they almost always grow out of. If the group's behavior runs toward the life-threatening—doing drugs, driving recklessly, having indiscriminate unsafe sex—it's best to seek professional help.

The teenage years are a time of extremely intense and binding friendships. It's a time when your son's or daughter's best friend may come to seem like part of your family. You may find that you have an extra body at the dining-room table and even on family trips. If you like the friend, the situation can be quite rewarding: your child will spend more time at home and you can keep an eye on her activities. She may also behave more warmly toward family members in front of her friend. You must, however, be careful to stay in contact with the other child's family, who may feel slighted by their child's new affections. Assure them that you enjoy her company and compliment them on the good job they've done raising her. You may even want to invite them to join you at a meal or some social activity.

If, on the other hand, *your* child has done the "adopting" of another family, try not to feel rejected. Realize this is just a stage. Refrain from criticizing the new family—even if their standards of behavior are far below yours. Instead, make sure that your home is a friendly, inviting, and safe place that welcomes your child and all her friends—

at all times. And try to encourage your child and her friend to divide their time between the two houses. If your child has a marked preference for her friend's house, stay cordial with the parents, even if you are weary of hearing from your child how incredibly great they are. You may also want to find out from your child what another family may be doing that impresses her and use this as a learning experience. Make sure your teenager pays her own way on outings and teach her to be sensitive to the other family's need for occasional time alone.

CURFEWS When your teenager goes out on a date (often teens don't formally "date" one-on-one but hang around in packs within which couples exist) she must have an agreed-upon curfew. Teenagers will stay out till the sun comes up if allowed to: they need to know their limits. You may want to talk to the parents of your child's friends to see if they will go along with you on a mutually acceptable curfew. Sometime between ten and one o'clock on a weekend or vacation night is reasonable for a sixteen- or seventeen-year-old. A ridiculously early curfew will only make your teenager doubt your trust and could lead him to resent your hold over him, causing him to rebel.

No matter what time your child is expected home, you should always know where he is going and with whom. If he's planning to be at a friend's house, he should leave you the friend's telephone number so you can call him in case of an emergency, or if he doesn't arrive home at the designated hour.

THE TEENAGER PARTY Giving a party is a big event for a teenager and a good learning experience. There will be, of course, all the usual anxieties just about everyone experiences when planning such an affair. Will everyone accept? Will they have fun? Will the food be good? If it's your teenager who is throwing the party, be helpful and understanding and don't be surprised if she suggests redecorating the entire house.

Before your child chooses a date for the party, she should make sure that no other friend is having one the same night. She can invite people by telephone or by asking them in person. However, if she sends out fill-in invitations (these can be found in stationery stores), it will make the party appear that much more festive an occasion. It's a good idea to put the time the party will end on the invitation so parents with children not old enough to drive will know when to pick them up, or at least when to expect them home. Ask your child to keep track of whom she invites and who accepts so you will know exactly how many guests to expect.

It's up to you and your teenager to decide what foods to serve at the party, based on how formal or informal an occasion it is. Under no circumstances should alcohol be served: in many states you, as host, are legally responsible if a person leaves your house intoxicated and is involved in a car accident. Nor is it ethically suitable to serve minors alcoholic beverages. If a guest arrives at the party carrying beer or slightly intoxicated, he should be asked to leave.

No matter how anxious you are to get away from the loud music or raucous voices, you must not leave the party even for a short time. While you don't want to appear intrusive, it's important for guests to be aware of the fact that there's an adult in the house. Your child may even be secretly relieved to have you present.

If you restrict the areas of the house to be used for the party, it will make it easier to clean up afterward. Your child should be responsible not only for seeing that everyone behaves well during the party but for helping with the cleaning up that follows.

You should end the party at whatever time was mentioned on the invitation. If the party is still in full swing at that time, you may want to ask your daughter to turn off the music and give her guests a nudge out the door.

DANCES AND PROMS A prom is often your child's first opportunity to practice what you've taught him about behavior in a formal setting. It is an exciting step into the adult world.

In certain cities and towns a teenager may need financial and organizational assistance from his parents in respect to attending a formal dance or prom. A girl may want a special dress and a visit to the hairdresser; a boy may need to rent or buy a tuxedo (better to rent at this age while he is still growing) and purchase flowers for his date. If he drives, he may want to borrow the family car; if not, he may need a ride. If it's cash he needs, arrange in advance against future chores or earnings.

Girls no longer wait around to be asked to a dance but often take the initiative. While this may be difficult for your daughter, it's worth taking the risk. Remember, boys have had to risk rejection for years; a girl can learn a lot about sensitivity to the male dilemma by putting herself in his shoes. If your child has someone in mind he or she'd like to invite to a dance, he should do the asking early on. It is not that unusual for a teenager to go to his (or her) prom solo. He may prefer it that way. Some teenagers even prefer to go in groups. And what's more, everyone not having a date will be hanging out together anyway.

Here are a few pointers for a teenager who is attending his or her first prom:

- About three or four months beforehand, a girl should start looking for a dress. A boy should start saving up for the big night out, budgeting the cost of the evening. Working out the financial details may mean taking an after-school job or a loan from parents. (If a girl plans to invite a boy, she should make plans to cover the expenses of the evening. Unless the boy insists, she should pay.)

- A month before the prom, plans should be made for pre-prom and after-prom parties. A girl must make an appointment with the beauty salon if she plans to get her hair or nails done for the event. If she has someone in mind she'd like to take to the prom, she should issue her invitation. A boy should ask his date now also. And he should get fitted for his tuxedo. This is the time to make transportation plans, especially if it involves renting a limousine.

- Two weeks in advance, a girl should pick up her prom dress (and after-prom party dress if there is one) and try it on to make sure it fits properly. New shoes can be worn around the house if they need breaking in. Now is a good time for the boy (or girl who wants to do so) to order flowers for his date, make dinner reservations, go over the arrangements with his date, both sets of parents, and any friends who will be involved.

- Prom day: a girl should pick up her date's boutonniere and get her hair and nails done (provided she made an appointment). A boy should pick up his tuxedo, his date's flowers, make sure he has enough cash for the evening, and confirm dinner and limousine reservations.

A boy always picks up his date at her front door. Merely honking the horn of his car outside is rude. He should ring the doorbell and say hello to his date's parents. (Teach your child to be respectful and courteous to his date's family.) If a girl is picking up a boy, she should go up to his door and introduce herself in a similar fashion.

Proms are traditionally all-night events. The dance ends late with the celebrants going to after-prom parties, then perhaps to a beach to watch the sun rise.

In some communities, prom night also includes an unsupervised group sleep-over at a hotel or someone's house. You alone can assess whether your child is ready for such a responsibility. For some teens, this will be a hilarious giant pajama party filled with laughter and pleasant memories. For others, it can be a huge experiment in peer pressure—exerted at a time when they can handle it least. Some teens live to regret that night. As a parent, do not be pressured into doing what other parents do. If you are the least bit hesitant, hold back. Your child will get over the disappointment.

VISITING A FRIEND If your teenager has been invited to visit a friend who lives some distance away, make sure she has enough money to get there and back and knows what it means to be a good houseguest. Remind her to make her own bed, help with the meals, observe the rules of the house, and see that she brings a present for her friend's parents with her. Explain to her that it is important to talk to any adults who are there and not spend all her time with her friend. She should also be reminded to write a thank-you note to the parents when she returns home.

SUBSTANCE ABUSE

Drugs, alcohol, and tobacco are substances that teenagers from all walks of life may eventually experiment with. The bad news is that many of those experimenters go on to become drug and alcohol users and abusers. The good news is that the majority don't. Though studies indicate that addiction may have genetic roots and that children of alcoholics and addicts may be at higher risk of addictions of any sort than the general population, nobody can yet predict with any certainty who will become addicted and who will not.

What *is* clear, however, is that many children learn to drink abusively at home—at the family dinner table or while watching parents down three scotches before a meal. Many see parents popping pills—a Valium here, a No-Doz there—for whatever ails them. And many are very susceptible to Madison Avenue's glamorization of addictive substances. Television and magazine ads and commercials imply that you'll have more fun, be more popular, more beautiful with every six-pack you imbibe.

Little wonder then that adolescents with very real and looming problems pick up the medicate-yourself message and run with it. Drugs and alcohol can make a self-conscious teen feel confident, handsome or beautiful, daring and carefree. Even teens well educated about the perils of drug use don't really believe their lives are in danger—because all teenagers feel they are immortal. So if you sense that your child is depressed or vulnerable to despair and anxiety, you need to reach out to him before drugs and alcohol enter his life. A nine-year-old with psychosocial adjustment problems will only become a nineteen-year-old with the same problems if he doesn't get help.

Here are some warning signals of drug and/or alcohol use:

- A change in sleeping patterns
- A change in appetite
- A change in grooming habits
- A sudden change of friends
- A dramatic drop in grade-point average
- A sudden need for money; money disappearing from around the house
- Furtiveness or excessive secrecy
- Memory loss
- More pronounced or wild mood swings
- Slurred speech, red eyes, enlarged or reduced pupils, weight loss or gain, skin problems, paleness.

Some of these symptoms may, singly and in moderation, also be indicative of normal teenage development, so study your child carefully before jumping to conclusions. There are hotlines you can call to discuss whether or not your teenager is abusing drugs or alcohol and you should make use of them.

Alateen and Narcateen are two twelve-step programs based on Alcoholics Anonymous that are specifically organized for teenagers with alcohol and drug problems. They cost nothing and can be extremely helpful to a teenager who wants to clean up his act. However, teenagers who have a troubled history, or who are resistant to the idea of giving up their addictions, may also need psychotherapy or a stay at a rehabilitation center.

Once parents confront their child's addiction problem and reach out they will find a whole community of help and support: self-help groups, therapy centers, classes, awareness programs.

In this very difficult and delicate time, do not neglect your other children. Remember that they still need your attention and love, and you certainly don't want to give them the impression that the best way to get you to notice them is to cultivate problems of their own.

CIGARETTE SMOKING Tobacco, when compared with drugs and alcohol, may not seem to be such a terrible "drug." But the fact remains that hundreds of thousands of people die every year from the resulting diseases, primarily cancer and emphysema. Many smokers start smoking in their teenage years. However, fortunately, most schools have instituted rather vigorous educational campaigns against smoking, and among many peer groups in high school smoking is now considered just plain stupid.

Studies prove, however, that parents who smoke are most likely to have children who smoke. The best way to keep your child from starting is to quit yourself. Then you can in all good conscience tell your teenager the truth: that cigarette smoking is not only dangerous to one's health and leads to lung cancer but that it's also smelly, expensive, inelegant, and unappealing. Don't allow smoking in your house or in your car.

If you find your teenager is already addicted to nicotine, you might send away to the American Cancer Society for pamphlets on the dangers of smoking and leave them in her room. Tell her how much you love her and that you don't want her to die young. Offer to help in whatever way you can. You may want to pay for a stop-smoking program and an exercise class if she tries to kick the habit.

If all else fails, you must teach your child to be responsible about her smoking habit. She must know that she cannot light up whenever and wherever she wants. She must always ask her host if she may smoke, and if there are no ashtrays around, and no one else is smoking, she should not even ask. She must not smoke during a meal, in bed (many fires are started this way), or around babies, young children, or people with respiratory problems. Smoking on the street has long been considered unattractive and remains so. Make her responsible for cleaning up her own ashtrays.

With new smoking laws going into effect each day, you will have to warn her to obey the laws as well. That means no smoking in theaters, on most airplanes, in certain hotel rooms, on the job in certain buildings, in certain restaurants.

RESPONSIBLE USE OF ALCOHOL　You can help prepare your teen for a responsible approach to alcohol by teaching him the following:

- Never feel that to be accepted by your peers you have to drink at a party.
- Avoid hard liquor. Stick to beer and wine, which have lower alcohol contents. But beware—quantities of either can still make you drunk.
- Drinking and driving don't mix. Never get in a car with someone who has been drinking.
- Never drink on an empty stomach. Food helps absorb some of the alcohol.
- If champagne is served at celebrations, one glass is sufficient. Overdoing with champagne can result in the same hangover or dangerous loss of control as comes from any other alcoholic beverage.

Once again, as with cigarette smoking, the best way to teach a child responsible behavior is by example. If you toss a few back every night to "unwind" you can bet your child will get the message and follow suit. If you drink to medicate depression, to hide from problems and reality, he will too. If you like a pre-dinner cocktail or wine with your meal, be moderate and consistent in your alcoholic intake. Older children can begin, as they do in France, with a bit of wine diluted with water. The point here is that alcohol should not be some naughty, dangerous thing that inspires curiosity and experimentation.

LETTING GO OF YOUR TEENAGER

The last of your child's teen years can be bittersweet. While it's rewarding to know you have raised your child successfully to the brink of adulthood, it is difficult to realize that now she is ready to fly. Sometimes you look forward to having the house to yourself. Other times you wonder when you do, how you will fill the void. Letting go of a child—so that she is free to make her own decisions, her own mistakes, develop her own interests and relationships—can make you feel both wistful and scared. Suddenly, or at least it seems sudden, the person you have nurtured since infancy, helped through the innumerable trials and tribulations of childhood, who turned to you for all her emotional needs will be leaving home. Some parents come to this with grace, wisdom, and a desire to meet new-found goals and challenges. Others struggle with a feeling of being left behind.

The best way to prepare for the empty nest is to start filling your own life with new interests, new friends, taking trips, and even rekindling the romance in your marriage. With an optimistic point of view, you will soon go from being the parent of a teenager to her important, trusted friend. It's in this new relationship that all your years of hard work will bear beautiful fruit.

BOOMERANG CHILDREN

The majority of young adults stop depending on their parents for financial support or housing once they finish school or marry. But today it's not uncommon for an adult child to return home, landing on his parent's doorstep with dirty laundry, books, stereo, computer, and an old jalopy to park in the driveway. Some children return home temporarily while looking for a job or apartment. Others may not have clear plans. In times of retrenchment or recession, many children return home for financial reasons—because they were laid off from a job or are in the process of switching careers.

The return home can be a positive experience—if you're both willing to make compromises. It can allow you and your child to develop an even closer, adult relationship. Although the parental urge to nurture is a natural one, it is essential that you treat your child as an adult, not as the child he once was.

Although there's no perfect solution for every family, these guidelines should help:

- Remind your boomerang child that he is once more living in your house and your rules, once again, apply. He should be expected to do his own laundry, clean his room, participate in (and contribute to) shopping and cooking.

- Charge a live-at-home adult child room and board. If he is unemployed, household chores can substitute for rent. Don't feel this is unkind. You are teaching a key survival skill: how to handle money and live within one's means. If you don't really need the money, without saying so, put it aside and give it back to him when he's on his own again.

- Set a time limit. Dependency can go on forever—and will—if you let it. Agree upon a departure date and stick to it. It could be through the summer months, until the end of the year, or two months, for example.

- Don't give your child significant amounts of money without asking for something in return.

- Finally, be supportive and empathetic to your child's situation, while at the same time encouraging his independence.

PRESERVING FAMILY TIES

When a young couple marry and start a family their responsibility to their original families doesn't end, it merely changes. This is especially true if getting married means moving out of town. Such a move signals the end of the family unit as everyone once knew it. And, when a member of the family marries, his loyalties must be expected to shift in the direction of his new spouse.

But marriage can also bring exciting new life changes and an opportunity to form new relationships and define new love bonds. A new son-in-law, for example, may share sports interests with his brother- or father-in-law; a new daughter-in-law may bring a family closer together on a regular basis by inviting everyone to her house for family dinners.

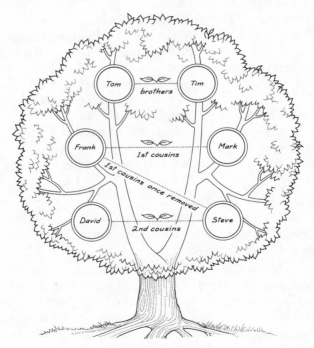

How cousins work.

COUSINS

Cousin relationships, especially when you start to talk about "once removed," can get confusing. Cousins are defined by the generation in which the relatives they have in common were born. Simply stated, the children of siblings are first cousins because they are of the same generation.

The children of first cousins are second cousins to each other because they are of the next generation. The children of second cousins are third cousins, and so on.

The child of your first cousin is your first cousin, once removed. The "removed" refers to the generation of the child, who is removed from your own generation. The child of your second cousin is your second cousin, once removed.

And remember, just because they're your cousins doesn't mean you have to adore them. Cousins, like anyone else, can be loving and wonderful or obnoxious and grating. Though you probably can't exclude them from your life, you don't have to surround yourself with them either. Pick and choose them as you would any friends—and always be as friendly as possible.

IN-LAWS

While marriage is a personal matter between two lovers, it is also the initiation of each partner into the family of the other. And in general the arrival of children tends to strengthen the ties to the in-laws. You owe it to your spouse and to your children to keep the relations with both sides of your extended family warm and friendly. This means remembering birthdays, holidays, and anniversaries with a card or a phone call, participating in family events, and being willing to help out if you are needed.

Though the problems that can occur with in-laws are the subject of hundreds of jokes, movies, and talk shows, they are, in fact, often very painful. The person caught in the middle of an antagonistic relationship between his family and his wife (or with a wife whose family dislikes him) has a definite problem on his hands. No matter whose side he takes, he'll upset—or chance alienating—someone.

But there are some possible solutions. If you sense that your in-laws are not crazy about you, don't force yourself on them. Just be as friendly and accepting as you can—to make it as easy as possible for your spouse. If you sense that they are trying to interfere in your life, talk it over with your spouse. It's important to be open about your concerns so he can try to help you work out these problems.

If, on the other hand, *you* are not crazy about *your* new in-laws, remember that you don't have to feel the same way your spouse does about them. But don't try to change his point of view. He may see them as loving and caring; you may see them as controlling and neurotic. As an outsider you will inevitably have a different—and possibly more objective—perspective from those closest to them. Your best course is to attend the important family ceremonies—Christmas or Hanukkah dinner, the June reunion—as required, with a graceful attitude. If you are not being asked to see your in-laws too frequently, or for too long at any one time, you can certainly get through periodic visits. If you are forced into frequent contact and can't take it, devise acceptable excuses. But don't stop your spouse from attending family occasions or taking your children. That is simply his choice.

And be sure never to bad-mouth your in-laws to your spouse or your children. Not only do children have an uncanny way of repeating things they've overheard—and at just the most inopportune moment—but your relationship with your in-laws might suddenly take a turn for the better and you don't want negative comments to come back and haunt you. Besides, it's only fair to let children make up their own minds about their grandparents. You may see their grandmother as someone who tries to run everyone else's lives. Your children may see her as a warm, lovable person.

If you do like your in-laws and you *do* become close to them, refrain from discussing with them any shortcomings of your spouse. No matter how justified your complaints may be, their loyalty will always lie with their child. And they may even take your complaints as criticism of them.

If you are the parent in-law who doesn't like your new son's or daughter's spouse you have two viable options. Act like an adult and grin and bear it—as you can bet the new family addition is trying to with you. Or maintain a separate relationship with your child. Arrange to see him alone for occasional lunches or dinners. And give your daughter-in-law an easy out. Make it clear to your son that, while you welcome his new spouse at every family event, you know she is *very* busy and you'll forgive her if she can't always make it.

A parent in-law who tries to pressure her child's mate into liking her, or who tries to turn her child against his wife, will in the end only be blamed no matter what happens. If you really love your child, make sure his interests, his happiness—at least as he sees them for the time being— are paramount.

UNMARRIED CHILDREN COMING TO VISIT

What about an overnight visit from your *unmarried* child who is living with someone? If parents feel uncomfortable with unmarried young adults sleeping together, then they may put them in separate rooms. Though there is no absolute rule, no one answer, it is clear that any host and hostess, even if they are the parents of one of the visitors, have a right to set the rules in their own house.

A child should accede gracefully to her parents' preferences while she is a guest in their house even though she may think her parents are horribly stuffy or old-fashioned. A child must also realize that the visit is not for more than a few days (or even just overnight), and that she will be free to return to her own life shortly.

When a child feels adamant enough to declare that she won't visit if not allowed to sleep in the same room with her boyfriend, parents must weigh the risks: alienate their child or adhere to moral principle. It is wise in such cases to consider the age of the child. The life style of an eighteen-year-old may be of more concern to a parent than the life style of one who is twenty-six. Also a child may simply be testing the parents' limits, maybe even hoping (secretly) that the parents will say no. A child may actually be responding to peer pressure and the parents' refusal could let her off the hook.

No matter which route you decide to take, it is critical that the subject be raised—and discussed—long before any guest appears on the doorstep. In the final analysis, if any one person—either a parent or child—feels very strongly and others don't, the person with the strong feelings should prevail.

THE ROLE OF THE GRANDPARENT

As all grandparents will tell you, they have the perfect arrangement: they get to give all the love and attention and don't have to do any of the disciplining. For children, grandparents can be the perfect object of love: they're the ones who bring them presents, who let them stay up past bedtime, and who never say no. If you are the parent, watching your own parents acting as grandparents may even bring about changes in your relationship with them. Now that you understand the tensions of parenthood first hand, you may be able to forgive your parents their perceived foibles and flaws.

Young children should be given a chance to get to know their grandparents. Whether the parents accomplish this with an annual visit or by weekly Sunday dinners does not matter: that depends on your geographical and emotional situation. If you live near your parents, you may want to leave the children with them occasionally, which has the added benefit of allowing you and your husband to get away alone. But don't overdo it or take for granted their kindness: grandparents are not unpaid baby-sitters.

On the other hand, if your parents are full of energy and really do want the children around, and they live nearby, you might talk with them about working out a mutually convenient childcare schedule. This might even involve money changing hands. If your parents refuse to be paid cash, you might instead buy groceries, pay utility bills, give them a generous present of some sort for a birthday, or treat them to dinner and the theater.

Above all, children must be taught to treat their grandparents with respect. Even a casual telephone call for no reason at all can make a grandparent's day. Children should address their grandparents with the appropriate name such as "Nanna" or "Grandpop" used within your family. When children call their grandparents by first names it takes some of the traditional coziness out of the relationship, although some grandparents may prefer this form of address. (Not everyone is thrilled with this generational milestone.)

Because older people have less tolerance for the chaos and noise that children bring, you might, if you are paying an extended out-of-town visit to your parents, give them a few evenings to themselves. Take your family out for pizza, bowling, or a movie. You might even take the children on an overnight camping trip or to a nearby historic site. A little break will leave both grandparents and grandchildren feeling renewed and excited about each other.

Children should follow the rules of the grandparents' house when visiting, no matter how unfamiliar to them those rules may be.

One of the saddest consequences of divorce is that many grandparents are dragged into the animosity and resentment that prevail. There are many cases of grandparents resorting to lawsuits to secure visitation rights with their grandchildren. Divorce is hard enough on children without their losing their grandparents as well. No matter what your private feeling about your ex-in-laws may be, you must try not to let it influence the relationship your children have with your former spouse's parents. Children of a divorce should understand that, whatever the new living arrangements, their mother will always be their mother and their father their father, and they should be assured that both sets of grandparents will always be there for them.

CARING FOR AN AGING PARENT

Though the miracles of modern medicine can prolong our lives significantly, it doesn't necessarily prolong their quality. As a result, more and more of us will find ourselves in the position of having to care for a parent or relative who is elderly and infirm. The strong, vital parent who once cared for and comforted you suddenly needs you to lean on. But just as he helped you through childhood, you are responsible for doing all you can to help him with the difficulties of old age.

If your parent suffers a catastrophic illness or physical incapacity, he may need your help to negotiate the maze of medical care and the tangle of insurance reimbursement that follow. In order to make things run more smoothly, siblings, if there are any, should convene a family meeting and decide together what to do. One child should be elected to handle administrative duties, another to handle medical care. Be sure that the child who lives nearest the parent does not get stuck with the largest portion of the responsibility; divide tasks as equally as possible and according to each person's strengths.

In your meeting you will want to discuss the issue of a "living will." Some older people who have already suffered a stroke or some other similarly incapacitating event may already have one, but most do not. This document, which may be obtained from almost any hospital, various right-to-die groups, or be drawn up by a lawyer, addresses the patient's right to die a natural death and the right not to be resuscitated. The document ensures that the hospital and its doctors will take no heroic measures to prolong an unsatisfactory life. Unless your parent is mentally incapacitated, he must sign his own living will. For that reason, and to ensure that he gets the amount of medical care he wants, you must sit down with him before the last moments and discuss his wishes—if he doesn't bring it up himself.

You will also want to discuss with him the course of treatment he prefers. Which nursing home would best suit his needs? Or would he prefer home care? Is that solution practical? In addition, you will need to talk about his financial situation. Will his insurance pay for round-the-clock nursing? (Some organizations, such as Cancercare, will provide home service free to patients with a terminal diagnosis.) Will you have to chip in?

And then of course there's the issue of his will. Does he have one? When was it last updated? (It should be revised every seven years or when the tax law changes.) Does he need to make any alterations? (If you don't have the money for legal fees, you can use one of the prepared will forms available at a local stationery store.) What about estate and inheritance taxes? An accountant can help you plan the most efficient and money-saving way to transfer assets gradually.

And what about his final wishes? Does he want to be cremated? Does he want a religious ceremony or just a gathering of friends? Where does he want to be buried? Macabre as it sounds, many elderly parents have already thought this one out and will be able to tell you exactly what their wishes are.

If your parent is widowed or divorced, you may even want to raise the subject of having him come to live with you. Though this may be easier for you, in terms of finances, than a nursing home, there are bound to be some adjustment problems. Not only will the old parent/child roles be reversed, but you will be thrust into a new kind of intimacy. Ideally, an elderly parent who comes to live with a child should have his own bedroom, sitting room, kitchen, bathroom, and separate entrance. (Some people adapt the area above a garage for this purpose.) This type of arrangement will give both of you the greatest degree of independence and privacy. If you allow your parent to pay rent, or pick up the bill for groceries, it may help him feel more a participant and less a burden. If, on the other hand, your parent cannot afford to help out financially, don't bring up the subject. If you don't have enough money yourself, ask siblings to pitch in.

If separate living quarters are not possible, be very careful about bringing a new, very dependent person into your household. It can create the same sorts of problems as bringing home a new baby. Who will cook for him on a regular basis? Who will drive him to the doctor? shopping? Who will clean his room and change his bed and do his laundry?

Will the burden fall on an already overextended working mother? Or on an already resentful spouse? Be careful to consider all such issues.

If your widowed or divorced parent decides to remain in his own home or to have a paid companion, you should call or visit your parent often to make sure he's getting the kind of care and attention he deserves. Treat the companion with professional respect; speak up only if you suspect something has gone awry. But don't be surprised if the companion is unhappy with your parent's behavior and asks you to intervene. You may be the only one your parent will heed. Invite the companion to family dinners if you wish, and include him on your gift-giving list.

You can make a parent's transition to a nursing home easier by showing up for frequent visits. Take the time to talk to the staff and ask how your parent is doing; some people adjust better than others to institutional life. If your parent is having difficulty, ask if there is anything you can do to help, such as moving him to a private room (and paying for it), or, if allowed, bringing a few pictures from home to hang on the walls of his room. You might want to set up regular appointments with a physical or psychological therapist. A visit to the masseuse, a relaxation specialist, a hairdresser, or a family counselor can also help.

A DEATH IN THE FAMILY

A death in the family can be devastating whether the one who dies is an elderly parent or a stillborn child. The shock and grief may go well beyond your verbal ability to describe. Words may be difficult for even your best friends as well. Though many will want to help you through this time, they may feel suddenly incapable and retreat. Or they may be trying to give you room to deal with your emotions. Do not be disappointed in them. Most will resurface after a time or after a small gesture from you indicating that the time is right.

If you are fortunate, the majority of your friends will be able to rise to the occasion and respond to the death with sensitivity and dignity. They may write letters of remembrance and comfort, or bring food to your house, and they should be thanked for their kindness in writing. Friends may also offer to help with child care or lend you a shoulder to cry on. It may seem impossible to thank such a friend, but a warm note of appreciation will get the message across.

And don't be angry or embarrassed if some family member doesn't express his emotion publicly. Many people deal privately with their grief when they are alone. Surprisingly, a death often brings out the humanity in people—and it is one of the few occasions when many feel they can **express their warmth and affection.**

COUPLES

THE INDEPENDENT SIDE OF A COUPLE'S LIFE

Fax, phone, television, Express Mail, CNN. Our increased ability to communicate means that we now live in a true global village. And because we travel thousands of miles across country to attend the college of our choice or our job transfers us to three locations in one year, we may date or marry on a global scale as well. A man in Iowa, for example, can interview potential mates living in Russia by videocassette; a woman in California can carry on a bicoastal relationship with a man living in Washington, D.C. Gone are the days when your choice for a mate was limited to the girl or boy next door! Gone, as well, is the homogeneous family unit. Today partners come together from across the country, from across the world. As a result, marriage is more likely than ever to cut across age, culture, religion, and politics. Even those who come from relatively similar backgrounds will find that there is much adjusting to a new spouse's habits, beliefs, family, friends, and career.

Both partners will benefit if they know how to compromise, how to give and take. Celebrate your differences. Bring up your children to respect and cherish each unique contribution to the family.

THE TWO-CAREER COUPLE

Sheer economics today dictates that, in all likelihood, both partners in a marriage will have careers or some kind of regular job. Even when children come along, many couples find that both of them must work part- or full-time. Unfortunately, old cultural ideas still prevail and many men, consciously or unconsciously, expect that their wives, working or not, will do the lion's share of the housework. Even the most liberated couples may find the scales tipping in that direction. The best way to avoid the problem—which can create quite a bit of domestic strife—is first to agree on what chores need to be done and when. Then tasks can be divided up or rotated between the couple. But if you find that your housekeeping standards are very different, that you squabble over the proper way to clean silver—and you have the money—a cleaning service may be a wise investment.

Food preparation can be another potential source of friction because most Americans raised on shows like "Father Knows Best" still believe it is solely a woman's responsibility. And while many men pitch in and prepare special meals, it's the day-to-day lunches, dinners, and breakfasts that can become burdensome. Many couples have found a good division of labor in letting one partner cook and the other clean up. Dining out once in a while also offers a great change of pace. You might even want to alternate which person picks up the check. Even if the money comes out of your shared bank account, it still feels great to be "treated" to dinner.

If one person works from home the question of who is responsible for domestic chores can become further confused. This is especially true if the person with the home office is the woman. Somehow there is a tendency to forget that her job is just as real and just as important as that of the man who leaves the house each day. She should not be expected to assume a larger part of the domestic duties.

Another potential flash point in a two-career marriage is when one partner believes that his or her job is more important than the other's because of a larger salary, greater prestige, or a more advanced level of education. Mutual respect is required here and neither partner should criticize or question the other's right to work, or the job they choose. Couples should take pride in each other's work, regardless of its position in the traditional spectrum of worldly success.

Because we spend more of our time at the office than at home, it is natural that each partner will want to talk about his job over dinner or before bed. Give each other a chance to talk out problems at work, and be your partner's supporter and ally. But try not to bring the office home every night—especially if you have children. They can sense if you are in the least bit distracted.

Talk is the key to making most two-career marriages work, or any marriage for that matter. Keeping the lines of communication open may not always be easy but every effort must be made to do so. Resentments allowed to build to an explosive point will only exacerbate a problem. Sometimes a note or card slipped under a pillow before bed can initiate a potentially difficult discussion. And humor will get you more positive results than bickering or nagging.

WORKING IN DIFFERENT CITIES It's no longer a given that when a husband gets transferred to a new city his wife will pack up the children and follow. Nowadays the wife will probably have a career of her own to consider, and such a sudden disruption could mean a serious professional setback. This being the case, a couple may decide to take up two residences, working in different cities during the week and commuting on weekends and holidays to be together. Though this solution is certainly expensive (there are telephone, car, airfare bills to consider), many fast-track couples have found that not only does such an arrangement work for them but in certain instances it actually improves their marriage. It injects back into it all the romance and anticipation of dating. Of course, such an arrangement also requires extra effort. It's a good idea for a couple to talk on the telephone at least once a day, to try to spend each weekend together, and to plan to live together as a family in the near future.

Children, however, may find such an arrangement too stressful, or it may leave one parent feeling disconnected. For that reason, each situation must be considered separately. Warning: couples who don't feel truly committed may find distance makes the heart wander. Those who do not have a strong relationship may feel that they are suddenly "available."

MONEY

History has proved that there are three major areas of conflict in marriage: sex, children, and money. Though the obvious money problems that surface in a marriage usually evolve because there is too little money, sometimes having too much can also create difficulties. For instance, if one spouse makes considerably more money than the other, the less solvent partner may feel beholden to the one who makes more. Or pressure to keep up. Or perhaps the high-wage earner may feel guilty for having used mutual savings to pursue his (or her) successful career. Whatever the cause of the friction, a frank discussion is in order. If you and your spouse cannot resolve your money conflicts, you can turn to a financial adviser who specializes in these issues or, if the problem is an emotional one, a family counselor.

Marriage is more than a pooling of assets, energies, and incomes if the whole is to be greater than the sum of its parts.

DIFFERENT RELIGIONS

If you marry someone of a different religion you have two clear-cut options: keep your own faith or convert to that of your spouse. Less clear cut are: Which religion should the children of this union be brought up in? What holidays and ceremonies should the household observe? The answer, of course, is that the decision is a personal one that only you and your spouse can decide on. Regardless of the choice you make, it is essential that you respect your partner's spiritual beliefs.

From the time of the Romans, religion has divided families and nations. Fortunately, interfaith marriages succeed every day all over the world.

DIFFERENT CULTURES

Partners from widely varying cultures may come together to create a rich and interesting union, with a mix of languages, foods, and life styles. The potential problem is, however, that one partner may, consciously or unconsciously, assert his or her own cultural heritage to the near exclusion of the other. Simply stated, this is not fair. Children's names, places of worship, holidays, and vacations should reflect a blending of the two cultures. Chinese Americans, for example, may want to celebrate both the January 1 American New Year and the Chinese one in February. A man of Italian parentage who marries a woman of Japanese descent may want to teach his children the language of his ancestors. (Children pick up languages quickly and the ability to speak several languages can be an asset in life.) And it goes without saying that grandparents who are proud of their heritage will be thrilled to communicate with grandchildren in their native tongue.

In any case it is crucial that language not be allowed to divide a family. Children forced to communicate in one language with their father and in another with their mother may end up deep in conflict. And one parent is bound to feel left out. If you live in the United States, make English the official language spoken inside the home. Nothing will hold a child back more in school and business than an inability to do the all-American thing: assimilate.

YOUR SPOUSE'S FRIENDS

When you get married, you, for better or worse, also marry your spouse's friends. After all, you and your spouse come to marriage with friends you have each cultivated over the years, often from early childhood. Since loyalty is what friendship is all about, think twice before telling your husband you'd rather not see a friend of his because your personalities don't mesh, or because he's not particularly friendly toward you. Not unlike marriage itself, think of this as a give-and-take situation where compromises must be made. What you can do is see his friend occasionally with your spouse, and at other times they can get together on their own, for lunch, a game of golf, or whatever.

Unquestionably, it's important to keep up with close friends after marriage. A husband and wife can't be all things to each other, nor should they be. Other relationships only strengthen the bond by allowing a couple to breathe, to express themselves as individuals.

THE SINGLE LIFE

LIVING ALONE

Provided you have the financial means, living alone is often more gratifying than sharing space with a roommate. It gives you a greater sense of freedom, as you are able to watch whatever television program you choose to when you choose to, receive telephone calls in the middle of the night, or have friends over when you want to—all without worrying about invading the privacy of someone living with you.

If you are looking for your own place, you should take extra care in finding a section of town that is not too isolated and one that is considered relatively safe. In a large city, it is best, until you have a feel for the various neighborhoods, to find an apartment in a building with a doorman or some sort of security guard. And always be alert when entering the building itself. If you live in a building without a doorman, have your keys readily available so you can slip in quickly. Never, ever hold open the door for a stranger or feel the least bit rude about closing the door in his face, even if it's someone who is well dressed. If it turns out that the stranger is a building tenant you have never seen before, he should be grateful to know you have the sense not to let someone unknown to you into the building.

If you live in a building with an elevator, don't enter it with a stranger if his behavior appears odd or if you're suspicious of his motives. If you are already in the elevator when he appears, step out—or if the doors are closing, push the button for the next floor and get out there.

If you ever have the feeling that you are being followed home, cross to the other side of the street and try to determine if you are still being followed. If so, move to the middle of the street, where there's a chance of stopping a passing car, and walk there until you have an opportunity to call for help or are able to duck into a store or other potentially safe place. Many single women living in urban areas have found it helpful to take a course in self-defense. It may be a good idea for men to do so as well.

ENTERTAINING

THE ROLE OF THE HOSTESS As a single person living alone, you'll enjoy entertaining from time to time, whether it's at a dinner for six or cocktails for sixty. In either case, you want to give special attention to your guest list, bearing in mind that it's more fun if you invite people with diverse interests. After all, variety is the spice of life! If you're inviting more people for dinner than you can accommodate at one table, you can have a buffet. Take ornaments and magazines off tables so guests will have some space to put their plates or glasses on. And the menu can be as simple as you like. People don't judge a dinner by the elaborateness of the food or the number of courses served. If you have a good friend, you can ask him if he'd be willing to help you out by acting as co-host, perhaps making drinks for the guests or bringing out food from the kitchen.

THE ROLE OF THE GUEST If you are invited to a dinner party, never ask to bring a date along. A hostess puts together her guest list based on the number of people she can accommodate and who she wants to have at her party, often asking a single man or woman to balance the number of men and women at the party. If, however, you are living with someone, and the hostess does not know this, you can either go alone, or you can call her to say, "I'd love to come, but I'm now living with someone. I realize you may not have room for an extra person." It's then up to her to say she'd be delighted to have you bring your live-in along or that she's tight for space but will invite both of you to another party she has. If it happens to be a cocktail party you're invited to and the hostess is a close friend, there's no reason not to ask if you can bring along your date for the evening.

Essentially, women no longer need an escort to attend a social event.

You may feel more confident with one in tow, but once you've been to a few parties on your own, you won't give it a second thought. One advantage to going places alone is that it allows you to arrive and leave whenever you choose to. Also, being on your own, you are apt to make more of an effort to meet new people.

(If you'd like to know more about giving parties, issuing invitations, etc., see Chapter 2.)

DATING

For single people of all ages who would like to make new friends, there are now options available that go way beyond the typical singles bars. By joining a social club or volunteer organization, or by taking a course, you have the opportunity to meet all sorts of interesting people. For the newly separated, divorced, or widowed, there are community support groups to turn to as well as organizations such as Parents Without Partners. While not created for the purpose of match-making, these groups can help you deal with feelings of insecurity and loneliness. By reaching out, you will meet people going through the same upheaval as you are going through, and a few may eventually become good friends.

The responsibility of asking someone out on a date has traditionally fallen on the shoulders of the man. But today, anyone can do the inviting. All it takes is courage, self-confidence, and practice. While it's true that whoever does the asking runs the risk of rejection, it's also true that being too afraid to ask may cause you to miss out on many of life's pleasures.

The best way for a man or woman to ask someone out is with a clear plan in mind. Present it up-front: "I have tickets to a play next week and was wondering if you might want to come and see it with me." Or, "There's this new Italian restaurant I've been dying to try. Would you like to join me?" Invitations phrased this way are less direct and the rejections (if they come) easier to rationalize than if you'd come right out and said, "Would you like to go out with me on Saturday night?"

Asking a man out, however, may be particularly difficult if you grew up expecting to be the passive partner. If you find it too nerve-wracking to telephone a man or ask him out face to face, try dropping him a note saying, "Dear Jack, I have tickets to the basketball game Wednesday and thought you might like to go. Please give me a call." Or, "I was wondering if you might be free this weekend to have dinner at my place?" Or you might instead want to leave a message on his answering machine at home or call him at his office at lunchtime when you figure he'll be out. You may feel better if you know he has time to think over your invitation before giving an answer.

The conventional dinner-and-a-movie still makes sense for a first date; it gives just about the right amount of time for conversation and something to talk about after the movie.

A man usually picks a woman up at her house, unless it's a date arranged through a dating service or a personal ad, in which case it's better to meet at a restaurant. If money is a problem, you can always take in a museum and have a snack afterward, rather than lunch or dinner and a movie. Other options include a lecture or band concert, ice skating, or playing tennis. Or you might consider going to a public beach or taking a walk in a state park.

The custom of a man *always* paying for a woman's meal is no longer the case. While much depends on the particular circumstance, certainly on the first date the person who does the inviting pays the restaurant bill. On a future date, it's up to the couple to decide who pays or whether they split the bill. (For further information on a woman paying, see "Who Pays the Restaurant Bill" under "Money—the Human Aspect" later in this chapter.)

A man should offer to see his date home, either by walking or driving her home. Or he should escort her to her car, bus, or train, or see her into a taxi.

As life becomes more harried and complex, more and more single people who wish to find a mate are turning to the various dating resources. These may be personal ads in a local magazine or newspaper or one of the many organized dating services. If you choose a dating service, always select one with care. As with any service, word of mouth is the best recommendation. Check with friends to see what their experiences have been. If you're at all skeptical about the service you're interested in, call your local better-business bureau and see if any charges have been lodged against them. And once you've decided on a dating service, be sure you understand their fees before signing up. That means reading the fine print on the contract.

When the dating service calls to say they have someone for you to meet, be realistic in your expectations. As with any first date, don't assume you'll be with the perfect person, but rather someone you may enjoy getting to know. In particular, if you are a woman, it's best to meet the person in a public place such as a restaurant or a club, instead of at your apartment. This is especially important if you live alone. And it is wise to be careful about giving out your telephone number and address. For that reason, many services make introductions only on a first-name basis. For security reasons as well, don't accept a car or taxi ride home until at least the second date.

If you're simply not interested in the person you've met, be polite and considerate of his feelings. Do not bolt from the table or climb out the powder-room window. Stay until the end of the meal and then say kindly but firmly something like "I've enjoyed meeting you very much. It was nice of you to take the time for lunch but I must be going now." If he suggests getting together again and you know you don't want to, say so, but as kindly as possible. Remember, you are rejecting the person. Try to put yourself in his shoes, imagining what it must feel like. Still it is far kinder to be honest than to raise the hopes of someone you have no intention of having a relationship with.

If you feel the person you've met would be a good match for a friend of yours, you can tell this to your friend, and if she likes the idea, arrange for the two of them to get together.

When you're single again

When you're divorced Today, divorce can happen to anyone, at any social or economic level. It is nearly always a sad affair, especially when there are children involved. And the repercussions of divorce often go way beyond the family itself—touching relatives, friends, even people you work with.

News of a divorce tends to spread quickly among friends and colleagues, so there is no reason to announce it formally. It would be wise, however, to inform close relatives and friends who may have been aware of the separation that divorce is imminent. Deciding whether or not to tell business acquaintances or casual social friends is a personal decision.

On a personal level, the two people who divorce will naturally suffer feelings of failure, loneliness, insecurity, and sometimes even depression. For that reason divorce is the time when really good friends should offer as much support and love as possible and when family members should try to be helpful and non-judgmental. When someone tells you about his divorce, aside from showing concern and sympathy, you may want to ask if there is anything you can do to be of help. An outpouring of excessive sympathy, however, can be upsetting. And don't say something tactless like, "Oh, that's too bad, I always thought you had the perfect marriage."

If a recently separated couple are invited to a party—the hostess not being aware of the situation—they may decide to go as a couple. If, however, they would feel uncomfortable being there together, one or the other may accept alone and make an excuse for the other, or both may decline the invitation by citing a previous engagement.

After a divorce, a woman will have to decide whether or not she wants to keep her ex-husband's name or go back to using her maiden name. If there are children involved, it makes sense for a woman to have the same last name as they do. A woman who keeps her ex-husband's name is addressed as Mrs. or Ms. Mary Smith.

When a spouse dies Losing a spouse to death is easily one of life's most crushing blows. Suddenly, the person who has meant the most to you over the years is no longer there. Even if you were married for only a short time, contemplating life on your own is difficult. Because family and friends can be enormously helpful and supportive at a time like this, you should not hesitate to call on them for comfort and advice.

For the majority of people, there are several stages of mourning, which include varying degrees of denial, despair, anger, sorrow, yearning for the deceased, coping, and, finally, acceptance. However, in some cases, time is not the healer we wish it was. If you find yourself unable to move beyond the first few stages of mourning, several sessions with a counselor may prove beneficial. Or you may find it comforting to join a support group that helps people deal with death. There you'll meet men and women who are also in the process of working through their grief. You can share your experiences, console one another, and at the same time make new friends.

One of the first steps you must take as a widow (or widower) is to cancel your husband's credit cards, driver's license, and other credentials held in his name. Taking charge of business matters and showing responsibility for your day-to-day affairs is a healthy sign as it indicates that you are on your way to accepting your spouse's death.

There is no particular time frame for disposing of your husband's personal effects. Many women find it comforting to see their husband's clothes hanging in the closet next to theirs for quite some time. Others find such reminders painful. When you are emotionally ready to take on the task of clearing out clothes and other personal belongings, you'll want to ask your children and grandchildren what they might like to have. And think about giving some personal mementos to a few of your husband's special friends. It will mean a great deal to them. But be cautious about giving away things too quickly: you don't want to regret your actions later. Before making any major life changes, like selling your house, it is always advisable to wait at least a year. When you have a more positive attitude toward life and see a ray of light in the future, things may look entirely different.

Once the funeral is behind you, you will need to get on with your life. Of course, there's nothing like having a job to take your mind off your loss and to occupy your time. If you don't have a job to go to, find some other way to keep busy and productive. If you belong to a church or synagogue, you can get involved with one of the many volunteer programs. There you will find not only spiritual solace but a sense of usefulness and fulfillment. There are other options, too. You might think about being a docent at a museum, helping out at your local library, or reading to the blind. Exercise is also always good therapy. It not only makes you feel healthy, but it helps to alleviate stress. You might think about taking up a sport you once played or even learn a new one.

There is no longer a designated mourning period which at one time every widow/widower went through. It is entirely up to you as to when you feel ready to accept social invitations. If at first you find it too difficult to be with couples, you can instead see one friend at a time for lunch or dinner. After a suitable period of mourning, the length of which only you can decide on, there is no reason not to remove your wedding ring if you want to and place it with any other valuables you have. This signifies that you are ready to move on to the next stage of your life.

When and if you remarry, your friends should not question your loyalty to your late husband. For, in fact, marriage—providing it doesn't come too closely on the heels of loss—may instead be a validation of the happiness and security that were so closely woven into the marriage.

OLDER PEOPLE LIVING TOGETHER

For various reasons having to do with finances and social acceptability, many older couples (whether single, divorced, or widowed), may decide to live together without getting married. Sometimes the grown children of either partner will resist the idea, finding the concept of a parent "moving in" with another person disturbing. Granted, your children have the right to disagree with you, but be firm in your right to the pursuit of your own happiness. If they don't want to see you with your partner around, invite them for a separate lunch or dinner outside the house, or meet them for a play or social event. Let them see how happy your new living situation has made you.

If you live with someone who has children who don't approve of you, allow him to maintain separate relationships with his children. Do not get in the middle of what can easily become a showdown of choices— between you and his children. Children who are more tolerant of a parent living with someone can smooth the transition by welcoming the new person into the family and including him in holiday plans and other family events.

PERSONAL APPEARANCE

No matter how much you say or believe you dress to please yourself, your appearance and the clothes you wear tell the world a lot about you. In fact, your appearance is what makes the first real impression when you walk into a room. What counts more than the clothes you wear, which in this day and age can be more a matter of personal rather than dictated style, is how well groomed you appear. If you are neat, clean, and pleasant-smelling it reflects not only your own sense of self-worth and self-esteem but your awareness of those around you. Good grooming and proper hygiene are everyday musts.

Grooming refers to the way in which you care for your body. And you should always have the highest standards. No one likes to look at—or live with—someone who has the air of having just crawled out of bed.

Hair, no matter what style, should always be clean and well cut. Men and women who color their hair should make sure to keep the roots recolored regularly. Any over-the-counter dandruff shampoo used regularly will keep hair flake-free. Men, unless they are affecting the "five-day stubble" Don Johnson look, should be sure their faces are clean shaven, their beards and mustaches neatly clipped. Women who choose to shave their legs and underarms should be sure to do so regularly, and to apply a moisturizing lotion to the legs afterward to keep them smooth. Both men and women should always use a deodorant.

Both sexes should pay attention to the care and cleanliness of their fingernails. Ragged cuticles and bitten, ripped-up nails are ugly. Men need only use a nail clipper and file to keep nails even and trimmed, although many salons offer male manicures—a cleaning, a clipping, an attractive buffing. Women who use nail polish should keep their nails in perfect condition, filling in chips when necessary. All nails should be of equal length. If you have long nails and one breaks off and cannot be replaced, the rest must be trimmed as well. False fingernails, now in natural or pale colors, or the newest glue-on "tips," which can be applied in a nail salon, are the fast modern approaches to great-looking hands.

Women who wear open-toed shoes in the summer should pay special attention to the look of their feet and toenails. A simple weekly cleaning, a once-over with a pumice stone, and a cuticle and nail trim will keep them in good shape. Once a month have a professional pedicure.

BEING NEATLY DRESSED

Almost as important as the grooming of your body is the grooming of your clothes. Be sure shirts, blouses, pants, jackets, and coats have all their buttons or hooks and eyes and the zippers work. Be sure there are no unsightly stains on your clothes. Make sure clothes are neatly pressed and that hemlines are even. Inspect stockings and socks for holes before putting them on. Neither socks nor stockings should bag. Be alert for any possible foot or shoe odor. Talcum powder sprinkled into shoes before wearing will keep feet not only dry and refreshed but also sweetly scented. Pet hair should be removed with a lint-removing brush before you walk out the door each morning.

GOOD POSTURE

Your posture—the way you stand or sit—also indicates to the outside world how you feel about yourself. If you walk with your shoulders hunched, head lowered, eyes cast to the floor, it conveys—either correctly or not—that you are shy, or timid, or don't have much in the way of self-esteem. If you sit up straight, shoulders back, chest out, eyes forward, meeting the world head on, others will perceive you as someone who is confident, with a healthy self-image and lots of self-respect. In addition, if you walk with a self-assured stride rather than shuffling along or rolling your feet on their edges, it indicates that you have a positive outlook.

Proper sitting posture is as important—for your image as well as for your overall health—as standing straight. Many of the new ergo-dynamically designed office chairs with special lumbar rolls and seats that tilt backward and forward are made to help you maintain the proper sitting position—spine straight, feet flat on the ground, head up and forward.

GOOD PUBLIC BEHAVIOR

There are, of course, some common courtesies that no one should ever ignore.

- Gum should never be chewed, or disposed of, in public. If you must get rid of it, bring a paper napkin or tissue to your mouth and spit the gum out like a pit; fold the paper up and toss it into a wastebasket.
- Always cover your mouth with your hand when you yawn.
- If you sneeze in public, cover your mouth and say, "Excuse me."
- Excuse yourself if you hiccup or your stomach rumbles.
- Curlers should never be worn in public, and it shouldn't be necessary today when there are so many types of quick electric rollers at your disposal.
- Toothpicks should not be used in public, ever.

COSMETIC SURGERY

While cosmetic surgery came into its own generations ago (with the nose job), face lifts, eyelid tucks, and implants, as well as liposuction, are rapidly becoming an accepted way of life for those who want to give a fresh look to their appearance and who have the money to do so. People who have cosmetic surgery, and this is particularly true of those who have face lifts, are often thought of as vain, even though getting rid of excess skin is no different from getting rid of excess body pounds, a physical improvement readily approved of. Aside from wanting to feel better about your appearance, there may be practical reasons for having a face lift—for example, looking younger may be a distinct advantage in your business life.

When contemplating any form of cosmetic surgery, it's crucial to find a skilled plastic surgeon who is board-certified. The best way to find such a person is through word of mouth. Your doctor may know someone he can recommend, as may a friend who had a similar operation and is happy with the way it turned out. You may want to confer with a number of surgeons so you can evaluate different approaches and techniques. But, when it comes to talking about the price tag for your operation, make no compromises. You'll only be shortchanging yourself if you do. Perhaps the soundest advice to give anyone signing up for cosmetic surgery is to have realistic expectations. If you are unrealistic in this sense, you are almost certain to be less than satisfied with the results.

Whether or not you go public with your procedure is up to you, although people today are less reticent in this respect than in the past. If you plan to have a face lift and want to keep it under wraps, be circumspect as to whom you tell. While friends you take into your confidence should know enough to be discreet about such a personal matter, it's still a good idea to make your wishes for privacy known when you give them the news.

HOW TO DRESS

Dressing has become a matter of personal style to which innumerable magazines and books have been dedicated. It is an individual decision whether you want to keep up with the trends and wear what's completely fashionable or stay with traditional looks. Most people choose something in between. Whatever you decide, there are some basics to remember.

No matter how wealthy a person is, he or she almost always needs a clothing budget. Whether this means buying two new expensive designer suits a season or two new pairs of jeans a year, it's best to make a realistic budget and try to stick to it. Hundreds of dollars can be wasted on impulsive buys that will just hang in the closet and never be worn. Try to develop a wardrobe that grows from season to season, year to year, has a color scheme that works with your life style, and flatters your figure. Give clothes to a charity if they haven't been worn after four seasons.

WOMEN'S CLOTHING It can be fairly said that anything goes in women's dress today. Country clothes have become city clothes; dresses, skirts, and pants have become interchangeable, and the very fashionable wear evening fabrics during the day. Nonetheless, there are some basic do's and don'ts. For instance, a woman who wears short skirts should be careful about crossing her legs in public, the skirt may ride up too high.

Blue jeans: Though blue jeans have broken all the dressing conventions and scaled the heights right into evening wear, generally jeans are still best for knockaround. This is true especially if they are patched, ripped, or well worn. If blue jeans are part of your overall dressing style, you may want to invest in two pairs: one for everyday use and one that stays pressed and fresh for evening. These "good" jeans must be dressed up with attractive shoes, an evening blouse, and/or jacket. Only in the most sophisticated cities can expensive designer jeans make it to a black-tie event—but they do. Before you attempt this look you must know exactly what you're doing and have a personal style that can carry it off. Otherwise, it's best to leave even the nicest pair of jeans for more casual affairs.

A few restaurants may still have the same restrictions against jeans as they do against shorts.

Gloves: Gloves were once de rigueur for white-tie affairs, with evening wear, for church, or for debutante teas and dances. Today they are worn as fanciful accessories whenever one wishes. There is no right or wrong time to wear gloves. And they now come in every length and fabric imaginable.

Older women who were brought up to wear gloves as part of a traditional costume may continue to do so if it makes them feel comfortable.

Each fall be sure to inspect all outerwear gloves for signs of wear and tear. Mend all torn or opened fingertips.

Fur coats: The question of fur has become politicized. In some areas of the country, anyone who wears fur will be subjected to insults and barbs from passing strangers who consider it their duty to make their politics known. In many cities, anti-fur activists have splashed fur wearers with red dye in order to discourage them. And often it's worked. One sees fewer and fewer fur wearers on city streets today.

Whether or not you wear fur is a completely individual decision.

If you do want to wear a fur coat, hat, stole, you may not want to wear it to the office, however. Some people think of fur as a genuine status symbol, a sign that you've arrived; but for just as many others it represents self-indulgence. And not all your coworkers will be able to afford a fur. Many corporate women, especially those on their way up the organizational ladder, leave their furs at home because they fear such signs of affluence and success will alienate the workers below them.

If the fur is attractive and well kept, it may be worn on any other occasion—from a casual walk in the country to a funeral (as long as the fur is dark colored) or a black-tie event. Of course, there are some women who choose to wear their furs on formal occasions only.

Keep in mind, too, that fake fur has come such a long way since it was invented that in most circles it's a perfectly acceptable, and politically correct, alternative. Fake fur is no longer a poor man's substitute for the real thing.

Jewelry: Like fur, jewelry was once something you wore only on special occasions. But today people invest in a few pieces of jewelry they can wear all the time—or nearly all the time. The feeling that good jewelry belongs hidden away in a vault seems to have changed.

The old rules about not mixing gold with silver or old with new or real with fake (or faux) jewelry have also relaxed. Women now mix and match whatever they like.

Jewelry in the office is the only exception to the modern free-for-all attitude. In a business milieu, jewelry should be carefully chosen so as not to draw too much attention to the wearer or to the jewels themselves. Lots of clanky, jangly necklaces or bracelets are highly inappropriate and may give the impression that you are more interested in fashion than in the business at hand. Unless you work in the fashion, advertising, or movie industry, big dangling earrings are inappropriate as well. Again, they may appear frivolous. Choose small, attractive pieces for work and wear them consistently. Save more flamboyant pieces for leisure hours.

Hats: Though hats are no longer mandatory—even in most churches or synagogues—they still play an important role in a wardrobe. The current vogue for baseball-type caps, in fact, requires some discussion. A baseball cap should never be worn inside. Period!

Black tie: In some conservative parts of the country "Black tie" on an invitation may still mean a floor-length dress for women. But in most regions it now means a dress or attractive evening suit of any length or style. Tuxedo pants, fancy culottes, or pajama-style trousers are also acceptable in most sophisticated settings.

MENSWEAR As with women's wear, the rules for menswear have loosened up considerably. Men are gaining more and more freedom when it comes to nonbusiness dress.

The business suit: The dark, neatly tailored business suit may come in any range of styles and looks. Each industry—in each different part of the country—has a subtle dress code, however. It may be appropriate for a banker in Chicago to wear a double-breasted suit with suspenders, whereas in Idaho the same clothing might be judged too flashy. In order to know what's appropriate, follow your boss's lead or the lead of one of the men above you. What they wear and what they avoid will give you the best sense of what is and isn't expected.

In any case, keep business suits quiet and subtly patterned—either solids or pinstripes or subtle checks and tweeds. You don't want what you're wearing to distract from or interfere with the business you're doing. When in doubt, err on the side of the conservative look, which is always appropriate.

Ties: Likewise, on the job your ties should not shout or scream about your fashion sense. Look for subtle patterns that give a bit of color but don't overwhelm. Save those funky ties for more casual dressing times.

Bow ties are appropriate for anyone who wishes to wear them. They may, however, cause you to be perceived as a bit professorial.

Ascots are a great way for men, young or old, to add a bit of color to an informal shirt. In some areas of the country an ascot is perceived as being an affectation.

Going without a tie is extremely casual. Be sure the restaurant or the event you plan to attend is relaxed enough to take it. When in doubt, wear a tie and take it off when you get there.

Shirts: Old-fashioned shirts with French cuffs that require cuff links are still considered appropriate and even elegant. Many men feel cuff links indicate a European style. Wear them if you like but shirts with buttoned cuffs are always correct.

Shirts with buttoned-down collars have a different appropriateness depending on where you work and live. Basic oxford cloth shirts with buttoned-down collars are always right. But in more creative fields (advertising, for example) such shirts can be abandoned for those with flat collars. Take note of those around you—and follow suit.

Short-sleeved business shirts are much more casual than those with long sleeves. In some circles they are a definite no-no. (It's far more attractive to wear a long-sleeved shirt and roll up the sleeves.) In very hot climates, however, they have become part of the everyday dress code. In some businesses, short sleeves are permitted on Fridays only. Check with your organization to see if they have any regulations about the look.

Blue jeans: Blue jeans for men tend to be very casual clothes. Even neatly pressed jeans, when worn by men, do not seem as dressed up as when they are worn by women. Keep them for comfortable, strictly casual times.

The blue blazer: Probably the one item every man, no matter where he lives, should have in his wardrobe is the classic navy-blue blazer. Though there are many variations on the theme, most come in a basic wool or wool blend and have elegant gold buttons. The blue blazer can go almost anywhere—with khaki pants and a tieless shirt to a Superbowl party, or to a more formal occasion, dressed up with a snappy tie and wool pants. With the right dress shirt and dress pants, it can even be worn to a semiformal event.

The sports jacket, usually in rough tweed or checks, is a more informal alternative. This is great for the country, worn over jeans and a T-shirt, or with a neatly buttoned-down shirt.

Jewelry: Jewelry on men is still an iffy subject. Much more than the classic wedding ring, in most areas of the country, is still taboo. An attractive, important watch, however, is always the exception. While some men will want one that is purely functional, others will want to make a status statement, for instance the classic Rolex, Cartier, or Brietling watches. Other men feel an antique watch has the same effect.

Rock stars, sports celebrities, and actors have revolutionized the traditions of jewelry on men. In certain circles, gemstone rings, necklaces, even earrings are acceptable. But unless the group you move in is extremely avant garde or trendy, it's best to take the conservative route and wear no excess jewelry at all.

Formal wear: When you receive an invitation that reads "Black tie" it means you are to wear specific formal clothes—a dinner jacket (nowadays commonly called a tuxedo, although they are technically somewhat different in style). A black jacket, rather than white, is the most appropriate color regardless of the time of year. If you live in a warm climate, purchase a black dinner jacket in a lightweight fabric.

The jacket is worn with a white formal shirt, a black bow tie, and a cummerbund around the waist. The shirt may have either a plain or pleated front; ruffled and flouncy shirts are not classic and are not considered in good taste, in the opinion of many. The shirt is worn with matching studs and cuff links. If you do not have studs and cuff links, you can make do by wearing a plain white dress shirt with a pointed (but never button-down) collar. However, if you attend several black-tie events a year, you may want to invest in a set of studs and cuff links.

Over-the-calf black socks in a lightweight fabric and black patent pumps or black patent laced oxfords complete the outfit. If you do not have black patent shoes you may wear well-polished black shoes with laces.

Many men enjoy wearing a cummerbund and matching bow tie in a dressy fabric such as silk, satin, or velvet, and some find a waistcoat more comfortable than a cummerbund. The waistcoat may also be of a dressy fabric, even a subtle print design, although most are of a black silky fabric.

A white linen handkerchief, either monogrammed or not, can be worn in the left breast pocket. If you're wearing a scarf or muffler, it should be of white silk, and gloves should be of a dressy gray suede.

No matter what other people choose to do, it is not correct to wear a dinner jacket or tailcoat before six in the evening. Some men wear colored dinner jackets with piping around the jacket collar, lapels, and pockets. The fact that they exist does not mean they are elegant. If you want to make certain you are properly dressed, buy or rent a conservative, well-fitting black suit.

White tie: White-tie occasions are rare today other than in diplomatic situations or at the most fancy debutante balls. When an invitation reads "White tie" men must wear the full evening regalia and women a floor-length gown with their best jewelry and gloves.

Most men rent a white-tie outfit because they are so seldom called upon to wear one. This means the pants and black patent shoes that go with a dinner jacket are topped with a stiff wing-collar shirt, studs, a white piqué waistcoat, white tie, and black tailcoat.

If you have received decorations from a foreign government or the military, you may wear them to a public white-tie event. However, do not wear your decorations to a private party unless the invitation reads "White tie and decorations."

MEN AND WOMEN INTERACTING

While certain customs have changed or become more relaxed with regard to the way men and women relate to each other socially, the rules of basic etiquette are always guided by the same two principles: do what is practical and considerate.

Gone are the days when it was customary for men to treat women as fragile objects. If you are, for example, a traditional type, you may consider it proper to open a door for a woman. If you take a more modern approach, you may let the woman, if she is ahead of you and her hands are free, get the door herself. Today a young woman may actually be insulted by overly solicitous behavior. She may think it suggests that she is incapable of taking care of, or providing for, herself. But, on the other hand, she may be charmed by old-fashioned courtliness, as long as it's done with a light touch.

However, tradition still prevails when it comes to a man being courteous toward a woman. For instance, a man:

- Helps a woman when she puts on or takes off her coat.
- Stands up when a woman enters the room.
- Goes through a revolving door first, pushing it for the woman.
- If convenient, allows a woman to enter and exit an elevator first.
- Gets into a taxi first (it can be difficult for a woman in a skirt to slide across the seat).
- Steps on an escalator behind the woman.
- Walks closest to the curb (to protect the woman from being splattered by water kicked up by a car).
- Offers his arm to a woman, if he feels she needs help (walking over rough terrain, etc.).
- Gives his seat to a pregnant woman on a bus (this applies to women, too).
- At the theater, lets the woman enter the row first.

BEHAVIOR IN PUBLIC PLACES

How you conduct yourself in a public place, such as a museum, theater, or restaurant, is important because your behavior can affect the people surrounding you. Mainly, you want to show respect for the others present, and in special situations to think twice before acting on impulse. For instance, if you're at a museum, don't stand directly in front of someone looking at a painting, and at the theater don't whisper or unwrap a package of mints. These actions may seem petty, but nonetheless they can be irritating to anyone trying to concentrate. The key to courteous behavior in public places is the same as in any place: be as considerate of others as you'd like them to be to you.

Restaurant

There are few places that allow a more perfect opportunity to show off your manners than a restaurant. The minute you walk through the door a whole set of etiquette procedures comes into play. While your everyday at-home table manners may be fine, in a restaurant there are other challenges such as ordering the meal and communicating with the staff to take into account. Whether you're the host or the guest at the finest bistro in town or the local luncheonette, if you master the material that follows, you'll feel at ease.

THE RESTAURANT STAFF

Each staff member in a restaurant has his or her specific duties. Although sommeliers are seldom seen today, they do exist in the finer restaurants. In a deluxe or first-class restaurant you'll encounter the following:

Maître d'	Headwaiter (in English); in charge of dining room; seats you at your table
Captain	Takes your order; supervises the service; fillets the fish, carves the meat, etc., at serving table
Sommelier	Wine steward
Waiter	Serves you
Bus boy	Fills water glasses; puts bread and rolls on the table; removes used plates, glasses

SEATING AT A RESTAURANT

The headwaiter or maître d' is in charge of seating customers at a restaurant. If he's seating a man and a woman, the woman follows him, then the man follows her. If a single man is hosting a dinner party, he goes first in order to seat his guests as they arrive at the table. There's no significance as to who sits where in banquette seating, but if you want to go by the rule book, the woman sits on the banquette on the man's right; if they sit opposite each other, the woman takes the banquette. If the party is two married couples, usually the women sit on the banquette, the men opposite. Because it's easier to talk across a table than side by side, it makes sense for wives not to sit opposite their husbands. If the seating is in a booth, the couple may arrange themselves as they do on a banquette or two women may slip in first opposite each other and let the men take the outside seats. In this case, husband and wife do not sit beside each other.

THE ROLE OF THE HOST

INVITING A FRIEND TO LUNCH OR DINNER AT A RESTAURANT

There are a number of things to keep in mind when you invite someone to be your guest at a restaurant. First, and most important, make it clear that you are the host. It won't be clear if you say, "Let's get together for lunch Wednesday." Be specific. "I'd like to take you to lunch Wednesday." If you want to go to an ethnic restaurant, ask your guest if he likes the type of food served. In addition, if you know your guest's an addicted smoker and you are not, either say to him, "Best for you to know in advance that I feel strongly about sitting in the nonsmoking section of a restaurant," or—which will please him a great deal more—"I know how much it means to you to light up, so I'm making the reservation in the smoking section."

MAKING A RESERVATION   When you make a reservation for lunch or dinner at a restaurant, give your name, the date, time, and number of people in your party. Also indicate whether you want to be in the smoking or nonsmoking section of the dining room. If it's a popular restaurant, it may be necessary to book at least two weeks in advance.

Here are a few hints having to do with reservations:

- If you've been to the restaurant before, you may want to request a table in a specific location.
- If your group will be six or more, it can save time if you order the meal in advance, particularly if you are going to the theater afterward.
- Call the restaurant if you're delayed for some reason. That way, they won't give your table away to another customer.
- If your plans change, cancel your reservation immediately. It's only fair to give the restaurant as much time as possible to rebook the table.
- Make sure the restaurant accepts whatever credit card you use. If it doesn't, ask if a personal check is acceptable.

WHEN YOU ARRIVE AT THE RESTAURANT   Arrive at the restaurant a few minutes in advance of the appointed hour so you won't keep your guest (or guests) waiting. You can wait in the area outside the dining room if there's a place to sit, or at the bar. Or, if you prefer, you can ask the headwaiter to show you to your table. If you don't like the location of the table or it's not the one you requested, this is the time to ask if you can be seated elsewhere. Always leave the better seat at the table for your guest (it's more desirable to look into the room rather than at a wall). Use common sense about ordering a drink while you're waiting for your guest. Although conventional etiquette says not to order until everyone is present, certainly if you're expecting a friend there's no reason not to go ahead and have one. Hold off on eating rolls and bread, however, until your guest arrives.

ORDERING THE MEAL   When ordering, keep in mind the following:

- Always offer your guest a cocktail. If you don't want one, to be sociable, order something nonalcoholic.

- When the captain or waiter brings the menu (some restaurants have two: one with prices for the host, the other without prices for the guest), he will tell you what the specials are. If he does not give the prices, it would be rude to ask in front of your guest (although if you're going Dutch treat, you certainly can ask).

- If the menu is written in a language you can't read, ask the waiter to interpret for you; you may also ask the waiter if there's a particular entrée he recommends.

- If you have eaten at the restaurant before and liked a certain dish, you may want to suggest it to your guest.

- If you plan to have three courses, it's practical to order from the prix fixe menu where the price of the entrée includes an appetizer and dessert. On the other hand, if all you want is an entrée and coffee, you're better off ordering à la carte, meaning each item on the menu has its own price.

- If you would like to substitute one vegetable for another, ask the waiter if this is possible; you may also want to ask to have your salad brought with your main course rather than being served it as a first course.

- While many hosts hold to the tradition of asking guests for their menu choices and then ordering for them, it's a lot simpler and equally correct if each individual speaks directly to the captain or the waiter.

- If your guest prefers to skip the first course, in order not to hold up the main course, you may choose to pass it up also. Still, if you have your heart set on a favorite appetizer, by all means order it.

- Once you've decided on the entrées, you can order wine. Gone are the days when red meat required red wine and fish white wine. Choose whatever pleases you. If you're not knowledgable about wine, tell the wine steward or waiter how much you want to spend and ask him for suggestions.

- Address the waiter as "waiter" (if it's a woman call her "waitress"). The captain is called "captain." If you need to get the waiter's attention and can't catch his eye, ask another waiter to send him to your table.

- Any complaints about food or service should be made discreetly to the waiter. It is better to send food back to the kitchen without making a fuss than to eat something not up to standard.

ORDERING THE WINE The best restaurants have a sommelier or wine steward who handles the selection and serving of wine, but in most the captain or sometimes even the waiter is trained to serve the wine.

Ordering and serving wine in a restaurant is, of course, slightly more complex than serving it at home.

After you select the wine, the wine steward will present the bottle to you. Do not take the bottle from him, but look at it carefully and check the label to make certain it is what you ordered. Then nod your approval. If it is a red wine, the bottle is uncorked and the cork is handed to you. Some people believe in sniffing the cork to see if it has dried out. Others say this is not necessary. In any case, you must test the wine to make certain it is fine. The wine steward will pour a small amount into your glass. You should then sniff it to check its bouquet, take a sip, and again nod your approval. If there was any loose cork in the bottle it will have landed in your glass. When this happens, the wine steward will replace the glass. Wine is then poured into each guest's glass, never more than about half full. The host's glass is the last one filled.

If you have ordered white wine, you should taste it, too, before serving it to your guests. Never sniff white wine; white wine, unlike red, does not have a bouquet and therefore there is nothing to sniff.

Never feel you must order a very expensive wine. There is nothing wrong with serving a modestly priced one as long as it is good. In fact, the house wine served in a carafe at good restaurants is often excellent. (If your guests are wine connoisseurs, you will want to order accordingly.) When ordering wine by the carafe, don't ask the waiter to pour any into your glass for approval. Doing so comes across as quite silly because, unlike a fine bottled wine, there's nothing to check, nothing to discuss.

If you are served a wine that has turned sour or vinegary, you certainly must send it back. First ask the wine steward or waiter to taste it. Most likely he will agree. If he does not, and you are certain you are correct, quietly insist on a new bottle, for which you should not be charged.

If you are hosting a number of people, you may ask them whether they prefer red or white. Or you may order white if most have ordered fish or fowl, or red if most are eating meat. If nearly everyone is drinking red, for instance, but one person prefers white, you may then order white wine by the glass for that person. With a large group, you may wish to order both red and white.

PAYING THE BILL When the time comes to pay the bill, look it over carefully to be sure it's correct (if you're splitting it, someone should be in charge of figuring out who owes what). As a tip, fifteen percent is customary, although in a first-class restaurant, if the food and service are outstanding, leave twenty percent.

If your meal and the service have been exceptionally good, make a point of telling the owner or manager. It will please him enormously and put you in good standing with the restaurant.

THE ROLE OF THE GUEST

Here are a few thoughts to keep in mind when you're someone's guest at a restaurant.

- If you arrive before your host, you may wait in the area outside the dining room (do not sit at the bar drinking) or the maître d' or headwaiter may escort you to the table. Unless your host is delayed an unreasonably long time, don't order a drink. What's more, leave your napkin as well as rolls and bread on the table untouched.

- You may order an alcoholic drink even if your host says he is planning to have soda water. If he offers you a second drink but does not want one himself, there's no reason not to accept, but stop with two.

- If you're a smoker and your host has made a reservation in the nonsmoking area of the dining room, you'll have to grin and bear it. It would be rude to object at that point.

- Be sensitive about what you order. As a general rule do not order the most expensive entrée on the menu unless the host recommends it to you and you know he can well afford it. Traditionally, you shouldn't order the least expensive entrée either, although it seems senseless not to if it's what appeals to you most.

- It's not up to you to address the waiter other than to ask him questions when you're ordering your meal.

- If you don't want wine when it's passed, all you have to say to the waiter is "No, thank you." Never turn the glass upside down.

- If you're not a dessert eater, tell your host. You can always have coffee while he eats his.

- If your host was given the coat check for both your coats, it's up to him to tip the coatroom attendant, although there's no reason for you not to suggest taking care of the tip. If you each have a coat check, handle your tips individually.

HOST AND GUEST ON PUBLIC VIEW

WHAT TO WEAR What you wear to a restaurant depends on the formality of the establishment and the community it's in. In the more fashionable restaurants, a woman customarily wears a conservative dress or suit. Many restaurants require that a man wear a jacket and/or tie. If a man appears without a tie, they lend him one. A man never wears a hat or cap in a restaurant, no matter how informal the setting is. If you are in doubt as to the dress code of the restaurant where you're planning to eat, call the restaurant and ask what's considered appropriate attire.

TABLE HOPPING It's the height of rudeness to leave your table to go talk to someone you know at another table. If you spot a friend you haven't seen in ages, wait until you are leaving the restaurant to say a quick hello. It must be really quick, as you don't want to block the aisle and make it difficult for waiters to serve. If someone stops by your table to speak to you, introduce that person to whomever you're with. A man seated at the table should stand or half rise from his dining seat when introduced to a woman. If on the way out you pass someone you see frequently, all you have to do is wave. If you do stop to say a word of greeting, the person with you continues on.

MISCELLANEOUS POINTERS

- Keep your voice as low as possible in a restaurant. Be cautious about saying something confidential; you might be within earshot of other diners. At the same time, don't eavesdrop on the conversation at the table next to you.

- Other than powdering her nose, a woman never applies makeup at the table. The worst is combing hair at the table (this applies to a man as well). It's simply not acceptable.

- You may be madly in love, but don't be overtly affectionate at the table; it can embarrass other diners.

- If a woman leaves the table, when she returns it's customary for any man she's with to acknowledge her presence by standing up or half rising from his chair.

- If you're seated on a banquette, don't take up more than your share of space by taking your coat, shopping bags, and packages with you to the table.

- It's pretentious to ask the waiter to bring a telephone to your table, except in very special instances. You can always use the restaurant's pay telephone.

- If you are carrying a pager, keep it on silencer unless you are waiting for an emergency call. You can check now and then to see if a call has come through.

- If you're a smoker, don't light up once the first course has been brought to the table.

- When a couple leave the restaurant, the man leads the way out of the dining room.

- If you're eating at a Chinese restaurant and don't use chopsticks, ask the waiter for flatware.

- A smorgasbord meal is very informal. People serve themselves from the buffet table, often beginning with fish, followed by hot dishes.

Because you are free to return for a second helping, don't pile your plate with food the first time around.

- Some restaurants refuse to check fur coats, in which case take your coat to the dining room and place it over the back of your chair.

- A dinner napkin is never shaken out or tucked into your shirt or blouse (unless the diner is a child). If you leave the table to go to the ladies' or men's room, place your napkin on your chair and push the chair in, close to the table. When the meal is finished, put your napkin to the left of the place setting, unfolded.

- If potatoes or vegetables are placed on the table in small dishes but you prefer to eat them on the same plate as your entrée, you may take a clean spoon and slide them onto your dinner plate. The same applies to salad.

- If you are eating with just one other person, it's permissible to let him taste something from your plate, but do so unobtrusively. Pass your plate to your dinner companion, who takes a clean fork and transfers the frog's legs or whatever from your plate to his, then hands your plate back to you.

- Doggy bags are pretty much a restaurant institution today. It's appropriate to ask for one, except at the most elegant restaurants, where they may be frowned on.

- Occasionally, an unforeseen embarrassment can arise at the table. For instance, if you discover some foreign matter in your mouth, put your fork or spoon to your mouth, remove whatever it is, and place it on your plate. So others don't have to look at the object, you can cover it with a piece of bread or a lettuce leaf. If the object happens to be a fly in your soup, or a caterpillar in your salad, remove it unobtrusively and quietly report it to your waiter.

- If someone nearby chokes, take immediate action (see Heimlich Maneuver later in "Behavior in Public Places" section).

DO'S AND DON'TS AT THE TABLE

DO

- Put your swizzle stick on the tablecloth unless your drink is placed on a plate.

- Leave the iced tea or iced coffee spoon in your glass if there's no saucer, holding it to one side with your finger. Do not put it on the tablecloth.

- Use flatware at your place setting from the outside in.

- Put the spoon or fork used with a stemmed compote glass on the service plate; never leave it in the glass.

- Never pick up a dropped utensil or anything else from the floor of a restaurant. Let it be and ask the waiter for a replacement.
- Put your fork and knife across the center of your plate on a diagonal slant when you have finished eating.
- Wait until you have finished your drink before picking an olive or cherry from the glass to eat.
- Sip from the side of a large soupspoon. To get the last remaining soup, tip the plate away from you, then scoop it up.
- Hold a two-handled soup cup by its handles; don't cradle the cup.
- Hold a wineglass where the stem and the bowl join.
- Pull pieces of French bread apart with your hands.
- Take small amounts of condiments and put them on your butter plate.
- Take a small amount of butter from a crock using the knife with the crock and put it on your butter plate. Return the crock's knife.
- Pour the oil and vinegar in cruets directly onto your salad.
- Eat ice cream with a spoon; if it is served with cake, use a fork and a spoon.
- Lift your tea bag and let it drain a little before putting it on the saucer or butter plate.
- Put sugar envelopes on the tablecloth or under the tea or coffee cup saucer.

DON'T

- Ask for ketchup at a first-class restaurant.
- Use a toothpick at the table.
- Take a drink if you have food in your mouth.
- Wipe a dirty utensil with your napkin; quietly ask the waiter to replace it.
- Put used flatware on the table or leave it in a cup.
- Pour coffee spilled onto your saucer back into the cup. If necessary, ask the waiter to bring you a clean saucer.

CAFETERIAS AND FAST FOOD ESTABLISHMENTS

When you go through a cafeteria line with your tray, try not to hold up the people behind you by lingering over the decision of what to eat. If you forgot something, the polite thing is to go back to the end of the line rather than cutting in between two people. If the eating area is crowded and you must join people at another table, before sitting down ask, "Do you mind if I sit here?" Once you are seated, it's not necessary to talk to the other people. If a bus boy brings you water and takes your tray away, which is the case in some cafeterias, you should leave a small tip. If there are trash receptacles in the area, it is a signal that you should clear your table for the next occupants.

LUNCH COUNTERS

If you and a friend are waiting for seats at a lunch counter and two become available on either side of a customer, you may politely say to that person (if he does not offer first), "Excuse me, but would you mind moving over one place so my friend and I can sit together?" Seldom do you find anyone so selfish as to refuse to move. If the sugar or ketchup is in front of the person seated next to you, rather than reaching, ask if he'll pass it to you, then thank him when he does. If there are people waiting for seats at the counter, don't linger too long over a cup of coffee.

THE HEIMLICH MANEUVER

By law every restaurant has and every kitchen should have posted on a wall somewhere a poster describing the Heimlich Maneuver. This is in case someone chokes on a piece of food and is unable to breathe. Because immediate action must be taken in such a situation, it's important to know how to administer this life-saving procedure.

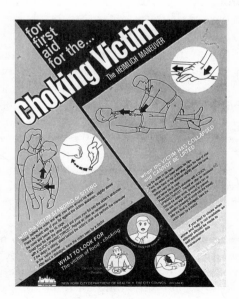

The Heimlich Maneuver.
By law this poster is displayed in every public eating place. You can obtain a copy for your home by contacting your local Department of Health.

Behavior in Other Public Places

AT A CHURCH OR SYNAGOGUE

While traditionalists still "dress" for church or synagogue, most houses of worship no longer have dress codes that require you to do so. The key is to be comfortable with your surroundings and to try as best you can to fit in. If you are attending the house of worship of a friend who belongs to a different denomination, ask ahead of time what you should wear and dress with the same degree of formality as he or she does.

But there are a few guidelines:

- Roman Catholic churches have relaxed their dress code. Women no longer have to have their heads covered.

- In an Orthodox Jewish synagogue, a woman cannot wear pants. And if she is married she must keep her head and arms covered. Men are expected to cover their heads as well. Conservative synagogues mandate headcoverings only for men and regular hats will do. In Reform synagogues there are no specific dress codes.

- Though some houses of worship have become so hip that they even offer "speed masses" during the summer months, it's still important to show respect for the institution by dressing with some care. Always appropriate: a dress or nice pants for a woman; for a man, a coat and tie. Save your jeans and shorts for play.

- If your reason for being in the house of worship is a wedding or funeral, again, you must wear clothes appropriate to the occasion, which means a suit and tie for men and a dress for women.

- Your conduct in an unfamiliar place of worship should be guided by your own religious feelings. You may kneel, sing, shake hands with a neighbor, read responses if you wish. Whether or not you want to take communion is a theological question and entirely up to you. If, for instance, you are the only Protestant in a Catholic family, inclusion in communion is important. Most houses of worship want to extend hospitality and good will, and assume that we all wish to take good care of one another.

- Each place of worship will undoubtedly have a different policy about children. In some, children are integrated into the entire adult service while at others they are kept at Sunday school. And some have them join the congregation once the service is under way. If you're new in town and attending an unfamiliar church, call and talk to the pastor or church secretary; he'll tell you their policy with children.

At a Football or Baseball Game, a Tennis or Polo Match, a Racetrack

At any public sporting event, and in particular at outdoor games, you need to be considerate of other spectators: you're not sitting alone in front of your television set! If you plan to eat at the ball game, purchase drinks and food at the concession stands before the game begins and take them to your seat.

If the national anthem is played, stand, and, if you wish, place your right hand over your heart. (If you don't rise it might be seen as a sign of disrespect; though if you don't like to sing, you don't have to.) A man should take his hat off and place it over his heart.

Everyone expects you to cheer enthusiastically for your team—so go ahead—stand up and root! Of course, at a tennis match you must be quiet at all times so as not to distract the players. But don't be rude, curse, or pick a fight with an opposing fan. Many of the lethal brawls you've seen on late night TV have been started just that way. Above all, have respect for the players, especially at more intimate sporting events such as tennis matches. Barbra Streisand had to get up and leave one of Andre Agassi's recent matches because the crowd started chanting "Barbra! Barbra! Barbra!" every time Agassi tried to serve.

In general, it's really not proper to try to sneak into better seats. But if the game is well under way and they remain empty, ask an usher or ticket taker if you may move up.

When the event is over, make a swift and orderly departure.

At the Beach

Because the beach is so many people's most cherished vacation spot, it can also be the most disappointing. Nothing is more frustrating than planning for a quiet nap in the sun and being subjected to Beach Blanket Bingo—with sand flying, dogs barking, radios blasting. Make sure the beach you plan to go to suits the level of activity or relaxation you're after. Many beaches, for instance, do not allow food, drink, animals, or four-wheeling. A few have surfboard and boogie-board restrictions; others require that you obtain a day badge from the town hall. It's best to call ahead or consult a travel guide.

Even if the beach is public, remember that each person there has a right to some private space, which usually extends at least to the perimeters of his or her blanket or towel. Respect those boundaries. Walk around towels when you see them. Don't run, because it kicks up sand. And, of course, never throw sand. When you pick your towel up to dry yourself off or to pack it at the end of the day, check that no one is downwind of you, so that the excess sand does not go flying into his face. And remember that you may love that new wave radio station you're listening to, but the people next to you may not. Best to leave the radio at home or bring along earphones or a Walkman unless there will really be no one else on the beach. And be courteous about tossing a football, flying a kite, or throwing a Frisbee.

Most important is to obey the lifeguard, pick up your litter, and put out your fire when you leave.

And if you're visiting friends with a house on the beach, be sure to rinse your feet each time you reenter the house. You'd be amazed at how quickly sand piles up indoors.

AT THE SWIMMING POOL

Treat any swimming pool, even a public one, as if it were yours. Shower first to remove excess body oils and dirt that can, over time, muck up the water. If you're visiting a friend's pool, be sure to take your own towel, sun tan lotions, grooming tools, and soft drinks. You might even want to take some extra sodas along for your host as a token of your appreciation.

For safety reasons, don't run, dunk other people, or splash. Don't dive off anything but the diving board, and then only when the coast is completely clear. Don't leave young children, or those who can't swim, unattended. And for goodness' sake, leave all pets at home—unless they are specifically invited. The only thing worse than your dog jumping in the pool is someone else's dog.

ATTENDING A CONCERT, THE BALLET, THE THEATER

As in most circumstances the best rule of thumb to follow when attending public entertainment is to treat people with the same respect and common courtesy you would like to receive yourself. Though there are no absolute rules of dress, you should, for the sake of those who will inevitably surround you, be clean and well groomed.

As for any public event, arrive with ample time to doff coats, check packages, undress small children. Have the tickets in your hand as you enter the door so you won't hold up those waiting behind you. Give the tickets to the usher or ticket collector and then, if you are a man, step back to allow the women in your party to move ahead of you. The woman always follows the usher and is followed by the man. The usher will give you one or more programs which you may hand out when seated. (It is not the custom in this country to tip an usher.)

Couples should seat themselves with the men on the ends, women in the middle. Be sure to place coats (if you did not check them) and handbags under your chair or in your lap so they won't be in the way when other seat holders pass by. Actually many theater seats are spaced so that simply swiveling your knees in one direction will allow newcomers to pass by easily, but if there isn't room, be quick to stand and lift your seat as soon as you see someone enter the aisle. When you are the one taking your seat and others stand to let you by, face the stage, not those standing.

Almost all concerts, ballets, and plays have at least one intermission. Be sure to wait until the curtain is all the way down and the applause has subsided before standing up or you will block the view of those behind you. Providing your coat is not a valuable fur, and that there is nothing of importance in the pockets, at an intermission you may feel free to leave it folded on your seat. Even if you are in a rush, do not push your way to the rest room. And if there is a long line at the ladies' room, women should be considerate enough of those standing in line to make sure adjustments of hair, makeup, or clothing are done outside the toilet stalls.

When the house lights flash it's time to return to your seat. And you must be quick. At certain theaters, and especially at the ballet, you will not be seated once the curtain goes up.

During any theater performance be conscious of the need for quiet and concentration. Do not rattle your program or fidget in your seat. And no whispering, please! You'd be surprised how far sound carries. If you are struck by a sudden uncontrollable series of sneezes or have a tickle in your throat, quietly leave your seat and head for an exit. An usher will often be there to help you. Though few people wear really big hats these days, if one of the few who does is seated in front of you, and your view of the stage is obstructed, you may gently tap the hat-wearer on the shoulder and say, "I'm so sorry, but I'm having a difficult time trying to see. Do you think you could remove your hat?"

ATTENDING THE OPERA

Until about the time of the First World War the opera was the most formal event in town. No one would think of showing up in anything but a floor-length dress or white tie. Today's dress is more relaxed, except at galas or opening nights when devotees still dress formally. But there is such a thing as being too informal, so keep in mind that a somewhat dressy dress for a woman and a jacket and tie for a man will add a sense of specialness to a night at the opera.

When the conductor takes the podium everyone should applaud. People often applaud after an aria and whenever the curtain comes down. One of the operagoer's pet peeves: people who stand up to applaud during the final curtain call so those seated can't see the stage as the performers take their bows. If you've brought flowers to toss to your favorite diva, wait for the final bows.

At intermission time, you may want to buy your host a drink at one of the bars. If you use a rest room, you should tip the attendant fifty cents to a dollar.

Sometimes friends get together and take a season subscription for box seats. Though in the past etiquette dictated that men never sat in the front row of a box, rules have eased enough to allow for switching seats at intermission. Or subscribers may prefer to switch seats halfway through the season.

AT THE MOVIES

Going to the movies in some theaters is like going to the zoo. There is so much talking and hooting, so much popcorn flying, so much soda spilling down the aisles, you wonder why you bothered.

Though it certainly costs less to go to a movie than to a ballet or a play, it is a no less respectable form of entertainment and should be treated as such. Tempting as it may be, don't talk to the person you're with. Keep popcorn in its container; do not rip into a candy wrapper during the silence of a love scene. Clean up your refuse at the end. Remove restless or noisy children to the lobby, where there are often video games or soda machines. If the theater is crowded, be aware that others may have difficulty seeing past you if you are constantly shifting in your seat or leaning on your movie partner.

AT A MUSEUM

Museums are generally quite formal, even awe-inspiring places. It is expected that visitors will keep their voices down and not touch works of art. In addition, never walk in front of people already looking at a painting. Though most museums allow strollers, many ask you to check yours and offer an infant backpack instead. If your child begins to talk too loudly, or cry, take her to the cafeteria or outside until she settles down.

AT AN AUCTION

In some ways an auction room is like a tennis court: certain conventions, certain prescribed rules of etiquette and courtesy, are always observed. However—as with a tennis match itself—the sport has become democratized and so has participant behavior. Today the only people who you know for sure will be dressed in formal attire are the auction house staff. They stand on tradition.

In the early days, an auction was a quiet if not dignified affair at which an audience barely murmured. No longer. In May 1990, when Vincent van Gogh's *Portrait of Dr. Gachet* sold at Christie's, New York, for a world record price of $82,500,000, scores of guests stood up, turned, and strained to see the seated bidder. And the traditional silence of the saleroom was shattered by enthusiastic applause.

If you've never been to an auction, the best introduction might be a daytime sale. They're free and open to the public. You don't have to bid; you don't even have to be well informed. You can consider it a learning experience.

Evening auctions, of which there are just a handful a year, are another story. Demand usually exceeds space and so a ticket, which is usually free, is necessary for admission. Tickets are issued for both seats and standing room. (At more informal "country" auctions it may be necessary to stake out and label a seat in the morning during the preview.)

At any auction, here are the basic rules of the game.

Bidding is done by paddle in most cases or by prearranged signals. You will not accidentally purchase a Renoir by scratching your ear, unless you and the auctioneer or bid-spotter have established this in advance as your bidding signal.

Low/high estimates printed in auction house catalogs represent the experts' assessment of the price range the work is likely to fall into.

The reserve or **reserve price** is the confidential price below which the owner will not sell the property. It is usually less than the lowest printed estimate.

By law the auctioneer can bid on the object until the confidential reserve level has been reached. After that he is prohibited from bidding on that piece. When the auctioneer says "Pass," that means that the work did not reach the reserve price and has been bought in by the auction house; it will be returned to the consignor.

When the auctioneer's hammer hits the rostrum at the end of bidding, that final bid is the **hammer price.** It is important for every buyer to remember that there is an additional **buyer's premium:** ten percent of the hammer price is automatically added on to determine the final sum to be paid by the buyer. This is the auction house's percentage. And you don't have to be in the auction room in order to bid. You can leave a written form or **order bid** that enables the auctioneer to bid on your specific instructions up to your stated maximum. Or you may arrange to bid by telephone.

A **silent auction** usually involves items on display with a kind of sign-up list. Each bidder signs her name to the list, upping the price on the line before. The last person to sign wins.

AT THE GAMBLING CASINO

Gambling, it seems, has become one of those great American pastimes. And like so much else, what used to be a very formal pastime meant only for the very rich who could travel to Monte Carlo with trunks full of expensive clothes has become a casual form of entertainment.

Though there still seems to be a great deal of glamour attached to the image of the casino, it is now in reality a place specifically aimed to attract and please Everyman. Dress is strictly a matter of personal preference, and it ranges from dinner jackets to tank tops and jeans. Some European casinos, such as those in London and Monte Carlo, still require jackets and ties. However, it's best to call ahead and find out what's expected. And, although in the United States, anyone can walk in off the streets of Las Vegas and pull on the handle of a slot machine, some European casinos are actually "clubs." This means you must sign up with the club and wait (usually forty-eight hours) before gambling. The reason? The club owners want to spare you the anguish and embarrassment of blowing everything on an impulse. Once you're registered, however, you can go in any time and play.

When standing at a gambling table feel free to talk to others at the table. But it is never appropriate to be loud or boisterous.

At some time you may want to take a gambling break. However, if the casino is busy the croupier may tell you that if you plan to return you may have trouble getting another place at the table. On very busy nights it's considerate not to hoard the slot machines by playing three at a time. Play just one.

Today many casinos offer smoke-free areas and rooms; one Las Vegas casino is completely smoke-free.

CAR ETIQUETTE

The courtly custom of a man opening the door for a woman to get in the car is still observed by some men. However, it is unusual for a woman to sit in the car and wait for the man to run around to open the door for her. When a woman is wearing a formal evening dress, the man should offer her a hand to help her out of the car. In bad weather he should remember to take an umbrella along and hold it over her as they walk from the car. Elderly people should be offered help in getting in and out of the car; but if they don't want to be helped, you must allow them their independence. Younger people traveling with the elderly should always offer to get into the backseat. If a couple are driving a single woman, it is a nice gesture for the wife to suggest that the single woman sit in the front. When two couples go out together it is up to them to decide whether they sit as couples or apart. There is no hard and fast rule.

CARPOOLING

Carpooling is a sensible way to reduce the number of cars wasting oil, gas, and space and adding to pollution. If you are about to join a carpool, remember a few of the niceties:

- Be ready at the specified location when the car comes to pick you up.
- If you will be absent, notify the driver in advance.
- Before opening a window, ask if the cold air will bother anyone or if the wind will be too much. Ditto for the heater or air conditioning.
- Offer to share the driving. This is or should be standard operating procedure of any car pooling.
- Be conscientious about paying your share of gas and tolls.
- You should assume that there is no smoking unless all the members of the carpool agree to it.

- Don't carry too much with you. A briefcase or one package or so is fine, but anything more can cause problems and delays if it has to be stored in the trunk.

- Don't bring another passenger without first asking the driver and/or the group.

- As the point of a carpool is to save time and resources, don't suddenly request that you be picked up or dropped off at another location unless you have discussed it with the group.

TAXI ETIQUETTE

Never enter a taxi unless the driver has proper identification. If you have an immigrant taxi driver who knows only a little English, be patient with him and try to communicate slowly, in well-modulated tones, using simple language. If he speaks English well enough to strike up a conversation and you don't want to talk, one-syllable replies (yes or no) can usually discourage conversational openings. Don't forget, a taxi driver is in a position to hear and see just about everything that goes on in the backseat, so behave circumspectly. And if you talk on your portable telephone in a taxi, remember, again, that you are not alone.

What follows are tips for taxi riders:

- If you see a taxi and hail it, don't jump into another one that pulls up first.

- Don't go after a taxi that someone else has already hailed.

- If you hail a taxi at the same time as someone else, it's good manners to cede it.

- A man should open the taxi door for a woman. It is considerate for him to slide to the far side of the seat, saving the woman from having to do so in a tight skirt or evening dress.

- If you feel the driver is taking a roundabout route, ask him politely why he chose that route (there may be road work he wants to avoid).

- Never eat or drink in a taxi, as you might spill something on the seat.

- Don't toss any litter onto the floor. Take trash with you.

- If the driver asks you not to smoke, respect his wishes. You can ask the driver not to smoke as well.

- If the radio is turned on too loud, or if the driver drives too fast or recklessly, speak up.

- Give the driver sufficient warning as to which side of the street you want to be dropped off on. Get out only on the curb side.

- The usual tip is fifteen to twenty percent of the fare. If the driver is rude, tip less.

HELPING PEOPLE WITH SPECIAL NEEDS

The biggest handicap in dealing properly with the physically challenged is not the person's impairment but others' awkwardness about it. Often we are so afraid of embarrassing, hurting, or insulting someone who is blind, deaf, or wheelchair-bound that we simply pretend not to notice the impairment at all. Even worse, our own fear of gawking—and embarrassing ourselves and them—may lead us to pretend that the handicapped are invisible. This is exactly the opposite of how they would like to be treated.

The handicapped, just like anyone else, like to have eye contact and they deserve the same respect, courtesy, and kindness you would offer anyone.

THE BLIND

Those with impaired vision are usually easily identified. Often they carry a white cane, walk with a Seeing Eye dog on a harness, or have another person walking close beside them. If someone is alone and seems to be lost or confused, approach him and say, "I'm John Smith. May I help you get to the corner?" If he says yes, ask, "Would you like to take my arm?" Touch his hand and direct it to your arm or offer your elbow. (Never reach out and grab anyone's arm without asking.) Or the person may prefer to link arms. Point out where steps go up or down or when obstacles such as a garbage can are blocking the path.

And remember, assistance must be related to the moment. If you see a blind person approaching a closed door offer to open it; if she is struggling with packages ask if she would like help. You might offer the same courtesy to a sighted person. Elevators that are not equipped with buttons in Braille or with sensors that ring at every floor or a voice that announces the floor can be problems for the blind. Often they will ask what floor the elevator is on; if not, you may offer the information.

THE WHEELCHAIR-BOUND

One problem people in wheelchairs sometimes encounter is the tendency on the part of others to talk down to them—literally and figuratively—because their faces are not at eye level. More than one person in a wheelchair has had the humiliating experience of a waiter asking a dinner companion, "And what will she have for dinner?"

If you see a person in a manual wheelchair trying to navigate thick carpeting, offer to help because it's hard on her arms. The same applies if someone is trying to work her way up a long incline or ramp or attempting to negotiate a muddy area.

When you approach someone in a wheelchair, don't assume she isn't independent. People in wheelchairs most often view the chair as an extension of themselves; they don't see themselves as confined. There is no need to focus on their disabilities.

TODAY'S CLUB LIFE

There are as many different types of clubs in this country—political, business, social, golf, beach, yacht, and athletic—as there are people. And each provides a whole range of different services. The structure and the amenities each club has to offer are often as formal or as informal as the people who run and belong to it. The classic country club, for example, may provide not only a swimming pool and, therefore, a great place for children to congregate, but also tennis courts, a snack bar, and a restaurant. It may also have public social rooms in which you may host special events such as wedding receptions, anniversary parties, luncheons, debuts, lectures, wine tastings. University clubs, however, which are often located within large cities in order to draw on the greatest number of alumni and members, may have fewer amenities and offer only a restaurant, a conference room, a reading area, and guest rooms for members. Even more loosely established clubs—chess, bridge, garden, book, or jogging—may be, in fact, nothing more than a mailing address or a phone or fax number to enable members to participate in group functions.

Some clubs will allow nonmembers to rent their facilities for functions because they help to defray the clubs' operating costs. Others simply will not.

While some clubs are open to the public and take anyone who wishes to join, others have strict requirements for membership and insist on applications being made through a formal process. Though there are still some all-men or all-women clubs, so many have come under fire from the public and antidiscrimination groups that most have grudgingly opened their doors to both sexes. Other clubs, such as the once selective Junior League, which does primarily charity work, now actively solicit members from all backgrounds and walks of life.

Many not-for-profit clubs now prohibit the exchange of business cards or business talk within their walls. This is to maintain their tax-exempt status.

JOINING A CLUB

The majority of public clubs are very easy to join: you simply call them up and give them your name and address and they send you an application. After you fill it out and pay your fee, you're in. Other clubs, especially the private, more "social" clubs, require that you apply for membership and many also require, as well, that a member sponsor you. If a close friend is already a member in good standing, and you feel comfortable doing so, you may simply ask him to sponsor you. The best approach is to be direct. Say, "I really love the Mainstreet Tennis Club and I understand that you're a member. Would you be willing to sponsor me?" Most of the time your friends will say yes.

If you don't know any of the members well it might be advisable to actively seek a few out to take to lunch. Or you might want to invite a member to dinner, a play, concert, or party. Once you know her better, you may feel you can ask her for her sponsorship in a more open-ended manner. Try: "I really love the Mainstreet Tennis Club. Do you know if they are accepting new members?" This leaves the member the option to jump in with, "Well, I can sponsor you," or to offer a more noncommittal, "I'm not quite sure. Why don't you ask Joe Smith?" Under no circumstances should you go to several members at once and ask to be proposed; if more than one says yes, it could prove extremely embarrassing both for them and for you.

A few clubs frown upon anyone who actively seeks membership as they gather new members by invitation only—in which case you just have to wait until they come to you.

The person who becomes your sponsor may have to write a letter of support proposing you to the board of admissions. Some clubs require that the sponsor also solicit letters from other members who can second the nomination. This may mean meeting those members, if you don't already know them, for lunch or drinks. Sometimes a personal interview with the admissions committee or the board of governors is required. On a set day and hour you appear, often with your sponsor, at the club for a formal or informal meeting or interview. Of course, it goes without saying that during these sessions you should be on your best behavior. Be outgoing, friendly, and show interest in the club's activities. If possible, try to get to know something about the committee members ahead of time— and try to talk with them about their personal interests. If you learn that Jake Jones is interested in car collecting, for example, and you often go to antique car auctions, bring up the subject. It will only help you two get to know each other better. At the same time, don't make it sound as though you've boned up on a subject to impress someone or compiled an FBI report on him. Mention of intimate details about someone's family life or work situation could be offputting.

Some committees will let you know of your acceptance right after the meeting, others may notify you by mail. Some clubs have yearlong waiting lists; many take six to nine months to complete the admissions process.

And each club has a different membership fee structure. Some require thousands of dollars up front, others a nominal initiation fee. All have annual dues. A few will let you pay monthly. And of course each club has different levels of membership: resident, nonresident (if, say, the club is located in a place you go to only on vacation), charter members (founders, etc.), lifetime members, honorary members (who are sometimes accepted without fees). Younger or junior members usually pay less dues than older members.

Be sure to research the fees and fee structures before you initiate the membership process. You don't want to embarrass yourself or your sponsor, by an inability—or unwillingness—to pay up.

It is always advisable, and just plain polite, to write a thank-you note to your sponsor.

PROPOSING A NEW MEMBER

Once you've joined a club, you may at some point be asked to propose a new member. If you like the person and think his interests and personality would work well with the style of the club, then you can go ahead and agree. But what if you're not quite sure that the person will fit in? The best way to handle this, and the one that's least likely to hurt the other person's feelings, is to say that you'd really love to sponsor him but that at the moment you are already sponsoring someone else. Or you may say that it would really be in the person's interest to ask someone else who has been a member longer, or who has known him longer, to be his sponsor. And that might be true: some clubs are more inclined to accept new members nominated by those who are very active on committees and the board of directors.

A number of clubs are very particular about adherence to their rules. A few even require that you handwrite your proposal letters and look negatively upon those who don't. Make sure that if you accept the role of sponsor you have the time and spirit to follow through; it can be a lot of responsibility. And once you're a sponsor, be careful not to overexpose your prospective member. Current members may resent a stranger appearing with you frequently for lunch or a club social event. It may look as though you're pushing him just a little too hard.

BLACKBALLING

There are many subtle ways by which committee or club members can blackball a proposed member. Some use the excuse that the applicant "doesn't know a sufficient number of members well enough to fit in." Others may maintain that he "did not follow admission procedures properly."

Unless you have a very good friend on the committee, it's unlikely you'll ever find out the truth about why you were blackballed. If you still like the club and are determined to join, it might be wise to wait a few years before trying again. Perhaps there will be some member turnover which will work in your favor.

BEHAVIOR AT A CLUB

Naturally, once you join a club you should do everything you can to uphold the club's rules and regulations. If the club allows guests, take only appropriate guests, and only to guest-oriented functions. Don't take the same guest too often as other members may be resentful wondering why that person doesn't take out his own membership.

Be sure to pay your membership dues on time. There is no need to tip for coat checks. But you may be expected to pay extra for tennis, squash, or racquetball courts and there may be greens fees. At the end of the year many clubs will send you a letter asking for donations which they will divide up among the club employees as a holiday tip.

If you give a guest club privileges and you are not able to be present with him, be certain to inform him ahead of time about the club rules. It is always best to accompany a guest if you can. Moreover, if you are given guest privileges at a club, respect and protect the reputation of the friend who brought you. Do not roam around by yourself—some rooms are for members only. If you want to thank your friend for having you to his club, offer to reciprocate and take him to your club. Or you can offer to take him to dinner.

MONEY—THE HUMAN ASPECT

BORROWING AND LENDING MONEY

> Neither a borrower nor a lender be;
> For loan oft loses both itself and friend.
> *Hamlet*, Act I, Scene 3

You would do well to keep Polonius's advice to Laertes about borrowing and lending in mind when you consider asking a close friend or relative to lend you money, or when you are asked for a loan. There may be a time, of course, when you are faced with financial difficulties. While the most logical place to borrow money is your bank, if you can't get a loan there, you may have to turn to a friend or family member. Before asking for a loan, be absolutely certain that the person you plan to approach can easily afford to lend you the money and that you will be able to pay it back within a reasonable amount of time.

Never ask anyone for money at a social gathering. Although you may be tempted to approach a relative or friend at a cocktail party when they may be feeling generous of spirit, it's not the time to bring up a personal matter, particularly one of a serious nature.

No one likes the idea of having to ask a friend or relative for money. To pave the way, write a letter to the person you hope to borrow from. Tell him why you need the money and ask if you may come to see him about a possible loan. By writing rather than approaching him in person, you give him time to think about your request, and if he decides to turn it down, he has the option of responding by letter, which can be less awkward than telephoning.

If after receiving your letter, the potential lender agrees to talk to you, when you meet come directly to the point. Say something like, "I am here as you know because I need financial help. I have found a new job but won't be starting it until the first of the year and am having trouble meeting my mortgage payments. It would mean a great deal if you could help me out until I get my first paycheck. Naturally, I'll pay you back with interest." Aside from giving the reason why you need to borrow the money, you must say how much you will need and for how long. It's also important to explain where you will get the money to pay the loan back.

If you are the person being approached to lend money, you may find yourself in a difficult position because you sense a loan from you will not remedy what may be a chronic problem and will at best plug the hole temporarily. For instance, a niece may come to you to ask if you will lend her money to help pay for her vacation or for furniture for her new apartment. You may have loaned her money before—and most willingly—but if you were never paid back there's good reason not to make a second loan. Explain to her that you were delighted to help her out the time before but the fact that she's asking you for money again must mean she's living beyond her means. If after listening to what she has to say in response, you feel she has a serious problem, and if you can afford the cost, you might offer to send her to a counselor or financial adviser, whichever seems more appropriate. If she rejects this idea, you have every right to say to her, "I'm sorry but I am not the answer to your financial problems. Coming to me for more money will only jeopardize our relationship." Beyond that, all you can do is hope that she will hear your message and reappraise her attitudes about money.

In particular, if you are the type who likes to help others, it can be very difficult to turn down a request for money. On the other hand it can be just as difficult, if you have made a loan, to collect. But you have to. If the person you have loaned money to does not make his payments on time, send him a reminder. Should your letter have no effect, try telephoning. What you want to try to avoid is having to take legal action, but in the end it may be your only recourse.

If you find yourself in any financial relationship—either borrowing or lending—with friends or relatives, make sure it's on a business basis. The arrangement should never be informal or casual. If no legal document is to be drawn up, you can get a standard loan note at your local stationery store. The note should include the date of the loan, the total amount being borrowed, the name and address of those involved, the dates that payments are due, the interest rate, and the final due date. Be sure the note is signed and dated.

BEING WITH THOSE WHO HAVE MORE MONEY THAN YOU

It's likely you'll find that friends who have considerably more money than you entertain in a manner commensurate with the amount of money they have. There's nothing wrong with this and, although you can't entertain them at the same level, it shouldn't embarrass you in the least. You will just have to make an extra effort to think of special, appropriate ways to repay your richer friends: invite them back to your house for drinks, coffee, and dessert after a concert or other entertainment, ask them for brunch or a light supper before the theater, for cocktails at a popular new bar, for a summer barbecue or picnic, or take them to a ball game. It's not how you entertain; it's doing something together that matters.

BEING WITH THOSE WHO HAVE LESS MONEY

When you have a friend who has considerably less money than you, you either change your style of entertainment—eat in a less expensive restaurant than you normally do or eat in a restaurant you usually go to and split the bill—or you can treat your friend. Probably you will end up doing a little of both.

If there are things that you and a particular friend would enjoy doing together but you know your friend won't be able to afford them, say it's your treat. If it's an invitation to the theater for instance, and he's uncertain about accepting your generosity, tell him you can well afford the price of the tickets and that it's seeing the play together that's important.

Money inequity, of course, can be a temporary situation—for example, if your friend is out of work or attending graduate school, you can offer to pay his way but reassure him that when he has a job he can take you.

Be sensitive about not making it a habit always to pay for a friend who has less money than you. Let him pay his way or treat you occasionally when you know the circumstances are right. In a good friendship it is as important to know when to take as when to give.

TALKING ABOUT MONEY

All of us from time to time think about the rising cost of living—from rent to food to health care—and sharing such concerns can be consoling. But, difficult as it may be, try to avoid talking about money more than is absolutely necessary. It becomes boring and can be offensive.

Whether the bore is the braggart, eager to divulge how much his car cost, the whiner who complains about not being able to live as well as he'd like, or the sharp dealer who wants to describe his latest acquisition, all social conversation centering on money is unattractive and unbecoming to people of any taste or character. Money matters should really be discussed only with your spouse or family, your banker or financial adviser.

Under certain circumstances, curiosity is a delightful characteristic but not when it comes to money matters. It is insensitive to ask even your best friend how much something cost. People often want to know the price of a house, a car, or some other personal possession and will come right out and ask. You absolutely do not have to tell the cost unless you want to. Instead, make a deflecting comment like, "I can't remember" or "It was a present." Another possible reply to the question is, "It's something I'd rather not think about. Everything costs too much today."

A parent should remember not to press an adult child of his for information about her salary (nor should one sibling ask another how much she makes). When you talk to your child about her job, if she wants you to know how much she's making, you can be certain she'll tell you so.

If a friend talks to you about her finances, perhaps asking your advice or opinion on a certain issue to do with money, you must keep whatever information she gives you confidential. Even if she does not tell you to, you're obliged to respect her privacy, and money is very definitely a private matter.

WHO PAYS THE RESTAURANT BILL?

Modern-day etiquette takes a more practical approach to the long-standing tradition of a man paying for a woman's meal when they go out socially. Now the roles are often reversed, with the woman reciprocating past dinner invitations by inviting the man to be her guest.

When you invite someone to lunch or dinner at a restaurant, phrase your invitation so it's absolutely clear to the person that he or she is to be your guest. You can get your point across by saying, "I'd like to take you to dinner Friday," or "Can you have dinner with me Friday? My treat this time."

When a man and woman have dinner together at a restaurant the waiter often assumes the man is the host and presents him with the bill. If you are taking the man to dinner, say to the waiter, "Please give me the bill." To be discreet, use a credit card instead of cash.

If you sense that the man you're taking to dinner will feel self-conscious if you ask the waiter for the bill—and some do—you have a number of options: when you make the reservation you can ask the owner or maître d' if it's possible to have the bill sent to you at home (if so, you must indicate in advance what percentage of the total bill should be added for a tip); you can give your credit card to the maître d' when you arrive at the restaurant and ask that it be brought to you at the end of the meal ready to be signed; on the pretext of going to the ladies' room, you can hand the credit card to the waiter, quickly and quietly saying the meal is on you.

When two couples go out for dinner together, usually the bill is split in half. If one couple orders entrees that cost considerably more than what the other couple orders, they should offer to pay a larger share of the bill. Couples who go out to dinner regularly can work out whatever system of paying seems best for them—they can split the bill, break down the bill so each couple pays for what they ate and drank, pay the total bill every other time, or when they place their order they can ask the waiter for separate bills.

The ordering of wine calls for special attention. The cost of a truly good bottle of wine can be a quarter of the price of an entire meal for four. If one couple wants a more expensive bottle of wine than the other, they should pay for it or at least pay a larger share.

Friends sometimes get together for an impromptu dinner, perhaps after a cocktail party or lecture series they have attended. In this kind of situation, it's usual to split the bill. There are times, however, when you may want to pay for a friend. If you do, give a reason—you received a windfall or you happen to be the one with a job. If your friend is firm about paying for his meal, don't force the issue. If you are going to pay, when the waiter brings the check, raise your hand, gesturing that the bill is for you.

A word of caution for anyone eating in a restaurant. Sometimes a mistake is made in the bill, unfortunately often in the restaurant's favor. Whether you do the treating or handle the check when it's to be divided, look the bill over carefully. If there's an error, whether it's in your favor or the restaurant's, it should be brought to the waiter's attention.

THE ART OF TIPPING

The word "tip" comes from England. Before the postal service was established, a businessman wishing to communicate with other business-men would hand letters to a stagecoach driver and offer him a shilling "To Insure Promptness." The idea of a reward for service of course goes back much further.

Despite its long history, few money issues cause as much anxiety as tipping, even among the most sophisticated. Partly this is because there are no hard and fast rules. Knowing when to tip and how much depends on such variables as where you live, the service rendered, and personal philosophy. Although there really is no right amount to tip, there are some general rules. The first is that many people, such as waiters, taxi drivers, and hairdressers, rely on tips to supplement their own minimal salaries. The second is that no tip is automatically required. It is a reward for good service. The third rule is that a generous tip will usually get you better service in the future.

When giving a tip, it's important to look the person in the eye and express your appreciation as you hand him the money. Kind words of gratitude are as important as the tip itself and will be remembered by the recipient long after the tip has been spent.

The suggestions that follow are averages. Feel free to adjust them to your inclinations, your income, and your locale.

AT A RESTAURANT

You will have to use your judgment to some extent when tipping in restaurants and take into account where you are dining and the type of service you receive (if the service is inefficient or unbearably slow, you have reason to reduce the tip to the minimal amount). In general, however, the more expensive and sophisticated the restaurant, the greater the number of people you tip and the larger the tips. Today, fifteen percent is standard in most restaurants, although in a first-class establishment, if the food is outstanding and the service impeccable, you might give twenty percent. At a lunch counter or in a self-service restaurant, on the other hand, you can leave between ten and fifteen percent to be shared among those helping serve the food and cleaning up. You should always leave something—even if you have a cup of coffee or a soft drink at a counter, give a twenty-five-cent tip.

When you dine at a first-class restaurant, you tip:

THE MAÎTRE D'HÔTEL, THE CAPTAIN, THE WAITER In a good, first-class restaurant you will usually be attended only by a captain and a waiter. However, at extremely elegant restaurants, including those given a five-star rating by the Michelin guidebooks, there will also be a maître d'hôtel.

If the maître d'hôtel merely shows you to your table, no tip is necessary. If you are a regular customer of the restaurant, however, then tip him approximately ten to fifteen dollars every few times you dine there. Hand the bills to him as you leave the restaurant and thank him for "everything." If it is your first visit to the restaurant, tip the maître d' before dinner—ten dollars is fine; fifteen is generous. He will see that you receive special attention and will doubtless remember you the next time you come.

Fifteen to twenty percent of the bill, minus taxes and wine, goes to the captain and waiter (leave one fourth to the captain and three fourths to the waiter).

In a more modest restaurant, leave only one tip—fifteen percent of the total bill, including the wine but not the tax—for the waiter or waitress. If you are paying cash, put the tip on the plate that's brought to you with the change from your bill.

THE SOMMELIER Give ten percent of the cost of the wine to the sommelier or wine steward; fifteen percent if you received extra attention or if you ordered a number of bottles. The sommelier is paid in cash as you leave the restaurant (if there is no wine steward to tip, then include the price of the wine in determining your tip to the captain and waiter).

THE BARTENDER Tip fifteen percent of the bar bill if you had drinks at the bar before going to your table.

THE COATROOM ATTENDANT One dollar or slightly more if you checked a briefcase, umbrella, etc. (When there's a charge for checking coats, the attendant should still be tipped, as that charge goes to the restaurant, not to the attendant.)

THE LADIES' ROOM ATTENDANT One dollar; two dollars if she did something special like sewing on a button (usually there's a plate on the washbasin counter in which to place tips).

THE MEN'S ROOM ATTENDANT Also one dollar.

THE DOORMAN One dollar for getting you a taxi (if it's raining, two dollars).

THE VALET PARKER Two dollars for getting your car.

PIANIST, STROLLING MUSICIAN Two dollars for a couple making a request (if several people are in the party, five dollars).

When the time comes to pay the bill check it for accuracy. If you are paying with a credit card, there's a space on the charge slip where you may fill in the amount of the tip. If you prefer, you may leave the tip in cash so the waiter will receive it immediately rather than having to wait until the credit card company reimburses the restaurant.

Two other points to keep in mind. If the restaurant totals the bill without indicating the tax, which is often the case if the slip is computer-generated, you may ask what the tax is, as a means of figuring out the tip. And, secondly, if the ink on the printed bill is so light that you cannot read it, ask the waiter to explain the various items and charges. As a consumer, you have a right to this information.

AT A DINNER HELD AT A RESTAURANT

If you are hosting the dinner, you may find that the restaurant has added a service charge, typically fifteen percent, to the bill. This is then divided among the waiters and waitresses and you do not need to add any more unless you wish to. However, it is standard after a large affair to give the maître d'hôtel or headwaiter a separate tip. Figure one or two dollars per guest.

If no service charge is added, then you must add the fifteen percent to the bill. It's nice to give it in cash to the person in charge and ask that he divide it among the waiters.

If you are a guest at a private party being held at a restaurant, although your host is paying for dinner, you are expected to tip the coatroom attendant, the ladies' or men's room attendant, and the valet parker if you arrive in your own car.

AT A CLUB

In most private clubs the personnel have been told not to accept tips, although sometimes they do. (However, if employees are discovered accepting tips the management may reprimand them severely or even fire them.) One of the convenient aspects of belonging to a club is that as a member you do not have to tip constantly; instead you are usually asked once a year to give to a special holiday fund for employees. At that time, some clubs consider it acceptable also for a member to give additional tips to those employees who have been particularly helpful throughout the year, such as the headwaiter or a locker room attendant. If you are uncertain about the club's policy, read the house rules or check with the club manager.

If you are the guest at a club, for a meal or special event, do not tip the coatroom attendant.

Many clubs have overnight facilities for members and their families or friends. If you stay in a club bedroom, service is usually added to the bill. If it is not, tip the chambermaid and others as you would in a regular hotel (two or three dollars a day). Again, if you have any questions about the club's tipping policy, ask the advice of the club manager.

At a beach club, do not tip the person who brings you an umbrella or gives you your towels (usually you give to the employees' holiday fund). Golf caddies receive about fifteen percent of the regular greens fees for eighteen holes; for nine holes, it is closer to twenty percent. Also, at some clubs the locker-room attendant is tipped periodically.

In the case of a health club, if you have a personal trainer, masseur, or masseuse, you will want to give him or her a tip or present at holiday time. This also applies to the locker-room attendant.

IN A TAXI, OR HIRED CAR

Plan to tip approximately fifteen percent of the total fare for most taxi rides; twenty percent in large cities. If you're lucky enough to find a driver who actually carries your bags to the curb or to the front door, tip him more generously. If you encounter a surly driver, you might undertip or give him no tip at all and tell him that you would have given him a tip if he'd been a little more pleasant. Nor do you have to tip a driver who willfully refuses to follow the route you suggest or is particularly argumentative or unpleasant.

Sometimes a really bad traffic jam, especially in a large city, brings all traffic to a halt. Bear in mind that your driver is losing money during these long waits on the road. If he's been pleasant, tip him a little extra and tell him you appreciated his good nature.

If you have hired a commercial limousine, in a large city tip twenty percent of the fare; in a smaller city, fifteen percent. If you use a limousine service regularly, you will be billed monthly, in which case you may ask the company to add the tip to the bill.

AT THE HAIRDRESSER

In some beauty salons there are so many people doing so many things that tipping can be quite overwhelming. One question that keeps coming up is whether or not to tip the owner of the shop. The guideline is really quite simple. If the owner charges more for his services than you would pay his employees, you do not need to tip him. In a small shop, whether it's in the city or country, if you are taken care of by the owner, he often charges the same as the rest of the staff. When that is the case, tip the owner the same way you would one of the employees. If you do not know whether the owner charges more, simply ask when making your appointment what the various fees are.

You may use these general guidelines and adapt them to your particular city or town:

- Twenty percent of the total bill to your hairdresser if you're having a cut, color, permanent, or other time-consuming treatment.
- Fifteen percent if you're just getting a wash and blow dry.
- Two dollars to the shampoo person.
- Fifteen percent of the cost of a manicure or pedicure to the manicurist, with a minimum of a dollar-fifty; the same for a facial or wax treatment.

Whether you have a regular weekly appointment or visit the hairdresser only now and then, your tip should be the same. After all, the staff is giving you the same amount of service whether it's once a week or once a month.

You should hand out your tips personally; if a stylist is with another customer when you are ready to leave, put the tip in the pocket of his jacket. Even if you are not pleased with your hair style or coloring, express your displeasure to the person in charge but leave a tip anyway as the staff depends on gratuities.

HOLIDAY TIPPING

The holiday season is the customary time to remember people who have made your life pleasant during the year. Of course, whom you tip or give presents to is very much a personal decision. However, your personal assistant, housekeeper, babysitter or nanny, cleaning woman, and hairdresser should head your list. How much you tip each depends on how close you are to the person, how long he or she has been with you and what the usual tip is for someone in that particular position.

As a standard rule of thumb, give your personal assistant, housekeeper, and nanny one week's salary if they've been in your employ a year or less; after that two weeks' salary is appropriate, or more if you choose to. A cleaning woman should be given a minimum of one week's salary and a babysitter the equivalent of two or more average sittings.

When it comes to your hairdresser, if you have a weekly appointment that costs thirty dollars, then thirty dollars would be your minimum holiday tip. If you have been going to the same hairdresser, you will want to give more generously than if you are a new customer. Those who live in cities such as New York, Washington, Dallas, and Chicago generally give larger tips because the cost of living is high.

Use new bills to tip with. Put them in envelopes each marked with the person's name. Add a short note thanking him or her for helping you throughout the year. "Many thanks for everything you do for me. I never would have gotten through the year without you. All best wishes for the New Year." If your relationship is less personal, you may simply write, "With appreciation and my best wishes for the New Year." Then sign your name.

IN AN APARTMENT BUILDING Those living in apartment buildings often face a large number of people to tip at holiday time. Aside from your superintendent, you may have several doormen, elevator men, and maintenance people to take care of. The amount to tip is based on a number of factors, such as how grand the building is, how long you've lived there, how often you use the services of the various employees, and if you tip them during the course of the year or just once at holiday time and of course the quality of service received. In some large apartment buildings, instead of each resident giving individual tips there is a locked collection box in the lobby with a narrow slit for bills and checks. In a smaller building, one resident may be in charge of collecting and distributing tips. If you are new to the building, ask the superintendent or a neighbor what the tipping policy is. Those who run their businesses from their apartments should tip more generously, especially if the doormen have the added responsibility of dealing with messengers and accepting deliveries. If you have small children whom the doormen occasionally keep an eye on or if you are elderly or infirm and require extra help, you also will want to be more generous in what you give.

What follow are a few tipping suggestions (amounts given are minimums).

$50 to $100	Superintendent
$25 to $40	Doorman
$20 to $50	Elevator operator
$20 to $30	Handyman

For those who remain in their same jobs, the amount should be increased by a few dollars each subsequent year.

IN A GARAGE If you keep your car in a garage, tip the equivalent of half of one month's garage rent. Of course, if you take your car in and out each day you should tip more generously than if you need it only on weekends or now and then. Tips may be placed in envelopes and given to the individual garage employees, or you may be asked to give a check made out to the Employees' Christmas Fund to the manager of the garage, who will then distribute the money among the men. In some garages, there is an intimidating practice of listing on a blackboard the amount each customer gives. Feel free to ignore such bad manners and tip as you wish.

WHOM YOU TIP AT HOLIDAY TIME There are a host of people you should tip whenever they perform a specific service, such as a waiter in a restaurant or the hotel doorman who gets you a taxi, and some people you may or may not tip regularly, but would at holiday time. This is not necessary though, if you deal with them only once or twice during the year. In the list that follows you might also want to give those marked with an asterisk a small present along with the cash tip. These are people who may be regularly employed by you or with whom you have a close working relationship. If they live in you might give something for their room, such as an area rug or a color television set that they can take with them should they leave.

- Personal assistant*
- Housekeeper/cook*
- Cleaning woman*
- Nanny/au pair*
- Babysitter*
- Chauffeur*
- Kennel operator
- Dogwalker
- Maître d' at your favorite restaurant
- Captain and waiter (these people are tipped at the time you dine at the restaurant; however, if you are a regular customer, you may wish to give them a holiday cash tip as well, but only to those who regularly wait on you)
- Health club trainer
- Health club locker room attendant
- Hairdresser

- Shampoo person
- Manicurist
- Barber
- Shoeshine person
- Gardener or lawn service person
- Regular snowplower or sidewalk shoveler
- UPS or other package delivery persons (it is illegal to tip the mailperson, who is an employee of the federal government)
- Private garbage collectors
- Newspaper carrier
- Building employees
- Garage personnel

TO TIP OR NOT TO TIP

The following are partial lists of people you do and do not routinely tip, although it should be noted that tipping procedures vary somewhat in different parts of the country. It would be impossible to list here every potential recipient of a tip, so only the more obvious ones are given.

DO TIP

- Headwaiter, waiter, bartender, wine steward, pianist or strolling musician, coatroom attendant, ladies' and men's room attendants, doorman if he gets taxi, and valet parker at restaurants
- Hotel concierge, bellboy, chambermaid, hotel doorman (if he gets taxi)
- Hairdresser (manicurist, etc.)
- Barber
- Personal trainer at health club
- Taxi driver/limousine service driver
- Employee who retrieves your car in public parking garage
- Car wash personnel who clean inside of car and wipe it dry (there is usually a receptacle marked TIPS)
- Moving men
- Those who deliver for the grocery or takeout food places, drugstore, dry cleaner, laundry, liquor store, florist. These people should be tipped a minimum of one to two dollars each time they make a delivery; if the package is large or heavy, if the weather is bad, or they have to walk up several flights of stairs, tip two to four dollars. Newspaper delivery people are tipped once a year at holiday time.
- Shoeshine person

- Building personnel, such as a handyman, when he performs a service.

Do not tip

- Professionals (doctors, dentists, teachers, lawyers, accountants, decorators, realtors, travel agent, etc.)
- Owners and managers of businesses
- Hospital staff members (a box of candy or basket of fruit is a kind thought for the nurses' station)
- Airline stewardesses
- Ship's officers
- Train conductors
- Municipal or long-distance bus drivers
- Employees of the federal government (i.e., mail carriers)
- Private club employees
- Maids or butlers at a dinner party in a private house
- Ushers in a theater, opera house, concert hall (except in certain European countries)
- Plumber, electrician, or other service employees (except if they come during off hours as a special favor because of an emergency)
- Busboy at a restaurant (exception: if a busboy is so efficient and affable that you notice him, it's nice to give him two to five dollars; many are working their way through school).

Special situations If your hairdresser comes to your house to do your hair, you would give him a tip. In the case of people who are self-employed, such as a masseur, exercise instructor, or yoga teacher, you do not give a tip, although if they come on a regular basis you should give them a present at holiday time.

Sometime you may find yourself in the embarrassing position of not knowing whether a tip is appropriate. For example, you get off a commuter train to find your car has a flat tire. Someone unknown to you comes by and changes it for you. If it's a young person, you probably won't hesitate to give him a ten to twenty-dollar tip. The dilemma comes when it's a man in a three-piece suit who looks a good deal more affluent than you. All you can do is call on your intuition, and in this case your intuition should tell you that this is not the right time to tip. If you are lucky enough to be carrying a bottle of wine or a gourmet delicacy you might ask him to please accept it with gratitude. Otherwise, all you can do is offer your profuse thanks.

Should you ever tip someone you normally do not tip? For instance, your oil burner gives out on New Year's Day. You call the owner of the plumbing company and he says he will come unless he can find one of his employees to send. Even though you will most likely be charged extra for a holiday service call, you still want to show your appreciation to the person who comes to your rescue by giving him a tip. If it's the plumber's worker who shows up, you can give him ten to twenty dollars, but if it's the owner who comes, do not tip him. Instead, if you have a bottle of scotch or other liquor on hand, give him that with thanks and good wishes for the New Year.

WORKING WITH A REAL ESTATE BROKER

Just the thought of dealing with the logistics that go with buying a new house or selling one can generate all sorts of anxieties, particularly if you are doing it for the first time. Questions such as "Will the real estate broker try to pressure me into buying a house I'm not absolutely wild about?" or "Will she talk me into selling my house for less than I need?" come to mind. Anxieties of this sort are perfectly natural when you find yourself on the brink of negotiating a real estate contract with very little knowledge of how such transactions work. What's comforting to know is that millions of other people have been through the same trauma and that the majority of brokers, far from wanting to do you in, have your best interests at heart.

If you are in the market to buy a house—or sell one—put yourself in the hands of a competent real estate professional. The best way to find such a person is through word of mouth. Ask a friend or colleague who recently had similar dealings what broker he used and whether he was satisfied. If you have a broker with whom you can maintain a good working relationship it can make a big difference. If you communicate well and respect each other, it all but guarantees that your search for a house or a buyer will be a happy experience. Should you find, after a few dealings, that you are not compatible with a particular broker, it's better to bite the bullet right away and tell her so: "I want to thank you for all your help, but I have decided I'd like to try another firm I've heard about."

Most people are not familiar with real estate terminology nor do they know all the fine points of negotiating an agreement, which vary from state to state. For instance, while it's customary for the seller to pay the broker's commission, in certain areas and in certain instances the buyer selects a broker of his own to represent him and pays that person a negotiated commission. Before meeting with your broker you'll feel a lot more confident if you do some advance research. Look into such matters as how does the broker determine the fair market value, what type of mortgage will you want, how does an exclusive listing work, where can you find a reliable building inspector, and what do "earnest money" and "contract sales" mean? If you have some familiarity with real estate terms you'll be better equipped to make intelligent decisions and less likely to be confronted with an unanticipated cost that's just been brought to your attention.

If you are buying a house, be as specific as possible when you tell your broker what you are looking for, and be honest about what you can afford. When you are selling, ask your broker about comparable recent sales in your area and then be realistic about an asking price. Be straightforward about answering any reasonable questions the broker asks you. For instance, if she asks whether you are using another broker as well, and indeed you are, tell her so. When it's your turn to ask questions, come prepared with a list. No matter how petty or ignorant they sound to you, do not feel embarrassed to ask them. She's the professional, you're the client. If it's possible, try to call your broker during her office hours, rather than at seven o'clock in the evening when she may be sitting down to dinner with her family. What's more, don't waste the broker's time by having her drive you all over town showing you places you know you can't afford. And once the deal has been cinched, write your broker a letter expressing your appreciation for all she has done on your behalf. Or, better still, take her out for a celebratory lunch.

Working With an Interior Designer

No matter how well you know your decorator, you must remember that she is a professional and is in business to make money. Often friends of a decorator either forget or ignore this important fact and expect her to get materials, wallpaper, or whatever for them at the decorator's discount. This not only puts the decorator in an embarrassing position, but it is not fair. After all, you don't ask your travel agent to forfeit her commission, nor do you expect a doctor friend to treat you for free.

Health-Related Matters

You and your doctor

Good health care, especially in large cities or urban areas, is no longer something you can count on your doctor to provide for you. You must be an active, informed participant who can speak up for—and direct—what you want. While it's good to treat your doctor with respect, it's equally good to remember that she is providing you a service, and should be sensitive to your wishes as well.

Your doctor, like any professional, has office hours and they should be respected. Always make an appointment and be on time. She may be seeing patients only at certain hours because she is going to the hospital for rounds or surgery. Never try to drop in or show up late. If your car breaks down so you're unavoidably delayed, give the doctor's office a call and let the secretary know what time you'll actually be able to get there. That way, she can plan around you or ask you to reschedule. Of course there are some doctors, such as obstetricians, who have very unpredictable schedules. If your doctor habitually runs forty-five minutes behind schedule and you don't like to wait, call before you go and ask if she is on schedule. Sometimes the answer will be "No, come at four-thirty instead of four." And be careful of "no shows." Not only is it inconsiderate not to show up for any appointment you've made, but some doctors will charge you for it.

When you get in to see your doctor, have a list of questions at the ready so you don't take up her time unnecessarily. Not only does this save you from last-minute jitters, it will also keep you from forgetting that one important point you thought of at three in the morning. Don't call your doctor on weekends unless it's an emergency or a very serious problem. Most have machines or answering services for after-office-hour calls. The latter will pass along a message and often can give you a referral. (But, of course, always feel free to call at any time if it *is* an emergency!)

It's not a good idea to ask any doctor, even one who's a friend, for free advice. And don't quiz her about her other patients; you want your doctor to respect the right to privacy of all her patients—including you.

The most common friction between any doctor and patient is about payment. Especially in this day and age, with all the different health care systems, from private health insurance to health maintenance organizations, it's a good idea to know your doctor's rules and regulations up front as well as those of your insurance provider. Ask if your doctor will bill the insurance company directly or if you must pay up front and be reimbursed. Should you expect to pay at the time of your visit or will she bill you? Ask your insurance provider if your doctor is covered under their plan. HMOs, for example, require that you see certain doctors they already have contracts with. It's also a good idea to ask for a list of your doctor's fees; she won't be insulted and you'll know what to expect.

These days, it's also quite standard to ask for a second opinion before undergoing any major surgery. Many insurance companies require that you do and many doctors will provide you with a list of other physicians to consult.

If you are unhappy with your care, with your doctor's bedside manner, or the way her office is run, you have every right to make a change. It's best to notify your doctor in person, but if you would rather not, you may write her a letter. The easiest out is to say you're switching to Dr. So-and-so because she is a specialist in the field in which you need care. In some states your doctor or your hospital will require you to sign a release before she sends your records to your new caretaker. But they have to do as you request. Just be aware that in small communities doctors tend to take care of each other, much like a large fraternity, and may become very territorial with their patients. Switching may be difficult in such a case—but you should never feel shy or embarrassed about doing it.

A HOSPITAL STAY

Before checking into a hospital, you want to give careful thought to what you take with you. For an average stay, you'll need one or two nightgowns or pairs of pajamas, a bathrobe and possibly a bed jacket, a pair of slippers, your cosmetics and toiletries. Often after surgery you are not permitted to take a bath or shower, so give thought to packing some bath gel, which will add a fragrant touch to your sponge bath. Also, a face cleanser and a dry shampoo are useful to pick up your spirits and appearance.

And don't forget to consider taking along the following: books, magazines, writing paper and/or postcards, pens, stamps, your address and telephone book, a clock, a radio. A small amount of cash comes in handy in case you want to buy the newspaper every morning and in some hospitals is necessary if you want to use the television set by your bed. Leave jewelry and any other valuables at home.

When you check into a hospital, make certain to use whatever surname is on your insurance company policy. Confusion can arise in the case of a woman who uses her married name socially and her maiden name professionally. Also be sure your doctor knows under what name you were admitted. One obstetrician tells a story about telling a patient to go directly to the hospital and he'd meet her there. He was unable to track her down until just before she gave birth because she'd checked in under her husband's name rather than her maiden name by which he knew her.

If you're sharing a hospital room, be as thoughtful and considerate toward your roommate as you hope she will be toward you. If your bed happens to be the one beside the only window, ask your roommate if she'd like to sit in front of the window occasionally. Or, if you're the one closest to the door and would like a crack at the window, ask first. Don't just walk over and sit down. Keep the volume of your television or radio low, do not talk endlessly on the telephone, and when you do use it, speak as quietly as possible. When you have visitors, ask them to keep their voices down. Abide by hospital rules. If there are limits to the number of visitors allowed in your room, don't try to sneak in others. And if your roommate's visitors are chattering away in loud voices, ask them to be quieter. This applies too if the night nurses' conversation disturbs your sleep. Ring your bell or go to their station and ask them politely to be a little quieter. In these situations, you have every right to speak up.

When you leave a hospital, you may want to express your gratitude to the floor nurses by giving them one big gift, such as a large box of fruit or assorted cookies; for a private nurse, a basket of gourmet food or a more personal present like a scarf is appropriate. But often just writing a short thank-you note is enough.

VISITING A PATIENT IN THE HOSPITAL

When a friend or family member enters the hospital, respect his wishes about whom he wants to see and when. Unless told otherwise, never just appear at the hospital assuming you'll be welcome. Call ahead of time or check with the family to find out the patient's wishes. After all, a person who feels poorly may not have the energy it takes to converse with a visitor, even for a short time. When you do visit a patient, be sensitive as to how long you should stay. In some cases, five minutes is enough. Keep the conversation light. If the patient wants to talk about his illness, be a good listener, but never volunteer information about someone you know who had a similar illness with bad complications. While you are there, it's thoughtful to ask the patient if you can get him anything from the hospitality shop or cafeteria. If he has a roommate, offer to bring him something also. Should the patient's doctor appear while you're there, leave the room so they can talk privately.

Instead of visiting the patient in the hospital, you might want to consider an alternative good-will mission: doing something for his family. Invite the patient's spouse to dinner or offer to take the children to lunch and the movies. You might even want to stock the family refrigerator with a casserole or two or with other foods they can make meals from.

Most hospitals discourage the sending of flowers as floor nurses don't have the time to care for them. Rather than sending flowers, you might want to rent the patient a television set for a day or two, or take him a sampling of the latest magazines.

THE TERMINALLY ILL

Never neglect or put off going to see a friend who is terminally ill. This is a time when she will need and appreciate all the love and support you can give her. The reason some people put off such a visit is not from lack of caring, but because the idea unnerves them; they are not sure what they should say to the patient or what questions to ask her. If you are about to visit a terminally ill friend, the best advice anyone can give you is: be your natural self. Talk about whatever you and your friend usually talk about, but by no means make unrealistic remarks like, "You look terrific," or "I'm sure you'll be just fine shortly." If the patient has faced up to her illness, then you must also. In addition, don't monopolize the conversation. If she wants to talk to you about her illness, be prepared to listen. It can be therapeutic for her.

Aside from taking your friend magazines or anything else you think she may like, you can offer to do errands for her or household chores.

If you live far away from your friend and can't get to visit her, call her on the telephone from time to time or send her frequent postcards with your news.

PSYCHOLOGICAL COUNSELING

Every life has many crossroads and at one point or another many of us feel the need to seek professional help. Sometimes we need counseling for a number of weeks or perhaps even a number of years. Fortunately, the stigma against psychological help has diminished as more and more people realize it's healthier to face problems head on than to deny them. The demise of the nuclear family, of community support systems such as the church and the neighborhood, all contribute to making modern life more difficult for everyone's psyche.

A good way to find a competent therapist is through the American Psychological Association (1-800-374-3120). They not only offer a free brochure called "How to Choose a Therapist" but will give you the telephone number of the psychological association in your state which you can call for a list of doctors' names. A personal referral is even better. Ask your doctor or a friend you know who is in therapy to suggest a therapist. But be aware that not everyone wants to speak freely about counseling. If you suspect someone is seeing a psychologist but hasn't told anyone, don't pry. This may be a very personal issue. On the other hand, if you're the one being counseled, don't talk endlessly about it to your friends. Like all health matters, they are of the utmost importance to oneself but less so to others.

If you don't believe in seeking psychological counseling, be tolerant of those who do. They may be going through a particularly difficult time and don't need criticism as well.

DRUGS AND ALCOHOL

Chemical dependency is a complicated disease and, despite what many people think, you do not have to drink or use drugs every day to be chemically dependent. What's more, someone with this disease may be able to hold down a responsible job and to maintain normal personal relationships. Certain individuals with a chemical dependency are cross-addicted to both alcohol and prescription or illegal drugs.

You may have reason to suspect a person is chemically dependent if he or she

- Shows an increase in alcohol or drug consumption;
- Has memory lapses or blackouts;
- Has many colds, sniffs constantly, or makes frequent trips to the bathroom;
- Brags about his drinking or drug exploits;
- Periodically goes "on the wagon";
- Has a personality change when under the influence of alcohol or drugs;

- Is secretive about his comings and goings;
- Spends more time with friends who drink or take drugs than with those who do not;
- Only goes to parties where alcohol or drugs are available;
- Often arrives at social occasions late and/or high;
- Refuses to turn over his car keys when he's incapable of driving safely;
- Is erratic or inconsistent in his behavior patterns;
- Has problems at work or frequently calls in sick;
- Spends money recklessly, borrows money from friends, and is unable to account for sums of money.

THE OFFICIAL SIDE OF LIFE

JURY DUTY

Every voting citizen in the United States is eligible for and has the duty to serve as a juror although lawyers or doctors or the self-employed are exempt in certain states. The way in which jurors' names are chosen varies from state to state, even from county to county. However, every jury panel is selected from a cross section of the community and, while certain temporary deferments are possible, most who are called must eventually serve.

It is a responsibility and a privilege to serve on a jury. How long you serve and how much you are paid depends on where you live and what type of jury you are called for—usually grand jury duty pays a bit more. When you receive your notice, read it *carefully*. If it is absolutely necessary that you request a deferment, and you must appear in person to do so, the notice will state a date, time, and place. Many people neglect to read the notice carefully and wait to ask for a deferment until they arrive at the courthouse on the day they are scheduled to serve. This upsets the entire system, as everyone without a prior deferral is counted on as a prospective juror.

Jury selection can be time-consuming. Each juror must satisfy the court, both litigants, and their attorneys. The questions you are asked as a prospective juror must be answered carefully and honestly. If you are questioned and not chosen for one jury, you go back into the pool and will be called for another. Once the jury selection is completed, the judge will instruct you on your duties and responsibilities. The judge must be treated with proper respect at all times. When he or she is talking, you should listen with close attention and not, as some have been known to do, leaf through magazines, write letters, or do needlepoint. Once the trial is under way, you must report promptly for each session, because the court can't convene until everyone is present. Never call in sick unless you really are. It wastes the court's time and the taxpayers' money. You must give full concentration to every question and answer during the trial. It is better not to try to take notes, even if you are allowed to, as you might miss important testimony. You will be asked not to discuss the case you're on with other jurors or with anyone else until it has been formally submitted to the jurors and you begin joint deliberations in the jury room.

Out of respect for the court, report for jury duty neatly dressed, as you would for business. Bring ample reading material or office work with you to fill up the time while you are waiting to be called for questioning. You will be able to call your home or office on one of the pay telephones, but out of consideration for those who may be waiting to make a similar call, make your calls brief. Once you are on a case, you can telephone only during a break. It's your responsibility to help keep the jurors' room free of debris. Get rid of used coffee cups and newspapers in the proper receptacles and keep the bathrooms neat.

Serving on a jury can be a boring or an exciting experience, depending on the case, but watching the process of justice in action is always impressive. Another positive note about serving on jury duty is the friendships that are formed. In fact, more marriages than you'd imagine have come about as a result of the jury system.

WHITE HOUSE PROTOCOL

Invitations to White House social events are engraved with the presidential seal embossed in white or gold; if it's a lunch or dinner your name is handwritten in the text by a staff calligrapher. Out of respect for the President and his wife, you should respond no more than a day or two after receiving the invitation. An invitation to the White House once took precedence over any other social invitation, but there is more leeway today and a family wedding or graduation, for example, would be a valid reason to refuse.

Two engraved cards are enclosed with a White House invitation; one tells you to go to the East Gate of the White House (if you were making a business call, you would be sent to the West Gate) and the other is your "admit" card. It is disrespectful to be late to any function at which the President will appear, so arrive at the gate at least five minutes before the time stipulated on the invitation. (It's best not to drive your own car as parking is limited.) After showing your "admit" card to the guard on duty, you enter the East Wing and will be directed to the area where coats are checked, after which you will be escorted to the reception room where the event is being held.

To a lunch or an afternoon reception, a woman should wear a short dress or a suit (if it is a late afternoon event, she may choose to wear a slightly dressier outfit). A man should wear a business suit. If you are

The President

requests the pleasure of your company
at a reception to be held at

The White House

on Wednesday, June 16, 1993
at five o'clock

In recognition of the
American Federation of
State, County, and
Municipal Employees, AFL-CIO

Please respond to
The Social Secretary
The White House
at your earliest convenience
giving date of birth and social security number

(202) 456-1414

Please present this card
with photo identification at
THE VISITORS ENTRANCE
The White House

NOT TRANSFERABLE

This is an example of a formal, engraved invitation to the White House. It includes an R.s.v.p. card and admittance card.

invited to the White House and are unsure of what to wear, call the Social Office (202-456-1414) and ask what the appropriate attire is for that occasion.

STATE DINNER With an occasional exception, state dinners are always black tie; a woman wears a short or long evening dress, a man his tuxedo. If you attend one of these dinners, when you arrive in the large entrance hall you'll be given a table number card, after which you will join the other guests in the East Room for cocktails. There you will notice a number of men in military uniform; they are the traditional White House social aides, who have regular jobs in the military services, but who also attend White House social events. Their job is to circulate among the guests, always on the alert to rescue someone who looks lost or is standing alone. The aides fulfill an important purpose because they are accomplished at making guests feel at ease and are able to answer practically any question.

At an appointed time the Marine Band, which has been playing in the entrance hall, will strike up a march, which is the signal that the President, the First Lady, and the honored guests are descending the staircase from the living quarters to join the party. There will be a short photographic session at the foot of the staircase, after which the group will proceed to the East Room while the band plays the fanfare called "Ruffles and Flourishes." At the entrance to the East Room the President and those with him stand at attention while a social aide announces in a loud, resonant voice the arrival of the President of the United States, the First Lady, and whoever the dignitaries may be. Immediately after the announcement they enter the room to the playing of "Hail to the Chief." There is a military posting of the colors by the honor guard, after which the President, the First Lady, and the guests of honor take their places in the receiving line. Next, the social aides assemble the guests for the receiving line. Introductions are made by a State Department protocol official or by a military aide at the head of the line. The line must move swiftly, so your greeting should be brief. If you have never met the President before, as you shake hands (a woman wearing long gloves removes the one on her right hand) you might say, "Good evening, Mr. President. It's an honor to be here," or "How do you do, Mrs. Adams. Thank you for inviting me."

After you pass through the line, you proceed to the State Dining Room. When you arrive there, look for the table with the number that corresponds to the one on your card and then find your place at that table. Do not sit down until the President and First Lady are seated. During dinner, talk to the guests to your left and right. At the conclusion of the meal, guests retire to the reception rooms where coffee and liqueurs are served.

A White House dinner is no different from any formal dinner party except that you may not leave until the President and First Lady go back upstairs to the family quarters. Once they have departed it's customary for guests to go home, although there's no reason not to stay on for about fifteen or twenty minutes if you want to, talking to friends.

After you have been to a state dinner or any function at the White House, you must write a thank-you letter. If you direct your letter to the First Lady, her name is written on the envelope as "Mrs. Adams" rather than "Mrs. John Adams" (according to protocol there is only one "Mrs. Adams," the President's wife) and sent to her at The White House, 1600 Pennsylvania Avenue, Washington, DC 20500.

SENDING GIFTS TO THE PRESIDENT AND FIRST LADY The policy for handling gifts sent to the White House often changes with each new administration. Currently, the President has the choice of keeping any gifts he receives (they are declared on his IRS form) or designating them as government property to be stored at the National Archives until his library is built, at which time they are displayed there. For reasons of security every package sent to the White House is X-rayed by the Secret Service. Food is always destroyed; even a salmon caught and crated by the President's closest friend must be disposed of.

You may want to think twice before sending a gift to the President or First Lady if you don't know them. The number of unsolicited gifts they receive is so great, it is not possible for them to see each one. For the same reason, it is impossible for them to send a personal acknowledgment for an unsolicited gift. Instead, a form letter or card is sent expressing gratitude "on behalf of the President and Mrs. Adams."

WRITING TO THE PRESIDENT AND FIRST LADY The White House receives approximately 50,000 letters a week, the majority of which are addressed to the President and/or his wife. Although the President and First Lady are interested in public opinion as expressed in these letters, they only have time to read a sampling of those received. Letters are turned over to the appropriate government agency or to staff members to be answered.

Family and close friends of the First Family are given a special code word to put on their envelopes so they can be delivered directly.

AN AUDIENCE WITH THE POPE

Many people, Catholic and non-Catholic, who go to Rome are anxious to see the Pope as well as visit Vatican City where he resides. At noon on Sundays, if the Pope is in residence at the Apostolic Palace in the Vatican, he appears at an open window in his private apartments to speak to the crowds of pilgrims in the square below. He speaks briefly in a number of languages, and when he pronounces the final benediction Catholics often make the sign of the cross and many kneel in the square.

GENERAL AUDIENCES General audiences with the Holy Father are held every Wednesday, except when the Pope is traveling. Usually these audiences take place at 11 A.M. in the Paul VI Audience Hall to the south of St. Peter's Basilica or, when weather permits, in St. Peter's Square. If you'd like to attend one of these audiences, tickets, which are given gratis, should be requested well in advance, particularly if you plan to be in Rome during the summer months. You can direct your request to Prefect, Pontifical Household, 00120 Vatican State, Europe, or to Visitor's Office, North American College (established by the National Conference of Catholic Bishops), at the same address. You must give the date and the number of tickets required; if you'd like the tickets delivered to you in Rome, give the name and address of the hotel where you'll be staying.

There are special reserved sections for people who have recently married, for invalids, and for the handicapped, which you may or may not qualify for. If you are a Catholic, you may want to include a letter of introduction from your parish priest. When you arrive in Rome, your tickets may be picked up after 5 P.M. the day before your audience at the Prefecture of the Pontifical Household, located past the bronze doors to the west of St. Peter's Basilica (if you requested your tickets through the North American College, these are picked up at Casa Santa Maria, Via dell'Umiltà 30).

Thousands of people attend the general audiences, so arrive early. There is no reserved seating, except for large groups who sit together in blocks. When the Pope appears, rise and remain standing until he is seated on his throne. The Holy Father speaks for sometimes fifteen minutes, sometimes much longer, and gives his remarks usually in Italian first, then other languages according to the nationalities of those in attendance. As the Pope finishes speaking in each language, people express their love and admiration for him by clapping and saying *"Viva il Papa!"* an international cry in Vatican City. Before the Pope leaves the hall he raises his hand to give the papal blessing. You should bow down at this moment; Catholics usually genuflect and make the sign of the cross. If you'd like a particular item blessed, hold it in your hand during this final benediction.

During the months of July and August, His Holiness usually resides at his summer residence, Castel Gandolfo, about twenty-five miles south of Rome. On Wednesdays he is taken by helicopter to St. Peter's Square for the general audience. If, however, you want to attend the Sunday noon audience at Castel Gandolfo, your hotel or a local travel agency will be able to arrange transportation for you.

SEMIPRIVATE AUDIENCES Semiprivate audiences with the Pope are held for groups of 50 to 200 people. Because of the number of requests received from all over the world, there's no guarantee you'll be one of the chosen few, even if you get your request in well in advance of the date. If you are going to Italy with a group from your city or town, or have a professional reason to be there, you may have a better chance of getting tickets by asking your city's bishop if he can arrange a semiprivate audience through the offices of the North American College in Rome or the Apostolic Nunciature, 3339 Massachusetts Avenue, N.W., Washington, DC 20008-3687.

PRIVATE AUDIENCES Private audiences are held for twelve or fewer prominent people, usually heads of state or ambassadors who are received with their families. At these private audiences, which usually last about twenty minutes, the Pope presents each person with a personal gift, such as a rosary, a small bronze medallion, or a holy medal. If a head of state calls on the Pope, there is an official exchange of gifts.

When the Holy Father enters the special room designated for private audiences, his guests are most often standing in a line. The Pope walks down the line as one of the assistants calls out the name of each person being presented. That person either goes down on one knee or bows low; if he is a Catholic he will take the Pope's right hand in his right hand and kiss his ring. A non-Catholic will simply bow low as a sign of respect and shake his hand. The Pope pauses to say something to each individual, giving special attention to children, and then he sits down on his throne to address the group. There is no need to be self-conscious about how to act. There are always friendly papal assistants and church assistants to instruct you on where to stand and what to do.

DRESS FOR AN AUDIENCE If you have a general audience you can wear your ordinary travel clothes, but they should be conservative in style and color. A woman is now admitted in pants, but not if she wears shorts or a sun dress. For a semiprivate or a private audience, a woman should wear a conservative dress of any color, with a minimum of jewelry and no gloves. A man should wear a dark business suit. A child should be dressed in his or her Sunday best. Some women, particularly if they live in a Spanish-speaking country, wear a black dress and lace mantilla to a private audience, a custom that is no longer obligatory.

THE POPE IN ST. PETER'S BASILICA On special religious feasts such as Christmas and Easter, the Pope often officiates at Mass in St. Peter's. Many thousands of *il popolo* crowd into St. Peter's Square to witness the proceedings. Admission to these Masses may be arranged in the same way as admission to an audience. On these occasions special stands for guests are erected close to the altar. These seats are reserved for members of the Vatican diplomatic corps, high church officials, titled individuals, and world social and business leaders. The Pope enters the basilica, at the end of the procession under a swirling gold canopy, and walks up the long center aisle to the altar. As he makes his entrance, the swelling shouts of the crowd in the square and the sounds of the majestic organ music fill the basilica. Slowly he makes his way to the altar that Bernini designed. The Swiss Guards stand smartly at attention, and the cardinals cluster in bright crimson robes. It is a most unforgettable sight.

THE FLAG AND THE NATIONAL ANTHEM

There are certain government rules and regulations having to do with the respectful use and display of the American flag. While these are not binding, they are set forth as a guide for citizens who wish to demonstrate the maximum respect for our national symbol.

INVOCATION AND SALUTE TO THE FLAG At a public lunch or dinner, or any occasion at which an invocation and a salute to the flag are given, the invocation precedes the salute—in other words, God and then country.

THE NATIONAL ANTHEM At the sound of the anthem, whether the flag is displayed or not, you rise and stand at attention (facing the flag, if there is one), unless you are physically unable to do so. If you choose to, you may place your right hand over your heart. A man wearing a hat removes it and places it over his heart. Whether you sing the anthem or not, stand quietly and respectfully until the anthem is finished and you can be seated. Men and women in uniform give the military salute at the first note of the anthem and hold it until the last note.

Here are a few guidelines concerning the display of the flag. They come from the National Flag Foundation, Flag Plaza, Pittsburgh, PA 15219.

- Never fly the flag upside down except as a distress signal.

- Don't let the flag trail on the ground or in the water.

- Display the flag out of doors only from sunrise to sunset. If a flag is flown at night, it should be lighted.

- Hoist the flag briskly but lower it slowly and ceremoniously.

- No other flag, city or state, is flown from the same staff above the United States flag.

- When other flags are flown in conjunction with the United States flag on adjacent flagstaffs, the United States flag is always hoisted first and retired last. The other flags should always be placed on the left of the United States flag.

- A flag flown from a staff fastened to a windowsill or balcony or fixed to the front of a building should be flown with the union, or blue field, at the peak of the staff unless the flag is at half mast.

- When a flag is suspended over a sidewalk on a cord between a building and a pole, the flag is hoisted from the building to the pole, union first.

- When a flag is displayed without a staff, it should lie flat against an upright support, indoors or out, never draped or festooned. (Use bunting for this purpose.) When it is displayed horizontally, or vertically against a wall or in a window, the union or field is uppermost, to the flag's own right (observer's left).

- A flag displayed over the middle of the street should hang vertically with the union to the north on an east and west street or to the east on a north and south one.

- The flag may not be draped on any vehicle. If it is to be displayed on a train, boat, or car it should be firmly fixed to a staff.

- The only exception to the rule about draping the flag occurs when it is used to cover a casket, union at the head and over the deceased's left shoulder. The flag must not touch the ground or be lowered into the grave. The casket is carried foot first.

- Flags carried in a mourning parade or procession are never put at half mast.

- The flag should not be carried horizontally in a procession, but should be aloft and waving.

- The flag must never be dipped to any person or thing. Only personal, state, regimental, or other flags may be used to render this honor.

- When the flag is flown at half mast, it is first hoisted to the peak, then lowered to half mast. Before retiring it, hoist it again to the peak.

- On Memorial Day the flag is flown at half mast only from sunrise until noon. At noon it is hoisted to full staff.

- In displaying the flag on a speaker's platform, place it above and behind the speaker, flat, union to the flag's right (observer's left). If it is flown from a staff, it should be placed in the place of honor (to the speaker's right) with the rope holding it run up the right side (audience's left) of the pole.

- A flag displayed in a public assembly (or house of worship) is flown from a staff, to the audience's right as it faces the stage (or pulpit). Service, state, or other special flags are flown to the left of the audience. If the flag is to be displayed from the chancel it is placed on the clergyman's right, to the congregation's left. Other flags are displayed on the clergyman's left.

- No lettering, marking, or imprint of any kind may be placed on the flag nor should the pole from which the flag flies ever carry advertising signs or pennants.

- When a flag becomes torn, tattered, faded, or otherwise unfit for display it should never be heedlessly discarded. An old flag deserves and must receive respectful destruction. It should be destroyed in one piece, privately, by burning it. Its fabric may not be reused for any other purpose.

GIFT GIVING

THE PHILOSOPHY OF GIFT GIVING

The spirit we bring to gift giving is most often instilled during childhood. Of course we are influenced by our culture and society, but it is the attitude of our family toward celebrating small and great occasions that shapes our emotional perspective on giving. If early experiences taught you to give and receive with gladness, without unrealistic expectations, chances are you look on the exchanging of presents as a happy and satisfying ritual.

The motive for giving a present can be powerful and subtle; all too often a present is given to win favor or gain approval. The ideal present, however, is one given with sincerity and generosity, and reflects the taste of the person you're giving the present to rather than your own.

Choosing an appropriate present takes time and thought, but not necessarily a lot of money. While a wildly extravagant present may be exciting to give and receive, a present does not have to be elaborate to convey your feelings. For instance, a handcrafted present has special significance as does an original poem. If the recipient of your present is secure in the knowledge of your affection, she won't measure your love by what you give her.

MONEY, STOCKS, AND GIFT CERTIFICATES AS PRESENTS

If the motive that prompts you to give money is a sincere and straightforward one, it can be a wonderful present. The person you give it to is free to go out and buy whatever he wants or needs most. Only you can decide whom to give money to and whether it should be in the form of a check or cash. If you decide to give money as a present, you can make it more personal if you include a token of some sort with it, for instance a pair of colorful socks, daffodil bulbs, or wild rice.

Stocks, U.S. savings bonds, and Treasury issues are often given in lieu of money for a graduation or a bar mitzvah. Both stocks and Treasuries can be bought through a stockbroker; savings bonds are sold at local banks at no charge. Zero coupon bonds are less expensive than regular bonds, because they are sold at a discount. When they mature (in from two to thirty years) the recipient receives the full face value.

A gift certificate is always a great idea. It not only has monetary value but guarantees that the person you give it to can choose a present compatible with her taste. You may want to give a gift certificate an entire family can enjoy, perhaps credit at an amusement park or a fast-food chain. You can personalize the giving of a certificate by putting it in a miniature shopping bag lined with tissue paper or a drawstring cloth pouch.

GIFT TO A CHARITY, ORGANIZATION, OR INSTITUTION

For the person who has everything, a donation to a college or local hospital can be the perfect present. When you send a donation to a nonprofit organization it's important to convey the following information: person in whose name the gift is being made, that person's address (if it is a memorial gift, the name and address of the family of the deceased), and the donor's name and address. The organization acknowledges receipt of the contribution to the donor. It will also send an acknowledgment to the person in whose name the donation was made without mentioning the amount of the contribution.

FLOWERS OR A PLANT

Flowers are appropriate for almost any occasion: Mother's Day, Valentine's Day, a debutante party, or an anniversary. Or a bouquet of violets or an armful of peonies can convey just the right sentiment when you want to express congratulations, gratitude, regrets, or consolation. If you are the guest of honor at a dinner party and want to send flowers to your hostess beforehand, call her well in advance (if you wait until the day of the party, chances are she will have placed her order), to find out what type of arrangement she'd like and what color flowers she prefers. If you decide to take flowers to a small, informal dinner, don't burden your hostess with the arranging of them; ask her for a vase and fix them yourself. Or even better, take her a plant.

Often the ribbons and furbelows of a florist's arrangement destroy the natural charm and simplicity of the flowers. Therefore, you should be firm about telling a florist you want a simple arrangement, or else ask for cut flowers or a plant. Some considerations when sending flowers are:

- If they are going to a home or office, make an effort to coordinate the color of the flowers with the décor of the room.

- For a funeral, it's wise to check with the church as to its policy on accepting flowers. As a rule, you do not send flowers to a Jewish funeral.

- A plant is a better choice than flowers for a hospital patient; it requires less care and can be taken home.

- Flowers are not only suitable for, but are greatly appreciated by, men.

- When sending flowers, a handwritten enclosure card is always preferable to one written by the florist.

- No matter how difficult it is to find fresh flowers or how expensive they are, never send plastic flowers.

When you place an out-of-town order for flowers, give explicit instructions as to what type of arrangement (or plant) you want. Should flowers arrive in less than perfect condition, the person you sent them to should let you know so you can ask the florist to send a replacement. There are subscriber services that offer flowers on a weekly or monthly basis. This can make an appealing present, but only if the service has been highly recommended or is well established. Of course, a gift certificate from a competent florist makes an excellent present.

GIFTS FROM A MUSEUM SHOP

A museum shop is a perfect place to find an original present. Most major museums carry a wide range of merchandise from postcards and posters to books on art and history, games and puzzles, scarves and ties, glassware and china products. Two exceptional museum presents are reproductions of an ancient artifact or a piece of antique jewelry, accompanied by a description of its history and original provenance. When you buy from a museum shop, you lend support to the institution and can benefit from a museum's discount if you're a member.

SPORT- OR HOBBY-RELATED PRESENT

A sport- or hobby-related present is an excellent choice for the person who has everything. Sports equipment such as golf clubs, snorkeling gear, skis, or a tennis racquet must be custom-fitted to the individual, and therefore should not be bought for anyone else. Instead, consider a gift certificate to a sports store or a sports-related present such as a compass for a skier or tickets to the U.S. Open. A gift certificate also makes a good present for the hobby enthusiast, the gardener, artist, gourmet cook, or other aficionado. When you give a sport- or hobby-related present, try to find something out of the ordinary, or new, something the recipient may not already own.

ORDERING FROM A CATALOG

Buying from a catalog is a practical and convenient way for the elderly, a person with no time, or someone with an aversion to shopping or who lives in an area with limited shopping facilities, to send a present. Most mail order companies charge for gift wrapping and will not wrap large or bulky items. And most do not deal with personal enclosure cards. Instead, a space is provided on the order form for you to write the message you want to accompany the present. (If you order by telephone, the message is given orally.) Many mail order companies have twenty-four-hour toll-free telephone service. Ordering by telephone not only makes processing the order quicker, it has the advantage of telling you immediately about stock availability. Also there are companies that offer special items at reduced prices for telephone orders. If time permits, you can have your order shipped to you. Then you can personalize the present by wrapping it and enclosing a handwritten card.

WHAT WOULD YOU LIKE FOR A PRESENT?

Children will answer quickly and honestly the question "What would you like for a birthday present?" but an adult is apt to be evasive. The common response, "Whatever you choose is fine," may be well intentioned but it does not help the giver. Whether to ask the question at all depends on how well you know the person you plan to give the present to. If it's someone in your family, you're likely to get a fairly direct answer. However, if it's someone less intimate, you'll have to trust your intuition. If you're the person being asked, don't suggest an item that is too costly or difficult to find. Your best response steers clear of specifics. You might suggest a present having to do with cooking, for example, or gardening, or art. Or you might want to suggest a number of items with a wide price range to choose from.

JOINT OR GROUP PRESENTS

There are occasions when it's practical for two or more people to give a present together, for instance for an anniversary or second wedding. When a number of people give a present jointly, each contributor signs the card that accompanies it. If you are asked to join in giving a present and would rather not, politely decline without feeling guilty.

WHEN AN INVITATION SAYS "NO PRESENTS, PLEASE."

The lower right-hand corner of an invitation may read "no presents, please" (another form is "your presence is your present"). Such a comment may apply to almost any occasion from a birthday to an anniversary or retirement party. The person for whom the party is being given makes this request because he does not want to accumulate any more possessions or does not want guests to feel obliged to bring something. If you want to give a present anyway, take it to the celebrant before the event. Taking a present to a party when specifically asked not to is unfair to the guests who have honored the request.

KEEPING A LIST OF ANNUAL PRESENTS

There is logic to keeping a record of presents you give to family and friends each year. If such a list is organized by month, it also serves as a reminder of forthcoming gift-giving occasions. But mainly a gift-giving record reduces the possibility of duplicating a present. Each entry on the list should be followed by the recipient's address, a description of the present, the occasion, the date it was given, and the cost. If applicable, include sizes.

COLLECTING PRESENTS THROUGHOUT THE YEAR

If you have an extensive, yearly gift-giving list and limited time to shop, it's less stressful if you accumulate presents throughout the year. Last-minute shopping can often end up costing more than anticipated and may result in a less than ideal present. If you are sufficiently tempted by a one-of-a-kind object in an antique store or a sale item in a current catalog, buy whatever it is and save it for the right person on the right occasion. If you're accustomed to giving clothes, carry a list, perhaps in a pocket address book, of sizes. Anyone with limited storage space can store presents in a suitcase or a laundry-type bag hung on a closet hook.

RECYCLING A PRESENT

It's not that uncommon to receive a present which is either identical to something you already own or is something you have no need for. If this happens, there's no reason not to pass the present on to someone you feel would appreciate it. You can put the present in an unmarked box or wrap it in tissue paper and put it in a decorative shopping bag. Best not to use the present's original box or the box of another store on the chance the person you're giving the present to decides to return it and asks you for the sales slip.

ELIMINATING SOMEONE FROM YOUR GIFT-GIVING LIST

There may come a time when it makes sense to reassess your gift-giving list. Only you can decide whether to trim it or not. Base your decision on the length of the list, the financial commitment it requires, and any change in your relationship with someone on the list. Often the easiest person to cross off is a good friend because you can be direct with her. All you have to do is bite the bullet and say, "Why don't we call a moratorium on birthday presents and instead treat ourselves to an extra special lunch each year?" Chances are your friend will feel exactly as you do, relieved to be able to shorten her list. Or if you are not very close to a particular person, on the next gift-giving occasion you might, in lieu of a present, send a card. Of course, a really effective way to cut down on your gift-giving list is to drop anyone who never thanked you for a previous present.

THE BELATED PRESENT

A present given after an occasion, in particular a birthday, never has the same impact as one that's given on the actual date. This is especially true for a child. If the number of different belated birthday cards in the stores is any indication, many people either forget birthdays or don't get around to sending their present on time. It's no crime to give a present after the fact, so just accept with good humor that it will be that way with certain individuals. If you keep an up-to-date gift-giving list, you're less likely to be the one to have the belated-present problem.

THE IMPULSE PRESENT

On occasion we are all taken with an irresistible urge to give a present for no other reason than to express a feeling of affection or appreciation or because, walking by a shop window or wandering through a bookstore, we find something perfect and can't wait. It's fun to give an impulse present—fun for you, the giver, and fun for the recipient. The gift could be cinnamon sticks for the fireplace or the latest book on rock stars; the pleasure comes from the spontaneity of the thought rather than the cost of the present. Naturally, you do not want to embarrass the person you're giving the present to by an overly elaborate gift or make her in any way feel an obligation to reciprocate.

THE INAPPROPRIATE PRESENT

An inappropriate present is one that shows poor judgment or bad taste, or gives the impression you are asking for a favor in return. For instance, it would be thoughtless to surprise a friend with a dog when she may not have the time or inclination to care for one. In addition, the gift of a secondhand car is of little use to someone who won't be able to afford the insurance. You should show discretion about giving expensive jewelry, especially to a young person, and common sense about giving something to someone you're in a business deal with. If you give careful thought to matching the present with the recipient, the chances of giving an inappropriate present are greatly diminished.

GIFT WRAPPING

The diversity in style and texture available in wrapping today makes it easy to find the right paper for the right occasion. There is handsome wrapping paper that comes in the form of a book with perforated sheets and is perfect either for you to use or to give as a present. Tissue paper, either plain or with a pattern, is easy to wrap with and inexpensive to buy. To add a dash of creativity, stick-on stars and circles, available at stationery stores, can be affixed to white or colored tissue paper. A glossy-paper shopping bag has become increasingly popular as a substitute for wrapping. Crunched-up tissue paper can provide a deep nest for the present and a gingham or velvet bow can be tied to the handles.

A well-wrapped present should have an air of simplicity and should be tied with a silk ribbon, yarn, or some other appropriate material. A self-sticking bow should not be used as a substitute for a ribbon. While a present that is wrapped by the giver has a personal touch, there are occasions when it is more practical to have a store send a present. However, instead of wrapping a package, many stores simply tie a ribbon around one of their signature boxes.

When daisies or other flowers are available, it is nice to entwine a few in the knot of any bow—at Christmas it might be a sprig of holly, or if the gift is for a child, some small toy such as a miniature teddy bear. The environmentally aware gift giver can wrap a present in newspaper or put it in a paper bag and tie it with colorful ribbon and/or decorate with stick-ons. Wrapping of this sort is not appropriate, however, for a formal gift-giving occasion, like a christening, wedding, or anniversary.

GIFT ENCLOSURE CARD

The engraved white or ecru calling card (a business card is never used for social purposes) is the most traditional gift enclosure card. If you use your calling card, your message should be written in either blue or black ink. If you know the person well to whom you're sending the present, to personalize your card, place a slash diagonally through your name and write your first name directly above. The envelope of a calling card is customarily left blank, but it's less likely to be misplaced if you write the recipient's name on it—without an address. The envelope is not sealed unless the message is a private one. With today's less formal style of living, most people don't have engraved calling cards, so they use an informal or a store's gift-enclosure card. For more casual occasions, a greeting card or a museum postcard makes an attractive gift card. There are times, of course, when you must order a present by telephone and have the store write your message. But it's always the card handwritten by you that means the most.

RETURNING OR EXCHANGING A PRESENT

Discretion is the key factor in helping you decide whether you should exchange a present. It is never worth the price of hurting someone's feelings. If you trust to instinct you'll know whether you can exchange a present without telling the giver you already have the identical item, or whatever your reason is. If a present arrives from a store broken, take it back without telling the giver. On the other hand, if it arrives through the mail broken, you have to decide whether or not to tell the sender. If it's a present of value you should, so she can alert the insurance company and have it replaced. When you are making a purchase, either for a present or your personal use, you should find out what the store's policy is in regard to returning a sale item or exchanging merchandise.

SUGGESTED GIFTS

Space limits the number of gift-giving suggestions we can list here, so if you are in doubt about what to give someone on a specific occasion such as a christening, bar mitzvah, retirement, etc., ask a friend who's recently attended a similar event or consult with a store about appropriate gift ideas.

Here are a few gift-giving thoughts to spark your imagination.

PRESENTS FOR A YOUNG CHILD
Pedal-controlled toy car
Starter train set
Child's table and chairs
Sleeping bag
Raggedy Ann and Andy dolls
Magic set
Subscription to a children's magazine
Book of wildlife stickers

STOCKING STUFFERS
Mickey Mouse sunglasses
Sweet and sour candy balls
Plastic finger rings
Monogrammed notepad
Chinese yo-yo
Socks with Christmas tree design
Glow-in-the-dark ceiling stars

Jacks
Rubber stamp and ink pad

PRESENTS FOR A TEENAGER

Portable radio/tape deck
Wallet with cash
Telephone service for his first year at college
Electronic dictionary
Gift certificate to video store
Array of bright-colored socks
Beach towel in tote bag
Weekender travel bag
Ankle weights

FOR SOMEONE YOU'RE DATING

Tickets to a sporting event
Bangle bracelets
Sports watch
Compact discs or tapes
Gift certificate to a health club
Reversible wool scarf
Cologne
T-shirt
Fun pair of socks or tie

HOSPITAL PATIENT

Tin of cookies or biscuits
Miniature jigsaw puzzle
A current best-seller
Postcards and stamps
Daily newspaper delivery
Worry beads
A dinner for the spouse
A stocked refrigerator before the patient returns home

PROFESSIONAL (DOCTOR, TEACHER, CLERGYPERSON, ETC.)

Dinner for two at local restaurant
Fruit-of-the-Month Club subscription
Two bottles of good wine
Woven rush "in" and "out" boxes
Flowering plant
Box of informal museum cards and envelopes
Homemade nutcake

CHAPTER 2
ENTERTAINING WITH EASE

INTRODUCTION

One of life's pleasures is getting together with friends—spending time with old, cherished friends, getting to know newer friends better, and introducing your favorite friends to one another. "Entertaining" friends implies that some form of food will be offered; at the least cookies and tea or coffee. Entertaining can be done almost anywhere—in a magnificent dining room, a one-room studio, or a restaurant or club—and it can be done on even the smallest of budgets. In fact, spending sizable amounts of money on wining and dining does not guarantee success. It may have exactly the opposite effect, making your guests feel they can never afford to reciprocate in kind. Instead, your warmth, enthusiasm, and overall spirit are what count. Although the food, wine, service, and setting are certainly key ingredients of a successful dinner party, just as important is an understanding on the part of the host and hostess that their guests need to feel special. They may not remember whether or not the wine was sparkling, but they will remember if the conversation was stimulating. All too often people forget this basic fact about human nature. So think of your dining room or backyard as a stage on which every guest has an important role with the wine, food, and staff as the supporting cast.

While entertaining can be fun, it is not necessarily easy, although some people, of course, find it easier than others. Yet it is a truly creative enterprise, and one that can be learned by anyone willing to take the time to do so.

As you read this chapter, you'll see that entertaining can take many forms: for the busy working woman it may be ordering dinner from the local takeout shop and serving it on her best plates. For the married couple, it may be giving a black-tie dinner dance at their club or a hotel. For the bachelor, drinks and a steak grilled in the backyard. Every host and hostess finds the combinations that are best suited to his or her lifestyle and budget. And, whether your friends sit on bales of hay at a barbecue or sip cocktails in your living room, your party will be a success if you follow the guidelines spelled out in this chapter. They will help you entertain with ease, whether you're a newlywed preparing your first dinner or a seasoned party giver looking for new ideas. Begin with the first section, "The Formal Seated Dinner With a Staff," even if you don't plan on giving one—the basics of entertaining and good manners are explained there. Then read on about the creative art of entertaining and how it can become an intrinsic part of your life, keeping in mind what Oscar Wilde had to say on the subject: "After a good dinner, one can forgive anybody, even one's own relatives."

THE FORMAL SEATED DINNER WITH A STAFF

Dinner jackets, long dresses, candlelight, and sparkling conversation— for many the most delightful type of entertaining is the formal dinner, served by a perfectly schooled staff. The easiest way to give such a dinner, of course, is at a hotel or club. Yet a formal dinner held in one's own house has a greater feeling of intimacy and specialness. The solution for many hostesses is to give smaller formal dinner parties at home and larger ones at a hotel or club. The logistics and procedures are, in fact, almost all the same. You'll find the text divided into three parts: the role of the hostess (or host), the role of the guest, and the role of the staff. The formal dinner described here is for twelve or more; given at home, with a staff, and it incorporates all the things you need to know to give your own party, although many of the procedural suggestions and all the tips on manners are equally applicable to informal entertaining.

The Role of the Hostess

The success of any party depends largely on the style and personality of the hostess. If you have a flair for talking with people, mixing friends, setting a beautiful table, and having a great time yourself, people will eagerly accept your invitations. Though many people are blessed with an innate sense of how to entertain, just as many are not. However, the ability to entertain well can be learned, especially if you're willing to observe those who do it with ease and panache and if you're well organized. Ideas can also be gleaned from books about party giving. Because a formal dinner party is more complex than an informal one, as a novice you might want to wait to give your first formal dinner until after you have entertained in a less grand fashion. However, once you have there's absolutely no reason why you can't give a formal dinner, carefully following the guidelines spelled out here. After all, the key ingredients that make for a successful party are not mysterious: the choice of guests, a carefully thought-out menu, good service, and a warm and welcoming atmosphere. In addition, the host *and* hostess are responsible for drawing out each guest and encouraging interesting and stimulating conversation. This means neither the host nor the hostess can indulge in long conversations with just one or two guests; instead you must both move around, introducing people to each other.

There are certain techniques that all great hosts and hostesses use which you, too, can incorporate in your party giving. First and foremost, remember faces and names. Not only are people flattered to be recognized, but it's the only way to introduce guests. Second, add a little something about each person to your introductions. For example, "Anne, I'd like you to meet Herbert Carter. You may remember I told you about his work with the Little League team. Herbert, this is Anne O'Brien, the absolutely number one tennis player at the club." This gives Anne and Herbert the seeds of a beginning conversation. Third, move people about. Take the shy person standing in the corner by the hand and literally move him/her into a group that's already carrying on a conversation. Or, if one of your guests is boring others with a long-winded story, let him finish but then break in and bring up a topic that everyone can join in on. By being forceful without seeming to, you can keep every guest involved and interested.

The overriding principle to keep in mind when entertaining is that there's much more to being a good hostess than preparing the house, the food, and the wine.

FIRST CONSIDERATIONS

THE PARTY BOOK To prevent repetition of menus and guest lists, keep an accurate record of each dinner party you give by writing the details in a special party book. Include the date, the guest list, whether it was black tie, who sat beside whom, the menu and the wines served as well as the costs. Then note any special hints that will be useful another time, such as the name of a wine that was particularly good or one that was not, a comment about cooking the meat fifteen minutes longer, or the fact that guests shied away from the richer hors d'oeuvres; these notes will be helpful in planning future dinners. Write down the name of the caterer and others who helped that evening, noting whether any did not live up to your expectations. If certain flowers looked particularly attractive or, unfortunately, wilted, put these facts in your notebook.

MAKING PLANS After deciding on the date and time of your dinner, the next step is to engage the necessary staff. How many people you need depends on how many guests are expected and whether you already have household help who will prepare and serve the meal. If the dinner is to be catered (see "Working With a Caterer" later in this chapter), make certain the caterer is available that evening before sending out invitations.

Prior to deciding on the number of guests to invite, check the size of the table or tables you will be using. To find out how many people can sit comfortably at the table, do a practice setting, measuring approximately two feet from the center of one place setting to the center of the next setting. You don't want to seat guests too far apart so they can't talk to their dinner partners easily or too close together so it's difficult for the waiters to serve.

THE GUEST LIST   Certainly a key element of any dinner party is the guest list. A compatible collection of people is essential to a good party. Avoid taking the easy way out—inviting people just because they know each other or share the same interests; such a list does not guarantee a fascinating evening. In fact, it can be deadly dull. Instead, interject a sense of surprise: mix and match people who know each other with some who do not, but who you think will be compatible or will create interesting combinations. For instance, a dinner party consisting primarily of teachers or doctors just about guarantees that the conversation will center around work, leaving out those who are not colleagues. Or if all the guests have children attending the same school, that will quickly become the focal point. The party will have much more spark if you blend office friends with neighbors, teachers with doctors, and out-of-towners with local residents.

When making out your guest list, think twice before asking someone who has refused an invitation from you as many as three times before, unless for very good reasons. It may be that person does not want to be put in the position of having to reciprocate social obligations.

POINTS TO BEAR IN MIND WHEN INVITING GUESTS
- When telephoning a formal dinner invitation, give the name of the guest of honor but not the names of the other guests. It's nice to have an element of surprise and you don't want to seem to be enticing certain people by the guest list. If a guest specifically asks who else will be attending the dinner, which is not considered good manners, there's nothing you can do but name the other guests.
- Many single women feel quite secure about entertaining on their own. However, asking a man friend to act as co-host for the evening can be helpful and reassuring. He can see that the guests at his end of the table are well taken care of and assume any other tasks you'd like to assign, such as introducing people to one another and keeping the conversation flowing. If you want a "host for the evening," line him up before you issue your invitations.
- While it is preferable to have an even number of men and women, it is not essential. It's far better to have an extra man or woman than to ask someone on the dull side just to make the number even. There is nothing wrong with two women sitting beside each other at the

dinner table. After all, as someone once said, you're being invited to dinner to be sociable, not for mating.

- It once was considered bad luck to have thirteen people at the dinner table, but no one pays attention to this superstition any longer.

- Refrain from asking a single woman to bring a man. If she does not know anyone suitable, it can be embarrassing for her. Instead, you might say: "If you'd like to bring a man, you can let me know. We have room for one more at the table."

- When a single woman living in the country accepts your invitation, ask if she would like to be picked up by another guest who lives close by. If she prefers to come alone, don't press the issue.

- If a single man or woman asks to bring a date (not someone he or she is living with) and you have taken single people into consideration when preparing your guest list, say to the person asking, "I've invited all the people I can handle and there'll be other single people coming alone."

- If a guest asks if she may bring houseguests and you do not have room, or you are not particularly fond of them, all you have to say is, "Unfortunately, we don't have room at the dining-room table for one more guest but I hope we can see the Archers some other time during the weekend."

- Any gay or straight couple living together are invited as a couple.

- If you don't hear from someone to whom you sent a written invitation, don't hesitate to call that person. For all you know, the invitation may have been lost in the mail.

- If a guest drops out of your dinner party at the last minute, ask only an extremely close friend or a family member as a replacement; in other words, someone you see frequently or invite for dinner on other occasions.

THE INVITATION

The most formal type of invitation to a dinner party is the engraved fill-in card, which has the hostess's (or the couple's) name/s on it. You can buy engraved fill-in cards at any good stationers. The printed fill-in card, of course, is less expensive than the engraved one. An invitation must include the date, time, place, R.s.v.p. (lower left-hand corner), and the words "Black tie" (lower right-hand corner). If there's to be a guest of honor, his or her name appears either in the upper left-hand corner or in the center of the card (see "Invitations" in Chapter 8). Instead of inviting guests for dinner at 8 P.M., it makes good sense to use the British style of inviting, which is to say, "Come at 7:45 P.M. for dinner at 8:30 P.M." In that way, guests know the exact time dinner will be served and you are much less likely to have late arrivals. Also, this form means that those who don't like a long cocktail hour can time their arrival accordingly.

An alternative to the engraved or printed fill-in invitation is a handwritten one on your personal notepaper. It is written in the third person: "Mr. and Mrs. Alex Smith invite you to dinner . . ." If the dinner is to be a small one, you can invite your guests by writing them a note on a letter sheet or informal. Envelopes are hand-addressed and hand-stamped. Instead of a written invitation, today many hostesses do the inviting by telephone, particularly when the party is less than two weeks away. If the dinner is to be held in the country in a hard-to-find location, include a map with each invitation.

WHEN TO INVITE Send the invitations at least three to six weeks before the date of the dinner. Naturally, the exact timing depends on your community and its customs. In a large city, for instance, where people lead busy social lives, invitations to formal dinners and other important events must be sent out at least six weeks in advance so guests can save the date.

This is to remind you that

René Dubois

expects you for *dinner*

on *Thursday, February 9*

at   *7:30*   o'clock

Apt. 4F
11 Scottsdale Drive   *Informal*

A reminder card is a useful follow-up to a dinner invitation.

THE REMINDER CARD Sometimes it's wise to send a follow-up card, which is just that—a reminder of the dinner. It is particularly important if the original invitation was issued by telephone. There's always the chance that a guest may have noted down the wrong date or time. Even when an invitation has been written, if it was sent four to six weeks before the party, send a reminder card timed to arrive approximately ten days before the dinner. The traditional reminder card is an engraved fill-in card, with or without the host's and/or hostess' names on it, although a printed fill-in card will do as well and is less expensive. If you wish to be less formal, write the reminder on your personal notepaper or informal. The reminder includes all of the essential information: your name, the date, time, address, apartment number, and "Black tie" and the name of the guest of honor if there is one (see "Invitations" in Chapter 8).

PLANNING THE DINNER

Once the invitations have been sent out, it's a good time to take care of the following details.

THE STAFF Whether you have hired the staff yourself or are working with a caterer, reconfirm the following details: date and time of the dinner, what the staff will wear, when they should arrive, and their exact responsibilities. For a formal dinner of twelve, two butlers are sufficient. (The word "butler" usually applies to someone who works in a household. Caterers refer to their staff as either butlers or waiters. In a restaurant, only the word "waiter" is used).

RENTAL EQUIPMENT If you don't have enough tables and chairs or other party necessities, you'll find rental companies (listed in the yellow pages of the telephone book) provide just about everything except the food. And, if any furniture must be moved out, note the day it should be picked up; preferably not the same day as the party. Among the items available from rental companies are:

- Tables
- Chairs
- Coatracks and hangers
- Umbrella stands
- China
- Glasses
- Flatwear
- Tablecloths
- Napkins
- Serving platters
- Serving trays
- Large chafing/heating dishes
- Coffee urns

CHINA, GLASSES, AND FLATWEAR Check to make certain you have on hand enough china place settings, serving platters and dishes, and demitasse cups and saucers. Also go over the glasses for cocktails, dinner, and liqueurs as well as the flatwear and serving utensils needed for each of the various courses (see "Table Settings" later in this chapter). The word "flatwear" is all-inclusive and refers to sterling silver, vermeil, bone-handled steak knives, etc. Only sterling silver or vermeil (silver gilt) is used for a formal dinner.

TABLECLOTH AND NAPKINS Look the tablecloth over carefully for spots or tears. A white damask cloth, which hangs over the edge of a rectangular dining-room table by twelve inches or more, is traditional for a formal dinner party. You can use a separate liner to protect the table. For round tables, pale-colored or delicately patterned tablecloths are popular. Count the dinner napkins, and if they are monogrammed, fold them so that the monogram is right side out. Dinner napkins measure anywhere from twenty-two to thirty inches square.

THE MENU The convention of serving five courses (soup, fish, meat or fowl, salad and cheese, and dessert) is rarely observed today, even at the most elaborate dinner party. Because people are increasingly health- and diet-conscious and don't have the time to spend endless hours at the dinner table, four courses with only one course instead of two being served before the main course have become standard. For cocktails, three hors d'oeuvres, hot or cold depending on the season, are sufficient. If you are using a caterer, he will suggest suitable menus along with their costs, or you can make your own suggestions. If you plan to hire a cook but do not have a specific person in mind, ask some reliable individual for a recommendation. Then consult with the cook carefully; have him prepare only food that he is familiar with rather than letting him use your dinner to experiment with a new recipe. When planning a menu bear in mind that if a guest is a recovering alcoholic he should not eat food containing alcohol, such as a soup to which sherry is added. Contrary to what many people believe, alcohol does *not* burn off completely in the cooking or heating process. A 1990 study by Washington State University found that alcoholic beverages retain five to eighty-five percent of their alcohol after cooking evaporation. The amount of alcohol remaining was determined by the type of heat and the length of cooking time. The National Council on Alcoholism and Drug Dependence suggests that you let guests know when you are serving something with liquor in it.

WINES, LIQUOR, LIQUEURS, NONALCOHOLIC DRINKS Make a list of all alcoholic beverages needed for cocktails, dinner, and after dinner. A knowledgeable wine merchant, when told the amount of money you want to spend and the number of guests you expect, can suggest specific wines which will complement the menu as well as the number of bottles needed. Unopened bottles can usually be returned, so it's better to have too many on hand than to risk running short. (For more on the subject, see "Wines" later in this chapter.)

Make certain you have proper liability coverage to protect yourself in case someone has an accident as a result of liquor served at your party.

FLOWERS Attractive flower arrangements add a festive look to any party. It's always nice to have them in your front hall, living room, and dining room. Remember that the flowers on the dining-room table must be low enough so that guests can see one another. Before calling the florist, you'll have to decide whether you want cut flowers that you will arrange yourself or prefer that the florist do the arrangements for you. When placing the order with your florist, remember to call him well in advance of the party date. At certain times of the year like Valentine's Day, Easter, or Mother's Day, when florists are at their busiest, several weeks' notice is advisable. Be specific when you speak with the florist. If you want him to prepare the flower arrangements, tell him what flowers and colors you particularly like, how many arrangements you need, how tall they should be, and where and when they should be delivered (preferably the morning of the party). If you have a special vase you'd like to use, take it to the florist so flowers can be arranged in it directly.

If your house tends to be on the warm side, keep in mind that certain flowers, such as iris, freesia, and some roses, wilt rather quickly, while carnations and any flower in the lily family stand up well. If the guest of honor sends flowers the day of the dinner, place them on a table where he will surely see them. Of course, what's best of all is when the guest of honor calls well in advance of the party to ask what type of flowers you'd like.

SEATING A DINNER

Of utmost importance to the overall success of a dinner party is the seating plan. The basic formula is to use your intuition about matching the guests. You may, for example, decide to put beside each other two people who are art buffs or two people who just returned from trips to the Orient. And, while it may seem logical to put a shy person next to an extrovert, it doesn't always work. In fact it may be disastrous, with one sitting quietly and the other carrying on an animated one-sided conversation. Best to put the shy person beside someone who knows how to draw people out. The easiest way to make a seating plan is to draw a diagram of the table (or tables) on a large piece of paper. Write the name of each guest on an individual slip of paper. You can then move the slips of paper around the diagram until you have just the right seating arrangement.

FOLLOWING PROTOCOL There are certain traditional rules the hostess tries to follow when seating a dinner, the first being that the host sits at one end of the table and the hostess at the other end. This tradition can be followed when seating a dinner for six, ten, fourteen, or eighteen people if there is an even number of men and women. With eight, twelve, sixteen, or twenty (numbers divisible by four), it is not possible for the host and hostess to sit opposite each other without two men and two women sitting beside each other. In this situation, to maintain the man, woman, man, woman formula, the hostess moves one place to the left, with the man on

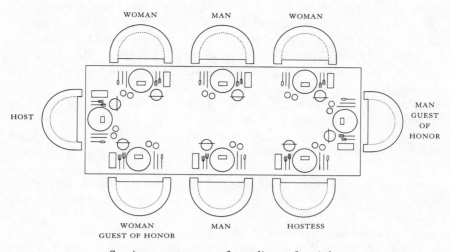

Seating arrangement for a dinner for eight.

her right sitting at the end of the table, opposite the host. If there are several round tables, the host and hostess sit at separate tables, seating themselves so they face into the room. That way they are able to keep an eye on the guests and the service. Regardless of the shape of the table, the places to the right of the host and to the right of the hostess are the places of honor. The woman to the host's right is the woman guest of honor, while the man to the right of the hostess is the man guest of honor. The second-ranking woman guest sits on the host's left and the second-ranking man on the hostess's left. If there are guests of official status, he and his wife or she and her husband are the honorees. In such cases, husbands and wives share equal rank. (A head of government, an ambassador, mayor, congressman, senator, city commissioner or representative, councilman, head of a government organization, etc., are regarded as "officials.") If there are no official guests, the place of honor is given to someone holding a prestigious position in the community, such as a college president, an author, a judge, or a director of a bank or museum.

Less formally, you might want to give a party for some friends who just got married, or a friend from out of town, or an aunt who is having a birthday. No matter who it is, when you tell someone you want to give a party in his or her honor, that person is highly flattered and pleased. When the occasion is simply entertaining good friends, the hostess chooses a man she would like to have sit on her right and, along with her husband, decides which woman guest will sit on his right; spouses at this type of dinner are not considered second-ranking guests and are seated in the exact same way as any other guests.

No matter how formal or informal a dinner party is, a husband and wife, an engaged couple, or a gay couple are not seated beside each other. After all, they see each other all the time and should be glad to have the chance to talk to others. If the party is large enough for round tables, seat each half of a couple at a different table; then when they get home they'll have lots to talk about: whom they sat beside, what those people do, what they said.

While only ten percent of the general population is left-handed, if you happen to know that a guest is left-handed, and it's convenient, seat that person at a corner of the table so his or her left side is free. That way, if the chairs are close together, elbows won't bump with the person to the left.

PLACE CARDS Place cards, used at formal or informal dinners for more than eight, help guests locate their seats at the table. They also save the hostess having to remember where each person is to sit or carrying a piece of paper with a sketchy diagram into the dining room as a seating reminder. When the host and hostess sit at the head and foot of the table, it is not customary for them to have place cards, but they generally do have place cards when seated at separate round tables.

There are two types of place cards: one (2″ × 3¼″) lies flat or is set in a place card holder and the other (3″ × 3½″ unfolded) stands up tentlike when folded in half. At a formal dinner, place cards are either plain or have a gold, silver, or colored border. A hostess who entertains frequently may have place cards with her monogram or, if entitled to it, a crest. For other than a formal dinner, there are place cards printed with a decoration on the upper left-hand corner of the card, such as holly for Christmastime use.

A guest's name is written legibly in black ink on a place card large enough to read easily from a reasonable distance. The protocol for writing a guest's name or official title on a place card is a set one. The title Honorable is not used; instead, it is Justice Benedict (not Honorable or Hon. Ralph Benedict), Senator Rosenthal, or Mayor O'Neill (see "Correct Forms of Address" in Chapter 8 for other examples). For guests without formal titles it is simply: Dr. Grant, Mr. Schmidt, Mrs. Franklin, Miss or Ms. Franz. When there are two people with the same surname, the cards read Mr. Richard Barker and Mr. James Barker. If it's a small dinner and the guests are all close friends, first names are used. When there are two people with the same first name, you can write Betsy Forster and Betsy Jordan or Betsy F. and Betsy J. If the dinner is large enough so that the use of first names only will be confusing, then first and last names are used throughout.

TABLE NUMBER CARDS When there are only two round tables in the dining room, a guest can find his or her table with no trouble. But when there are a number of tables it's less confusing and more practical to have a table number card for each guest. In that way, when dinner is announced, if a guest's table number card says "5," he knows to go to the table marked "5." There must also be place cards so guests will know where to sit at their table.

There are two types of table number cards; one (3″ × 3½″ unfolded) stands up tentlike when folded in half. The name of the guest is written on the outside of the card and the table number on the inside. The other (2″ × 4″) is a single card with an envelope and has the table number on the card inside. Each guest's name is written out on the envelope exactly as it appears on the place card.

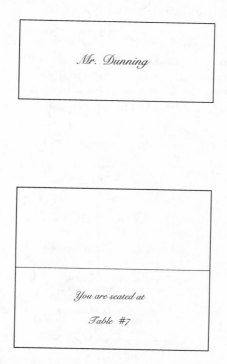

Table number cards are a convenience for both hostess and guests when there will be three or more tables.

Table number cards are arranged alphabetically and placed on a table, usually in or near the front hall, where guests can pick them up as they arrive. Occasionally, at a small formal dinner party, you see in the front hall a round or rectangular seating chart, known as the *plan de table*. It's usually made of leather and has an easel back. Each guest's name is handwritten or typed on a white card that is inserted in its proper place on the chart. In years past, the *plan de table* was very much a part of social entertaining. One of its uses was to let guests know who their dinner partners would be, giving them the opportunity to talk to other guests before dinner.

Numbering the tables At a large benefit or other party where there may be as many as fifty tables, stanchions with numbers affixed to the top are placed in the center of each table. These metal holders are tall enough and the numbers large enough so they can be seen from a distance.

For smaller affairs, you can make your own numbered cards for each table. Use simple white (5″ × 7″) cards with the numbers written in black large enough to be easily read. After the table is set, you can place the cards wherever seems most convenient—perhaps against the centerpiece, or against a candlestick or other table decoration. After the guests are seated, butlers remove the cards from the tables.

Menu cards Although traditionally seen at only the most formal dinners, menu cards are occasionally used in less formal settings, often as a memento for guests, particularly the guest of honor, to take home. Written on the menu card are the courses and the wines that are to be served at the dinner. The menu may be written entirely in English or, if a typically

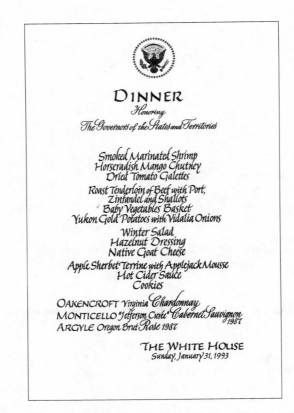

DINNER
Honoring
The Governors of the States and Territories

Smoked Marinated Shrimp
Horseradish Mango Chutney
Dried Tomato Galettes
Roast Tenderloin of Beef with Port,
Zinfandel and Shallots
Baby Vegetables Basket
Yukon Gold Potatoes with Vidalia Onions
Winter Salad
Hazelnut Dressing
Native Goat Cheese
Apple Sherbet Terrine with Applejack Mousse
Hot Cider Sauce
Cookies

OAKENCROFT *Virginia Chardonnay*
MONTICELLO *"Jefferson Cuvée" Cabernet Sauvignon 1987*
ARGYLE *Oregon Brut Rosé 1987*

THE WHITE HOUSE
Sunday, January 31, 1993

A menu card shows what food and wine will be served at a very formal dinner. In most instances, the date is also mentioned.

French or Italian dish is to be served, the name of that dish may be written in the native language of the cuisine—a decision made by the hostess.

Menu cards are white or ecru and approximately 4½″ × 6½″ in size. The most formal type is engraved with a monogram or, if applicable, a crest. If it is not engraved, it may be printed in black ink or handwritten. For less formal menu cards, you can make your own by cutting them out of any heavy white or cream paper.

Menu cards have the date of the party written in the upper right and the word "Dinner" at the upper center. If it's a party to celebrate an anniversary or a birthday, that specific date can be added at the very top of the card, along with the name of the guest of honor. There may be just one menu card between two place settings, or there may be cards only for the women guests. Sometimes there are only two menu cards, in which case they stand upright in a menu card holder, one at each end of the table.

FINAL PREPARATIONS

The savvy hostess makes a check list, well in advance of the dinner, of all pre-party preparations she must take care of. This guarantees that no detail will be forgotten. It also makes for a more relaxed hostess.

A WEEK BEFORE THE PARTY

- Reconfirm time of dinner and other arrangements with hired help or caterer.
- Reconfirm delivery of rentals.
- Reconfirm delivery of liquor.
- Reconfirm delivery of flowers.
- Buy nonalcoholic beverages.
- Count and check all china to be used.
- Count and polish silver (flatware and candlesticks).
- Count and wash glasses.
- Check number of serving dishes, platters, utensils.
- Count and check tablecloths and napkins.
- Buy new candles for candlesticks (they should be above eye level so as not to shine in guests' eyes).
- Make sure an umbrella stand will be available.
- If there won't be coatracks, decide where coats will be left. If in closets, make space and check number of hangers on hand. (When coats are to be left on rack in apartment house lobby, hire a coatrack attendant.)
- Write out the menu cards.

- Make preliminary seating plan.
- Give thought to the lighting of the rooms (i.e., will candles give sufficient light to the dining room?).

THE DAY BEFORE THE PARTY
- Order ice.
- Press tablecloth and napkins, if necessary, then place directly on table.
- Set the dining-room table/s.
- Set up the bar area.
- Set up after-dinner coffee and liqueur trays.
- Rearrange any furniture for seating groups.
- Put coasters on tables where needed; if all-purpose wineglasses will be used, coasters aren't necessary.
- See that there are a few ashtrays around for any smokers.
- Write the place cards and table number cards.

THE DAY OF THE PARTY
- Arrange flowers.
- Put guest towels and fresh soap in bathrooms.
- Put table number cards on hall table.
- Put place cards, menu cards, and cards with individual table numbers on each table in dining room.

NOTE: Since many people like to sit during the cocktail hour, furniture in the living room should be arranged so that there are two or more small seating groups. This is not as important at a large party where people often prefer to stand so they can move around the room, mingling.

JUST BEFORE THE GUESTS ARRIVE
If there are any last-minute instructions to give the head butler, now's the time to do so. It is also the time to take a last "look-through" at the various rooms, to see that the lighting is right, the sofa pillows are plumped up, and the outside lights are on. You are now ready for the cocktail hour, which should last no longer than that amount of time.

THE COCKTAIL HOUR
As the hostess you should be near the entrance to the living room, so you can greet guests as they arrive. Introduce each new arrival to whomever you have been talking to as well as to others in the general vicinity. If the party is not too large introduce each person to all the guests he or she does not know. The host serves as a kind of roving ambassador. He sees

that everyone has a drink, talks to friends, introduces people, and helps set the tone of the party. If you spot two guests who will be sitting beside each other at dinner, and see that they have been talking for some time over drinks, you may want to give them the chance to talk to others. There is no reason why you can't go up to them and casually say: "Just want to let you know that you are sitting next to each other at dinner and will have lots of time to talk then. I'd love for you, Jane, to meet Frank Green, and for Herbert to meet our old friends the Whitsons." If Jane and Herbert would rather continue talking to each other and one says, "We're having a great time catching up; we haven't seen each other in ages," take them at their word and say nothing more.

GOING IN TO DINNER

When the butler announces that dinner is served, you may wait about ten minutes for a guest who is late, but for the sake of the food and the other guests who have arrived on time, it should not be any longer than that. If the guest of honor is the one who is late, and has not called to say so, you might wait a slightly longer time. Having been given the dinner signal, find the guest of honor, or whatever man will be sitting on your right and say to him, "Dinner's ready, let's go in." As you lead the way into the dining room, motion to others to follow. The host, who brings up the rear, should do his part to encourage guests to move along. If the guest of honor is a woman, tell the host when dinner is announced and he in turn will get the guest of honor and lead the way into the dining room with you as the hostess bringing up the rear. Sometimes guests are so engrossed in conversation that they miss your dinner signal, not out of rudeness but because they are distracted. Therefore, you may have to do a little nudging to get people moving, but it can be done easily with a little humor. At a formal dinner, unlike an informal one, do not suggest that unfinished drinks be brought to the table. The wines at a formal dinner are an intrinsic part of the meal, chosen with care and served shortly after the guests are seated. In addition, the look of a well-set formal dinner table with its crystal wine-glasses can be spoiled by the sight of half-empty cocktail glasses.

AT THE TABLE

On arriving at the dining room, you may tell your guests where to sit from memory, or, you can have the seating diagram on a piece of paper and take it with you to the dining room. When there are place cards, help guests out as best you can by gesturing in the general direction of their seats. When you're ready to sit down, the man on your left or right pulls out the chair for you.

The hostess who entertains regularly feels completely at ease at the dinner table. Because she knows the best time to give her toast and no longer worries about what she will say or do if "that" fateful glass of red wine is spilled, she is able to focus her attention on her guests and the dinner conversation. Such a hostess is relaxed and has a wonderful time at her own party. But as most of us give a formal dinner party only occasionally, the following pointers are the fruits of other people's experience. Use them and you'll find the fifth or sixth or even the first formal dinner party a great deal easier than you may have anticipated. And you certainly will be a more relaxed hostess.

- Should a man guest arrive late, after you are at the table, he will undoubtedly come up to you to offer his apologies. You can remain seated, giving him a brief warm hello: "Don't give it a second thought. I felt you'd want us to go ahead and start." Ask him to sit down and introduce himself to his dinner partners. If the late arrival is a woman, the host rises and greets her, takes her to her seat, and pulls out the chair for her.

- Once you are seated, initiate the conversation at your table, talking to the men on both sides. The traditional, almost ritualistic convention of the hostess talking to the guest of honor during the first course and then turning to the man on her left for the second course, with all the guests turning their heads in unison, is fortunately archaic. It certainly did nothing to foster spontaneous conversation. Today, you may talk to either dinner partner at any time. You can also engage three or four others in conversation—particularly easy to do at a round table and the reason why many hostesses prefer round tables when entertaining (the standard rectangular dining-room table is too wide to talk across without shouting). At a rectangular table, where guests are more or less limited to talking only to their partners, some hostesses will ask every other person to move two or three seats to the left or right after the main course. This would only apply at a dinner for ten or more people.

- When there are ten or more guests at the dining-room table, once the first three or four have been served, you can suggest they start eating while the food is still hot.

- If several guests get into a heated argument, don't hesitate to intervene to bring it to an end and introduce a new, more neutral topic of conversation.

- If only one guest has taken seconds, when the platter is passed to you, it's sociable to take a small amount "to keep him company," unless, of course, you still have some food on your plate.

- Should a guest knock over a glass filled with red wine, don't jump up and take charge. The butler is trained to know what to do and will come to the rescue. Even if it is your favorite tablecloth, stay cool so as not to upset the guest further. Make some consoling remark like, "I've done the same thing so I know how you feel." This would also apply when a guest knocks over and breaks a glass at the table.

- If a bone or piece of meat gets stuck in someone's throat, it is up to you to take immediate action. It takes only a few minutes for someone to choke this way. Every household should have a copy of the Heimlich Maneuver on hand (see "The Heimlich Maneuver" under "Behavior in Public Places" in Chapter 1).

- Although you and the staff have spent considerable time and care on the food, never ask a guest why he or she is not eating the soup, the fish, or anything else. It is embarrassing to the guest. Most likely it's because of an allergy or medical or religious dietary restriction. Don't make a fuss or offer a substitute.

- A minor cooking disaster is bound to occur now and then; the meat may be overdone or the fish undercooked. Try to take it in your stride and carry on as though you have not noticed. Don't draw attention to any flaws in the cooking which in all likelihood have not been noticed by the guests.

PROPOSING A TOAST   Toasts always add an element of festivity to a dinner party and those being toasted feel flattered by the compliment being paid them. It's fun to think up an appropriate toast to a friend and with a little practice it's easy to give one well. You may want to write out your toast beforehand and rehearse it in front of a mirror until your timing is perfect. While there's no reason why you can't read your toast, one given by heart (and from the heart) is more expressive.

Traditionally, the host proposes the first toast of the evening, although there is no reason why the hostess can't go first. Toasts are generally made to the guest of honor, who may be an out-of-town friend or a family member celebrating one of life's special occasions—a birthday, anniversary, retirement, birth of a child or grandchild, etc. Ideally, the first toast is made after the main course has been cleared. It's a good time to start toasting as the guests will have had plenty of time to talk to one another. Also, it's a time when people are still drinking their wine. The technique in giving a toast is a simple one. The host stands up. If he has a problem getting the guests' attention, he may rap on a glass with an unused fork or spoon. Speaking slowly and distinctly so everyone can hear, he may tell an amusing anecdote about the guest of honor, or he may congratulate him on a recent achievement in his life. Whatever he says, he should avoid potentially embarrassing remarks and he should be brief, particularly if there will be other toasts. When he finishes, he turns to the person being toasted and raises his glass in recognition, and then takes a sip of wine. Before sitting down, the host may call on a friend to say a few words about the guest of honor. "Frank, I know you have a few stories up your sleeve about Harry." To avoid putting guests on the spot by suddenly asking them to make impromptu remarks, the host should ask a possible toast giver well in advance of the dinner party if he or she is willing to say a few words. This gives the person time to think about and to prepare a toast, or to refuse as the case may be.

WHEN THE MEAL IS OVER At the most formal, traditional kind of dinner, at the end of the dessert course, put your napkin on the table, rise and tell the women sitting closest to you to follow you into the living room for after-dinner coffee and liqueurs. On the way, stop to ask if anyone would like to use the bathroom.

At the same time, the host tells the men guests whether they will stay at the dining-room table for coffee and liqueurs (only occasionally do men smoke cigars today) or move to the living room to join the women. One of the primary reasons for the long-established practice of men and women being separated after dinner was so that men could discuss business, a subject that was taboo at the dinner table. While the separation of men and women at a formal dinner party still takes place occasionally, the custom has pretty much given way to the friendlier, more popular practice of men and women gathering together over after-dinner coffee. It's more congenial and gives guests a chance to chat with people they did not talk to at cocktails or dinner. Because most women (and some men) are less than enthusiastic about the smell of cigars, when the men join the women for coffee, many hostesses do not offer cigars.

Many hostesses today serve only decaffeinated coffee after dinner. However, if it's possible to serve both regular and decaffeinated, it's thoughtful to offer guests a choice.

Sometimes the conversation at the table is so animated and spirited, you may decide to have the coffee served at the table so as not to break the mood. If this is the case, alert the butler to the change in plans. (For the exact procedure for serving coffee at the table, see "The Dinner Service Begins" under "The Role of the Staff" later in this chapter.)

AFTER COFFEE
Having finished coffee, guests continue to socialize with friends, perhaps savoring a glass of brandy. Although playing games after dinner, with the possible exception of bridge, is not usually part of the formal dinner party, sometimes an energetic, game-loving host or hostess will suggest playing charades. While charades can be great fun, it's important to know your guests well before proposing such an idea. Many people are shy about performing in public, particularly when they don't know the other guests all that well. If the party coincides with a television program of national news interest, the hostess may ask her guests if they want to watch it in another room.

It's usual for the first guests to start going home about forty-five minutes after getting up from the dinner table, particularly if it's a weeknight. Sometimes it's you who must get up to go to work the next day and it can seem that the last two or three people at the party will never leave. There's not much you can do to encourage party enthusiasts to go home aside from not offering them any more drinks.

The question of a single woman going home alone is something that should be discussed when she accepts the dinner invitation, not in front of others at the party when it might be embarrassing to her. If a woman who has planned to leave on her own changes her mind and decides she does want to be escorted home after all, you can ask someone who lives in the same direction to give her a lift.

If one of the guests has had too much to drink, he or she must be prevented at all costs from getting behind the wheel of a car, not only because of the likelihood of a serious accident, but also because the host can be sued for serving liquor to an intoxicated person who ends up having an accident (see "The Problem Drinker" under "Cocktail Parties" later in this chapter).

It's up to the host or hostess to tell the butlers when they can go home. There's no particular reason why they have to stay after removing the coffee and liqueur trays and cleaning up the dining room and kitchen. The host can always take care of any after-dinner drinks guests may want. When a caterer has provided the waiters, he will either bill the host for their services or ask him to pay them directly. If you have hired the waiters, they are usually paid at the end of the evening. In either case, if the service has been outstanding, it is nice to give each waiter a tip as a sign of appreciation.

The Role of the Guest

When you accept an invitation to a dinner party, you automatically assume a responsibility to the host and hostess: that of making a positive contribution to the success of the evening. By understanding the "rules of the game" and knowing what to expect, you will be more at ease; it's the unknown that tends to undermine our self-confidence and composure. Sometimes even for those for whom socializing and making conversation are easy the formality of this type of dinner can be intimidating.

REPLYING TO AN INVITATION

Convention says that when you respond to an invitation you follow the same form the hostess used. In other words, if the invitation is in the third person, then you reply on your personal stationery in the third person. If the invitation is extended by personal letter, you reply by letter. When the R.s.v.p. gives a telephone number, you reply by telephone. While you can never go wrong following convention, in today's world you may feel like replying by letter in response to a third-person invitation, or calling a close friend to say why you must regret her written invitation. It's a matter of using your own good sense to decide what is right.

BEAR IN MIND WHEN REPLYING Never treat an invitation casually. An invitation to a dinner party should be answered promptly, preferably within two days after it's received. The host and hostess have given a great deal of thought to the guest list and it's thoughtless not to respond as soon as possible. It's even more thoughtless to cancel at the last minute, unless you have a very good reason.

What follows are observations that have to do with replying to a formal or informal invitation. How you react to a given situation depends on your own intuition, how well you know the hostess, and other factors.

- Before replying, confirm the date with your spouse.

- It's rude, either before or after accepting, to ask who else has been invited. It implies that your main concern is whether people of importance or good friends of yours will be there.

- Don't hesitate to call the hostess if you're uncertain as to the degree of formality of dress. It can be particularly difficult if you are in a strange city or town to know whether the dress code for a formal dinner is the same as where you live.

- Do not ask if you may bring a date to a dinner party. The hostess may ask, "Would you like to bring someone?" But it should come from her.

- An unmarried man, asked alone, but living with a woman, may tell the hostess, "I'm sorry I can't come as I am now living with Susan Arensberg. Perhaps some other time the four of us can get together." It is then up to the hostess to say either, "Please do bring Susan with you. We'd love to meet her," or, "I'm afraid space at the table is tight but we'll ask you both for a meal very soon." The same thing applies, of course, in the case of an unmarried woman or someone living with a person of the same sex.

- Unless the hostess is a very close friend and she knows your house-guests, do not ask to bring them to dinner. Instead, be firm about refusing and explain, "I'm so sorry we can't make it but my old college roommate and her husband will be staying with us." If the hostess has room at the table, it's up to her to extend the invitation to include your friends.

- If you're a houseguest and are taken to a dinner party, be sure to write the hostess afterward, thanking her for including you.

- If only one member of a couple can attend the dinner, the hostess should be told, "Sorry, we can't come as Henry will be in Phoenix on business." It is then up to the hostess to say, "Come any way," or, "What bad timing! Let's get together soon."

- If you'll be flying back from a business trip the day of the dinner, tell your hostess. Then, if you are delayed for some reason, she will know not to wait dinner for you.

• Never accept an invitation and later cancel because a better invitation has come along. It's not fair to the hostess who has spent time putting her guest list together.

• If, having declined a day or two earlier, you find you can attend a dinner, call your hostess to explain the situation and ask her if she has already filled your place. She will be flattered that you cared enough to inquire.

• Be sensitive about accepting an invitation to dinner if you have already refused an invitation for the same evening. If the hostess who extended the first invitation finds out you went elsewhere, her feelings can be understandably hurt.

• If you turn down a dinner invitation, and hope you will not be invited again, do not make too convincing an excuse or you'll certainly find another invitation in your mailbox. Be brief but polite when refusing. "Jim and I have another engagement that evening. Thank you for asking us," is all you need say.

• Should some last-minute emergency prevent you from attending a dinner party, call your hostess. Speak directly with her, explaining your situation. Aside from offering your apologies, you may want to send flowers or a plant.

• If you are asked to dinner and you regret, you are under no obligation to respond with a return invitation.

• An invitation to your daughter's wedding would not be considered a payback for a dinner invitation.

• If you are on a strict medical diet, tell this to your hostess when accepting the invitation, so she will understand why you are not eating certain foods. Guests who require kosher food or follow other religious dietary laws should do the same. Don't, however, discuss the fact that you are a vegetarian or have food allergies—your hostess may feel obliged to change an already planned menu just for you. If you anticipate a food problem related to your allergy, have a snack before you leave home and then eat what you can at dinner.

THE COCKTAIL HOUR

The exact time you should arrive for a dinner party varies depending on the custom of the community. The general rule of thumb, however, is to arrive not more than twenty minutes after the time called for on the invitation. New Yorkers tend to run up to a half hour late, while San Franciscans are much more punctual, usually arriving at the exact time specified. In some Western and Midwestern areas, however, when a dinner invitation says 7 P.M., guests begin to arrive at 6:30 P.M., assuming they will sit down to eat at seven or shortly thereafter. The guest of honor, of course, should be punctual, ideally the first to arrive.

At a formal dinner, don't show up with a bunch of cut flowers because the hostess and staff will be too preoccupied to arrange them. Instead, it's thoughtful to call your hostess several days before the dinner to say you'd like to send her flowers and to ask what are a few of her favorites as well as her preference in color. In that way you'll be certain she has an arrangement she can use that evening and one to her liking.

When you arrive at a dinner party, a butler or maid will greet you at the door and either take your coat or tell you where to leave it. If there's a table in the front hall with table number cards, pick up yours before going into the living room. (Instead of table number cards there may be a seating chart, a *plan de table*, to show your seat at the table.)

As you enter the living room, your hostess in all probability will be standing near the entrance. If she's not, find her so you can say hello. If a butler offers you a drink before you've had a chance to find her, refuse; it's only good manners to speak to your hostess before accepting her hospitality. Sometime shortly after your arrival, you should also find an opportunity to say hello to your host.

Having been given a drink, if there is a coaster on a wooden table, it means you should put your glass there so the finish won't be damaged. Should you want a second drink, it is perfectly all right to say to a butler, "May I please have another drink?" When hors d'oeuvres are passed, take one at a time from the plate—not three or four. It is not necessary to ask a butler for another hors d'oeuvre as his job is to see that they continue to be passed. If an hors d'oeuvre is served with a toothpick (not a very practical idea in this situation), discard the toothpick in an ashtray or in your cocktail napkin. Whatever you do, don't put a toothpick back on the serving plate.

During cocktails, make a concerted effort to meet people you don't already know. Husbands and wives should mingle; when they only talk to one another it appears insulting and exclusive. If the hostess notices you have been talking for some time to the person you'll be sitting beside at dinner, she may suggest you each join another group of guests for the remainder of the cocktail hour. It's an idea that makes sense but if you and the person you are talking to would rather continue your conversation, all you have to do is say so.

GOING IN TO DINNER

When dinner is announced and the hostess asks you to follow her into the dining room, try not to linger in the living room, drinking and talking. The food is obviously ready and slow-moving guests cause problems for the kitchen. Guests make their way into the dining room at random with this exception: if you are the woman guest of honor, you are escorted in by the host; if you are the man guest of honor, the hostess will escort you. At a formal dinner you will not be asked to bring your unfinished drink with you to the table. Wines are an important feature at this type of party and are served shortly after guests are seated. You can either leave your evening bag behind in the living room or, if you prefer, you can take it into the dining room to place under your chair. A small evening bag can rest in your lap.

AT THE TABLE

Once you arrive in the dining room, the hostess will tell you where to sit or, if there are place cards, look for your seat at the table. Traditionally, a man pulls out the chair for the woman on his right. Today, however, life is more relaxed and a woman arriving at the table before her dinner partners can seat herself. Men guests remain standing until the hostess is ready to sit down. At that time her chair is pulled out by the man on her left or right.

If you are a man and for some unavoidable reason you arrive after the guests are all seated, go up to the hostess to say hello and offer your apologies. Do not linger but go directly to your place and sit down. If you are a woman, the host will get up to greet you and take you to your place at the table.

Once you are seated, take care not to tip your chair back, a habit some people picked up as children or teenagers. Sometimes the chairs at the table are too close together, in which case move slightly to the side to make it easier for the waiter to serve you. It's fine to rest your wrists on the table but, just as your mother probably said, no elbows on the table! Unfold the dinner napkin in half; it should not be shaken out in its entirety. Then place it on your lap. Never tuck it into your neckline!

Guests frequently wonder when they can start eating. In general, watch the hostess and begin when she does. Once three or four people have been served, she may tell you to start eating so the food won't get cold. If not and you are at one large table, say for ten or more people, it's fine to begin eating when a majority of the guests have been served. If there are several round tables, each seating six or eight people however, wait until all the guests at your table have been served.

If you are being served by a butler you know, say hello quietly but do nothing to detain him. When you take food from the platter, use both the serving fork and spoon. Use your judgment as to how much to take. You certainly don't want to pile your plate with food. As a general rule, two small pieces of meat are considered an average helping. You may take some garnish from the platter such as a few sprigs of parsley or watercress, or a piece of lemon for the fish. If the meat has not been sliced all the way through, the butler will help cut it. If the platter is divided into sections, take the meat, fish, or chicken first, then the vegetables. After being served, as you're putting the fork and spoon back on the platter, it's nice to say a quiet thank you to the butler.

At a very formal dinner, seconds are not always passed, the reason being that there are enough courses so that guests will have plenty of food.

If seconds are passed, keep in mind that there are others to be served after you. And remember to keep pace with other guests in order not to delay the butlers in clearing the table for the next course. When the butlers do clear the table, don't assist by handing them anything. It's their job to remove whatever it may be from the table. You can, of course, help them by leaning to one side, if chairs are so close together that clearing is difficult. Should you not want wine, gesture toward your wineglass and say, "No, thank you," to the butler; don't turn your wineglass over to indicate "No." There once was a custom whereby the ladies placed a glove over the wineglass; today that would cause a few smiles! If you want more wine, wait until it is passed; it will be periodically.

Eating should not be your sole interest at the table. It's important at any dinner party to talk to both your dinner partners—the person on your left and on your right. Introduce yourself if you didn't meet at cocktails. Initiate the conversation. Try to draw both of them out and show an interest in what they have to say. If you feel you are not on the same wavelength with one of them, don't let it show. By making an effort, you'll find something to talk about that will interest both of you. At a round table, it's easy for three or four people to join in a single conversation—the reason why most hostesses favor round tables over the traditional rectangular dining-room table.

FOR WOMEN ONLY Many women instinctively reach for their lipstick at the end of a meal. Whatever you do, resist the urge. When the hostess gives the signal that dinner is over, that is the time to retire to the bathroom to fix your face. Never primp at the table and try your best not to smear lipstick on your napkin or wineglass.

PROPOSING A TOAST If the host or hostess does not make a toast first, you may do so after the main course. Rise to your feet and, if you have trouble getting everyone's attention, rap on a glass with an unused spoon or fork. Your toast may be a word of thanks to the hostess for a splendid evening or an anecdote or story about the guest of honor. It may have been prepared beforehand or not, but in either case it should be short and either amusing or touching. After finishing the toast, raise your glass to the person you are toasting and take a sip of wine. If toasting is informal, guests stay seated when raising their glasses. For more commemorative occasions, such as toasting a couple on their wedding anniversary, all the guests rise to their feet and raise their glasses. The person being toasted remains seated and does not drink or raise his glass—to do so would be to drink to oneself! He acknowledges the toast by an approving gesture and a "Thank you." The gracious honoree stands up and says a few words in response, either directly after he is toasted or a little later, perhaps near the end of the dessert course. Nondrinkers may toast with a glass of water, although some people raise an empty glass, believing that to toast with water is bad luck. While it can be unnerving to be called upon to make a toast without any warning, if you're asked, you have little alternative but to rise to your feet. You need not say more than a few words, such as: "Here's to Harry. No one could be a better friend."

WHEN THE MEAL IS OVER   Once the dessert course is finished and the hostess gets up, indicating that the meal is over, place your napkin in a casual fashion on the table to the left of your plate. A used napkin is not refolded nor is it left on a chair or on a plate. The hostess usually asks the women guests to follow her to the living room where after-dinner coffee and liqueurs will be served (occasionally after-dinner coffee is served at the table). On the way to the living room, she'll ask if anyone wants to use the bathroom.

It's up to the host to tell the men guests whether coffee, liqueurs, and cigars will be served at the table or whether they will move into the living room. While separating the sexes after dinner is a longstanding custom, today most hostesses like a more congenial approach, with the men joining the women in the living room for coffee. When this is the case, cigars are not always passed, the smell being less than popular with most women and even some men.

When the butler serves the after-dinner coffee, it's perfectly all right to ask if it's decaffeinated. If it's not, and you choose not to have any, just say "No, thank you," and leave it at that. (For the exact procedure for serving coffee, see "After-Dinner Coffee and Liqueurs" under "The Role of the Staff" later in this chapter.)

AFTER COFFEE

Once the coffee tray has been removed, guests mingle, talking to those they have not spoken to earlier in the evening. Although games, with the possible exception of bridge, are not played at a formal dinner, on occasion a hostess may suggest a game of charades. If you are a guest and eleven out of twelve people want to play, there is nothing much you can do but summon up your courage and join in. You may be a great deal better at it than you thought. Unless there's a game, in which case you would stay until it is over, you should not think about going home until approximately forty-five minutes after leaving the table. If you leave too early, it gives the impression that you haven't had a good time. Unless the guest of honor is a high government official, there is no reason why you can't leave the party before he does, provided you go up to him and say goodbye. You can explain that you have to get up for an early meeting or to take the children to school. If you're the guest of honor at a dinner party, keep in mind that some people will feel they shouldn't go home until you do. Just how long the guest of honor should stay after dinner is impossible to say, as much depends on the mood of the party and whether it's a weeknight or a weekend. But be sensitive to the fact that, if you are the guest of honor, many guests will take your leaving as a lead and go home when you do.

After saying goodbye to the host and hostess, leave right away. A guest who lingers can be most exasperating for the host and hostess who want to go back to their other guests. It can also break up the party.

THE NEXT DAY

If you were the guest of honor at a dinner, and didn't send flowers to the hostess before the party, do so now with a note of thanks. Each guest (if a couple, one of them) should call the following day or within a day or two to thank the hostess. A word of caution, however. If the dinner party was a particularly large one, the busy hostess may be driven to distraction by all the telephone calls. If you think this will be the case, a brief thank-you note is much easier on her than a telephone call.

TIPS TO FOLLOW AT THE DINNER TABLE

When you're not sure where to put your soup spoon, you can always watch what the hostess does. But you'll feel a lot more relaxed at the table if you know already. Here are a few reminders about conventional table manners:

- Knives and forks are used for eating European (continental) or American style. Either style is correct. In the European style, the fork remains in the left hand, tines down, and the knife in the right hand at all times. In the American style, the food is cut with the fork in the left hand; before eating, the knife is placed on the plate and the fork changed from the left to the right hand, with the tines up (if left-handed, the fork remains in the left hand).

- Flatware at a place setting is used by working course by course from the outside in, toward the plate.

- Used flatware is never placed on the table or left in a cup, with one exception: in the case of a large soup plate resting on a service plate, the spoon is left in the soup plate, unless there is room for it on the service plate.

- To indicate you have finished eating, the fork and knife are placed across the center of the plate, or on a diagonal slant, the sharp side of the blade facing in, fork tines up, to the left of the knife.

- A soup plate is always used at a formal dinner. Since soup served in a plate requires a large soup spoon, you sip the soup from the side of the spoon rather than attempting to put such a large utensil into your mouth. To spoon up the last remaining soup, tip the plate away from you (it's less awkward this way) and scoop it up. Then, leave the spoon in the soup plate, or on the place plate if there's room.

- A two-handled soup cup is used for jellied soup or consommé. You can drink the soup from a handled cup as well as spooning it. If there are vegetables or a garnish floating on the top, eat these with a spoon before drinking the soup. Hold the cup by its handles, rather than cradling it. And, when you have finished, leave the spoon on the service plate.

- True wine connoisseurs hold long-stemmed glasses where the stem and the bowl join so their hands won't warm the wine. However, unless you're a perfectionist, hold the glass wherever it feels most comfortable.

- When asparagus or mushrooms are served on toast, take the toast as well.

- Cut one piece of meat, fish, or chicken at a time on your plate and eat it before cutting the next piece.

- Do not season food before tasting it. To do so shows a lack of confidence in the cook.

- Individual open salt (and occasionally pepper) dishes are usually accompanied by small sterling silver or ivory spoons. If for some reason they are not, use the tip of your clean knife blade to take a little salt or pepper, or take a pinch with your thumb and forefinger.

- In the past, at a formal dinner there were no butter plates and hard rolls were placed in or on the napkin or directly on the tablecloth. Today, however, butter plates are used either for prebuttered soft rolls or for hard rolls. In the latter case, there will be butter and a butter knife. If there are no butter plates, the larger of the two standard dinner plates (10¾ inches in diameter) should be used to make room for rolls. (NOTE: Butter on butter plates is intended for rolls only. It is not put on vegetables or potatoes.)

- When mint jelly, horseradish, cranberry sauce, or some other condiment is passed, take a small amount and put it on the side of your dinner plate. When presented with a gravy boat, only put a modest amount in the ladle. Don't drown your meat.

- If you are served dessert in a stemmed glass on a service plate, the spoon is placed on the service plate and never left in the glass, even while eating. If dessert is in a plate that resembles a soup plate or sauce dish, leave the spoon in the dish or put it on the service plate if there is enough room.

- Ice cream is eaten with a spoon, but when served as part of baked Alaska or with cake, it is eaten with a dessert fork and spoon.

- If finger bowls are used, the butler places each on a dessert plate with a doily underneath it and a fork and spoon on either side. It is then brought to you at the table. Remove the finger bowl and doily from the plate and place them on the table at the eleven o'clock position above your dessert plate. Then put the dessert fork to the left of your plate, the spoon to the right. When using the finger bowl, dip the tips of your fingers in the water one hand at a time and dry them on your napkin. If you like, touch your lips lightly with moistened fingers and wipe them as well with your napkin. (NOTE: Occasionally finger bowls are presented after dessert, in which case flatware is omitted.)

PROBLEMS AT THE DINNER TABLE

The perfect guest is one prepared for any mishap. Here are a few guidelines to ease your way through some common problems that may arise at the table.

- If you are missing a piece of flatware or anything else, don't trouble your hostess; instead catch the eye of a butler and ask him in a quiet voice for what you need.

- If you are allergic to something on the menu, take a very small portion and leave it on your plate. You do not need to say anything to your hostess unless it's very obvious to her that you are not eating the lobster she has had flown in from Maine. In that case, wait until after dinner and then tell her about your allergy.

- If you find there's something in your mouth you cannot eat, like a piece of gristle, do not spit it into your napkin. Instead, put your fork up to your mouth and remove the inedible object; replace it on your plate where you can bury it under some food so it is not visible.

- If someone swallows the wrong way, causing a temporary coughing attack, don't stare. It often takes a minute or so to recover one's voice. Of course, if a bone or piece of meat is stuck in someone's throat, immediate action must be taken. Someone can die that way in a matter of minutes (see "The Heimlich Maneuver" under "Behavior in Public Places" in Chapter 1).

- If you taste something unbearably hot—soup, for instance—do not spit it back into the soup plate, but quickly take a sip of water to cool your mouth off.

- If you spill jelly, gravy, or sauce on the tablecloth, take your knife and scoop it up, putting it on the side of your plate. If you spill it on your shirt or dress, take an end of the napkin, wrap it around your finger, dip it in your water glass, and rub the spotted area. If something is spilled while you are being served, the waiter will take care of it.

- If you knock over a wineglass and it breaks, do your best to find out where the glass was bought and replace it the following day.

- If you spill wine on the tablecloth, quick action must be taken to save the cloth and the wood finish of the table. Use your napkin as best you can to soak up the wine until the waiter arrives with towels to place between the tablecloth and the table. To take out the wine, he'll sprinkle the tablecloth with salt or soda water or other cleaning substance.

- If there are no ashtrays on the table, you can safely assume that the hostess does not want smoking at the table. That being the case, there is nothing you can do but resist. Respect her wishes. Don't use your dessert plate, or saucer as a substitute ashtray. If ashtrays are on the table, light up only after the dessert course is finished.

The Role of the Staff

Expert service is one of the three basic ingredients that guarantees a successful dinner party. You may have the perfect guest list and the most accomplished chef, but if the last ingredient, a well-trained, efficient, and caring staff, is missing, in all probability the party will fall short of your expectations. Do not compromise when it comes to service. An effective staff that anticipates the needs of host and guest and knows how to meet those needs is worth the time and effort it may take to find them and whatever the cost may be.

BEFORE THE GUESTS ARRIVE

Shortly before the guests arrive, the head butler, the one in charge of the other butlers (and waitresses, if there are any), should go over any last-minute details with his staff. He may also want to reconfirm with the hostess what time to announce dinner.

THE COCKTAIL HOUR

When guests arrive, the butler stationed at the front door greets them, calling by name those he recognizes. He either takes their coats or directs them to a room where they can be left. If there's a table in the front hall with table number cards, he tells the guests, seeing that each person picks up his or her card before going into the living room. Other butlers, during the cocktail hour, make and serve cocktails and pass hors d'oeuvre trays. After an arriving guest has said hello to the hostess, a butler goes up to that person and asks, "May I get you a drink?" The trained butler keeps an eye on guests throughout the cocktail hour, replenishing their drinks and seeing that they are not lacking for hors d'oeuvres. If there are smokers in the room, he empties ashtrays when necessary.

BEFORE THE DINNER BEGINS

Before dinner is announced, a butler lights the candles in the dining room and fills the water glasses. If there's sufficient help, the hostess may prefer that the glasses be filled after the guests are seated. When everything is ready, the head butler goes up to the hostess and tells her, "Dinner is served." The guests then move into the dining room.

If there are table number cards, each table in the dining room will have its own number (1, 2, 3, etc.) written on a card and standing on the table. Once the guests are seated, these cards are removed from the tables by the butlers.

THE DINNER SERVICE BEGINS

Today, the truly traditional style of service at a formal dinner has been somewhat modified to accommodate changing times. People don't have the space to serve thirty-four guests at one table, or enough trained help to serve them. Queen Victoria's dinners required three servants for each six guests. In those days of lavish entertaining, the head butler stood behind the hostess's chair, only leaving his post to give instructions to the footmen or to pour wine. Also, in those days, liveried footmen presented dishes with the right hand always behind the back. They wore white cotton gloves, because of the danger, as one writer put it, of a dirty thumb in the soup. Today, even the word "footman" is obsolete; we talk of butlers and waiters, the latter being most often associated with a restaurant.

The actual service at a dinner is much as it always has been. The butler serves the woman on the right of the host first (in this country the hostess is never served first). He then moves counterclockwise around the table, serving the host last. While tradition once called for the hostess to be served after the host, it's seldom seen today. It slows up the service and has no practical purpose. To speed up the serving there may be two complete services going around the table at the same time. If that's the case, one butler begins with the woman on the right of the host and the other butler begins with the man on the right of the hostess.

The only time during a dinner when there is no plate in front of a guest is just before the dessert is served. When guests arrive at the table, there is a place plate (also known as a charger) at each setting. Sometimes there is another plate on top of it, as in the case of, say, a crabmeat cocktail which would be in a stemmed glass, or stemmed double container, a "supreme" glass (sometimes silver) surrounding the "liner," on a small service plate. The complete unit is set on the place plate. When that course is finished the unit is cleared although the place plate remains and the soup course— always in a flat dish—is served. At the end of the soup course, place plate and soup dish are removed together, and a warm plate for the fish course (if there is one) is put down, or a heated dinner plate for the main course.

A butler brings one plate at a time to the table, serving each guest from the left. He removes from the right or it can be the left, whichever side is most convenient; as an example, a butter plate is removed from the left. He takes away one plate at a time, never putting one on top of another. In a somewhat less formal style, and to speed up the service, a butler brings in two soup plates (and later the dessert plates), one in each hand. Standing between two guests, he places the plate in his left hand in front of the guest on his left and the plate in his right hand in front of the guest on his right. He removes the plates exactly the same way when the course is finished. It takes some dexterity to carry two plates filled with soup or two dessert plates each with a fork or spoon, but it can be done with a little practice.

Butlers always pass a serving platter with the left hand, steadying it if necessary with the right. If there are sauces or gravies, these are passed by a second butler who follows immediately. Ladles for sauces are in the sauce when it is served, and the bowl or "boat" is on a serving plate. When serving any hot food, the butler places a napkin under the serving dish to protect his hand. The serving spoon and fork are placed face down on the serving platter or vegetable dish with the handles facing in the direction of the guest (with a vegetable like peas, a fork is not necessary). All serving dishes and platters are held at a comfortable level for the guests— not too high or so far away that they must twist around to reach them. Dinner rolls are passed in a shallow serving dish or basket lined with a napkin. Water, wine, and champagne glasses are filled from the right without lifting the glass from the table; to prevent dripping, a napkin is wrapped loosely around the neck of a champagne or wine bottle with the label exposed.

The butlers wait until all the guests have finished eating before removing plates, with one exception: in the case of a noticeably slow eater, they can start removing plates as unobtrusively as possible and return to the slow eater at the end.

The salad course is served after the main course. Since there are never more than three forks at a place setting at one time, if an additional fork is needed for salad and cheese it is brought when the salad is served. Before dessert is served, a butler removes the salts and peppers and unused flatware on a small tray. Only glasses remain on the table. The table is then crumbed. For this the butler uses a folded napkin and, from the left of each place setting, brushes any crumbs onto a small tray, a clean plate, or into a "silent butler," a lidded silver receptacle with a short handle.

Finger bowls, although rarely seen today, are placed on the dessert plate with a doily underneath and the dessert flatware (a fork and spoon) on either side of the bowl. The finger bowl is filled three quarters full with cold water; a few flower petals often float in the bowl. The dessert plate is placed directly on the tablecloth with no service plate under it.

If after-dinner coffee is served at the table, demitasse cups on a silver tray are placed by a butler to the right of the guests and a second butler follows with the coffeepot (or pots, if both regular and decaffeinated coffee are being offered), cream, and sugar. Or demitasse cups already filled are placed by a butler to the right of the guests and cream and sugar are passed by another butler. Chocolate thin mints or other mints are passed just after the coffee has been served. The butlers do not remove the demitasse cups or wineglasses until the guests have left the table.

DURING THE DINNER SERVICE   While the guests are at dinner, one of the butlers straightens up the living room, removing cocktail glasses, emptying ashtrays, and plumping up pillows. He sees that the room is in perfect order for when the guests return.

AFTER-DINNER COFFEE AND LIQUEURS

When guests have their after-dinner coffee in the living room, there are a number of ways it can be presented. Unfilled demitasse cups, the sugar, and the cream are carried in on a silver tray by a butler, who is followed by a second butler with the coffeepot. The second butler hands each guest a cup and saucer and fills the cup, and the guest helps himself to cream or sugar. Or the butler brings in a tray with pre-filled demitasse cups, the sugar, and cream and the guests serve themselves from the tray. If both regular and decaffeinated coffee are being offered, the butler will ask guests which they prefer. Less formally, the coffee tray is placed in front of the hostess on a coffee table or other low table and she pours the coffee. She then hands the cup and saucer to the butler, who takes it to a guest on a tray along with the cream and sugar.

After coffee has been served, liqueurs are passed in a similar fashion, with the butler asking each guest his or her preference. Sometimes a tray with glasses and liqueurs is set up on a table in the living room, and the host offers and pours the liqueurs.

THE STAFF GOES HOME

It's up to the host or hostess to tell the head butler when the staff can go home. It may be that they will want one butler to stay on until the last guest leaves.

THE INFORMAL SEATED DINNER WITH A MAID

While formal dinner parties with everyone splendidly dressed in their finest attire create a special atmosphere of glamour and festivity, these days we are more used to entertaining in a far simpler, less elaborate fashion. Small seated dinners for six or eight are a lovely way to bring friends together in a relaxed, friendly setting. With six or eight guests, there's room for everyone to sit down before dinner and for everyone to talk to everyone else. Most hostesses can handle a seated dinner for six alone, but when there are as many as eight it's that much nicer for you and your guests if someone serves the dinner and cleans up as she goes along. It allows you the rare privilege of being a guest in your own house.

When you stop to think about it, there are not all that many differences between a formal and informal dinner aside from the service, which varies considerably. The roles of the host and guest, and courtesies they show each other, are basically the same no matter what the style of entertaining.

What follows are those elements of an informal dinner that are different from a formal one. If you have not read the previous pages on the roles of the host and guest, and perhaps the service, you may want to do so now. You will then have the complete story on formal and informal seated dinners.

THE ROLE OF THE HOSTESS

- When you are to cook and also serve, the meal should be kept simple—no more than three courses. If you plan to have help with the cooking, the meal can be slightly more elaborate.

- Complicated dishes that need last-minute attention should be avoided.

- Unlike a formal dinner, you may ask your guests to bring their unfinished cocktails to the dinner table.

- Whenever you need to get the maid's attention—for example to signal that a course is finished—you ring a bell on the table or, if there is one, press a buzzer on the floor.

THE INVITATION

Invitations to an informal dinner are almost always extended over the telephone, although an invitation written on personal notepaper or an informal or correspondence card is equally correct. If time is of the essence and the person can't be reached on the telephone, the invitation can be faxed or left on an answering machine, but it must *always* be followed up with a telephone call. How far in advance to do the inviting depends on what's customary in your community. In general, ten days is minimum advance notice. If a couple do the inviting, either can extend the invitation or, if both are out of town, a secretary may do it. But if this happens, it's courteous for the husband or wife to call the invitee later to reiterate the invitation.

THE ROLE OF THE GUEST

REPLYING TO AN INVITATION Because an informal invitation is most often extended over the telephone, the response is usually given at the time. Otherwise, the invitee checks the date and calls the hostess back.

AT THE TABLE Here are a few pointers to consider if you are a guest at an informal dinner:

- At an informal dinner, it is unnecessary to take a bottle of wine as a present. However, if you choose to, your hostess can save it for some other occasion. Flowers are not as convenient a present, since the hostess has to take time to arrange them.

- At a large dinner party, guests often start eating before the hostess, but at a small one they should wait until she begins, unless, of course, she says the soup will get cold and they should start.

- If there's a bottle of wine at the hostess' end of the table, the man on her right may offer to pour it.

- If the hostess does not get around to offering a second glass of wine, it's all right to ask for one provided there is plenty in the bottle. You should, however, not ask for a third glass.

- Salts and peppers are passed as a pair; a pepper grinder, however, can be passed separately.

- Celery and radishes are placed on the butter plate with your fingers. Salt to dip them in is also placed on the butter plate, not the tablecloth.

- When a condiment such as mint jelly or chutney is in a dish (usually on a small service plate) on the table, the spoon or fork, on or by the plate, is placed in the condiment by the first person picking up the dish.

- While you don't help the maid as she clears the table, if something like the salts and peppers are beyond her reach, of course, you can hand them to her.

THE SERVICE

An experienced maid will have no problem serving six people at the table. She follows the same procedures as described in the formal dinner service with one exception: if two vegetables are being served in separate dishes, she can hold a dish in each hand, offering first the dish in her left hand and then the one in her right. When there are eight people, to speed up service, the gravy boat may be put on the table to be passed around by the guests.

In a less formal setting, the host does the carving. A carving set with a sharpener along with a serving spoon for the juices is placed to his right above his place setting. The maid stands to the left of the host and helps with the service. In one form of service, there is a hot dinner plate at each place setting. The host fills the plate in front of him (he includes some garnish from the platter). The maid then picks up the plate with her left hand and takes it to the person sitting on the host's right. She removes the empty plate in front of that person with her right hand and replaces it with the filled plate in her left hand. She returns to the host, putting the empty plate in front of him. When that plate is filled, she serves it to the next guest, continuing around the table counterclockwise until everyone is served. The host serves himself last.

In another form of service a stack of hot plates is put in front of the host. The maid, again standing at his left, passes each plate one at a time as it is filled. Or, when there are no place plates, which usually is the case at an informal dinner, she can take two plates, one in each hand.

Still another form of service is for the host, starting with the woman at his right, to pass the filled plates down the right side of the table and then the left, serving himself last. In this case. the maid brings in the vegetables from the kitchen and serves them.

You may prefer to do the serving or the host may serve the meat or fish while you serve the vegetables. If you add the vegetables, the serving fork and spoon are at your right. The maid takes the plate from the host, who has put the meat on the plate, and brings it to your left for you to add the vegetables. The maid then serves the woman to the right of the host and continues around the table, serving in the regular order. When you are doing the serving, you serve yourself last, after which the maid takes the food back to the kitchen where it is kept hot until seconds are served; if additional carving is necessary, the maid attends to this in the kitchen.

Wine at an informal dinner with one maid is seldom passed. Instead, the wine bottle or a decanter is placed on the table on a wine coaster. There may be two bottles of wine, one at each end of the table, in which case the host serves one bottle and you ask the man on your right to serve the other or you can pour the wine yourself. When the table is cleared, the wine is left on the table.

While the guests are eating the main course, the maid straightens up the living room, removing the cocktail glasses and hors d'oeuvre plates, plumping up sofa pillows, and emptying ashtrays.

THE INFORMAL SEATED DINNER WITHOUT A MAID

Undoubtedly, this type of dinner is the most popular today. Four, six, or eight guests are manageable, but if you have more than eight you really need a maid to serve your guests comfortably and graciously. When there is no help both host and hostess have to be well organized and willing to fill in as cook, bartender, server, and cleaner-upper. With practice it's not difficult to handle a dinner for eight. The trick is to serve a meal that does not call for last-minute preparations, or one in which there is no first course. A one-dish main course is ideal for this type of entertaining. You can serve it with a salad and follow it with dessert. When a meal needs only last-minute reheating, you are free to concentrate on your guests and to have fun yourself.

THE ROLE OF THE HOSTESS

If there is no maid to help, before going in to dinner, you should light the candles in the dining room and fill the water glasses. You also tell the guests when dinner is ready. While there's little time to put the living room in order for after-dinner coffee, the host may do a quick "pickup" job and at the same time go in to dinner with the guests. Very often at the end of the meal, friends ask to help clear plates. Thank them but firmly decline, saying, "Thanks so much but I have my own system that works really well." Or in advance of the party you might ask a son or daughter to help you with the clearing.

THE SERVICE

There are two ways to handle a first course without help. You can serve it in the living room or have it ready on the table before the guests go into the dining room. Advocates of eating the first course in the living room feel that clearing the dishes on a tray from the living room before seating the guests for dinner is simpler than having to clear the first course in the dining room. When the first course is served in the living room, you might have a cold soup or scalloped fish in shells. An alternative to a real first course can be substantial hors d'oeuvres such as stuffed mushrooms, pâté, and crudités.

The most practical way to serve dinner without help is to put the food on hot trays on a sideboard or buffet table in the dining room and let the guests help themselves (see "Buffet Lunches and Dinners" later in this chapter). There's no order as to men and women helping themselves, although the host and hostess are the last to go through the line. If there's no sideboard, then the host can do the serving at the table. When all the guests have been served, if there are no hot trays the food is taken to the kitchen to be kept hot until seconds are offered.

People who live in small apartments sometimes feel they cannot give dinner parties because the serving space is too small. All you need is a little inventiveness. If there's no room for the serving dishes on the dinner table, you can fill the plates in the kitchen and bring them in two at a time. Rolls and salad are brought in separately for the guests to pass to one another; the salad bowl is held for the person on the right. If there's no space on the table for salad plates, use dinner plates that are large enough to allow room for the salad (place plates because of their size are a good choice in this case). Choose a main course that does not include a sauce or gravy that will run into the salad. The dessert can be served at the table or filled plates can be brought in from the kitchen.

When the dining area is a part of the living room, dessert plates should be taken to the kitchen and the table tidied up when the meal is finished so guests don't have to spend the rest of the evening looking at a messy table and dirty dishes.

THE FORMAL SEATED LUNCH WITH A STAFF

The word "luncheon" is seldom used in conversation, as it is generally reserved for formal and ceremonious use; you might, for example, speak of going to a luncheon at the British Embassy. On formal occasions a butler may announce, "Luncheon is served," but you would turn to your guests and say, "Let's go in for lunch." While hotels and restaurants often use the word "luncheon," most people talk about "having lunch" or "lunching."

The formal lunch is pretty much a thing of the past except in diplomatic or official circles. When one is given, invitations are extended in the same way as for a formal dinner. But the two forms of entertaining differ greatly, except for the service. At a formal lunch cocktails include drinks such as Bloody Marys, spritzers, Lillet, daiquiris, and Virgin Marys, soda water, and ginger ale for those who do not drink liquor at lunchtime. The table is usually set with placemats instead of a tablecloth. If a tablecloth is used, it should hang only about eight inches over the edge of the table. When there are round tables, it is not necessary for the tablecloths to match each other as is customary at a formal dinner. A lunch napkin is used instead of the larger dinner napkin. Traditionally, candles are not put on the table at lunch. If they are used for decoration, they should never be lit. While four courses is the maximum for a formal lunch (soup, main course, salad, dessert), three is much more usual. Soup at lunch is traditionally served in two-handled soup cups, although it is not incorrect to use soup plates. It was once *de rigueur* to serve sherry with soup, but today, when many people drink less alcohol, the hostess often eliminates it. No more than two wines are served, although one is more likely.

THE INFORMAL SEATED LUNCH WITH
OR WITHOUT A MAID

Invitations to an informal lunch are almost always made by telephone. When there is a large group, a buffet-style meal is the easiest and best solution. The menu is less elaborate than the formal lunch and only one wine is necessary. In the summer, iced tea or iced coffee is served in glasses placed on a china saucer, iced-tea spoon to the right of the knives. Either the maid pours the iced tea or coffee or a pitcher is placed on the table. Sliced lemon, sugar, and cream are passed or placed on the table. Extra ice should be available.

TABLE SETTINGS

Formal dinner table setting.
The place plate is placed one inch from the edge of the table. If the first course is already on the place plate, the napkin is placed to the left of the forks. The handles of the flatware are aligned at the bottom. The forks (no more than three) are at the left of the place plate, placed in order of use, working from the outside in; the oyster fork is the only fork on the right side with the knives, tines of the fork placed upward, across the soup spoon or parallel with the knives. The knives (no more than three) are at the right of the place plate in order of use, with the cutting edge toward the plate. The only spoon (for a first course) is placed to the right of the knives. The dessert fork and spoon are above the place plate, the bowl of the spoon facing left, the fork below facing right; in the most formal setting, the dessert fork and spoon are brought in on the dessert plate. No more than four glasses are set on the table, in order of use, for water, white wine, red wine, and champagne. The butter plate (optional) has the knife placed across the top of the plate, handle to the right, edge of blade toward the user. The salt and pepper are above the place plate, the pepper to the left of the salt; larger salts and peppers to be shared are placed slightly below the wine glasses and between every two place settings.

THE FORMAL DINNER TABLE SETTING

The chairs around a table, whether it is rectangular or round, should be spaced far enough apart so butlers can serve with ease, but not so distant as to inhibit conversation. Spacing of chairs depends on the size of the table and of the chair; a ballroom chair will take up less room than an antique chair with a high back. As a guideline, approximately two feet from the center of one place setting to the center of the next setting is recommended.

TABLECLOTH The traditional formal tablecloth is made of white damask and hangs over the edge of the table by twelve inches or more. A damask cloth is sometimes overlaid with an antique lace runner set. A padding is placed under the tablecloth to protect the table. A lace tablecloth does not have a padding; it is made to be seen through. Pastel-colored tablecloths, with or without a pattern, are popular for round tables. They may be made of such materials as glazed chintz, linen, or brocade and look best when floor length.

DINNER NAPKIN The traditional dinner napkin is anywhere from twenty-two to thirty inches square. It is centered on the place plate, except when the first course is already on the place plate or the place plate is too rare or beautiful not to be seen. Then the napkin is placed on the table to the left of the forks. When folding a monogrammed napkin, make certain the initials are on the outside and that the initials face the guest.

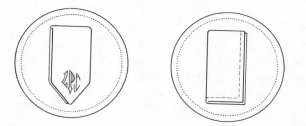

The folding of napkins.
While there are many imaginative ways to fold a napkin, here are two classic examples. Left: Fold napkin into quarters, turn the top left point down and the points to the left and right of it over the top point. Turn the napkin over and place it on the place plate. Right: The square is folded over to the left into a rectangle and placed flat on the plate, with the edge either on the left (more convenient) or the right. When folding a napkin with a monogram, be sure that the initials are on the outside of the napkin and that it is placed right side up so it faces the guest.

CENTERPIECE AND OTHER TABLE DECORATIONS The centerpiece is placed in the direct center of the table and should be in proportion to the size of the table. A decorative china bowl filled with beautiful flowers, carefully arranged, is the conventional centerpiece and one that suits any occasion. Still, there are many other possibilities. You may have inherited a silver epergne which you can fill with flowers or fruit, or a lovely Meissen or Chinese porcelain figurine which can bring an air of originality to the table. When choosing a centerpiece, bear in mind that it should not be too tall or guests across the table will not be able to see one another. Other decorative items can be placed on the table according to the space available. These might include compote dishes filled with candy, miniature crystal vases with tiny flowers, crystal cones and obelisks, or small hurricane lamps.

CANDELABRA While a candelabrum is the most elegant candle holder on a formal dinner table, ornamental candlesticks are equally appropriate; often both candelabra and candlesticks are used. The number is determined by the size of the table and how much light is needed. At a formal dinner candles are traditionally white and always brand-new. They must be sufficiently tall or guests will be bothered by their glare.

MENU CARD There may be a card between each two place settings, cards for women guests only, or no more than two cards placed one at either end of the table in menu card holders.

PLACE CARD Placed either on the center of the napkin, provided the napkin is on the place plate, or on the table directly above the center of the place plate.

PLACE PLATE (ALSO KNOWN AS A CHARGER) The plate is on the table when you sit down to dinner (standard size twelve inches in diameter). It is placed one inch from the edge of the table. If it has a representational motif, the design on the plate should face the guest.

SERVICE PLATE (ALSO KNOWN AS A LINER) A plate placed under a cup or a bowl, for example a two-handled soup cup or a dessert bowl.

DINNER PLATE The china used at a formal dinner need not be the same for each course but should be similar within a course; the one exception is a rare set of dishes which do not match but are compatible in style. When a dinner plate does not have a matching butter plate, a fine-quality glass butter plate can be used. A dinner plate is 10¼ or 10¾ inches in diameter, the larger size being more practical when there is no butter plate.

BUTTER PLATE Longtime custom excluded butter plates from the formal dinner table; the hard dinner roll was put in or on the napkin or to the left of the service plate. Today, practicality has overruled convention and a butter plate is often placed above and to the left of the place plate. The butter knife is placed across the top of the plate, handle to the right, edge of blade toward the user, or it may be placed on the plate at a slight angle with the handle pointing downward. If butter is offered, it is rolled into small balls or molded into flower shapes and placed on the butter plate.

FLATWARE Flatware used at a formal dinner is always sterling or vermeil (silver gilt). While vermeil has a special elegance, it is difficult to maintain and, therefore, not often seen. In general, flatware placed on the table should match; an exception is sharp knives with bone handles. The spoon and fork brought in on the dessert plate need not match the silver on the table, and demitasse spoons are often of a different pattern. When flatware is placed on the table, the handles are aligned at the bottom.

Knives: Set on the right of the place plate in order of use (working from the outside in), with cutting edge toward the plate. There are never more than three knives at a place setting—for appetizer, fish, and meat, or for fish, meat, and salad, if cheese is served with it. If more than three knives are necessary, the additional one is put in place at the time the course is served.

Forks: Placed to the left of the place plate, forks are used from outside in also. An exception is the oyster fork, which is not placed with the other forks but on the side with the knives with the tines of the fork placed, upward, across the soup spoon or parallel with the knives. Forks are also limited to three; if a fourth fork is needed for salad, it is placed on the table when the salad is served.

Spoons: The only spoon placed to the right of the knives is a spoon for a first course, such as soup or melon.

Dessert fork and spoon: In the most formal style, when there are sufficient waiters, the dessert fork and spoon are brought in by the waiter on the dessert plate, fork to the left, spoon to the right. Less formal but also correct is to place the fork and spoon above the place plate, the bowl of the spoon facing left, the fork below facing right.

GLASSES No more than four glasses are set on the table (for water, white wine, red wine, champagne). The sherry glass, once an integral part of a table setting, is rarely seen today.

Wineglasses are placed on the table in order of use, above the knives. The glasses need not match but all the glasses for a particular wine should be the same. If you do not have sets of wineglasses, it is not necessary to buy a different type of glass for each wine. The all-purpose glass is appropriate for either red or white wine. A champagne glass may be either a flute, the more popular today, or tulip-shaped or wide and shallow.

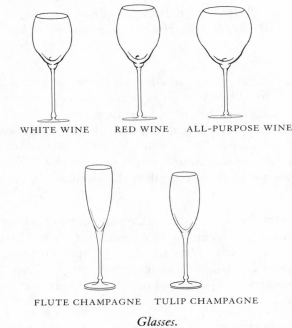

WHITE WINE   RED WINE   ALL-PURPOSE WINE

FLUTE CHAMPAGNE   TULIP CHAMPAGNE

Glasses.

SALTS AND PEPPERS Silver or silver and crystal salts and peppers may be placed above the place plate, pepper to the left of the salt. Larger salts and peppers, which are shared, are placed slightly below the glasses and between two place settings with the pepper slightly above and to the left of the salt. Open salts and peppers require little sterling, ivory, or mother-of-pearl spoons. (A salt cellar with a silver top must have the top removed and the threading washed completely free of salt after it has been used a number of times or the threading will corrode and the user will get more salt than bargained for.)

ASHTRAYS Guests rarely smoke at dinner today but, when ashtrays are used, they are brought in by a waiter after the dessert is served.

THE FORMAL LUNCH TABLE SETTING
The tablecloth for a formal lunch need not be white and may be linen, cotton organdy, embroidered Madeira cloth, or some other material. It should hang over the edge of the table by approximately eight inches. The napkins may be the same color as the tablecloth or a contrasting color. Today, placemats are more frequently seen on the lunch table than tablecloths. Some of the more formal placemats are made of linen, lace, embroidered cotton, or mother-of-pearl. Particularly popular are English lacquered wood placemats with center panels depicting flowers, hunting scenes, birds, etc. When round tables are used, a cloth may be floral or

paisley in design and is floor-length. The lunch napkin is traditionally smaller in size than the dinner napkin and varies in size from fourteen to twenty-four inches square. The centerpiece at a formal lunch should be elegant, perhaps a vermeil basket filled with flowers or a china soup tureen or crystal bowl with flowers floating in it. Candlesticks by convention are not placed on a lunch table. However, it is not incorrect to have candles on a lunch table so long as they are not lit.

THE INFORMAL DINNER TABLE SETTING

The logistics of setting an informal table are similar to those of the formal table. The difference between the two styles is that a formal table requires classic flatware, china, and crystal, while the informal setting may be less conventional, allowing you to mix and match more freely, use bolder colors, and a wider variety of textures. Napkins need not match tablecloths; geometric designs may be combined with stripes so long as they are color coordinated. Cork, rattan, or quilted placemats are quite appropriate at an informal table. The centerpiece may be a pottery bowl with a pyramid of apples. You may have a collection of objects which can make for interesting and unusual centerpieces, such as art pottery, ceramic figures, even Chinese and Japanese lacquerware. Stainless steel may be used instead of silver with nonwhite candles adding a touch of color to the table. Many different types of salts and peppers may be used: china, earthenware, cut crystal, smooth glass, or wooden salt and pepper grinders.

WORKING WITH A CATERER

A creative, knowledgeable caterer can be an invaluable asset if you have no household help or have limited time to plan and organize a party. A caterer with an established reputation can almost guarantee the success of that aspect of a party and means you can give undivided attention to your guests. If you happen to live in an area where there are no caterers, you can often get a restaurant or gourmet food shop to do some or all of the catering, whether for a simple or grand meal. Sometimes these places are also helpful in finding waiters and waitresses.

The best way to find a caterer is by word of mouth. Ask a relative or friend who has had firsthand experience with one or, when you go to a party where the food and service are outstanding, ask for the name of the caterer. Unless the recommendation is a reliable one, don't commit yourself to a caterer without first sampling his food and observing his staff in action. Choosing a caterer from an ad in the newspaper or because the price seems right is at best risky and might even be disastrous.

Full-service caterers such as Glorious Food in New York City, one of the best-known and respected caterers in the country, are equipped to handle all your entertaining needs. As well as the food and waiters, they will also supply tables and chairs, linens and place settings, ice, soft drinks, arrange for flowers and other decorations, engage the music, and, if necessary, find people to park cars. If the party is held outside your home, for instance in a garden or a public building, they will bring serving tables, warming ovens and containers to keep things cold, and screens to hide their working area. And the food will taste as though it had just been prepared in your own kitchen. While some caterers are willing to use your china, glassware, and flatware, many prefer to bring in their own because they feel that is more efficient. It also means they are less likely to break one of your treasured plates.

In a large city it is necessary to book a caterer as much as a year in advance, especially during the wedding and holiday seasons. On occasion, a hostess with a cook or one who plans to cook the meal herself will call a caterer just to book waiters. For the most part, caterers are reluctant to agree to this type of arrangement since they may need these waiters to take care of a full-service event.

Once you have hired a catering outfit for a dinner, a representative of the firm will come to your apartment or house to talk over your specific requirements for the evening. You will need to discuss among other things:

- What menu suggestions the caterer has in mind and their relative costs (while you can make your own menu suggestions, you don't want the chef to experiment with a recipe he is not familiar with).
- What wines the caterer feels will complement the menu. It is more economical to buy your own wines.
- Whether liqueurs will be served with after-dinner coffee.
- Whether the caterer should provide any rentals, such as chairs, tables, coatracks, china, flatware, etc.
- What time guests are expected and what time dinner is planned for.
- Whether someone is needed to take the guests' coats when they arrive.
- The number of waiters needed—a dinner for twelve requires two waiters; a dinner for twenty, four waiters. (It's not practical to settle for fewer. You don't want to risk poor service.)
- What the waiters will wear. The conventional outfit for a waiter at a dinner party is a tuxedo (black trousers, black jacket, plain white shirt, black tie); a waitress wears a black skirt and white or black blouse or a tuxedo (a skirt may substitute for trousers). In the most conservative setting a waitress wears a black dress with a white apron. If you have a particular preference as to what you would like your waiters and waitresses to wear, such as red jackets at a

Christmas or Valentine's party, the caterer can make the necessary rental arrangements at your expense.

On the initial visit, the representative will check out your kitchen, noting the amount of counter space available as well as other factors related to the preparation and serving of the meal. He will also want to see the layout of the dining room—how the table or tables will be arranged, the amount of space between chairs for serving purposes, whether there is a sideboard on which to place the dessert plates, flatware, and other necessities related to the dinner service.

After the terms of the service have been agreed upon, the caterer will send you a written agreement or contract to sign. It is important to read the contract carefully so that everything contained in it is itemized and clearly understood. Check not only on the menu and service that's to be provided but also the insurance proviso to make certain the catering company has the proper general liability as well as liquor liability insurance as protection against the odd disaster. And ascertain whether waiters' gratuities are included or if you are expected to give tips. When you sign the contract, a usual deposit of fifty to seventy-five percent is required, with final payment due the day of the party or whenever you have agreed. A day or two before the dinner you must tell the caterer how many guests you expect and guarantee to pay for that number. After the guarantee has been made, the cost remains the same whether or not a guest cancels at the last minute. The cost increases, of course, if any additional guests are added. If a party is canceled, the deposit is forfeited, although there are always exceptions to this rule, depending on the circumstances. Caterers have different billing policies. Some break down the costs and others charge an all-inclusive price. As a common practice, waiters are paid for by the hour, with a customary four-hour minimum fee. In planning a party of any kind, it should be remembered that, as the guest list increases, the cost per head decreases.

The caterer cooks the food at his own kitchen and brings it to your kitchen in special warming ovens. He will reheat it on the spot before it's served. The kitchen must be cleared of all clutter before the catering staff arrive so they can work efficiently and with ample counter space. If any of your pots, pans, dishes, etc., are to be used, lay them out in advance. When the waiters arrive they should be shown to a room where they can leave their coats and, if necessary, change clothes. Now is the time to give any last-minute instructions to the headwaiter or to answer any questions he may have. Caterers must work within a certain time frame, so it is important that they not be interrupted unnecessarily. While children love the excitement of a party, they must not be allowed to interfere with the waiters' preparations. The same holds true for pets; they should not be underfoot. If you have a question, or a request, it should be directed to the headwaiter, the person in charge of coordinating all phases of the evening.

Once the guests arrive, you can relax and let the catering staff take over. They are professionals and you have hired them for their expertise. Whether greeting guests on their arrival or serving cocktails and later the meal, the waiters are adept at seeing that the evening runs smoothly. Some catering companies even send their waiters equipped with a corkscrew, a paring knife, and matches so they are well prepared for a variety of needs. (For specific details regarding the service of a dinner, see "The Formal Seated Dinner With a Staff" earlier in this chapter.)

After dinner, when the waiters have cleaned up the dining room and kitchen, there is no reason why they should not go home, even if a few guests still remain. It is up to you, as the host or hostess, to tell the headwaiter when the staff is no longer needed. If you have hired the waiters directly, and have not paid them beforehand, you would do so now, adding a tip if you're satisfied with their service. If the caterer has provided the waiters, whether you pay them directly or are billed for their services is something you would have discussed earlier while making the party arrangements. However you are paying, if you have been impressed by the staff's service, it is always nice to give a tip.

The day after the dinner party, it is thoughtful to call the caterer to report on the evening and to express your thanks. And, too, if the meal or service was less than perfect, he should be told so. After all, any praise or criticism is in his best interests.

MENUS

When giving a lunch, a dinner, or a party of any kind, remember that a meal does not have to be elaborate to satisfy the palate or to show off your entertaining skills. Planning a meal, however, does require a certain amount of time, a degree of inventiveness, and a lot of attention to detail.

A well-thought-out menu means choosing courses that balance each other; if the main course is a rich roast duck, then consommé is a better choice for the first course than cream of tomato soup or pâté. What you want to do is create a meal that will please the more indulgent eater as well as the health- or weight-conscious one, but never a meal that is too rich or too bland. We don't always associate the word "texture" with food but it should play a part in the planning of a menu. For instance, if you are serving a mint sauce with leg of lamb, asparagus with hollandaise would probably be a poor choice as an accompanying vegetable. Two sauces running together on the dinner plate are definitely less than appetizing to see or taste. Something else to keep in mind is color. Vegetables in particular can add color, whether it be green beans or spinach, red cabbage or broiled tomatoes. What you want to avoid at all costs is a menu that even approaches being all white. Nothing could look duller or more boring. There are many ways to add color to a meal: a sprinkling of chives, a bit of minced parsley or dill or a sprig of watercress on the platter, or red peppers used as garnish.

Here are a few tips to remember when planning a menu:

- If you have a budget for your meal, it is necessary to plan the menu carefully before shopping.

- Don't skimp on the amount of food you buy; nothing's worse than to be caught short.

- Party time is not when you experiment on a new dish.

- Buy fruits and vegetables in season; they are cheaper, fresher, and taste much better.

- If it's a buffet, keep it simple. Don't feel you have to go overboard with variety, as long as you have enough.

- If you are doing the cooking, don't choose a dish that has to be prepared at the last minute.

- If pressed for time, buy one dish at a gourmet food shop and arrange it attractively on your platter.

- Substantial hors d'oeuvres with cocktails can substitute for a first course.

There are many great cookbooks and books on entertaining you can consult for good menu suggestions. Newspapers and magazines are also sources of new and innovative recipe ideas. When you see a recipe that sparks your imagination, cut it out and save it for the right occasion, testing it of course on yourself or family before serving it to guests. You can file prospective menus and recipes in folders or put them on the computer. In that way, they will be instantly available when you are faced with the prospect of giving a party.

The menus that follow are suggestions for a number of different entertaining occasions.

1. The Formal Seated Dinner (for twelve with a staff)

First Course:
Wild mushroom soup

Second Course:
Crown roast of lamb
Rosemary potatoes
Garden vegetables

Third Course:
Bibb lettuce and endive salad

Fourth Course:
Cold lemon soufflé with a lemon sauce
Tuiles cookies

2. The Informal Seated Dinner (for eight with a maid)

First Course:
Cold asparagus vinaigrette

Second Course:
Braised short ribs
Pommes de terre Anna
Frenched green beans

Third Course:
Arugula salad

Fourth Course:
Strawberry sorbet with fresh strawberries

3. The Informal Seated Dinner (for eight without a maid)

First Course:
Broiled swordfish marinated in soy sauce and herbs
Brown rice
Creamed spinach

Second Course:
Green salad

Third Course:
Tarte Tatin

4. The Formal Seated Lunch (for twelve with a staff)

First Course:
Melon and prosciutto

Second Course:
Poached red snapper
Broiled tomatoes with basil-mustard sauce

Third Course:
Watercress and endive salad

Fourth Course:
Peaches with raspberry sauce topped with crushed pistachios

5. The Informal Seated Lunch (for eight with a maid)

First Course:
Rosemary roasted chicken
Wild rice
Sautéed snow peas

Second Course:
Tomato salad vinaigrette

Third Course:
Chocolate roll with sauce

6. The Informal Seated Lunch (for eight without a maid)

First Course:
Artichokes with melted cayenne butter

Second Course:
Broiled salmon steak
Chicory salad with hot bacon vinaigrette dressing
Corn sticks with sweet butter

Third Course:
Cantaloupe halves filled with cantaloupe and honeydew balls

7. Buffet Dinner

Cold baked ham with a fruit mustard sauce
Cold roast turkey
Hot ratatouille
Salades composées
Basket of French bread
Chocolate mousse
Chocolate lace cookies

8. Buffet Lunch

Vitello tonnato
Rice primavera
String-bean salad
Tomato salad with basil vinaigrette

Sliced country bread
Individual fruit tarts
Pound cake

9. Cold Summer Lunch

Jellied madrilène
Curried turkey salad
Parsley potato salad with green beans
Yellow and red tomato salad with basil
Assorted breads
Rhubarb crisp with thick fresh cream
Iced tea and lemonade

10. Brunch

Orange juice
Brioches with marmalade
Quiche Lorraine
Steamed artichokes
Canadian bacon
Fruit salad
Sparkling cider or champagne
Tea and coffee

WINES

The subject of wine fascinates some and intimidates others. Whether you believe that a day without wine is like a day without sunshine, or you simply want to know what wine to serve with what food, you will find that a great deal of information is available—so much, in fact, that you may be a bit overwhelmed. The secret, of course, is not to be intimidated by those who know more, and to realize that there are really only a few simple rules about the selection and serving of wine. Craig Claiborne, in his classic *New York Times Cookbook,* put it well: "For some obscure reason, some authorities seem bent on making the drinking of wine a ritual more complicated than chess. They have succeeded in inhibiting a large section of the public and depriving them of one of the greatest pleasures known to man."

You will learn from what you read here the basics—how to select and serve a wine properly. Then, if you wish to know more about how wine is made and labeled, which specific wines from each country are the best, and how to set up your own wine cellar, you may want to read Hugh

Johnson's *How to Enjoy Wine* or his *Pocket Encyclopedia of Wine* as well as *Windows on the World Complete Wine Course* by Kevin Zraly. *Pick the Right Wine* by Daniel McCarthy is a complete guide to matching specific wines with specific foods.

In the opulent Victorian and Edwardian eras, every gentleman of wealth knew all about wines—how to select, store, and serve them. He and his head butler stocked and watched over his full wine cellar, serving and replacing each bottle with loving care. Although not many Americans maintain extensive wine cellars anymore, we have become increasingly interested in wine for special occasions. And the success American wine producers have had in recent years has not only helped increase Americans' interest in wine, it has also made a wide selection of good wines available at moderate prices. In fact, some American wines now rival those of Europe. California still and sparkling wines, in particular, are excellent, as are New York State sherry and port. Of course, great wines continue to come from France as well as Italy and Germany, and Spanish sherry is still among the best. And fine wines are also imported from Chile and Australia.

TYPES OF WINES

The best way to discover wines you like is to experiment and keep notes. Don't be afraid of making a mistake. If a selection is disappointing, you can always use it the next time a recipe calls for a cup of wine.

There are five basic categories of wines and, within each category, a number of variations.

APPETIZER WINES, OR APÉRITIFS Wines served before the meal include vermouth, Campari, Dubonnet, Lillet, and sherry. True sherry is produced in Spain but sherry-like wines also come from Australia, Cyprus, England, California, and New York. The four types of sherry are: fino (pale, light gold, and very dry); manzanilla (light and tart); amontillado (darker and not as dry); and oloroso (usually sweet, such as cream sherry).

WHITE WINES French white wines include Chablis, Macon Blanc, Meursault, Pouilly Fuissé, Pouilly Fumé, Riesling, and Graves. American whites include Chenin Blanc, Pinot Chardonnay, Riesling, Sauvignon Blanc, and White Zinfandel. Italian white wines include Soave, Verdicchio, Orvieto, and Pinot Grigio. Among the German whites are Rhein, Liebfraumilch, and Mosel. Dry white wines are often served before dinner at cocktail time and with lighter foods, such as fish, chicken, veal.

A word about Chablis. Because the French did not take the necessary steps to protect the use of the name, it has over time become a general term for many ordinary wines from other countries. However, French Chablis continues to be among the finest of wines and is ranked from Petit Chablis (ordinary) to Chablis Grand Cru, the most expensive. There are only seven vineyards in Chablis that qualify to have their wines use the appellation "Chablis Grand Cru."

RED WINES French red wines include Beaujolais, Burgundy (such as Nuits St. Georges, Pommard, and Volnay), Bordeaux (such as Graves, Médoc, Pomerol, and St. Émilion), Rhône Valley (such as Côtes du Rhône and Châteauneuf du Pape). American red wines include Merlot, Pinot Noir, Zinfandel, Cabernet Sauvignon. Among the Italian reds are Chianti, Bardolino, Valpolicella, and Barolo. Spain's most popular red wine is Rioja.

You may see a wine called Beaujolais Nouveau. This refers to a light red wine officially released for consumption every November 15. The new Beaujolais is picked, fermented, bottled, and delivered to stores, all within a few weeks. It should be drunk within six months. Regular Beaujolais can be kept from one to two years.

Red wines are traditionally served with meat, game, and cheeses.

Rosé is a lighter variety of red wine. Although it is not regarded as a great wine, it is often very good and may be served with light foods. Among the better rosés are Tavel from France and Lancers and Mateus from Portugal.

DESSERT WINES Because people are drinking less and watching their diets more, dessert wines, which include port, sauternes, and sweet sherry, are simply not as popular as they once were. When they are offered, however, port is served at room temperature while sauternes and sweet sherry are served chilled.

Port, as you might have guessed, was originally from Portugal. Most ports are red and all are sweet. The four main types are: vintage (aged for two years in wood, then in bottles for years); ruby (young); tawny (less sweet than ruby port); and white (made from white grapes).

SPARKLING WINES Heading this group, of course, is champagne. The word officially refers to the sparkling white wine made from grapes grown in the French province of Champagne. It is a mixture of black Pinot Noir and white Chardonnay grapes and is named for the vintners and shippers responsible for each blend. An American sparkling wine called champagne is made in New York and California. Other sparkling wines include sparkling Burgundy, sparkling rosé, and Asti spumante. The latter, from Italy, is too sweet to accompany the main course but can be served with dessert or after dinner. Champagne is wonderful served throughout the entire meal—if you don't mind the expense.

Champagnes are categorized by how dry they are: brut is the driest, extra dry is less dry, sec is sweeter, and demi-sec is the sweetest. Vintage champagne, made from the best of that year's grape harvest, is more expensive than nonvintage. Among the leading brands of champagne are Bollinger, Charbaut, Piper Heidsieck, Deutz, Henriot, Krug, Lanson, Laurent-Perrier, Moët & Chandon, Mumm, Perrier-Jouet, Pol Roger, Pommery, Roederer, Ruinart Père & Fils, Taittinger, and Veuve Clicquot. A good medium-priced choice is Korbel.

Opening champagne: The pressure in a champagne bottle is about ninety pounds per square inch, so it's wise to open it correctly and carefully, always pointing the bottle away from your guests and anything breakable.

STEP 1. Remove the foil from the top of the bottle.

STEP 2. Untwist the wire cage over the cork and slide it off.

STEP 3. Remove the metal disk over the cork.

STEP 4. Wrap a towel around the bottle in case the champagne bubbles up and spills. Hold the bottom of the bottle against you with the mouth pointing in a direction where the cork won't hit anybody or anything.

STEP 5. Put your hand over the top of the cork. Do not remove your hand until the cork has been pulled out completely.

STEP 6. Remove the cork very gently by slowly rotating the bottle with your right hand while holding the cork fixed with your left. In other words, turn the bottle, not the cork. Take time to ease the cork out rather than pull it quickly, which could cause the champagne to foam up.

STEP 7. Before pouring, let the carbon dioxide escape. Then tilt the glass slightly so that when the champagne is poured it doesn't fizz too much.

WINE AND FOOD

We are not so rigid as we once were about what wines should be served with what foods. It is no longer written in stone that red meat calls for red wine or that fish and poultry must be accompanied by white wine. However, wine and food should complement each other. That means that with wines, as with foods, it is preferable to serve lighter wines before heavier ones. So, at a dinner, white wine is served before red, and dry before sweet. You'll find these general guidelines helpful in making decisions about what wines to serve when:

- Cocktail time: an apéritif, such as Dubonnet, Campari, Lillet, or champagne, dry white wine, or dry sherry.

- With soup or consommé: at a formal dinner, sherry may be served with certain soups and all consommés. (You would not serve sherry with a cream of chicken soup, for instance, but it goes nicely with black bean soup and any soup that is seasoned with sherry.) Sherry is often poured into an attractive decanter and left at room temperature until served.

- With fish: white wines go well with fish but a rich fish, such as salmon, may be accompanied by a light red or dry rosé.
- With chicken, veal, pork, and mild cheeses: because these tastes are lighter, serve a light red, such as a Beaujolais or Pinot Noir, or, of course, a white wine.
- With baked ham, turkey, sausages: use medium-bodied reds, such as Pinot Noir, Cabernet Sauvignon, Zinfandel, Beaujolais, or Chianti.
- With lamb, game, strong cheeses: best with Bordeaux, Cabernet Sauvignon, Burgundy, and other flavorful reds.
- With desserts: Riesling, Sauternes, muscatel, champagne, port, or any sweet or fortified wine.

WINEGLASSES

Although each type of wine has its own type of glass, today the trend toward simplified living has led to the "all-purpose glass" which can be used for either red or white wine. It holds eight to ten ounces and has a large bowl which tapers slightly at the rim to capture the bouquet. The glass is filled just a little over halfway, leaving room to swirl the wine about so its aroma may be enjoyed. If you are serving an apéritif in the all-purpose glass, fill it about one third full.

For champagne, you use a special champagne glass rather than the all-purpose glass. There are three: a flute, which is currently the more popular today; a tulip-shaped one; and a wide and shallow glass. The latter, sometimes called a coupe, is the least desirable because it lets the bubbles escape. Champagne glasses are filled a little more than halfway.

The legend is that the first champagne coupe, modeled after the breasts of Helen of Troy, was rather small in size. Then Marie Antoinette decided to have a glass molded to the shape of her breasts, which changed the size entirely since she was considerably bustier than Helen of Troy.

If you have matching glasses—water, red wine, white wine, sherry, and champagne—by all means use them. They add a touch of elegance to any table. At a formal dinner, these glasses are placed in a grouping above the knife at each place setting. At a formal dinner, sherry is served with consommé, white wine with the fish course, red wine with the meat, and champagne with dessert.

STORING AND SERVING WINE

The flavor of a wine will be enhanced if it is stored and served at the correct temperature. Most red wines are served at room temperature, about sixty-five degrees. However, light red wines, such as Beaujolais, are served just slightly chilled, at about fifty-five degrees. Red wines should be uncorked and allowed to "breathe" for at least a half hour before serving to improve their taste. If for some reason a bottle of red wine becomes too cool, you can warm the wine and bring out its flavor by cradling the bowl of the wineglass in your hands.

White wines and rosés, like light reds, are served just slightly chilled at about fifty-five degrees. This generally requires placing the wine in the coldest part of the refrigerator for about two hours. Champagne, too, must be chilled well in advance. Most champagnes and other sparkling wines taste best if served quite cold—about forty-five degrees.

Sometimes we forget to chill wine before guests arrive. It's tempting to put the wine in the freezer—but don't: it can ruin the flavor. Instead you can speed up the chilling process by putting the bottle into a bucket of ice to which salt has been added. Unfinished bottles of wine can be recorked and kept successfully for a short time. Keep unfinished red wine in a cool place, but not in the refrigerator. It will probably turn bitter in about three days. A recorked bottle of white wine may last well for two to three days in the refrigerator.

OPENING A BOTTLE OF WINE   The best wines are sold with corks, not screw caps, which means everyone needs a good corkscrew. One of the easiest to use is the kind with arms that rise outward from both sides when the spikelike metal piece, called the worm, is screwed into the center of the cork. You then press the two arms down and the cork comes out quite easily.

SERVING WINE AT DINNER   When your guests arrive at the table, the wine bottles are already there, on coasters to avoid getting the tablecloth stained, or it may be in decanters. If you are serving a white wine with the first course and a red wine with the second course, only the bottle or decanter of white is on the table at the beginning of the meal. Bottles of red have been opened and left to breathe on your sideboard or serving table. When the first course is finished, the white wine bottles or decanters are taken to the kitchen, by either the maid or the host, and replaced with the red wine bottles.

After the host has poured and tasted a little wine himself, the wine is served first to the woman on the host's right and then, moving counterclockwise, to everyone else at the table. If the host is serving, once he has filled each guest's glass, he is then responsible for refilling glasses at his end of the table. You or the male guest of honor to your right will keep the glasses filled at the other end. If you are entertaining on your own, serve wine in the same manner.

A FEW SERVING POINTERS TO KEEP IN MIND
- When wineglasses are being filled, they are left on the table and not lifted up.

- When serving wine, in order to avoid spilling, try turning the neck of the bottle before lifting it away from the glass. If you are unable to prevent the wine from dripping as you pour, then wipe the bottle neck with a napkin after you fill each glass.

- If you are serving a very fine vintage wine, place the bottle in a slanted straw basket specially made for this purpose. The basket keeps the bottle in a semihorizontal position. Leave it this way for a day to let any sediment settle. Vintage wine is opened and then served from the basket, with the label showing.

- Wineglasses are held where the stem and bowl join. This keeps white wine and champagne cool and, with red wine, allows you to enjoy its color.

- Although it's permissible to ask for ice in your wine at a cocktail party, you would never do so at a dinner party where the host or hostess has given special thought to the wines that are served.

MEASURE FOR MEASURE

On December 31, 1979, the sizes of liquor bottles in this country were converted to metric measures. Here's what happened to bottle sizes:

SPIRITS

Old name	Old size	New size	New size
miniature	1.6 oz	1.7 oz	50 ml
half pint	8.0 oz	6.8 oz	200 ml
pint	16.0 oz	16.9 oz	500 ml
fifth	25.6 oz	25.4 oz	750 ml
quart	32.0 oz	33.8 oz	1 liter
half gallon	64.0 oz	59.2 oz	1.75 liter

WINES

split	6.3 oz	187 ml
tenth	12.7 oz	375 ml
fifth	25.4 oz	750 ml
quart	33.8 oz	1 liter
magnum	50.7 oz	1.51 liter
jeroboam	101.44 oz	3 liters

HOW MUCH WINE DO YOU NEED?

Daniel McCarthy, author of *Pick the Right Wine*, has devised this foolproof formula for determining how much wine to buy for large parties.

For 25 or more people, if the party lasts:

1–2 hours	6 ounces per person
2–3 hours	8 ounces per person
3–4 hours	10 ounces per person
a dinner	12 ounces per person

This formula can be used for any number; here it is based on 50 people:

1. Determine the number of hours
   (e.g., 3 hours or 8 ounces per person)
2. Determine the number of people
   (e.g., 50 people)
3. Multiply the number of ounces times the number of people
   (e.g., 8 ounces × 50 people = 400 ounces)
4. Divide the total ounces by 25.4 ounces (per 750-ml bottle)
   (e.g., 400 divided by 25.4 = 15.7 or 16 bottles)

Another useful measurement to help you determine how much wine to buy for smaller groups:

HOW MANY DRINKS IN A BOTTLE?

	750 ml	1 liter	1.5 liter	1.75 liter	3 liter
Liquor (1.5 ounces each)	16	22		39	
Wine or champagne (5 ounces each)	5		10		20

BUFFET LUNCHES AND DINNERS

The word "buffet," which dates back to the eighteenth century, referred to a sideboard or a side table. Today it is commonly used to describe a type of party at which the meal is placed on a side table and the guests serve themselves. This way of entertaining allows you to feed many guests with one maid or even with no extra help. Any occasion lends itself to a buffet, from a black-tie supper dance to an outdoor lunch for a few close friends.

The buffet dinner, which typically consists of drinks, a main course with a vegetable, salad, bread, dessert, and coffee, has many advantages: it requires only a few dishes, for serving and for eating; it is a godsend to the working person who doesn't have time to organize a formal dinner party; and it is also an easy solution for a couple without a formal dining room, for anyone living in a small apartment, or for those gregarious souls who know more people than their dining table can comfortably accommodate. The buffet is also, by its very nature, informal, which many people like.

An ideal type of buffet on a hot summer day is a clambake or lobster party. Seafood, a tossed salad and/or potato salad, rolls, and a simple dessert, along with beer and wine, can be served at long tables set up on the lawn or at the beach.

Yet its primary advantage—that you can serve many guests without much help—can turn into a distinct disadvantage if you invite more people than you can comfortably accommodate. The cardinal rule for a successful buffet is that every guest must have a chair and a place for his or her plate and drink. This means you must avoid the temptation to ask everyone you know. The purpose of any social gathering is for people to meet and talk—which is difficult if the rooms are too crowded and guests are perched precariously on the arms of sofas or sitting cross-legged on the floor, balancing plates on their laps while holding a wineglass in one hand and a fork and knife in the other.

It is easy to give a successful buffet for twelve or more people if you follow these guidelines:

INVITATIONS

An invitation to a buffet is extended in the same manner as for an informal lunch or dinner, using informals, printed fill-in cards, or the telephone. (Ideally you should give your guests at least two weeks' notice.) You may want to try this idea thought up by a Connecticut hostess who gives large parties: she buys museum postcards of paintings that show food or people eating, writes her invitations on the cards, and sends them in envelopes printed with her return address.

ELECTING THE TYPE OF BUFFET

There are two basic types of buffet—the classic buffet and the seated buffet. The amount of room you have as well as the number of guests you invite will determine which type is best for your gathering.

THE CLASSIC BUFFET   At this type of party, the guests form a line and pass in front of the buffet table, filling their plates with food. They then go into the living room or den and sit down wherever they want, holding their plates on their laps. Although men tend to hold back and let women go through the line first, it is not impolite for both to go at the same time. In fact it is preferable so that there will be a mix of men and women when they sit down.

Each guest should have a table, or a portion of one, available for his or her plate and glass—an end table, TV table, or coffee table will do. Although it's easy to sit on the floor at age twenty, it becomes increasingly difficult with each passing decade. So if your guests are older, make certain that each one has a chair even if it means renting or borrowing folding chairs. If the event is a large family gathering, ask the younger people to leave the chairs for their elders.

The napkins, often wrapped around the flatware, are put out at one end of the buffet table or placed strategically about the living room. Have stacks of extra napkins in each room too. It's nice to have two napkins per guest—the extra one to spread on their laps.

To make it easier for your guests, have already filled glasses on the serving table or sideboard. At a brunch, pitchers of Bloody Marys, mimosas, or sangría may be on the serving table. And always include ice water or a bottled sparkling water as well.

THE SEATED BUFFET At this type of buffet, the guests serve themselves from the buffet table and then sit at the dining-room table or at smaller tables set up in the living room or library. Place cards are helpful if there are eight or more guests.

If there is more than one table, it's best if all those at one table go through the line together. One way to do this is by giving all the guests assigned to one table the same color cocktail napkin during the cocktail hour. When it's dinnertime, you ring a bell and ask all the guests with red cocktail napkins to proceed to the buffet. The other guests wait until you call out their colors.

Since you will serve yourself last, when you arrive at your table, the man seated on your right should rise and pull out your chair.

The seated buffet is much more comfortable than the classic type. The tables are set exactly as they would be for a seated informal lunch or dinner, with tablecloths, flatware, napkins, and glasses. The water glasses are on the table and filled before the guests sit down. An open bottle of wine is placed at each table but it is never poured until the guests are seated. Then the host pours the wine or, if there is more than one table, he may designate a man to serve the wine at each table. You may ask one of the men to fill the wineglasses at your table or do so yourself.

THE BUFFET TABLE

A careful arrangement of the buffet table as well as the items on it eases the task of feeding a large number of people. First and foremost, the table should not be too cluttered—guests should be able to reach plates, flatware, and dishes easily without dipping an elbow or jacket sleeve into a casserole or salad. If there's room, flowers and/or a candelabrum can add to the ambiance, it should never overwhelm the table, and if your table is quite small, you can eliminate flowers and candles altogether. Regardless of the size, use a formal linen or damask tablecloth for special evening buffets and more casual cloths for lunches, brunches, and outdoor affairs. All-purpose wineglasses are preferable to glasses without stems for this type of setting because they eliminate the need for coasters. Use the largest dinner plates you have or, if you have them, place plates (also called chargers), which because of their size make excellent buffet plates.

If the group is large, place the table in the middle of the room so two lines can go around it at once. Duplicate the serving dishes and have two groups of plates, glasses, napkins, and flatware. Leave enough space between serving platters and casserole dishes so guests can put their plates down on the table and use both hands for serving. Although a salad course may be served separately at a seated buffet, it is set out with the entree.

If the buffet table is against the wall, place it where people can pass by easily. Try to position it so guests who have taken their food do not have to double back past those who are in line, creating a bottleneck. After you have set up the table, walk through yourself to see if you've left enough room for people to serve themselves with ease.

Popular layout:

Table setting for a classic buffet.

At a buffet table, plates are stacked in a location convenient to where the guests will approach the table. If you expect a large number of people and have a table of appropriate size, you can duplicate each dish so guests can form two lines, one on either side of the table. Flatware, glasses, and napkins are placed after the food so guests will have both hands free to serve themselves. An alternative to placing flatware directly on the table is to tuck individual sets into the folds of the napkins. Flowers, candles, or other decorations can be placed on the table, provided there is sufficient room and they will not interfere with guests who are filling their plates.

1. Stack of plates (no more than twelve high) near main course
2. Main dish (often in a chafing dish or a casserole on a hotplate); serving spoon and fork
3. Second dish, if there is one, with serving fork and spoon
4. Vegetable dish with serving spoon
5. Salad bowl with serving pieces
6. Condiments, salt, pepper
7. Flatware and napkins at the end of table (unless they are on the tables where guests will sit)
8. Wine, water, other beverages; may be pre-poured in glasses at one end of table or on a separate serving table
9. Coffee cups, dessert plates; may be on a separate table
10. Separate table for used plates.

THE MENU

Buffet menus should be carefully thought out well ahead of time. Food that requires a knife should not be served at a classic buffet because people have to hold their plates on their laps; dishes that are runny should be avoided at all types of buffets. Casseroles are always suitable and easy to keep hot.

THE ROLE OF THE HOSTESS

The buffet lunch or dinner is usually preceded by a cocktail hour. After cocktails are over, announce that dinner is ready and ask the guests to go through the buffet line, gesturing them toward the buffet table, which may be in the dining room, a corner of the living room, or even in the kitchen. If they linger, encourage them to move along. You can say, with a touch of humor, "Come on in or we'll all be eating cold food."

When most people have finished the entree, say to the guests: "There's lots more food, so do have seconds if you like." If there's a maid, she can offer to get seconds for guests. In most cases, however, guests go back to the buffet and help themselves. It is proper for a man to offer to get a woman seconds and for younger people to serve older guests.

Dessert and coffee may be served from the buffet table, in which case the guests help themselves and return to their seats either at tables or in the living room. You may eliminate dessert plates by passing trays of cookies, miniature pastries, or seedless grapes, along with small napkins. Liqueurs may be offered with coffee at a dinner buffet.

SERVING A BUFFET WITH A MAID

A buffet often involves moving large numbers of hungry people around the house. You and the maid, each attending to specific tasks, should work closely together to help insure the success of the party.

As the cocktail hour comes to a close, check with the maid, making certain that the food is on the buffet table, that the hot trays are turned on and, if it is a seated buffet, that the water glasses are filled. If it is a dinner, the candles should be lit. (Although candles are never lit at lunch or brunch, they may be on the table, along with flowers, as a decorative element.) At the classic buffet, where guests aren't seated at tables, make certain the maid has filled the water glasses and wineglasses on the buffet or sideboard for guests to pick up.

If the guests have had cocktails in the living room but are eating elsewhere, during dinner the maid removes the cocktail glasses, empties the ashtrays, and puts the room in order. If the guests are to eat in the living room, she can tidy up while they are in the buffet line.

If coffee and dessert are to be served in the living room, she sets up the cups, saucers, plates, forks and spoons, sugar and cream on the appropriate table.

THE ROLE OF THE GUEST

As a guest at a buffet you'll find yourself taking a more active role than at a more formal occasion. For instance, you will get your own food and drinks, take the initiative for getting seconds, and, if it is a classic buffet, find your own place to sit. And, if you notice your hostess is busy, ask if she'd like help removing the dirty plates. If she says no, take her at her word. Not everyone wants guests helping to clear.

Sometimes another guest may offer to bring you a plate filled from the buffet. If you'd rather select your own food, feel free to say, "Thanks very much, but I'd like to see what the choices are." In fact, that's one of the pluses of a buffet—you can take just the foods you enjoy. Although if the hostess notices you skipping over a dish and says, "Do try my crab casserole," take a small amount to be polite. If you really don't care for crab, you can always leave it on your plate.

Never, tempting as it may be, switch place cards to sit next to a friend. The party may be informal but the hostess will have put a great deal of time into the seating plan. It's not up to you to rearrange it. If you are to choose your own seat, however, it's thoughtful to ask someone who is alone to sit with you.

BRUNCHES

The English came up with the idea of combining breakfast and lunch and invented the brunch. The word, combining BR(EAKFAST) and (L)UNCH, was introduced by Guy Beringer in the 1890s in the publication *Hunter's Weekly*. Now, around noon on almost any Saturday or Sunday, people in America can be found having brunch at home, in restaurants, and in hotel dining rooms. In some parts of the country, for instance the Southwest, hotel brunches can be very elegant. Brunch is also a fashionable way to celebrate certain occasions such as Easter Sunday. They are also often given the day after a big event, such as a wedding or a big homecoming sports event, especially if a number of out-of-town guests have not yet left for home.

Because brunch is, almost by definition, casual, invitations can be extended practically at the last minute, in person or by telephone. Sometimes a brunch is planned at someone else's dinner party: "Why don't you come over for brunch tomorrow around twelve?" Or, "How about coming by for brunch tomorrow after church?"

Bloody Marys, mimosas, and/or screwdrivers are often served at a brunch but, since many people do not like alcohol that early in the day, it is important also to offer juice, consommé, and soft drinks. The meal is generally served buffet style and choices will include both breakfast- and lunch-type foods. For example, scrambled eggs, sausages, hashed browns, waffles, chicken hash, eggs Benedict, and eggs Florentine are popular choices. So are pancakes or waffles with yogurt and syrup and perhaps fresh fruit. In the spring and summer, a compote of whatever fruit is in season is delicious. Include special breads, muffins, or Italian breakfast breads, such as panettone. Pitchers of orange or other fruit juices and hot coffee and tea should be on the buffet table or, if there is not enough room, on a separate table.

Dress for brunch is usually informal—slacks or skirts and sweaters for women; slacks, shirts, and sweaters for men. Sunday brunch, however, may be slightly more formal in some areas, in which case men wear blazers or sports jackets, especially if they are coming directly from church.

TEAS

The daily ritual of afternoon tea is no longer a common occurrence. In our fast-paced world, the majority of men and women are at work between the hour of 4:30 and 5:30 P.M., the traditional teatime. Still, it takes no more than two tea bags, regular or decaf, and two cups and saucers to share a break in the workday with a friend (those who prefer can have coffee instead). The custom of a "spot of tea" in the afternoon has a relaxing effect and is not as time-consuming as the drink after work often is.

A formal tea is most likely to be given for an official function or to honor a debutante. Invitations are engraved or written by hand. Women dress for such an occasion according to local custom, most commonly in a simple dress or suit; definitely not in dressy evening attire. A less formal tea might be given for a relative who comes to visit or for no better reason than to gather together a few friends in a relaxed atmosphere. Invitations to this type of tea party may be extended over the telephone. A tea party, because of the nature of the occasion and the time of day it is given, is mostly attended by women who don't work outside the home, although many men enjoy the custom of having tea in the afternoon, especially if they have traveled in Great Britain. There are many books that describe the different kinds of tea parties as well as the history and ritual of tea drinking.

THE TEA TABLE

For a large tea, the table must be big enough to accommodate two services (see diagram) at opposite ends of the table: one for tea and one for coffee. The table, whether the dining-room table or one improvised for the occasion, should be located in an area of the room where it won't interfere with the mobility of the guests, who will want to move around serving themselves. The table is covered with a traditional white linen or lace tea cloth, which falls approximately a foot over the edge of the table. Tea trays, usually silver, are not covered and, as with all silver, must be beautifully polished. It is never correct to use tea bags at a formal tea party, but at an impromptu party, to save time and effort, you may place bags in a pot and pour boiling water over them.

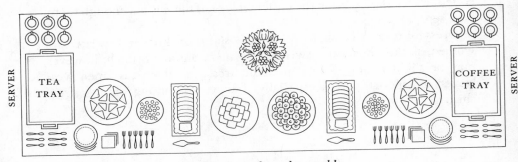

Setting up a formal tea table.
For a formal tea, the table is set up with symmetry and ease of service in mind.
Cups, saucers, and spoons should be within easy reach of the persons pouring.

For the tea tray you will need:

- A teapot filled with freshly brewed tea, kept warm with an alcohol lamp beneath it
- A pitcher or pot of very hot water (for those who like to dilute their tea)
- A tea strainer set and a separate bowl to dispose of the tea leaves (or an infuser)
- A pitcher of milk (never cream)
- A bowl of lump sugar with tongs, or a bowl of sugar with a spoon (low-calorie sugar substitute should also be available)
- A small saucer with lemon slices and a small fork
- Cups, saucers, and teaspoons

Cups and saucers are placed close to the server, preferably to the left of a right-handed person and to the right of a left-handed person; this makes pouring more convenient.

At the end of the table opposite the tea tray is the tray with the coffee urn, a bowl of lump or loose sugar, a pitcher of cream, and coffee cups and saucers (the coffee cup is straight-sided and lower than a teacup).

If there is room for tea plates on the tea tray, they are placed there, otherwise they go on the table. Small folded, usually white, tea napkins, approximately eleven inches square, are set beside them, or a napkin can be folded on top of each plate within the stack. If cake is served, dessert forks should be on the table.

The food for a tea party is placed on the table buffet style. There is a wide variety of foods suitable for a good tea, including tea sandwiches, which are made from paper-thin slices of white or grain bread. The crusts should be trimmed off before cutting both ways on the diagonal to make four tea sandwiches. Fillings might include minced chicken or ham salad, cucumber with dill, cream cheese and watercress, or anything small and dainty. Toast, cut into strips and topped with butter and cinnamon sugar, is another favorite, as are scones, butter cookies, pound cake, tiny fruit tartlets, even rich chocolate cake. And some people always have plain bread and butter at their tea parties, a very traditional touch.

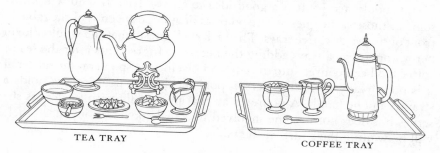

TEA TRAY   COFFEE TRAY

Setting up a tea tray and a coffee tray.
For a smaller tea, the accoutrements may be placed on the tray.

THE MAKING OF GOOD TEA

Good tea is easy to make properly if you follow these directions. It is important to take the chill off the teapot by half filling it with boiling water, swishing the water around, and then discarding it. Measure one teaspoon of tea for each cup to be served into the warmed pot, then add another teaspoonful for good measure. Pour *boiling* water over the tea leaves, cover the pot, and let it steep three to five minutes. Tea made with water at less than the boiling point will not have its flavor liberated and will be flat and insipid. Stir the tea before serving the first cup. Since tea gets stronger the longer it stands, keep a pitcher of boiling-hot water available (preferably on an alcohol burner) for those who like weaker tea. If more tea is needed, it is best to repeat the entire procedure rather than try to "top up" the pot with tepid water. However, if you make the tea at the tea table and are keeping the water at a boil over a spirit lamp, you may add the actively boiling water to the leaves in the pot when half the tea has been poured.

THE ROLE OF THE HOSTESS

If there is enough space in the room where the tea is being held, you should place chairs so as to make several seating arrangements. If you do not have enough chairs, you can rent them for the afternoon. Ornaments should be removed from the tables to make room for cups and saucers and tea plates.

At a large tea party, you should circulate around the room, talking to friends and in general seeing that everyone feels at ease and is enjoying the party. When there is a guest of honor, you stand at the entrance of the room to introduce that person to each guest as he or she arrives. Before the party, you can ask two friends familiar with the protocol of serving tea to stand in for you at the tea table, pouring tea and coffee (there's no reason not to ask a man to pour, but if he refuses don't force the issue). If you like, two sets of pourers may spell each other every half hour or so. Since it is a compliment to be asked to pour, unless there is a good reason not to, a friend should accept. It is a good idea to choose friends who will know some or most of the guests. The pourers sit at opposite ends of the table in front of the tea or coffee trays. They ask each guest what she would like in her tea or coffee, always adding the necessary ingredients after the tea or coffee has been poured into the cup and placing the spoon on the saucer, if it is not already there (the person pouring the tea, if necessary, holds a strainer in one hand). A pourer may chat informally with a guest as she serves but does not become involved in a real conversation since others will be waiting their turn at the table.

The role of the guest

You should try to mingle with the other guests, including those you do not know. You may help yourself to whatever food is on the table, or take what you like from the maid passing food on a silver tray. If there are chairs and tables around, you may take your teacup and saucer and tea plate with food and sit down to chat with other guests. If there are not enough places to sit, you must stand, doing your best to balance your cup and saucer, with perhaps a sandwich on the edge of the saucer. Not the easiest feat for even the most accomplished tea-goer, but it *can* be done!

You may return for more tea or coffee as often as you wish but only after everyone has been served. When you have finished drinking, put the cup and saucer on the tea table or hand it to a maid. After staying at the party an hour or so, you are free to leave, after thanking the hostess first and saying goodbye to the guest of honor.

COCKTAIL PARTIES

A cocktail party can be a practical way to entertain a large number of people. However, an invitation to a cocktail party is not a "pay back" for a dinner invitation. The nicest cocktail parties are smallish ones—given in honor of someone or as an informal gathering of friends. Often cocktail parties are given before an event such as a benefit, a theater party, or a dinner dance at a club.

Cocktail party hours are generally from 6 to 8 P.M. but if it is a weeknight and guests are coming directly from work, you can invite them for five-thirty. The time also depends on the customs of the community. If the invitation is to a cocktail buffet, it states the time the party starts but, unlike the standard cocktail invitation, it does not give the ending time because guests are expected to stay on for the buffet.

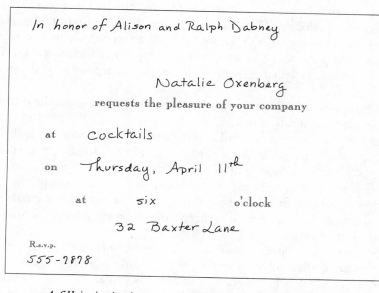

A fill-in invitation to a cocktail party honoring friends.

THE INVITATION

You can extend a cocktail party invitation by sending printed fill-in invitations bought at a stationery store, or informals, or you may invite everyone by telephone. It's always a good idea to include on your invitation the hour the party's to end. That way guests have an indication as to how long they are expected to stay. When the party is in honor of someone, add that person's name to the invitation. It's up to you as to whether you include an R.s.v.p.; if you don't, it indicates the party is a fairly large one. If you put "Regrets only" on an invitation, you'll find that most people don't bother to reply at all.

THE SETTING

If the party is at your house, it's best to put away any fragile objects or prized antiques in a closet or the attic. Coffee tables and end tables should be cleared of ornaments, books, and magazines so guests will have space for their drinks or, if a cocktail buffet, for their plates. Also, put away tripper-uppers, such as tiny tables, footstools, baskets, and scatter rugs. Your dog, cat, and/or children also come under this heading.

If the party is a small one so that coatracks are unnecessary, guests' coats can be laid on beds—men's in one bedroom; women's in another—if you have two bedrooms. If it's a rainy evening, put an umbrella stand in the hallway or, in an apartment building, just outside the front door.

If you are giving a large party in your apartment, after checking with the building superintendent or your neighbors, you may borrow from the building or rent elsewhere coatracks to place in the hall just outside your apartment front door or, if the hall is too small, in the main lobby of the building. If the coatrack is in the lobby, have a responsible person watch the coats during the party. Women wearing expensive fur coats should be given the option of leaving them in a closet or bedroom in your apartment.

The success of a cocktail party depends on two key factors: the number of guests and the location of the bar. People are often tempted to invite everyone they know to a cocktail party. When they do, no guest feels like a special friend but more like a member of a mob. Ideally, you should invite just enough people to fill the space comfortably; if you're inviting only a few guests, arrange the furniture in such a way that people are able to sit down and talk in small groups. Regardless of how many guests you invite, there should be enough chairs so older people or anyone tired of standing can sit down.

At a cocktail party people tend to stick together, often near the bar, and don't venture forth to other areas of the room unless there is a table with food there, or another bar. Keep this in mind as you arrange your party; if you're expecting a lot of guests it may be necessary to place food and drinks in several locations—in a second room, on a balcony or porch, or possibly in a garden. On the other hand, if it's a small party, choose your space accordingly. Being too spread out makes it more difficult for people to communicate.

If you give cocktail parties, it's important to check with your insurance broker about appropriate liability coverage—to protect yourself should someone have an accident as the result of liquor served at your party. A host and hostess can also be sued for serving liquor to minors, something you really should not do anyway.

THE BAR

An important factor in giving a cocktail party is the location of the bar or bars. People, especially women on their own, do not like elbowing their way through a crowd to get a drink. If it's a large party, set up two bars— one in the dining room, say, and one in the library. If there's not enough space to set up a bar, drinks can be made in the kitchen, in which case the waiter or waitress asks the guests what they would like to drink and then brings the drinks to them on trays. Although this method means more floor space is devoted to guests, it also means more dirty glasses because every time someone asks for another drink his or her empty glass is returned to the waiter's tray.

THE BARTENDER

How many people you hire to help with your party depends mainly on how much service you need and can afford. The rule of thumb, however, is that a couple or a single host or hostess can handle a party of up to twenty guests—slightly fewer if mixed drinks are served and more if only wine is offered—provided they ask the guests to make their own second drinks. Once a party goes over twenty, it's time to hire a bartender so you will be free to introduce guests to one another, if that is necessary. As a guide, a hundred guests require three bartenders and three waiters. If you have only a few guests, the waiter/bartender can both make and serve the drinks. If you have one bar and two helpers, one acts as waiter, asking each guest for his or her drink order, relaying it to the bartender, and then delivering the drink to the guest.

Discuss with your bartender what drinks will be offered, if any extra help is required, and if so who will provide it. Although you are the one to decide where the bar (or bars) should be located, let him set it up the way he likes. If the bartender is new to your house, when he arrives show him where to find your glasses, serving trays, water pitchers, towels, and cocktail napkins. Also, aside from the liquor, see that he has lemons, limes, a bar knife, a bottle opener, a jigger, and a corkscrew on hand. Depending on the size of the party, have at least one large clean garbage can for bags of ice. A large ice bucket may be used if the group isn't too large.

The two traditional glasses used for cocktails are the highball and the old-fashioned. The taller highball glass is used for scotch, bourbon, or other type of whiskey when they are mixed with water or soda, for gin or vodka and tonic, beer, and all soft drinks. The shorter old-fashioned glass is used for apéritifs, martinis, manhattans, and scotch or bourbon on the rocks. In addition, an all-purpose wineglass is essential today because so many people are drinking wine at cocktail parties. Because this glass has a stem and can be placed on wood and marble without creating a water mark, it is often used for all types of drinks, to eliminate the need for coasters.

Discuss with the bartender how strong you want him to make the drinks. You certainly don't want to offer drinks that are too weak; on the other hand, you don't want to make them too strong. What you should do is ask the bartender to measure the drinks, using about 1½ ounces of liquor per drink (an experienced bartender can pour that amount without using a jigger).

When the party is winding down and only a few guests are left, you may tell the bartender you no longer need him and take over the making of drinks yourself. You do not close the bar at your own house as you might do at a business cocktail party.

THE DRINKS

Plan on about three drinks per person. One bottle of whiskey will make about twenty-five drinks and one bottle of wine has about five glasses in it. Use a liquor store that will take back any unopened bottles so you'll feel free to order more liquor than you may need. Limit what you serve to drinks that are popular among your friends. That way the bartender will be able to work more quickly and efficiently. At a standard cocktail party there is no need to offer elaborate mixed drinks such as piña coladas, tequila sunrises, or pink ladies. Drinking habits vary somewhat from place to place, but the standard drinks are presented in our checklist at the end of this "Cocktail Parties' section. Regular and low-calorie soft drinks, bottled waters, and wine (especially white wine) should be included.

Of course, on special occasions you may want to serve traditional drinks. For example, at Christmastime, a bowl of eggnog or wassail. Or, if you are having a party to watch the Kentucky Derby, mint juleps; in celebration of a birthday or anniversary, champagne. (But remember, many people don't like champagne, so have at least one alternative kind of drink available.)

THE FOOD

When you are planning your menu, keep in mind that a cocktail party is not a substitute for dinner, although some guests may try to make it so. On the other hand, it is important to give your guests enough to eat so they are not drinking on empty stomachs. Experienced hostesses have learned what types of food work well for them, but if you are a novice at entertaining, you may want to look at some party-giving books for food suggestions and recipes. There are also lots of special books devoted solely to canapés and hors d'oeuvres. In general, three hot hors d'oeuvres and two or three cold ones will be sufficient, although it depends in part on the weather. Among the most popular choices are: cheeses (include a low-fat, low-sodium one, such as a goat cheese), cold shrimp with a cocktail sauce, crudités (raw vegetables cut into bite-sized pieces served with a dip), deviled eggs, tiny hot meatballs, bacon wrapped around chicken livers or artichoke hearts, and stuffed mushrooms served hot or cold. If the hors d'oeuvres require toothpicks or skewers, the waitress should carry an extra plate for collecting them. Don't forget that it is difficult, if not impossible, for guests to hold a cocktail in one hand and spread cheese on crackers with the other; which says a lot about serving finger foods at a cocktail party.

PLASTIC GLASSES AND PAPER NAPKINS

Controversy rages between those who subscribe to the "use and throw away" theory and those who recycle. Plastic glasses, in most cases, should be avoided. They are unattractive and appropriate only for outdoor parties, picnics, or if you're young and on a tight budget. Or at fundraisers when the purpose of the party is to raise money, not to spend it renting or buying glasses.

If you don't own enough glasses, you can rent them, or, if you expect to give lots of cocktail parties, buy glasses in quantity from a wholesaler or when they're on sale at a department store.

THE PROBLEM DRINKER

Every host and hostess should be prepared for the possibility that someone at a cocktail party may have too much to drink. There are several ways you can try to forestall this happening at your party: one is not to serve drinks that are too strong and the other is to be sure to serve enough food, because people become inebriated much faster on an empty stomach. However, no matter what precautions you take, the serious drinker *will* drink. If a guest becomes obnoxious or difficult, ask whomever he or she came with to help get him or her home. If the drunken guest came alone, ask your husband or another man to help you get him into a taxi or to a bedroom to recuperate. You may even want to discuss in advance with your bartender what to do with a drunken guest. One well-known New York caterer instructs his bartenders to stop serving drinks to anyone on the way to becoming obnoxious. If the person becomes drunk, they try to get him to eat something and to drink black coffee.

It's imperative that you never let a guest who has had too much to drink get behind the wheel of a car. Don't hesitate to take away his or her car keys, or to ask someone else to drive him home. Or, if you live in the city, call a taxi. If it is literally impossible to find a way to get the person home, put him to bed at your place overnight and let him sleep it off. The next day don't gloss over what happened; suggest that he get help with his problem.

If you know a friend has a drinking problem, it is probably wisest not to ask him or her to a cocktail party at all. Invite the person instead for lunch or dinner where you can better control the alcohol content.

COCKTAILS BEFORE A DINNER DANCE

An easy way to entertain friends is to invite them to cocktails before a dinner dance at a club you belong to. You can invite people by telephone or by writing a short note on your informal: "Hope you can come for cocktails at 6 P.M. before the Piping Rock Dinner Dance on May 15. Give me a call at 977-5748." At this kind of affair, you serve drinks for about an hour, figuring into your schedule the amount of time you will need to get to the dinner.

If you're invited to a cocktail party of this sort, it's taken for granted that you are buying your own ticket/s to the dinner. In other words, the hostess is only providing drinks beforehand—unless of course, she specifically asks you to be her guest for the evening. If you are not planning to go to the dinner, tell her so as a reason for not accepting her invitation. You may, however, find she will ask you to come for cocktails anyway.

ENDING A COCKTAIL PARTY

Even when you put the ending time of your cocktail party on the invitation, you usually find that there are a few hangers-on who are having such a good time that they forget, or want to forget, it's time to go home. If it's getting late and you want to end the party, there's not much you can do to encourage people to leave—it's unfriendly to close the bar and just as unfriendly to say you are weary and want to go to bed. Really, the only viable solution is to suggest to the last remaining guests that you all go somewhere nearby for a quick bite to eat. This gets the message across that the party's over and those who want to can join you while others may prefer to go their own way. Everyone who comes along pays for his or her own meal at the restaurant.

THE ROLE OF THE GUEST

Many people feel it's unnecessary to reply to a cocktail party invitation, so they ignore the R.s.v.p. entirely. This simply should not be. Any social invitation with an R.s.v.p. should be answered within three or four days. In addition, the R.s.v.p. is there for a purpose—to give the hostess an indication of how many people to plan for. If the invitation says "Regrets only," you're not obligated to respond, but if you do, you can be certain the hostess will be glad you bothered.

Here are a few comments on being a guest at a cocktail party:

- Do not bring a friend along without first asking the hostess. If she says you may, introduce whoever it is to the host and hostess when you arrive.

- Don't be standoffish. Make an effort to introduce yourself to guests you don't already know. If you're talking in a group and someone close by is standing alone, ask that person to join you.

- Don't stand at the bar talking once you've been served your drink. Move to a less congested area so others can have their turn at the bar.

- If you get stuck talking to one person, which often happens at a cocktail party, excuse yourself on the pretext of going to the bar to get a drink or to speak to a friend you haven't seen recently.

- Don't overstay your welcome; if an ending time was given on the invitation, leave shortly after the time indicated.

- Always say goodbye to your host and hostess, thanking them for including you. It's not necessary to write a thank-you letter after a cocktail party, unless of course you were the guest of honor.

CHECKLIST FOR A COCKTAIL PARTY

- Glasses
- Cocktail napkins
- Jigger
- Stirrer
- Ice cubes

- Ice tongs
- Trays for passing and collecting glasses
- Paring knife
- Bottle opener
- Corkscrew
- Several dishtowels
- Lemons, limes, and lemon peel (precut)
- Plain water
- Perrier, soda water, tonic
- Diet and regular soft drinks; tomato juice and/or orange juice
- Beer
- Scotch, bourbon, vodka, gin, rum, sherry, Campari, Dubonnet, vermouth
- Red wine
- Chilled white wine

RECEPTIONS

Receptions, which are often public or semipublic events, are generally held to honor a specific person, such as a celebrity, political figure, an award winner, or a visiting dignitary, or they may be held for groups of people to recognize their special achievements or contributions to the community. For example, when visiting companies of performing artists come to town, often the sponsoring group will hold a reception after their performance to honor the artists. Or when an important community event takes place such as the launching of a new recreational center or the opening of a new wing of a museum or theater, a preview reception is often given for members and donors.

Official receptions, which are often held at a faculty or social club, the mayor's official residence, an embassy, or hotel, usually last two hours at most and guests should not stay longer than the time stated on the invitation.

Although receptions are usually hosted by a group rather than an individual, they are sometimes given by and for a single person. The most common sort of private reception is the one given after a wedding ceremony. Or, if the wedding takes place in the bride's hometown, the groom's family might hold a reception in their hometown as a way of introducing their new daughter-in-law to friends and relatives who might not have been able to attend the wedding.

Most receptions are held in the late afternoon or early evening, although times vary. A school-sponsored reception might take place in the afternoon, whereas a reception given after a theatrical performance would be in the evening.

Sometimes a reception is given instead of a cocktail party because the hostess doesn't wish to serve liquor. In lieu of alcohol, punch, iced tea and coffee, one or two soft drinks, and bottled water may be served, although typically a reception offers white wine, or champagne, or a light apéritif such as Campari and soda or Lillet.

The food served at a reception depends entirely on the formality of the occasion. At a more formal reception, a buffet table is covered with a floor-length white tablecloth and platters of elaborate finger food as well as tea sandwiches and small cookies and pastries are set out, along with napkins and plates. Waiters, besides passing drinks, might also pass plates of food.

The food at a smaller, simpler reception might consist of cheeses and crackers and mixed nuts. At this type of affair, drinks and punch are served from a bar or passed around by a waiter.

When a reception is being given to honor someone, which is almost always the case, there is a receiving line in which the host, hostess, guest or guests of honor, and committee or board president stand. If a town or civic organization is involved, for instance to celebrate a centennial, one or two officials are included in the receiving line.

BALLS AND DANCES

The grand private ball to which men wore white tie and tails, women their fanciest ball gowns, and champagne flowed well into the early hours of the morning is all but a thing of the past, not unlike the private railroad car and ladies' maids. It belonged to an era of opulence and extravagance when balls were given to honor an occasion or for no purpose other than to entertain friends in an elegant setting. Today, when we speak of a ball, it most often means a group undertaking, such as a charity ball, a ball commemorating a historic event, or a hunt ball. While almost no one now indulges in the opulence and trimmings of a private ball, there are still plenty of opportunities for an individual to give a dinner or supper dance. It may be that you have some special cause for celebration, such as a major birthday or wedding anniversary, a mid-life college graduation, a family reunion, a holiday, or to honor a young woman making her debut. A dinner dance usually begins at 7:30 or 8 P.M., while a supper dance, which is held after dinner, begins at 10 or 10:30 P.M.

Unless you have a house or apartment with plenty of space to entertain a large number of people, it is more practical to hold a dance at a club or hotel. These are good choices not only because they have the space but also because such places can handle the major arrangements of the evening, including food and liquor, flowers, waiters and waitresses, rest room attendants, and car parkers, if needed. Because clubs and hotels are so convenient, they are also very booked up. Therefore, reservations must be made well in advance of the occasion, often as much as a year ahead of time.

Whether you are giving a dinner or supper dance at a club or hotel or at home, the logistics of planning the event are very similar. The dance described here, by way of illustration, will be one given at a private house where you supervise all aspects of the party. A cautionary note: one of the first things you should do when planning to entertain at home, expecially if you'll need a tent, is to check with your insurance broker as to the extent of your general liability as well as liquor liability insurance. If necessary, you may need to make a policy adjustment for that evening. (For more comprehensive details and information concerning the giving of a formal party, making preparations, the role of the host(ess), the guest, and the staff, refer to "The Formal Seated Dinner With a Staff" earlier in this chapter.)

THE INVITATION

A formal engraved or printed invitation to a dance is sent out a month or more in advance of the date. Exactly how early depends on the town or city where you live, the time of year, and your social world. An invitation to a formal dance always means formal dress. However, if you feel it is necessary, "Black tie" can appear on the lower right-hand corner of the invitation.

Women wear their fanciest evening dresses to a formal supper dance; at a dinner dance, which is slightly less formal, they wear a short or long evening dress, a long skirt, or evening pajamas.

If you'd like to offer a single man the option of bringing a date, you can write "and guest" on the invitation or the envelope; for a single woman add "and guest" or "and escort."

THE PARTY COORDINATOR

Often it is worth the expense involved to hire a party coordinator to take charge of all aspects of a dance. Under your direction, the party coordinator takes care of the invitations, finds a competent caterer, hires the orchestra, sees that the piano is tuned, helps seat the dinner, arranges for the car parkers, and much more. The night of the party he or she is on hand to oversee the running of the party and to handle any problems that might come up. The party coordinator essentially relieves you of all the literally dozens of details involved in giving a large party. With expert knowledge of entertaining costs and logistics, the coordinator can also often save you as much money as trouble.

Party coordinators have different ways of charging. It may be on a percentage basis, an hourly or flat fee, or a sum based on the number of guests invited. The best way to find a party coordinator is by asking around among your friends; sometimes a caterer can give you a reliable referral. Because you will have to work closely with this person, only hire someone whom you like at your first meeting. If he or she comes across as too much of a takeover type, consider this a warning to look elsewhere for the right person. After all, it's your party and you want it run your way.

THE CATERER

If you are not going to use a party coordinator, a full-service caterer can take on many of the same chores and responsibilities as a party coordinator in addition to providing the food and staff. A caterer will take care of any necessary rentals, such as tables, chairs, coatracks, table linens, china, flatware, glasses, and can also recommend a florist and help find a photographer. It is vital to book a caterer well before sending out invitations because the most sought-after ones are booked months ahead. (For more complete details, see "Working With a Caterer" earlier in this chapter.)

THE ORCHESTRA

The most important consideration when giving a dance naturally is the choice of an orchestra or band. The music sets the mood for a party and can make all the difference. Never hire an orchestra if you are unfamiliar with their repertoire, unless of course a friend whose taste you trust vouches for them. If you can't listen to them in person, you can ask an orchestra representative to provide you with recorded cassettes of their playing. While this is not the same as hearing an orchestra live, it can still be helpful in making a decision. It is customary for an orchestra to charge for a minimum of four hours' playing time, after which there is a per-hour overtime fee. Orchestras have different overtime policies, so this should be discussed at the time of the booking. How many musicians you will need depends on how many people are expected at the party and the size of the dance floor. For an indoor dance of a hundred to a hundred and fifty people, you need a minimum of five or six players; two additional players if the party is outside under a tent.

Once you have decided on the orchestra, you will sign a contract and put down a deposit of up to fifty percent with the balance due on the night of the party. Each orchestra has its own policy about cancellation charges. After you've signed the contract, you'll want to discuss various details with a representative of the orchestra. He'll be able to suggest specific songs once you've given him an idea of the kind of music you'd like played and what the age group or groups will be. If the ages are mixed, the band usually plays old favorites and standard classics in the early part of the evening and then, as the night progresses, breaks into a faster pace for the younger dancers. If you like, you can also request special songs. In addition, you'll want to talk about acoustical equipment, whether a microphone is needed, what the musicians will wear, how often they will take a break (usually once every hour for ten to fifteen minutes). If you expect there will be toasts and you would like the orchestra to play a trumpet fanfare or drumroll to get the attention of the guests, they should be told. This is also true if you want the orchestra to alert the guests that dinner is about to be served.

It is customary for the dancing to start between the first and second courses. If you want the orchestra to play while the guests are eating, the music must be very low—more background than dance music. Nothing is more irritating or likely to spoil a party than trying to make dinner conversation in competition with a loud band. An alternative to having the orchestra play while guests eat is hiring a trio to serve as roving musicians. In the case of a supper dance, the musicians start playing at the exact time the dance is called for.

A room in the house should be made available to the members of the orchestra in case they need to change their clothes. They should also be offered the same food that is being served at the dinner or supper, as well as sandwiches and soft drinks during their first break. While individual members of an orchestra are not tipped, a letter of thanks to the manager or orchestra leader is always appreciated. It can serve as a future recommendation.

THE PHOTOGRAPHER

If the party is of special significance to you or the honored guest, it's very nice to have a photographer on hand. You'll naturally have to give him a list of the key people to be photographed—guest or guests of honor, your family, and any close friends. You might caution the photographer about not taking pictures while the guests are eating, although if he is a professional such advice probably isn't necessary.

AN INDOOR DANCE

Very few people have a large enough living room or dining room to accommodate both an orchestra and dancers. If you do, you'll need to clear out most of the furniture, maybe even store it with a moving company. Also it is extremely important to the success of a dance that a professional floor waxer make sure the floor is in proper condition for dancing. If the dancing is to be in the living room, tables and chairs can be set up in the dining room, library, and perhaps the front hall for eating. While this arrangement can work well, keep in mind also that using more than one room has the potential to divide a party, often making it less successful, less cohesive and congenial.

TENT

If a dance is being held under a tent, choose the flattest site possible. Since you can't be sure about the weather, you may want a canvas awning and carpet (traditionally red) put down from the driveway to the front door as well as one connecting the house to the tent. The tent should have side flaps, and heaters or fans must be readily available in case there's a sudden storm or change in the weather. You may also need a few floodlights, placed either in trees or on the ground, to guide your guests. The company you rent the tent from can make arrangements for the dance floor and determine the size of the tent and the floor by the number of guests expected and their ages; younger people tend to fill a larger dance floor more readily than the older generation does. It's important that the ratio of guests to the floor space be correct as a half-filled dance floor looks dreary and an overcrowded one can be discouraging to the less aggressive dancers. If it is to be a supper dance, the buffet tables should be placed in an area convenient to the kitchen of the house; the caterer can tell you how many buffet tables and bars will be needed once he knows how many people are expected.

FLOWERS

Flowers are an absolute must for almost any kind of celebration, and at a dance you'll want flowers and other decorations for the tables in the tent, the front hall of the house, the living room and, if there's a receiving line, somewhere close by it. A lovely touch and one quite commonly used is to decorate the tent poles with some kind of colorful material or with garlands of flowers.

CAR PARKERS

Be sure to have plenty of parkers on hand to handle the cars; off-duty policemen and college students are good sources to tap. The police can be helpful to the party giver in arranging parking and they will often direct traffic on the main road. For security reasons, most local police like to know when a party of any size is given in their area anyway.

When a guest arrives at the entrance to the house, one of the parkers takes the car and gives the guest a numbered ticket. When the guest is ready to leave, he gives the ticket to a parker, who goes to retrieve the car (to facilitate the procedure, walkie-talkies can be used so a dispatcher at the house is able to call in car requests to coworkers in the parking area). Sometimes in places where the weather is warm and it seldom rains, golf carts are used to transport guests between the parking area and the house.

THE ROLE OF THE HOSTESS

If you decide to have a receiving line, you and your spouse, and anyone who will receive with you (a guest of honor, someone of official standing, family members, a debutante daughter), stand in the hall or living room of the house. If the party's in a tent, the receiving line can be either directly inside or just outside the entrance. If you have hired someone to announce the guests, that person stands beside you at the head of the receiving line, which may flow from left to right or right to left depending on what's most convenient. As a guest arrives, the announcer asks his or her name, then turns and repeats it to you. If you choose not to have an announcer, you can greet guests yourself, introducing each person to whoever is standing next to you. If there's no receiving line, you introduce a new arrival to those standing closest to you.

Once the guests have arrived and it is time for dinner, the band plays a march or some other attention-getting music, and you, with the guest of honor, or whoever will be seated on your right, lead the way into dinner. Guests follow, with the host bringing up the rear. Host and hostess sit at separate tables, in fact all couples, married or otherwise, are split up and seated at separate tables. The attentive host and hostess need to pay close attention to their guests throughout the evening, making introductions, if necessary, talking to as many people as possible, trying to see that everyone is having a good time.

You and the man who is seated on your right lead off the dancing between the first and second courses. While the host and/or hostess can toast the guest of honor whenever they feel it is appropriate, toasts are generally given after the first course is finished.

Throughout the evening, pay attention to the sound of the music and don't hesitate to tell the orchestra leader if the tempo is too slow or too fast, or the music too loud. The age of the guests is the main factor in deciding the tempo of the music and how loud it should be. It's up to the host and hostess to decide whether to ask the orchestra to play overtime or whether it's better to end the party on a high note, sending the guests home full of enthusiasm and wishing the evening would go on forever. To keep a party going, just for the sake of doing so, or because you're having fun, is not always the best decision.

At the end of the party, the host and hostess stand near the entrance to the tent, or some place where guests can easily find them to say good night.

THE ROLE OF THE GUEST

The one time a single woman needs an escort is at a supper dance. She is not in the same position as a single man, who can ask women to dance or cut in at will. She needs someone to accompany her to the party, to dance with her, and, since supper is not seated, to eat with her. If the hostess omits "and escort" or "and guest" on the invitation, a single woman can call the hostess and bring up the subject by saying, "Would it be possible for me to bring a date? I'd feel a lot better not arriving alone." An understanding hostess will surely agree; if she does not, then the woman has the option of going to the party alone or graciously regretting the invitation.

At a dinner dance, a table in the front hall or just outside the entrance to the tent is set up with alphabetically arranged cards assigning each guest to a table. Guests pick up their cards as soon as they arrive and, when dinner is announced, go to their table, where place cards will indicate who is to sit where. If a guest is not happy with the seat his hostess has given him, he makes the best of it; it would be extremely rude to switch place cards. A woman needn't wait to be escorted to her seat. If her escort isn't close by, she finds her own place and sits down.

Once the hostess has taken to the dance floor, after the first course, guests can dance whenever the orchestra plays dance music. It is customary for a man to dance first with the woman on his right, then with the woman on his left. After he has met this responsibility, he can dance with the woman he came with, the hostess, the guest of honor, or anyone he wants to. As a courtesy and as a gesture of thanks for being invited to the party, he should dance at least once with his hostess. After coffee has been served at a dinner dance, guests are free to move around from table to table, chatting and sitting with friends at other tables. A man should try to be attentive to all the women at his table and never leave a woman sitting alone.

Unlike a dinner dance, at a late evening supper dance a man dances the first and last dance with the woman he came with. Again, as a courtesy, he dances with the hostess of the party as well as his hostess for the dinner before the dance, if there was one.

At a supper dance, the food is placed on the buffet tables and the guests make up their own small groups and sit at any available table after serving themselves.

Although there are no hard and fast rules, dinner dances and supper dances last approximately four hours. How long you stay depends on your age, whether you have to work the next day, and, of course, whether you are having a good time. Young people with lots of energy love to stay up and dance until the last note of the orchestra. No one, however, leaves a dinner dance until the orchestra has played several pieces after dinner. And at a supper dance you ought at least to stay until supper has been served.

Perhaps the best answer as to whether to thank your host and hostess before leaving the party is to use your best intuition at the time. If you are sitting at a table with one of them, you most definitely say good night. Otherwise, when you think about it, if each of a hundred and fifty guests said their goodbyes while the evening was still in progress, the host and hostess would constantly be interrupted. If they are on the dance floor, you probably will not say goodbye, but if they are sitting at a table you might stop by and say a brief word of thanks or wave from a distance. If you stay until the end of the party, of course you say goodbye along with others as you leave. Regardless of whether or not you have said your thanks at the party, you should follow up with a note reiterating your thanks. In the case of a dance, it's more thoughtful to write rather than telephone. If everyone telephoned the hostess, she'd be inundated with calls!

ABOUT CUTTING IN A man may cut in on any woman but, generally speaking, he does not cut back in on the man who cut in on him. Sometimes people "double cut," exchanging partners on the dance floor. There is nothing wrong with double cutting provided it's done among good friends and with tact. The problem with double cutting is that a woman might feel slighted if a man suggests changing partners in the middle of a dance.

THE SERVICE

The service at a dinner dance is exactly the same as that described for "The Formal Seated Dinner With a Staff" earlier in this chapter. At a supper dance, the food is usually placed on the buffet tables around midnight. It may be simple (scrambled eggs or omelets, bacon, sausages, and rolls) or more elaborate (creamed chicken, cold salmon, lobster Newburg, cold meats, salads, and desserts). Depending on the number of waiters, coffee may be served at the table; otherwise guests get their own coffee from the buffet table and take it to wherever they are sitting. The bars should stay open as long as the orchestra is playing and as long as the host wants to continue serving drinks. It's up to the host to tell the bartenders when to close down.

BENEFITS

Benefits, events given to raise money, are becoming increasingly important as sources of income for nonprofit organizations and charitable causes. A benefit, which can be great fun to organize as well as attend, is a practical way to raise money and you can tailor the event to a certain age group or specific happening. Many private individuals, not just corporations, take tables or buy seats for a benefit because they feel it is important to be seen there for a business or social purpose; others go to have fun with friends or to meet people or to enjoy the special entertainment. Whatever the guests' motives, fund-raisers serve a useful purpose.

When you start thinking about the benefit you'll be giving, take into account what time of year the event will take place. This will help determine how far in advance you have to start making plans. In a large city, timing is crucial. It can be disastrous to compete with another worthy benefit. In order not to choose a date that conflicts with another local event, call the style page of your newspaper. It often has a list of forthcoming events.

Almost any event can be used as a benefit; it may be a full-scale ball held on the stage of an opera house, a boat cruise, a lunch to meet a group of well-known authors, a cocktail party for a performing arts group, a lunch at the zoo, an auction, a Designer Showcase, a house tour, or a community chest picnic. There is even the nonevent fund-raiser. The invitation reads: ". . . invites you to a Stay-at-Home dinner . . . because we feel that your total gift should be applied directly to support every aspect of our mission!" With a little thought you can come up with all sorts of ideas for a benefit party.

Planning a benefit, particularly a ball or an auction, requires an enormous amount of time and energy. Great care and attention must be given not just to the date but to every aspect of the event, from the decorations to staffing. Unless you know someone with experience in running a benefit, it makes sense to hire a professional benefit or party consultant who can make all the arrangements; this person may have an office staff, or someone may come to your office and work there with your own staff. A benefit consultant will know how and where to cut costs in order to save money for the client and will also be able to suggest a suitable event and the time and place to hold it, can produce a well-thought-out and up-to-date invitation list, knows when to send out invitations, has good press contacts, can hire a caterer and orchestra, will see about flowers, arrange entertainment, and more. His or her job is to pull everything together tastefully and efficiently within a certain amount of time. The best way to find a benefit consultant is through word of mouth, although you might also ask a local caterer. When you book a benefit consultant, ask how he charges. Like a caterer, he may work on a percentage basis, an hourly flat fee, or he may charge a figure based on the number of people attending. Be cautious, however, about a fee that is keyed into a percentage of the money raised at the benefit.

If you decide not to use a benefit consultant, then the committee chairman handles all arrangements. (If this person is a woman, she is called "chairwoman" or "chairperson," if she prefers.) The chairman acts as the liaison with the organization being benefited and has a special contact there—someone who will help encourage board members to spread the word about the benefit, and who can help find underwriters and performers.

The chairman must first put together a benefit committee, whose names will appear on the invitation. He does this by making a list which includes board members of the organization being benefited, well-known people in the community who will attract attention to the event, and people who enjoy working on a benefit and have the time to devote to its planning. It is expected that committee members will take tickets, although a chairman should not force the issue. In the case of younger committee members or those on a tight budget, it is thoughtful to offer them free or discounted tickets, particularly if they have given a great deal of their time and effort to planning the occasion.

The chairman will most likely need one or two cochairmen on the committee to help share the organizational responsibilities. They in turn will engage other committee members, putting each person in charge of one aspect of the event: invitations, tickets, program, food and drink, music, entertainment, getting items for an auction or raffle, finding a

YOU ARE CORDIALLY INVITED TO CELEBRATE

THE 100TH ANNIVERSAY
OF
THE TRUSTEES OF RESERVATIONS

SATURDAY, JUNE 1, 1991

A GALA BIRTHDAY PARTY

9:00 P.M.

THE GREAT HOUSE AT CASTLE HILL
ARGILLA ROAD
IPSWICH, MASSACHUSETTS

PLEASE RESPOND ON THE ENCLOSED CARD
BLACK TIE

This evening's celebration at Castle Hill marks the 100th birthday of The Trustees of Reservations, the oldest land trust in the world.

In honor of our founder, Charles Eliot, whose vision inspired the land trust movement worldwide, the Charles Eliot Award will be presented to two individuals who have demonstrated extraordinary commitment to the preservation of our natural heritage.

WE GRATEFULLY ACKNOWLEDGE
THE GENEROUS SUPPORT OF
THE STATE STREET BANK AND TRUST COMPANY
AND
THE KINDNESS OF
THE CRICKET PRESS OF MANCHESTER.

MRS. CORNELIUS CRANE
HONORARY CHAIRMAN

MRS. KENNETH A. IVES, JR.
CHAIRMAN

MR. AND MRS. GORDON ABBOTT, JR.
DR. AND MRS. NILE L. ALBRIGHT
MRS. ROBERT E. BELLIVEAU
MR. AND MRS. ADOLFO BEZAMAT
MRS. WILLIAM R. CALLENDER
MRS. NATHANIEL B. CLAPP
MR. AND MRS. FERDINAND COLLOREDO-MANSFELD
MR. AND MRS. ALBERT M. CREIGHTON, JR.
MR. AND MRS. JAMES N. ESDAILE, JR.
MRS. JOHN J. GLESSNER III
MR. AND MRS. HENRY R. GUILD, JR.
DR. AND MRS. BRANDON HART
MR. AND MRS. ARTHUR C. HODGES
MRS. STEPHEN G. KASNET
MR. AND MRS. JONATHAN M. KEYES
MR. AMD MRS. PETER E. MADSEN
MR. AND MRS. GEORGE R. MATHEY
MR. AND MRS. WILHELM M. MERCK
MR. AND MRS. FREDERICK S. MOSELEY III
DR. AND MRS. ROBERT T. OSTEEN
MR. AND MRS. RICHARD D. PHIPPEN
MR. AND MRS. DAVID J. POWELL
MR. AND MRS. G. NEAL RYLAND
MR. AND MRS. PRESTON H. SAUNDERS
MR. AND MRS. DAVID W. SCUDDER
MR. AND MRS. EDWARD C. SHOTWELL III
MR. AND MRS. NORTON Q. SLOAN
MR. JOSEPH P. SPANG
MR. AND MRS. THOMAS J. G. SPANG
MR. AND MRS. RICHARD D. THORNTON
MR. AND MRS. HERBERT W. VAUGHAN
MR. AND MRS. CHRISTOPHER M. WELD
MRS. FREDERIC WINTHROP, SR.

PRINTED ON RECYCLED PAPER.

An example of a well-worded, well-designed benefit invitation (note the uniform style in which the names are listed).

Champagne, a dessert buffet and Illyrian coffee will be served. The historic rooms of the Great House will be open and decorated as if the Crane family were in residence. Entertainment by the Classic Jazz Ensemble and the Copley Chamber Players will highlight the evening.

This benefit helps support our centennial year celebrations. We hope you will join us as we launch a second century of land conservation.

I/We Accept the Invitation to

THE 100TH BIRTHDAY CELEBRATION
OF
THE TRUSTEES OF RESERVATIONS
SATURDAY, JUNE 1, 1991

Enclosed is my check, payable to The Trustees of Reservations
_____ Individuals at $125 each
         (Includes a $45 tax deductible gift to The Trustees of Reservations)
_____ Sponsors at $250 each
         (Includes a $170 tax deductible gift to The Trustees of Reservations)
_____ Patrons at $500 each
         (Includes a $420 tax deductible gift to The Trustees of Reservations)
_____ Benefactors at $1000 each
         (Includes a $920 tax deductible gift to The Trustees of Reservations)

Sponsors, Patrons and Benefactors will be acknowledged
in the evening's program.
A guest list will be held at the door.

Name(s): _____
Address: _____
                _____
Telephone: _____
☐   I am unable to attend but enclose a tax deductible donation to help defray
      the expense of the centennial year celebrations.

PRINTED ON RECYCLED PAPER.

The reply card.

photographer, etc. The chairman can also put together an honorary committee made up of the board members of the organization and others whose names will add prestige to the invitation and entice people to buy tickets. The committee may be headed by an honorary chairman or honorary cochairmen who will have no responsibilities beyond lending their names. While the honorary committee is not required to work on the benefit, it is assumed they will attend, buy tickets, take tables, and encourage friends to attend. Occasionally, a person of official standing or prominence, such as a governor, senator, or celebrity, is asked to be honorary chairman. As a way of thanking that person for lending his name, he is given a free ticket or tickets.

You can learn a lot serving on a benefit committee: how tickets are priced, where to find good entertainment talent, how to plan a menu for a large number of people, how to create an appealing invitation. Being on a committee is also a good way to meet new people and learn more about your community. If you are invited to join a committee, before you accept you should ask yourself the following questions: "Is this a charity that means a great deal to me? Do I have the time to make the necessary commitment? Am I willing to take tickets? Do I have friends who will take tickets?"

Only people who have agreed to serve on a committee can be listed on the invitation. Some nonprofit organizations solicit committee members with a letter which in essence says, "If we do not hear back from you shortly, we will assume that you agree to be on the committee." This is not legitimate. You cannot use someone's name based on such a letter. You must have confirmation of a potential committee member's acceptance either in writing or from talking directly to that person or his or her office.

Very few people still adhere to the protocol of proper address, so when you ask committee members how they would like to be listed on the invitation you will get a wide variety of responses. For instance, a single woman may ask to be listed as Miss or Ms. Helen White or simply Helen White. A divorced woman may be Mrs. or Ms. Jane Brighton or Jane Brighton. A married woman has the choice of Mrs. James Klein or Mary Klein, while a married woman who has kept her maiden name may be Ms. Sally Pack or Sally Pack. A widow may be Mrs. Allen Mayers or Mary Mayers. A woman doctor uses her title as does one in the clergy or military. A couple may prefer Helen and Robert Graves or Mr. and Mrs. Robert Graves and a man's name is used without a title unless he is a doctor or a member of the clergy or military. It is the responsibility of the chairman to ascertain how each committee member wants to be listed on the invitation. While uniformity in style is visually appealing, committee members who have devoted time and money to the benefit should be allowed the courtesy of being able to list their names as they wish.

It is up to the organization or charity to give the committee chairman a ball park figure as to how much money the benefit is expected to bring in. The figure is based on the organization's or charity's current or long-term needs. Given a net target goal, the chairman decides what type of event to hold, when and where to give it, and how much to charge for tickets. To decide how much to charge for tickets you have to take into account the age group you are gearing the party toward, the competition, the economic status of those living in the community—and even the general state of the economy. The organization's public appeal must also be taken into account as a factor in the sale of tickets. A chairman faced with an annual benefit must ask herself, "Should we give the same type of party as last year, or do we try something different which may attract even more people?" There is no set answer; many organizations give the same kind of party year after year with great success, others experiment with new ideas, which either do or don't succeed.

One of the major roles of the committee chairman, or the chairmen of particular subcommittees, is to approach companies and ask them to underwrite the benefit; to solicit florists, liquor stores, and other merchants for donations or for party favors and gifts; to look up printers who might absorb the cost of the benefit program; and, if there is to be entertainment, to find appropriate entertainers. In return for their participation, the names of the companies are listed in the benefit program and often in advertising and publicity materials. When a company has made a particularly generous contribution, as added recognition, its owner's name may be listed as a committee member and he or she may be given complimentary tickets to the benefit. And at the event a word of thanks to the underwriting company is particularly appropriate; the president of the organization benefiting may say a few words of appreciation, often in the form of a toast at dinner, to the president of the underwriting company.

There is nothing more important to the sale of benefit tickets than a supportive and enthusiastic press. The committee chairman should approach those on the board of the organization or charity, as well as committee members, and ask them to contact friends in the press and try to get them interested in writing about the event before it takes place. Long before the invitations go out, the chairman should talk to the city or style page editors of area newspapers, or the managing editor if it is a small-town paper, or even the publisher/owner. She tells them any interesting facts about the party and the organization it is to benefit—what makes it different from other events or organizations. The members of the honorary committee may also be of interest to the papers. The same editors should receive a press release several weeks before the benefit. If the newspapers write a glowing report of the party it's a good publicity tool for the next year's benefit.

You may not want to serve on a committee but you can still contribute to a charitable event by buying one or more tickets or by buying enough tickets to make up a table and inviting friends to be your guests. Or you can tell friends you will be going to the event and hope they will buy tickets and make up a table with you. Asking people to help make up a table is a good way to stimulate ticket sales. However, when you broach the subject to friends, you must be very clear as to whether you or they will be paying for the tickets.

Buying a ticket to a benefit doesn't mean you have to attend. People often give benefit tickets away to friends or, instead of buying tickets, they fill out the portion of the ticket request form which says, "I cannot attend but wish to send a contribution," and return it with a check.

There are many rewards from attending a benefit beyond the obvious one of helping a good cause. It is an easy (if expensive) way to get good seats to a popular play, concert, or athletic event. Or it may present the opportunity to do something entirely different, such as seeing a rodeo, going up in a hot-air balloon, taking a tour of San Simeon, attending a preview or premiere, or visiting some site not generally open to the public.

Since a nonprofit organization has an IRS tax-exempt status, a portion of the cost of a benefit ticket is always tax deductible. It is the responsibility of the beneficiary to list the deductible amount. After you fill out the benefit invitation form and send in your payment, generally tickets are sent to you. If the charity is not going to send tickets, it should say so on the invitation along with alternative instructions, such as "Your name will be on a list at the door." Keep your canceled check or the receipt of payment from the organization for your tax records.

If you have had an especially good time at the benefit or feel it was particularly well run, it is thoughtful to write a letter to the chairman praising her efforts. You'll be surprised how much such a gesture will mean to her.

SURPRISE PARTIES

One of the greatest (and most expensive) surprise parties ever was given by an inventive, and very wealthy, husband for his wife's fiftieth birthday: he chartered the Concorde, filled it with her friends, and flew everyone to Paris for a week of partying. He had arranged ahead of time for all the invitees to board the plane early and to have their heads buried behind newspapers and magazines when he and his wife got on board to take their seats. He told his wife that her birthday present was at the back of the plane and was too large to bring to the seat without her help. She went with him, only to find the present was her nonflying best friend, who hadn't wanted to miss the celebration.

But tread carefully. Since not everyone likes being surprised, give this type of party only if you're certain the person will welcome it.

What you can do is tell the person you're planning to take her to a restaurant or a friend's house for dinner. That way, she will be suitably dressed for the occasion, and still be surprised.

An invitation to a surprise party may be extended by telephone, fill-in invitation, or personal note. If you receive such an invitation, whatever the form, the important thing for you to pay attention to is the time you are told to appear. The surprise may hang on that. For instance, the host may tell you to get to the appointed place at five because the guest of honor will be arriving at five-thirty. If you get there late and are seen by the guest of honor it could well ruin the surprise. So be punctual.

COSTUME PARTIES

A costume party is a wonderful opportunity to enter a world of fantasy for one night and be anyone you choose to. The football fanatic can turn into Joe Montana for the evening and the would-be actress can play Sarah Bernhardt for a magical few hours. It's a good way to release pent-up aspirations.

An invitation to a costume party may be a printed fill-in type or a commercial one created specifically for a costume party. If a prize is to be given for the most original costume, it may or may not be mentioned on the invitation.

Costume parties are usually held in the evening. The occasion is likely to be a dinner followed by dancing to an orchestra or tapes or records, or a dance, with friends giving dinners beforehand. Often it's a family affair, with all ages attending. While a costume party may be to celebrate a birthday, an anniversary, or college graduation, it may also be given for no better reason than to have a party.

Generally speaking, costume parties are designed around a theme and guests are asked to come dressed accordingly. The invitation may say to come as your favorite storybook character, your favorite song, a famous person, someone you would like to be, or to dress as if you were from a particular era—the twenties, colonial days, the French Revolution—or as a character in a play or opera. For a couple celebrating a tenth wedding anniversary, an entertaining idea is to ask people to come as you were at the age of ten, or the way you looked ten years ago, or how you think you'll look ten years from now. Sometimes costume parties are given with no theme specified, which means you can dress any way you like, maybe just wearing a mask or a bright wig.

While a lot of people enjoy dressing up, there are those who are less than enthusiastic about the idea. So, before deciding to have a costume party, give careful thought to some of the following questions. Will your friends enjoy the idea? What about the time and expense involved in planning a costume? Is there a convenient rental company for those who do not want to make a costume? To lessen the obligation of having to put together a full-scale costume, you might add on the invitation, "If you'd prefer not to wear a costume, put on a festive hat or mask and come." This option is particularly appealing to older people and to those hard-pressed for time. But once you enter into the spirit of a costume party, chances are you will find it an amusing change.

GAME PARTIES

Parties at which friends get together to play games such as bridge, canasta, poker, mah-jongg, or Trivial Pursuit are a popular form of entertaining. When you give a party of this type, in order for it to work well and be fun for everyone, players should share a common interest in the game and play at the same level. These games require concentration. The person who likes to sit around the table chatting and exchanging gossip does not belong with the more serious players and should limit his or her participation to less committed groups.

If, for instance, your friends play bridge or poker and you decide you want to learn the game, find a professional teacher who will give you private lessons, or join a beginners' group. If you find it impossible to master the intricacies of the game, no matter how many lessons you've had, give it up (no one will consider you a social outcast just because you don't play). You can always meet friends for lunch or tennis instead.

To be well prepared for your game party, it's important to have comfortable chairs at the table for your guests. You may also need bridge table covers, if the surface of the tables is too slippery and cards would slide all over them. If it's a bridge party, at each table have two packs of unused or at least very fresh cards; if it's a poker party, have chips and so on. Also, each player needs a score pad and a well-sharpened pencil with an eraser.

Proper lighting is important when playing any game; a standing lamp provides the best illumination. Lastly, you will want two small tables so players will have a place to put their cups and saucers or glasses.

Many groups ban smoking at the table. If you're one of those who can't bear smoking while playing, that's fine, but it's only fair to tell people so when you extend the invitation.

The food you serve at a game party depends on lots of variables such as the time of day and whether it's all women or a mixed gathering. If your party is in the afternoon, tea and small sandwiches and cookies are appropriate. Some parties are held in the evening and dinner is served first, or you might invite friends to come for dessert and then play your game. If your party is an after-dinner one, arrange the dessert and any other foods on the dining-room table and have players help themselves buffet style. They can eat before sitting down to play or between games. Whether or not you serve food, soft drinks, coffee, tea, and, if you wish, beer and alcoholic drinks should be offered.

If a friend calls to invite you to a game party and you've never played with her group, be up front as to your standing as a player. If you honestly feel you can't measure up to the group, then politely decline the invitation. Or you may qualify as a player but not like to gamble (if stakes are involved) or not be able to afford to. If this will be an issue for you, before accepting the invitation discuss the stakes openly and frankly. If the stakes the group plays for are too high, tell your friend. She may want to lower them or she may want to "carry" you, which means she will honor any losses you may have above those you are willing to incur. What you don't want to do is put yourself in the position of playing for stakes that are too high for you. If you can't afford to lose, don't play for money. And, if you do lose, pay your debt immediately.

In some areas of the country people play games for prizes, not stakes. There may be prizes for the man and woman with the highest scores. These might be a pack of cards or a score pad, a book or a jar of homemade jam—something that's appropriate for either a man or a woman winner. Another idea for nongamblers is to have each player put a dollar or two in a prize pot.

As with all competitive games, there are rules of sportsmanship and manners to observe. Some are:

- Spouses who don't get along well as partners should play at separate tables.
- Don't ever criticize your partner's or opponent's playing.
- Try not to take longer to play than absolutely necessary.
- Don't spend too long rehashing a point or hand or move just played.
- Chest your cards so your opponents don't have to resist the temptation to look at your hand.
- Don't drum your fingers on the table.
- Women should not wear dangling bracelets.

INSTRUCTION GROUPS

Book clubs, discussion and singing groups, sewing circles, collectors' associations, and investment clubs are only a few interesting ways to get together with friends and learn or practice some special skill. Such groups usually meet at the house of one of the members. If all the members of the group work at home and/or are at home raising children, the meeting might be in the morning when the children are in school. They may meet to learn something specific like needlepoint, quilting, or a foreign language. Or they may get together to discuss a prearranged topic such as a book they have all read. Groups of people who work outside the home are more likely to meet on a Saturday morning or in the evening.

Depending upon the time of the meeting, coffee, tea, and sandwiches, cider and doughnuts, cookies or coffeecake might be served. Each group establishes its own style and preferences. Some prefer low-calorie snacks such as fresh fruit and juice, others make it a rule not to serve anything except coffee and tea. As the hostess, you actually have little to do except perhaps send out (or telephone) notices of the meeting, arrange the food, and make certain the group adheres to the agenda (this includes discouraging those inclined to gossip from doing so until after the book reviews have been given, the French lesson completed, the poetry read, etc.).

If the group is meeting to do needlework, have extra needles, thread, and several pairs of scissors on hand. If the group is learning about investments, then paper, pencils, and one or two small calculators are helpful. Those studying political issues, books, or foreign languages require good light, paper, pencils, and possibly a tape recorder. Writing groups will need a dictionary and thesaurus as well as paper and pencils.

COOKOUTS

The word "barbecue" originally referred to roasting a whole animal over an outdoor fire. The animal was spitted from whisker to tail: in French, from *barbe* to *queue*.

This mode of entertaining gained great prominence when Lyndon Johnson was President. The Johnsons often cooked and served ribs, chicken, and roast pig for several hundred guests at the LBJ Ranch in Texas. You don't need a huge ranch, however, to have a barbecue. A portable grill will do. In fact, about 50 million grills are fired up every Fourth of July with 1.5 billion charcoal briquettes. On our nation's birthday, 200 million steaks and 154 million hamburgers are grilled, to be washed down with 46.1 million gallons of beer.

To give a great cookout you will need in addition to a grill a separate table for food, plates, cooking utensils, and sauces. Have ample seating for guests—picnic tables and benches, bales of hay, cushions for cement or stone walls, or yard chairs and tables.

You can be creative about decorating your barbecue table. Think about large arrangements of wildflowers in wicker baskets or old copper or tin pitchers, or husks of corn, pine cones, gourds, pumpkins, or purple cabbages. Checked or striped tablecloths with matching napkins are popular. They may be linen or cotton, or, if you like, this is one occasion at which recyclable paper cloths and plastic plates and glasses will not be frowned on. If you use paper plates, however, buy good-quality, plastic-coated ones so the food won't seep through. If you serve hot coffee, make certain your paper cups have handles.

Decorate the patio or outdoor area with Chinese lanterns, strings of Christmas tree lights, or candles. Remember to have enough light so the chef can see to cook and the guests to eat. If insects are likely to join the party, set out candles or torches that contain insect repellent or stick tall insect-repellent wicks into the ground.

At most barbecues the host is also the cook, although if he does not like cooking or is no good at it, there's no reason why the hostess cannot fill in. The most popular barbecue items include hamburgers, hot dogs, beef, lamb, or seafood kebabs, grilled swordfish, spareribs, and steak. Baked beans, baked potatoes, coleslaw, potato or green salads, and French bread are good accompaniments. For dessert, watermelon slices, fresh fruit, cookies, pie, or shortcake are good choices. When buying produce, be guided by what's freshest in the market.

Although you may serve cocktails while the meal is cooking, copious hors d'oeuvres are unnecessary because barbecue foods are so substantial. Bowls of potato chips and raw vegetables with a dip are sufficient. Beer, sangría, soft drinks, iced tea, iced and hot coffee may also be served.

If you and your guests like some kind of party activity, a barbecue is perfect for square dancing (on a patio, driveway, or even in your garage), swimming if you have a pool or are located on the water, softball, badminton, tennis, Frisbee, or croquet.

It's a good idea to tell your guests that they will be eating outdoors so they can dress accordingly. In addition, keep a supply of shawls and sweaters for anyone who forgets to bring one. And let your guests know too how formal or informal the party will be; dress can vary from shorts to long country skirts.

PICNICS

The word "picnic" is adapted from the French *piquenique* (*piquer*/to pick and *nique*/a small thing). It was actually what we might now call a potluck supper. The picnics we know today come in a wide range of styles—from the brown bag lunch hour picnic in the park to the tablecloth picnic on the lawn at Tanglewood in the Berkshires, where the Boston Symphony performs in the summer.

Most of us look back on childhood family picnics with nostalgia. There's every reason to, because taking off for the beach or the lake, the mountains or park meant a happy carefree outing. When you plan a family picnic, let each child take turns choosing a favorite picnic spot. The one whose turn it is may also pick the route the family will travel to get there. It's fun for the child and also a good way for her to learn how to read a road map.

When you are inviting friends for a picnic, make sure to ask only those who like the outdoors and are not averse to a little sand in their sandwiches. You may invite people to a picnic by fill-in invitation or telephone, whichever seems most appropriate for the occasion. You may want to give a rain date, just in case the weather doesn't cooperate. At the time you are inviting, let your guests know whether there will be a baseball game after lunch or a long walk on the beach, so they will have an idea as to when they may expect to get home. Also, tell them if there is anything special they should bring along such as a flashlight for when it gets dark or a fishing rod or snorkling equipment. As for your guests' comfort, folding beach chairs and small collapsible tables are a plus at any picnic no matter where you go. And if it's a beach picnic, have an umbrella and a few straw hats for the less ardent sun worshipers. For a touch of exercise, take along a Frisbee or a kite to play with, or a volley ball or horseshoes, and for quieter moments, a pack of cards. If, after you have settled down for your picnic, the weather turns chilly or a family of mosquitoes invades your territory, it's best to head home and not stick it out just to prove you can withstand nature.

The food served at picnics varies enormously, from sandwiches to cold lobster salad. For ideas on picnic foods, cookbooks can set the imagination in action. There are delicious cold soups and summer salads that can be put together without a great deal of effort, as well as cold casseroles that are a meal in themselves. What you eat will depend on where you plan to picnic, what equipment you have on hand, the time of year, and whether you are feeding children, adults, or both. If children are included, peanut butter and jelly sandwiches, potato chips, and sodas are reliable standbys.

If you are taking a grill along, it opens up all sorts of choices for a meal. While you can never go wrong with the standard picnic fare of hot dogs and hamburgers, there are other options such as grilled chicken, steak, or lobster, corn on the cob, and baked potatoes. Also popular at picnics are crudités, with or without a dip, to nibble on, potato salad, macaroni salad, deviled eggs, apples, peaches, and pears, and cookies and brownies. If the picnic is on a beach and you have a fire, as a finale to the day's activities it's always fun to toast marshmallows.

When preparing the food for a picnic, remember that sandwiches made with tomatoes may be soggy by the time you eat them. Instead of eliminating the tomatoes altogether, you can take them already sliced in a snap and seal storage container and add them to the sandwiches at the last minute. Sandwiches or salads made with mayonnaise must be kept refrigerated until shortly before they are eaten: mayonnaise spoils easily, particularly in summer heat, and can cause food poisoning. And milk sours in hot weather. So, if you are traveling any distance to a picnic, foods that may spoil should always be kept in a cooler.

All styles of picnics are correct and it's totally a matter of personal choice as to whether you want to eat off plastic plates or real china. You can improvise with empty food jars and plastic containers from your kitchen or you can go all out and buy a fully equipped wicker picnic basket. Actually, the style of the picnic is far less important than the food and the company, and of course the weather.

If your picnic takes place at a site along a highway, any trash should be put in the receptacles placed there for that purpose. Naturally, the same applies for a picnic at the beach or any public place. If you won't be at a spot where trash cans have been provided, take along a large plastic bag to throw the garbage in. If you have done any cooking over a grill or in an open pit dug in the sand, be particularly careful to extinguish the fire completely before leaving the area. Douse it, scatter it over, and feel it with your hand to be sure all the coals are out; people walking on beaches can be burned by stepping on sand that covers hot coals.

Tailgate picnics do not differ from other picnics. They, too, can be simple or elaborate. They evolved with the arrival of the station wagon: the tailgate is let down and becomes a table from which to serve the food. While the first tailgate picnics usually took place at football stadiums, today almost any event can be the occasion for a tailgate picnic. And you no longer need a station wagon: all you need are folding chairs or a blanket to sit on, the picnic food, and a few good friends.

Since a picnic is not a daily occurrence in any of our lives, it helps to make a checklist of exactly what food and equipment are needed. There is nothing more disastrous than to drive a good distance only to discover that something as important as the corkscrew or bottle opener has been forgotten. Such a list should be made out a few days in advance of the picnic to allow for any last-minute shopping.

CHECKLIST FOR A PICNIC

- Picnic basket
- Food
- Salt and pepper
- Butter
- Beverages
- Water
- Ice
- Plates
- Glasses
- Cutlery (including a sharp knife)
- Bottle opener
- Corkscrew
- Thermos
- Tablecloth
- Napkins
- Wet wipes
- Plastic bags for trash
- Insect repellent
- Suntan lotion
- Matches
- Flashlight
- Beach towels
- Blankets
- Beach chairs
- Folding tables
- Umbrella

POOL PARTIES

A close cousin of the barbecue is the poolside party, which is also held outdoors and usually includes swimming and lunch. If children are invited, as they often are, your menu should reflect this and include hot dogs, hamburgers, and sandwiches plus milk, soda, and fruit juices. Beer for the adults and soft drinks should also be available.

Word your invitation to a pool party very carefully. Don't expect your guests to guess. "Come over any time for a swim and lunch" will leave them wondering whether you mean 10 A.M. or noon. Instead, state the time they should arrive and when lunch will be served. For example, you can say, "We'd love to have you and the children for lunch tomorrow. We'll eat about 12:30, and if you'd like to have a swim, come an hour earlier."

You should make it clear when you are inviting friends to your pool whether they may eat lunch in their bathing suits or if they'll have to change into dry clothes for an indoor lunch, and whether children and houseguests are welcome. (Dogs, incidentally, are never welcome at someone else's pool.) To accommodate those who plan to swim, a stack of towels should be available. If you invite people for a Sunday, suggest they bring the newspaper or, better, have several copies on hand for guests to read. The considerate hostess also supplies insect repellent, paper tissues, extra sunglasses, bathing caps, sun hats, suntan lotion, and Band-Aids.

If you do not have a pool house, set aside bedrooms and bathrooms in the main house for your guests to change their clothes in. Tape "men" and "women" signs on the bedroom doors.

Sometimes people issue an open invitation to close friends to "come over and swim any time." Even if you have been given such a privilege, call first. Your friends may have a houseful of relatives on that particular day, or they may be planning a quiet afternoon alone. And if you do go, be sure to take your own towels.

Considerate parents ought to explain basic swimming pool manners to their children before they visit someone's pool. Remind them not to splash water on others, not to dive in near anyone, not to cannonball or do any other wild dives, and not to jump up and down or shout around the pool. They should also refrain from playing water polo around other swimmers. Encourage them to use the bathroom before jumping into a pool. And the edge of a slippery pool can be very dangerous, so warn children not to run. Although parents should supervise their own children, if a problem arises, you can certainly intercept, asking guests' children to keep their voices down or to stop running.

COFFEES

Coffees are traditionally associated with the South and Midwest, but women who are at home during the day in any part of the country enjoy this casual way of spending time with other women while their children are in school and husbands are at work. They are also ideal for senior citizens or groups of neighbors, with men often included. Coffees are held midmorning and are usually quite simple—coffee and Danish, bagels and cream cheese, or muffins. You might also want to include orange juice and fresh fruit.

Invitations are almost always made by telephone, unless the coffee is being held in honor of a new neighbor or someone else, in which case invitations may be handwritten. In some towns, coffees are given for a bride or mother-to-be. Guests may wish to bring a small gift to such gatherings.

POTLUCK SUPPERS

In certain parts of the country, covered dish or potluck suppers are very popular. The tradition goes back to the first Thanksgiving in 1621, which was in fact a three-day celebration of a good harvest. Each Pilgrim family contributed something. The hunters brought wild turkeys, partridges, geese, and ducks. Others brought clams, eels, and fish. The women made breads, Indian pudding, pies, and hoecake. Ninety Indians accepted Governor William Bradford's invitation to share in the celebration. They and their chief, Massasoit, killed five deer for the feast and also introduced the settlers to oysters.

The potluck supper is today's equivalent. And, both because so many women are working full-time and such suppers are easy on the budget, they are gaining in popularity all over the country.

You do not really *give* a potluck supper, you organize it and then serve it at your own house. You provide the setting, cocktails, coffee, and often the main dish. Those who are invited bring the rest of the food—hors d'oeuvres, a first course, vegetables, salad, potatoes or rice, rolls, and dessert. It must be made clear that everyone is to bring a dish. You can do this by writing "potluck" on the invitations or, if invitations are extended by telephone, by saying, "We're getting the group together Friday after work. If you're free we'd love to have you come. Everyone is bringing something." When the guests accept, suggest an assignment: "Perhaps you'd like to bring the dessert." The wine can be the host's responsibility or, if someone in the group is a real connoisseur or doesn't want to cook, that person can bring the wines. Because each person or couple are responsible for part of the meal, "Regrets only" on the invitation simply won't work. You need to know who is coming and what food they are bringing.

Everyone should bring his or her offering in an attractive container, ideally one that can go from refrigerator to oven or stove, and onto the table.

Potluck suppers may be given a theme, such as international cuisine, and everyone brings a dish that is Italian, Spanish, French, Chinese, Scandinavian, etc. A variation is the gourmet club, in which a group of people who enjoy elaborate cooking meet on a regular basis and contribute their best culinary efforts. The cooks then share recipes and culinary secrets. They take turns playing host (so that no one household has all the dishes and cleaning up).

THE BRING-YOUR-OWN PARTY

Yet another shared entertaining experience is the BYOB (Bring-Your-Own-Bottle) party, a wonderful idea for young people on tight budgets who would like to entertain but could not do so otherwise.

At a typical BYOB party, people call their friends and invite them over for a meal (something inexpensive like spaghetti, pizza, or chili). The hosts make clear that they will also provide drink mixes but that each guest must bring his or her own alcohol. If the invitation is written, the letters BYOB are added on the lower right-hand corner. At some BYOB parties, the bottles are shared; at others each person or couple drink only what they brought, in which case the bottles are marked with the owners' names. At the end of the evening, each person may take home his own bottle.

Some young people give Bring-Your-Own-Barbecue parties. The host or hostess provides the cocktails, salad, vegetables, dessert, and wine, and the guests bring whatever meat or bird they would like to put on the host's outdoor grill. To avoid having various cooks fighting for grill space, one person can be asked to take charge of all the cooking.

OPEN HOUSE

An open house—when people are invited to stop by for a short visit and refreshments during certain hours—is traditionally associated with Christmas Eve or New Year's Day. It's a wonderful way to entertain a large group of friends without too much fuss at that time of year, although there's no reason you can't have an open house at Thanksgiving, the Fourth of July, or after a local football game. An open house is very much like a large cocktail party, although liquor is not necessarily served. The invitation states both the beginning and ending hours, for example, 4 to 6 P.M. or 1 to 3 P.M. Invitations are written on informals or on fill-in cards purchased from a stationer. There is no need for an R.s.v.p. on an open house invitation. Grown or well-behaved children may be included in holiday open house invitations with their parents. In very small towns, open house announcements are sometimes placed in church or club newsletters.

Because you do not know exactly how many people are coming, it's best to keep the food simple. Platters of small sandwiches, cookies and cupcakes, mixed nuts, cheese and crackers, and potato chips and dips, along with a punch (alcoholic or not, or both), are common, although if you wish you may serve individual drinks. A baked ham or turkey, already carved, along with buttered bread slices, encourages guests to make their own mini-sandwiches. Guests are expected to stay a half hour or forty-five minutes, just long enough to greet the host and hostess, wish everyone a happy holiday, and have a bite to eat.

HOUSEWARMINGS

The first written use of the word "housewarming" is found in a letter dated 1577: "The shoemakers of London, having builded a newe Hall, made a royall feast for their friends which they called a howes warming."

If you have "builded a newe Hall" or simply moved to a different one, quite naturally you'd like to show it to your friends. The easiest way is to invite them to a housewarming party. If you have a great many friends, you may want to give several small parties so the house will never be too crowded. Most housewarmings are cocktail parties, although some people prefer a Sunday lunch or evening buffet.

You may invite people to a housewarming informally either by written note or an attractive fill-in invitation from a stationery store. Telephoning such invitations is also perfectly acceptable. If children are included, this should be stated on the invitation.

It is customary for each guest, or each family, to bring a small present, such as a local road map, perhaps, with a magnifying glass or a subscription to the local paper. These can be left on the front hall table with your name on the card. The host and hostess will open them after the party. If the housewarming is for people new to town, it's a good thought to have a guest book at the front entrance so people can write in their names and addresses. Later on, the couple can look over the names of the new neighbors they have met.

Keep in mind, however, that if someone has moved from a larger house to a smaller one or into an apartment, they most likely are not interested in accumulating more possessions. In this case, take something edible (a bottle of wine, a good cheese, some special preserves) or a plant as a present.

FAREWELL PARTIES

When good friends are about to move away, it's nice to hold a farewell party in their honor, to let them know how much they will be missed. A farewell party may take many of the forms mentioned in this chapter, from a buffet dinner to a summer pool party. As far as presents are concerned, most people don't want to accumulate more possessions when they're moving. Therefore, you can put on the invitation, "No presents, please," or "Your presence is your present." Or the guests may join together to give one major present.

There should be only one major farewell event for a couple, although good friends may want to give separate farewell parties for the departing ones.

THE HOUSEGUEST

Having houseguests for a night, for a cozy winter weekend, or for a leisurely summer weekend is a wonderful way to catch up with friends in the relaxed atmosphere of your home. Planning a house party can be great fun provided you put your organizational skills to work well in advance, to see that the guest room is in good order, meals planned, walks or tennis and golf games organized. If you know your guests well, you'll be able to judge how much in the way of social activities they might want. It could be that having a few local friends over for dinner one night is all that's called for. It's up to you to settle the question of how much entertaining to do, and certainly for some friends a quiet, restful weekend will be preferred to a more socially active one.

THE ROLE OF THE HOSTESS

If you have a guest room, you immediately become a potential host or hostess to a houseguest. If you haven't had a great deal of experience with overnight or weekend visitors, you'll find it useful to keep the following in mind.

- Invitations to spend a weekend are almost always telephoned, although if your friends live out of town or are away at the time you call, you may, of course, invite them by letter.

- If you're asking friends for Labor Day or some other holiday weekend, be sure to ask them well in advance, so there's a better chance they'll be able to accept.

- If you are inviting a number of people who don't know one another, do as you would for a dinner party—consider each guest's interests and temperament, and mix those you think will fit well together.

- Think twice before asking someone you don't know well or aren't particularly fond of to spend the weekend. Two days with anyone who bores you or who needs constant entertaining can seem like forever.

- If you must entertain relatives or business associates you don't get along well with, invite a good friend or couple too; it will help relieve any underlying tensions.

- If friends say they cannot come for the weekend unless they bring their children, and you can't work them into your plans, tell them it's not a children's type of weekend. Say you'll give them a rain check.

- If a guest asks to bring a pet, and you don't want an animal in your house, don't feel guilty about saying no in a nice way. Many hosts and hostesses don't appreciate having pets in their house, which is why most dog or cat owners have the sense not to ask to bring theirs along.
- Should friends call to say they will be vacationing in your area and would like to spend a night, if it's not convenient or you just don't want them, any excuse will do: "The guest room's being painted"; "My mother-in-law's coming"; "The house will be bursting to the rafters."
- So as not to encourage an unwanted guest who may be hinting for an invitation, never make even the most casual reference to your house, the area, or the possibility of his coming to stay. Completely innocent statements can be taken as an opening. "Not this weekend, but perhaps another time," may elicit yet another telephone call. Keep in mind that it's your house, and whom you invite to share it is completely your choice.
- Tell your guests just when you expect them to arrive and leave. Send them train, plane, bus, or ferry schedules, or, if they are driving, a road map and directions. Also, let them know if you will meet them at the station or wherever or, if you won't meet them, how they can get from there to your house.
- Be specific about clothing. Don't leave it to your guests to figure out what to bring. Tell them exactly what the dress code for the weekend is. A houseguest will feel terribly out of place if he or she is dressed differently from everyone else.
- If you are inviting friends for the first time, ask them if they have any special dietary needs and what they usually have for breakfast.
- If you don't allow smoking in your house, be sure to tell this to smokers when you do the inviting.
- If you have extra sporting equipment, such as fishing and hiking gear, or tennis rackets and golf clubs, tell your guests so they have the option of bringing or not bringing their own.

AFTER YOUR GUESTS ARRIVE

- Your guests will undoubtedly ask if they can help you with household chores. Some people welcome help in the kitchen, but if you're like many hosts and hostesses who prefer to unload the dishwasher or do the grocery shopping themselves, just say so.
- If the hot water supply is a problem in your house, when it comes time to take baths, tell your guests so they can help conserve what hot water there is.

Most guests enjoy having part of the day, either a morning or afternoon, to themselves—to read or just relax. Tell your guests in advance (perhaps at breakfast) just what the day's schedule will be. Don't expect every guest to participate in every activity. Above all, no guest should be forced to participate in a game or sport he's not interested in.

When you feel the time has come for the evening to wind down, ask your guests if they would like a nightcap. Once you've finished yours, you are free to go to bed, asking those who stay up to turn off the lights when they retire.

THE GUEST BEDROOM

The best way to be certain that your guest room will satisfy even the most meticulous guest is to give it a test run by sleeping in it yourself. You'll quickly discover if the radiator pounds incessantly or a loose shutter bangs in the wind—and, most important, whether the mattresses are too soft or too hard. Before a guest arrives, see that the room is aired out, that there's an empty drawer or two with clean liners for the guest's use, that the windows can be opened easily, and in the summer that screens are on. Check the fan in case it needs cleaning and be sure that the bulbs in the reading lamps are bright enough. If there is a desk in the room, the blotter should be spotless and a pen, notepaper, envelopes, and a few stamps placed in one of the drawers.

The ideal guest sleeping arrangement consists of twin beds separated by a night table. Some couples or friends may prefer separate rooms. If you are not certain about your guests' sleeping habits, ask the one you know best if he or she would like to sleep in the same or in separate bedrooms. If you have only one guest room and two women or two men will have to share it, tell them at the time you extend the invitation.

Many houses and apartments are not large enough for a room to be set aside for guests, but with a little imagination there are ways to improvise sleeping arrangements. Children can double up and give over a room, or the living room or library may have a convertible sofa, in which case a folding screen around a pull-out bed adds privacy. Either of these arrangements is preferable to your having to move out of your bedroom. Not only is it disrupting for you, it will make the guest who caused the move feel guilty. An exception to the rule about moving is when a single person who sleeps in a double bed invites a couple to stay. Then the best solution may be for her to give the couple her bed while she sleeps in the living room or den.

CHECKLIST FOR THE PERFECT GUEST ROOM
- Alarm clock
- Few carefully chosen books
- Recent magazines

- Pencil and pad by bedside table
- Sewing kit
- Notepaper and stamps
- Thermos or pitcher for water
- Radio and/or TV
- Bedside reading lamp/s
- Vase with fresh flowers
- Extra pillows for reading
- Extra blankets
- Opaque window shades
- Fan and/or heater
- Flashlight
- Luggage rack
- Two empty bureau drawers
- Closet space
- Hangers (not wire ones); skirt/pants hangers
- Mirror

CHECKLIST FOR THE PERFECT GUEST BATHROOM

- Face towel, bath towel, washcloth, bath mat
- Beach towel (if applicable)
- New soaps for basin and bathtub, plus liquid soap
- Bath oil and bath powder
- Hand cream
- Two glasses
- Toothbrushes and toothpaste
- Mouthwash
- Shower cap
- Shampoo and conditioner
- Comb
- Blow dryer
- Heating pad
- Hair spray
- Disposable razor and shaving cream
- Box of tissues
- Aspirin
- Band-Aids

- Sun block
- Sanitary napkins/tampons
- Extra roll of toilet paper
- Wastebasket
- Room deodorant
- Sponge and cleansing powder
- Night light

THE GUEST'S DRAWER If you have frequent overnight guests, you may want to set aside a drawer that includes the following:

- Extra set of house keys
- Local and area maps
- Subway and bus routes
- Telephone directories
- List of museums, suggested restaurants, tourist attractions
- List of specialty shops
- Places to take children
- Location and hours of nearest library
- List of churches and synagogues
- List of municipal golf courses and tennis courts
- Names of hairdresser and barber
- Folding umbrella

THE GUEST'S BREAKFAST

Houseguests seem to be divided between those who like a 6 A.M. jog on a weekend and those who like to luxuriate in bed until nine o'clock or later. As the hostess, you should not attempt to legislate the breakfast hour for your guests but rather tell them they are welcome to fix their own breakfast whenever they get up. The night before, you can show the early risers where the dishes, glasses, flatware, and other utensils are kept. You can leave out trays for anyone who wants to have his breakfast in his room. Cups, plates, cereal bowls, cold cereal, sugar, marmalade, and jams can be put out on the kitchen counter the night before with milk, cream, butter, and juices left in plain sight in the refrigerator. If you are up early enough, you can organize a part of the breakfast, making a large pot of coffee and perhaps leaving scrambled eggs and bacon on the hot tray. Guests can then get their own orange juice, make their toast, and heat up rolls.

If guests are visiting on a weekday, breakfast must be quick and simple so everyone can get off to work or school on time. Generally a family has its own morning routine which the guest should willingly fit into.

However, if a guest does not have to get up early, there's no reason for her not to stay in bed as long as she wants and then get her own breakfast.

If your household has a number of people in staff, guests may be asked if they'd like to have breakfast in bed. They should be asked the night before what they'd like to eat.

THE ROLE OF THE GUEST

When friends invite you for the weekend it's important to reply as quickly as possible so they can ask someone else if you can't make it. If you have to check with your spouse before accepting, explain that to your hostess and say you'll get back to her promptly. If for some reason you can't give her an answer when you said you would, call her and explain why and ask if she can hold off a few days longer. Chances are she'll be delighted to wait if she feels there's a good possibility of your accepting. A houseguest present is a must; in addition you may want to bring a small present for any child in the family. If you don't know your host and hostess that well, you can always wait until you get home to send a present, tailoring it to their tastes and interest. While any hostess appreciates a bunch of flowers or a plant, they are not considered house presents. If you will be staying with friends who don't have help, call and ask if you can bring something in the food department, perhaps for a specific meal—fresh pasta is always a good thought, or you may want to make something yourself such as good bread or a casserole.

Once you accept an invitation to spend a weekend with friends, you assume responsibility for contributing to the success of the weekend. It's up to you to make an effort not only with your host and hostess but with other houseguests and everyone you're introduced to. It's important to give the impression that you are having fun. Even if you're bored to tears, don't let on. After all, two days is not forever and you don't have to accept a future invitation.

While some people are born to be houseguests, not everyone knows how to behave in someone else's house. If you follow the tips given here, you're on your way to being the well-thought-of popular houseguest every hostess hopes for.

- After you have accepted an invitation, ask your hostess when she'd like you to arrive, how long she expects you to stay, and what's the best means of transportation. With this information in hand, you can make your travel arrangements. Reservations should be made early, particularly during the summer months and on holidays when airline flights and rental cars get booked up well in advance.
- Ask your hostess what clothes you should bring and pack accordingly; don't bring too many clothes, which we all have a tendency to do. Also find out if you should bring your tennis racket or any other sports equipment.

- Never ask if your children are included in a weekend invitation. Assume they are not unless your host or hostess specifies otherwise.

- Unless it's one of your most intimate friends who loves your dog, don't ask to bring him. Dogs often misbehave in a strange environment.

- If you can't eat certain foods, tell your hostess when you accept her invitation. If you are allergic to shellfish, for example, she should know this in advance.

- If you don't want to have to creep around the kitchen in the predawn hours, but need your caffeine to wake up, come prepared. Bring an electric water heating unit, a cup, instant coffee or tea bags, powdered milk, sugar, and a spoon. That way no one will care at what hour you begin your day.

- If you don't feel well at the last minute, call and cancel. Being sick away from home is no fun for you or your hostess.

AFTER YOU ARRIVE

- Be on time for meals and other activities.

- Be considerate of someone else's house; don't sit on furniture in a wet bathing suit; keep your feet off the furniture; don't hog the bathroom.

- If you must smoke, ask the hostess if she minds your doing so in her house; if she does, then smoke only out of doors. *Never* smoke in bed.

- Keep your room neat. Make your own bed unless you've been told a maid will. Be sure the bathroom is kept tidy as well. Before taking a bath, ask your hostess if there's any limit to the hot water supply and, if there is, use the hot water sparingly so others will get their fair share. After your bath, clean the tub.

- If you are sleeping on a pull-out convertible sofa bed, take the sheets and blanket off each morning, fold them, and put them along with your pillows away in some out-of-the-way place (you can leave the sheets on the mattress before folding the bed). When it's time to go to bed, it's up to you to turn the sofa back into a bed.

- Ask your hostess if you may help with any household chores. If she says she likes to do things her way, herself—and many hostesses do—take her at her word.

- If there is no maid, wash your own breakfast dishes or put them in the dishwasher; few hostesses will object to this.

- If you want to have breakfast in your bathrobe that's fine, provided you come to the breakfast table looking neat, hair combed, and wearing bedroom slippers.

- Don't tie up the telephone; if you make a long-distance call be sure to charge it to your credit card or ask the operator for charges and reimburse your host in cash.
- Be a bit independent. Don't rely entirely on your host and hostess for entertainment; they'll appreciate time to themselves to do chores or whatever. If there are other guests staying in the house, think up things you can do together that may not necessarily include your host or hostess, such as playing backgammon or bridge or walking into the village.
- If you have friends in the area who invite you over to their house, tell them you'll have to check with your hostess before accepting their invitation and be sure to ask if it's all right to bring your host and hostess with you. If your hostess has no specific plans, there's no reason she shouldn't agree to the idea. If she prefers not to accompany you, and doesn't offer to drive you there, your friends will have to come and get you or you'll have to call a taxi.
- If you break a glass or a piece of china, tell your hostess. If it's something valuable, take it home and have it repaired. If you accidentally leave a stain on a bureau or table, again tell your hostess and offer to pay whatever the refinishing charges will be. If you stain upholstery, rugs, or other fabric, insist on paying the cleaning bill.
- If you stay longer than a weekend, offer to take your host and hostess out for dinner one night. If there are other houseguests involved, you can all split the cost.
- If your hostess asks you to stay an extra day, think twice before accepting. It's better to leave while you're still appreciated rather than to wear out your welcome.
- On the day you leave, take the sheets, blankets, and pillowcases off the bed, fold them, and leave them neatly on the top of the bed.
- Check your bedroom and bathroom before leaving to be sure you haven't forgotten anything. Then check it a second time. It's a bore for a hostess to have to mail something you've left behind.

IF THERE'S A MAID If you visit friends with a staff, a maid may ask if you'd like her to unpack your suitcase. Say yes if indeed you would, in which case she will put your underwear, sweaters, etc., in the bureau drawers, hang up your dresses, pants, suits, and skirts in the closet, and put your toilet articles in the bathroom. If you'd rather do your own unpacking, all you have to do is tell her so. Among other things the maid may do for you is press any clothes of yours and bring you breakfast in bed. You should not ask her to take on other personal chores without checking first with your hostess.

If the maid is going to bring you breakfast in bed, she will ask you the night before what you'd like to eat and at what time she should bring the tray—or she may suggest you ring for your breakfast when you wake up. Sometimes the maid wakes up guests at a given time, drawing back the curtains, pulling up the shades, and, if necessary, turning on the heat. In the evening, while guests are at dinner, she turns down the beds, lays out nightgowns and pajamas, and puts bedroom slippers on the floor beside the beds. She also puts a small tray with a thermos of ice water and glasses on the bedside table.

TIPPING THE HELP How much you tip the staff depends on the length of your visit and what services were performed. Rewarding someone else's servant is one of the diciest of all types of tipping. Unlike a restaurant, where it's easy to figure fifteen percent of the total bill, here there is no weekend total to deal with. Apply these general guidelines and your own good judgment. If you simply can't decide what's best to do, talk it over with your hostess; undoubtedly she's had previous experience.

- If the maid unpacks your bag, presses your clothes, or does anything else for you, leave a minimum of ten dollars a day.
- If the cook prepares a number of meals, leave a total of twenty to forty dollars, depending on the length of your visit.
- If a chauffeur drives you a number of places, then a total of twenty dollars is reasonable.

You give the help their tips in person when you leave. Put the money in envelopes with the recipient's name on each envelope, along with a brief note thanking him or her for all that has been done for you (it's not a bad idea to take along notepaper and a few envelopes for this purpose). If you can't find a maid or other staff member, give the envelope to your hostess to pass on to the appropriate person.

THE BREAD AND BUTTER LETTER Whether you spend a night or a weekend at someone's house, you must always send a thank-you letter to your host and hostess within a week of your return home. Take time to write an enthusiastic and appreciative letter, mentioning something you did that particularly appealed to you or people you met who impressed you. If you did not take a present with you when you visited, now is the time to send one with a gift enclosure card reiterating your thanks.

CHAPTER 3
WEDDINGS

INTRODUCTION

The wedding ceremony is unquestionably one of the most spiritually moving and profound of life's rituals. Aside from its religious significance, the service formalizes the love and respect two people have for each other and their commitment to a long and intimate relationship.

The traditional wedding has survived the passage of time and many of the customs observed throughout the centuries are still with us: the ring, the veil, the breaking of the wineglass in the Jewish ceremony, the bridal flowers. Depending on the couple's preference and what the budget will allow, the wedding may be a small, intimate affair with only family and close friends invited, or it may be an elaborate celebration involving many attendants preceding the bride up the aisle and a four-course seated dinner for two hundred guests.

Planning a wedding can be tremendous fun, despite the time and effort required. If the bride feels she and/or her mother won't have the time or energy to cope with the vast number of details involved, they may want to hire a professional wedding planner. But, armed with good organizational skills, a taste for detail, a sense of humor, and imagination, there is no reason you can't put together the ideal wedding on your own. No matter who is in charge of the arrangements, this chapter will guide you through all aspects of this notable occasion from a practical and personal perspective. Follow it and the result will be a wedding perfect in every way: for you and your betrothed, your family and friends, and for you to look back on with pride and pleasure.

ENGAGEMENT

You have just announced your engagement. The love you and your fiancé feel for each other is all the more intense because of the long-term commitment you have made to share yourselves and your lives forever.

And now you have a wedding to plan and the delightful knowledge that the future is no longer a dream.

Life is a great deal easier today for an engaged couple. If you compare what was once considered standard "etiquette for being engaged" with what is done today, you will see how much more freedom there is about observing traditional conventions. For example, almost no one would suggest that a man ask a father's permission to marry his daughter. Nor is it necessary that the young man explain his financial prospects to his future father-in-law, unless there's a real problem that necessitates such a discussion—for instance, if both he and his fiancée are still in school or out of work. The days are also long since over when an engaged couple had to be chaperoned every moment. In many cases, the couple announcing their engagement will have been living together for quite some time. Despite all of these changes, there are still some valuable customs regarding an engagement for couples to consider. During this time of heightened emotions and much decision making, if the woman understands some of the possible choices before her, she will be better able to cope with the unexpected feelings which may suddenly surface as she and her fiancé go public with their love for each other. Being forewarned about what an engagement entails is being forearmed, so there will be less likelihood of undue stress or of misunderstandings arising among all those involved in the wedding plans.

TELLING YOUR PARENTS

Once you and your fiancé decide to announce that you plan to be married, you should tell both sets of parents before telling anyone else. No matter how tempting it may be to let a close friend in on your secret, resist the urge. Your parents would have a right to feel deeply hurt and angry if they got the news via the grapevine. Both sets of parents should be told of the engagement on the same day, even if they live in different towns or cities. If one or both sets of parents are divorced, decide which parent to tell first, and then contact the other parent immediately. If you reach an answering machine, you can always leave a message saying you have some exciting news, so please call back right away. After you have told your families, feel free to tell the whole world you're engaged, if you like, by telephone or by letter. It is never acceptable to send out engraved or printed cards announcing your engagement. To do so might give the impression that you're expecting presents.

AN INTERFAITH OR INTERRACIAL ENGAGEMENT

You may find it difficult to accept the fact that your child is marrying out of the family's religious faith or is marrying someone of a different nationality or race. In most cases this has nothing to do with not liking the actual spouse-to-be, but with feelings of disorientation that come from contemplating a break in tradition. Fear of the unknown can be deeply disturbing to a concerned parent. "Will my daughter convert to her husband's faith?" "Will my grandchildren be brought up with completely different cultural practices?" It helps if you ask yourself the question, "What's more important to me, my daughter marrying out of her religion, or my love for my daughter?"

If your child tells you he or she is planning to marry someone of a different religion, race, or nationality, don't react hastily. Keep an open mind and take a positive approach to the subject. Before being critical or judgmental, get to know the bride- or groom-to-be. Remember, your child loves this person. Often any doubts or reservations will be resolved once you get used to the idea that new beliefs and customs do not have to be threatening to the emotional well-being of your family. Most important is to keep lines of communication to your child open. You may need to learn about another religion, study a new language, or take a course in the history of a foreign culture. If you approach the learning process in the right spirit it can be fun and stimulating as well as educational. And it will mean a great deal to the engaged couple that you took the time and made the effort to learn about whatever is different in their backgrounds.

CLEARING THE AIR FINANCIALLY

If there are any financial problems that should be taken into consideration, now is the time to do so. It's important for a marriage to start off on a sound financial footing. If you or your fiancé will be in school when you get married, or you'll need to furnish an apartment or house from scratch, you might have to plan a smaller wedding than you'd dreamed of. The money that would have gone toward a lavish wedding reception can then be used for future living expenses. Or, if they're able to, your parents or your fiancé's parents might make you a loan which you can pay back when you're better off. Remember, a couple old enough to get married is old enough to accept the monetary responsibilities that come with marriage.

Hardly romantic, but necessary to mention, is the prenuptial agreement, which is most often drawn up by older couples who are marrying for the second or third time. The subject is a sensitive one; it must be handled with delicacy and diplomacy. If a young couple think a prenuptial agreement makes sense, which it does in certain cases, it should be discussed before the engagement is officially announced. All the particulars of the agreement need to be worked out with legal advice. If the discussion of the prenuptial agreement becomes so heated that the relationship falls apart, it is obviously better to have it happen before rather than after the engagement is announced.

WHEN A PARENT OR FRIEND DISAPPROVES

Regrettably, it *can* happen that a parent (even both) may not approve of your choice of a spouse. This can cause a great deal of heartache for everyone. It may also happen that a sister or brother or a best friend may not approve, or at least not feel happy about the choice. This can also be very painful and the only recourse is to try to behave like an adult, to stick to your decision and support your new commitment. After all, when Bess Wallace became engaged to Harry S Truman in St. Louis, Missouri, Truman was not quite on the same social level as the Wallaces, and Bess's mother warned her daughter that Truman would never amount to anything. In most cases, if the choice was a correct one, the parent will eventually have a change of heart and come to see the person in a different and better light.

What should you do if *you* have a friend (or sister or brother) who you truly think is making a bad choice? It may be wrong to say you should *never* reveal your true opinion, but telling a friend you think he or she is making a mistake may very well compromise your relationship irrevocably and nothing will be gained because your opinion will most probably not change your friend's mind. If you have solid proof that the intended spouse is already married, or has been charged with a criminal offense, and such a fact is not known to your friend, then of course you must speak up. Otherwise, if the friendship is important to you, it's best to keep your thoughts to yourself and your mind open. If you want to stay friends, try to be cordial and to get to know the intended better. Assume a positive attitude; eventually you may change your opinion. The best possible outcome might be that you even find you have gained a new friend.

PARENTS MEET PARENTS

After the parents have been told about the engagement, it's traditional for the future groom's parents to contact the prospective bride's parents to introduce themselves and to express their happiness over the forthcoming marriage. If they are not close friends and distance doesn't make it impossible, the groom's mother should initiate a meeting between the two families so the parents can get to know each other. The engaged couple should also be invited. The groom's mother may write a letter to the bride's mother suggesting that they meet for lunch or dinner, or she may telephone. If the bride's mother and father are divorced, then the groom's mother contacts both the bride's mother and father and there will have to be two separate meetings, the first with the parent with whom the bride lives or spends the most time. Even though it may not be possible for the two families to get together immediately, the groom's mother should still make written or verbal contact with the bride's parents as soon as she learns of the engagement. If she and her husband aren't familiar with the convention of contacting the bride's parents (and many people aren't), then the bride's parents should not stand on ceremony but take the initiative, after a week or so, and make the call or write the note. This is a good example of thoughtfulness and kindness taking precedence over social customs.

Even if the couple are well suited, there is no guarantee that the chemistry between the two sets of parents will be compatible. What everyone must remember is that how one mother or father feels about the other mother or father is not what is important. What matters is that they make a sincere, dedicated effort to get along, not only for the sake of their children, but also to create a friendly atmosphere for when it is time to make various decisions about the wedding arrangements. Although the bride's family, as hosts for their daughter's wedding, set the style and tone for the celebration, everyone involved in the preparations must work together with good humor, flexibility, and plenty of civility.

WHAT TO CALL YOUR IN-LAWS

During the engagement period you will both have a chance to get to know your future in-laws, provided they live within a reasonable traveling distance. As you all become better acquainted, your relationships will become more relaxed. At some point, the mother of the bride-to-be, for example, may ask her future son-in-law to call her by her first name. Such a gesture has significance because it shows that the relationship has progressed to a point where a special friendship has developed. It must be remembered, however, that it is the older person who must take the initiative by saying, "I wish you'd call me Louise." Sometimes a young person feels awkward or embarrassed at suddenly switching to a first name, but after taking a deep breath and forcing yourself to say "Louise" it will soon be automatic.

It's important for any young man or woman to remember that some older people are more bound by convention than others, or may just be more formal and may prefer to be called Mr. and Mrs. In no way should you feel the least bit slighted by this or have hurt feelings. (When grandchildren come along, the problem disappears as they usually come up with some sort of name like Gran, Pop, Gaga, even Grumpy, for grandparents. Then everyone can adopt that name.)

INVITING WEDDING ATTENDANTS

It's natural for a future bride and groom to want their key attendants—the two people who will stand beside them at the wedding ceremony—to be longtime friends or family members to whom they feel particularly close.

After you have told both families about the engagement, you may tell your closest friends, and at the same time ask them to participate in what will certainly be a joyous occasion for all. No bride or groom must ever feel compelled to ask someone to be an attendant just because he or she was in that person's wedding. Conversely, friends should understand that the bride and groom may have a number of relatives they'd like to have in the wedding party, and beyond that, it's desire, never a tit-for-tat obligation, that determines the choice.

When you invite people to be in your wedding party, you should try to be in touch with as many of them as possible at approximately the same time. This way you eliminate the risk of anyone feeling slighted, wondering if he or she was invited as an afterthought or as a substitute for someone who was unable to accept.

The age of a best man or maid/matron of honor, or for that matter any wedding attendant, is not nearly so rigidly prescribed as it once was, when all attendants had to be close in age to the bride and groom. Today, it's fine if the couple want to choose an attendant considerably older than the rest of the wedding party. But before asking someone older to be in your wedding, give some thought to whether that person will feel at ease walking up the aisle with a much younger member of the wedding party. Usually the chief attendant will also be the legal witness who will sign the marriage certificate. Since a person must be eighteen years of age to sign a legal document in most states, if either you or your fiancé want to choose someone younger than eighteen as a chief attendant, you can always ask an older bridesmaid or usher to serve as the legal witness.

How many bridesmaids and ushers you ask to be in your wedding depends on the size and formality of the occasion; quite often there are more ushers than bridesmaids, if it's a large wedding. As a general guideline, there should be one usher to seat every fifty or so guests at the church or synagogue. The groom will want to ask one of his ushers to serve as head usher. This will be someone other than his best man. It can be a brother, a friend, or a close relative. At the church, the head usher gives special seating instructions to the other ushers and often escorts the bride's mother up the aisle. While the ratio of bridesmaids to ushers really isn't important, there are a couple of reasons for having more or less the same number—it's more fun for the bridesmaids and ushers if the numbers are fairly equal; it lends a pleasing symmetry to the wedding procession. And when it comes to walking up the aisle, the clergyperson will know exactly how to line up the assembled group. Still, it's not incorrect to have uneven numbers.

Since it's a bridesmaid's responsibility to pay for her own dress and accessories, if you have a good friend you want as a bridesmaid but you think she might have trouble meeting the expenses, talk to her about it. After all, if she is a good enough friend that you want her in your wedding, it should not be that difficult to have an open discussion about this. Depending on the circumstances, yours and hers, you might offer to pay all or half her expenses. Whatever the arrangement, it's a private matter between you and your friend and something that neither of you should discuss with other members of the wedding party.

Sometimes it happens that a friend who is asked to be a bridesmaid is pregnant. If the bridesmaid-to-be knows she will be well along at the time of the wedding and probably quite large, she should tell you so you can then decide whether you want her in the wedding. The very pregnant bridesmaid, of course, may participate in all the pre-wedding activities. It's only the ceremony she'll have to miss out on.

In addition to the maid and/or matron of honor, best man, bridesmaids, and ushers, the bride and groom may choose to have one or more of the following attendants in the wedding.

JUNIOR BRIDESMAID If there's to be a junior bridesmaid, there is usually only one. She should be somewhere between the ages of nine and fourteen, and may be a younger sister of the bride or groom or some other relative of the couple.

FLOWER GIRL The flower girl (there are sometimes two) is in the age range of four to eight. She's usually a relative of the bride or groom but might also be the daughter of a close family friend.

JUNIOR USHER Occasionally a relative of either the bride or groom is chosen to be a junior usher (there are sometimes two). It is preferable for him to be in his mid-teens so that he will be able to perform the duties of a regular usher.

RING BEARER The ring bearer is a young boy aged four to eight, either a relative of the bride or groom or the son of a close family friend.

RINGS

The custom of giving a diamond engagement ring to the bride-to-be seems to have begun in the fifteenth century when the Archduke Maximilian of Austria proposed to Mary of Burgundy. Maximilian was told that he had to give her a ring set with a diamond. So he did, and from that time on diamonds have been associated with engagement rings. While a diamond solitaire is, and probably always will be, the traditional engagement ring, many women prefer other stones, such as emeralds, rubies, or sapphires. Semiprecious stones, such as aquamarines, topazes, or tourmalines, are also popular. These semiprecious gems can be quite beautiful and usually cost much less than precious gems, so that you can get a much larger stone for the same amount of money. Birthstones are also popular as engagement rings. How much a man spends on the engagement ring depends on how well off he is financially. It may be helpful to know that two months' salary is considered a general guideline when estimating the cost of a ring.

If the engagement ring is a diamond, a round solitaire is the preferred cut, although personal choice always is, or should be, the decisive factor. When buying a diamond, there are four "Cs" to consider: clarity, color, cut, and carat. The weight of jewels is measured in carats. (The American Gem Society [213-936-4367] can give you the names of certified gemologists in various parts of the country, if you feel you would like an appraisal before buying a diamond ring.)

One of the most thrilling moments in any woman's life is when she's given her engagement ring. It's up to her fiancé to decide how and where to give the ring. Only he knows what will please you most. He may take you out to dinner at a special restaurant you like and give you the ring then—perhaps dropping it into your champagne glass when you're not looking. Or, if you are ardent hikers, he may take you off on a day's outing and present you with the ring at the top of some mountain with a magnificent view. With a little thought and imagination, the presentation of the ring can be very romantic. The only possible drawback to giving a surprise ring, as opposed to one you have picked out together, is that your fiancé can't be absolutely certain you will love the ring enough to wear it the rest of your life. If he wants to take a more practical stance he will have to forfeit some elements of romance or surprise, but there's no reason why a more pragmatic approach should not be equally as exciting.

What your fiancé can do is go to a jeweler and pick out a number of rings that appeal to him and are within his budget. Then he can take you to the store and ask you to pick out the one you prefer. If you're not wild about any of the rings, the jeweler, knowing the price range, can show you others. Remember that an engagement ring is a present from your fiancé. If your eye lights on a ring that costs more than he can afford, you should not give away your feelings. Of course, if he has an unlimited budget, he needn't go to the jeweler's in advance. The two of you can go together and choose whatever ring pleases you the most.

An heirloom ring that has been in your fiancé's family makes a beautiful as well as sentimental engagement present which can be passed down to future generations. There's always the possibility, though, that you might not like it. If you don't, it's best to be diplomatic about it, rather than ruffle the feathers of your husband-to-be's family. You should put on a good face, be gracious and gratefully enthusiastic about having been given a family treasure. As you grow used to the ring, you may become attached to it. If after you have worn it for a few years you're still not fond of the ring, you may ask your husband how he would feel if you took the stones and had them reset or made into a pin, or whatever you want. But you should always take his feelings into account. The ideal way to deal with a family ring is for the man to show his fiancée the ring and then give her the option of wearing it as is, having it reset, or getting the ring of her choice.

Some women would rather have a different piece of jewelry, like a pearl necklace or a diamond pin, rather than an engagement ring. Others might not get a ring until they have been married a few years and their husbands can afford to give them a really nice one. Some brides prefer to wear just one ring and rather than an engagement ring, opt for a more elaborate wedding ring, often encircled with stones and usually wider than a regular wedding band.

When buying the engagement ring, thought should also be given to the woman's wedding ring. In this country, the wedding ring is worn on the third finger of the left hand and at the ceremony is placed on the finger before the engagement ring. The most popular wedding rings are made of yellow or white gold or platinum. Only the wedding ring, not the engagement ring, is engraved with the couple's initials and the date of the wedding; sometimes a sentimental phrase is included.

Wedding rings for men have been commonplace in other parts of the world for years and have become increasingly popular in this country. If you want your husband-to-be to wear a wedding ring, and he prefers not to, you should not force the issue. A man's wedding ring is wider than a woman's, usually gold, and worn on the third finger of the left hand. It may be engraved as a gift from the bride: "G.L.C. to D.A." with the date of the wedding. If you want to, you may add a phrase or motto with special meaning for both of you.

BIRTHSTONES

January	Garnet
February	Amethyst
March	Aquamarine
	Bloodstone
April	Diamond
May	Emerald
June	Pearl
	Moonstone
	Alexandrite
July	Ruby
August	Peridot
	Sardonyx
September	Sapphire
October	Opal[a]
	Tourmaline
November	Topaz
	Citrine
December	Turquoise
	Zircon

[a] The opal is said to bring good luck to those born in October; bad luck to those born in other months of the year.

THE ENGAGEMENT ANNOUNCEMENT

Ideally, the engagement announcement in the newspaper appears the day after the engagement party, if there is one. Otherwise, the timing of the announcement is at the bride's discretion, although most large urban papers make no promise as to the exact day the notice will appear. Before sending an engagement announcement to the newspaper, call the society news department to find out their policy as to engagement announcements: what the lead time is; what their style is in the use of titles; anything in particular that ought to be included. For example, newspapers usually want to know whether you or your fiancé have been married before. The announcement should be as complete as you can make it because the newspaper does not have the time to help you write it. If the groom comes from a different city or town, the announcement should also be sent to his local newspaper. Or, if he once lived in another city for a good many years, the paper in that city might run the announcement.

The easiest way to find out how to word an engagement announcement is to read a number of them in the newspaper where it will run and then choose the style that appeals to you and best suits your situation. A submission to a newspaper should always be typed with double spacing. Newspapers often want to call to verify specific details or to ask questions, so it's important to include your and your fiancé's telephone numbers, both at work and at home, as well as the telephone numbers of both sets of parents. If the telephone numbers aren't easily available to a newspaper, they may decide not to run your announcement.

If there's been a recent death in either of your immediate families, you will have to decide whether to postpone the engagement announcement in the newspaper and, if so, for how long. It's a decision that can only be made by you and your families.

If you and your fiancé have been living together and you decide to be married, announce your engagement the same way as any other couple.

Here's an example of an engagement announcement in the newspaper (including information for the newspaper at the top).

Date:

Bride's business telephone number:
home number:
Mother's or father's numbers:

Groom's business telephone number:
home number:
Mother's or father's numbers:

(HOLD FOR RELEASE TUESDAY, JANUARY 12)

Gail Lee Cramer to wed David Alexander, Jr.

Mr. and Mrs. Arthur Cramer of Santa Fe[a] have announced the engagement of their daughter, Gail Lee Cramer,[b] to David Alexander, Jr., a son[c] of Mr. and Mrs. Alexander[d] of Springfield, Mass. A June wedding is planned.

Ms. [or Miss] Cramer, known as Gigi, is a graduate of Samuel Kent High School and Sarah Lawrence College. She is a senior editor at Devon Publishing Company in Chicago. Her father, who is retired, was chief counsel for the Rathborne Corporation. Her maternal grandfather, Rufus Harland, was president of Continental Investing from 1968 to 1983.

The prospective bridegroom is a graduate of Princeton University and received a Master of Architecture degree from Harvard University. He is with Abrams & Abrams, a Chicago-based architectural firm. His mother is a reporter for the *Evening Standard* in Springfield. His father is a civil engineer with Tuscan Engineering Company.

[a] If the announcement is in a local paper, it's not necessary to include the name of the state.
[b] In the case of a doctor, minister, etc., the title would precede the name (i.e., Dr. Gail Lee Cramer).
[c] If there is only one son in the family, the announcement is worded "*the* son of . . ." If there are two or more sons in the family, it's "*a* son of . . ."
[d] Since the father is "Sr.," his first and middle names are not repeated. Otherwise, full name of father is needed.

(If David Alexander was married before, it is stated in the announcement: "He is with Abrams & Abrams, a Chicago-based architectural firm. His first marriage ended in divorce.")

A variation to the first paragraph is:

The engagement of Gail Lee Cramer to David Alexander, Jr., has been announced by Mr. and Mrs. Arthur Cramer of Santa Fe, parents of the bride. Her fiancé is the son of Mr. and Mrs. Alexander of Springfield, Mass. A June wedding is planned.

It's customary to send a photograph along with the engagement announcement but it's important to check with the newspaper to find out if they want a picture of the couple or just the fiancée. Usually the paper will ask for an 8 × 10 black and white glossy photograph. Taped to the back of the glossy should be information identifying the photograph as well as a telephone contact number.

It's a good idea to call the newspaper a few days after sending the notice, to be sure that it was received, to find out if any further information is needed, and to get a general idea as to when the announcement might appear in the paper.

SPECIAL ANNOUNCEMENTS Different newspapers have different policies when it comes to the use of titles in engagement announcements. In the following examples, titles are used with parents' names.

Deceased parent or parents: If both parents of the bride are dead, the engagement can be announced by a close relative or a friend. The word "late" precedes any reference made to either of the parents. If one parent has died and the one living is not close to the bride, the announcement may be issued by another relative, but mention of the living parent should be made. If the father or mother is deceased, and the other parent has not remarried, the announcement might be worded:

Mr. Frank Weinberg of Webster Groves, Mo., announces the engagement of his daughter, Mary Ellen Weinberg, to Allen Farmer, a [the] son of Dr. and Mrs. Julian Farmer of Seattle, Wash. Ms. [Miss] Weinberg is also the daughter of the late Mrs. Weinberg. . . .

An announcement giving some information about the deceased may read as follows:

Mr. James Figiola of Saratoga, Calif., announces the engagement of his daughter, Julia Figiola, to Edgar Allen Finley, Jr., a [the] son of Mr. and Mrs. Finley of Independence, Mo. Ms. [Miss] Figiola's late mother was Geraldine Figiola, founder of the Rocky Mountain Opera Company. . . .

If the father is deceased and the mother has remarried, the announcement may read:

Mr. and Mrs. Paul Johnston of Salt Lake City announce the engagement of Mrs. Johnston's daughter, Althea Frances Warren, to Alfred Martin Otis, a [the] son of Mr. and Mrs. Benjamin Otis, also of Salt Lake City. Ms. [Miss] Warren is also the daughter of the late Peter Warren. . . .

If the bride has never known her mother and has been brought up by her father and stepmother, the announcement may read:

Mr. and Mrs. Ralph Eggleston of Portland, Me., announce the engagement of their daughter, Felicia Eggleston . . .

Divorced parents: When parents are divorced, the engagement may be announced by both of them in the following way:

Mrs. Ruth Westland of Framingham, Mass., and Mr. Joseph Westland of San Jose, Calif., announce the engagement of their daughter, Sally Ann Westland . . .

If only one of the divorced parents makes the announcement, it is most usually the mother, but the father must be mentioned in the story. A typical announcement by a divorced mother who has not remarried follows:

Mrs. Gretchen Weeks of 1125 Park Avenue announces the engagement of her daughter, Pamela Weeks . . . Ms. [Miss] Weeks is also the daughter of Mr. Albert Ransom Weeks of Ashville, N.C. . . .

If this form is used, no mention of the word "divorce" is necessary as it is clear that the parents are divorced and it is assumed, unless otherwise noted, that Ms. Weeks lives with her mother.

If parents are divorced and the mother has remarried, the announcement reads:

Mr. and Mrs. Clifford Jones Stoddard of Unionville, Pa., announce the engagement of Mrs. Stoddard's daughter, Pamela Weeks . . . Ms. [Miss] Weeks is also the daughter of Mr. Albert Ransom Weeks of Ashville, N.C. . . .

If the parents of the groom have been divorced, the announcement reads:

Mr. Grissom is a [the] son of Mrs. Prudence Beers of Atlanta, Ga., and Mr. Morris Seale Grissom of Nashville, Tenn.

In rare cases, when the father makes the announcement of his daughter's engagement, it is worded the same as when it is announced by her mother.

If a bride whose parents were divorced and whose mother has subsequently died has been brought up by her aunt and uncle, the announcement of her engagement reads like this:

Mr. and Mrs. Seth McClure of Reno announce the engagement of their niece, Sally Dexter, to Penn Snyder, Jr., a [the] son of Mr. and Mrs. Snyder also of Reno. Ms. [Miss] Dexter is the daughter of Mrs. McClure's late sister, Joan Dexter [in this case a title is omitted], and of Dr. Joseph Dexter of Denver, Co. [This indicates that Sally's father was divorced from her mother at the time of her mother's death.]

Separated parents: When parents are separated, the bride's mother is legally Mrs. Joseph Marron until the divorce is final. Therefore, the announcement is worded:

Mrs. Marron of Pittsburgh, Pa., and Mr. Joseph Marron of New Orleans, La., announce . . .

Adopted children of a single parent: When a bride has been adopted by a single parent, the announcement reads:

Dr. Bernard Masters of Washington, D.C., announces the engagement of his daughter Carolyn Webber . . .

Legally changed name: Occasionally you see an engagement announcement or a notice of a marriage in which mention is made of a legally changed name. For example:

Mr. and Mrs. Josef Greenberg of 50 Robinson Drive announce the engagement of their daughter Dorothy to Robert Harris, a son of Mr. and Mrs. Chaim Hirsch, also of this city. Mr. Harris changed his name legally.

This clears up Mr. Harris's status but is not strictly necessary so long as the notice states that he is the Hirsches' son. The reader will assume he changed his name.

The mature, divorced, or widowed woman: If you are in your late thirties or even older, and have never been married, you may have your parents or, if they're not living, another relative such as a brother announce your engagement in the newspaper; it makes no difference whether or not your fiancé has been married before. Or you may want to forgo a regular announcement and inform your family and friends by word of mouth or by letter. When a divorced or widowed woman plans to remarry, it's not usual to announce the engagement in the newspaper. She may, however, send the announcement of her marriage to the newspapers.

ENGAGEMENT PRESENTS

A bride is usually given an engagement present by members of her family, their closest friends, grandparents, and godparents, and in most instances her future mother-in-law. While her own friends may want to give her a present, they should not be made to feel they have to. After all, what with buying shower presents and a wedding present, there's a limit to what's financially feasible for any young person, no matter how close he or she may be to the bride. Engagement presents of a personal nature such as lingerie, a pocketbook, cosmetic case, or a silk scarf are all popular choices. Linen also makes a good present, although you don't want to be too adventurous about color without consulting the bride. If the bride needs more practical items such as an ice bucket or bathroom scales, she should not hesitate to say so, if asked what she'd like. Money of course is always welcome.

The man gives his fiancée an engagement ring, and she may want to reciprocate with a jewelry-like present of sentimental value such as a tie clasp, cuff links, or a silver letter opener engraved with the couple's initials and the date they became engaged. Actually, there are no limits as to the choice of a present: a new golf putter, a sport jacket, a barometer, a night on the town. Whatever the woman knows will please her fiancé is the right present and only she can decide that.

ENGAGEMENT PARTY

Not every couple will have an engagement party, but when there is one, it's given by the bride's parents. If they are divorced, the parent the bride lives with or spends the most time with usually hosts the party. If the future bride lives a great distance from her family, it may make sense for her parents to come to the city or town where she is to hold the engagement party. This way, friends and business associates who won't be able to attend the wedding will have a chance to participate in a wedding-associated festivity.

An engagement party should be a joyous event. Divorced parents on both sides should put aside any grievances they may have and celebrate the occasion.

An engagement party can be held in a variety of places: at the house of the bride-to-be's parents, a club, a hotel, or in a private room at a restaurant or country inn. The invitations may be specially engraved or printed, or they may be handwritten on a fill-in invitation or on one's personal stationery. It all depends on how formal and how large the party will be. While there are no restrictions as to size or kind, an engagement party is often a late afternoon cocktail party.

If family and friends don't already know about the engagement, they certainly will when they open an invitation saying, "To meet Gail and David." But some engaged couples want to make the official announcement at the party and invited guests should play along with the so-called secrecy of the event and act surprised. Of course, if the invitation is worded, "To meet Gail's future husband, David Alexander, Jr." it means the engagement is common knowledge to all.

Here's an example of a fill-in invitation for an engagement party:

In honor of Gail and David[a]

Arthur and Louise Cramer
invite you to
cocktails
on *Saturday, January 12th*
at *six-thirty* o'clock
at *40 Alta Mira Drive*
Santa Fe

R.s.v.p.
(505)-xxx-xxxx

[a] *Italic* type indicates handwriting.

A woman used to wear her engagement ring for the first time at her engagement party, but that tradition has fallen out of favor. Many women have the engagement party weeks or months after becoming engaged and, therefore, have been wearing their rings for quite some time before the party.

Generally speaking, an engagement party, whether it's a dinner, a cocktail party, or outdoor barbecue, is handled like any party of its sort. There may be decorations unique to the occasion, such as blown-up photographs of the couple at various stages in their lives, or a banner with their names and the date of the party written out on it. Balloons, with their initials and the date, can also add a festive air to the party. To mark the occasion, there are often paper cocktail napkins or paper coasters or matchbooks specially marked with the couple's initials and the date.

Instead of a receiving line, the bride-to-be, her parents, and her fiancé stand informally near the door of the room to greet the guests as they arrive. Introductions are made as they seem appropriate. Of course, the young man should be introduced to any guest he does not know already, and he in turn should introduce any friends of his, who are not known to his fiancée or her parents, to them. The host and hostess should keep a careful eye on their future son-in-law's mother and father and make certain they meet people and have a good time. Guests also have a responsibility to mingle and talk to the young man's family and any out-of-towners they do not know already. Brothers and sisters of the future bride should also make a special effort as far as introductions and socializing are concerned.

It will mean a lot in the future if a photographer has been on hand to record the occasion. This may be a professional, hired for the evening, some family member, or a talented friend.

At some point during the party the father of the future bride will formally announce his daughter's engagement in the form of a toast. He makes the toast even if the couple's engagement has been made public many months before. If it's a cocktail party, he proposes the toast when the majority of the guests are present. At a dinner party, a good time to give the toast is during the dessert course. The father may say something like, "This may be the happiest moment in Gail's life but it's also one of the happiest moments in the life of her mother and me. If we had handpicked a husband for Gail, we could not have come up with anyone we admire or respect more than David. We welcome him into our family knowing he will bring great happiness to Gail always. I hope you will join me in drinking a toast to Gail and David and their future together." As a response to the toast, David says a few words of his own: "It means so much to Gail and me to have you all with us today and I particularly want to thank Mr. and Mrs. Cramer [Louise and Arthur, if on a first-name basis] for planning this celebration." While this is not a toast-making occasion, if a good friend or relative of the couple wants to make a remark or tell an anecdote, it's perfectly appropriate for him to do so.

No one should feel obligated to bring a present to an engagement party. In fact, if a present is given to the bride-to-be, it's usually in advance of the party. If some of the guests do bring presents, they should be put aside and opened after the party to avoid embarrassing those who did not bring anything. The next day, or as soon as possible, the bride-to-be should write each person who brought a present a note of thanks. A typical letter might say:

Dear Cousin Arthur,
I just this moment opened your present and can't tell you how much I love the place mats and napkins. At this point we haven't either one so you could not have chosen a more ideal present. Also, the colors go perfectly with the china we've picked out. David and I were very happy you could be with us last night. It meant so much to have you there. With so many thanks,

Love, Gail

If the groom's family live some distance from the couple or from where the wedding will take place, they may want to give a party of their own to introduce the bride-to-be to members of their family, as well as to some of their hometown friends who won't be able to attend the wedding. If the party can't be given before the wedding, it can always be held at some later date at everyone's convenience.

LENGTH OF ENGAGEMENT

There's no formula for the perfect length of an engagement. It all depends on the couple and their particular situation. If one or both are in graduate school, they may not be able to get married until their studies are over and they've found jobs. And, even if they've found jobs, they may still have to wait until they've saved some money. The length of the engagement is something each couple must work out themselves. What's far more important is setting a date for the wedding. A firm date set at the time of the engagement reinforces the commitment the couple have made and gives them a goal to look forward to.

Another factor entering into the length of an engagement is the booking of the church and the place for the reception. If a couple have their hearts set on holding the reception in a certain location, they may have to lengthen the engagement period.

It's no one else's business how long a couple is engaged. Never ask anyone why she's been engaged for so long. The reason, which is a personal matter between the engaged couple, may be one they want to keep private.

SHOWING AFFECTION IN PUBLIC

While there's nothing wrong with a couple indulging in a spontaneous gesture of affection, a more passionate display of emotion is embarrassing, even annoying, for those who have to observe it.

HAVING DINNER WITH AN OLD FRIEND

An engaged couple do not have to drop single friends of the opposite sex. If the bride-to-be has to attend a business dinner or take a business trip, there's no reason her fiancé shouldn't have dinner with a female friend—a colleague at work or an old school friend—provided there was never a romantic link between the two and his fiancée has been informed. If his fiancée is not happy about his seeing the friend, he should forget it.

BREAKING AN ENGAGEMENT

Almost all engagements lead happily to marriage, but if an engaged couple are having serious troubles they should be acknowledged. If they can't be resolved, breaking the engagement might be the smartest course. Of course, breaking an engagement can be one of life's most stressful and emotional experiences for a man or woman. There's bound to be a lot of disappointment and heartache, not only for the couple themselves but for those who love them and care about their future happiness. But far better to end a relationship that's gone sour before a final commitment has been made. Going through with something you know won't work out in the long run is a bad mistake. What's important to remember is that the word "failure" should never be identified with the breaking of an engagement. Agreements entered into with the best intentions often don't work out the way we hope.

It's not easy to announce the breaking of an engagement, yet it's a reality that has to be faced. You'll probably want to tell close friends on the telephone or in person and write notes to those you don't know so well. Never send out printed or engraved cards. And remember, it's no one's business why the engagement was broken, so no explanation need be given. What's more, most people realize that it's insensitive and rude to ask. When the breakup is in the open, and you talk to people, never publicly criticize your fiancé/ée, nor should he or she criticize you. If anything, try to think of something positive to say.

You must return your engagement ring and any other jewelry you received from your fiancé and his family. Many stores will take back an engagement ring and give a full refund within two or three months of purchase. If your fiancé insists on your keeping something of sentimental value, the decision is yours, but it's best to return everything and make a clean break. Any wedding presents received must also be returned. In the case of an initialed present, write the person who sent it to you, saying, "I would like to return the leather-bound scrapbook you sent me, but since it is monogrammed with my initials, I thought I should ask you first what you would like me to do." If you're the person being asked this question, by all means say to keep the present.

WEDDING PLANS

Many couples have a good idea of the kind of ceremony and reception they'd like by the time they talk to the bride's parents about the wedding plans. If you have not given much thought to the subject you and your fiancé, soon after your engagement is announced, must decide how elaborate a wedding you want and, most important, where the ceremony and reception will take place. If a couple wait too long the bride's mother may set into motion all sorts of plans of her own which may be quite different from what the bride has in mind. What's most important for everyone to remember in this situation is that a wedding is a celebration of the love and commitment marriage signifies. The bride and groom are the central figures; their wishes are what are really important. It is *their* wedding, not their parents', and it's *their* joy and happiness that matter most of all.

WHO PAYS FOR THE WEDDING?

In order to prevent any misunderstandings or resentments later on, it's important to establish who will pay for what wedding expenses before any plans get under way. By tradition, the bride's family give the wedding reception and the groom's family the rehearsal dinner the night before the ceremony. While this was once a hard and fast rule, today there are a number of realistic variations, depending on the financial circumstances of the bride and groom and their families. Men and women are marrying later (twenty-eight on average for the bride and thirty-two for the groom in urban areas) so they are more likely to be able to contribute to the costs themselves. If a couple want a more elaborate wedding than the bride's parents can afford, and they have well-paying jobs, there's no reason they shouldn't defray a major part, if not all, of the expenses themselves. Certainly no family should go into debt over an extravagant wedding. For instance if the bride's parents are divorced, her father may be raising a new set of children and financially unable to bear the cost of an elaborate wedding. Or parents with financial responsibilities to their own parents or to other children still in school may not have sufficient money in reserve to pay for a daughter's wedding, much as they might like to.

If it happens that the groom's family have a great deal more money than the bride's, they may want to offer to pay for the entire wedding, or a major part of it. This kind of situation can be embarrassing to the bride's mother and father unless handled tactfully. Usually the groom is the best one to decide who should transmit his family's offer. He may feel he and the bride should talk to her parents, or that his mother should call the bride's mother and talk to her directly. If the subject is approached with logic and diplomacy and if the bride's parents are self-confident, mature people, there's no reason why having the groom's family pay some or all of the expenses can't be arranged to everyone's satisfaction. Including their names on the formal wedding invitation can be a way for the bride's family to show appreciation for their generosity.

There are many other possible ways of handling the wedding expenses, if everyone contributes a little effort and understanding. For instance, the total cost of the wedding might be divided in thirds, with each family paying a third of the expenses and the couple the other third. If one set of parents is divorced, the cost could be divided four ways. Or the parents might work out some other acceptable arrangement according to their particular circumstances. As an example, the bride's family might pay for everything to do with the ceremony, such as the clergyperson and the organist's fee, a donation to the church, the flowers, and then split the other wedding expenses with the groom's family. If this is how you decide to arrange things it usually works out best if the bills for whatever items or services each family are responsible for are sent directly to them. If the expenses of the wedding are being shared, all contributors must be willing to compromise when necessary, whether on the choice of flowers, music, the style of the invitation, or any of the other multitude of details.

No matter how many people are contributing to paying for the wedding, it's much less complicated and more efficient if one person is in charge of making all the arrangements. The logical person in almost all instances is the bride's mother, who works directly with her daughter on coordinating all features of the wedding.

HOW WEDDING EXPENSES ARE TRADITIONALLY DIVIDED These are the traditional expenses paid for by the bride and groom and their families:

Bride and family:

- Invitations and announcements, including mailing costs
- Bride's wedding outfit and, in special circumstances, a bridesmaid's dress, if she cannot afford to pay for her own
- Bride's formal wedding portrait photograph and the wedding photographs. A small selection of wedding photographs may be given to the groom's family as a present; other guests may order on their own
- Wedding consultant, if used
- Wedding reception
- Bride's bouquet (in some communities the groom pays for this) and bouquets for bride's attendants. Also flowers and all decorations for the place where the ceremony will be held
- Fees for off-duty policemen to direct traffic, if needed; parkers at reception, if needed

- Rentals (i.e., tents, awnings, carpet runners, etc.)
- Presents for the bride's attendants
- Lunch party for bridesmaids, if bride gives one
- Music at the church and at the reception
- Any church fees, except the clergyperson's
- Transportation for bridal party from house to ceremony and from ceremony to reception
- Groom's wedding ring, if he plans to wear one
- Bride's wedding present to groom, if she gives one
- Wedding present of substance (i.e., silver or wedding trip) from bride's family to couple
- Hotel accommodations for bride's out-of-town attendants not staying in private houses

Groom and family:
- Bride's engagement and wedding rings
- Groom's wedding present to bride, if he gives one
- Rehearsal dinner
- Bachelor dinner, if groom gives one
- Marriage license
- Boutonnieres for best man, ushers, groom's father, bride's father, and himself (in some communities, also the bride's bouquet)
- Best man's and ushers' wedding ties and gloves (today these are most often included with the rentals of the attendants' outfits)
- Presents for the groom's attendants
- Clergyperson's fee
- Transportation for groom and best man to church, if bride's family have not included this in their transportation arrangements
- Transportation and hotel accommodations if groom's family is from out of town
- The wedding trip, unless this is a present from the bride's parents; if not the wedding trip, then some other present of substance
- Hotel accommodations for out-of-town ushers not staying in private houses

WORKING OUT A WEDDING BUDGET Considering the number of expenses connected with a wedding, if you don't have a carefully thought-out budget to work with, there's a good chance you'll end up spending a *lot* more money than you thought you would. There's no way you can make an educated guess as to how much a wedding will cost. You have no past experience to draw on. Therefore, whether you're thinking in terms of a wedding that costs $5,000 or $500,000, you need an estimated budget that includes *every* projected expense down to the last rose petal tossed at the reception. It should also allow some leeway for an unexpected expense or two.

If you're planning to hire a wedding consultant, he'll be able to help you prepare a budget; otherwise you can inquire of some caterers, rental companies, florists, etc., what their charges are. It's always helpful to talk to a friend who was recently married or who has recently given a wedding. She may even be able to give you tips on how to save money. One thing to keep in mind when allocating money for food, music, or whatever is that you should maintain a consistent style throughout. In other words, invitations, tablecloths, the cake, the band, even the brides-maids' presents should reflect the same degree of distinction.

Once you have a final budget, if the total should be less than you anticipated, you'll have the fun of spending the extra money any way you want to, such as on a lunch party for your bridesmaids. Or you may want to put the money aside to spend on your honeymoon. If the total comes to more than you planned for, you'll have to decide how and where to cut expenses. Maybe you can do with fewer musicians in the orchestra or a less expensive caterer. With a little ingenuity and some juggling of costs, you should be able to pare down expenses and still have the wedding of your dreams.

While it's all well and good to have prepared a practical budget, it serves no purpose unless you keep a detailed account of all your expenses—deposits made, bills paid. Many wedding planning books include a section for keeping such a record. Or use a looseleaf notebook.

The following is a list of wedding expenses to consider when preparing a budget:

- Wedding invitations and announcements (including addressing and postage)
- Bride's stationery
- Bridesmaids' lunch
- Lunch, day of wedding (if given, may include out-of-towners/plus bridal party/and some family)
- Dinner, following afternoon wedding (if given, same as above)
- Professional wedding consultant or secretarial help
- Bride's wedding dress and accessories
- Mother of the bride's dress
- Bride's going-away outfit (clothes/lingerie for honeymoon)
- Bridesmaid's dress (if bride chooses to assume this expense for a particular bridesmaid)

- Wedding ring for groom (if he's to wear one)
- Bride's wedding present to groom (if she gives one)
- Bride's presents to her attendants
- Bride's bouquet
- Bride's attendants' bouquets
- Outside canopy/chuppah/canvas runner for church or synagogue
- Organist's fee
- Flowers at church or synagogue
- Flowers at reception
- Music at reception
- Photographer (plus formal wedding picture and candids)
- Videographer (plus tapes)
- Caterer for reception (per person cost, plus any additional charges)
- Reception (per person cost at club, hotel, or wherever reception will be held, plus any additional charges)
- Rentals: tables, chairs, glasses, china, tablecloths, etc.
- Insurance
- Any special decorations at reception
- Outdoor wedding (tent, heating or air conditioning of tent, dance floor, canopies, special lighting)
- Other reception expenses (place cards, table number cards, hiring off-duty policemen, car parkers, movers, someone to watch house when wedding takes place, someone to polish dance floor, etc.)
- Wedding cake (or cakes)
- Paper rose petals or confetti
- Limousines
- Hotel rooms for any wedding attendants
- The wedding trip (if this is to be a present from the bride's parents)

WHEN AND WHERE TO HOLD THE CEREMONY

RELIGIOUS ASPECTS OF WHEN TO BE MARRIED Neither Christians nor Jews generally want to be married on their own Sabbath (religious Jews may not be married on the Sabbath—Friday sundown through Saturday sundown—or on High Holy Days or days of major festivals). Therefore Saturday is the usual day of choice for Christians, Sunday for Jews. Catholics seldom get married during Lent. Actually, it is not considered proper for any Christians to have a large wedding during

Lent, although very simple marriages with or without a clergyperson do take place.

WHAT TIME OF YEAR TO BE MARRIED It makes absolutely no difference which month you decide to get married in, although about fifty percent of all weddings take place in the spring and summer. June is the most popular month, followed by August. The month in which a wedding is held often varies according to the region or community where it will take place. In the South, for instance, weddings are likely to be in the early spring and late fall when the weather will not be too hot.

Compromises may be necessary when choosing the ideal wedding date. Vacation time from work may be the determining factor, or it may be a date when relatives and friends are most likely to be able to come. If a couple want to spend their honeymoon in a special place, that too can make a difference in their plans. If their hearts are set on Alaska, they'll want to think twice about going in the middle of winter. When choosing a date, it's worth bearing in mind that, if the wedding reception is to take place in a hotel or restaurant, you can often get a better rate during the nonpeak wedding months. The same is true if the wedding is in the middle of the week rather than on a weekend. Of course, if you plan a weekday wedding, you have to bear in mind that people who work may not be able to take time off, so it should probably be in the evening.

WHAT TIME OF DAY TO BE MARRIED The time of day to be married varies in different parts of the country and depends in part on how much money you have to spend on the wedding. An afternoon reception will cost less than an evening one with a full-scale dinner. In general, Protestant and Catholic weddings take place in the late afternoon. There's no restriction as to the time of day a Jewish wedding takes place, although many are held in the evening.

WHERE TO HOLD THE CEREMONY Weddings don't have to be only in churches and synagogues. They can be held at a hotel or club, the office or home of a justice of the peace, at a city hall, a dear friend's house, in a garden, on a boat, on the beach—almost any place. It doesn't matter where, so long as it's not too inconvenient for guests to get there.

WHAT TYPE OF RECEPTION TO HAVE, WHEN, AND WHERE Where you hold your wedding reception and what kind it is will depend on several things: how many people you want to invite; how formal you want to be; the time of year; and how much money you want to spend.

Naturally, the time of the reception must be coordinated with the time of the ceremony. Ideally, the reception should be immediately after the service, as it's most convenient for guests to go directly on to the reception.

Catholic weddings are occasionally held in the early morning, followed by a breakfast reception or brunch. A reception for a bride of any religion who is married at 11:30 A.M. or noon is referred to as a wedding breakfast, although it is actually a lunch. This may be buffet style or seated. But late afternoon or evening are the most popular times for receptions. A late afternoon celebration may be either a cocktail party which ends by eight o'clock, or a buffet or seated dinner that goes on into the late evening. The evening reception, particularly popular in the South, where it's hot in the daytime, is usually a buffet or seated dinner. If the wedding has been a civil ceremony, the bride and groom may choose to have any type of reception, large or small.

The majority of wedding receptions are held at a hotel, a club, or at the bride's family's. Most hotels and some clubs offer all-inclusive wedding packages in different price ranges. The manager or banquet manager will be able to answer all your questions from whether you can substitute one item in the package for another to what range of sample place settings and different-colored tablecloths you can choose from. A full-service caterer can supply the same services as a club or hotel for a home wedding. Understandably, however, a wedding at home requires more time and effort on the part of the bride and her mother than one given elsewhere.

If you don't want to or can't have the reception in one of the above places, there are plenty of alternatives. For instance, many restaurants have private rooms where receptions can be held, with a meal ordered in advance. The parish house of a church or the community room at a synagogue is always a good thought and has the added advantage of being less expensive than other locations. Sometimes the church or synagogue will cater the event or you can supply your own food and drinks. Be aware that alcoholic beverages may not be permitted at a parish house.

Some museums rent out space for social events, as do other institutions or nonprofit organizations such as public libraries or schools. Private men's and women's city clubs often have ideal spaces for rent, as well as facilities to provide the services needed. Many civic groups have spaces, such as the lodge at a town park or a local historic house, available for rent or in return for a contribution which may or may not be tax-deductible. Mansions and historic houses are extremely popular as wedding reception sites—so much so that many are booked up more than a year and a half in advance of the wedding. Or you might have a reception at sea on a yacht, in a municipal park, at a roller skating rink, a gallery—just about anywhere your imagination takes you.

It's fine to be original as long as the place you settle on will be comfortable for guests of all ages. Romantic as it may seem, you don't want to have a reception at a ski lodge on the top of a mountain if elderly guests would have to arrive by ski lift. Before making a final decision on the reception site, think of the guests' comfort: how far they'll have to travel from the ceremony to the reception, for instance. If the reception's to be in a tent, it may be necessary to have heaters in the winter or fans in the summer.

SECOND OR DELAYED WEDDING RECEPTIONS If the bride is living in a city other than the one she comes from, and the groom not only works there but also comes from that same city, they may decide to get married there in a small ceremony attended by the couple's immediate families and a few local friends. The groom's family may offer their house for the reception or it may take place elsewhere. A second reception may be given later in the bride's home city or town, so that all those who were not invited to the wedding or could not make it will have a chance to meet the groom.

Conversely, a second reception may be given in the groom's hometown if the couple plan a trip there after their honeymoon. This gives the groom's family the opportunity to introduce the bride to relatives and friends of theirs who didn't attend the wedding.

Such "second receptions" are almost always informal affairs held in the late afternoon with tea or cocktails. Guests may be invited by telephone, or informal, fill-in invitations may be sent. There may or may not be a receiving line, depending on the number of guests invited. The bride and groom wear clothes appropriate to the time of day the party's being given.

RESERVING THE CHURCH/SYNAGOGUE

It's never too early to reserve the church or synagogue for the wedding. Many are booked on weekends—the most popular time of the week for weddings—as much as a year in advance. Once you have decided on the date and approximate time you want to be married, call the office of the church or synagogue to find out if the time is available on the date of your choice. If not, you may have to change the date or the hour of the ceremony. On this initial call, you will also want to find out whether the minister, priest, or rabbi is free to marry you at that particular time and whether the church or synagogue is available for the rehearsal the afternoon of the day before the wedding.

Before making a firm commitment the minister, priest, or rabbi will most likely want to know whether either of you has been married before and whether you are both of the same faith (if you or your fiancé has been divorced, or if you are of different faiths, some clergypersons will refuse to marry you). In addition to papers documenting the divorce, if there has been one, they may also want to see your birth and baptismal certificates.

As soon as the church or synagogue confirms the marriage date, you and your fiancé will want to make an appointment with the clergyperson to talk about the type of service you have in mind and to find out what premarital counseling he requires. If your fiancé is of another faith and you want a clergyperson of his religion to officiate in the ceremony too, this is the time to discuss such a possibility.

You will also want to make an appointment to talk with the person at the church or synagogue who is in charge of the logistics of the wedding ceremony.

MEETING WITH THE CLERGYPERSON While every house of worship has its rules and regulations, these vary from faith to faith, sometimes even among congregations of the same faith. Naturally, every clergyperson must conform to the doctrine of his or her religion but there are times when a minister, priest, or rabbi is allowed to use discretion in granting special requests.

When the time for your appointment with the clergyperson comes around, remember to take along whatever documents you and your fiancé have been asked to bring. At your meeting, the wedding service will be the main focus of your discussion. You and your fiancé may want to write part or all of the ceremony (sometimes a bride and groom each writes a segment with neither hearing the other's words until they are spoken at the wedding), which is a fine idea, provided the clergyperson thinks so too.

The clergyperson may also talk to you about premarital counseling. It is required by the Catholic Church, and many Jewish and other Christian denominations offer it as well. This seems to be a personal matter of choice, depending on the minister or rabbi. While the purpose of premarital counseling is to examine religious opinions, other aspects of life, such as careers, children, family life, and money, may also be dealt with. If premarital counseling is necessary, it may mean a session or more with your clergyperson or someone he refers you to, or attending one of the church's or synagogue's weekend group counseling programs. If one of you is converting to a different faith, special religious instruction is required before the conversion is complete. What faith the couple's children will be brought up in is an important factor here.

If your clergyperson will not marry you because one of you has been married before, you have no choice but to accept his decision and find some other clergyperson who is willing to perform the wedding. It is also up to the clergyperson to decide whether to allow another clergyperson—who might be a relative or a close friend of yours or your fiancé's or his clergyperson for instance—to conduct or coparticipate in the ceremony.

There has been a marked rise in the number of interfaith marriages, most likely because of greater religious and ethnic tolerance. Recent figures show that forty percent of Catholics wed in the United States married outside their denomination; among Jews, fifty-two percent married gentiles. The clergy of most Christian denominations are willing and usually happy to participate in an interdenominational service. Marriages between Jews and Christians sometimes take place in Christian churches or on "neutral" ground like a hotel or club. Orthodox rabbis will not perform interfaith marriages, nor in most cases will Conservative rabbis.

Many Reform rabbis do, however, preside at interfaith marriages; some allow a clergyperson of another faith to coofficiate at the ceremony. If you are unable to find a rabbi to officiate at your wedding, you can call the Rabbinic Center for Research and Counseling (908-233-2288). They will be able to provide you with the names of rabbis who will marry couples of different faiths.

In some churches or synagogues, you speak to the sexton, deacon, or other church official, not the clergyperson, about the following:

- The logistics of the ceremony.
- An estimate of all fees related to the service—minister, priest, rabbi, visiting clergyperson (who may receive a present instead of a fee, depending on his relationship to the couple), sexton, altar boys, cantor, organist, choir, soloist, use of facility, any necessary rentals.
- Confirmation of the time of rehearsal.
- Whether a canopy is available for outside the church in the event of inclement weather.
- Whether a chuppah is provided.
- Appropriate flower arrangements and when they may be delivered and arranged.
- Any restrictions as to music played.
- Whether it's possible to have a choir or soloist sing at the wedding.
- Whether you can provide your own organist and, if so, whether you still have to pay the church or synagogue organist.
- Whether you can hire a group of musicians (i.e., a string quartet, a brass quintet), or any other kind of musicians.
- Policy as to taking photographs and videotaping during any part of the ceremony.

THE MARRIAGE LICENSE

You and the groom will have to go to your local license bureau or city hall to obtain a marriage license. You'll need to bring your birth certificates or some other proof of identification, such as a passport or driver's license, with you. If you were not born in the United States, proof of citizenship will be necessary. Different states have different regulations for issuing a marriage license; some require a waiting period or a blood test. In addition, the length of time the certificate is valid varies from state to state. You should contact your marriage license bureau to find out just what their rules are for obtaining a license, what form of payment is acceptable, and what hours they are open for business. When you receive your license, put it away for safekeeping as you'll need to take it with you when you get married.

To obtain information on getting married in certain foreign countries, contact the Office of Overseas Citizen Services, U. S. State Department, Room 4817, 2201 C Street N.W., Washington, D.C. 20520 (telephone: 202-647-5226). Or contact the embassy or consulate of the country in question. Some religious ceremonies that take place in foreign countries are not considered legal by the United States Government. Also, in certain situations, an American marrying a foreigner in that person's country may risk losing his or her citizenship. Because laws differ from country to country, in order to protect yourself, you should seek legal advice on this subject.

PRACTICING DANCING

Imagine this is your wedding day. It's time for the first dance and the orchestra has just struck up a spirited rendition of "I Married an Angel" or another favorite wedding song. You're about to take to the dance floor with the groom and all eyes in the room are focused on you. Do you picture yourself gliding gracefully across the floor following your husband's step, self-assured and loving every moment? (You should, as dancing is one of the more romantic aspects of any wedding.) If your answer to the question is anything short of a resounding "yes," it means you need to brush up on your dancing. You can do this by finding a dancing teacher to give you individual instruction in the fox trot, waltz, samba, ethnic dances, or whatever type of dancing you've planned for the reception. There are also dance studios where you can take group lessons. How much instruction you need depends on how experienced a dancer you are. If you're a novice, you'll want to start your instruction at least six months before the wedding. If there's no teacher or dance studio in your area, or you can't afford the cost of lessons, you can rent videotapes which will give you the fundamentals in dancing techniques. Or ask a friend who's a good dancer to help you.

Regardless of whether the groom has the time or inclination to sharpen up his dancing, the two of you should spend some time dancing together to music that will be played at the reception. Wear shoes similar to the ones you plan to wear the day of the wedding; although not the exact pair, as you don't want to get them scuffed up.

ELOPEMENT

"Elopement" is a word seldom heard anymore because couples no longer feel they must have the approval of their parents to get married.

Sometimes a man and woman can't bear the idea of having to face all the complexities and pressures of a big wedding and, once they have announced their intentions and received the blessings of their parents and friends, they go off with two friends as witnesses and get married in a civil or religious ceremony. This is all well and good if the parents understand about not being at the wedding. Otherwise it's best if the couple get married some distance from their hometown. This will make it less upsetting for the parents who can't be there.

After the couple have been married, they may want to send out formal wedding announcements, always with the place of the marriage, the date, and the year stated. If the reason for the elopement was pregnancy, the couple may not want to reveal the date they were married. In that case, they should not send out announcement cards. The announcement may be made by the bride's parents or, if their disapproval is so strong that they refuse to, then the couple may send out their own announcement.

Often, after an elopement, the bride's parents give a party to celebrate the marriage. It can be as simple or as elaborate as they and the couple want it to be. It's up to them whether to have a receiving line and a wedding cake. And everyone should wear whatever is appropriate for the time of day.

MISCELLANEOUS DETAILS

There are a number of miscellaneous details to attend to before the wedding. Perhaps not all the ones mentioned below will apply to you and/ or your groom, but some certainly will.

- Making a new will.
- Adding bride's or groom's name to the apartment lease, if one is moving into the other's apartment. Or adding name to title deed to house, if it's to be owned jointly.
- Arranging for any necessary insurance (i.e., if reception is being held at home, extra liability coverage may be required).
- FOR THE BRIDE: changing name with bank, credit card companies (keep your own credit card history separate from the groom's), magazine subscriptions, on driver's license, passport, etc.
- FOR THE BRIDE: ordering social stationery to use after the wedding (personal stationery and stationery to be used jointly with the groom).
- If wedding trip is out of the country, checking on what documents will be necessary.
- Sending wedding announcement and photograph, if one's to be used, to newspaper/s.
- Physical checkups.
- Picking up wedding ring/s.
- Checking out suitcases for wedding trip; buying new ones, if necessary.
- Reconfirming arrangements with caterer, photographer, floral designer, etc. (wedding consultant will do this for you, if you're using one).

- Checking that bridal dress and groom's outfit will be ready as scheduled.
- Contacting wedding attendants to make sure they have followed through with their fittings, rentals, etc., and to give them any final instructions as to wedding activities.
- Getting marriage license.
- FOR THE BRIDE: making hairdressing appointment for wedding day.
- Breaking in wedding shoes (wear them around inside for a week or ten days).
- Making arrangements for someone to watch wedding presents at the time of the ceremony and reception.
- Asking someone to be in charge of the signing of the guest book at the reception, if you have one. You can ask the junior bridesmaid, if there is one, or two friends of yours to take turns at the signing table until all the guests have gone through the receiving line.
- Asking someone to mail wedding announcements the day after wedding.
- Hiring car parkers and/or police for home reception.
- Making arrangements for transportation when leaving reception.
- Taking care of clergyperson's fee; putting it into an envelope to give to best man.
- Seeing to the polishing of the dance floor, if reception is at home.
- Buying place cards and table number cards.
- Making reserved seating list for church (guests can be notified of pew numbers by telephone, in writing, or by being sent engraved pew number cards. Each usher should have a typewritten list of guests who are being specially seated along with their pew numbers).
- Putting together a "care package" to take to church in case of a last-minute emergency—extra pair of pantyhose for bride or brides-maids, needle and thread, safety pins, straight pins for ushers' boutonnieres, scissors.

WEDDING ATTIRE FOR WOMEN

BRIDE'S WEDDING DRESS

Every bride has a romantic image of just how she wants to look when she walks up the aisle on her wedding day. Therefore, your wedding dress may easily be the aspect of the ceremony to which you devote the most time and thought and the single greatest expense connected to the wedding.

In some families a dress for the bride may have been handed down from her mother or grandmother, an aunt or other female relative. If you like the idea of wearing the precious satin and lace wedding dress your grandmother wore and the style of the dress suits you, wear it with pride and pleasure. On the other hand, if you want to choose your own dress, and many brides do, no family pressure should be brought to bear. What you may decide to do, depending on the formality of the wedding, is wear a veil that has been in your family. If so, you will want to wear an ivory rather than a pure white dress because the veil will have yellowed a bit over the years.

No matter whether you plan to make your own dress or buy it, you will find it helpful to browse through the different bridal magazines to get an idea of the current style in dresses (according to BRIDE'S magazine, ninety-two percent of the brides being married in the nineties wear long dresses).

If you plan to buy your dress through the bridal department of a store, allow no less than six months from the time the store orders the dress to its delivery. That six-month period takes into account any delay in the manufacturer's shipping schedule as well as the possibility that further alterations may be necessary once the dress is finished. Another reason for ordering your dress well in advance of the wedding date is that if you want a picture of yourself in your dress to appear in the paper along with the wedding announcement, you may need the dress to meet an early newspaper deadline.

The style of the dress you choose and the material it's made from depend on the formality of the wedding (see "Wedding Attire" charts later in this chapter), the time of day the wedding will take place, whether it's a country or city wedding, and the weather. For the most formal wedding, you would wear a full-length wedding dress in a variety of possible materials: satin, velvet, taffeta, chiffon, organza, tulle, or lace. Any of these fabrics except velvet and heavy satin can be worn for a summer wedding, plus a wide variety of summer cottons, such as eyelet and organdy. For a less formal wedding, a dress may be knee length (covering the knees), mid-calf or ballerina length (at the center of the calf or slightly below), or high-low (reaching slightly below the knee in front and to the ankle in back).

The color of the traditional wedding dress ranges from pure white and deep ivory to blush pink, so you will want a color that complements your skin tone. You also want to be sure the dress you choose is becoming from the back as well as the front: it's your back that will be on view during the entire ceremony. While some brides favor a high neckline, others prefer the more decolleté look of an off-the-shoulder dress, or perhaps a strapless dress worn with a bolero jacket. If you like the decolleté look, don't go overboard if the dress is to be worn in a house of worship.

If money is tight or you're the practical type, and if you have the time, you can often save a considerable amount of money by buying your dress off season, for instance, a heavy satin dress on sale in June to wear in a winter wedding. If you're lucky, you may be able to fit into a sample dress; these are often sold at reduced prices. Borrowing a dress is always an option as long as you won't have to make major alterations to it. The only problem with borrowing is that you can't help but worry about spilling. If, however, you do accept the offer to borrow a dress, it must be cleaned before being returned to the lender and you must ask the lender if she wants the dress returned to its pre-alteration state. You will also want to give a present of some sort to the lender to thank her for her thoughtfulness and generosity.

Many brides can find their ideal wedding dress at a rental company. For the bride who only wants to wear an expensive dress but hasn't the money to pay for it, renting a dress can be a practical solution. There are places in most cities that specialize in renting wedding dresses. Before renting, find out what alterations can be made to the dress and who is responsible for making them. Then examine the dress carefully to make sure there are no noticeable spots or other imperfections. You'll also want to know whether there's any possibility of the dress being rented out to some other bride before the date of your wedding; if there is, think twice before putting down a deposit on a dress that may not be in the same perfect condition when it's your turn to wear it.

THE BRIDE'S ACCESSORIES It is no longer the rule that a bride wear a traditional wedding dress with a veil and train, although veils in particular are still popular. What follows is the terminology for different veils and trains:

- Veils—bouffant (to the shoulder); elbow; fingertip; ballet (to the ankle); long (to the floor or as long as the train).

- Blusher—worn over the face and headpiece, and may be attached to a longer veil. A birdcage falls below the chin and may be attached to a hat. A flyaway has several layers brushing the shoulders.

- Trains—the sweep train is the shortest, barely sweeping the floor; the floor-length train fully brushes the floor; the court train extends 1 foot longer than the sweep train; the chapel train (most popular) extends 1⅓ yards from the waist; and the cathedral train extends 2½ yards from the waist.

- Lace is often used to decorate a wedding dress. The most common lace is Alençon (curving floral elements, distinctively outlined with cord on a net ground); Chantilly (exuberant scrolls and floral patterns on a lacy net ground). Heavier laces include Venise (with floral sprays, foliage, geometric designs) and guipure (large needlepoint on a mesh ground).

- While gloves aren't mandatory, if the wedding dress has short sleeves you may want to wear long gloves—or, with three-quarter sleeves, short gloves. If you wear short gloves, you may remove the left-hand one at the altar for the ring ceremony. If you wear long gloves, the underseam of the ring finger can be slit so the top half can be folded back when it's time to receive the ring. If you plan to wear your engagement ring at the ceremony, you should put it on your right hand, under the glove.

- Bridal shoes are of silk or satin and match your dress (you should wear them around the house before the wedding to break them in).

- The jewelry you wear on your wedding day should be understated. Eyes are meant to be on you, not on your jewelry. BRIDE'S says that ninety-one percent of women wear earrings and fifty-seven percent wear pearl necklaces (single-strand and multistrand chokers being popular choices). Choose one or the other; if you want dramatic earrings, don't wear a necklace and vice versa. Instead of pearls, you may wear a simple gold necklace, perhaps one given to you by your parents or the groom.

- For bouquets, see "The Floral Designer" later in this chapter.

Many brides still follow the old folk adage about wearing "something old, something new, something borrowed, something blue" for good luck. If you borrow a piece of jewelry from your mother, or a friend's veil, the "old" and "borrowed" will be covered. With new gloves or dress and a blue garter you're all set.

THE PREGNANT BRIDE-TO-BE Occasionally it happens that a bride-to-be in the midst of planning her wedding, finds out she's going to have a baby. How she and her fiancé deal with the emotional and practical aspects of this news only they can determine.

If the wedding is to be a large, formal one, there's no reason why the couple can't go ahead with their proposed plans, provided the bride will be able to fit into her wedding dress when the time comes to wear it. What she must not do is walk up the aisle in a traditional wedding dress or wear a veil (traditionally a symbol of virginity), if her pregnancy will be very apparent. To do so is quite poor taste; considering her condition, and would probably be interpreted as an act of defiance or rebellion on her part. If the wedding is planned for so far in the future it's certain she'll be noticeably pregnant, she and her fiancé can cancel their original plans in favor of a smaller, less formal wedding at an earlier date. She may still wear a long dress if she wants to, although a pale color would be more appropriate than all white. But, other than the dress she wears, the pregnant bride's wedding is no different from anyone else's.

(If the bride decides to take her parents and/or a close friend into her confidence, they must honor her wishes if she wants to keep her pregnancy a secret. If a parent is upset about the pregnancy, he or she should keep quiet about it. It would be sad to jeopardize a relationship with one's daughter over a situation that can't be changed. What the pregnant bride needs most at such a time are the love and support of the people who mean the most to her.)

WHEN A TRADITIONAL WEDDING DRESS IS NOT WORN If you are being married in a rectory or in a civil ceremony, you should wear a short dress in a flattering color or a dressy suit.

BRIDE'S ATTENDANTS' DRESSES

It's customary for the bride's wedding attendants to pay for their own dresses and accessories. Therefore you should try to find dresses that are reasonable in price and, ideally, can be worn again. If you have your heart set on your bridesmaids wearing a particular dress, and it happens to be expensive, there's no reason not to choose that dress provided your family is in a position to pay for all the dresses. If not, you'll have to compromise and give up the idea of that dress in order to find one that all your friends will be able to afford.

The dress or dresses you choose for your attendants should match the formality of your own. Try to choose a dress that will be becoming to all the women in the wedding party. When deciding, bear in mind your attendants' coloring—a shade that looks great on a fair-skinned attendant may be all wrong for someone dark. Figures are another factor to take into consideration. Again, you'll find it helpful to look in bridal magazines for ideas.

Naturally, the only way to be sure all your bridesmaids will want to wear their dresses again is to have each bridesmaid choose her own. This is only possible when the wedding is not strictly formal. If the bridesmaids are to buy their own dresses, establish some regulations to maintain a coordinated look.

When discussing the dresses with your bridesmaids, be as specific as you can about the color, design, and style you want them to wear. All black is probably the easiest color to coordinate, although black is appropriate only for an evening wedding.

Once you have settled on a particular dress, before making it final you may want to show it to your maid or matron of honor to get her opinion. See if she likes it as much as you do and whether she feels the cost of the dress is reasonable. The decision having been made, you'll want to find out your attendants' dress sizes and any other measurements required to order the dresses. Ideally, of course, each bridesmaid should have a fitting, if it's convenient.

If you have the time to act as the liaison between your attendants and the store's bridal department, you can keep track of those who have sent in their dress sizes and be in touch with those who need further nudging. If you don't feel you have the time or inclination to take on this assignment, your maid or matron of honor may be free to help out. Or you can give the attendants the name, address, and telephone number of the person in the store who is in charge of your order and have them deal directly with the bridal department. If you prefer to handle the ordering of the dresses this way it's fine, but be sure to check periodically with the bridal department to make sure all the dress sizes have been sent in.

Your maid or matron of honor may wear the same dress as your bridesmaids or one that's slightly different, perhaps the same dress in a different shade of the same color. If there's a maid and matron of honor, they may be dressed alike or the dresses may be of the same design but a different color, or the same color but a slightly different design. Or all attendants may dress alike but with different flowers or headdresses distinguishing the maid or matron of honor. Attendants' dresses should be made in fabrics that complement that of your dress. For instance, if the dress is silk, the attendants' dresses should not be cotton. The bridesmaids may wear white, perhaps with a colored belt or colored trimming. The maid of honor and bridesmaids may wear short dresses even though the bride's dress is long. It is not correct, however, for the bridesmaids to wear long dresses if the bride is in a short one. The shoes of all attendants are alike in fabric, style, and color; if the maid or matron of honor wears a dress that's a different color from the bridesmaids', the color of her shoes should match her dress. If the dresses are short, they should wear the same shade of pantyhose. Short white gloves are optional. The attendants wear similar jewelry, whether it's a pair of gold earrings and/or single- or double-strand pearls.

If there's to be a junior bridesmaid in the wedding party, she may wear the same dress as the bridesmaids. If the style of the dress is too sophisticated for her, she wears one that blends well with the other bridesmaids' dresses.

A flower girl may be dressed in a white or pastel party dress that complements the bridesmaids' dresses. She wears white or colored slippers to match or contrast. She may also wear white cotton gloves.

A ring bearer wears a white Eton jacket with short pants. A slightly older boy wears a navy-blue suit, navy socks, and black shoes. In summer, he wears a navy-blue blazer and white pants. In certain foreign countries, pages and train bearers often participate in the most formal of weddings wearing satin and velvet suits.

DRESSES FOR MOTHERS AND STEPMOTHERS
OF THE BRIDE AND GROOM

The bride's mother with the bride decides what she will wear at her daughter's wedding and then tells the groom's mother so she can coordinate her dress. Neither mother should wear black or white. Their dresses should complement the bridesmaids' dresses and not be too decolleté. White kid or leather gloves are worn at very formal weddings. The mothers may wear hats or bands or bows on their heads but the two mothers don't have to match. Even if the bride's mother wears a hat, the groom's mother may go hatless if she prefers.

If a stepmother will be attending the wedding, she should be told what the mothers will be wearing so she won't outdo them by choosing a more elaborate outfit.

WOMEN'S WEDDING ATTIRE

	BRIDE	MOTHERS	WOMEN GUESTS
Formal Daytime (before 6 P.M.)	**MOST FORMAL:** traditional floor-length white or ivory dress; cathedral, chapel, or sweep train, matching-length veil; if sleeves are short, long white gloves are optional. **LESS FORMAL:** traditional floor-length dress, chapel or sweep train, shoulder or fingertip veil; gloves optional. (Short dress is optional; may have detachable train).	Short or long dress in dressy daytime fabric such as silk; matching accessories, hat, and corsage optional.	Short dress or suit in dressy daytime fabric such as silk; hats optional.[a]
Informal Morning or Afternoon	Short afternoon or cocktail dress or suit (white optional).	Short dress or suit in daytime fabric; matching accessories; hats and corsages optional.	Short dress or suit in dressy daytime fabric such as silk; hats optional.

[a] Women guests do not wear corsages.

	BRIDE	MOTHERS	WOMEN GUESTS
Formal Evening (after 6 P.M.)	**MOST FORMAL:** Traditional floor-length white or ivory dress, cathedral train; matching-length veil; if sleeves are short, long white gloves are optional.	Short or long dress or suit (not too decolleté), in dressy evening fabrics such as taffeta or velvet; matching accessories; corsages optional.	Short or long dress or suit in dressy evening fabrics such as taffeta or velvet.
	LESS FORMAL: Traditional floor-length dress; chapel or sweep train; matching-length veil; if sleeves are short, long white gloves are optional.		
Semi-formal Evening	Short or long dressy outfit; chapel or sweep train.	Short dress or dinner suit; corsages optional.	Short dress or dinner suit.
Informal Evening	Same as informal Morning or Afternoon		

WEDDING ATTIRE FOR MEN

GROOM'S ATTIRE

Together the bride and groom decide what type of wedding outfit he will wear. The degree of formality of his clothes (see "Men's Wedding Attire" chart later in this chapter) depends on what the bride is planning to wear and, like hers, depends on the time of day of the wedding, whether it is taking place in the city or country, and on the weather.

Today, almost without exception, the outfits for the groom and his attendants are rented from one company (not only is it more convenient, there's less chance that the colors of the suits, collars, etc., will vary). If the wedding's to take place in June at the height of the bridal season, it may be necessary to place the rental order as much as two or three months in advance.

The best man and ushers pay for the rentals of their suits. While traditionally the groom bought the ties and gloves for the best man and ushers, today these are usually rented along with the rest of the outfits.

Men's Wedding Attire

	GROOM[a,b]		MALE GUESTS[c]
Formal Daytime (before 6 P.M.)	SUIT:	**MOST FORMAL:** Black or oxford-gray cutaway, striped black or gray trousers, gray waistcoat. (These are only worn during the day, never at night.)	Dark suit.
	SHIRT:	Wing-collar shirt with lie-down collar.	
	TIE:	Ascot (gray with checks, stripes, or paisley), or four-in-hand (striped or checked).	
	SHOES:	Black kid shoes.	
	SOCKS:	Black silk socks.	
	SUIT:	**LESS FORMAL:** Black or gray sack coat or stroller, striped gray trousers, gray vest.	Dark suit.
	SHIRT:	White pleated shirt.	
	TIE:	Striped or bow tie.	
	SHOES:	Black kid shoes.	
	SOCKS:	Black silk socks.	
Informal Morning or Afternoon	SUIT:	Navy-blue, gray, or black suit.	Dark suit.
	SHIRT:	White, colored, or striped shirt, turn-down collar.	
	TIE:	Silk tie.	
	SHOES:	Black shoes.	
	SOCKS:	Socks to match suit color.	
Formal Evening (after 6 P.M.)	SUIT:	Black tail coat (full dress), Black satin-trimmed trousers, white piqué waistcoat.	Black tie (tuxedo) or white tie (tails).
	SHIRT:	White piqué wing-collared dress shirt.	
	TIE:	White piqué bow tie.	
	SHOES:	Black patent leather pumps or black kid shoes.	
	SOCKS:	Black silk socks.	

[a] At a Southern or summer daytime wedding, if the groom is to wear a cutaway (these are never worn at night), it should be of lightweight material. Otherwise, he may wear a stroller and striped trousers. Less formal is black tie, worn with a dinner jacket and black trousers. If it's an after 6 P.M. wedding, ties and cummerbunds should be black. If it's a daytime wedding, four-in-hand ties are worn.

[b] Fathers of the bride and groom dress as the groom and ushers do, but may substitute dark suits for cutaways, if they won't be standing in the receiving line.

[c] Male guests do not wear boutonnieres.

		GROOM[a,b]	MALE GUESTS[c]
Semiformal Evening	SUIT:	Black tuxedo or dinner jacket with matching trousers (jacket may be white or ivory in summer with black trousers); single- or double-breasted black vest or cummerbund.	Black tie (tuxedo) or dark suit.
	SHIRT:	White pleated or piqué shirt.	
	TIE:	Black bow tie.	
	SHOES:	Black patent-leather pumps or black kid shoes.	
	SOCKS:	Black silk socks.	
Informal Evening		Same as Informal Morning or Afternoon	

The best man's and ushers' outfits will be the same as the groom's, so as soon as he knows what he's wearing, he should get in touch with his attendants. He asks for their measurements or he gives them the name of the person to contact at the rental company. He must keep on top of the situation, as the rental company cannot set aside the suits until they have the men's measurements. As soon as possible, the attendants will need to try on their suits, since there is always the possibility that alterations may be necessary. Trousers, for example, should break slightly above the shoe tops, the jacket collar should hug the neck, and for a well-turned-out appearance at least one and a half to two inches of white cuff should show below the sleeve of the jacket. Most rental companies are accustomed to out-of-town ushers arriving the day before the wedding and are prepared to make last-minute adjustments to suits that don't fit properly.

Sometimes the best man handles the rental arrangements, particularly if he lives near where the wedding will take place. Regardless, it's usually the best man's job to see that all the rentals are returned to the company afterward. If he's leaving the area immediately after the wedding, the groom will have to delegate someone else, the head usher for example, to return the clothes. Whoever has this task must make sure *all* clothes are returned.

APPROPRIATE WEDDING ATTIRE FOR ATTENDANTS

All men in the wedding party, including the fathers of the bride and groom, if they are to stand in the receiving line, are dressed in a similar style, except for the ties and boutonnieres. The groom and best man wear the same tie, different from the ushers. The best man wears a different boutonniere from the groom but it may or may not be the same as the ushers'. If the fathers won't be standing in the receiving line, and the bride's father chooses to dress as the ushers in a cutaway, it does not mean the groom's father has to wear a cutaway as well.

While ushers, including junior ushers, dress in the same style as the groom and best man, variations in fabric are permissible. In the men's outfits, not only will the ties vary from those of the groom and best man, but lapel facings, stripes on trousers, and shirts may also differ slightly. The ushers' identical ties may be gray four-in-hands worn with a turned-down collar which may be attached to the shirt or separate. An attached collar is soft and a little less formal than a detachable collar, which is starched. An attached collar should be a plain, rolled one, not buttoned-down.

GLOVES

If it's a formal wedding and the men are wearing gloves, the ushers may keep theirs on during the entire ceremony. The groom and best man wear their gloves until they get to the altar. The best man takes off his right glove so he can pass the ring to the groom at the correct moment. The groom takes off his right glove to accept the ring. Each man holds his glove in his left hand or places it in his inside breast pocket. The clergyperson or other church official will explain the glove procedure at the rehearsal.

WHEN THE GROOM DOES NOT WEAR A TRADITIONAL SUIT

If the wedding is in a rectory or it is a civil ceremony, the groom wears a dark business suit and silk tie.

WHEN THE GROOM IS IN THE MILITARY

If the groom is in the military, he may want to be married in uniform. But if the majority of his ushers are not military men, he may prefer to be married in civilian clothes for the sake of uniformity in dress. If he does wear a uniform, he should adjust the formality of his uniform to the formality of the bride's dress. The rule of thumb is that "full dress" uniform is equivalent to civilian "white tie and tails," and "mess dress" equals "black-tie" attire. Both of these are considered very formal and should not be worn before six o'clock in the evening. The "service blue" uniform is the equivalent of a conservative business suit and is the best choice for a daytime wedding. Although a civilian usher cannot wear a military uniform, a military usher *can* wear civilian clothes to match the groom's. If the groom and some of the ushers are in uniform, whether service blues and whites or evening dress, civilian ushers dress with the same degree of formality. Military personnel never wear boutonnieres, even at weddings.

PUTTING TOGETHER THE INVITATION LIST

Once the date and size of the wedding have been decided upon, serious thought must be given to the guest list. If, as is customary, the wedding is being given by the bride's parents, the mother of the bride is in charge of putting together the invitation list, even if the couple or the groom's family are paying part of the wedding expenses. The list—certainly if the wedding is to be large—takes a considerable amount of time and thought. A hastily put together list might mean omitting someone you really want to be there, such as a favorite college professor or a beloved former babysitter.

There's usually only one guest list, made up of people being invited to the ceremony and reception. It would include family members, social friends, and professional friends, but not unless they truly are friends. If, however, the church or synagogue is too small to accommodate everyone or the bride and groom prefer a more intimate ceremony, two lists will be necessary: one for those being invited to the reception only, the other for family and close friends who will attend both the ceremony and the reception. There may also be a third list of people who will receive an announcement of the wedding, with or without an "at Home" (couple's married address) card enclosed. The including of an "at Home" card with the wedding announcement is up to the bride.

Not every bride sends out wedding announcements, but they do serve a useful purpose. For example, if a couple have had a very small wedding or been married in a civil ceremony, they may send out wedding announcements as a way of telling friends they have not been forgotten even though they were not invited to share the happiness of the occasion. Or the bride may feel it's more tactful to send wedding announcements to people who live a great distance away, knowing they could not accept the invitation and not wanting them to feel they have to send a present (a wedding announcement carries no obligation to send a present). Family members and close friends, however, should be sent invitations, no matter how far away they live.

It was once the custom to invite certain people only to the ceremony; a reception card was not included with their invitations. In the category of those invited just to the ceremony were the bride's and groom's less intimate friends, family servants, friends' servants, and tradesmen. Today it would be insensitive, if not impolite, to ask someone to the ceremony and not to the reception.

Traditionally, the bride and her family and the groom and his family each may ask the same number of people to the wedding. It's a somewhat more involved situation, however, when both families have been divorced and remarried, and not just two families are producing guest lists, but possibly four. It's up to the couple to work out a satisfactory formula for how many people each family may invite.

When the groom's family lives a great distance away, it's assumed that many of their relatives and friends who receive invitations will not come. The groom's family may give the bride's mother an estimate of how many people they think will actually attend the wedding so that the bride's family have the opportunity to invite more of their own friends. This brings up the question of the groom's family sending invitations to people they know won't be able to accept and putting them in the position of having to send a wedding present. Family or very close friends will want to feel part of the wedding by receiving an invitation and will probably want to send a present to the couple whether or not they can attend. Some may even accept and use the wedding as an excuse for a trip away from home. People the groom's family are less close to may be sent wedding announcements, which gives them the option of sending a wedding present or not.

A decision the mother of the bride will have to make is how many people to invite to the wedding over and above the number of guests agreed upon. As a rule of thumb, she can count on a fourth to a third of the invited guests regretting. The actual figure will depend on a number of factors such as what percentage of the invitees are out-of-towners, or whether the wedding is being held at a time when a lot of people will be away on vacation.

What both families must remember as they start compiling names of relatives and friends to invite is that there has to be a certain amount of give and take. The bride's father may want to invite his somewhat boring college roommate, only to discover that his wife does not want him there. Or perhaps the groom's mother will feel her tiresome great-aunt must be invited while her husband thinks it's more important to ask a business colleague instead. There's bound to be an occasional difference of opinion because each person contributing to the list will have his own feelings and obligations to deal with. If everyone involved keeps that in mind and is willing to compromise, it will make the whole process a great deal less stressful. And not least important is the fact that it's the bride's and groom's wedding and they get the last word about who is invited to *their* wedding.

Collecting and coordinating lists is made much easier if the mother of the bride is blessed with good organizational skills and has access to a computer. The master list for everyone being invited to the ceremony and reception should be computerized and, if wedding announcements are being sent out, that list should also be entered. If the bride's mother does not have access to a computer, it's well worth the expense for her to hire someone to do the work for her. Or the bride or the groom or a friend may be willing to take on this assignment.

The master list must be in alphabetical order, so the bride's mother should ask everyone contributing names to alphabetize their lists before sending them to her. She should also ask that ZIP codes appear with addresses. Each list is then added to the computer's master list as it is received. If an invitee has been asked to bring a guest, his or her name is also put on the list: "Grossman, Philip (guest of Gretchen Greene)"; or, if the name is not known: "Gretchen Greene and guest." It will also be helpful if the initials of the person who supplied the invitee's name are included beside that name. Once the master invitation list is completed, it is printed out and those who supplied names are given copies. Later, when replies to the invitations are received, the bride's mother marks beside each name on the master list A (for accept) or R (for regret).

The bride's mother may also want to keep a reserve list of names of people to be sent invitations. As regrets come in, she can send out invitations to those on the reserve list. While this may seem like a perfectly reasonable practice, it's not very complimentary to people on the second-string list. It's common knowledge that wedding invitations are mailed four to six weeks before the wedding, so the person receiving an invitation two weeks before will realize he's a second choice for someone who regretted. Instead of sending an invitation, it's much more thoughtful and tactful for the bride or groom to call to explain the situation. He or she can say, "David [or Gail] and I are getting married a week from Saturday. Could you come? We would be so happy if you would, as it looks like there'll be plenty of room." Inviting someone this way shows you care about that person's feelings. He'll be flattered and pleased that you wanted to invite him, albeit at this late date, even though he was not a close enough friend to have been on the original list.

When preparing the wedding list, these are some considerations to keep in mind:

- An invitation is sent to:

   the groom's parents (tell them you are sending it as a memento of the wedding, not because you expect a reply).

   the wedding attendants (spouses and "live-ins" included).

   the clergyperson and his or her spouse.

   the attendants' parents. (The bridal couple may want to invite parents they know well to the reception; parents who don't know the bride or her family wouldn't expect to be asked to the reception. If a bridesmaid says it would mean a great deal to her parents to see her in the processional, if there's no space problem tell the bridesmaid her parents are welcome to come to the church or synagogue.)

- A wedding invitation should not be considered a payback for a dinner invitation or other social obligation.
- If you are having a small wedding, you are not obligated to invite anyone just because you were invited to his or her wedding.
- When several members of a family are invited, children thirteen and older are not included in the invitation sent to their parents. They receive their own invitations.
- An unmarried couple living together are invited as a couple.
- If you know a friend is dating someone steadily, you may want to offer her (or him) the option of bringing that person to the wedding. Ask your friend for the person's name and address and send an invitation. That's the most formal, polite way to handle the situation. Or you can enclose a handwritten note with your friend's invitation saying you'd be delighted if she wants to bring her friend. You could even write on the invitation envelope "and guest." Remember to put the guest's name on the invitation list.
- Don't hesitate to ask someone in mourning to the wedding. It will please the person to be remembered and it may give him a lift to be a part of a happy occasion.

INVITATIONS

Your wedding invitation is something to be given special thought. The texture and weight of the paper as well as the style of the engraving are all important factors. When invitees first see the invitation you can be certain they will give it more than a passing glance. What you want them to see is an invitation you're proud of, one that reflects your taste and style. The invitation also serves the practical purpose of indicating how formal an event you're planning. It sets the mood and tone of the wedding.

THE TRADITIONAL INVITATION

The most popular wedding invitation is the one that's folded along the left-hand side so that it opens like a book. Invitation sizes vary somewhat but, as a point of reference, 5½ × 7½ inches is standard. The traditional color is ivory or ecru. Pure white is popular in Europe but is not often used here. While a wedding invitation is traditionally engraved, if it doesn't fit your budget you might want to consider thermography, which resembles engraving but is less expensive. Thin pieces of tissue paper, once placed on top of the engraving to prevent oil-based inks from smearing, are no longer necessary since the water-based inks used today dry more quickly.

Lettering on a traditional invitation is always in black; English script and Shaded Antique Roman are the most popular typefaces. If your

Mr. and Mrs. Arthur Cramer

request the honour of your presence

at the marriage of their daughter

Gail Lee

to

Mr. David Alexander, Jr.

on Saturday, the eleventh of June

at half after four o'clock

St. James Church

Four Main Street

Santa Fe

Reception

immediately following the ceremony

The Westerly Hotel

1112 Costa Mesa Terrace

R.s.v.p.
40 Alta Mira Drive
Santa Fe, New Mexico 12345

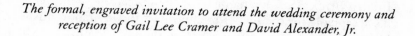

The formal, engraved invitation to attend the wedding ceremony and reception of Gail Lee Cramer and David Alexander, Jr.

family has a coat of arms, it can be blind embossed at the top center of the invitation.

Unfolded invitations are less formal than the folded ones but equally correct to use.

THE STATIONER

At least three months before your wedding, you'll want to talk to a stationer, one who has been recommended by a friend or other reliable source, about the invitation. He'll be invaluable in helping you decide on a style and will be able to show you a variety of paper samples, either plain or with a blind embossed panel, and in different weights. He'll also be able to advise you on the color of the paper, the type of lettering, the wording of the text, and how to set it up. When placing your order, ask for a dozen or so extra invitations and envelopes in case you add names to your list before the invitations go out. Envelopes should be sent to you before the invitations so you can get a head start on the addressing. Order extra envelopes to take care of any addressing errors. Once you have decided on the invitation, be sure the stationer sends you a proof for your approval.

SOME WEDDING INVITATION TIPS

Before seeing your stationer, it will help to know the following:

- The traditional wedding invitation is issued in the third person and follows a prescribed wording.

- If the bride's parents or other relative/s of the bride issue a formal invitation, traditionally no title—"Doctor" for instance—is used in front of the bride's name. It's different when the invitation is issued by friends of the bride or the bride and groom send out their own invitation. Then the bride has the option of calling herself Miss or Ms. or Doctor (most correctly spelled out in a formal invitation). If the bride has a doctorate in a field other than medicine or dentistry, and uses her title professionally, she may choose to use it socially as well. However, it is somewhat pretentious for people who are not medical doctors or dentists to use "Doctor" on wedding invitations or announcements.

- If the bride's mother or father, or whoever is issuing the invitation, has a title, it is used in the invitation. For instance, "Justice and Mrs. Bernard Graham Walinsky" or "Senator and Mrs. Cyrus Kingsley." When it's the mother who has a professional title and she uses her maiden name both professionally and socially, she and her husband are correctly addressed as "The Reverend Jane Bogden and Mr. Francis Brinkman" (her name comes first because of her title). While it's acceptable for the names to appear on the invitation this way it looks awkward. How much better on this occasion to use "Mr. and Mrs. Francis Brinkman," a form of address more in keeping with the use of titles on a traditional wedding invitation.

- "The pleasure of your company" replaces "the honour of your presence" when the ceremony is held at home or at a club or hotel.

- When it's a Catholic wedding, it's optional to include the information that it's a nuptial Mass. Some guests may like to know this, however, because it gives them a better idea of how long the service will be.

- Most formally, the date is written out on a wedding invitation, "on Saturday, the eleventh of June." Less formal but equally correct is "on Saturday, June eleventh." Sometimes the "on" is omitted, but simplification of the form reduces its dignity.

- While the year does not usually appear on a wedding invitation, it is always on a wedding announcement and is written out in full. Either "One thousand nine hundred and ninety-five" is correct or "Nineteen hundred and ninety-five."

- The wording for a noon wedding is "at twelve noon," or "at twelve o'clock."

- If the wedding is on the half hour, the invitation reads, "at half after four o'clock," not "at half past four o'clock."

- When a reception following an afternoon wedding includes dinner, it should be stated on the invitation ("reception and dinner immediately following the ceremony"). If it is not spelled out, guests may make other dinner plans and the bride will end up with half the number of people expected.

- When the town or city where the wedding is to take place will be obvious to the invitees, it's not necessary to include it in the body of the invitation; for example, "The Harbor Inn, 32 Main Street."

- A house or apartment number is written out through the number ten on the invitation; all street numbers are written out.

- If the name of the state appears on the invitation, it is written out in full.

- The ZIP code does not appear after the name of the state in the body of the invitation. It does, of course, appear with the address below the R.s.v.p.

- Instead of the usual "R.s.v.p." or "R.S.V.P. [*Répondez s'il vous plaît*]," a more formal version is "The favour of a reply is requested" (the word "favour" is always spelled with a *u*).

- The R.s.v.p. is to an address, never to a telephone number.

- While it's not necessary to put the address under the R.s.v.p. if it is on the back flap of the envelope, it's practical to do so because many people throw the envelope away before answering the invitation.

- If a reply card is enclosed with the invitation, R.s.v.p. does not appear on the invitation.

- If the wedding will be black tie, "Black tie" is engraved on the lower right-hand corner of the invitation. (Note that black tie is never worn before 6 P.M.)

- When a wedding is held outdoors there's always a chance of rain, so alternate plans should appear on the lower right-hand corner of the invitation:

In case of rain
the wedding will be held
at St. James Church
Four Main Street
Sante Fe

- Wedding presents are sent to the address to which you R.s.v.p. If the bride would rather they were sent elsewhere she's out of luck as there's no way to indicate this on the invitation.

THE ENVELOPE

Once almost every bride used the traditional two-envelope wedding invitation. The addressing of the envelopes was done by a social secretary or a calligrapher was hired. Even if the envelopes were addressed by the bride and her mother, in the days when few women had jobs they had plenty of time for the added chore of writing guests' names on the inner envelope and stuffing it into the outer one. Today, it's up to the bride to decide whether she wants to simplify her life by using only one envelope. If there will be a number of enclosures, such as maps, included with the invitation, an inner envelope may add to the postage cost, a consideration the bride may want to take into account. When there are two envelopes, the inner one is not gummed and is left open.

RETURN ADDRESS Traditionally, the return address is blind embossed on the back flap of the envelope. Often people don't notice the blind embossed address when they open an invitation, and for that reason you may prefer to use black ink. The post office prefers that the return address appear on the upper left-hand corner of the envelope rather than the back flap because this makes it more convenient for them to return misaddressed envelopes. Once more, it's up to the bride to decide whether to follow tradition or go for practicality. The latter ups the odds for a misaddressed envelope to be returned to her.

ADDRESSING ENVELOPES There is nothing so harmful to the look of a beautiful invitation as an envelope addressed in sloppy handwriting. Good penmanship means you care—that the overall look of the invitation is important to you. If your handwriting is only mediocre, find someone with handsome writing to do the addressing, perhaps a sister or a friend. If no one comes to mind, a party coordinator can always find you someone to hire. Tell whoever does the addressing to use black ink and a proper pen, not a smudgy ballpoint. Should it occur to you to address the envelopes on a typewriter, think again—it's just not done.

Traditionally, full names were written out on the envelope of a wedding invitation. However, this is no longer a hard and fast rule. People who use the middle initial only may certainly be addressed that way.

Abbreviations are not used except in the case of "Mr.," "Mrs.," "Dr." (or "Lt." combined with "Colonel," etc.).

The word "junior" is written with a small *j*. When it is abbreviated, which is more usual, the *J* is capitalized ("Jr."); II, III, IV may also be written 2nd, 3rd, 4th, although most people with suffixes prefer to use Roman numerals. (Note that there is a comma between the last name and "Jr." but no comma between the last name and Roman numerals.)

House and apartment numbers and street numbers are rarely written out anymore because the post office can sort more efficiently and accurately when it is dealing with numerals. The same is true when it comes to the state. The two-letter abbreviation is acceptable.

(For examples of the correct forms of address for envelopes, see "Addressing Envelopes," in Chapter 8.)

When you address an envelope to a friend and want to include his or her fiancé/ée or "live-in," rather than writing "and guest" on the invitation, it's politer to find out the name of the other person and send a separate invitation. Or you can make your point known by including a note with the invitation you send your friend. When "and guest" is used, it appears on the inner envelope if there are two envelopes, otherwise on the outer envelope.

Addressing envelopes to children: The names of children through age twelve appear on the envelope beneath their parents' name (avoid using "and family").

> Mr. and Mrs. George Bullock
> Amy Bullock [or Miss Amy Bullock]
> Alexander Bullock

It's customary to address a wedding invitation to a girl thirteen and over as "Miss" (when she becomes twenty-one you have the option of addressing her as "Miss" or "Ms."). However, it's not improper to include "Miss" at an earlier age if you choose to. A boy acquires the title of "Mr." when he reaches eighteen, although it's not improper to use "Mr." if he is slightly younger.

INNER ENVELOPE On an inside envelope, write "Mr. and Mrs. Bullock"—no given name or address. As with the outer envelope, children are listed under their parents' name: "Amy Bullock" or "Miss Amy Bullock"; "Alexander Bullock."

(For the uses of "Messrs." and "Misses," see "Addressing Envelopes" in Chapter 8.)

ENCLOSURES

While it was once customary to send maps and information on hotel accommodations and transportation as a separate mailing to invitees who had indicated they would attend the wedding, today these extras are almost always enclosed with the invitation. It's a lot more practical to have just one mailing; it saves time and eliminates the cost of additional envelopes and postage. What's more, if out-of-towners are given information on hotels and transportation when they receive their invitation, it may influence their decision to attend the wedding.

THE CEREMONY CARD When the majority of people are being invited just to the reception, a smaller card on the same stock as the reception invitation is included in the envelope for those being invited to the ceremony as well. (If very few people are being invited to the ceremony a card is not necessary. Handwritten notes may be sent.)

THE CHURCH CARD If the wedding is to be held in a large church or cathedral which might ordinarily be filled with sightseers, it is sometimes necessary to close the church to the public for the duration of the ceremony. If this is the situation, church cards on the same stock as the invitation are sent to wedding invitees. Only bearers of the cards are admitted. Such cards read:

> Please present this card
> at St. Patrick's Cathedral
> Saturday, the fourth of August

THE "AT HOME" CARD "At Home" cards are often included in wedding announcements, less often in wedding invitations. Traditionally, the couple's name does not appear on a card accompanying the wedding invitation because the bride will not have taken her new name. If an "at Home" card is being included with a wedding announcement, and the bride is keeping her name, both names appear on the card. Actually, this is a good way for the bride to make clear that she's planning to keep her name after she's married.

When name is not used:

> at Home [or this may be omitted]
> after the fifteenth of August
> [Capital "A" for "After" if first line is omitted]
> 42 Anderson Avenue
> Charlottesville, Virginia [ZIP code]
>
> Telephone number [optional]

When name/names are used:

> Mr. and Mrs. David Alexander, Jr.
> [or]
> Gail Cramer and David Alexander, Jr.
> will be [optional] at Home
> after the fifteenth of August
> 42 Anderson Avenue
> Charlottesville, Virginia [ZIP code]
>
> Telephone number [optional]

THE REPLY CARD Reply cards were initially devised to simplify business entertaining and for that purpose they were practical. But, reply cards have now worked their way into the world of social entertaining. They first appeared as enclosures in debutante party invitations and the excuse was that young people were no longer taught by their parents how to handwrite a formal reply to an invitation, or else they weren't taught that it is good manners to answer all invitations.

Brides today have to decide whether to go with tradition—meaning no reply card—or to include a card, thus bettering the chance of invitees answering quickly. When a reply card is included with the invitation, it should be on the same stock as the invitation and follow the same style. The envelope is hand-stamped, first class, and must conform to post office regulations, which say that an envelope smaller than 3½″ × 5″ will not be accepted in the mails.

Here are two examples of reply cards. Note that they do not ask how many people will be attending the wedding. If that question is raised, it might give invitees the impression that they are free to bring along children or houseguests.

> The favour of a reply is requested
>
> M _____
>
> will _____ attend

> M _____
>
> will _____ attend
>
> The favour of a reply is requested
> by the first of June.

A third reply card with the words "Please respond" at the top allows the invitee to write a formal acceptance or regret on the card itself. Or a short note may be written on the card instead.

THE PEW CARD The purpose of pew cards is to notify special guests that they will be seated in reserved sections of the church. While it's not incorrect to enclose pew cards with the wedding invitation, it's more usual for the mothers of the bride and groom to call or send notes to those who are being specially seated, after their acceptances have been received. By waiting until the responses are in, everyone will have a better idea of how many pews to reserve and who should sit where. When pew cards are sent with the invitation, the paper stock and engraving should match that of the invitation. A pew card generally says, "You will be seated in pew number _____."

TRANSPORTATION AND ACCOMMODATION INFORMATION When there are many out-of-towners on the wedding list, it makes sense to include information on hotels and transportation with the invitation. The paper stock used should be of a high quality that complements the invitation.

MAP If the wedding will be a country or suburban one, it may be necessary to include a map showing how to get to the church or the reception. That way you won't be bothered by guests calling for directions. As with other enclosures of this nature, the map must be reproduced on quality paper.

INSERTING INVITATION IN ENVELOPE When there are two envelopes, the invitation is inserted into the inner envelope folded edge first with the writing facing the back flap of the envelope; that way, the writing will be face up when the recipient removes it from the envelope. Enclosures like maps and hotel information are inserted in front of the invitation in order of size (larger ones first). Just like the invitation, the lettering faces the back flap of the envelope. The one exception to this rule is the envelope of the reply card. It is inserted so the return address is face down, with the reply card face up, under its flap. The inner envelope is inserted so the names on the front face the back flap of the outer envelope; that way the names face the recipient when the inner envelope is removed. If there's only one envelope, the insertions are placed in it exactly as they are in the inner envelope. (See illustration on following page.)

MAILING INVITATIONS AND ANNOUNCEMENTS

Invitations are mailed out four to six weeks before the wedding to allow relatives and friends ample time to save the date. Announcements are not sent out until after the wedding, preferably the day after.

Envelopes are hand-stamped with first-class postage. Stamps must be affixed carefully, not stuck on haphazardly. If enclosures such as a ceremony card, an "at Home" card, or a map are to be included with the

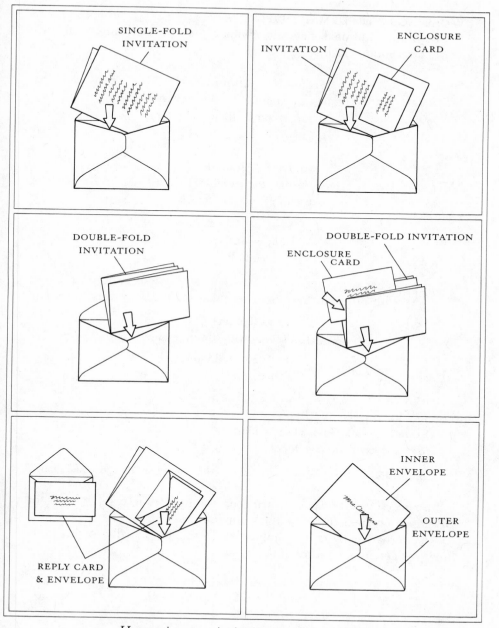

How to insert an invitation into its envelope.

invitation, be sure to stuff and weigh a sample envelope so you will know what the correct postage should be.

WORDINGS FOR FORMAL INVITATIONS

The most traditional wedding invitation is to the ceremony and includes a reception card.

Mr. and Mrs. Arthur Cramer
request the honour of your presence
at the marriage of their daughter
Gail Lee
to
Mr. David Alexander, Jr.
on Saturday, the eleventh of June
at half after four o'clock

St. James Church
Four Main Street
Santa Fe

RECEPTION CARD

Reception[a]
immediately following the ceremony

The Westerly Hotel
1112 Costa Mesa Terrace

R.s.v.p.
40 Alta Mira Drive
Santa Fe, New Mexico [ZIP code]
[or reply card and envelope]

[a] If guests are expected to stay for dinner, then the wording is "Reception and dinner."

Instead of the R.s.v.p. appearing on the invitation, a reply card and envelope may be included with the invitation.

An alternative invitation, slightly less formal but equally correct, combines the ceremony and reception.

Mr. and Mrs. Arthur Cramer
request the honour of your presence
at the marriage of their daughter
Gail Lee
to
Mr. David Alexander, Jr.
on Saturday, the eleventh of June
at half after four o'clock

St. James Church
Four Main Street
Santa Fe

and afterward at the reception
The Westerly Hotel
1112 Costa Mesa Terrace

R.s.v.p.
40 Alta Mira Drive
Santa Fe, New Mexico [ZIP code]
[or reply card and envelope]

When everyone is invited to the reception but only family and intimate friends to the ceremony, the invitation is to the reception with an enclosed card for those invited to the ceremony as well (if it will be a very small ceremony, handwritten notes are appropriate). Note that "the pleasure of your company" is used here since it's a social occasion.

INVITATION TO RECEPTION

Mr. and Mrs. Arthur Cramer
request the pleasure of your company
at the wedding reception of their daughter
Gail Lee
and
Mr. David Alexander, Jr.
on Saturday, the eleventh of June
at half after four o'clock
The Westerly Hotel
1112 Costa Mesa Terrace
Santa Fe

R.s.v.p.
40 Alta Mira Drive
Santa Fe, New Mexico [ZIP code]
[or reply card and envelope]

INVITATION TO CEREMONY It is not necessary to repeat "Santa Fe" because it is on the invitation to the reception. It is also unnecessary to include an R.s.v.p. because it appears on the reception invitation.

Mr. and Mrs. Arthur Cramer
request the honour of your presence
at the marriage of their daughter
Gail Lee
to
Mr. David Alexander, Jr.
on Saturday, the eleventh of June
at half after four o'clock
St. James Church
Four Main Street

Here is an example of an invitation to a house wedding (note that "the pleasure of your company" replaces "the honour of your presence" when the ceremony is held at home or at a club or hotel). No mention of the reception is made, as it is assumed that guests will stay on for the reception. If the ceremony is being held out of doors, alternate arrangements, in case of rain, should be engraved on the lower right-hand corner of the invitation.

Mr. and Mrs. Arthur Cramer
request the pleasure of your company
at the marriage of their daughter
Gail Lee
to
Mr. David Alexander, Jr.
on Saturday, the eleventh of June
at half after four o'clock
40 Alta Mira Drive

R.s.v.p.   In case of rain
40 Alta Mira Drive   the wedding will be held
Santa Fe, New Mexico [ZIP code]   at St. James Church
[or reply card and envelope]   Four Main Street
                                                         Santa Fe

[or reply card and envelope]

When the wedding takes place at a club or hotel, the reply is sent to the bride's mother and father at home.

Mr. and Mrs. Arthur Cramer
request the pleasure of your company
at the marriage of their daughter
Gail Lee
to
Mr. David Alexander, Jr.
on Saturday, the eleventh of June
at half after four o'clock
The University Club
350 Cyprus Drive
Santa Fe

[or reply card and envelope]

R.s.v.p.
40 Alta Mira Drive
Santa Fe, New Mexico [ZIP code]
[or reply card and envelope]

When the wedding is held at the house of a friend, the bride's parents still issue the invitation:

Mr. and Mrs. Arthur Cramer
request the pleasure of your company
at the marriage of their daughter
Gail Lee
to
Mr. David Alexander, Jr.
on Saturday, the eleventh of June
at half after four o'clock
at the residence of Mr. and Mrs. John Percival
56 Garde Street
Santa Fe

R.s.v.p.
40 Alta Mira Drive
Santa Fe, New Mexico [ZIP code]
[or reply card and envelope]

Occasionally, the couple have been married in a town or city other than where the bride's parents live, and the reception is taking place at a later date. Either fill-in or engraved invitations may be sent out, depending on how formal an occasion it is. Here is an example of a formal invitation.

In honour of
Mr. and Mrs. David Alexander, Jr.

Mr. and Mrs. Arthur Cramer
request the pleasure of your company
[at dinner, cocktails, etc., optional]
on Saturday, the eleventh of June
at seven o'clock
40 Alta Mira Drive

R.s.v.p.
40 Alta Mira Drive
Santa Fe, New Mexico [ZIP code]
[or reply card and envelope]

When sisters are being married in a double wedding, the elder sister is mentioned first and the invitation reads:

Mr. and Mrs. Arthur Cramer
request the honour of your presence
at the marriage of their daughters
Gail Lee
to
Mr. David Alexander, Jr.
and
Patricia Lind
to
Mr. Leonard Whitney
[etc.]

In a double wedding of cousins or friends, the elder bride may be mentioned first or the order may be alphabetical. However, if one bride's invitation is being issued by her grandparents, the older sponsors take precedence.

Mr. and Mrs. Nicholas Kraft
request the honour of your presence
at the marriage of their granddaughter
Theresa Kraft
to
Mr. John Guggenheimer
Mr. and Mrs. Arthur Cramer
request the honour of your presence
at the marriage of their daughter
Gail Lee Cramer
to
Mr. David Alexander, Jr.
[etc.]

SPECIAL SITUATIONS AND THE ISSUING OF INVITATIONS

The bride's parents being legally separated, the invitation is issued in the following way:

> Mrs. Arthur Cramer
> Mr. Arthur Cramer
> request the honour of your presence
> at the marriage of their daughter
> [etc.]

When the bride's mother and stepfather issue the invitation, the bride's last name is included in the text of the invitation because it is not the same as her mother's. If the bride has been brought up by her stepfather (her father may be dead or she's had little contact with him), the invitation below may read "at the marriage of their daughter" instead of "Mrs. Behr's daughter."

> Mr. and Mrs. Joseph Behr
> request the honour of your presence
> at the marriage of Mrs. Behr's daughter
> Gail Lee Cramer
> [etc.]

When the bride's father has remarried and he is issuing the invitation, the bride's stepmother is included:

> Mr. and Mrs. Arthur Cramer
> request the honour of your presence
> at the marriage of Mr. Cramer's daughter
> Gail Lee
> [etc.]

In the following examples the bride's mother and father are divorced and only her father has remarried. Her mother and father are issuing the invitation to the ceremony and her father and stepmother are giving the reception so the stepmother's name is included on the invitation to the reception.

INVITATION TO CEREMONY

> Mrs. Joan Cramer
> Mr. Arthur Cramer
> request the honour of your presence
> at the marriage of their daughter
> Gail Lee
> [etc.]

INVITATION TO RECEPTION

Mr. and Mrs. Arthur Cramer
request the pleasure of your company
at the wedding reception of Mr. Cramer's daughter
Gail Lee
[etc.]

When the bride's mother and father are divorced and both have remarried, a joint invitation should include the bride's last name for clarity.

Mr. and Mrs. Joseph Behr
Mr. and Mrs. Arthur Cramer
request the honour of your presence
at the marriage of
Gail Lee Cramer
[etc.]

If the bride's mother is a widow (the same form applies for a widower), the invitation reads:

Mrs. Arthur Cramer
requests the honour of your presence
at the marriage of her daughter
Gail Lee
[etc.]

Only if the wedding is being given by a close relative is the relationship shown on the invitation. The bride's last name is included here again for clarity.

Commander and Mrs. Charles Simonson
request the honour of your presence
at the marriage of their granddaughter
Gail Lee Cramer
[etc.]

This is an invitation issued jointly by the bride's and groom's parents. In the first invitation the bride's last name is given, for clarity.

Mr. and Mrs. Arthur Cramer
Mr. and Mrs. David Alexander
request the honour of your presence
at the marriage of
Gail Lee Cramer
to
Mr. David Alexander, Jr.
[etc.]

or

Mr. and Mrs. Arthur Cramer
request the honour of your presence
at the marriage of their daughter
Gail Lee
to
Mr. David Alexander, Jr.
son of
Mr. and Mrs. David Alexander
[etc.]

It is most unusual for the groom's family to issue the invitation, but if the bride has no living adult relatives the groom's family may give the wedding. On such invitations a title is used before the bride's name. Responses should be sent to the Alexanders at their home address, which should be listed below the R.s.v.p. on the invitation.

Mr. and Mrs. David Alexander
request the honour of your presence
at the marriage of
Miss Gail Lee Cramer
to their son
Mr. David Alexander, Jr.
[etc.]

When the bride and groom issue their own invitation, titles may or may not precede their names, titles being the more formal usage. Here's an example of a modern style invitation:

[Miss] Gail Lee Cramer
and
[Mr.] David Alexander, Jr.
request the honour of your presence
at their marriage
[etc.]

or more traditionally

The honour of your presence
is requested at the marriage of
Miss Gail Lee Cramer
and
Mr. David Alexander, Jr.
[etc.]

THE SELF-DESIGNED INVITATION If you have a creative flair and like the idea of designing your own invitation, or perhaps have an artist friend and can put his talents to use, a self-designed invitation can be charming as long as it's done well and in good taste. A nontraditional invitation does not necessarily mean an informal wedding. It may just mean it's worded differently but still engraved on good paper stock, perhaps in an unusual color ink, or it may include some color artwork. What distinguishes a self-designed invitation from a conventional one is the personal touch it brings to the act of inviting.

This is an example of the wording of an invitation less formal than the traditional wedding invitation.

> Louise and Arthur Cramer
> have wonderful news.
> Their daughter Gail Lee
> will marry
> David Alexander
> on Saturday, June 11th
> at four-thirty
>
> Please join us
> at St. James Church, 4 Main Street, Santa Fe
> and afterwards at the reception
>
> The Westerly Hotel
> 1112 Costa Mesa Terrace

R.s.v.p.
40 Alta Mira Drive
Santa Fe, New Mexico (ZIP code)
[or reply card and envelope]

The reply to a less traditional invitation such as this would be either a formal acceptance or regret or a personal note, whichever seems most appropriate.

MILITARY INVITATIONS

Noncommissioned officers and enlisted men often prefer to use their names with the branch of service immediately below (if the bride is in the military, no title, as in civilian invitations, is used before her name).

> Mr. and Mrs. Grant Kingsley
> request the honour of your presence
> at the marriage of their daughter
> Nora
> to
> Andrew Cass Bowers [note, not "Mr."]
> United States Marine Corps
>
> or
>
> Andrew Cass Bowers
> Staff Sergeant, United States Marine Corps

In the case of a regular officer in the U. S. Armed Forces, only where the officer's rank is captain or above in the Army, Air Force, or Marines (or commander or above in the Navy, Merchant Marine, or Coast Guard) does the title appear first:

Captain [or Capt.] Andrew Cass Bowers
United States Navy

The rank of junior officer is placed below the name:

Andrew Cass Bowers
Lieutenant, United States Army

Officers in the Reserves use their ranks on wedding invitations only when they are on active duty. Otherwise, they are "Mr."

FOREIGN WEDDING INVITATIONS

It would be quite impossible here to go into full details of the national wedding customs of every country. However, in many foreign countries one invitation is printed with the bride's family issuing their invitation on the left-hand side and the groom's family issuing theirs on the right. If, for example, the bride is French, her invitation is in French and if the groom is American, his is in English. Each family sends out invitations to their own list.

INVITING BY LETTER

If the wedding will be a small one of not more than fifty people, many of whom are couples, the mother of the bride may want to invite people by writing them notes on her personal stationery. Such a note might read:

Dear Clarisse,

Gail and David are being married on Saturday, June 11th at 4:30 P.M. at St. James Church (4 Main Street) in Santa Fe. Following the ceremony, there'll be a reception at The Westerly Hotel, 1112 Costa Mesa Terrace.

Mr. Cramer [or Arthur to a contemporary] and I hope you will be able to be with us that day, and of course it would mean a great deal to Gail and David to have you there. You can call me at (505) 000-0000 to let me know your answer, which we all hope will be yes.

Sincerely,
Louise Cramer

INVITATIONS FOR SECOND MARRIAGES

When a young widow or divorcee remarries it is usually at a private ceremony attended by a few family members and intimate friends, invited by personal note or telephone. The invitation to the reception may be issued by the bride's mother and father or by the couple. When the bride's parents issue the invitation, their daughter's title appears on the invitation (in the case of a widow, she continues to use her husband's full name); when the couple issue their own invitation, titles may or may not be used.

PARENTS ISSUE INVITATION

Doctor and Mrs. Scott Blankharn
request the pleasure of your company
at the wedding reception of their daughter
Mrs. Mary Blankharn Franklyn
to
Mr. Richard Carpenter
[etc.]

COUPLE ISSUE INVITATION

[Mrs.] Mary Blankharn Franklyn
and
[Mr.] Richard Carpenter
request the pleasure of your company
at their wedding reception
[etc.]

ACCEPTING A FORMAL WEDDING INVITATION

When you accept a formal wedding invitation, write it in the third person. Use blue or black ink on your personal letter sheet or half sheet, or on plain, conservative notepaper. You reply to the address below the R.s.v.p. on the invitation. When answering an invitation from a couple whose name is followed by "Jr.," "II," or "III," if you omit the hosts' given name, you also omit the suffix. In your acceptance, you repeat the hour designated for the reception.

Dr. and Mrs. Bernard Rosenberg[a]
accept with pleasure
the kind invitation of
Mr. and Mrs. Arthur Cramer
for Saturday, the eleventh of June
at half after four o'clock

or

Dr. and Mrs. Bernard Rosenberg
accept with pleasure
Mr. and Mrs. Cramer's
kind invitation for
Saturday, the eleventh of June
at half after four o'clock

[a] *Italic* type indicates handwriting.

When a husband and wife receive an invitation and only one can attend, the acceptance comes first and the regret follows:

Mrs. Bernard Rosenberg
accepts with pleasure
the kind invitation of
Mr. and Mrs. Arthur Cramer
for Saturday, the eleventh of June
at half after four o'clock
Dr. Bernard Rosenberg
regrets that he will be unable to accept
owing to absence from town[a]

[a] While this line is optional, it is a polite gesture.

REGRETTING A FORMAL WEDDING INVITATION

In regretting as in accepting a formal invitation, there's a standard protocol to follow. A formal regret usually states briefly the reason for the refusal—"because of their [her] absence from town," "owing to a previous engagement." Avoid giving illness as a reason since the host and hostess will feel obliged to respond in some way. If you are a very close friend of the hostess, it's no breach of etiquette to call or write her a note explaining why you cannot be there. In fact, it's exactly what you should do.

When you send your regrets to an invitation, give the date; it's not necessary to repeat the time.

Dr. and Mrs. Bernard Rosenberg
regret that they are unable to accept
the kind invitation of
Mr. and Mrs. Arthur Cramer
for Saturday, the eleventh of June

or

Dr. and Mrs. Bernard Rosenberg
regret exceedingly
that owing to a previous engagement
they are unable to accept
Mr. and Mrs. Cramer's
kind invitation for
Saturday, the eleventh of June

or

Dr. and Mrs. Bernard Rosenberg
regret that
owing to absence from the city
they are unable to accept
the kind invitation of
Mr. and Mrs. Arthur Cramer
for Saturday, the eleventh of June

BRIDAL REGISTRY

Two terms long associated with weddings are almost never heard anymore; one is "trousseau" and the other is "hope chest." In most instances, a girl started to plan her trousseau when she was fairly young, perhaps in her early teens. It was very carefully thought out, down to the last hat or bonnet. And the "hope chest" was literally a chest or antique trunk in which trousseau items were stored in anticipation of a future proposal and subsequent marriage. Fashions are continually changing, so we tend to buy what we need when we need it. When clothes become worn or go out of style, we discard them and buy new ones. In the past, a trousseau made perfectly good sense because a bride's wardrobe was designed to last for a long time, often beyond her life. Embroidered sheets, towels, and tablecloths were saved and passed down from one generation to another.

Today's bride-to-be in all probability has been living on her own or with her fiancé. What they together will bring to the marriage, in a material sense, are the household possessions they've acquired over the years. In order to supplement what they already have, they sign up with the bridal registry department at one or more stores that cater to their particular needs. Table settings are nearly always on most couples' lists for wedding presents; in fact brides account for almost half the silver, china, and crystal sold in this country every year.

While the concept of a bride-to-be suggesting wedding presents is a relatively new one, it's a practical and efficient innovation for both the couple who are planning to get married and their guests. For the couple, it reduces the likelihood of receiving eight crystal vases or five spice racks. For their friends, it solves the dilemma of what to give that the couple might need or will be in keeping with their tastes.

The best time to register for wedding presents is before the wedding invitations have been sent out. Where to register is a matter of preference and will depend in great part on your needs. As there is no charge for the service the store provides, you may want to register at two stores, one for silver, china, and crystal and the other for household items of a more functional nature. If you live in one city but will be married elsewhere, it may make sense to register at stores in both places. Even though a store may not have an official bridal registry, chances are it will be delighted to set one up for you, for the added business it will bring.

Most large department stores already have bridal registry departments. As the bride-to-be, in most cases accompanied by your fiancé, you meet with the store's bridal registry consultant to compile a list of suggested wedding presents. A knowledgeable consultant is invaluable when it comes to choosing flatware, china, and crystal (now is the time to discuss the lead content in any china or crystal you are considering). He or she can help you decide what patterns and textures will best suit your tastes and life style; how to coordinate silver, china, and crystal; how many and which pieces of each you need to start with, and how long it will take to fill an order, if the item is not part of the store's regular stock. This last point is quite important, as merchandise that's specially ordered from another country can take as long as a year for delivery. If you want your wedding presents sent to other than the address on the R.s.v.p. of the invitation, be sure the consultant notes this.

After your initial meeting with the consultant, you and your fiancé are free to wander around the store familiarizing yourselves with the merchandise, picking out what you'd like. What you choose should range widely in price so that family and friends will be able to select a present for the amount of money they want to spend. Anything you'd like to have monogrammed, whether it's flat silver, a leather picture frame, or linen cocktail napkins, should be noted accordingly on the list beside the specific item. It will be necessary to make a list of the number of pieces of silver, china, and crystal that are needed. Most stores have their bridal registries on computer, so it's easy to keep count of any pieces still outstanding.

Since it's scarcely good manners to take for granted that a wedding guest will send you a present, you should wait to be asked what you'd like before mentioning where you're registered. To get the word around, you can tell your family and close friends where you're signed up so that they'll have this information on hand if asked by others. You shouldn't assume, however, that every guest will give you a wedding present from a store where you're registered. Many people would rather give a present they have chosen themselves, either because they have a specific idea for you or just because they think it's more fun to give something with an element of surprise to it.

In general, a woman who is divorced or widowed and then remarries does not sign up for a bridal registry at a store. By the time her second marriage comes around, she probably does not need the same wide variety of household necessities. Also, it's unlikely that she will want friends who gave her a first wedding present to feel they have to give her a second one. If friends ask what she'd like for a present, she may suggest that several of them band together to give her something special that she needs or wants, such as a new set of demitasse cups and saucers or a croquet set. The woman most likely to use a bridal registry for a second marriage is one who had a very small first wedding or eloped.

CHOOSING YOUR FLATWARE

Silver has been associated with weddings since the time of ancient Greece. The finest silver is sterling. For the sake of durability, sterling silver consists of 925 parts pure silver and 75 parts copper. You can readily identify sterling as it has a stamp on it with the logo and name or initials of the maker. The word "sterling" also appears on the piece itself.

People often confuse the word "flatware" with "silverware." "Flatware" is applied to any set of forks, spoons, and knives, regardless of what they're made of. "Silverware" means sterling silver or silverplated flatware only. What's confusing is that in conversation we often say "Will you put the silver [or silverware] on the table?" whether it's sterling or not.

If you're lucky, your family may provide you with sterling silver flatware that's been passed down from one generation to the next. Or it may be that your fiancé's parents will present you with silver flatware that's been in their family. Sometimes lost pieces are replaced with ones in a slightly different pattern, which doesn't matter so long as the pieces are sufficiently similar to make a set table appear uniform. As for serving pieces, many people choose ones that harmonize with the place settings rather than having them match.

Silver styles change very little. Heavy embossed or repoussé silver takes a little more time to clean than simpler, more modern patterns, although the plainer patterns may show scratch marks in time. You often hear people say that keeping silver clean is a lot of trouble. This was true years ago, but today there are many effective silver-cleaning products on the market that are fast and easy to apply. And you should store your silver in a drawer lined with a specially treated tarnish-preventing cloth and cover it with more of the same cloth.

Your silver pattern is strictly a matter of preference. When deciding, though, keep the rest of your place setting in mind so the silver, china, and crystal will look well together. Of course, if you've inherited elaborate sterling silver flatware there's nothing that says you have to have gold-rimmed china to go with it. As long as the china and crystal are compatible in texture to the silverware, your table setting will appear coordinated. If it's out of the question to have even a starter set of sterling silver, there is plenty of good-looking stainless steel flatware on the market.

But a word of warning for every bride-to-be who turns down an offer of sterling silver because she feels household furnishings are more important: *if you don't get your sterling flatware now, you may never get it.* Once you have a child or two, their constant needs too often absorb funds you thought would be available for something as basic as sterling flatware. So you make do over the years with inexpensive cutlery that continually wears out and needs replacement. Never again in your lifetime will your family and friends be in such a giving and sentimental mood as they are at the time of your wedding. Even if you start married life with only the barest of household essentials, if you have sterling place settings for four people, you can add to these pieces as you and your fiancé become more financially secure.

MONOGRAMMING SILVER Monogramming, while expensive, adds distinction to any sterling flatware. Your bridal registry consultant or whomever you are buying your silver from can show you different monogramming designs that will go well with your flatware pattern. You'll find that ornate initialing has given way to simpler markings. If at all possible, have all your silver engraved at the same time to prevent any variation in the look of the engraving.

In hope chest days a girl began collecting her silver piece by piece long before she had a suitor. It was monogrammed with her initials or the single letter of her last name—or with her family's crest—and it remained her personal property. After she was married, any silver she received was marked with the initials of her first name, maiden name, and her husband's last name, or just the initial of her husband's last name or his crest. This meant variously marked silver was used on the same table. While this can still be the case if a woman has inherited family silver, most brides-to-be, given a choice, would rather have all their silver monogrammed the same way.

What initials you choose to have engraved on your silver is entirely a matter of personal preference. Say you are Gail Cramer marrying David Alexander. You may want only one initial—that of your fiancé's last name (*A*). Or you may want three initials; those of your first and last names, and your fiancé's last name (*GCA*). Another choice would be to use the initials of your first names in combination with your fiancé's last name (*GAD*).

If you plan to keep your maiden name after you're married, you have a number of choices. You may use the initial of your last name only on the silver (*C*) or the initial of your fiancé's last name (*A*). Or you may want both your initials on the silver in the style below. There's basically no right or wrong way to initial silver; any combination of initials is correct.

CHOOSING YOUR CHINA

Some couples have a complete set of everyday china by the time they get married. If they don't, they can also sign up for a less formal, less expensive pattern for their daily use when they register for their fine china. Here again, the bridal registry consultant can be very useful. If you've never studied or read up on china, it can be mind-boggling suddenly to have to choose among earthenware, stoneware, porcelain, and bone china. A consultant, on the other hand, will be able to guide you in many ways once he knows your life style, your surroundings, your taste in textures and patterns, and what type of flatware or crystal you already have to work with. He'll tell you which china patterns are in open stock so you can replace a cup or plate that gets broken; which materials are microwave- or regular ovenproof, and which will resist the detergents used in the dishwashing process. For instance, plates decorated with gold are not meant to be put in the dishwasher as the gold will eventually wear off.

People mix their china table-setting patterns all the time, which is fine as long as the colors blend. For example, your salad plates may contrast in style and color to your lunch or dinner plates, or your dessert plates may differ from but complement your demitasse cups and saucers. While you can always use the same pattern plates for dessert as you used for the first course, if you can afford to, you may want to have two sets of plates in the same pattern, one with a plain center to be used for the first course and the other with a design in the center to be used for dessert. For reasons of style, all plates for the same use (i.e., all dessert plates) are identical and the textures of plates for different courses should be coordinated. In other words, don't set a table combining earthenware with fine bone china.

You can get by nicely with five-piece china place settings, which include a dinner plate, bread and butter plate, dessert plate (which can also be used as a salad plate), and a cup and saucer. Eventually, you'll want to add to these basic requirements with soup plates, demitasse cups and saucers, and whatever else you need. The place plate, also known as a charger, has become increasingly popular. Larger than a dinner plate, the place plate was originally set on a table when the guests arrived and the first course was placed on it. Now it is more frequently used as a buffet plate.

CHOOSING YOUR GLASSWARE

Only you can decide how many different styles of glassware you need for everyday use. The minimum is two types: double old-fashioned glasses that can be used for juices and cocktails and highball glasses for water, soft drinks, iced tea or coffee, and mixed drinks. It's always best to have more glasses on hand than you think you'll need in case the odd glass slips off the table and breaks. If you don't already own many everyday glasses, you may want to register for these as well as the stemmed glasses you'll want for formal entertaining.

It's easier to choose your crystal stemware after you've decided on your china and glassware; the style should be in keeping with the rest of the table setting. While the different types of glasses on a formal dinner table need not match, the glasses for the same use should be identical.

You'll want to start off your stemware collection with water goblets, white wine glasses, and red wine glasses. For less formal entertaining, you can always use the all-purpose wineglass. Later, you can add classic flute or hollow stemmed champagne glasses, martini or margarita glasses, brandy snifters, and liqueur glasses. Crystal is particularly thin, so remember, these glasses must be washed by hand, not put in the dishwasher.

CHOOSING YOUR BED LINEN AND BATH TOWEL SETS

There's such a wide variety of sheets and pillowcases on the market today that there's a color and style for every person's taste. The same is true for bath towels, hand towels, and washcloths. If you don't know exactly what the décor of your bedroom and bathroom will be when you send out your wedding invitations, it's best not to register for bed linens and towels.

MONOGRAMMING BED LINEN AND TOWEL SETS Monogramming, which appears to be having a rebirth, accents simplicity in design and is most often stitched by machine rather than by hand. You can have your sheets and towels monogrammed with almost any combination of initials—your given, middle, and last initials, your given, last-name, and future husband's last-name initials, or your first-name initial and your future husband's first- and last-name initials. If you prefer, you can have one last-name initial only. Since a woman who keeps her maiden name after she remarries uses her own initials, today many couples have his and hers towels, each with their own initials.

BRIDE'S WEDDING PLANNER BOOK AND OTHER BRIDE'S BOOKS

To keep track of the multitudinous details that go into organizing a wedding, every engaged woman should head straight for the nearest stationery or bookstore and buy a wedding planner book. It will give advice and information on the specifics of planning a wedding from the time you become engaged until the time you leave the wedding reception. For instance, it will remind you to call your bridesmaids about having their dresses fitted; to take out a floater insurance policy on your wedding presents; help you decide what the musicians should wear, and so much more. With the wedding planner book at hand, you won't be haunted by a dread that you've forgotten some vital detail.

It's most important to keep an up-to-date list of the wedding presents you've received. Some wedding planner books include a section where you can list the wedding presents you receive and who sent them to you. If not, you can buy a book that's specially designed for this purpose, or keep a list in a ring binder for that matter. But a handsome leather book is more in keeping with the spirit of the occasion and makes a nice keepsake. Also, this list will help you keep track of whom you have written thank-you notes to.

Another book you may want to have is a leather-bound album for guests at the wedding reception to sign. Even if you have a printout of the guest list, you may want a more personal and pleasing reminder of the people who came to celebrate with you. Any attractive bound book with sufficient space for all your guests to sign in is suitable, although books designed specifically for this purpose are available.

THE WEDDING CONSULTANT

There's no reason why you can't plan the perfect wedding on your own. But if you and your mother both work, there's a real advantage to hiring a wedding consultant to handle all details of the wedding. The number of wedding consultants in this country is on the upswing, indicating that more and more people either do not have the time it takes to coordinate a well-planned wedding or are calling on consultants because of their knowlege of the wedding scene and their expertise. An experienced consultant can advise you on which florist, caterer, or orchestra will best suit your needs and your pocketbook, will know how to hold down prices, and can even serve as a mediator when there are differences between the bride and groom or other family members.

While you can find a wedding consultant through the Yellow Pages or by contacting the Association of Bridal Consultants, 200 Chestnutland Road, New Milford, CT 06776, a far more reliable and satisfactory way is through word of mouth—a friend who recently got married or a caterer who may know of a good one. Regardless of who recommends a wedding consultant to you or what the consultant's credentials may be, before making any commitment, you will want to ask yourself the following questions: "Will she reflect my style and taste, rather than her own?" "Will she try to talk me into doing things her way?" "Will she be fun to work with?" To answer these questions call the person you are considering as a consultant and make an appointment. Tell her she's been recommended to you, but before committing yourself you would like to talk with her. When the two of you meet, be explicit about what type of wedding you have in mind and approximately how much money you have to spend. Ask her how she charges for her services and what the charges include. If after your meeting you sense that you are on the same wavelength and her fee is in line with what you have in mind, you can happily sign her up. On the other hand, if instinct tells you this is not the right person for you, there's no reason to feel any sense of obligation just because you've taken up her time. When the appointment's over, all you need say is, "Thanks so much for seeing me. Before making up my mind, I'd like to look into one or two other options." You are then free to interview other consultants until you find someone compatible.

Wedding consultants have various ways of charging. While the majority charge an hourly fee or a flat fee, or some combination of both, there are some who charge a fee based on the number of guests attending or a fee based on the percentage of the cost of whatever wedding arrangements are made. A lot depends on the size of the wedding and the amount of responsibility the consultant takes on. Before signing a contract with a wedding consultant and putting down a deposit (and you must have a contract) be sure you understand exactly how you will be charged and what the estimated bill will cover. Make certain the consultant has listed all the expenses on the estimate, otherwise you may be surprised to find an added charge or two on the final bill.

THE HOTEL OR CLUB BANQUET MANAGER

A hotel or private club with a reputation for good food and service is an excellent place to hold a wedding reception. As well as providing you with food and drinks, the manager may assume other responsibilities that have to do with planning a reception. When a social event of any kind is held at a hotel, the banquet manager is in charge; at a club, the club manager himself handles, or supervises, the preparations. Some hotels and clubs have all-inclusive wedding packages which are considerably less expensive than the total per person rates would be. Before signing a contract, be sure you know exactly what the estimated cost includes and whether gratuities and taxes have been figured into the amount.

If you're planning to have your reception at a hotel or club, ask the manager to show you photographs of parties that have been held in the room you will be using. That way you can get an idea of how the space is utilized and the management's taste in colors, flowers, and other decorations. Should their taste not jibe with yours, don't hesitate to say so. If you don't like the color of the seats of the ballroom chairs or the tablecloths, perhaps you can rent others; if you feel the candelabra on the sideboard are too ornate, you may be able to bring in your own. Remember, it's *your* wedding, and therefore *your* taste should be reflected in every aspect of the reception. If you want your own florist or anything else, ask the manager if there is any reason why this can't be arranged.

Since the food is one of the more important features at any wedding reception, you'll want to pay special attention to the suggested menus that the hotel or club offers. You'll also want to discuss with the manager what wines and liquors to serve and ask to see pictures of cakes they've created before. Then you can decide whether to use their facilities or have your own baker make the cake.

Other subjects to bring up are location of the bars and orchestra, whether you need to take out any special insurance, and what you foresee the reception's agenda to be, such as when toasts will be made, when you will cut the wedding cake, etc.

If it's a seated lunch or dinner be certain there will be an adequate number of waiters and/or waitresses on hand so the service moves along at a systematic pace (for example, at a round table for ten, ideally there should be two waiters). In addition, you'll want to find out about reserving rooms where you and the groom can change into your going-away clothes and, if necessary, a room where members of the orchestra can change and relax during their breaks.

THE CATERER

If you are planning to have your wedding reception at home, or some place such as a historic house, museum, or municipal park, where food is not usually served, in all likelihood you will need the services of an experienced caterer to give you various menu suggestions and other food-related advice. In many of the larger cities, it's often necessary to book a caterer as much as a year in advance, particularly for a wedding during the height of the season. If there is no caterer in your immediate area, you may find that a local restaurant or gourmet food shop will be delighted to do the catering for you.

There are many excellent caterers who do a great deal more than supply food and drinks. Known as "full-service" caterers, they take on many of the responsibilities associated with a wedding consultant or a party coordinator. While a full-service caterer may not get involved with invitations, he can supply all the necessary rentals, find you a tent for the reception, parkers for the cars, someone to polish the dance floor, and limousines for the bridal party. At the reception, he will know when to bring out the wedding cake and when the dancing should start.

But though it may be a lot more convenient for you to have a full-service caterer take care of your reception rather than one who only supplies food, don't compromise on food for the sake of convenience. You want to choose a caterer for the food he serves. Once you know how much help the caterer can give you, in addition to providing the food, you'll know whether it will be necessary to hire a wedding consultant. It may be that you can do nicely on your own or with the help of a part-time secretary, a relative, or a good friend.

As with a wedding consultant, the best way to find a competent caterer is through word of mouth; a reliable friend or perhaps the chef at your club or at a good restaurant may be able to recommend someone to you. If you have to choose a caterer on your own, ask to sample his food before making a firm commitment, and ask for references.

If you are interested in reading more about using a caterer at home, see "Working With a Caterer" in Chapter 2.

THE FOOD

The choice of foods and the way they are prepared and presented reflect the overall style of the wedding. Some of these decisions will be dictated by the formality of the occasion, the season, the number of guests expected, and your budget. The knowledgeable caterer, hotel or banquet manager, given these facts, will be able to suggest a variety of menus in different price ranges for you to choose among, often arranging a tasting session so you can sample the chef's culinary skills. With regard to the menu, it's a lot safer to stay with the chef's suggestions than to ask her to experiment with a recipe you've heard or read about or an ethnic dish she's unfamiliar with.

There's a tendency for people to think they should go overboard in the variety and amount of food served at a wedding reception. The quality of the food is what counts, not the number of different types of hors d'oeuvres or buffet dishes. Two simple but well-prepared courses are far more satisfying than three courses of mediocre food. Naturally, however, there must be plenty for all to eat. There's something unappetizing and pretentious about large platters filled with assortments of ten or more different kinds of hors d'oeuvres. All you'll ever need for cocktail hors d'oeuvres are three cold and two hot (reverse the numbers for cold weather).

Essentially, there are three types of wedding reception: the lunch reception (the wedding breakfast is actually a lunch), the late afternoon reception, and the dinner reception.

For the seated lunch reception, the caterer or chef may suggest beginning with a cold or hot soup depending on the weather (if it's a buffet, the first course is usually omitted), followed by a second course which might be breast of capon or beef tenderloin, and then a dessert to go with the wedding cake—perhaps homemade peach ice cream or berries with a raspberry sauce. At a late afternoon reception, hot and cold hors d'oeuvres are passed and there is usually one or two buffet tables offering more substantial foods such as small quiches and cold hams and turkeys. If guests are invited to stay on for dinner, foods such as seafood Newburg, beef Stroganoff, or cold salmon with a sauce are placed on the tables along with salads and buttered breads and rolls. Later, individual plates with slices of wedding cake are brought out. For a seated dinner reception, three courses are usual today. The first course might be soup, shrimp, or pâté; the second course something on the order of cornish hen or tenderloins of beef, and lastly the wedding cake with ice cream or some other accompanying dessert.

Coffee is served or made available at any wedding reception at which a meal is involved; at a wedding lunch tea may be offered as well.

THE CAKE

The history of the wedding cake can be traced to the Romans, who made a wheat cake which was crumbled over the bride's head to assure her of fertility. Today the cake still plays a prominent role at any wedding. Guests gather around to admire it and to watch the bride cut the first piece and feed it to her groom. It's a matter of personal style and preference as to what type of wedding cake a bride chooses. Some like the idea of an ornate, heavily decorated cake prepared by an innovative baker; others prefer a simple, homemade cake baked by the bride's or groom's mother or a friend.

If your wedding is being catered, the caterer can supply the cake. Before arriving at any decision as to what kind you want, ask to see color photographs of cakes she's produced for other weddings. Also, look through magazines and books. You may find the ideal cake in a gourmet magazine and decide to have it duplicated. There are three things to keep in mind when arranging for your wedding cake: be sure the color of the icing and any decorations on the cake blend with the color scheme of the reception, and in particular the colors of your bouquet; if the wedding's outdoors, that the icing is a type that won't melt in warm weather; and that the cake will stand up well if it has to be transported any distance.

A wedding cake can have as many tiers as you want, although three or four is about average. The top tier of the cake is most often kept intact and later frozen so the bride and groom can eat it on their first wedding anniversary, either alone or with friends. The size of the cake depends on the number of people you plan to feed, although you don't want a cake that's so enormous it appears pretentious. If your wedding will be a particularly large one, you can have a good-size cake that's brought out for you to cut, and a second cake that's cut in the kitchen and served to the guests from there. Sometimes, if a bride has her heart set on a cake the design of which is so complicated that even the most talented baker would have difficulty constructing it, a "dummy" cake can be the solution. The layer the bride cuts is real, the rest is made of Styrofoam and frosted. Also it might be worth considering a "dummy" cake if it has to be transported a great distance.

The traditional wedding cake is all white, perhaps a sponge cake with a cream filling and white icing. Today, however, brides often break with tradition and have cakes with more colorful icings and decorations and that are more tempting to the palate. Carrot and chocolate hazelnut cakes and nut tortes are popular, as are mocha praline, chocolate mousse, and raspberry fillings. Fresh flowers are frequently used to adorn the top of a wedding cake or to form a wreath around its base. Or, when miniature white columns are placed between layers of the cake to give it added height, flowers can be placed within the spaces. You have to be careful in your choice of flowers, as you don't want any that secrete oils that might seep into the icing or that will wilt too quickly. Tiny, pastel-colored satin bows, randomly placed on the cake, also make attractive decorations.

Instead of the customary replicas of a prim-looking bride and groom, or bells, bedecking the wedding cake, couples are showing greater imagination and self-expression by crowning their cakes with porcelain figures and decorative accessories that mean something personal to them. For instance, if the groom is an obstetrician, the figure may be a doctor in operating clothes holding up a newborn baby; if the bride's an editor, the companion figure may be a woman holding a book. Often you see a sports- or hobby-related object on top of the cake. Whatever the couple choose will add originality to the cake and be a conversation piece for the guests.

If the baker or pastry shop doesn't carry the sort of decorative object you want to top your cake with, you can always look for something that appeals to your aesthetic sense, your sense of humor, or whatever, by browsing through local antique shops or flea markets.

There is a second kind of cake associated with weddings, the groom's cake. It is a dark fruitcake covered with boiled white icing (in the South, it's the preferred cake at the reception). Traditionally this cake was cut into small pieces and placed in white boxes lined with wax paper and tied with a white satin ribbon. The initial of the groom's surname appeared in silver on the top of the box, either alone or with the bride's first-name initial to the left and the groom's first-name initial to the right (these two initials were slightly smaller than the surname initial). Each guest as he left was given a box to take home to place under his pillow to dream on. If the guest was an unmarried woman, she was supposed to dream of the man she'd marry. Unfortunately, because of the high cost of producing these boxes, this charming custom has all but disappeared. However, groom's cakes are still served, although instead of a fruitcake they are usually a rich chocolate cake now. In the South, they are served at the reception along with the bride's cake; elsewhere, if there is a groom's cake, it's served at the rehearsal dinner or at a gathering with friends when the couple return from their honeymoon.

THE LIQUOR

What wines and liquors you serve at your reception more or less depends on your budget. Should you decide to go all out and give your guests the very best, you'll want to serve brand-name liquors and French champagne. Often, however, the very people who can afford top-of-the-line brands see no reason to go to this expense, particularly at a large gathering, when there are many excellent brands available that cost considerably less.

If you're having your reception at home, you'll want to talk to a knowledgeable wine merchant who will be able to recommend a variety of wines and liquors in different price ranges. He'll tell you what the current trend is in drinks; how much liquor and champagne you'll need (based on the number of guests expected and the number of hours the reception will last); the number of ounces to put in a drink (to help prevent guests from becoming intoxicated) and whether you may return unopened bottles for credit. Even if you're having your reception at a hotel or club, it's good to know something about wines and liquors when you talk to the manager about the drinks that will be served.

Some couples serve only punch (alcoholic or nonalcoholic) because they prefer it or because it is less expensive than mixed drinks and wines. Light on the alcohol is the password for punch, which can be lethal. Punch should be well chilled and not too sweet.

Whatever you do, don't skimp on the amount of liquor you order. It would be embarrassing to find yourself running short on such a special occasion.

Also talk to your insurance broker about necessary liability coverage for serving alcohol. You want to protect yourself against a suit by an intoxicated guest who was in an accident caused by the liquor you served. Also, it's important to remember that you can be sued for serving liquor to a minor.

For further information on wines, see "Wines" in Chapter 2.

THE FLORAL DESIGNER

Unless you have a creative flair and a feel for color, your best bet is to put the flowers for your wedding in the hands of a floral designer, one you already know or one who has been recommended for her style and taste *and* the freshness of her flowers. A floral designer, who may or may not have her own retail shop, differs from an ordinary florist in that she does more than just flower arrangements. She advises on the choice of tablecloths and other linens, the color of the waiters' jackets, and just about every other decorative aspect of a wedding. In most instances the floral designer works with the wedding consultant, although some floral designers—like some caterers—are capable of taking over all aspects of the wedding arrangements.

Be sure to sign up the floral designer (a contract must follow) as soon as you know your wedding date. If you procrastinate, you may find she's already been spoken for by someone else getting married on the same day. Before making an appointment with her, look at pictures of flower arrangements in home decorating books and magazines. It will give you a better idea of the types of flowers and what colors appeal to you. And show the pictures you particularly like to the designer.

She will need to know certain details right away: what time of year the wedding is planned for, where the ceremony and reception will take place, approximately how many people are expected, and, most important, how much money you have budgeted for flowers. Later on, in order to know exactly what flowers are needed, she will want to see the place where the ceremony and the reception are to be held.

Think about the time of year you will be married and what flowers will be in season. While you can import flowers from almost anywhere in the world, they'll be a lot less expensive if you buy them locally. If it's a spring wedding, branches of dogwood or masses of peonies can do wonders to offset the open look of large spaces. In the fall, hydrangeas are lovely, and in winter, in cold climates, you can save money by substituting velvet ribbons or bowls filled with fruit for flowers. No matter how difficult it may be to find flowers that fit the season or your pocketbook, *never* compromise by substituting fake flowers for the real thing.

Before going ahead with the flowers for the church or synagogue, find out if another bride is being married there on the same day. If so, you may want to be in touch with her to find out if she would care to join forces with you, choosing flowers both of you will like. Not only is it less wasteful but you can save a considerable amount of money by sharing the cost of the flowers.

Give careful thought to the colors of the flowers you have in the church or synagogue. Most often, churches are dimly lit, so you want to think twice before using colors like deep blue or lavender, unless they are contrasting colors in a lighter arrangement. And check with the church office to find out if there are any restrictions as to where flowers can be placed. At a small wedding or in a small space, there may only be two arrangements on the altar. Sometimes only the aisle posts of the reserved pews are decorated with flowers, even for a very formal wedding. At a Jewish wedding, the chuppah may be designed as a magnificent arch of fresh flowers. There's no set protocol when it comes to decorating a church or synagogue. It's all a matter of personal taste and style, although you'll want to avoid flower arrangements so garish and lavish that they aren't in keeping with the dignity and spirit of a house of worship.

In general, florists are able to supply small trees and other greeneries which can be rented for a wedding. If there's a problem because the church is unusually large for the number of guests attending the ceremony, a clever florist can do impressive things with boxwood, other shrubs, and trellis screens to create a feeling of intimacy and warmth within the area that's to be used.

If you want to have a white canvas runner rolled down the aisle just before the processional begins, it's sometimes provided by the church, but more often by the floral designer.

At the reception there is usually some kind of background decoration, perhaps pots filled with plants or topiary trees, behind the receiving line.

These give the line a focal point and a finished appearance. If the receiving line forms in front of a fireplace, the mantel may be decorated instead. You may or may not want flowers on the buffet tables, depending on how much room there is. The bride's table usually has a floral centerpiece and when there are small round tables for the guests, if you can afford it, each table has its own centerpiece. The color of the flowers should coordinate with the tablecloths, the bride's and bridesmaids' dresses and their bouquets. Remember, too, that the centerpieces must not be so tall that the guests are unable to see each other across the table. Take time to discuss this point with the floral designer. If the reception is being held at home, flowers in the halls, bedrooms, and bathrooms, in addition to the rooms where the guests congregate, add a welcome touch of warmth and color.

Certainly the most important flower arrangement at any wedding is the bride's bouquet, a symbol of love and romance. Every bride has her own vision of the perfect bouquet, its style, size, and shape. Orchids, tulips, freesia, roses, stephanotis, and daisies are popular choices as is lily of the valley, a symbol of lasting love, and baby's breath, a symbol of fertility.

Traditionally, there are three types of bouquet—the nosegay, which is round with flowers tightly clasped together with ribbons or in a holder; the cascading bouquet that flows downward along the front of the bride's dress; and the presentation or arm bouquet, which lies along the bride's arm. A newer style is the unstructured bouquet, which is irregular in shape and made with different wild and garden flowers such as asters, cornflowers, and delphinium, rather than hothouse blooms. Because of its casual look, this type of bouquet is most often seen at outdoor weddings. Sometimes a bouquet is made so that the bride can remove a small cluster of flowers from the center to wear as a corsage when she leaves the reception.

The bride's bouquet should complement the bride's height, her dress, and the climate. It would look ridiculous for a petite bride to carry a mammoth bouquet. And a cascading bouquet works well with a long, bouffant dress. Then think about the weather. You may have your heart set on carrying a particular flower, but if it doesn't stand up well in summer heat, you may be left holding a wilted bouquet.

Some brides prefer to carry a white prayer book, with or without a bookmark made of grosgrain, silk, or satin ribbons, rather than a bouquet. If the book has ribbons, tiny flowers may be tied at their ends.

The maid's and/or matron's of honor and bridesmaids' bouquets should be designed to complement their dresses as well as the bride's bouquet. They don't have to be exactly alike, although they should be similar in formality and style. If cost is a factor, the floral designer can always create an attractive bouquet using fewer flowers and more green leaves. Or a small bouquet of trailing ivy is inexpensive and will stand up well in hot weather. Sometimes you see bridesmaids holding a single flower in place of a bouquet. This looks rather insipid, though many brides may not agree, favoring it for its simplicity.

A junior bridesmaid may carry the same bouquet as the bridesmaids or, depending on her size, a smaller rendition of it. If her dress is a younger version of the bridesmaids' dresses, the bouquet may be slightly different in style, to conform with her dress and age.

A flower girl often carries a tiny nosegay or a small basket filled with flowers. If the church doesn't mind picking up afterward, she may carry a basket filled with real or paper rose petals, to scatter along the aisle ahead of the bride. A small head wreath of flowers is always becoming on a young child.

If the bride or her attendants are to wear flowers clipped to their hair, or wreaths, the flowers must be coordinated with the bouquets and must be of a type that won't start to droop or wilt halfway through the wedding. For wreaths to be made to fit properly the designer will need to know head-size measurements.

The groom's boutonniere is traditionally a spray of the flowers from the bride's bouquet worn in his left lapel. His boutonniere will be different from those of the best man and the ushers. The best man can wear another kind of flower from the bride's bouquet or the same boutonniere the ushers wear.

No mother of the bride or groom must feel compelled to wear a corsage; in fact, corsages are not nearly so popular today as they once were. If the bride's mother does not plan to wear a corsage, she should tell this to the groom's mother, but give her the option of wearing one if she wants. These corsages must be coordinated with the colors of the wearer's dress. It's nice for the bride and groom to give corsages to a few favorite people like a grandmother, stepmother, half sister, or aunt, but only if they know they'd like to wear one. Corsages may be pinned to the left shoulder, to the waistline of a dress, to a purse, or made into a wristband. If there's a possibility of a pin making a permanent mark on a dress, it's best to pin the corsage to a purse.

Fathers of the bride and groom wear the same boutonnieres as the ushers. Stepfathers, younger brothers, and stepbrothers may also be given boutonnieres by the groom.

ROSE PETALS

If the bride and groom are true traditionalists, they'll want to be pelted with rice, symbolic of fertility, when they leave the reception. Many hotels and clubs, however, won't permit the throwing of rice for a number of good reasons: a misguided handful of rice might hit the bride, the groom, or an unsuspecting guest in the eye; rice is slippery underfoot, and it is difficult to clean up. At most weddings today, paper rose petals are used instead of rice. Real rose petals, aside from the expense, aren't practical as they might stain the floor or be ground into the carpet. While paper rose petals usually replace rice, sometimes paper confetti is used instead.

MUSIC FOR THE WEDDING

Choose the music for your wedding ceremony as carefully as you do the music for your reception. Music creates a specific mood for the ceremony. When guests arrive at the church or synagogue, slow, quiet music produces a reflective mood. When they leave the service, a stronger, more exhilarating beat sets them up for the reception.

Today's brides no longer depend on the traditional wedding processionals and recessionals, the best known of which are Wagner's "Wedding March" from *Lohengrin* (commonly called "Here Comes the Bride") as the processional and Mendelssohn's "Wedding March" from *A Midsummer Night's Dream* for the recessional. Instead one might hear classical or religious music (popular music could detract from the dignity of the occasion) that reflects the couple's own personal tastes and style. When choosing music for the processional or recessional, bear in mind that you want music with a beat that will be easy for you and your attendants to walk to.

If you'd like to have your own organist play at the ceremony, check first with your church or synagogue. In some instances, you have to pay the in-house organist whether you use his services or not.

The music for your reception depends on how many people you're inviting and how much money you want to spend. If you're planning a small wedding and need to keep expenses down, use your own taped music. Should you want a more sophisticated presentation, you can hire a disc jockey, who will bring in special equipment and tailor the selections to your preferences.

While you can have a first-rate wedding reception using tapes, there's no substitute for live music. The mere presence of a musician adds a festive note as well as a touch of glamour to any gathering. The music a musician chooses varies according to the mood of the guests; he knows when to play soft, romantic music and when to switch to a more upbeat rhythm.

If you're having a reception for fifty people or fewer, you can do nicely with just a piano player, although a trio makes for livelier dance music. If you're planning a wedding with all the trimmings, though, you'll want an orchestra; the number of players depends on the number of guests you expect. Start thinking about the orchestra as soon as you know your wedding date, as the more popular ones are booked up as much as a year or two in advance. If you don't have an orchestra in mind, the most reliable way to find one is through word of mouth. A friend who has good taste in music may know of one, or a reputable caterer may have a suggestion. If all else fails, and you find yourself in the position of having to contact an orchestra you know nothing about, before making any commitment, hear them play or, if that's not possible, at least listen to them on tape. Choose an orchestra with a broad repertoire so there will be a diversity to the type and tempo of the music. This is particularly important at weddings where the ages of the guests can range from eight to eighty. In addition to the orchestra, you may want to hire an accordionist or other soloist to play when the orchestra takes a break.

If you are told the orchestra leader will appear in person at the reception and this is important to you, have it written into the contract. Unfortunately, and all too often, a bride will arrive at the reception only to find that the orchestra leader has sent someone to replace him.

You and the orchestra leader will need to get together to discuss the music that's to be played and other specifics related to the orchestra's participation. In general, it works well to start off the reception with light dance music; standards by Cole Porter and George Gershwin are always popular. Later, as the guests become more relaxed and the spirit of the reception gains momentum, you can quicken the pace of the beat, perhaps with some rock or Latin rhythms.

You will also want to discuss some or all of the following variables:

- The color of the jackets the players will wear (if you want a certain color, you may have to rent the jackets).
- The song you want played when you and the groom have your first dance.
- Your mother's (or the groom's mother's) favorite song if you'd like to surprise her with it.
- What type of easy rhythmic music to play when you or the groom take to the floor with any young child unfamiliar with dancing.
- Whether you want the orchestra leader to play a trumpet fanfare to get the guests' attention when toasts are to be made or when you are ready to cut the cake or throw your bouquet (a trumpet fanfare is always played when the bride and groom have their first dance).

If you want to read more about working with an orchestra, refer to "The Orchestra" under "Balls and Dances" in Chapter 2.

THE PHOTOGRAPHER

Whatever amount of time you put into finding the right photographer for your wedding, it will have been well spent. Since you can only take the pictures once, you want to do your best to find someone who will do the occasion justice. Don't put off looking for a photographer either, particularly if you are getting married on a Saturday or Sunday, when most weddings take place. Many of the more popular and accomplished photographers have bookings well over a year in advance.

It takes a special talent and know-how to produce really good wedding pictures, so you need someone who has had experience in this particular area. Whether you'd feel less self-conscious being photographed by a man than a woman, or the reverse, is something you may want to consider. Many brides have a distinct preference. As to finding a photographer, that should not be too difficult. If you have a friend who was recently married, ask her who took the pictures at her wedding. Or one of your parents' friends, or a caterer, may know of a photographer. With a little networking, you are bound to find just the right person.

Videotaping, with or without sound, is very popular today. The photographer who is taking your still photographs should be able to recommend a professional videographer to you. Before making any decision, ask to see a sample of her work and also discuss how long a tape you want; an hour and a half is usual. Videotaping is costly, so you need to know the charges and whether they include editing the tape. The only problem with videotaping is that any professional videographer, with her reputation to consider, may insist on using terribly bright lights to get the best possible results. Very bright lights can be annoying and distracting and can turn a meaningful occasion into a media-type event. If you want your wedding videotaped, you might think of handling it this way. Hire a professional photographer to take the still pictures, but ask a friend or family member to do the videotaping, perhaps for a token fee or a present of some sort. An amateur can do a perfectly acceptable job of videotaping without using the brightest lights, and even if the tape doesn't turn out to be of the finest professional quality, it will still be fun to look at over the years and to show to your children and grandchildren. It will probably be more fun if it *isn't* too professional.

A friend or relative may offer to take your wedding pictures as a wedding present. While it sounds like a good idea and a cost-saving one too, still pictures taken by an amateur photographer won't compare in quality with those taken by a professional. Of course, there's no reason not to have a relative as well as a professional photographer take pictures. In all likelihood he will know many of the guests, which of course the photographer won't, and will be able to provide you with pictures you may not otherwise have. If a relative does take some pictures, it's nice to offer to pay for the film.

Before you decide on a particular photographer, call and make an appointment to go see her. When you meet, give her an idea of the type of wedding you're planning; how many guests are expected and how formal or informal it will be. See how well you get along together before making any commitment. You want a photographer you feel at ease with, whom you won't mind taking directions from, who will help you overcome any feelings of nervousness whenever she clicks the camera—basically, someone you will enjoy working with and have fun with.

When you go to see her, she will show you her portfolio of wedding photographs. Look them over carefully. Are they in proper focus? What about the color? How well does she organize group pictures? Does it appear that she takes so many pictures she might be an annoyance to the wedding party and guests? Do her pictures include the major happenings at a wedding, like the cutting of the cake or throwing the bouquet? If after studying the photographs you feel satisfied with the quality of her work, you will then want to find out how she charges for her services. Photographers charge in a number of different ways. Some charge by the hour, with a charge for each print made (often you have to order a minimum number of prints); others charge a flat fee for a minimum number of hours, with a fee for every additional hour, and a charge for each print. Still other photographers offer a package proposal which includes their time as well as one or more albums of photographs.

Before you actually sign the contract, you want to be certain you have satisfactory answers to the following questions: What's included in the estimate? Will the photographer definitely be there in person or is there a possibility of her sending someone else? How many rolls of film will she shoot? When can you expect to see the contact sheets? How long will it take to get the pictures once you have placed the order? Can you buy the negatives and what will the cost be? How is the cost affected if there's a problem with the camera or if some of the film doesn't come out?

Once the contract is signed, you and the photographer will need to decide when your formal bridal picture will be taken. It can be taken whenever you have your dress, although you should check with the newspapers as to when they will need the picture, if you are planning to send them one with your wedding announcement. You will also want to discuss with the photographer how much lighting she plans to use so that the makeup you apply will look natural. Then decide where the picture will be taken. Some bridal salons have photographic equipment just so the photograph can be taken there (the thought being that there's less risk of the dress being wrinkled or spotted if it's not moved). Otherwise, the dress is taken to the photographer's studio and the picture taken there.

It's up to you to tell the photographer just what pictures can or cannot be taken in your church or synagogue. You'll have to find out from the minister, priest, or rabbi who is marrying you just what's permitted, as each house of worship has its own set of rules and regulations, and make sure the photographer conforms to them. Some houses of worship let the photographer go halfway up the aisle, allowing her to take a picture of the bride and groom at the altar with a zoom lens, while others require the photographer to remain behind the last pew, which is probably preferable as it means people in the back of the church can concentrate on the service rather than the photographer. Should your church allow a photographer to take a picture or two at the altar, don't look on this as a possible photo opportunity. Nothing is less in keeping with the sanctity of the marriage ceremony than a photographer at the altar, no matter how discreet she may be. Permission must be asked to use a flash and for videotaping the ceremony. The least conspicuous place for the video equipment to be set up is in the balcony of the church or synagogue.

Sometimes the clergyperson will allow the bride and groom to have photographs taken at the altar after the ceremony when the guests have left the church. If you do this, the picture session should be kept short so guests arriving at the reception won't have to wait an unduly long time for the receiving line to form.

Talk to the photographer about other pictures to be taken the day of the wedding; it's important that you brief her on any sensitive family relationships. For instance, if your parents are divorced and you know they won't be happy appearing with their present spouses in the same picture, tell her so. That way, she can orchestrate any group pictures so the two couples are never photographed together. You'll also have to let her know when you want your first and last pictures taken. Some brides want the photographer to take pictures from the time they are getting dressed for the wedding until they wave farewell from the honeymoon car; others, either out of preference or to save money, ask the photographer to begin with their arrival at the church or synagogue and to end with the throwing of the bouquet.

Some of the traditional photographs taken to commemorate a wedding are: getting dressed for the wedding, leaving for the church, arriving at the church, waiting for the processional to start, starting up the aisle, coming back down the aisle, getting in the car to drive to the reception; group pictures taken before the receiving line forms, such as bride and groom, bride and groom with each set of parents, bride with her attendants, groom with his attendants, bride and groom with all their attendants (at a Jewish wedding the ceremony and reception are usually held at the same place so the group photographs are most often taken before the ceremony); the receiving line, dancing, toasts, cutting the cake; bride feeding groom cake, bride throwing bouquet, groom throwing garter; bride getting dressed to go away, groom getting dressed to go away, leaving the reception, waving from the honeymoon car. Aside from these photographs, you may want to ask the photographer to take other special pictures, such as your mother and father walking out of the church together or dancing together.

A word should be mentioned about group photographs of family and attendants taken before the receiving line forms. Try to make this session as snappy as possible. Even though the guests can mingle with each other and sip champagne, you don't want them to have to wait around endlessly for the receiving line to form. In order not to waste time, pay attention to the photographer when she does the posing for these pictures. You and the groom can help her organize the different groupings by asking family members and attendants to listen to her instructions and to line up as quickly as possible. It saves a great deal of time if everyone is alert and cooperates to the best of their ability. An alternative to having the picture session before the receiving line is to have it directly afterward. That way, guests go through the line as they arrive at the reception and then are free to socialize.

At the reception, you'll want some pictures of the wedding guests. If the guests are to be seated at small round tables, the photographer will have a chance to photograph most of them by taking a picture of each table. Since she can't be expected to know who each person is, ask someone in your family to point out other family members and close friends for her to photograph. Your groom should do the same for his side of the family. In addition, you may each want to ask a good friend to point out other friends and colleagues you would enjoy having pictures of. When it comes time to cut the cake or toss your bouquet, have someone alert the photographer if she's not within sight. It would be sad to have her miss any key photos.

You might want to give the guests an opportunity to play a part in the picture taking at the reception by placing disposable cameras at a number of tables. Put a small stand-up sign by each camera that says, "We'd be happy if you'd use this camera to take any pictures you think we'd like. Gail and David."

Sometime after the wedding, usually a number of weeks, the photographer will send you the contact sheets. When you place your order, you may want to have a few prints made for your husband's family, just as a friendly gesture. It's not the least bit necessary, however, as the groom's family is responsible for ordering their own wedding pictures. If you and your husband can afford to do so, it's nice to send each wedding attendant a print (8 × 10 or smaller) of one of the posed group pictures in which they appear. Putting the pictures in frames, which need not be expensive ones, adds a nice finishing touch to the present.

TRANSPORTATION

There's no reason not to ask a bridesmaid or usher to pick up an out-of-town guest arriving at the airport or train station. While most people are perfectly able to get around on their own, an elderly person in particular may be grateful for some assistance. Or it may even be an able-bodied relative to whom you want to pay a little extra attention, for instance a favorite uncle. If there are a good number of out-of-towners on the wedding list, for their convenience it's often a good idea to enclose in their invitations a printed card with the names and telephone numbers of local limousine and taxi services.

Not everyone by any means hires limousines for the wedding. Oftentimes transportation is provided by friends, or the brother of the bride may be the one to drive his sister and father to the church or synagogue. However, given the choice, it's a safe bet that just about any bride would rather set off for her wedding in a chauffeur-driven limousine, even if it means economizing on some other wedding expense. This is a time when a touch of glamour is called for.

Assuming you are not restricted in the number of limousines you can hire, you may need one (in some instances two or more) for the following people:

To the church or synagogue:

- Bride and father
- Groom and best man
- Bride's mother and any family members accompanying her (as an alternative, bride's mother may go to church with bridesmaids)
- Groom's mother and father
- Bride's attendants (not too many to a limousine or the dresses will get crushed)
- Ushers
- Stepparents, grandparents, and any other special guests

From the church or synagogue to the reception:

- Bride and groom
- Bride's mother and father
- Groom's mother and father
- Bride's attendants
- Best man and ushers
- Family members (those who accompanied mother of bride to church)
- Stepparents, grandparents, and any other special guests

You'll need to give the limousine service a well-organized, typed list of instructions so transportation arrangements will run smoothly.
Here is an example:

LIMOUSINE #1
    Pickup point:
    Pickup time:
    Names of passengers:
    Destination:
    Telephone contact:

Each limousine should have its own number plainly visible on one of the windows and each person traveling in a limousine should be sent a note with the number of his or her limousine. This will especially facilitate leaving the church, as passengers will know exactly which limousine to look for. Also, if each driver has a list with the names of his passengers, there's less likelihood of his driving off and leaving someone behind. Passengers should be told when and where they will be picked up and given the telephone number of the limousine service in case they need to be in touch with the driver.

It's up to the bride and groom how they want to leave the reception: in a limousine, a car driven by the best man, or a car they drive themselves. Or they may want to be more adventuresome and depart by hot-air balloon, horse and carriage, a golf cart, or a dogsled. It's all a matter of how far you want your imagination to take you.

RESERVING HOTEL/MOTEL ROOMS FOR OUT-OF-TOWN GUESTS

If there are a good many out-of-town guests on your wedding list, you will want to reserve a number of rooms at a local hotel or motel well in advance of the wedding, certainly before the invitations are sent out. Since it's customary for guests to pay for their own rooms, try to choose a hotel that's comfortable but also reasonably priced and relatively close to where the ceremony and/or reception will take place. You can alert out-of-town guests as to where the rooms have been set aside by enclosing in their invitations an engraved or printed card (suggested plane flights, limousine and taxi services may be included as well) with this information or by writing a personal note. To get across the point that guests are expected to pay for their own hotel rooms, give the number to call for reservations. Guests can then make reservations with their credit cards. If you or your fiancé decide you want to pay for the accommodations of any friends, let them know in advance rather than waiting until the time comes for them to pay their bills. You should also tell the hotel which guests you are paying for and how you want to be billed.

There's an advantage to housing out-of-towners in one location as it makes the logistics of sending cars or friends to pick them up a great deal easier. It's also more fun for those arriving for the wedding to have the companionship of others, perhaps breakfasting or sightseeing together. If, however, you don't feel it's necessary to reserve a block of rooms or if you want guests to have a choice of hotel rooms in different price ranges, you may enclose a card in the invitation, giving the names, addresses, and telephone numbers of suggested hotels and motels in the area or wait to send this information to those guests who accept. You may find that some guests will prefer to stay at a hotel other than the ones you recommend, and of course there's no reason to dissuade them.

As for out-of-town bridesmaids, if there's room at the bride's house they might stay there; if not, the bride may arrange for them to stay with neighbors or friends of hers. The same is true for the groom, if his family lives where the wedding's to be held. If any of the attendants are to be put up in a hotel, it's customary for the bride's family to pay the cost of the rooms for her attendants and the groom's family for his.

THE HONEYMOON

For a bride and groom, the honeymoon—the beginning of married life together—has come to be almost as ritualistic as the wedding ceremony. Whether the honeymoon consists of a weekend at a ski lodge, a two-week luxury cruise, or a three-month trip abroad, its very real purpose is to give the couple time to bask in their newfound happiness and to unwind after the wedding festivities. It's a time they will look back on always with more than a touch of nostalgia.

The word "honeymoon" refers to a custom among Germanic tribes whereby the couple, after the wedding, celebrated their marriage from one moon to the next, drinking honey-sweetened mead each day—hence, "honey moon." Pleasant as this tradition may have been, modern-day honeymooners don't usually have time to sit back and savor this type of ritual. Nor do they subscribe any longer to the more recent custom of the groom whisking his bride away from the wedding reception without her having any knowledge as to where she was being taken on her wedding trip. All she was told was whether she was headed for a warm or cold climate so she could pack accordingly. In our less conventional, more practical society, the bride and groom decide together where to spend their honeymoon, with both helping to make the arrangements and often sharing expenses.

In order to have the honeymoon you've dreamed about, start making plans well in advance, particularly if you are being married at the height of the wedding season and you have your heart set on going to Bermuda, Hawaii, or some other popular honeymoon site, where hotels are booked up as long as a year in advance. If you are smart, you'll put yourselves in the hands of a knowledgeable travel agent, one who will be able to give you all sorts of ideas on where to go, according to the time of year and the amount of money you have to spend. She'll be able to tell you about all-inclusive tours, which hotels have special rates for honeymooners, plane schedules, and just what travel documents you will need. She can also spare you the time-consuming job of making reservations, and remember, there is no charge for her services (see "Planning Your Trip" in Chapter 6).

While you may be bursting with energy when you first start talking about where to go on your honeymoon, chances are your energy level will be somewhat diminished by the time the wedding has taken place. What with planning the wedding, pre-wedding parties, and all the excitement that goes with these activities, you may end up being a great deal more tired than you ever expected. With this in mind, it can make a lot more sense to collapse on some Caribbean island than to fly off on a ten-city European tour.

If you and your intended spouse have unrelated vacation interests—for example, one of you is a passionate snorkeler and the other a passionate hiker—you may want to honeymoon at a place where neither of these activities is available to tempt either one of you, or a place that offers both. Or you may decide to go off snorkeling with the understanding that the next vacation will be spent on the hiking trails. Two people who care about each other enough to get married should be able to decide on the perfect honeymoon spot without either one feeling slighted or compromised. When it comes to paying for the honeymoon, traditionally, the bride's or groom's family gave the honeymoon as their wedding present to the couple. Today, there's no set protocol as to who pays for the honeymoon. It may be that the bride's or groom's family does pay for it, or splits the cost, but increasingly it's the couple themselves who pay for their honeymoon, sometimes using money they have received as wedding presents.

PRESENTS

KEEPING A RECORD OF PRESENTS

It's important to keep an accurate record of the wedding presents you receive so there's no chance of not remembering what the mother of one of your bridesmaids gave you or, even more important, so you won't forget to thank someone. The day will come when you'll be glad you kept a record, and you'll probably refer to it many times during your married life. When former wedding guests come to your house, they'll be flattered if you point out a present they gave you which you've been using—particularly twenty or thirty years after the wedding! Many wedding planner books have a section for recording presents. Otherwise you can use anything from a plain spiral notebook to an elegant leather-bound album.

When you receive presents, enter them in your book under the following headings, which should appear across the width of the page, with appropriate spaces in between: Name/s of Sender/s, Address, Present [with brief description], Store, Date Received, Date Thanked. Presents are then listed below, with numbers (#1, #2, etc.) added to the left as needed.

You need to know the name of the store a present comes from, in case you decide to exchange it or return it for credit. Don't be too hasty about throwing the box away, either. It will be necessary if you have to return the present. When you record your presents, put a numbered sticker on the bottom of each one; the number on the sticker should correspond to the number of the entry in your record book. That way, if you receive two scrapbooks and three sets of old-fashioned glasses, you'll know exactly who gave you which.

MONEY AS A PRESENT

If a couple have been living on their own and have enough possessions between them to start married life, money can be the best wedding present of all. It can go toward a more extravagant wedding trip, a cappuccino machine, or perhaps some much-needed landscaping around the house. Giving money as a present is a common practice in certain religions and cultures. In other cultures it's traditional to give a tangible present. If you belong to one of these, it's not likely you'll receive money as a present, except perhaps from grandparents or other family members to whom you have made your wishes known. When the custom is to give presents other than money, it would be bad manners to ask wedding guests for cash. If someone asks your mother what you want and she can get the message across discreetly, money is fine. But she must be tactful in phrasing her message and discriminating about whom she gives it to. You don't want to put anyone in the awkward position of having to spend more than he can afford; for example, a useful or decorative present can be found for $35, whereas a check for $35 can appear skimpy.

WHEN PRESENTS ARE BROUGHT TO THE RECEPTION

From a practical standpoint, it's a lot more convenient for a bride to receive her wedding presents at home before the wedding than to have them brought to the reception. At the reception, there's the question of security, and someone has to be responsible for taking them home afterward. Furthermore, brides like to receive presents before the wedding so they can get a head start on writing thank-you letters. Nonetheless, in certain areas of the country and in some cultural groups it is not unusual for a guest to show up at a reception bearing a present. If you anticipate receiving presents at your reception, try to arrange with the coatroom attendant to have her keep them; otherwise, you'll need a table to put them on and possibly someone to keep an eye on them. You'll also have to make arrangements for the presents to be taken back to your or your mother's house once the reception is over.

Wedding presents are not opened at the reception as the bride and groom are busy socializing and dancing. Also keeping the packages intact eliminates the possibility of cards being misplaced or possible breakage when transporting the presents home.

When checks are brought to the reception, which is the case at some weddings, one person should be in charge of their safekeeping so that they aren't mislaid or lost. The banquet manager of the hotel or club may even have a place where they can be safely put away until the reception is over.

DISPLAYING YOUR WEDDING PRESENTS

Displaying wedding presents is an old-fashioned custom that is still popular in many areas of the country. If there's space to exhibit your presents and you choose to do so, you'll most likely find that family and friends will be delighted to be invited to see what you've been given. You might ask two or three friends at a time to stop by, or you might invite a group of people to come around for tea or cocktails some afternoon close to the date of the wedding, after you have received a majority of the presents.

When wedding presents are displayed, it's usually at the house of the mother of the bride. Depending on the number of presents expected, it may be necessary to rent one or more tables to put them on. It's usual to cover the tables with floor-length tablecloths of white damask, although plain white sheets will serve the purpose nicely if you haven't any tablecloths on hand. White satin ribbon can be used to make bows for the corners of the table.

Some brides like to display their presents by category: china, crystal, housewares, kitchen accessories, etc.—each in its own grouping. Others like to arrange presents in a random fashion, thus eliminating the possibility of a guest feeling embarrassed when she spots her six cork placemats beside a dozen embroidered linen ones. With silver, china, and crystal, it's only necessary to put out one place setting. Checks are never displayed. Larger articles, such as a small table, a picnic basket, or a suitcase, may be placed on the floor against the skirt of the tablecloth.

It used to be that the sender's card was placed beside the present, but most brides today prefer not to identify the givers. And with good reason, as many people see the viewing of the presents as an opportunity to find out who gave what—calculating how much So-and-so spent. If you do want to put the card by the present, and someone has given you a check, write the name/s of the person who gave the check on a white 3" × 5" file card and place it on the table. The amount of the check is not given. The card simply says, "Mr. and Mrs. Rodney Tyler—Check."

You'll need some sort of floater insurance policy for the wedding presents, and you'll want to have someone guard them while the ceremony is going on and during the reception. Leaving presents unattended at any time is asking for trouble.

EXCHANGING AND RETURNING PRESENTS

Use discretion when exchanging a wedding present. No replacement is worth hurting someone's feelings. Wedding presents from your family and your fiancé's should not be exchanged unless they've told you it would be all right to do so or there is an excellent reason why you need to make an exchange. You may certainly return a duplicate present for credit or exchange, and a present that arrives broken should be returned to the store for replacement, without telling the sender. If the broken present came directly from the sender, you'll have to decide whether to tell her it's broken. If it was insured there's no problem, but if it wasn't, in all likelihood she'll feel obligated to send you another present. For obvious reasons, presents that have been initialed can't be returned.

PRESENTS AND THE WEDDING THAT'S CALLED OFF OR DOESN'T LAST

If you call off your wedding, all presents must be returned directly to the senders, with the exception of those that are monogrammed. You should include with the present a handwritten note on your personal stationery (you don't have to mention the wedding's cancellation because people were informed of this when the invitation was rescinded). You're not expected to go into any details about why the wedding was called off and the note can be as short as, "Dear Meg, Since David and I are not getting married, I am sure you can understand why we are returning your lovely crystal vase. David and I are sad things didn't work out the way we had hoped they would, but it's better that we arrived at our decision now rather than later on. I hope to see you before too long, Love, Gail."

If a wedding has been postponed for some reason, presents are not returned unless, after a reasonable length of time, it still does not take place. Only if the prospective bride or groom has died is it proper for the fiancé or fiancée to keep wedding presents. In the event that the marriage lasts only a brief time, ending in an annulment or divorce, the presents legally belong equally to the bride and groom. Whether they return any presents depends on how long they were married and their personal feelings in the matter. The bride, however, should return any jewelry or heirlooms she received from the groom's family.

PRESENTS RELATING TO WEDDING PARTY AND FAMILY PRESENTS

Traditionally, the bride and groom give each other a wedding present of sentimental significance, something that will serve as a lasting reminder of their love and the occasion. If one has more money to spend than the other, the more affluent of the two should scale down his or her present. When money's no object, the groom may give the bride a piece of fine jewelry, perhaps a pair of pearl earrings or a gold rope necklace. She in turn may give him gold cuff links with matching studs or a gold watch with his initials and the date of the wedding on the back.

Naturally, what a bride and groom give each other depends on the couple's finances. They certainly don't want to sacrifice a wedding trip or buying needed furniture just so they can give each other lavish presents.

Something in sterling silver or gold is great if you can afford it, but if you can't, there are plenty of meaningful presents that fall within the limits of almost any budget. The groom might give the bride a piece of costume jewelry or a lovely silk scarf; she might give him a good edition of his favorite book or a cashmere-lined silk scarf. Some brides and grooms, by mutual agreement, choose to postpone giving each other presents until their first wedding anniversary or whenever they feel financially secure. This is not a bad idea, as they can then spend more on what they give each other without suffering any guilt feelings.

It once was traditional for the bride's parents to present the couple with sterling flatware or to pay for the wedding trip; if the bride's parents didn't pay for the wedding trip, then the groom's parents did. Wonderful as both these presents are, few parents today can afford such expenditures. Actually, there's no reason for parents to feel obligated to give the couple a present if it's a financial strain. After all, they will have put out a great deal of money for the rehearsal dinner and the wedding itself. When the parents of the bride and groom do give something it should be commensurate with their means, whether it's china place settings or something more practical such as a microwave oven.

It's always nice if the bride and groom can afford to give their attendants some small lasting memento to commemorate their role in the wedding. Often the bride gives her maid or matron of honor a slightly more elaborate present than the one she gives to her bridesmaids, and the groom does the same for his best man. It's customary for the bride to give her attendants their presents at the bridesmaids' luncheon. If no luncheon is planned, she may present them at the rehearsal dinner. The groom gives his presents to the best man and ushers at the bachelor dinner or at the rehearsal dinner.

It's worth repeating here that stores require a minimum of two to three weeks for initialing. At Christmas, or some other major holiday times, it can take even longer.

Here is a list of suggested presents:

GROOM TO BRIDE
Gold flower or animal pin
Silver locket on chain

BRIDE TO GROOM
Two-piece matching luggage set
Gold tie bar

MOTHER AND FATHER OF BRIDE TO BRIDE
Money toward wedding trip
Set of demitasse cups and saucers

MOTHER AND FATHER OF GROOM TO BRIDE
Silver box engraved with facsimile of wedding invitation
Brass table clock

BRIDE TO MAID OF HONOR
Sequined evening bag
Hand-painted porcelain box

BRIDE TO BRIDESMAIDS
Initialed silver picture frame with wedding date
Initialed silver heart-shaped key ring

BRIDE TO FLOWER GIRL
Gold heart locket
Zodiac charm

MAID OF HONOR TO BRIDE
Silver compact
Crystal perfume flask

BRIDESMAIDS TO BRIDE
Gold heart pendant
Silver bangle bracelets

FLOWER GIRL TO BRIDE
Sonnets from the Portuguese by Elizabeth Barrett Browning

GROOM TO BEST MAN
Silver belt buckle
Leather credit card or business card case

GROOM TO USHERS
Silver pen or money clip
Silver letter opener

GROOM TO RING BEARER
Swatch watch
Swiss army knife

BEST MAN TO GROOM
Silver flask
Initialed waterproof lined toiletry case

USHERS TO GROOM
Gold belt buckle
Binoculars

RING BEARER TO GROOM
Personalized luggage tags

THANK-YOU LETTERS

If possible, try to keep current with your thank-you letters, writing them as the presents arrive. Granted, it's not always easy to keep up with the influx of presents, but if you make an effort to set aside half an hour each day just for this purpose, you'll be glad in the long run. No matter how hectic your life is, a thank-you letter should be written within two to three weeks after receiving a present, certainly no more than six to eight weeks later. There are good reasons for writing prompt thank-you letters; it's good manners, there will be a spontaneous tone to your writing, and the sender won't start to wonder whether the present ever arrived.

Formerly, when fewer women worked outside the home, it was their sole responsibility to write thank-you letters for wedding presents. Today, when both men and women work, the groom should participate in the writing of the letters. While the bride may write the greater number of letters, he should make an effort to share the load, writing to members of his family and some of his friends.

Thank-you letters should be written on good-quality stationery. Before the bride is married, she uses stationery engraved or printed with her maiden name or monogram. After she's married she uses stationery with her married name, unless she's planning to keep her maiden name. If she doesn't have her own personal writing paper, she may buy plain letter sheets or informals. The paper can be white or some other pale color, with or without a border, and with matching envelopes. The groom uses his personal stationery before the wedding; after the wedding, he can of course continue to use it, but if the bride has ordered joint stationery, he may use that if he prefers. (Refer to "Stationery" in Chapter 8.)

Commercial "thank-you" cards, which have a message of thanks printed on them, so all you have to do is sign your name, are designed for people who don't know how to say "Thank you." Surely any bride or groom can find the time to think up and write a few words of thanks to a wedding guest who has gone to the trouble and expense of sending a present. There are also prepackaged notes with envelopes you can buy in upscale stationery stores; "Thank you" is printed on the top page and inside you write your own message of thanks. However, there is no substitute for a letter of thanks written on your personal stationery.

If your wedding is particularly large, and hundreds of presents must be acknowledged, an engraved or printed card may be sent immediately upon receipt of the present. It reads:

> Miss [Ms.] Gail Cramer
> wishes to acknowledge the receipt
> of your wedding present
> and will write a personal note of
> appreciation at an early date

If the card's to go out shortly after the wedding, your married name appears on the card:

> Mrs. David Alexander
> wishes to acknowledge the receipt
> of your wedding present
> and will write a personal note of
> appreciation at an early date

And a personal note *must* be written at the first possible opportunity. The card is not a substitute thank-you letter. It merely informs wedding guests that their presents have been received.

Never write a thank-you letter that merely says, "Thank you for the wonderful present..." Not mentioning what the present is shows a slipshod and lazy attitude on your part, and what's more the giver of the present will be left with the impression that you actually don't remember what he sent. How much more thoughtful and polite to say, "Thank you for the wonderful four-slice toaster..."

When you write a thank-you letter for money, don't mention the amount given: "A million thanks for your most generous check. David and I have been wanting to buy a canoe for quite some time, and now you and Mr. Slater have made it possible..."

If a number of people have sent you a joint wedding present, each person should receive an individual letter of thanks.

You close a thank-you letter as you would any other letter you write: "Sincerely," "Affectionately," "Love," etc. It depends on how well you know the person you're thanking. Whether you sign your last name again depends on your relationship to the person you're writing. You do not sign your letter "Gail and David," although you should mention David in the text: "Your dog-barking burglar alarm is by far the most unusual present David and I have received..." Or, at the end of the letter, "...David joins me in sending you our thanks. We do hope to see you soon. Love, Gail."

An example of a thank-you letter:

Dear Aunt Lydia and Uncle Frank,

How can David and I ever find words to thank you for the magnificent coaching prints? We never dreamed we'd be given a present we both love so much. Last night we had great fun talking about where to hang them and finally decided on the living room. It's where we will spend most of our time and where they will best be seen and admired by everyone who comes to our house. All I can say is that you could not have thought of a more perfect present, or one that will bring us greater pleasure over the years.

Once we are settled, I'll give you a call to find out when you can come by to see us. In the meantime, I hope it makes you happy to know what happiness you have brought David and me.

With many thanks and lots of love,
Gail

When you don't want to go overboard with thanks for a present you feel is pretentious, in poor taste, or just plain tacky, you can say something like this:

Dear Fiona:

Thank you for the plastic reindeer for our lawn. It was thoughtful of you to think of David and me and we look forward to seeing you at the wedding. It's hard to believe we'll be a married couple in barely two weeks' time!

See you then,

All the best,
Gail

WEDDING ANNOUNCEMENTS

The wedding announcement is issued by the bride's mother and father or by the couple themselves. Unlike the wedding invitation, the announcement includes the year, which may be written out as "one thousand nine hundred and ninety-five" or "nineteen hundred and ninety-five."

PARENTS ISSUE ANNOUNCEMENT

Mr. and Mrs. Arthur Cramer
announce the marriage of their daughter
Gail Lee
to
Mr. David Alexander, Jr.
on Saturday, the eleventh of June
One thousand nine hundred and ninety-five
Santa Fe, New Mexico

COUPLE ISSUE ANNOUNCEMENT

(Miss) Gail Lee Cramer
and
(Mr.) Richard Carpenter
announce their marriage
[etc.]

NEWSPAPER ANNOUNCEMENT OF WEDDING

When preparing your wedding announcement for the newspaper, follow the same guidelines as those for the engagement announcement, given earlier in this chapter. With the wedding announcement, however, you will need to include some or all of the following details, depending on the requirements of your newspaper: date of wedding; name of church or synagogue or wherever ceremony will take place; name of minister, rabbi, or priest; place where reception will be held; names of attendants; relationship of any attendants to you or groom; description of your dress and bouquet, as well as the attendants' dresses and bouquets; where you will honeymoon; where you and the groom will live; whether you will keep your name after you marry.

Newspapers differ in the amount of space they allot for their engagement and wedding announcements. Major metropolitan papers usually print only the basic details of a wedding, whereas local papers are apt to elaborate more fully.

The sample wedding announcement of Gail Lee Cramer and David Alexander that follows is modeled after the style of their engagement announcement, given earlier in this chapter.

Gail Lee Cramer, a daughter of Mr. and Mrs. Arthur Cramer of Santa Fe, was married yesterday to David Alexander, Jr., a son of Mr. and Mrs. Alexander of Springfield, Mass. The Rev. John Witherspoon performed the ceremony at St. James Church in Santa Fe. A reception followed at the home of the bride's parents.

The maid of honor was Arabella Cramer, sister of the bride. Bridesmaids were Susan Schwartz, Lucinda de Mello, Katharine Longley, and Rebecca Sanger. The flower girl was Julia Cramer, niece of the bride. The groom's best man was Francis Sullivan. Ushers were Ralph Cramer, brother of the bride, Robert Green, James Johannsen, Ricardo Salmona, and Trevor Scott.

The bride, who will keep her name, is a graduate of Samuel Kent High School and Sarah Lawrence College. She is a senior editor at Devon Publishing Company in Chicago. Her father, who is retired, was chief counsel for the Rathborne Corporation. Her maternal grandfather, Rufus Harland, was president of Continental Investing from 1968 to 1983.

The bridegroom is a graduate of Princeton University and received a Master of Architecture degree from Harvard University. He is with Abrams & Abrams, an architectural firm based in Chicago. His mother is a reporter for the *Evening Standard* in Springfield. His father is a civil engineer with Tuscan Engineering Company.

(If David Alexander was married before, the announcement reads, "He is with Abrams & Abrams, an architectural firm based in Chicago. His first marriage ended in divorce.")

MARRIED WOMAN AND HER SURNAME

A woman has various options about the name she uses after she marries. If she doesn't work outside the home, she will probably take her husband's name. While many professional women also take their husbands' names, the increasing tendency to keep one's surname after marriage is among the most profound changes in our social customs over the past decades. The basic reasons for doing so are: the woman feels a strong connection between her name and her identity; it's a link to her family heritage; or it's the name business associates know her by. No matter how valid any of these reasons may be, however, many people are still unable to accept the fact that a married woman has a right to hold on to her maiden name.

Every woman must weigh the pros and cons of keeping her surname. It's certainly something she'll want to talk over with the man she's planning to marry long before they're officially engaged. While you can assume that two people who love each other enough to get married will be able to resolve the issue, it still has to be dealt with, and better to do it before any commitment is made.

If a friend of yours who's about to be married says she's planning to keep her name and you don't approve, make no comment. She's not breaking any marriage law, and she's entitled to her own opinion, just as you are to yours. It would be sad to create friction between the two of you over a matter of no consequence, other than to your friend and the man she's to marry.

Sometimes a man's parents are upset when they learn that their future daughter-in-law is not planning to take their son's name. They read all sorts of messages into her declaration, such as "Our name is not good enough for her," "She doesn't like the sound of it," "Our son is marrying a domineering feminist," and they ask, "What will our friends think?" They must realize that her decision to keep her name has nothing to do with their family name or her wanting to control their son, but rather is a personal decision. They should not try to dissuade her but accept her conviction with good spirit.

POSTPONING A WEDDING

It doesn't happen often, fortunately, but there are times when it's necessary to postpone a wedding. The reason for doing so is usually an illness or a death. In the case of the sudden death of the bride's or groom's mother or father, or one of their siblings, the grief-stricken family would certainly not want to go ahead with a wedding, nor would anyone expect them to. For how long to postpone the wedding is a decision only the family can make but, as a sign of respect for the person who has died, they should wait at least six weeks. The future date will, of course, depend on the availability of the church or synagogue or the place where the reception was planned. If the circumstances should be, for instance, that the groom's father dies from a prolonged, terminal illness, the bride and groom, along with the groom's mother, may decide to carry on with the wedding—often a dying parent will request this. If the couple do follow through with their plans in spite of a tragedy, it would be wrong to be critical or disapproving of their decision. You can be certain that they will have been through a great deal of emotional anguish while making up their minds. What they need now is all the love and support they can get.

If you have to postpone your wedding, you want to alert the guests as quickly as possible, particularly those from out of town who will have to cancel their travel arrangements. While you may send a printed card announcing the postponement, this is not a time for formalities. You can get the news out much faster by mailgram (if it's only a day or two before the wedding, you may have to call on family, friends, and bridesmaids to help by telephoning). In the mailgram, you should include the new wedding date. If, on such short notice, it's impossible to confirm a specific date, mention in the mailgram that you will be in touch later, once the date is firm.

Here are two suggested mailgrams. You will note that in each case the reason for the postponement is given. You'd better give a reason, or you can be certain your telephone will be ringing off the hook, with guests wanting to know what's happened.

We regret that because of [our daughter] Gail's recent appendectomy, her marriage to David Alexander has been postponed from Saturday, June 11th, to Saturday, August 9th. If we do not hear to the contrary, we will look forward to seeing you then. Louise and Arthur Cramer.

We regret that [our daughter] Gail's marriage to David Alexander on Saturday, June 11th, has been postponed because of the death of David's father. We will be in touch shortly to give you the new date of the wedding and hope you will be able to join us then. Louise and Arthur Cramer.

Whether you reinvite family and friends who were unable to accept the original wedding invitation depends on whether the reception area is large enough to handle extra guests and, more important, whether you can afford the additional expense. If you do decide to invite those who regretted originally, you must include all of them. If you decide not to reinvite everyone, you can still make an exception in the case of a favorite aunt or close friend who originally regretted. Because the decision not to reinvite those who regretted is based on space and money, no one should feel the least bit slighted by not receiving a second invitation.

In the frenzy of other details that have to be attended to when postponing a wedding, don't forget to call the newspaper/s to say the wedding's been postponed and that you'll let them know when you have a new date.

CANCELING A WEDDING

As with postponing a wedding, if you have to cancel one, it's important to get the word out to the guests as quickly as possible. Mailgrams are a far more expedient form of notification than announcement cards, which take time to print and time to go through the mails. If the cancellation happens only a few days before the wedding, family, friends, and members of the wedding party should be asked to lend a hand by telephoning guests to alert them of the change in plans. And don't forget to have someone call the newspapers to cancel the wedding announcement.

What follows is an example of a mailgram:

We regret that Gail's [or our daughter Gail's] marriage to David Alexander on Saturday, June 11th, has been canceled by mutual agreement. Louise and Arthur Cramer.

Even though it's most unlikely the cancellation was by "mutual agreement," it's the tactful way of characterizing the breakup and makes the mailgram sound less abrupt. Also, if you add these words guests are less likely to telephone to ask what happened.

When a couple decide to cancel their wedding, family members and close friends should show their loyalty by not discussing the matter with other people who want to know the "true story" of what went sour in the relationship. What you can say is, "They both felt it was not right to go ahead with the marriage." If you are pressed further, be firm in your reply: "This is something I'd rather not discuss."

THE ROLE OF THE GUEST

Most people aren't invited to more than one or two weddings a year, so they tend to forget from one event to the next certain formalities that go with being a wedding guest. These formalities are not difficult to understand or follow. They are all based on practical procedures and common courtesies. If you know what to expect and what's expected of you as a guest you will never have to worry about where to sit in the church or when to leave the reception. You will feel at ease in your role as a guest and be able to enjoy the wedding festivities to the fullest.

Here's a list of reminders to help you brush up on your wedding-guest etiquette:

- Never ask to be invited to a wedding, no matter how well you know the bride or groom.
- A wedding invitation must be answered promptly, no more than a week after receiving it.
- Answer the invitation with the same degree of formality with which it's extended. In other words, an invitation issued in the third person warrants a third-person reply (see "Accepting a Formal Wedding Invitation" under "Invitations" earlier in this chapter). There is an exception, however. If you are regretting a formal invitation to the wedding of a close friend, you may want to write a letter explaining why you can't be there.

- Send your reply to the address beneath the R.s.v.p. on the invitation. If no address is given, look for it on the back of the envelope the invitation came in. If a reply card and envelope are enclosed with the invitation, then return the card with your acceptance or regret.

- Sometimes an invitation says "reception and dinner [or supper] immediately following the ceremony." When accepting the invitation, if you know you'll be unable to stay for dinner, let the bride's mother know. Below your formal acceptance, you can write, "Unfortunately, owing to a previous engagement, I/we will not be able to stay for dinner." It's important for the bride's mother to have a good idea of how many people will be eating dinner at the reception so she can order the proper amount of food and will have the necessary number of tables and chairs available. In addition, she will have to pay for the dinners ordered for any no-shows.

- If after accepting an invitation you find you have to regret, do so promptly by telephone or by sending a note. In either case, explain why you will be unable to attend.

- Do not ask to bring a friend to a wedding.

- If you are engaged or living with someone, and the bride is unaware of this fact, it's permissible to ask her if you may bring that person with you to the wedding. However, use discretion about making this request. If the bride knows you are engaged or living with someone, and has not sent that person an invitation, do not ask if you may bring him or her with you. It probably means that it is a very small wedding, and guests are limited to those the bride and groom know well.

- If you are invited to a wedding as the guest of a bridesmaid or usher or because you are living with someone, and you receive your own invitation, even if you don't know the bride or groom, you should send a wedding present. It need not be expensive as long as it's suitable.

- If your children have not been invited to the wedding, do not ask to bring them.

- If your young children are invited to an evening wedding, think twice before taking them. It's likely they'll become restless and cranky as the hour gets later.

- Since the ceremony is the most important feature of any wedding— certainly as far as the bride and groom are concerned—it's not only disrespectful but rude to skip it for no good reason, and attend only the reception.

- While you are not obligated to send a present if you refuse a wedding invitation, if you know the bride or groom well, you will undoubtedly want to anyway.

- If you are sent a wedding announcement, a present is not required, although most people do send one if the bride or groom is a good friend.

- There is a popular misconception that you have a year's grace before sending a wedding present. This is not so. Unless there's a special reason for not doing so, the wedding present is sent before the wedding. Taking presents to the reception has drawbacks; someone has to watch them during the reception, and someone has to be responsible for seeing that they are transported home.

- You may ask a bride what she'd like for a wedding present if you want to, but keep in mind there's always the possibility she may suggest something that costs more than you are prepared to spend and you'll find yourself in an awkward position.

- If you plan to buy your present through the bridal registry department of a store, you'll be smart to do so soon after receiving your wedding invitation. That way you will have a greater number of presents to choose from and a wider price range.

- Never send a wedding present that is on sale, unless you know it can be exchanged or returned for credit.

- Don't take it upon yourself to have a wedding present monogrammed, because that means the bride will not be able to exchange it if she wants to. The best way to handle monogramming is to ask the store to enclose a note with your present saying, "The customer has requested that you bring this gift to the store, if you would like to have it monogrammed." If the bride does decide to have the present monogrammed, you will be billed for the charges. Of course, if you buy your present through a bridal registry department, they'll know just which items the bride and groom would like monogrammed and with what initials.

- As a gift enclosure card, you may use your personal calling card (not your business card) or the store's card. To personalize your own card, put a diagonal slash through your name and above it write your message, "Best wishes to you and David for your happiness always, Love, Tory Whipple." A couple use their "Mr. and Mrs." calling card and sign it, "Love, Tory and Jack Whipple."

- A wedding present is addressed to the bride and sent to her care of whoever issued the invitation, usually her mother and father. Even if she would rather have presents sent to her at some other address, there's no way she can get this message across on the invitation without giving the impression that she's soliciting gifts. If you think the bride would rather have presents sent to her own address, ask her, or ask her mother. Of course, if you are dealing with a bridal registry department there's no problem, as they will have this information on file. Should you for some reason have to send the present after the wedding it is addressed to the bride and groom and sent to them at home.

• Among certain religious and ethnic groups it is common practice and perfectly proper to give money as a present. You may send a check to the bride at home or put the check in an envelope and take it to the reception. If the latter, hand the envelope to the bride or groom when you go through the receiving line or when you are saying your goodbyes just before you leave the reception. Checks sent before the wedding are made out to the bride; when they are taken to the reception, they may be made out to the bride (Gail Alexander, if she takes her husband's name), or to the groom, or to the bride and groom (Gail and David Alexander).

• If you don't receive a thank-you letter within two months of sending a present, feel free to get in touch with the bride. Even though you may think your present deserved an earlier acknowledgment, the letter you write should be friendly in tone because, at this point you don't know whether the present was ever received. What you can say is, "Dear Gail, Having not heard from you, I am worried that you never received the crystal pitcher we sent you from Haliby and Wexler on May 3rd. While I know how busy you must be, it would relieve my mind to know it arrived safely. I hope you and David had a great time in Hawaii and that we'll see each other before too long. All my love, Aunt Allie."

• If the bride and groom invite you to their house after the honeymoon and your wedding present is not in evidence, don't embarrass them by asking where it is.

• If you're an out-of-town guest at a wedding, you are responsible for paying your hotel bill. The bride's mother will in all probability send you the names of a few hotels or motels in the area along with their rates, or a card may be enclosed with the wedding invitation listing hotels and motels. You then choose the hotel you want to stay at and make your own reservation. On the other hand, she may write saying she has blocked off rooms for out-of-town guests at a particular hotel. In that case, all you have to do is call the hotel and give them your name and credit card number. If the hotel she chooses is more than you can afford or doesn't appeal to you for some reason, you are not obligated to stay there. You can look into other hotels that may be more to your liking.

• As an out-of-town guest, you may or may not be invited to the rehearsal dinner. It depends entirely on how large the dinner will be and how many other out-of-towners are attending the wedding. If you haven't been invited, don't solicit an invitation.

- If you are attending a wedding in a city or town other than your own, and are not certain what to wear, ask the advice of the bride or her mother. That way you won't have to worry about being underdressed or overdressed.

- A man does not wear a tuxedo before six o'clock in the evening.

- At a Jewish wedding, particularly if it's Orthodox or Conservative, if guests are expected to wear headcoverings, a man who arrives without one is given a yarmulke, a woman without a head covering is given a handkerchief.

- If you are a relative or close friend of the bride or groom, you may be asked to sit in one of the reserved pews at the front of the church (there is no seat assignment within the pew itself). The mother of the bride or groom will inform you of this either orally or by sending you a handwritten note or an engraved pew card. Sometimes, instead of a pew number card, a card that says "Within the Ribbon" is sent. This means ribbons will be placed before the ceremony along the aisle posts to mark the reserved pews.

- Arrive at the wedding ceremony approximately fifteen minutes before it's to begin. If you are to sit in one of the reserved pews and were sent a note with the pew number on it, hand the note to an usher; if you were told orally, give the usher your name and he will refer to the seating list he's been given. If you have not been specially seated, the usher who greets you will ask whether you are a friend of the bride or groom so he will know whether to seat you on the left side of the aisle, which is the bride's side, or the right side, which is the groom's. (At a Jewish ceremony the two sides are often reversed; it varies according to tradition.)

- A woman being seated takes the usher's arm and walks up the aisle with him. As you walk, make light conversation, perhaps commenting on how lovely the church looks or asking him how the rehearsal dinner went off. If you see a friend, and there is space in that pew, you may ask the usher if you may sit with your friend. While the custom is for a married woman to take the usher's arm and her husband to follow behind them, rather than tagging along, there's no reason for him not to walk at his wife's right side (it's certainly a lot friendlier that way). If the couple are accompanied by children, the husband walks behind with them. When an usher escorts a single man, they walk up the aisle side by side. Usually, when the groom is from out of town, there will be fewer guests on his side of the aisle than on the bride's side. If this is the case, to give the church a balanced look, ushers ask guests who are friends of the bride if they would mind sitting on the groom's side—to which the guests should readily agree. At a large wedding, if there's a long line of people waiting to be escorted into the church, guests can help the ushers out by seating themselves.

- Ushers do not seat any guest who arrives at the church after the mother of the bride has been escorted up the aisle. If you arrive late, either stand at the back of the church during the ceremony or slide into one of the back pews as inconspicuously as possible.

- Occasionally the white canvas runner is already in place on the center aisle when guests arrive. If so, the two side aisles are used for seating guests.

- If you're smart enough to arrive in time to get an aisle seat, meaning you'll have a choice view of the wedding procession, you have every right to hold on to it. When other guests are ushered to your pew, they slide past to reach their seats.

- Once seated, you can talk quietly to the person beside you.

- The bride's mother is always seated last. When she is in her seat the organist will start the processional. At the sound of the first chords, the congregation rises. If you are at all uncertain as to when to stand, watch what the people in front of you are doing. Once you are on your feet, you can turn and face the back of the church to watch the wedding party as it starts up the aisle.

- If you attend a wedding of a faith different from your own and are not familiar with the service, watch others so you will know when to stand up or sit down. Non-Catholics are not expected to cross themselves or genuflect, and if it is a nuptial Mass you do not have to take communion.

- Do not take pictures in either a church or synagogue.

- After the recessional, guests are expected to remain seated until those in the reserved pews have walked all the way back down the aisle. When white satin ribbons have been strung along the aisle posts of the nonreserved pews, they are removed by two ushers once the special guests have reached the back of the church. You can then leave your pew; you are not escorted out by an usher.

- Once you arrive at the reception and before the receiving line forms, you may talk to the other guests and perhaps sip a glass of champagne if it is being passed.

- At some point you must go through the receiving line (in the case of a couple, the woman goes first). If the line is particularly long, wait until it's eased up a bit. It's not good manners to go through the line carrying a drink, so give it to a waiter or put it down on a table. When there's an announcer at the head of the line, give him your name: "Oliver Frost." He will repeat your name to the bride's mother, who is first in line. If there is no announcer, announce yourself. Don't assume the bride's mother, who perhaps has seen you only a few times, is going to remember your name at a time like this. Help her out by saying, "Mrs. Cramer, I'm Oliver Frost."

The receiving line is not a place for long conversation, so once you have told the bride's mother how pleased you are to be there, or how lovely her daughter looks, she will introduce you to the groom's mother. If you're a relative of the bride, as you shake her hand tell her so. Otherwise you might say, "I'm so glad finally to meet you. I hope we'll have a chance to chat later." After you've said a few words, move right on, so as not to hold up the orderly flow of the line. The next person you speak to will be the bride. If she is talking to another guest, you'll have to wait your turn, even though you may feel somewhat self-conscious standing there with no one to talk to. When your turn does come, extend your hand and say, "Gail, I'm Oliver Frost, a colleague of your father's." If you are a relative or close friend of the bride, instead of a handshake give her a kiss on the cheek. While it was once considered improper to congratulate a bride (the implication being that you were congratulating her on finding a husband), it is no longer a breach of etiquette. However, there are other things you can say to the bride that would be more personal, for instance, "I've never seen you look more beautiful," or "Your mother's so happy you are wearing her wedding dress."

After you've exchanged a few words with the bride, the groom will be next in line. You can offer him your congratulations followed by a remark or two—maybe commenting on how calm he appeared during the ceremony; any short remark that comes to mind is appropriate. Next in line will be the bridesmaids. Instead of stopping to say hello or shaking hands with each, you can give a collective greeting, saying, as you move along, how well they performed at the ceremony and how much you like their dresses. If you happen to know one of the bridesmaids, stop and shake hands with her or kiss her as you exchange a few words.

- If there's a guest book, a man or woman signs his or her name without a title. A couple sign their name "Adelaide and Oliver Frost."

- No one at a wedding dances before the bride and groom. They have their first dance together and the guests congregate around the dance floor, applauding them. Once the bride's and groom's parents and their wedding attendants have taken to the dance floor, any couple may join in.

- If it's a dinner reception, the orchestra will play a trumpet fanfare to get your attention. You will then know it's time to be seated. No matter how much you'd like to sit beside a particular person at dinner, it is the apex of rudeness to switch place cards.

- The reception, unlike the rehearsal dinner, is not a toast-making occasion. While the best man, the bride's father, or a few other key people may make toasts, do not make one yourself unless you are called on.

- When the time comes for the bride and groom to cut the cake (sometimes the orchestra plays a trumpet fanfare) you'll want to gather around with the other guests to watch.

- As a general guideline, don't leave the reception until after the bride and groom have cut the cake. However, if they delay the cutting of the cake, and you've been at the reception a few hours, you may certainly slip out, without drawing attention to your leaving. Later, you can write a letter to the bride's mother and father thanking them and saying what a good time you had.

- When the bride throws her bouquet, a woman guest does not leap for it. The bride is probably throwing it to her maid of honor or one of the bridesmaids.

- If you stay at the reception until the bride and groom leave, you'll usually be given paper rose petals to throw at the couple as they make their getaway. Their departure signals that the reception is over. You should find the bride's parents to tell them how much you enjoyed the wedding and to thank them for including you.

- It's customary at any reception held at a hotel or club for the gratuities to be included in the overall cost of the event. Therefore, you do not tip the coatroom attendant.

- While it's not obligatory to write to the bride's mother if you thanked her at the reception, you can be certain that a letter would mean a lot to her. Describe some of the highlights of the wedding and tell her what a success it was—how everyone thought so. End the letter by saying, "So many thanks to you and Arthur for including us." Of course, if you didn't thank her at the reception because you left a bit early, you certainly *must* write to her afterward.

THE ROLE OF THE WEDDING ATTENDANTS

It's very exciting to be asked to be an attendant in the wedding of a friend or relative. It's a compliment plus, of course, there's the delight in knowing you'll be playing a part in this once-in-a-lifetime day for someone you've shared a great deal with. There's very little responsibility associated with the role of a bridesmaid or usher, although the maid or matron of honor and the best man do have certain functions they have to see to. But, for the most part, all that's required of the attendants is to surround the bride and groom with good cheer and merriment and to add an element of cameraderie to the wedding festivities.

When a good friend announces his or her engagement, don't take it for granted that you will be asked to be an attendant just because that person was in your wedding. If you aren't asked, it may be for a good reason, such as that your friend is having a smaller wedding than yours with fewer bridesmaids and ushers, or he or she has more relatives or friends to include.

If you're asked to be an attendant and would rather not accept—you may not feel as close to the bride or groom as he or she feels toward you—there's no easy answer. You're pretty much limited to giving a lame excuse, which in all likelihood will be seen as such. So, unless the idea is totally unacceptable and you don't care whether or not your excuse is believed, it's best to accept such an invitation with good grace and a positive attitude.

Once you have made the commitment to be an attendant in a wedding, do not cancel out except for a significant reason: serious illness, the recent death of a family member, or a sudden and unavoidable business obligation.

Although it may not happen often, occasionally a bride or groom will ask a relative or friend to substitute for a bridesmaid or usher who has suddenly dropped out of the wedding because of illness. The reason the substitute was not invited to be in the wedding in the first place is perhaps because his or her relationship to the bride and groom is not as close as that of the other attendants, who may be relatives or longtime friends. If you are asked to fill in as a bridesmaid or usher at the last moment, you don't have to accept unless you like the idea well enough to enter into the spirit of the occasion. Of course, there's no way a woman can fill in at the very last moment unless she can fit into the dress of the bridesmaid she's substituting for.

If you're worried about whether you can afford to be in a wedding, don't say anything to the bride about the cost when she first asks you to be a bridesmaid. That's hardly the appropriate time to bring up such concerns as it puts her in an embarrassing position. Also, at this point, it's doubtful that she'd have any idea of what the attendants' expenses will be. The best thing to do is accept the invitation, wait a bit, and then have a chat with the bride about your concerns. Once the topic is out in the open and a discussion in the works, chances are some compromise can be made—perhaps you can pay the expenses in installments or perhaps the bride and her family will share the expenses with you. If that is the case, you should consider this a private matter between you and the bride and not discuss it with anyone else. You do not want to put her in an awkward situation with other members of the wedding party.

Should you become pregnant after you have agreed to be a bridesmaid, discuss your condition with the bride. If you are able to have your bridesmaid's dress altered so it fits properly there's really no reason why you shouldn't be in the wedding. Not being in the ceremony, however, does not mean you can't participate in whatever wedding festivities are planned.

Lastly, and not the least important, it's your responsibility as an attendant to show up on time at the wedding rehearsal and ceremony, not to be late for any pre-wedding parties, and to make sure you thank your host or hostess before leaving a party. If you are the houseguest of a friend of the bride or groom or their parents, when you get home write a letter thanking your hosts for having put you up.

THE MAID AND/OR MATRON OF HONOR AND BRIDESMAIDS

The maid and/or matron of honor and the bridesmaids are responsible for buying their own dresses and other accessories. While they pay their own travel expenses to and from wherever the wedding is held, if they are not housed with friends or relatives of the bride, which is usually the case, the bride or her family pick up the cost of the hotel or motel bill. Bridesmaids also have the expense of a shower present and a joint wedding present to the bride. Generally, the maid or matron of honor, or perhaps one of the bridesmaids, gives a shower for the bride. While it's not necessary to do so, if the bride's attendants live in the same town or city as she does, sometime before the wedding they may decide to entertain her at lunch or dinner. Those who can should offer to put up out-of-town attendants or other wedding guests.

The primary role of the maid or matron of honor is to be a devoted and loyal friend to the bride. The bride may need her to run interference when wedding plans go awry or to soothe her frazzled nerves as the magical date draws near. In a lighter vein, the maid of honor is there to share with the bride all the excitement that goes along with the wedding plans: who's accepted the invitation, what the bridal bouquet will look like, who will sit beside whom at the bridal table, whether the groom will wear a wedding ring, and all the rest of the fascinating trivia that have to do with the upcoming event.

As the bride's chief attendant, the maid or matron of honor should ask the bride or her mother what she can do to help with the wedding plans. Aside from her ceremonial duties (see "Official Duties of the Attendants" later in this section), she

- Suggests a joint bridesmaids' present for the bride, taking into account what she feels the bridesmaids can afford. After the bridesmaids agree on the present, collects the money to pay for it and buys it.
- May give a shower for the bride.
- Gives a toast to the bride or bride and groom at the rehearsal dinner.
- Helps the bride get dressed before the wedding.
- Is in charge of the groom's wedding ring, if he will have one.

- Serves as an official witness, signing the marriage certificate at the church or synagogue.
- Helps the bride get ready to go away after the reception.
- Alerts the bride's and groom's parents when the couple are ready to leave the reception.

THE BEST MAN AND USHERS

While ushers have no specific responsibilities other than escorting guests to their seats, they should ask the best man if they can assist him in any way and make themselves available for whatever requests he may make of them.

The best man and ushers pay for the rental of their suits. While the groom traditionally gives them their ties and gloves (if gloves are to be worn), today they are most often rented along with the suits. Ushers are responsible for their transportation to and from the city where the wedding is to be, but if they will not be staying with family or friends of the bride or groom and need hotel accommodations, the groom picks up the tab. Other usher expenses include the joint wedding present to the groom and possibly a shower present, if they attend one. Also, if the groom does not give a bachelor dinner, the best man and ushers may chip in to give their own dinner for the groom. At the actual wedding and reception, aside from their ushering duties, they must make a point of dancing with the bride, the maid and/or matron of honor, and each of the bridesmaids at the reception. An usher who knows the mother of the bride or groom particularly well should dance with her also.

In an earlier edition of this book, the best man was described as adviser, messenger, valet, secretary, and general factotum to the groom. Today, a best man does not have that much time to play secretary to the groom, although there are certain pre-wedding chores he should be willing to help with and a number of wedding customs to participate in. These below are in addition to his ceremonial duties (see "The Best Man" under "Official Duties of the Attendants" later in this section). The best man

- Suggests an ushers' present for the groom, taking into account what he feels the ushers can afford. After ushers agree on a present, he collects the money and buys the present.
- Often oversees ushers' suit rentals and fittings. Makes sure that ushers pick up their suits the day before the wedding so there's time for any last-minute alterations.
- Makes first toast to the bride and groom at the rehearsal dinner.
- Makes certain ushers have their ties, and gloves, if any.
- Helps the groom get dressed before the wedding and sees that he gets to the ceremony on time. (The best man may drive the groom to the ceremony, if a limousine has not been reserved.)

- Is responsible for holding the bride's wedding ring at the ceremony.

- Makes sure that the groom has the clergyperson's, the organist's, and any other fees in his pocket to take to the wedding or takes them himself.

- Makes sure that the groom has the wedding license with him.

- Serves as an official witness to the wedding, signing the marriage certificate.

- Makes the first toast at the reception and reads any congratulatory mailgrams.

- When the dancing starts, led by the bride and groom, the father of the bride cuts in on the groom. After the bride and her father have danced together briefly, the best man then cuts in on the father of the bride. Sometime during the reception the best man should also dance with the maid and/or matron of honor and the bridesmaids. He should also ask the mothers of the bride and groom for a dance.

- Makes certain the groom has the suitcases for the honeymoon, the tickets, and any reservations safe and at hand.

- Puts the suitcases in the going-away car. If possible, keeps the car hidden from pranksters. (The all but obsolete custom of tying old shoes to the going-away car and throwing others after it is said to represent the stones thrown at pursuers when marriages were achieved by capture.)

- Makes sure the car is at the proper location when the couple are ready to leave the reception. May drive them to the airport or other destination.

- Places an order for champagne to be waiting in the couple's honeymoon hotel room.

- Sees that the ushers' suits are returned to the rental company after the wedding.

OFFICIAL DUTIES OF THE ATTENDANTS

THE MAID OR MATRON OF HONOR The maid or matron of honor serves as an official witness to the wedding and the bride's chief attendant. During the ceremony she holds the bride's bouquet. She is also responsible for the bride's veil and straightening the bride's train just before the recessional. If the groom will be given a ring, the maid or matron of honor hands it to the bride (for lack of a better place, she may wear it on her thumb). When there are two honor attendants (a maid *and* a matron of honor), they may walk beside each other in the processional, or one may precede the other. In the latter case, the one that the bride has designated as her chief attendant comes last so she will be next to the bride when they reach the chancel.

THE BEST MAN The best man is also an official witness to the wedding and may be asked to take the clergyperson's fee (and any other fees) with him in envelopes to the church or synagogue, giving them to the clergyperson or one of his associates either before or after the service. He is also in charge of the bride's wedding ring. He should keep it in his vest pocket, or wear it on his little finger, until he hands it to the groom during the ceremony. In the recessional, he walks back down the aisle with the matron or maid of honor (if there are both he escorts the matron of honor, the head usher the maid of honor). Once he has reached the rear of the church, he may or may not retrace his steps to escort the mother of the bride back down the aisle.

THE HEAD USHER The head usher should be given instructions (preferably written) about any special seating arrangements for relatives or honored friends of the bride and groom. He alerts the ushers about these instructions. He may also ask an usher to tell the groom when the bride's party has arrived. As the church fills up, the head usher watches to see that the pews on either side of the aisle are more or less equally filled. If not, and it happens that there are fewer people sitting on the groom's side, the usher asks some of the guests, even if they are friends of the bride, whether they would mind sitting on the groom's side. The head usher also often escorts the bride's mother up the aisle. After he has seated her, and if the canvas runner is now to be laid down, he and another designated usher walk up the aisle to the foot of the chancel steps (or wherever the runner starts) and each takes an end of the runner holder and they roll it back down the aisle to where the processional begins. After the service the head usher may or may not be the one who escorts the bride's or the groom's mother back down the aisle.

THE USHERS The ushers should arrive at the church an hour before the ceremony is to start. In the vestry they are given their boutonnieres, and the head usher goes over any special seating instructions with them as well as the list of guests who are to be escorted to the reserved pews (sometimes the guests are sent notes with the pew numbers on them, or engraved pew number cards, to hand to an usher). When an usher approaches a guest waiting to be seated, he asks, "Are you a friend of the bride or groom?" That way he will know whether to seat the guest on the left side of the aisle, which is the bride's side, or the right side, which is the groom's (at a Jewish ceremony, the sides are often reversed, depending on custom). An usher offers his right arm to a woman. As they walk up the aisle, they chat politely—he may remark on what a great occasion it is or ask her how she knows the bride or groom. In the case of a married couple, the husband may either walk behind the usher and his wife (the traditional way) or, which is more sociable, at his wife's right. If any children are accompanying the couple, then the husband walks behind with them. When an usher escorts a man to his seat, the man walks beside him but does not take his arm. If he escorts a guest to a pew where someone is sitting next to the aisle, he does not ask that person to move over a seat. Anyone who arrives early enough to get an aisle seat—the choice spot from which to watch the processional—is entitled to keep it; other guests can slide by as they enter the pew. If, as the church or synagogue fills up, it appears that more pews are filled on one side than the other, ushers ask arriving guests if they would mind sitting on the more sparsely filled side, regardless of whether they are friends of the bride or of the groom.

A preassigned usher escorts the mother of the groom up the aisle, after which the head usher or a brother of the bride, if he's an usher, escorts the mother of the bride to her pew. Any guest who arrives after the mother of the bride has been seated is not escorted up the aisle. After the mother of the bride is seated, if there's a white canvas runner, it's rolled back down the aisle by two assigned ushers, one usually being the head usher. If there are to be white satin ribbons laid along the aisle posts of the pews, two designated ushers walk together up the aisle to the last reserved pews, the point where satin ribbons have been carefully laid alongside the posts. They pick up the entire bundle of ribbon and, in step, walk back the length of the pews, as rehearsed, drawing the ribbons inside the aisle posts in a straight line, and finally placing the loop at the end of each ribbon over the furthest aisle post. The ushers are then ready to take their places for the processional. Ushers go up the aisle in pairs, but in the recessional it is optional for them to pair with bridesmaids. If there's an unequal number of ushers, one may walk between two pairs of ushers. After the recessional, the pew ribbons are left in place until the mothers of the bride and groom and reserved pew guests have reached the back of the church. The ribbons are then removed by two ushers. Ushers do not escort guests back down the aisle.

THE RING BEARER When there's a ring bearer, for safety's sake, the ring may be tacked to the pillow with a very fine piece of thread, or a fake ring may be substituted for the real one, which the best man carries in his pocket.

WHEN AN ATTENDANT DROPS OUT

If an attendant has to drop out of the wedding party for some very good reason, such as illness, a death in the family, or, if working abroad, being unable to make the trip back home, the bride or groom may either find someone to fill in for the absent attendant or leave the wedding party as it is. It is not that easy to find an appropriate stand-in. Most people you'd think of asking would wonder why they weren't asked to be in the wedding in the first place. What's more, if it is a bridesmaid who has dropped out and the substitute can't fit into the dress the original attendant was to wear, she probably won't be able to get a dress of her own on short notice.

Since replacing a missing attendant presents problems, the simplest solution is to leave the bridal party as it is—and there is absolutely no reason not to do so. A lone usher can walk between two pairs of ushers or, if there are now only three ushers, they can walk single file in the processional (the clergyperson will know what looks best). If it's a bridesmaid who will walk alone, she precedes the maid or matron of honor.

PRE-WEDDING PARTIES

Once the wedding preparations are well under way and plans are moving along as scheduled, you and your fiancé can relax and look forward to whatever pre-wedding parties are being given in your honor. For you, it's a time to get together with the people you care about most but may not see that often and to share your happiness with them. For family and friends, it's an opportunity to express their love and admiration for you both and to commemorate the occasion with congratulatory toasts.

While you may have many friends who want to entertain you royally before the wedding, it's best not to load your calendar with too many social activities, or you and the groom may arrive at the altar feeling somewhat bedraggled. If you explain that you have a busy schedule ahead of you and don't feel you can add to it, in all probability your friends will understand—or at least they should. Perhaps they will want to give you some kind of a celebration later on, after you return from your honeymoon, when you'd appreciate a party much more.

What follows are descriptions of the traditional pre-wedding parties:

SHOWER

According to legend, the first wedding shower was given for a maiden whose father so disapproved of her beloved that he withdrew his daughter's dowry. Today's wedding shower might be considered a modern replacement for the hope chest and dowry of former years, although most contemporary women enter marriage with a good number of possessions of their own. Still, every bride-to-be enjoys being given at least one shower—perhaps not so much for the presents it brings as for the chance to get together, often for the last time as a single woman, with her closest friends.

A wedding shower is never given by the bride's mother, sister, or grandmother. It's considered poor taste, for the good reason that it might seem as though the bride and her family are asking for more presents. A shower is most often given by a close friend of the bride, possibly the maid of honor or a bridesmaid. It's not always one person alone who gives a shower; it can be a couple or a number of friends of the bride who band together to give a shower. Seldom are more than two showers given for any bride. And if there are two, different friends should be invited to each. That way no one has to buy more than one present.

There's no set custom that says when, in relation to the date of the wedding, a shower should be given, although most take place at least two weeks before. Later than that the bride will probably be too busy. As to the time of day a shower is given, it's up to the hostess and the bride to make this decision. They may like the idea of inviting guests to a brunch or an after-dinner dessert shower. Or they may prefer a lunch, tea, or cocktail party. While showers were once the private domain of women, today men often attend.

Generally, presents are simple, practical items that are relatively inexpensive, costing anywhere from five to twenty dollars. They aren't intended to be more than small tokens because everyone attending a shower will also be invited to the wedding, which means another present.

Guests at a shower bring presents based on the theme indicated on the invitation. If the bride has a certain color request, that too appears on the invitation. There's no set rule about themes for a shower. There are showers for the bedroom, kitchen, bathroom, closet, or garden for instance. And there are lingerie or pillow showers, or anything else the bride and hostess think up. A very popular type is the "round-the-clock" shower. The invitation indicates a specific hour of the day for which the guest should bring a present. For example, if the time given is 7 A.M. two coffee mugs or a box of bath soap would be appropriate presents. Those who are clever and witty have fun with this theme—whatever the hour chosen.

In some communities it's customary to have a "wishing well" at the shower. If there will be one, it's stated on the invitation, ("Please bring a present for the 'wishing well' "), and a small present is then brought to the shower to be placed in the "well." Since guests will already have the responsibility of buying a wedding present, it doesn't seem right to burden them with the expense of still another present. However, for those brides who favor the "wishing well" gimmick, it should be assumed that guests will bring only a token present, like a ball of twine, Scotch tape, a spool of thread—some small useful item that can be put in the "wishing well," wrapped or unwrapped, with or without a card identifying the giver. If it's not possible to find a "wishing well" at a party rental service, with a little creative ability one can be designed from a large box or other suitable receptacle.

THE ROLE OF THE HOSTESS If you are hosting a shower, ask the bride when she would like it to take place, if necessary asking her for a choice of two or three dates. You should also ask her if she has a preference as to the time of day it's held. If she works, in all likelihood it will have to be the late afternoon, evening, or a weekend. You can either give her an idea of how many people you feel you can accommodate comfortably or, if space or cost is of no concern, you can ask her to give you a number to work with. With a little give and take, you'll be able to work it out to your mutual satisfaction.

While there's nothing that says you can't give a surprise shower, how much more fun for the bride to be in on the plans, deciding the friends she'd most like to invite and the type of shower she'd most enjoy. Also, when the shower is a surprise, it's not possible to ask the bride her color choice in kitchen utensils, linen, or whatever the theme of the shower is.

You can invite guests to a shower by sending printed, fill-in invitations, specially designed for the occasion, which are available in any quality stationery store. If the shower is to be a relatively small affair, and you have the time, you can extend the invitation by writing a note to each guest on your personal stationery or informal. Or, since it's an informal event, there's no reason not to telephone the invitations. In addition to the usual information contained in an invitation, give the theme of the shower and the bride's color preference, if she has one.

THE ROLE OF THE BRIDE It's assumed that the friend who is giving you the shower will ask you to give her a few dates when you'd like to have it held. She will also want to know what time of day is best for you. Be receptive to any suggestions she may have about the number of people or type of party she has in mind. You don't want to put her in the position of having to give a more elaborate party than she wants or can afford.

When deciding on the theme of your shower, give some thought to how well off your guests are. Presents for a linen shower are bound to be more expensive than those for a kitchen shower. Bear in mind, too, that each guest attending will also have the expense of a wedding present. Be particularly cost-conscious with regard to your attendants, who will have to pay for their dresses, accessories, and a bridesmaids' present. If you're at all worried about their finances, you may suggest that they get together and give you just one shower present. And if, for some reason, a bridesmaid is to attend a second shower, tell her that she was more than generous the first time around, and that you'd be most upset if she gave you another gift.

When you make out the guest list for the shower, remember that no one should be invited who is not also being invited to the wedding. You will want to invite your mother and the groom's mother. Even if she lives some distance away and won't be able to attend, she'll be pleased to have been thought of. Others to invite are your wedding attendants, family members, good friends, and anyone else you're close to. If men are being invited, you'll want to include your father, the groom's father, the groom's attendants, and any other male relatives and friends who can be accommodated. If two showers will be given for you, you will have to figure out how to divide the list so each person is invited to only one.

When you give the guest list to the hostess, be sure to include all ZIP codes with the addresses. Also, it will be much easier for her if the list is typed.

There's not a hostess who doesn't appreciate the luxury of flowers in her house, particularly when she's having a party. As an expression of gratitude for giving you the shower, it's thoughtful to send her flowers or a plant. You should call her several days before the party to find out what her favorite flowers are and what colors would look best in her living room. If you are in touch before she gets around to calling the florist, you'll save her the expense of buying her own flowers.

At the shower, you open your presents whenever you feel it's opportune, but not before all the guests have arrived. Although you will, of course, thank each guest for her present as you open it, be sure to keep a list of who has given you what. That way, you can write a note of additional thanks, if not to everyone who attended the shower, at least to those who brought something special. Since you'll be busy opening presents and thanking people, ask your sister or one of your friends if she'd mind keeping the list for you.

Sometimes, just for fun, the bows and ribbons from the shower packages are fashioned into a hat, which the bride then puts on and is photographed in. The hat is made by stapling bows and ribbons to a paper plate; the ribbons tie under the bride's chin. Or the bows and ribbons may be made into a bouquet which the bride may carry at the wedding rehearsal. The bows are stapled to the plate and the ribbons are drawn through slits in the plate.

After the shower, you should write a letter to the hostess, thanking her for her thoughtfulness and generosity. If you did not send her flowers or a plant before the shower, this would be the time to do so. Or, instead of flowers, you may want to give her a present of some sort.

THE ROLE OF THE GUEST

- Do not expect to be asked to a shower unless invited to the wedding.
- You may reply to a shower invitation by letter or by telephone.
- If you are single, do not ask to bring a date to a shower unless couples are being invited, in which case you may ask to bring someone you are engaged to or living with.
- A shower present is not a substitute for a wedding present.
- Do not buy a shower present that's more extravagant than is called for. It isn't fair to the other invitees who have gone along with the guidelines. The only exception to this might be the bride's mother, grandmother, or some other older relative, who may choose to give a somewhat more substantial present.
- The shower present you give should be wrapped, with a card or tag attached, saying, "Here's to your future happiness. Lots of love, Helen," or whatever other message you choose.

- If you are invited to a shower and must decline, it's not necessary to send a present, although if the bride's a good friend you'll probably want to anyway. You can deliver the present to the hostess' house any time before the shower or you can mail it to her.
- Should you be invited to two showers for the bride, there is no reason you have to attend both, unless you want to. However, if you accept the first invitation, it would be impolite to regret it later just because the second invitation you receive appeals to you more.
- If a wedding is called off after the shower has taken place, don't expect the bride to return your present, unless it was an item of considerable expense.

BRIDESMAIDS' PARTY

It used to be that as part of the pre-wedding festivities the maid and/or matron of honor and bridesmaids gave a lunch for the bride a week or so before the wedding, at one of their houses. At that time, they often gave their bridesmaids' present to the bride and she, in turn, gave them her presents. Other than that, it was a purely social occasion, with conversation centering around the bride and the forthcoming nuptials.

As women became a part of the work force, life's patterns changed, and the bridesmaids' lunch lost popularity as a wedding ritual. Today, however, if the majority of the bridesmaids are living in the same city or town as the bride, they often do entertain her, perhaps at lunch on a weekend, or at dinner some evening, either at someone's house or at a restaurant. If they live or work any distance away, there's little chance for them to have a party for her, particularly if they won't be arriving in town until the day before the wedding. If there is no bridesmaids' party, presents between the bride and her attendants can be exchanged at the rehearsal dinner.

BRIDE'S PARTY

Rather than the bridesmaids giving a lunch or dinner for the bride, the bride may want to honor her attendants with a similar party. If the groom has a bachelor dinner, she may choose that night to invite her bridesmaids to dinner.

BACHELOR DINNER

The motive for giving a bachelor dinner used to be very different from the motive today, if indeed one is held. The bachelor dinner was intended to bolster the groom's flagging courage in the face of the responsibilities he was taking on. It was also more or less a swan song to his bachelorhood—a chance for a final fling before he tied the knot. The party often turned out to be raucous, including plenty of drinking, and culminated in breaking champagne glasses to honor the bride.

Today, the groom views the bachelor dinner differently: as a chance to get together with close male friends, to honor their friendship, and to celebrate with them his forthcoming marriage.

If bachelor dinners are no longer so prevalent, it's for lack of opportunity. The best man and ushers don't always live within commuting distance of the groom. In fact, in most cases, they arrive at the wedding scene only the day before, in time for the rehearsal. When there is a bachelor dinner, it may be given by the groom, or his father may host the event at his house or at a restaurant or a club. The affair is no different from any dinner party, except that at sometime during the evening the groom presents a toast, in champagne, to his bride. After his toast, any guest is free to follow suit.

The groom and his attendants may exchange their presents at the bachelor dinner or at the rehearsal dinner. This is the time for the groom to give his best man and ushers their wedding ties and gloves (if they have not been rented along with their suits).

Ushers' dinner

Sometimes, instead of the groom giving a dinner, the best man and ushers give one for him. If there's to be a party, it's immaterial as to who gives it.

Pre-wedding lunch

It used to be considered bad luck for the groom to see the bride on their wedding day, before they met at the church or synagogue. This superstition was observed at any cost until fairly recently, when brides decided to throw caution to the wind and attend pre-wedding lunches with their about-to-be spouses. Actually, there's something to be said in defense of the old custom; by the day of the marriage, the bride's and groom's nerves tend to be stretched out and it only takes one lover's quarrel to disrupt the happiness of the day.

Often a relative or friend of the bride or her family will offer to give the pre-wedding lunch. This is about the most thoughtful gesture any friend can make, as it spares the bride worrying about how the wedding attendants and out-of-town guests will occupy themselves and where they'll be fed. It also helps her fill up her day, which in all probability will be going by less quickly than she'd like it to. The guest list should include, in addition to the bride and groom, their parents (the bride's parents may want to stay home attending to last-minute wedding details), the wedding attendants, and any other special guests the couple want to include, such as out-of-towners.

Not every bride may want to attend a pre-wedding lunch, and if she does not, the person hosting the lunch must not have hurt feelings. This is not only an exciting day for the bride, but it is also an emotional one, and it may be that she'd rather spend the remaining hours before her wedding quietly, in the familiar surroundings of her home—attending to last-minute details. What she might choose to do, as a courtesy to the hostess, is drop in at the start of the lunch party for half an hour or so, and then go home for a leisurely lunch with her parents, and possibly her maid of honor and siblings.

OUT-OF-TOWN GUESTS AND PRE-WEDDING PARTIES

When the bride and groom are expecting out-of-town relatives and friends at their wedding, they should make a special effort to see that these guests are included in one or two of the pre-wedding parties. Since most out-of-towners arrive only the day before the event, a pre-wedding party is probably the only chance they will have to spend some time with the couple.

When the bride and groom make out the guest list for the rehearsal dinner, they should take into account any out-of-towners they're expecting for the wedding, particularly those staying in hotels. Some out-of-towners, such as grandparents and godparents, may already be on the dinner list, but if there's room for others, it's that much more fun for all involved. If not, it is nice if some close friend of the bride's mother, or even the mother of a bridesmaid, knowing the couple can't invite every out-of-towner to the dinner, offers to have a number of them to her own house that evening.

There are two other occasions when out-of-town guests may be at loose ends. The first is lunchtime, before an afternoon wedding. If the bride has a favorite aunt, or someone else she's close to, living in the area she may feel she can ask that person if she's willing to have a few of those out-of-towners over for an informal brunch or lunch. The other loose-end time happens when the reception is at midday or early in the afternoon. Then the guests will not be fed dinner. In this situation, the bride's parents may want to give thought to having a simple buffet supper for those remaining in the area.

If the bride and groom do not have friends who can entertain their out-of-town guests, it's not the end of the world. The guests will, or should, understand if there's not enough space at a pre-wedding party for everyone from out of town. And because in all probability most of the guests will be staying at the same hotel they can get together for their meals.

WHO ACCOMPANIES THE BRIDE UP THE AISLE?

It's customary in a Protestant ceremony for the bride to be given away by her father. In the Roman Catholic and Jewish ceremonies giving the bride away is not a part of the service, although the father does accompany his daughter up the aisle.

Many brides today like the idea of walking in the processional unescorted. That's fine, except for one important concern. If a bride senses that her father might be hurt and won't understand why she prefers not to go up the aisle on his arm, then she should think twice before making the decision to go it alone.

Circumstances and the bride's personal preference should determine who accompanies her in the processional. For instance, the bride may want both her mother and father to walk up the aisle with her (this is the custom at Jewish weddings). If she does, she walks between the two, her father on her left, her mother on her right. If she has been brought up by her stepfather and has had little communication with her own father, then her stepfather may be the one to take her up the aisle. If the bride's father is dead, she may be escorted by a male relative—a brother or uncle—or a close family friend. If she decides to have her mother escort her, she does not take her mother's arm. Sometimes the bride may walk escorted or alone in the processional until she reaches her mother's pew, at which point her mother accompanies her to the chancel steps.

THE PRE-REHEARSAL BRIEFING

There are a number of nonreligious customs having to do with the wedding ceremony that you and the groom will want to have clear before the rehearsal takes place. While the following questions and answers have all been covered in their appropriate entries, this summary comprises a sort of rehearsal checklist.

- Does the bride go up the aisle on the right or left arm of her father?

  The bride can be on her father's right or left arm; the right is more convenient as it places her father on the same side of the aisle as the pew he will sit in. Also, if the bride has a train, it means he won't have to cross over it to get to his pew.

- In what order do the bridesmaids and ushers walk up the aisle?

  They may walk single file or in pairs, the shorter ones preceding the taller (they walk in time to the music, slowly, left foot first up the aisle, each pair approximately four paces behind the couple ahead).

- Where will the bridesmaids and ushers stand during the ceremony?

  A lot depends on the size of the church and the number of bridesmaids and ushers. The clergyperson will have performed many weddings, so you should ask his opinion as to what makes the most pleasing arrangement.

- Which is the bride's side of the aisle?

  In Christian ceremonies, facing the front of the church, the left side of the aisle is the bride's, the right the groom's. In the Jewish faith, the two sides are often reversed.

- When there are two main aisles?

When a church has two main aisles, one may be used for the processional, the other for the recessional. If it is decided that one aisle is to be used for both, the other aisle is used only for seating guests. If one aisle is chosen, the grouping at the chancel will be on that aisle's side. If both aisles are used by the bridal party, the grouping at the chancel is as it would be for a church with a center aisle. The bride's family may either be seated in the pews on the far left or a dividing ribbon may be placed down the middle of the center pew and the bride's and groom's families can share the center front pew.

- How many reserved pews should there be?

It depends on the size of the wedding, how many people can fit in a pew, and how many relatives or close friends of the bride and groom will be given special seating. Sometimes there are only one or two reserved pews on each side, although at a large wedding there may be as many as six on each side. If the groom is an out-of-towner, it's likely there will be fewer reserved pews on his side.

- Who sits in the reserved pews?

It's up to you and the groom and your parents as to who has special seating. Along with your parents, siblings, and grandparents, you may want to include other relatives, and perhaps a few close friends.

- How are guests informed that they are to be seated in reserved pews?

Guests who are to be specially seated are most often informed after they have accepted the wedding invitation. They can be informed by telephone or sent notes saying, "This is to let you know you will be seated in pew #3." (There is no specific seat assignment within the pew itself.) Or they may be sent an engraved pew number card or one that says "Within the Ribbon."

- Where are family members and special guests seated?

The mother of the bride is escorted to the aisle seat of the left front pew. Later, when her husband (or whoever escorts the bride) joins her, she moves over one seat, giving him the aisle seat. The groom's mother and father sit beside each other in the right front pew, the father at the left of his wife in the aisle seat. Siblings or grandparents can also sit in the front pew, depending on how much room there is. Other special guests are seated in reserved pews behind the front pews at the discretion of the bride and groom.

• How are divorced parents seated?

It's impossible to set rules for seating divorced parents. It all depends on how well they get along—if they do—and whether they are willing to put their grievances aside for this one day for the sake of their child. Unless the anger is intense, the biological parents sit together in the front pew with their present spouses if they have remarried. Should the parents be on such bad terms that they refuse to sit together, then the father sits in the second or third pew. If you or the groom are worried about seating your divorced parents, particularly if new husbands and wives are involved, the best solution is to talk the subject over with both parents. Who knows? They may be the ones who come up with the idea of sharing a pew.

• Who escorts the mothers of the bride and groom to their pews?

The groom's mother is escorted up the aisle by an usher. If a son of hers is an usher, he may do the honors, otherwise it may be an usher she's known for a long time and is particularly fond of. While it's traditional for her husband to follow behind her, it's a lot more sociable if he walks at her right, but she does not take his arm. After all the wedding guests are seated, the bride's mother is brought up the aisle by the head usher unless she has a son she'd like to have take her up the aisle. If she has two sons who are ushers, she may want both of them to escort her, one on either side. No guests are escorted up the aisle after the mother of the bride has been seated.

• Are grandparents and siblings escorted by assigned ushers?

Not necessarily, but it's a nice gesture on the part of the bride and groom to ask ushers who will recognize grandparents and siblings to be on the lookout for them when they arrive at the church. That way they can greet them by name and escort them to their pews.

• If there's to be a white canvas runner, which usher joins the head usher in rolling it down the aisle?

After the bride's mother has been seated, the head usher with another appointed usher takes the runner and rolls it down the aisle from the front of the church to where the processional will start. Usually the runner is used only at formal weddings. Its purpose is to keep the hem of the bride's dress clean, a mostly symbolic gesture.

• If white satin ribbons are to be placed over the posts of nonreserved pews, which ushers are given this assignment?

This honorary function may be performed by any two ushers. If there's a junior usher, he would be a good choice for one of them, and probably thrilled to be asked.

- Who escorts the mothers of the bride and groom back down the aisle after the recessional?

  If the mothers of the bride and groom don't walk with their husbands, the bride's mother may be escorted by the best man and the groom's mother by the head usher. Or, if either mother has a son who's an usher, he may be asked to take his mother down the aisle.

THE DOUBLE WEDDING

Usually a double wedding occurs when sisters marry at the same time, although occasionally the marriage involves cousins or very close friends. If each bride and groom have separate attendants, the dresses of the attendants should be, if not identical, at least in harmony. Each bride may act as maid of honor for the other, or they may have other attendants. Each groom, too, may act as best man for the other, or each may have his own best man.

There are two sets of ushers in a double wedding. The ushers of the elder bride's wedding party lead off the processional, paired by height, and are followed by the second set of ushers. Then come the elder bride's bridesmaids, her maid and/or matron of honor, and the bride herself on her father's arm. Next come the attendants of the younger bride, then that bride on her father's arm. If she happens to be the sister of the elder bride, a brother or male relative escorts her, or the father may escort his elder daughter up the aisle and return to escort his younger daughter. In the recessional the elder bride, the one married first, leads the recessional with her groom and is followed by the younger bride with her groom. The attendants return as they did in the processional or they may be paired up, with the elder bride's attendants coming first.

When two mothers are involved, they are escorted up the aisle by ushers in the usual way, with the mother of the elder bride coming first. The mother of the younger bride is then escorted to the seat closest to the aisle. The grooms' parents may either sit in the same pew or, if one set of parents is to sit behind the other, they have to decide between themselves who will sit where.

When the two grooms enter the main part of the church to take their places at the chancel, the groom of the elder bride stands closer to the center aisle, facing the aisle itself, his best man to his left and slightly behind him. Next come the second groom and his best man.

THE MILITARY WEDDING

Military ushers, because their swords are worn on the left side, offer their right arms to the bridesmaids, and as in any other wedding the bride stands at the right of the bridegroom in full dress uniform. All ushers, civilian and military, in the recessional must be on the right if they are paired with bridesmaids.

In a service wedding, if the groom is a commissioned officer and it's good weather, brother officers in uniform acting as ushers make an arch of swords for the bride and groom outside the church, after the ceremony. If the wedding is a naval one, the naval officer wears only his sword belt, not his sword. At the end of the ceremony the ushers proceed down the aisle before the wedding party, assist the guests outside, then buckle on their swords and, when the head usher issues the command "Draw swords!" unsheath their swords (blades up) and make the ceremonial arch for the bride and groom—and only them—to pass through. Then at the command "Return swords!" they sheath their swords.

Since military wedding etiquette is so complex and so specific, it's best to consult the particular branch of the service for detailed information.

THE REHEARSAL

What time the wedding rehearsal takes place is determined by when the church is available; the most convenient time is probably late afternoon of the day before the wedding, by which time any out-of-town attendants will have arrived on the scene.

In addition to the bride and groom and their attendants, the mother of the bride attends the rehearsal. The bride's father or whoever will escort her up the aisle must be there too, as well as the clergyperson, the sexton or church wedding director, and the organist. If there's to be a vocal soloist, she too must be on hand, so she will know when she is to perform her part at the service and where to stand or sit. The groom's parents do not attend the rehearsal.

Out of respect and consideration for the clergyperson, members of the wedding party arrive at the church not one minute later than the hour the rehearsal's called for. When the clergyperson appears, the bride and groom introduce their bridesmaids and ushers to him. Later, as he explains the ceremony, they must pay close attention to what he says, so that the following day's ceremony will run as smoothly as possible. Often attendants come to the rehearsal dressed in the clothes they will wear to the dinner that follows. If not, whatever they choose to wear must be in keeping with the formality of the setting—in other words, conservative.

The church sexton begins the rehearsal with the processional, lining up the various members of the wedding party according to protocol. While it's the rare wedding that includes all categories of attendants, the following list shows the order of the processional, ending with the bride and her father.

- Ushers
- Junior usher/s
- Bridesmaids

- Maid of honor
- Matron of honor
- Junior bridesmaid/s
- Ring bearer
- Flower girl
- Bride and father

While the processional is being rehearsed, the groom and his best man stand at the chancel steps waiting for their instructions. They will need to know who will give them the signal to enter the main part of the church the following day, where they should stand and in what position at the chancel.

Once the wedding party has reached the chancel, the clergyperson or the sexton will tell them where to stand. While the entire wedding ceremony is not read at this time, the clergyperson will explain the service and tell each key member of the wedding party at what point he plays his role. For instance, the bride's father is told when the bride is given away, if this is part of the ceremony; the best man is told when to produce the ring from his vest pocket or from the ring bearer's pillow; the maid or matron of honor is told when to take the bride's bouquet or prayer book and, if the groom's to wear a wedding ring, when to give it to the bride.

The bride and groom lead the recessional down the aisle, the bride taking the groom's right arm. It's optional as to whether the bridesmaids and ushers follow in the same order as in the processional or whether they pair up. If they pair up, the maid of honor is escorted by the best man; if there are two main attendants, the matron of honor is escorted by the best man and the maid of honor by the head usher. A junior bridesmaid may either walk alone or be paired with an usher (if she's small, the usher should not be too tall).

Before leaving the rehearsal, the clergyperson or sexton will give the bride and groom the information they need about arriving at the church the next day, telling the groom which entrance to use and showing him the room he will wait in. It may be, too, that the clergyperson will ask the couple to sign the marriage certificate so that detail will be taken care of.

THE JEWISH REHEARSAL

There is no formal Jewish rehearsal or "rehearsal dinner" as there is at Christian weddings. The Jewish wedding ceremony most often takes place at the hotel or club where the reception is being held, with the rabbi instructing the wedding party as to their specific roles in the service just before the ceremony begins.

THE REHEARSAL DINNER

The rehearsal dinner is usually held in the evening of the day before the wedding, directly after the rehearsal itself. It's customary for the groom's family to give the party but, if they can't afford to or for some other reason, it can be given by a relative or a godparent of the bride or groom. Or the bride's family might take over planning and paying for the dinner. If the groom's parents are divorced and both remarried, either can give the party, or they may give it jointly, depending on the circumstances and their relationship. There's no directive as to the formality of a rehearsal dinner, although the groom's mother must be certain that her party does not overshadow any aspect of the following day's wedding reception, whether in the food that's served, the music, or the decorations. Other than that, the dinner can be a simple, buffet-style party or a formal black-tie affair.

Invitations to the rehearsal dinner are sent out any time after the wedding invitations have been mailed—the sooner the better, so guests can save the date and make their plans accordingly. Invitations may be issued in a variety of ways, depending on the formality of the occasion and the number of people being invited. If cost is not a consideration, the groom's mother may want to order printed invitations.

In honor of
Gail Cramer
David Alexander, Jr.

Mr. and Mrs. David Alexander
invite you to dinner
on Friday, June tenth
at seven o'clock

Fairview Country Club
33 Starling Drive
Santa Fe

R.s.v.p.
10 Stuart Place
Springfield, MA [ZIP code]

(On a formal invitation, "dinner" is used, not "rehearsal dinner." If it's to be a black-tie affair, "Black tie" is engraved on the lower right-hand corner of the invitation.)

Otherwise, she may use engraved or printed fill-in invitations which can be found in any quality stationery store. On the top left-hand corner of the card she can write "Rehearsal dinner for Gail and David." If the dinner's a small one, instead of fill-in invitations, she may prefer to extend the invitation by sending out handwritten notes on her personal stationery or informals:

Rehearsal dinner for Gail and David

Mr. and Mrs. David Alexander[a]
Friday, June 10th
7:00 P.M.

Fairview Country Club
33 Starling Drive
Santa Fe

R.s.v.p.
10 Stuart Place
Springfield, MA [ZIP code]

[a] Name is engraved or printed on informal—rest of invitation is handwritten.

Before going into details about the rehearsal dinner, it's important to emphasize that it's the groom's parents who are giving the dinner and are in charge of the arrangements, and therefore the bride and her parents should stay out of the planning of this event. If the groom's mother asks the bride's mother for her opinion, she should by all means give it. Otherwise, she should keep quiet.

It's up to the groom's mother and father, and of course the bride and groom, to decide how many people to invite to the rehearsal dinner. The list must include the bride's parents (stepparents, if there are any), the bride's and groom's brothers and sisters (step-/or half brothers and sisters), other close relatives, and wedding attendants (including spouses, live-ins and fiancé/ées). Because of their age, young children taking part in the wedding ceremony are not customarily invited to the rehearsal dinner. When cost or space isn't a problem, and the officiating clergyperson is close to the bride or groom, he and his spouse may be included on the guest list. If it's a question of inviting either local or out-of-town guests, the out-of-towners should be given preference, not only because they made the effort to come to the wedding, but because this may be their one chance to spend time with the bride and groom.

Details that have to do with planning the rehearsal dinner have already been written about in this chapter, so they are not repeated here. In addition, you may find the previous chapter, on entertaining, helpful. What follow are concerns specific to a rehearsal dinner:

- Before deciding on the dinner menu the groom's mother should confer with the bride's mother to make sure she will not duplicate any foods that will be served at the wedding reception. She must use caution so her party does not give the impression of competing with the reception.

- It's always fun for the couple to have a few photographs commemorating the occasion. It doesn't have to be a professional photographer who takes the pictures—if a sister of the groom or a member of the wedding party is a camera buff, she may be delighted to take pictures and will most likely consider it a compliment to be asked.

- Again, as a memento of the evening, it's nice to tape the toasts.
- It makes good sense to have place cards as there's some protocol to the seating at the rehearsal dinner. If it's a large party with six or more tables, table number cards will help the guests find their seats (see "Seating a Dinner" under "The Formal Seated Dinner With Staff" in Chapter 2).
- If there will be dancing, this is the opportune time for the bride's mother to brief the bride and her father, the groom and his parents, and the best man on the exact order of dancing at the reception— when the dancing begins, who dances with whom and when, and who does the cutting in and when (see "Dancing" under "The Wedding Reception" later in this chapter). Giving these instructions close to the wedding day means the participants will be better able to remember their specific roles.
- This is customarily the time when the bride and groom exchange wedding presents with their attendants.

Seating the rehearsal dinner is no different from seating any dinner party, except for the following protocol: at the bridal table, the bride sits on the right of the groom with the best man on her right. The matron of honor sits on the groom's left. Other members of the wedding party are seated to the right of the best man and to the left of the maid of honor, alternating men and women. If there are round tables for six or eight for people other than the wedding party, the groom's mother is the hostess of one table with the bride's father on her right. The groom's father hosts another table with the bride's mother on his right. A stepparent may or may not be seated at the same table as his or her spouse. If the clergyperson and his or her spouse attend the dinner, they are considered honored guests, with the clergyman usually seated on the left of the groom's mother (if a clergywoman, on the left of the groom's father). If not there, the clergyperson should certainly be given a choice seat. Other guests should be seated as they would be at any dinner party. The bride and groom, in conjunction with the groom's mother, must take into consideration individual personalities and match people according to their mutual interests or some other governing principle. It may take time to work out the seating arrangements but it's time well spent, as congenial dinner partners are the basis of a successful dinner party.

Toasts are very much a part of the rehearsal dinner, giving family members, wedding attendants, and others an opportunity to express their affection and admiration for the couple. The rehearsal dinner lends itself to toastmaking more readily than the wedding reception, when it's difficult to attract people's attention.

At one time, toasting at the rehearsal was left to the man, but modern age etiquette allows for women friends and relatives to pay tribute too. It's customary for the best man to act as toastmaster. He leads off with a toast to the couple and is followed by the groom proposing a toast to the bride. If the best man knows a certain guest is planning to give a toast, he can call on that person, saying, "I think it's time we heard from David's old roommate." What he does not want to do is call on someone who is unprepared, who will be put in an embarrassing position. Guests are free to offer a toast without being called on. Sometime during the evening the bride toasts the groom, the groom's mother and/or father toast the bride, welcoming her into their family, the bride's mother and/or father toast the groom's parents and at the same time thank them for dinner.

The groom's parents should make a point of ending the dinner at a reasonable hour. If necessary, they can tactfully let the guests know that they feel the time has come to break up the party so everyone can go home and have a good night's sleep in preparation for the big event. While the wedding party (especially when they're young) may feel the evening has just begun, chances are the following morning they'll be grateful to have been sent home early. As for the bride, if she wants to leave the dinner before the other guests, there's no reason for her not to.

THE WEDDING CEREMONY

Each religion has its own rituals and procedures concerning wedding formalities and they may vary depending on practices the particular clergyperson prefers. It is important, therefore, that the bride and groom discuss the service with the clergyperson at the time that they reserve the church or synagogue for their wedding. They will then know whether or not they may write their own marriage vows or include a favorite poem or text in the service. The wedding rehearsal is very important because that is when the bride and groom and their attendants have their particular roles in the ceremony described to them.

THE CHRISTIAN CEREMONY

In Christian ceremonies, just before the bride walks up the aisle on her father's right arm, the groom and best man enter the main part of the church from a side door and join the clergyperson at the chancel steps. The groom stands at the clergyperson's left, facing the center aisle and the approaching processional; the best man stands to the groom's left and slightly behind him. When the maid of honor reaches the chancel, she stands on the left (looking toward the altar) in line with the best man. Bridesmaids and ushers take whatever positions were assigned to them at the rehearsal. The ringbearer stands to the right of the best man and the flower girl stands to the left of the maid of honor.

Christian wedding processional.
(*From the top down): bride and her father; flower girl; ring bearer; junior
bridesmaids (if there is one, she walks alone); maid or matron of honor (if
there are both, they may walk next to each other, or whoever is the chief
attendant may follow the other); bridesmaids (paired according to height;
shorter ones precede taller); junior ushers (if there is one, he walks alone);
ushers (paired according to height; shorter ones precede taller);
best man and groom; clergyman.*

In Protestant ceremonies the father of the bride stays at the chancel until the "Declaration of Consent" part of the service, if there is to be a "presenting" or "giving" in marriage. If this is included, the clergyperson will say, "Who gives this woman to this man?" or words to that effect. In response, the bride's father says, "I do," or "Her mother and I do." If it is left out, the father goes to his pew as soon as his daughter has joined the groom. This is also the time in the Roman Catholic service (where there is no giving away of the bride) that the father leaves his daughter.

If the bride's father is dead, and a grandfather, brother, or family friend gives her away, he stands at his appointed place with the bride and answers, "I do," or "On behalf of her mother, I do." If the bride's mother is giving her away, there are a number of alternatives: the bride's mother may walk up the aisle with her daughter (the daughter does not take her mother's arm); the bride may walk in the processional with her brother or other male relative and have her mother join her as she reaches the left front pew where her mother has been seated, or the bride may walk up the aisle alone and again have her mother join her as she reaches the front pew. Another option is for the bride to be escorted to the chancel steps by her brother or other male relative and, when the clergyperson asks who gives the bride away, her mother may nod in response. Or, just before the words are spoken, the best man may go to get the mother and escort her to the chancel.

Once the bride arrives at the chancel, she lets go of her father's arm and takes her place beside the groom. Her father remains a few steps behind her. After her father responds to the "Declaration of Consent," he steps forward and places the bride's right hand in the hand of the clergyperson. Then he joins the bride's mother in the front pew (if she wishes to, the bride may turn and kiss her father as he departs). The clergyperson, after taking the bride's hand, places it in the groom's left hand. The groom then places the bride's hand on his left forearm or—if the couple prefer—they can hold hands, with arms to their sides.

In the Episcopal and Roman Catholic ceremonies, the bride and groom follow the clergyperson up to the altar and may kneel at an indicated point in the ceremony. They are followed by the maid of honor (if there is a matron of honor as well, both women go to the altar with the one the bride has chosen as her chief attendant standing next to her). The best man, on the groom's immediate right, is followed by the ring bearer, if there is one, who stands to the best man's right and a few feet behind him. Once the bride and maid of honor have taken their places, the bride hands her bouquet to the maid of honor so that her left hand will be free to receive the ring (during the ceremony, the bride wears her engagement ring on her right hand). When the clergyperson asks for the ring, the best man produces it from his vest pocket, his little finger, or from the ring bearer's pillow. In the Catholic service, the best man gives the ring to the groom, who hands it to the acolyte, who in turn gives it to the priest, who blesses it.

Christian grouping at the altar.
(From left to right): ushers (4), junior ushers (2), ring bearer, best man, groom, bride, clergyman, bride's father, maid or matron of honor, flower girl, junior bridesmaids (2), bridesmaids (4). Note: In the Roman Catholic ceremony the bride's father joins her mother in the first pew as he reaches it; he does not give the bride away. It is optional where the ring bearer and the flower girl stand, although the customary positions are ring bearer at best man's right, flower girl at maid of honor's left (if they are very young, at the conclusion of the processional, they may return to their parents' pew).

In the Protestant ceremony (the Episcopal service or some variation of it is often used in Presbyterian and Congregational churches), the best man gives the ring to the groom, who either hands it to the minister or places it on his prayer book. When it is a double ring ceremony, the maid of honor hands the bride the groom's ring after the bride has been given her ring.

After the vows have been said, the clergyperson says a few prayers which are followed by the blessing. Then the ceremony is over. He congratulates the bride, offering his hand to assist her in rising, and then congratulates the groom. Once the bride is on her feet, if she is wearing a veil, the maid of honor lifts it from her face. The couple then turn toward each other and, if they have decided to do so, kiss. The bride then turns to face the back of the church, takes back her bouquet from the maid of honor with her right hand, and takes the groom's right arm with her left. After the maid of honor has adjusted her train, the couple lead off in the recessional.

If they choose to, as they reach the front pews, they may stop briefly to greet their parents for the first time as man and wife.

DIFFERENCES IN RELIGIOUS CEREMONIES

It is interesting to note how essentially alike the marriage services of different religions are. Most Christian ceremonies differ in only minor details. As the Christian ceremony evolved out of the ancient Jewish one, there is also a definite similarity between the Jewish and Christian ceremonies.

THE ROMAN CATHOLIC CEREMONY There have been so many changes in the Roman Catholic ceremony, and such a variety of options are now available, that it would be impossible to list all of them. The options each couple in consultation with their priest choose to incorporate into the new Rite of Marriage may vary from one part of the country to another, as well as from one parish to the next. Civil marriage involving a Catholic is not recognized by the Catholic Church, but an interfaith marriage may take place in a Roman Catholic church under certain circumstances, with a Protestant clergyperson (or a rabbi) as an assisting celebrant. Or, with the consent of the local bishop, a priest may participate as a guest in another faith's church.

There are options as to where the wedding party is placed during the ceremony. Sometimes they are grouped in front of the altar rail; in larger churches, sometimes they stand in the sanctuary area.

Music plays a prominent part in the wedding ceremony. Hymns from both traditions are permitted in an interfaith marriage. The couple may select the readings and the people to read them. These could be the maid of honor and best man. Altar boys are no longer usual.

JEWISH CEREMONIES There are four major Jewish movements in the United States which differ in their interpretations of tradition: they are Orthodox, Conservative, Reconstructionist, and Reform. Orthodox Judaism is the most traditional and adheres to a rather strict interpretation of the legal standards of the Bible and later rabbinic sources. Reform Judaism, at the other end of the spectrum, is more liberal and follows an approach based on a progressive interpretation of Jewish law. Conservative and Reconstructionist Judaism fall between these two, more liberal than Orthodox and yet more traditional in their practice than Reform.

Orthodox and Conservative rabbis do not officiate at a mixed marriage, nor will many Reconstructionist and Reform rabbis. Though Judaism does not actively seek converts, the non-Jewish partner in a proposed mixed marriage may go through a period of instruction and conversion and then be taken into the congregation as a Jew; then a rabbi may perform the marriage ceremony. Questions of conversion and intermarriage, such as "Will the rabbi officiate at the ceremony?" "Can the ceremony be held in a synagogue?" or "Can the ceremony be held without a rabbi officiating?" must be discussed with the rabbi.

An Orthodox or Conservative rabbi will not marry divorced persons who have received only civil decrees. A religious divorce document (in Hebrew a *get*) is also necessary. Some liberal rabbis require only the civil decree.

At a formal Jewish ceremony the bride wears the traditional wedding dress and veil. She has attendants, maid and/or matron of honor, and bridesmaids if she wishes; the groom has a best man and ushers. The bride and groom walk separately in the processional, each accompanied by his or

Jewish wedding processional.
(From top down): bride's mother, bride, bride's father, flower girl, maid
or matron of honor, bridesmaids and ushers, groom's mother, groom, groom's
father, best man, and rabbi.

her parents. Grandparents may also join the processional. In fact, there is no prescribed limit in the Jewish faith on the nature or number of attendants the bride may choose to have. In the recessional, both mothers and fathers may walk together side by side. However, a bride should remember that a particularly large number of attendants will only serve ultimately to distract the guests' attention from her.

Jewish grouping at chuppah.
(From left to right): ushers (3) groom's father, groom's mother, best man, groom, rabbi, bride, maid or matron of honor, bride's mother, bride's father, flower girl, bridesmaids (3). Note: The arrangement of the wedding party is not a matter of rabbinical law but of social custom; hence it varies. For example, parents may be under the chuppah *if there is room. Sometimes only the fathers take part, and their placement is optional.*

At Jewish weddings there is usually music for the processional and recessional. A cantor is not necessary but he frequently does take part in the ceremony, chanting, not singing, especially if it is a big wedding. The music selected and the instruments it's played on depend on the couple's taste. Most often it's traditional Israeli or Hebrew music. Sometimes the music is on tape.

Before the ceremony the bride usually receives the wedding guests in an anteroom at the place where she is to be married. Seated with her attendants, she sees all but the groom before the ceremony. In liberal temples, however, she may even see him.

Often the right side of the synagogue or temple, as one enters, is where guests of the bride are seated; the left, those of the groom. However, this varies; in Reform practice, the right side is the groom's and the left the bride's (in Orthodox synagogues men and women do not sit together). The couple are married under a canopy (in Hebrew, *chuppah*) supported on standards which symbolizes a home. The bride stands on the groom's left. Also under the canopy stand the rabbi and, usually, the couple's two principal attendants. If the canopy is large enough, the bride's and groom's parents stand beneath it also, otherwise they stand outside the fringe of the canopy (in the Reform service parents never stand with their children). The rabbi, who faces the bride and groom, has beside him a small table covered with a tablecloth on which are placed two cups of ritual wine and one glass wrapped in a napkin.

The traditional service is in Hebrew, and some Aramaic may also be included. It begins with the invocation, which is followed by the two betrothal benedictions, after which the rabbi passes a glass of wine to the groom, who takes a sip and passes it to the bride. Then comes the ceremony with the ring, a traditional gold band. The best man hands it to the groom, who, with a traditional declaration, places it on the bride's right index finger. Any time after the ceremony she may remove it and place it on what our society considers the traditional wedding ring finger: the fourth finger of her left hand.

The ring ceremony is sometimes followed by the reading of the marriage contract, which is usually in Aramaic but may be in English. The rabbi then delivers a short address in English, or whatever the language of the congregation is, to the couple on the sanctity of marriage and his personal concern for their future welfare. Next, the seven blessings are recited, or chanted, at the end of which the bride and groom drink the ceremonial second glass of wine. This is followed in the traditional service by the bridegroom crushing the wrapped glass beneath his foot to symbolize the destruction of the Temple of Jerusalem. It represents an admonition to the congregation that, despite the happiness of the occasion, all should remember and work for the rebuilding of Zion. Other interpretations have also been given to this custom.

At most Jewish weddings men must cover their heads, although this is optional among Reform Jews. Men wear the traditional skullcaps (yarmulkes) or their own hats. Synagogues have skullcaps available in the vestibule. At Orthodox weddings, married women must always cover their heads. The reception that follows Jewish weddings is exactly like other receptions, except that at Orthodox receptions, at most Conservative receptions, and at some Reform receptions kosher food is served. And a special nuptial grace is offered after the meal.

CHRISTIAN SCIENCE CEREMONY Christian Science services are conducted by lay people elected by the rest of the congregation. They are not legally empowered to perform marriages, so when members of the Christian Science faith get married the ceremony is performed by an ordained minister or someone else with the proper legal authority. Since Christian Scientists do not use alcoholic beverages they will not serve them even in the mildest form at wedding receptions.

EASTERN ORTHODOX CEREMONY   The Orthodox Christian Church —the One Holy Eastern Orthodox Catholic Apostolic Church—is comprised, in this country, of adherents from different ethnic backgrounds, such as Albanian, Antiochian, Bulgarian, Greek, Romanian, Russian, Serbian, and Ukrainian jurisdictions. The marriage ceremony of the Church is considered a sacrament in that it is believed that the Triune God is the celebrant through the priest or bishop. A mixed marriage is permitted only between an Orthodox Christian and a person baptized in the name of the Trinity.

The ceremony is actually two services in one: the betrothal and the sacrament of matrimony. The service takes place before a table called an anti-altar placed in the center of the chancel. Marriages can be celebrated on any day, although the great majority take place on Saturday or Sunday. There are, however, certain times of the year, such as periods of fasting, when marriages are not permitted. Special wedding hymns are a part of the service, as is chanting.

In the Slavic tradition the priest greets the bride and groom at the narthex (entrance) of the church and there conducts the official betrothal, using the wedding rings. He then escorts the couple up the aisle to the chancel area where the sacrament of matrimony takes place. Some Greek churches have adopted the Western Christian tradition of the bride being escorted by her father up the aisle to the chancel where the double service takes place. When the father of the bride gives his daughter over to the groom at the chancel, the groom, as a gesture of respect, kisses the hand of the bride's father. As the father joins his wife in their pew, the bride and groom are given lighted candles that symbolize the light of the Lord, which they hold as they stand before the anti-altar.

In the Eastern Orthodox service, the mystical number three, representing the Trinity, has great significance. The wedding bands (a double-ring ceremony is used) are blessed on the Gospel Book by the priest, then, with the rings in his hand, he blesses the couple by making the sign of the cross on their foreheads: three times from the groom to the bride and then three times from the bride to the groom. He then places the rings on the right index fingers of the groom and bride and finally the sponsor of the wedding, who may be the best man, removes the rings and replaces them three times on the fingers of the groom and bride.

The first significant act in the sacrament itself is the joining of the right hands of the bride and groom, symbolizing that they will become one. This is followed by the crowning. The Slavic tradition uses metal crowns, signifying royalty, while the Greek tradition uses crowns of white pearls. The priest blesses the crowns, then blesses the couple's foreheads, as he did with the rings. He then places the crowns on the couple's heads, thus acknowledging their new status as husband and wife in the household of God. The sponsor then comes forward as the official witness of the sacrament to exchange the crowns on their heads. Next there are scriptural readings, followed by the partaking of the common cup. In this ritual, a small amount of sweet wine is placed in a cup from which the bride and groom drink, thereby affirming the fact that they share the "cup of life." Finally a symbolic dance of joy takes place in which the priest leads the groom and bride around the anti-altar. This is done three times in honor of the Holy Trinity.

These are only the highlights of this richly impressive, ancient ceremony, usual in all Eastern Orthodox marriages.

QUAKER CEREMONY Today a bride being married in a Quaker ceremony may wear a traditional wedding dress and veil, although these plain people, as they call themselves, believe in the renunciation of worldly display. Their ceremony is as unadorned as their meeting houses and impressive in its quiet sincerity.

A Quaker wedding may take place in the meeting house or in a private home, with notice of intention to wed being made by the man and woman two monthly meetings or more in advance of the wedding date. It is necessary for at least one of the couple to be a member of the Society of Friends. It is not unusual for the parents' permission to be appended to the letter of request, even when the couple are of age. After the letter of request has been read at monthly meeting, a committee of two women and two men, known as the Clearness Committee, is appointed to discuss with the bride and groom, respectively, "clearness to proceed with marriage." The Clearness Committee may discuss marriage and its obligations with the couple just as a minister would, for originally the Quakers had no appointed ministers but instead gathered together in Quaker silence, speaking up in meeting as the inner spirit moved them to express themselves. (In some meetings, especially in the West, there is now a regularly appointed minister.)

The Clearness Committee submits a report on its conferences with the couple at the next monthly meeting. Then the congregation appoints a committee of overseers to advise the couple on marriage procedure and legal requirements, and to attend the wedding.

On the wedding day, the bride and groom come up the aisle together— or there may be the usual wedding procession—and take the "facing seats," the benches that face the meeting. After a period of silence, the couple rise and take hands. The groom says words to the effect that "in the presence of God I take thee . . . to be my wedded wife, promising with divine assistance to be unto thee a loving and faithful husband as long as we both shall live." The bride repeats the answering vow. The couple are then seated again and the ushers bring forward a table on which they place the marriage certificate. When the bride and groom have signed the certificate, it is read aloud. Regular meeting for worship follows. After the rise of meeting, all present sign the certificate as witnesses to the marriage. The overseers later officially register the marriage.

At the next monthly meeting the overseers report that the marriage "was carried out in the good order of Friends."

MORMON CEREMONY There are two kinds of marriages among the members of the Church of Jesus Christ of Latter-day Saints (Mormon). The first are those performed in temples of the Church by those holding the holy priesthood. In pronouncing the couple man and wife, the officiator declares them wed "for time and for all eternity," instead of "until death do you part." Children born to a couple so married are believed by the Mormons to belong to their parents in the eternal world by virtue of such marriages. These marriages are always referred to as temple marriages. All brides married in the temple dress in white and wear veils, although they may have previously been civilly married.

There are also civil marriages performed by bishops of the Church or any other accredited person. Later, if couples married in civil ceremonies have complied with the requirements of the Church in their daily living, they may enter a temple of the Church and be married "for time and all eternity."

Following temple or civil marriages, the reception for the bride and groom is usually held in the cultural hall of the church or at the home of the bride's parents. In some communities there are special centers where such receptions are held.

Mixed marriage, although not encouraged, is permitted. The church takes no stand against remarriage.

HOME CEREMONY

If there's sufficient space, it's lovely to have a wedding at home. The largest room, usually the living room, is cleared of furniture for the ceremony with the "altar" improvised before the fireplace or some other focal point, preferably at some distance from the entrance to the room. Two large flower arrangements can be placed on the floor to mark off an "altar."

As with a church wedding, the bride's family sit on the left, the groom's on the right. Usually a small section for family members and special guests is roped off with ribbons on either side of the altar. Chairs may or may not be provided for the guests, although they should be if the ceremony lasts more than ten minutes or so.

As guests arrive, the mother of the bride greets them at the front door and asks them to go into the living room and to sit wherever they please. While the bride and groom may have only a maid of honor and best man as their attendants, if there are ushers, they do not seat the guests.

If the house has a staircase and the bride is descending it, she does so as soon as the wedding march begins; otherwise she and the wedding party assemble outside the living room before the music starts. At a very small wedding, there may not be any music, in which case the bride enters the room on the arm of her father or, if she prefers, alone, after the clergyperson and groom have taken their places. The service that follows is no different from one held in a church. At a home wedding there is no recessional unless a formal receiving line is to form elsewhere in the house or garden. If the reception is being held in the same room, the bride and groom simply stand in place and receive informally with or without their mothers, or mothers and fathers, standing with them.

A wedding ceremony, of course, may take place out of doors, provided the climate is sufficiently dependable and alternative plans have been made in case of rain.

RECTORY CEREMONY

Sometimes a couple are married in the rectory of the church, either because they choose to or because some overriding reason prevents their being married in the church itself. This simple ceremony takes place in the clergyperson's study or his living room. A few guests may be present, but usually the group is limited to witnesses and parents. After brief preliminary instructions, the bride and groom stand before the clergyperson, the bride to the groom's left. If the bride's father or someone substituting for him is present, the giving-away part of the service may be included, but it does not have to be. When the ceremony is over, the clergyperson congratulates the couple and they kiss if they choose to. If there's no best man, it's up to the groom to leave an envelope with an appropriate fee for the clergyperson.

A couple being married in the privacy of a small rectory wedding may like the idea of having a fairly large reception afterward, perhaps at a hotel or club. Or they may prefer to keep the whole occasion low-keyed and invite those attending the ceremony back to the bride's house or to a restaurant for a celebratory drink and meal.

CIVIL CEREMONY

For a civil wedding, the couple must have two attendants to act as witnesses; if they don't bring along their own attendants, the justice of the peace, judge, mayor, ship's captain, or other officiant will provide the witnesses.

A civil wedding may or may not be followed by a religious ceremony, which may be a private service or a traditional church wedding with the bride wearing a long white dress. Of course, the latter would be followed by a reception. But if a reception is held after the civil ceremony, a second one would not be in order.

THE WEDDING RECEPTION

As you read about the reception, certain questions may come to mind, such as, "Who should videotape the reception?" or "How can you be sure the orchestra leader will appear in person?" or "What's the traditional wedding cake made of?" Since information of this sort has already been covered, it will not be repeated here. If you're to attend a wedding reception, refer to "The Role of the Guest" earlier in this chapter to help make yourself a more self-assured and responsive guest.

THE RECEPTION BEGINS

While the wedding party are having pictures taken, guests arriving from the church or synagogue stand around informally chatting with one another. Because the bride's mother will be involved in the picture taking, she might ask a good friend to act as interim hostess until she's free. In this role, her friend stands near the entrance to the room, hall, tent, or wherever, to greet the guests as they arrive at the reception and to introduce them to one another. As a welcoming gesture, and so that guests won't stand around empty-handed, waiters pass glasses of champagne on silver trays.

THE GUEST BOOK

If there's a leather-bound book for guests to sign, the table it's placed on should be near the entrance to the reception area where it can be easily seen by guests as they arrive but won't get in the way of the receiving line. The junior bridesmaid, if there is one, may be stationed at the table and put in charge of the book; otherwise, a cousin of the bride or groom or two friends of the couple can spell each other until the receiving line breaks up, an indication that most of the guests have arrived. The person in charge of the book has the responsibility of giving it to the bride's mother to keep for the bride.

THE RECEIVING LINE

The main reason for having a receiving line is to give the bride and groom a chance to greet and say a few words to each guest who comes to the reception. It also allows the guest an opportunity to admire the bride and to offer congratulations to the couple. At a relatively small reception of no more than seventy-five people, where it's possible for the bride and groom to mingle easily, there's no real necessity for a receiving line and often there isn't one.

The receiving line at a hotel or club forms in a location that won't inhibit the flow of traffic in the room; often the choice place is in front of a fireplace. At a home reception, the receiving line, if there is one, is best located in a room such as a hall or dining room with both an entrance and exit, again to facilitate the flow of traffic. There should be one or two tables close to the receiving line where guests can put down their drinks before going through the line. Or waiters can be assigned to that area so guests can hand them their glasses.

The bride's mother, as hostess, stands first in the receiving line with the groom's mother next, followed by the bride, the groom, the maid or matron of honor, and the bridesmaids. While the fathers of the bride and groom usually play the role of hosts, socializing with the guests, they may stand in the line, but usually just for a short time. If the bride and groom feel that too many people in the receiving line will slow it down they may ask only the maid and/or matron of honor to stand with them. Or they may ask the bridesmaids to take turns standing in line. It's completely up to the bride and groom to decide how they want it to work.

SPECIAL SITUATIONS If the bride's mother is dead, her father comes first in the receiving line. Quite often, someone close to the bride, such as an aunt or cousin, stands next to him. In the case of divorced parents neither of whom has remarried, there is no reason why they can't stand in the line together, even though it's not necessary for the father to be there. If the bride's father has remarried and he and his wife are the ones giving the wedding reception, the custom is for the stepmother to be the first in line, followed by the groom's mother. As for the bride's mother, she too may be in the receiving line, provided any existing differences between her and her ex-husband can be set aside for this one day. If she does stand in the line, the order is: the bride's stepmother, the groom's mother, the bride's mother. When the bride's mother is giving the reception on her own or sharing the reception expenses with her ex-husband, this is a case when the bride's stepmother should step aside in deference to the bride's mother. If, however, she's asked to join the line, then the grouping is the bride's mother, the groom's mother, the bride's stepmother.

HOW THE RECEIVING LINE WORKS If there's an announcer—and there sometimes is at a formal wedding—he stands at the head of the receiving line, which may flow from left to right or right to left depending on the layout of the room. When a guest approaches he asks the name and, turning to the bride's mother, repeats it in a soft voice. When there is no announcer, the guest greets the bride's mother, giving his name if they do not know each other. The bride's mother, in turn, may say, "I'm delighted you could make it, Oliver. Gail said she couldn't imagine getting married without your being here." After the two shake hands (those who know each other well kiss on the cheek) and exchange a few words, the bride's mother turns to the groom's mother and says, "Helen, this is Oliver Frost, one of our oldest and dearest friends." If the bride's mother does not have a chance to make this introduction before the guest directly behind Oliver Frost greets her, it's up to Oliver Frost to take the initiative and introduce himself to the groom's mother. If the guest is known to the groom's mother but not to the bride, she introduces the person to her new daughter-in-law. As for the bride, she tries to acknowledge each guest's greeting in a warm and friendly tone; "Hello, Mr. Frost, I'm so happy you're here. David's heard so much about you and can't wait to meet you." While the bride is not expected at this moment to remember who gave her which wedding present, if she does match a present to a face, it will please a guest enormously to hear, "Thanks again"—she's already thanked by letter—"for the magnificent weather vane. Without a doubt, it's David's favorite present." She then introduces the groom to Oliver Frost. The groom expresses his pleasure at meeting him: "The entire Cramer family has talked about you often. I'm so glad to finally have the chance to meet you." When he gets to the bridesmaids, Oliver Frost, in order not to hold up the line, can give them a general greeting as he walks by. If one of the bridesmaids knows him, they may shake hands and say a few words. As Oliver Frost leaves the receiving line, he is offered a glass of champagne from the tray of a waiter.

THE BRIDE'S TABLE

At a formal wedding, the bride's table is usually rectangular in shape. The bride and groom sit together in the middle of the table on the far side so they face into the room, the bride on the right of the groom. On the bride's right is the best man and on the groom's left the maid or matron of honor. Other members of the wedding party are seated to the right of the best man and to the left of the maid or matron of honor, alternating men and women. Place cards are used except for the bride and groom, who have no place cards at their seats. Even if it's a buffet-style meal, the bride's table is waited on, with the bride served first and then the groom.

If there's space, spouses, fiancé/ées, and live-ins of the wedding party are also seated at the bride's table, among the bridesmaids and ushers. If the table is not large enough to include them, they may be seated together at a separate table in proximity to the bride's table.

At a small wedding, in addition to the wedding party, the bride's table may include the parents of the bride and groom, grandparents, and a few honored guests.

WHEN THERE'S NO BRIDE'S TABLE Sometimes, particularly at a less formal wedding, the bride and groom may prefer not to have a bride's table but they will still need their own table for six or eight people to sit at and eat and to which they can return between dances. When there is no set seating plan the bride and groom are free to leave their table whenever they want to go sit with friends at other tables, and guests may take turns joining them at their table. To distinguish their table, it should have a more elaborate centerpiece. So no one will sit at their table while they are in the receiving line, a "reserved" sign can be placed on it.

THE PARENTS' TABLE

When there's a bride's table, there's almost always a table for the parents of the bride and groom. It is larger than the guests' tables but is otherwise the same except for place cards. Seating is as follows: the bride's mother, as hostess, has the groom's father on her right. On her left may be one of the groom's grandfathers or a male relative of hers. Opposite the bride's mother is the bride's father with the groom's mother on his right. On his left he may have a grandmother or godparent of one of the couple, or some other honored guest. If the clergyperson who performed the ceremony and his or her spouse attend the reception, they are seated at this table; the clergyperson usually sits on the left of the bride's mother (if a woman, on the left of the bride's father). If not in that spot, the clergyperson should be given some other choice seat at the table.

If the bride has a stepmother, her father and stepmother may or may not sit at the parents' table depending on what the relationship is between the bride's mother, her ex-husband, and his wife. If relations are strained, her father and stepmother can always form their own table, with some of her father's relatives and close friends sitting with them. The same situation applies to the groom's family.

DANCING

The bride and groom are the first to dance together at the reception. At a formal, seated lunch or dinner reception, the traditional time for dancing to begin is after the wedding toasts have been made—in other words, after dessert has been served. The modern-day bride and groom, however, have all but done away with this tradition and start dancing either before the first course or before the main course. Since guests love to dance at a wedding and good music inspires them to do just that, there's no reason to hold off the dancing any longer than necessary. At an afternoon, buffet reception, the bride and groom can have their first dance as soon as the receiving line breaks up, once they've had a chance to sit and relax with friends for a short time.

It's necessary for those who start the dancing—that is, the bride and groom, their parents, and the best man—to be well versed on who dances with whom and when, and who does the cutting in and when (the rehearsal dinner is a good time for the bride's mother to brief everyone). Timing is most important so that no two people end up dancing together for more than two or three minutes. What you want is a spontaneous effect, and this can only be achieved when each person performs his expected role.

When it's time for the couple to dance, the groom leads the bride, her hand in his, to the dance floor. At the same time the orchestra issues a trumpet fanfare so guests will know to gather around and watch. The bride's and groom's parents and the best man must be ready to make their way to the dance floor as soon as they hear the signal that the bride and groom are about to dance. Once the couple reach the dance floor, the orchestra starts playing the song they've requested for their first dance together. At this point, the bride's and groom's parents and the best man should be standing at the edge of the dance floor.

This is how the dancing works:

- The bride and groom dance.
- The bride's father cuts in on the groom and dances with the bride.
- The groom brings his mother out onto the floor and dances with her.
- The father of the groom brings the bride's mother onto the floor and dances with her.
- The best man cuts in on the bride's father and dances with the bride.
- The bride's father cuts in on the groom's father and dances with his wife.
- The groom's father cuts in on the groom and dances with his wife.
- The groom cuts in on the bride's father and dances with the bride's mother.
- The bride's father cuts in on the groom's father and dances with the groom's mother.

When the best man has cut in on the bride and danced with her for a minute or two, bridesmaids and ushers may start dancing and after that any couple may take to the floor.

THE WEDDING TOASTS

At a formal lunch or dinner reception it's customary to start the toasting after the dessert has been served, when people for the most part have finished their meal. At an afternoon reception, toasting takes place after the bride and groom have had their first dance. At a large wedding, it may be necessary to have a microphone set up for the toast makers. Consider having the toasts taped. The bride and groom will have the fun of listening to them in later years, as will their children and grandchildren.

The best man should be the toastmaster and ask the bride's and groom's parents, grandparents and siblings if they'd like to make a toast. He should ask well in advance of the wedding so the prospective toaster will have plenty of time to prepare himself. Unlike the rehearsal dinner toasts, the toasting time at the reception is kept short, so as not to tax the attention span of the guests. Only a few people need speak, and those who do should be told to limit what they say to no more than a minute or two. As to the tone of the toasts, it's up to the person doing the toasting to decide whether he wants to be sentimental or clever. However, since this is a formal affair, it's best to leave suggestive remarks that may embarrass some of the older guests for another occasion.

The best man leads off the toasting with a toast to the bride. This is followed by the groom toasting the bride, the bride toasting the groom, and the bride's father toasting the couple. If there are to be other toasts, it may be the mother of the bride and/or mother of the groom toasting the couple or the bride toasting her parents and the groom his. When the bride is being toasted, she remains seated and the groom stands; when they are toasted as a couple, they both remain seated. They do not drink to the toast at the same time as others do, but a minute or two later. As soon as the toasts are finished, the best man may read congratulatory mailgrams that have been sent to the bride and groom at the reception. Any mailgrams should be saved and given to the couple, not only for their wedding scrapbook, but so they can thank the people who sent them.

CUTTING THE CAKE

At a formal lunch or dinner reception the cake-cutting ceremony starts before the dessert course is served. At an afternoon reception the cake is cut after the toasts have been made. Because guests aren't supposed to leave the reception until the cake is cut, as a courtesy the couple should not put off this ritual too long—two thirds of the way into the reception is a good time. Usually guests are told, either by an announcement or a signal from the orchestra, when the moment has arrived so they can stand around and watch.

A silver cake knife is used to cut the cake. Its handle is often decorated with a streamer of white satin ribbons knotted with flowers. (If the groom is in uniform, the cake is cut with his dress sword.) The bride, standing at the groom's left, cuts the first piece with the groom assisting her, his hand on top of hers. She feeds him a tiny piece of cake with her fingers, and he in turn feeds her a piece. After that they can go back to their table or the dance floor while the cake is cut for the guests, usually by the caterers.

THROWING THE BRIDE'S BOUQUET

The bride traditionally throws her bouquet to her attendants just before she changes to go away. She may throw it from the entrance of the reception room doorway unless there's a staircase or balcony to throw it from. Since legend claims that the woman who catches the bouquet will be the next to marry, the bride often throws her bouquet in the general direction of a friend who's engaged or one she'd like to see engaged. If she doesn't want to single out a particular bridesmaid, she can turn her back on all of them and throw the bouquet over her shoulder.

At some weddings a garter is also tossed. After the bouquet has been thrown, the groom removes the garter (usually blue) the bride wears below her knee and tosses it to his ushers. The one who catches the garter is supposedly the next to get married. It's up to the bride to decide whether to include this in the reception proceedings.

THE RECEPTION ENDS

When the bride and groom decide it's time to leave the reception, the bride, accompanied by her maid of honor and bridesmaids, goes to change into her going-away outfit. The groom does the same, accompanied by his best man and ushers. As soon as they are ready, the maid of honor goes to tell the bride's and groom's parents that the couple are about to leave. Parents and guests will then know to congregate in the hallway to cheer the couple on their way.

As the bride and groom depart, they stop to say goodbye to their parents. By this time the guests are stationed near the door, their hands filled with paper rose petals to throw at the couple as a good-luck gesture. Once the couple have driven off, guests return to the reception for a final dance or drink. When the music stops, it's a signal for them to go home. As they leave, they may each be given a small white box which contains a piece of the groom's cake.

WHEN DINNER IS NOT SERVED

If the reception is one where dinner has not been served, the bride's mother and father may ask out-of-town guests and some family members back to their house for a light supper.

HOW THE DOUBLE WEDDING RECEPTION WORKS

At a double wedding ceremony, the elder bride comes first in the processional. If the two brides want to share equal honors (which seems only fair), then the younger bride comes first in the receiving line. It actually makes no difference who comes first. It's something the brides can work out between themselves.

Assuming the brides are sisters and the younger sister will come first in the line, here is the order in which the nine people stand: mother of the two brides, mother of groom of younger sister, younger sister, younger sister's groom, younger sister's maid or matron of honor, mother of groom of elder sister, elder sister, elder sister's groom, elder sister's maid or matron of honor.

If it's a double wedding of cousins or friends, then of course there are two mothers but only one receiving line consisting of ten people. The order of the receiving line for each bride is the same as the one described earlier when there is only a single bride.

Because of the number of people in the line, it makes sense for the fathers to circulate among the guests rather than stand in the line. For the same reason, bridesmaids do not stand in the line.

At a double wedding there may be one bride's table or two, depending on the size of the two wedding parties, the same for the parents' table. When there are four sets of parents, in all probability two or three tables will be necessary.

When it comes time for the dancing to begin, each bride takes to the dance floor with her groom. Cutting in is exactly the same as in a single wedding, except in the case of sisters. The father cuts in on his elder daughter first, and once she's cut in on by the best man, the father cuts in on his younger daughter.

Each bride has her own wedding cake; other than that, the reception is like any other.

WHEN THERE IS NO RECEPTION

At a small church wedding not followed by a reception the bride often receives with the groom, her mother, the groom's mother, and the maid and/or matron of honor and the bridesmaids in the vestibule of the church or, at a country wedding, on the church porch. The father of the bride may or may not stand in the line; the groom's father rarely does.

GETTING MARRIED AGAIN

Divorce and remarriage—at least until the last two or three decades in this country—were considered unpleasant subjects. A woman divorced was an object of some contempt, derision, and disapproval until fairly recently. But, as times have changed and divorce has become more prevalent, and therefore acceptable, society's attitude has changed radically. As it has toward widows, who, it used to be assumed, would spend the rest of their lives sitting in a rocking chair, content and rightly so with widowhood. Happily, this is no longer the case.

Since traditional wedding customs have been written about in detail in this chapter, here we will simply deal with how these customs differ for subsequent marriages. The most important point to note is that the previous marital status of the bride is the primary factor to consider in talking about second weddings. The groom's previous marital status is of little consequence in terms of the etiquette associated with a second wedding.

PRENUPTIAL AGREEMENT

The subject of a prenuptial agreement is a sensitive one; it must be handled with delicacy and diplomacy. It used to be that prenuptial agreements were only for those with great wealth. This is no longer true. Today a prenuptial agreement is most often drawn up for couples who have been married previously and have children they want to be sure will inherit all they are entitled to. It might also be that one of the couple is much older or much richer than the other.

While we have come to accept the practical aspects of the prenuptial agreement, the mere mention of it (especially if it is a first marriage) can give rise to many anxieties and apprehensions. It's easy for thoughts such as "Does she really love me?" "Is he marrying me for my money?" or "Maybe she's not sure it will work out," to surface. For that reason, the couple planning a prenuptial agreement should start talking about it sooner rather than later—in other words, before they announce their engagement. If the ramifications of the agreement become so heated that the relationship falls apart, it's obviously better to have it happen before rather than after their plans have been made public.

If you decide to have a prenuptial agreement it is crucial to find a good lawyer who will be able to guide you both legally and emotionally through the agreement process. The prenuptial agreement is no less a private document than a will and should be discussed only with your fiancé and your lawyer. The agreement is no one's business but your own. It is very poor taste for anyone to ask if you are planning to have one, but if someone does, you can answer, "That's a personal matter that I prefer not to discuss."

OTHER FINANCIAL CONSIDERATIONS

Sad but true, it's well known that money is the major cause of the breakup of a second marriage (the other is children). Therefore, anything having to do with monetary matters should be openly discussed with the man you plan to marry, preferably before you make a commitment to each other. If either or both of you has children, it's important to reveal all your financial responsibilities having to do with their care. It would be unfair, after five years of marriage, to spring the news on your spouse that you promised to pay for your daughter's education—it might even put your marriage on the line. If both of you are working, you must sit down and figure out who will pay for what out of each one's own money and what will be paid for jointly. At the same time you will want to discuss the making of new wills, bank accounts, credit cards, insurance policies, and other matters of this sort.

WHO PAYS FOR THE SECOND WEDDING?

By the time a second marriage comes around, the couple most often pay for the wedding themselves. But there's nothing that says they have to. The bride's father may want to pay for his daughter's second wedding or contribute to the expenses, although he certainly has no obligation to do so, particularly if he paid for the first one. If there's a dinner the night before the wedding (in this case it's not called a rehearsal dinner), the groom's parents are not expected to pay for it. However, if their son has not been married before, they may want to.

TELLING PEOPLE YOU ARE REMARRYING

Never talk about remarrying with your friends or relatives until both divorces are final if this applies. If one of you has a divorce that drags on, you will be fending off questions like "What's holding it up?" or "Why can't he speed things along?"—putting a strain on the relationship between the two of you. Worse yet, the news could have an adverse effect on ongoing divorce proceedings.

When the time comes to spread the word, the first people to tell are your ex-husband and your children. Next to know should be your parents and close relatives. Chances are you will also want to tell your former in-laws, if for no other reason than to maintain good relations with them for the sake of your children.

After the key people in your life have been given the news, you may tell anyone you like. Or you might have a small party to announce it. As you tell people you're to be married, remember one thing: no matter how you feel about your ex-husband, don't bad-mouth him. It won't change how you feel about him but reflects poorly on you, and can hurt your children.

WHEN A WIDOW REMARRIES

Out of respect to the memory of her late husband, traditionally a widow (the same is true for a widower) does not remarry until a year after his death. If the widow is older and was married to the same man for fifty or sixty years, her children may feel that if their mother really cared about their father she would wait longer than a year before even considering marriage. It can be difficult for children when a widowed mother or father remarries, but they should try to accept that their parent is happy and be pleased. They should also be able to understand that an elderly couple are entitled to whatever happiness lies ahead of them sooner rather than later.

CHILDREN AND REMARRIAGE

Only you can know when and how to tell your children you are planning to remarry. Everything depends on your particular situation—the age of your children, if you are divorced or widowed, if you're marrying someone you've known a long time, and how you feel your children will react. If you're a divorcée and get along reasonably well with your ex-husband, it's better to tell him about your plans before you tell your children, so he can be ready for any questions your children may ask him. If he's supportive of your decision to remarry and of your choice of a new husband, he can be the greatest comfort to your children—encouraging them to accept their stepfather and helping them overcome any fears they may have.

Generally it's best to tell a child you are remarrying when the two of you can be alone. That way he's more likely to express any anxieties he may have. Of course, if he knows the man you're to marry well and is fond of him, there's no reason he shouldn't hear the news from both of you.

It's wonderful when young children participate in second weddings. Aside from having the fun of getting dressed up and being a part of the festivities, it gives them a sense that they have played a role in a major event in a parent's life. If you have a young daughter, you may have her as your flower girl or an older daughter can be your witness. Or you can ask a teenage or older son to escort you up the aisle. If, however, your child says he does not want to take part in the ceremony, he should not be forced to do so.

Under any circumstances, remarriage causes major changes in the life of a child. Therefore, in the best interest of your child, you must do everything you can to help him establish a good relationship with your new husband. At the same time, your child must never feel that his stepfather can replace his own father. He needs his father more than ever during this period of adjustment and his father must reassure him that he will always love him and be there for him.

While your child is adapting to life with a stepfather, his grandparents—your parents or your ex-husband's—can be an enormous help to him. Children love their grandparents, not only because grandparents love them in return, but because the love of grandparents is unconditional. If you keep in touch with your former in-laws (and you should if at all possible), it will give your child a sense of continuity, which can only help him feel secure.

When a widow (or widower) remarries, the grown children may be concerned that their new stepparent has designs on the family's money, perhaps threatening their future inheritance. It can be hard for the children to broach this subject with their mother or father without appearing greedy or self-serving. Therefore, the caring and considerate parent will bring up the subject at the time of the marriage. All questions having to do with the estate and the children's inheritance should be discussed openly, although this is never an easy task. However, it is crucial to assure children that they will not be deprived of what is justly theirs, and that their rights will be protected.

RINGS AND THE DIVORCED OR WIDOWED WOMAN

When a bond of marriage is broken and a woman divorces, it's up to her to decide what to do with her engagement and wedding rings. She may want to throw her engagement ring in the river (not advised!), save it for her children, make the stones into earrings, or she may feel perfectly at ease changing the ring to the third finger of her right hand. However, because of the symbolism inherent in the ring, it's doubtful she'd want to continue to wear it on her left hand. If the engagement ring belonged to her ex-husband's family, she might want to return it. Or, if she has a son, she could save it for him to give to his fiancée when he gets married.

When she's no longer married, a divorced woman takes off her wedding band, as does a divorced man. A woman does not wear an engagement ring given to her by a man she's planning to marry if either of the couple has a divorce pending; she must wait to wear the ring until the divorce is final. A widow may continue to wear her engagement and wedding rings as long as she wants, although many widowed women, particularly those widowed at an early age, prefer to take off their rings after a respectful amount of time, to show that they're back in circulation and ready to date. The same, of course, is true for a man. When a widow remarries, she removes her first husband's engagement and wedding rings. Whether her new husband gives her an engagement ring is something they decide together. She may prefer some other present or a more elaborate wedding band. These are very personal choices to be made by the individuals involved. Whether or not the groom wears a wedding band is something only the couple can decide.

WHOM TO INVITE

It's up to you and the groom to decide whom you want to invite to your wedding ceremony and reception. In addition to your family and friends, you may want to invite your former in-laws, if you are fond of them, because your children would enjoy having them there. Before asking them, talk it over with the groom to see how he feels. If he objects to the idea of their being at the wedding, say nothing more. If, however, you do agree to invite them, be prepared for them to decline your invitation. They may be delighted to be asked but decide it's best not to attend out of regard for their son's feelings. Although it's not unheard of to invite an ex-husband, it's rather unusual.

INVITATIONS AND ANNOUNCEMENTS

WEDDING INVITATIONS What type of invitations you send out depends on the size and formality of the wedding. If it's to be small, invitations may be extended by letter or even by telephone. For a more formal wedding, you may want to send out engraved or printed invitations. If the bride is fairly young, say in her early thirties, her parents may extend the invitation, particularly if they are paying for the wedding. Otherwise, the bride and groom do the inviting.

If you are asking only a small number of people to the ceremony, you may send a handwritten note:

[date]

Dear Helen and Bob:

Richard and I are being married at St. Andrew's on Friday, October 6th at 4 P.M. We're only inviting family and a few friends and hope more than anything that you can be with us. You'll soon be receiving an invitation to the reception.

You can reach me any morning at (415) 000-0000. Please come!

Love,
Mary

Parents' invitation to reception:

Doctor and Mrs. Scott Blankharn
request the pleasure of your company
at the wedding reception of their daughter
Mrs. Mary Blankharn Franklyn[a]
and
Mr. Richard Carpenter
on Friday, the sixth of October
at five o'clock[b]

Hotel Carlton
Fifth and Grant Streets
San Francisco

R.s.v.p.
15 Shady Road
Belvedere, CA [ZIP code]
[or reply card and envelope]

[a] The bride's title does not appear on the invitation for a first wedding, but in this case it does. In the case of a widow, she continues to use her husband's full name.

[b] If the reception is being held after 6 P.M. (a tuxedo is never worn before that hour), "Black tie" is written on the lower right-hand corner of the invitation.

Couple's invitation to reception:

[Mrs.] Mary Blankharn Franklyn[a]
and
[Mr.] Richard Carpenter
request the pleasure of your company
at their wedding reception [etc.]

[a] When the couple issue their own invitation, they have the option of using or not using titles. In the case of a widow, she continues to use her husband's full name.

WEDDING ANNOUNCEMENTS Wedding announcements are customarily sent out the day after the ceremony takes place, never before. Unlike the wedding invitation, the announcement includes the year.

Parents' announcement:

Doctor and Mrs. Scott Blankharn
announce the marriage of their daughter
Mrs. Roger Franklyn [widow]
Mrs. Mary Blankharn Franklyn [divorcée]
to
Mr. Richard Carpenter
Friday, the sixth of October
One thousand nine hundred and ninety-five[a]
San Francisco, California

[a] The year is always written out.

Couple's announcement:

Mrs. Roger Franklyn
or Mary Franklyn [widow]
Mrs. Mary Blankharn Franklyn [divorcée]
[or Mary Blankharn Franklyn]
and
Mr. Richard Carpenter
[or Richard Carpenter]
announce their marriage [etc.]

"at Home" card: You may or may not include an "at Home" card with the wedding announcement.

After November first
at Home
Mary and Richard Carpenter
41 Paradise Road
Belvedere, California [ZIP code]
[Telephone number]

Newspaper announcement: It's not customary for a bride who has been married before to announce her engagement in the newspaper. However, if the bride has never been married but the groom has, the wording is the standard bride's engagement announcement.

When a bride is marrying for the second time, the wedding announcement she sends to the newspaper is similar to that of the bride marrying for the first time, except that the text also mentions her previous marriage: "The bride's previous marriage ended in divorce" or "The bride has two sons from a former marriage." If the bride and groom have both been married before, the announcement may end with "The couple's previous marriages ended in divorce."

ATTENDANTS

Usually an older bride and groom will have only one attendant each to serve as witnesses. An older bride, in addition to her main attendant, may have her young daughter participate as flower girl. When an elderly widow remarries, she may ask a favorite granddaughter to be her witness. An attendant at a second marriage is given a token present as a remembrance of the occasion.

WHAT TO WEAR

What the bride wears at her second wedding depends on her age, the season, the time of day the wedding is to be held, and the formality of the occasion. For an informal daytime wedding she may wear a silk or shantung suit or a short dress. For a more formal afternoon or evening wedding she may wear a long dress in any color that's becoming to her. It can even be a white dress so long as it does not resemble a traditional wedding dress. The second-time bride may carry a very simple bouquet or a prayer book, perhaps with a flower marker. She does not wear a veil, but if she likes the idea of wearing something on her head she may wear flowers, a bow, or a simple hat of some kind. The bride's attendant wears a dress that complements the bride's in style and color, although if the bride wears a long dress her attendant's dress does not necessarily have to be long also.

The groom's clothes should be keyed to the degree of formality of the bride's dress. At an informal afternoon wedding he might wear a dark business suit or, in summer, a light or even white suit; at a formal evening wedding after six o'clock he wears a tuxedo. The groom's attendant dresses exactly as the groom does and each wears a boutonniere.

Guests at a second wedding, including children, wear clothes suitable to the time of day, just as at any first wedding.

WEDDING PRESENTS

FROM THE BRIDE'S POINT OF VIEW   If you've been married before you should not expect wedding presents the second time around. Still, you may find that many people you invite to the wedding will want to send you something—those who gave you a present the first time perhaps opting for something less expensive now. It's not customary when you remarry to sign up with a bridal registry. The woman most likely to use a bridal registry for her second marriage is one who had a very small first wedding or eloped.

If you are fortunate enough to have all the worldly goods you need or have room for, and no desire to accumulate any more possessions, you may be tempted to put "No presents, please" on the invitation. Practical as this sounds, you'll have to pass over the idea, as it's not done on a formal wedding invitation. About all you can do is tell any friends who ask, that you're grateful for the thought but the only present you want is their presence. Or you may suggest that a group of friends get together and give you a joint present. You can make a few suggestions as to items you might find useful and practical.

Writing thank-you letters for second wedding presents is no less important than it was for the first. Because you won't be receiving as many presents this time, you and the groom have no excuse for not getting your letters out promptly. With the experience gained from the thank-you letters you wrote before, you'll be much more adept—in fact, you'll probably enjoy the letter-writing process a lot more this time.

FROM THE GUEST'S POINT OF VIEW If you're invited to a second wedding, you are not obliged to send a present. However, if you're invited to the reception and accept, you'll probably want to send something; if you sent a present to the first wedding, the present need not be extravagant. If you get a wedding announcement, there is no obligation to send a present, but if you are a close friend of the bride or groom you will probably want to send something.

If the couple seem to have everything they need, you could ask the bride's mother what they might like for a present. If you're a relative, money is always a good second wedding present. Or you might consider sending the bride any of the following: bath towels that have her new initials on them; one or two more pieces of her existing china pattern; a few bottles of really good wine; or a gift certificate to a restaurant. Another possibility might be to get together with a few friends and give one special present such as a framed Audubon print or some new indispensable electronic gadget.

PRE-WEDDING PARTIES

There are seldom showers for second weddings since their purpose is to help the bride furnish her house or apartment, and a divorced or widowed woman presumably has all the household possessions she needs by the time she marries again.

There are, however, often small parties before second weddings. They may be cocktail or dinner parties given by relatives or close friends of the couple. Because the bride and groom do not rehearse for the second religious ceremony, a party given the night before the wedding is not referred to as the rehearsal dinner. If the groom has not been married before his parents may give a dinner—otherwise, anyone can give a party for the couple or they can give it themselves.

THE CEREMONY

If the bride is in her late thirties or even older but has not been married before (though the groom has) there's no reason why she shouldn't have a wedding ceremony similar to that of any first bride. When the bride has been married before, however, most often she and the groom invite only their families and a very few close friends to the service, and have a larger reception right after the wedding or at another time. If the wedding does not take place at a church or synagogue, it may be held at a hotel or club or perhaps at the house of the bride's family or her own house. Or it may be a civil ceremony with only the couple and their witnesses present.

If you or your fiancé has been divorced and you want to be married in a church or synagogue, you'll need to find out from your clergyperson what the policy is on marrying divorcés. It may be that he's unwilling to conduct the ceremony in the church or temple proper but will agree it can be held in one of the reception rooms. He may suggest having the wedding at a club or a hotel. If he says he's unable or unwilling to marry you under any condition, he may know of a clergyperson of some other denomination who will perform the ceremony.

When a second wedding takes place in a church, there is no formal processional or recessional—no traditional Lohengrin or Mendelssohn music—although there may be music. White satin ribbons are not placed along the pew posts and no canvas runner is laid on the aisle. There are no ushers to seat the guests. There is usually no more than one bridal attendant and a best man for the groom.

A bride who's been married before is not given away. The question, "Who blesses this marriage?" may replace "Who gives this woman to be married?" If the bride is reasonably young, her father or a relative of hers may escort her to join the groom either up the aisle or into the room where the service is to be held. An older woman may ask her son to do the honors, if he's a teenager or older. If she chooses not to be escorted, she may walk alone, possibly preceded by her attendant. If only a few people are attending the ceremony, the bride and her fiancé usually enter the church from a side door preceded by the clergyperson.

THE RECEPTION

It's entirely up to the bride and groom as to how large a reception they want. There's really no restriction on the size of the party, unless the bride is a widow being married only a year or so after her husband's death. While each situation has to be considered on its own, a smaller rather than a larger reception is generally more appropriate. Where the reception takes place is up to the couple. It may be held at a club or hotel or at home if one of them has a house that lends itself to the occasion.

A reception for a second wedding is really no different from one for a first, apart from one or two details. The bride and groom will still have to decide whether or not they want a receiving line and, if they do, who if anyone will stand in it with them. If there's dancing, they are the first to take to the floor. The bride is then cut in on by her father; if her father is not present, or she prefers, her son or the groom's son may cut in. After that, all the guests are free to dance. Any type of cake is appropriate, including a tiered one with or without a decoration of some sort on the top. You would not, however, have the traditional all-white cake decorated with confectionary rosebuds or other ornaments so associated with a first wedding. If the bride is carrying a small bouquet of flowers—and it should be small—she may toss it to whomever she likes when it comes time to leave the reception. And, of course, there can be paper rose petals to throw at the couple as a final good-luck gesture.

REMARRYING EX-SPOUSE

Occasionally people who have been divorced remarry each other. When this happens, no formal announcements are sent out, and no announcement is sent to the newspapers. Friends are informed orally or by letter. In such cases, when the couple celebrate an anniversary it is based on the number of years since their first wedding. In other words, the years they were separated are put to rest, as they well should be.

REAFFIRMATION OF MARRIAGE VOWS

In some Christian communities it's become popular for couples to reaffirm their marriage vows after a number of years, in most cases twenty-five or more. This service may include just the couple, their family, and the clergyperson, or several couples reaffirming their vows at the same time, not necessarily on the wedding anniversary of any one of them. The renewing of marriage vows can be held during a regular church service or it can be arranged as a special, private service. There is really no standard ceremony for this, so the clergyperson can suggest the form of service that will include the repeating of the marriage vows.

The couple's children are often present, as are the best man and maid or matron of honor from their wedding. No one stands up for the couple, nor do they walk up the aisle as in a regular wedding. If they want to, they may replace their old wedding rings with new ones during the service. For this ceremony, the couple wear whatever they would ordinarily wear to church. If the reaffirmation is made at a regular service, no donation to the church is necessary. However, if the service is a private one and the church has been opened specially for the occasion, a donation is in order. The ceremony may be followed by any celebration or reception the couple want. The wedding cake may be a duplicate of the original one and toasts with champagne are offered. In all of this, it's important to talk to the clergyperson involved before making plans.

Some couples would rather renew their wedding vows privately, without benefit of clergy. A couple in Connecticut renew their wedding vows every seven years on the top of a hill overlooking a peaceful New England valley. It's a joyous time for them as well as one filled with nostalgia and romance. In honor of the occasion they dress up in their best clothes. They bring a picnic supper in a basket, a bottle of champagne, their wedding certificate, and the prayer book used at their marriage ceremony. They take turns reading the marriage service in the prayer book, repeating their vows when indicated. Afterward they eat and drink a toast to the next seven years.

CHAPTER 4
OTHER CEREMONIAL OCCASIONS

INTRODUCTION

From the beginning of time, every group of people has conducted ceremonies, great and small, religious and secular. Man's earliest rituals were conducted to appease the unknown, to deal with the mysterious forces of nature. Today our most important ceremonies have to do with beginnings—baptism, circumcision, first communion, and confirmation; with continuations—birthdays and marriage; and with the finale—death.

We take time to celebrate these and other major passages of life with special foods and the giving of presents. Rituals not only acknowledge the passing of time and celebrate happy moments, they also provide protection in times of emotion, particularly in the face of death. Forearmed with information and knowing we won't have to extemporize enables us to act gracefully, say the right thing, and deal calmly with emotionally charged moments. Here, then, are guidelines for handling the rituals surrounding the major occasions of life.

CHRISTENINGS

Christenings, like so many of our social and religious customs, have changed radically in the last two decades. For example, whereas they once were private ceremonies, now multiple baptisms are often performed as part of a regular service to emphasize the role of the congregation and liturgy in a child's spiritual life. The child of a single mother or unmarried parents is now routinely welcomed into the Christian community; this would have been unheard of not too many years ago. A friend who belongs to a different faith altogether is now permitted to assume the role of godparent, although usually with the title "sponsor" or "witness" instead of godparent. And some denominations now encourage parents themselves to act as godparents to their child. While these sorts of modifications have been made, many of the old customs and traditions for baptizing a child are still observed.

In the Catholic Church today a baby is still usually christened within two to six months after his or her birth and has two godparents; one a man, the other a woman. One of the two must be a Catholic. In Protestant churches a child is christened at any age starting after about two or three months. Most Episcopalians have three godparents: two of the same sex as the child and one of the opposite sex, although some Episcopalians favor only one sponsor or, as Baptists do, no sponsor.

Christenings, particularly ones held during a church service, must be planned weeks or even months in advance. Both Catholics and Protestants have become more emphatic about the seriousness of baptism, so now many clergypersons require parents and sponsors to attend a counseling session before a baby is baptized. If for some reason the godparents are unable to be present for the baptism, the subject of proxy godparents, who will stand in for the true godparents at the ceremony, must be brought up. Because customs vary somewhat from church to church, it's important for parents to discuss all aspects of a baptism with their priest or minister.

Parents choose a baby's godparents from among their relatives or closest friends, sometimes asking them if they will assume the responsibility well in advance of the birth. Godparents may be any age, often it's a much younger sister or brother of one of the parents. While asking a relative to be a godparent is fine, at the same time selecting someone outside the family will expand a child's circle of close relationships.

The responsibility conferred upon the relative or friend chosen to be a godparent remains as solemn as ever. Sponsoring a child in baptism means taking a vow to support the child's spiritual life with prayer and with example.

While a godparent is, in theory, responsible for the spiritual guidance of a child, in practice his obligation may be no more than that of any close friend of the family. It's customary to give a godchild a present at Christmas at least until he's grown up and, if the godparent chooses, on his birthday as well. The extent of a godparent's involvement with a godchild depends entirely on their relationship.

If you're asked to be a godparent, and feel you already have as many godchildren as you can handle, be candid and tell the parents so. Explain that you do not feel it would be fair to their child to add this responsibility to your present commitments.

Parents may extend an invitation to a christening by writing a note on their personal stationery, their informal (in this case a couple's informal), or by telephone. A note might say something like this:

Dear Sally,

Andrew is being christened on Sunday, June 11th at St. James' Church at noon. Don and I hope you can be there and that you will come back to the house afterward for a glass of champagne and a little lunch.

Love,
Martha

If the baptism, which includes family and close friends, is to be followed by a large reception, a more formal engraved or printed invitation for the reception only may be sent. Christenings most often take place in the late morning or late afternoon. An officiating priest is always invited to the christening party that follows, as are a minister and the minister's spouse.

Traditionally, the baby wears a long white christening dress for the baptism. It can range from a simple white cotton smock to an embroidered dress, trimmed in lace and worn over layers of organdy petticoats. A christening dress for a small baby is often passed down from one generation to another, and boys as well as girls wear the same one. The baby may wear white booties or white silk shoes and, when the weather is cold, a cap and coat. Baby jewelry, especially of a religious nature, may also be worn to the ceremony. A blanket should be brought along to wrap the baby in once the cap and coat have been removed. It's best not to dress him until just before it's time to go to the church so his clothes will not get mussed or soiled. It's also a good idea to see that he's well fed and rested before the service; that way, he won't make a fuss in the church.

The baby's mother wears whatever she would to church but she should avoid black. In fact, church attire is appropriate for anyone attending a christening: the father, godparents, and guests.

Seating in the church varies according to church procedures and the number of people invited. Traditionally, the godmother holds the baby during the ceremony (if there are two godmothers, the child's mother decides which will hold him). If he becomes restless because he's been handed over to someone he's unfamiliar with, then his mother should take him. When the clergyperson asks what the baby's to be called, the mother, or it can be the mother and father together with the godparent (this will be discussed beforehand with the minister or priest), answers with the child's first and middle name, if there is one, not the surname. The clergyperson has to repeat the name, so if it is a complicated one, it should be written down and given to him.

After the ceremony, the baptismal certificate is signed. It should be taken home and put away in a safe place with other family documents. It may very well be needed at a later date for the child's first communion, confirmation, or marriage.

While the church does not set a fee for christening a child, a donation is given to the officiating clergyperson, usually after the ceremony. The donation may be in the form of cash or a check, placed in an envelope and handed to the clergyperson by the mother or father of the child. The donation may range from twenty-five to one hundred dollars, depending on what the parents can afford. As a guideline, the amount of the donation should be in keeping with the general expenses of the christening.

When a christening is held in the late morning, it's usually followed by a buffet lunch; in the afternoon it's most apt to be a tea, with or without cocktails. The food and drinks are similar to those served at any lunch or tea party, except that there's champagne to toast the baby with. Traditionally, a white cake with the child's initials or name and the date, written in icing, is also served. It's traditional for the godfather to propose the first toast to the baby, although there's no reason the godmother shouldn't do so. Once this toast has been made, the parents may propose a toast, followed by anyone else, including a brother or sister of the baby.

The christening is a time for family and friends to be aware of, and sensitive toward, young siblings of the baby. It's only natural for brothers and sisters to feel somewhat jealous of all the attention the new baby is receiving. To help them feel more special they may be given a featured role in the proceedings: carrying flowers or the special missal or prayer book. Guests, too, should make a fuss over young siblings of the guest of honor, perhaps giving each a small present, or it may be a combined present.

The godparent gives the baby a christening present which is traditionally something of fine and lasting quality. It may be a sterling silver mug, a porringer, or a napkin ring with the baby's name and the date of the christening engraved on it. Baby jewelry, such as a gold cross and chain, is also popular. Guests at a christening usually give the baby a present, although those who gave one at birth should not feel obligated to give another. Presents are ordinarily opened after the guests have left the lunch or tea. You should keep a list of everyone who gave presents and write a note thanking each person for being a part of such a special day in the baby's life as well as for the present.

Not all clergypersons will christen a child at home, nor are home christenings so common as they once were. When the ceremony is held at home, all that is required is a waist-high table on which to place a bowl (usually silver) to be used as a font. The base of the bowl may be encircled with a wreath of delicate flowers, such as daisies, sweet William, white violets, baby's breath, or lily of the valley. If the table is a particularly beautiful one, it may be left bare; otherwise it is covered to the floor with some fabric such as a white cloth or piece of rich brocade.

The service at a home christening does not differ from one in a church. All those attending gather around the font with the parents and godparents and the priest or minister. When the service is finished, a reception usually follows.

BRITH MILAH

Brith milah is the Hebrew phrase for the covenant of circumcision, an ancient ritual performed on Jewish males eight days after they are born. (*Brith* means covenant; *milah* means circumcision. In Hebrew the ceremony is referred to as a "*bris*," while in Yiddish it is pronounced "*brit*.") The ceremony marks the initiation of the male child into Judaism. He is formally named, circumcised, and given godparents.

The ceremony is usually held at the parents' home or that of the grandparents, since few babies remain in the hospital longer than two or three days. However, if circumstances make it necessary, the service can be held at the hospital. Most hospitals provide a special room for this.

Close friends and family are invited to attend, usually by telephone because there is such a short time between the birth and the ceremony. Guests wear the clothing they would to a synagogue, which means that men usually wear yarmulkes. The host must be sure to provide yarmulkes for non-Jewish or forgetful guests. In some congregations, women are required to cover their heads too. Non-Jewish women should check with their hostess as to whether this custom prevails.

There are usually a *kvater* (man) and a *kvarterin* (a woman) appointed to bring the child officially into the room for the circumcision. These people fill the role of godparents and, should the parents be unable to, it is their responsibility to see that the child is educated and lives according to the rules of the Torah. In addition to the *kvaterim*, traditionally a *sandek*, or holder, is also appointed. This man, sometimes referred to as the godfather for the day, does not have the same long-term responsibilities as the official godfather. He first holds the baby during the circumcision. Very often the *sandek* is the boy's paternal grandfather. The *mohel* (pronounced MOY-el), who is often but not always a rabbi, actually performs the circumcision.

If small children are present, they are usually asked to stand in back of the room while the circumcision is being performed and the mother often prefers not to watch either, so she too may stand toward the side or rear of the room. As the ceremony is quite short, guests usually stand.

The ceremony traditionally takes place in the morning and is followed by breakfast or brunch. Typical foods include challah (egg bread), herring, lox, bagels, egg kichelach, honey and sponge cakes, nuts, and dried fruits. Often friends and relatives bring much of the food. Although gifts are given to the baby, they are not a central part of the occasion and are usually modest.

Baby girls are officially named and welcomed into the Jewish community at the ceremony of *simhat habat*, or rejoicing for a daughter. The *simhat habat* is held on the Sabbath shortly after the child's birth. In an

Orthodox family this naming ceremony is held at the synagogue although neither the mother nor the child is present. Her father, however, is called up to the Torah. A special prayer is recited on her behalf and her Hebrew name is officially announced to the congregation. After the services a celebration, similar to the one for a boy, is held at home and attended by friends and family.

In Conservative and Reform services for baby girls, both parents come to the synagogue as soon as the mother feels well enough and often the baby is also brought along. (In some Reform congregations, boys, too, are named in the synagogue and also have a ceremony at home.)

BABY SHOWERS

A baby shower is a wonderful way to celebrate the anticipated birth of a child while at the same time helping out the parents-to-be with all sorts of practical presents for the baby's layette and nursery.

Usually a baby shower is given by friends rather than family, and most often it takes place about a month before the baby is due. In some communities the tradition is to give a baby shower after the baby is born, so it's a good idea to ask an expectant mother which time she'd prefer. There is no standard time for baby showers but usually they are held in the afternoon, with tea and refreshments served, or at midmorning and followed by a light lunch. Such showers, once the exclusive province of women who didn't work outside the home, now often include men and take place on a weekend or after work at the cocktail or dinner hour.

You may invite your guests to a shower by a fill-in invitation (available in most stationery stores), by a note on your personal stationery or informal, or by telephone. One big change in baby showers is that these days parents often know the sex of their expected child. If they do, invitations may say something like, "Please come to a baby shower in honor of Alice Smith, who is expecting a son." Another more subtle way to pass the word along is by drawing a ribbon on the invitation, using pink or blue ink, or highlighting the words "baby shower" with pink or blue marker.

If you are planning a baby shower, ask the mother-to-be what sorts of things she needs for the baby. She should give you a list of articles that vary in cost so that, when a guest asks you what to bring, you can come up with a range of suggestions. A number of friends may want to contribute toward the purchase of a special, much-needed present, such as a collapsible stroller, a crib, or a changing table. Moderate-priced presents might include undershirts, drawstring nightgowns, receiving blankets, bibs, and socks. A mother cannot have too many of these, the basics of any layette.

A classic book on child rearing such as Dr. Spock's or Penelope Leach's also makes an excellent and inexpensive present.

A baby shower is not usually given for a second or third child because the mother already has certain essentials left over from her first child and may not want to put friends who came to the first shower in the position of having to give a second present. Instead of a shower, a small gathering of close friends at a lunch or tea is a good way to celebrate. If a guest wants to bring a token present, in this case an article of clothing is the best choice.

Parents who are adopting a child will appreciate a baby shower too, even if the child is already a few months old. After all, the arrival of a child is always a cause for celebration. It makes more sense, though, to give this shower after the adopted child has been brought home. If the child being adopted is no longer an infant, the invitation may include his birth date as well as the date of the adoption, so guests will have a better idea of what kinds of presents are appropriate.

If the mother-to-be is single there's a very good chance she may be financially less well off, and therefore more in need of presents, than a married mother. For those who can afford it, a check for the prospective single mother, enclosed in a letter congratulating her on the forthcoming blessed event, can be the most meaningful present of all.

While the expectant mother thanks her friends for the presents as she opens them at the shower, she should follow up with short notes reiterating her appreciation. The notes should be written and sent soon after the shower, because once the baby arrives she'll have little time to sit down and take pen in hand.

First Communion

First communion is an important religious event in the lives of young Catholics and for members of some other Christian churches which observe communion as part of their service. Communion is the rite in which the symbolic body and blood of Jesus Christ are given to the congregation in the form of bread (usually a wafer, called the host) and a sip of wine. When a child makes his first communion, he partakes of the host for the very first time. Catholic children make their first communion at age seven or eight. They attend a class in simple religious instruction, then receive their first communion together.

Individual churches may give parents instruction about what the first communion child should wear. Generally girls dress all in white with veils and boys wear white or dark suits. (In some communities, boys wear white suits with shorts.) Parents and guests dress in clothing appropriate for a church service.

During the Mass, the children go up to the altar in a group to receive their first communion. Then the adults in the church take their turn. In a Catholic Mass, small children and non-Catholics do not normally receive communion, though some priests do indeed welcome non-Catholics to the altar.

Only relatives, very close friends, and the child's godparents are invited to the church service. After the first communion, the parents may give a brunch or lunch in honor of the child. The parents and godparents and sometimes close friends give the child a religious present, such as a Bible, a biography of a saint, a prayer book, a crucifix, or a rosary. Parents should make sure their child writes a short thank-you note for each present received.

CONFIRMATION

Confirmation is a Christian ceremony in which a person is confirmed in the faith into which he or she was baptized. The ceremony normally takes place in early adolescence to signify that the child is now adult enough to make his own commitment to the faith in which he was baptized. (Anyone who was not baptized as a child or who changes faiths may, of course, be baptized and confirmed at any age.) In order to be confirmed, a candidate must first take a course of religious instruction; when the ceremony is over, the candidate officially becomes a member of the congregation.

A girl being confirmed may wear all white if she wishes (this was required by some churches until recently) or simply a good Sunday dress. A boy wears his best dark suit with a tie.

At the ceremony the person being confirmed is typically presented to the congregation and to the minister or priest, or in some cases to a bishop or other high church dignitary. Many churches require that the candidate be presented by a sponsor: either one or both of his godparents or a member of the congregation chosen expressly for this purpose. In some churches, the sponsor stands up with the person being confirmed and presents him or her by name during the ceremony; in others, the sponsor's role is merely symbolic.

Confirmation is not a social occasion so much as a religious milestone and it is usually celebrated quietly. The child's godparents and close relatives may give a present—perhaps money enclosed in a special card, or a gold cross, a Bible, a piece of religious jewelry, or a pen and pencil set with the date engraved. Following the church ceremony, the parents may give a brunch or lunch at a restaurant or at home for members of the family, close friends, the godparents, and sponsor.

BAR AND BAT MITZVAH

Bar mitzvah is an ancient and very special ceremony officially marking the passage from childhood into manhood for a Jewish boy. The phrase means "son of the commandment" or "man of duty."

The bar mitzvah typically is held on the Sabbath (Saturday) closest to the boy's thirteenth birthday, although the ceremony may also be held when the Torah is read on Monday or Thursday evenings. Young women were originally excluded from this rite of passage into adulthood; today girls who are members of Conservative and Reform congregations may have a *bat mitzvah* and become a "daughter of the commandment." In some congregations a bat mitzvah may be scheduled for a Friday evening.

In preparation, the young person studies Judaism and Hebrew for about five years in order to answer questions about the religion and learn to speak the language. Toward the end of his studies he devotes some nine months preparing for the bar mitzvah itself. During the ceremony, the boy and girl read aloud in Hebrew from the Haftorah and then recite a prayer, also in Hebrew. Although congregations vary with regard to how much the boy may participate in the ceremony, in most he gives a short original talk, often thanking his parents and teachers and saying a few words about what kind of adult he hopes to be.

After the service the boy is now a man in the eyes of God and the congregation and a very simple reception may be held at the synagogue to which all members of the congregation are invited and at which they congratulate the young man. Following this gathering, many parents give a private lunch or dinner at home or in a restaurant or club. Only those who have received invitations may attend this private celebration.

Because the bar or bat mitzvah is a religious ceremony, the food conforms to the ancient dietary laws known as *kashruth* set forth in the Old Testament books of Leviticus and Deuteronomy. These rules govern the slaughter, preparation, and consumption of *kosher* or permitted foods and *trayf* or forbidden foods. Orthodox Jews carefully abide by all such laws; Conservative Jews may keep the dietary laws at home or in principle but are less rigorous; Reform Jews do not keep kosher, although many prefer not to eat pork or shellfish.

Non-Jews should be aware that dietary laws forbid serving meat and dairy dishes together, which means there will be no butter on the table or real milk, only a dairy substitute. Therefore don't ask for milk or cream for your coffee. And no one should start to eat until the special blessing, the *hamotzi*, is said.

If a bar or bat mitzvah is held on a Friday night, which may now be the case among Reform Jews, hors d'oeuvres may be served first because the ceremony lasts several hours. Following the ceremony, a dinner is served.

Invitations to a bar mitzvah are sent out at least six weeks in advance of the occasion. They may be as formal as an engraved wedding invitation or as informal as a handwritten note. If it is to be black tie, this is stated on the invitation. Although some parents regard their child's bar mitzvah as a time to entertain business associates, it's important to keep in mind that this really is the celebrant's day and he should be surrounded primarily by loving relatives, classmates, and friends with whom he's grown up. The bar mitzvah is one of the most important events in a Jewish boy's life—more important than the comparable Christian confirmation.

> *Mr. and Mrs. Jacob Cohen*
> *request the pleasure of your company*
> *on the occasion of the Bar Mitzvah*
> *of their son*
> *Noah Elkon*
> *who will read Maftir and Haftorah*
> *at Temple Beth-El*
> *on Saturday, the eighth of July*
> *at ten o'clock*
> *and afterward at*
> *The Cumberland Hotel*
>
> *R.s.v.p.*
> *64 Cypress Avenue*
> *San Antonio, Texas 78265*

An example of a formal, engraved invitation to a bar mitzvah.

Guests should reply to an invitation immediately, because the preparations for a large bar or bat mitzvah are often elaborate. Clothing should be appropriate for a religious service, although if the ceremony is in the evening women may wish to dress up a bit more, as often there will be dancing at an evening reception.

Guests should attend both the ceremony and the reception or neither—to skip the ceremony and attend only the dinner or lunch is as rude as attending a wedding reception but skipping the ceremony. However, it is permissible to attend just the ceremony. Because a bar mitzvah is often a long day, beginning at 9 A.M. at the synagogue, not everyone can devote that much time to the occasion. If you plan to attend only the ceremony, let your host and hostess know.

Everyone who receives an invitation is expected to give the bar or bat mitzvah candidate a present whether or not they attend the ceremony. Money is traditional, tucked in an envelope, inside a book, or in a new wallet. Other gifts suitable for a thirteen-year-old include a bond, a *kiddush* cup, prayer book, religious jewelry such as a Star of David, a *chai* (the symbol of life) charm, or binoculars, Polaroid camera, tickets to a sporting event. It's thoughtful to send your present to the family's house before the event rather than take it to the party.

The child should write thank-you notes for every gift received. When money is the present, it is in keeping with the teachings of Judaism that he give some of it to charity.

SWEET SIXTEEN PARTIES

The sixteenth birthday is a major milestone for teenagers, particularly girls (in Spanish households it's the fifteenth birthday). The young man or woman is now on the brink of adulthood, good cause for celebration.

A sweet sixteen party for a girl is usually given by her parents, although an aunt or godmother could just as easily do the honors. A surprise sweet sixteen party isn't the best idea—given the unpredictability of adolescents, there's no knowing what the reaction to the party will be. So it's important to include the celebrant in the planning of the occasion.

Sometimes a sweet sixteen party is given at a club or restaurant but most often it takes place at home. The style of the party may range from a formal dance to a backyard barbecue, depending on the sixteen-year-old. The trick is to work out an agreement between your pocketbook and the teenager's wishes.

Parties with a theme or activity are always good for putting young people at ease. You might invite your guests to "Come as you hope to look ten years from now" or "what you looked like ten years ago," and give prizes for the funniest or most original idea or costume. Or you might give a square dance, provided you can find an experienced caller. There are all sorts of group activities to base a party on: roller skating, ice skating, or a round robin tennis match. You might take the group to an amusement park or on a boat cruise or a beach picnic. There are now, in many cities, "sober clubs" which feature dance music, a nightclub-like atmosphere, and serve no liquor. One of these can be an excellent place for a party.

Food at a sweet sixteen party may be anything from pizza, the teen staple, to an international smorgasbord, followed by a make-your-own sundae buffet. Whatever you serve, given the notoriously huge appetites of that age group, be sure you have plenty of food. You also want to have plenty of soft drinks on hand and perhaps a punch of sorts.

Invitations to a sweet sixteen party may be extended in a number of ways depending on the formality of the party. If it's an informal event, you may use one of the many inventive fill-in invitations found in stationery stores or you may write a note or simply telephone. Always word the invitation so guests know what to wear: "You're invited to a pool party" or "to a dance." If the party is a formal dance, you may still use fill-in invitations, although you may want to send printed or engraved ones, the latter being considerably more expensive. On an informal invitation, just give the telephone number so that guests can call their acceptances or regrets. If the guests are to have an option of bringing a date to the party, on the lower right-hand corner of the invitation write, "Bring a date if you like." Don't just say, "Bring a date," because that sounds like an order and could be awkward for someone. If you are inviting known couples, send each of them an invitation. In this, as in all other teen etiquette questions, solicit the advice of the birthday girl. You don't have to do exactly as she says, but do ask.

The honoree will doubtless receive birthday presents, which may or may not be opened at the party, depending on the size of the group. Opening presents at a party can be time-consuming and distract from the main purpose of the celebration: for everyone to have a good time. If it's a small party and everyone has brought a present, there's no reason not to open them while all are together. What you don't want is for presents to be opened in front of someone who did not bring one. The honoree thanks the guests for the presents soon after the party, either by note or by telephone.

THE ROLE OF THE GUEST

When you are invited to a sweet sixteen party, you should reply to the invitation as soon as possible and follow its form. If the occasion is a dance and the invitation does not say, "Bring a date if you like," do not ask to. Bring a birthday present—to a girl, something like a scarf, a cosmetic case, bath oil, costume jewelry, cassette tapes, or a beach towel in a tote bag; to a boy, a disposable camera, a computerized pocket address book, a gift certificate to a movie theater, great socks or ankle weights. If you have any doubts about what to wear to the party—how formal or informal it will be—don't hesitate to ask. As a guest at a sweet sixteen party, you thank the host and hostess as well as the birthday person before you leave. A follow-up letter expressing further thanks is always appreciated by those who put so much effort into making the party a success.

GRADUATION

Graduation is an occasion for great pride and happiness, marking as it does a milestone in life. High school graduation is a move into adulthood; the years of mandatory schooling are over. College graduation, of course, represents the completion of years of hard work. It's not surprising, then, that graduates often regard the day as the most significant in their lives to date. If you are the parent or stepparent of a graduate, remember it is important to them that members of their family be with them. To make sure they will, let them know the date a few months in advance. (If the graduation is out of town, knowing the date in advance is essential so hotel reservations can be made at an early date. Often there is a shortage of rooms in college and prep school towns.)

Most schools must limit the number of guests who may attend the graduation ceremony to four or six per graduate; therefore only the closest relatives are usually invited to the ceremony itself.

If the graduate has stepparents, grandparents, and a number of close friends, choosing four or six guests could be difficult. The dilemma may be resolved by inviting parents and a grandparent from each side, or by drawing straws, or perhaps by using a rotation system if there are several graduates within one family. If you are not invited keep your disappointment to yourself. The graduate should not have to worry about family politics on his big day.

If parents are divorced, the question of who attends becomes more complicated. If a graduate gets only six tickets, for instance, and wants to ask his natural parents and both sets of grandparents, his stepparent or stepparents will not be able to attend. A thoughtful stepparent will make it easy for the graduate by volunteering to stay home and perhaps help with the preparations for the lunch or party afterward. One understanding stepmother, seeing the conflict her stepson was having, smoothed things over by sending him a handwritten invitation to a special graduation dinner. The two of them celebrated later that week at his favorite restaurant. Several years later he told his stepmother he'd completely forgotten what the speakers said at his graduation but he remembered every detail of their dinner together.

Divorced parents who do not get along must also put aside any feelings of acrimony for the day and be civil. To minimize conflict, they may wish to sit at opposite sides of the auditorium or seating area. Each should allow the other a private moment with their son or daughter after the ceremony as well as time for pictures to be taken. Divorced parents who are on friendly terms can add to their child's joy by sitting together on graduation day.

Because tickets are limited, many schools provide printed announcements with a space for the graduate to fill in his or her name. These announcements are sent after graduation to those who would have been invited had there been room and to other close friends and relatives. In order to avoid having the announcement look like a request for a present, the phrase "No presents, please" may be written in the lower right-hand corner. Of course, if someone wants to send a present he is free to do so. A student who does not graduate with his class may save his announcements and use them when he has fulfilled the school's requirements. He then crosses out the original date and fills in his own graduation date. If the school does not provide announcements, parents may have them printed formally or the graduate, if he likes, may design his own.

Most graduations are held in May or June, a lovely time of year in which to celebrate, with the freshness and beauty of spring adding to the joyful feelings of the graduate and his family. At many boarding schools and colleges, the week between finals and graduation is designed to be a whirlwind of parties, theatrical events, dances, and other social functions, some of which will be open to guests of the graduate. Guests and members of the graduate's family may want to spend a day or two near the campus to participate in these activities. While a college graduate may assume the responsibility for making hotel reservations for his family, this should not be expected of a high school senior. Often, the school will send parents on request a list of nearby accommodations and they can make their reservations directly. Regardless of who actually makes the reservations, they should be made well in advance, often as much as a year. If a hotel is out of the question for some family members, the college graduate must try to make other arrangements, perhaps putting guests up in a spare dorm room or at a friend's house or apartment. The parents or other adults attending the graduation pay their own hotel bill and, if they are bringing along a friend of their son or daughter, they pay for that person's room as well.

The school generally provides a list of events open to parents and friends, their times and locations. In some cases, individual invitations are sent to each event. If you are not sure from the invitation about what to wear, telephone the school. Attire for the baccalaureate service and the graduation ceremony is always slightly on the dressy side, what one wears to church or synagogue. For men, that means a jacket and tie and, for women, a suit or dress and perhaps a hat. Out of consideration for those seated behind you, however, remove your hat during the ceremony. If the graduation is to be held outdoors, bring a small umbrella and a sun hat.

Parents and grandparents should not expect the graduate to spend all his time with them. He will want to party and say goodbye to his fellow grads as well. On the other hand, the graduate must remember that his parents made it possible for him to attend school and quite naturally they want to share some of the happiness of the day.

Parents often like to give a party for the graduate, as well as for family and friends if geography allows. It is also a way to entertain those for whom there were not enough tickets. Invitations are mailed or telephoned far enough in advance to give out-of-towners plenty of time to make hotel reservations—at least three weeks before the event. Graduations are frequently held in the morning, so a lunch following the ceremony works particularly well. Lunch is also unlikely to conflict with a graduates-only party, because those are in the evening. However, it's wise to consult with the graduate before setting the time for the gathering so it won't conflict with his plans. By the same token, as soon as the graduate knows he will be attending a party with contemporaries, he should tell his parents.

Lunch, of course, is not the only possibility. A graduation party can be a simple picnic or backyard barbecue, a dinner, or even a dinner dance. If it's a lunch or dinner, it can be held at the graduate's home if he lives near the school, or at a nearby restaurant, hotel, or club. Regardless of the type of party, the parents and the graduate should stand together and greet their guests as they arrive. If it's a seated dinner, the graduate sits in the place of honor: a male graduate, to the right of his mother; a female graduate, to the right of her father. It's a nice touch if one or both parents toast their son or daughter sometime during this party and if the graduate then responds and thanks his parents for their help and support.

Certain family members and friends will want to bring the graduate a present. For those who don't have a particular idea in mind, his parents or brother or sister may have suggestions. Traditional graduation presents include money, a gift certificate, savings bonds or shares of stock, luggage, miniature television set, simple jewelry, initialed silver key ring, sporting or computer equipment, a clock or clock-radio, a reference book.

A word about drinking. Although high school seniors are usually not of legal drinking age, this does not always stop them. Some put pressure on their parents to serve liquor; others sneak liquor into no-liquor parties. Whether you are the host at such a party or know that your child is attending one, your stand should be firm: it is against the law for those under twenty-one to drink. It's too dangerous and the legal liabilities of serving liquor are severe. Don't veer from your position. The statistics on the number of teenagers hurt in automobile accidents on graduation night because they had been drinking should be persuasive and help make your stand unalterable.

After the festivities have ended, the graduate should take time to send handwritten thank-you notes to everyone who gave him a present. These notes need not be lengthy but they should be sent within a month of the date of graduation. For example:

Dear Aunt Beth,

Thanks so much for the generous check you sent me for graduation. I plan to put half of it in my graduate school savings fund and to use the rest for a short vacation in California.

When I get back from my trip, I hope we can have lunch so I can tell you all about it.

Again, many thanks for your present and for being the greatest aunt ever.

Much love,
Thad

DEBUTS

The original purpose of a "debut" was to make known to the world that a daughter was ready to accept suitors for her hand in marriage, usually at about age eighteen. But the "coming out" party eventually became the elite's celebration of its own exalted status. In this country the snobbishness reached its peak in the Gilded Age when Vanderbilts vied with Astors to produce the most spectacular displays of wealth and ostentation.

Since those days the coming out party has more or less mirrored the spirit of the times. During the turbulent, antiestablishment 1960s, young women began shunning the idea of making a debut. But the pendulum then began to swing in the opposite direction. Young women once again became interested in making their debuts but the new debutantes are more concerned with their education than with their prospects for marriage. And their parties are geared to a more realistic, contemporary style of entertaining.

Not every young woman is cut out to be a debutante. Many have no interest whatever in being debs while others heartily disapprove of all the affectations and costly excess. While it may seem hard to believe, there are always some parents who encourage, in fact push, their daughters into a debutante season just to advance their own social status in the community or to impress business associates by showing off their wealth or their connections. No matter what the reason—political or social—if a young woman chooses not to make a debut, it's unfair to force her into a situation that will make her unhappy. Being debutantes should be left to those more party oriented.

Traditionally, the debutante season takes place during the Thanksgiving and Christmas holidays, after a young woman has graduated from high school, when students are home from college, although occasionally a debutante will be given a private dance in June before the season begins, usually in the country.

Few parents today can afford to give a private dinner or supper dance for their debutante daughter. Instead, they give a joint dance, sharing expenses with the parents of two or three other debutantes. Sometimes the dance is held at the house of one of the debutantes, often outside in a tent, but it is more likely to be at a hotel or club where all arrangements can be taken care of. (If you're interested in knowing more about the planning of a dinner or supper dance: the caterer, the orchestra, the flowers, the tent, etc., see "Balls and Dances" in Chapter 2.)

THE DEBUTANTE TEA

In some places, particularly in the South, a debutante is given a tea, with or without dancing, by her parents, her grandparents, or a friend of her parents. A debutante tea is usually held from five to seven. It's customary for the invitation to read "at Home" even if the tea is going to take place at a club or hotel. If there's to be dancing, the word "Dancing" is written on the lower right-hand corner of the invitation. Tea sandwiches and any other foods served at a formal tea are offered with tea and coffee. Cocktails are also available, with bars set up in the room or waiters passing drinks. Sometimes, even though it's still daylight, the curtains in the room are drawn and the candles lighted. Of course at Christmas it will probably be dark already.

ASSEMBLIES AND COTILLIONS

If a young woman isn't planning a private debut or one shared with a few friends, she might come out at a debutante assembly or cotillion. (There is no reason, of course, that she cannot have her own party as well as attending a group ball.) Cotillion balls are usually quite large, with perhaps a hundred young women making their debuts at the same time. The oldest and best known of the debutante balls are the Cotillion in Boston, the Junior Assembly in New York, the Passavant Cotillion in Chicago, the Delta Debutante Ball in Greenville, Mississippi, the Harvest Ball at the Piedmont Driving Club in Atlanta, the Beaux Arts Ball in Oklahoma City, the Fiesta Ball in San Antonio, the Idlewild Ball in Dallas (a debutante does not pay to go to this particular party and may attend only if she promises to give a ball of her own), and the Ak-Sar-Ben Ball in Omaha. Participation in some balls is strictly by invitation; for others, a young woman applies for membership, often years before she plans to make her debut. The ball committee decides who will be privileged to come out at the ball. If a young woman's parents are well known in the community, particularly to committee members, the likelihood of her being accepted is enhanced. A debutante brings one, or more often two, escorts to these balls, and is responsible for the cost of any tickets involved. Once the young men have agreed to be her escorts she gives their names to the ball committee, who in turn send them invitations. Usually the committee will have its own list of single men to whom invitations are sent.

Another type of debut party is a ball at which a number of debutantes are presented for the benefit of some organization or charity. One such is the National Debutante Cotillion and Thanksgiving Ball, Ltd., of Washington, D.C., which benefits Children's Hospital National Medical Center. If the party serves a useful purpose, it gives less cause for people to say that coming out is a waste of money and time.

While a dance automatically implies formal attire, which customarily means that men wear tuxedos, sometimes a debutante assembly or cotillion calls for "White tie," meaning a stiff wing collar and shirt, evening studs, white piqué waistcoat, white tie, and black tail coat worn with black patent leather pumps. However, because it may be difficult for many of the men invited to put together full evening regalia, "Black tie" is also acceptable.

What follows here are certain formalities that pertain specifically to debutante parties.

THE INVITATION

The invitation to a private debutante dance reads, "at a dance," or it may say "at a small dance" even though the party will be large. In other words, you don't invite people to a "debutante dance." If the word "dancing" is not mentioned in the body of the invitation, it appears on the lower right-hand corner of the invitation.

Mr. and Mrs. Arthur Taylor White

request the pleasure of your company

at a small dance

in honour of their daughter

Miss[a] Pamela Timmins

on Tuesday, the third of May

at eight o'clock

The National Hunt Club

11 Greene Street

R.s.v.p.
Ms. Marie Linstrom
11 Main Street
New Orleans, Louisiana 12345

An example of an invitation to a debutante party.

[a] A woman uses the title Miss until she is twenty-one, at which time she may change to Ms. if she so chooses.

REPLYING TO AN INVITATION   An invitation to a debutante party, like any invitation, should be answered, if not immediately, then certainly within a week. Putting off or forgetting to answer an invitation is extremely rude because the hostess must know the exact number of guests to expect. If you accept an invitation to a coming out party and for some reason find you can't make it, get in touch with the hostess immediately, particularly if it's a dinner dance. Caterers, hotels, and clubs all charge for a guest who has accepted an invitation even if he doesn't show.

In the case of an invitation whose wording says, "at a small dance," you accept or regret "at a dance"; the word "small" is never repeated.

THE UNINVITED GUEST It's amazing that some people have such bad manners as to go where they're not invited and apparently see nothing wrong with crashing a party. *Never* go to a party uninvited or use someone else's invitation. And never bring a friend along with you no matter how entertaining or attractive you feel the person is.

DRESS

At your own debut, you wear a long white or pastel-colored dress with white kid gloves either to the elbow or above. As a guest at someone else's debut, you may wear a dress of any color, although light shades are more traditional. At a tea dance you wear a short cocktail-type dress. If a number of girls are having a joint party, you can decide together whether you want to wear white or how you want to coordinate the colors of your dresses. The mother of a debutante dresses according to the formality of the occasion: a long dress for a ball, a short dress for a late afternoon party. The man who presents you, usually your father, though it may be your stepfather or some other family member, wears white tie and tails with white kid or chamois gloves if it's a formal ball. Your escort or escorts also wear white tie and tails. While traditionally all men attending a debutante ball wear white tie and tails, often these are not available to young men today and they wear black dinner jackets with white shirts. If in doubt as to the evening's proper attire, ask the debutante or committee chairman.

THE ESCORT

Any man should be complimented to be asked by a debutante to be her escort for her coming out party. While your role is not the least bit complicated, you do have a few responsibilities. To begin with, you must find out if the debutante would like to wear a corsage the evening of the party and, if so, what her preference in flowers and color is. If she prefers not to wear a corsage, you may send her cut flowers instead, either before or after the party. It's important for you to be on hand when the debutante has the first dance with her father, because you are supposed to cut in on the two of them.

Beyond these two specific duties, your role is to introduce the debutante to your friends, see that she's danced off her feet, and if the party is a supper dance, to escort her into supper and sit at her table. Although you do not pay for your ticket to a subscription ball, you should still have some cash on hand to pay for taxis or drinks if there's an open bar. And if a group of friends go on for a post-party drink, you pay her share as well as your own.

FLOWERS

A debut is not really a present-giving occasion. While your family may give you a piece of jewelry and close friends personal accessories to celebrate your debut, in most communities, family, friends, and some-times business associates of your parents send flowers to you the day before or the day of your party. The best choice is cut flowers, which can be placed in vases and banked behind the receiving line. The names of the senders should be kept track of so you can write and thank them after the party. Whether or not you want to wear a corsage is your decision. If you want one but prefer not to pin it to your dress, you may pin it to your evening bag or wear it around your wrist. Or, instead of a corsage, you may prefer to carry a bouquet. When a number of girls are being presented together, they often carry similar bouquets.

THE RECEIVING LINE

Your mother, or whoever is giving the party for you, stands at the head of the receiving line with you beside her. While your father may or may not stand on your other side, most often he chooses to play the role of the host, welcoming and chatting with guests as they arrive. As guests pass by, your mother introduces you to anyone you do not know. Conversations should be brief, no more than, "I'm glad you could come. Let's get to-gether later," so as not to hold up the line. A receiving line lasts until a majority of the guests have arrived, perhaps as long as an hour.

DANCING

At a private dance, you and your father are the first to take to the dance floor once the receiving line has disbanded. After you have danced for a few minutes, you are cut in on by your escort. Your father then dances with your mother. If your father and mother are divorced, it's hoped for your sake that they can put aside any lingering disagreements and dance together once at the party. Each man at the dance should dance with you, with your mother, and naturally with his date for the evening. If the party is a dinner dance, he also dances with the women seated on either side of him. If a woman has danced so many dances that her feet are starting to give out, she may say to the next person who asks her to dance, "Thanks, but I've been dancing so much I'm exhausted. I think I'll take a breather." Once she's made such a remark, she must sit awhile, long enough so that the man who asked her to dance does not think she was singling him out. If a woman feels she has been dancing an unbearably long time with the same man, she may suggest going to get something to drink or joining friends at a table. Of course, the same applies for a man. As to cutting in, one quite firm rule is that a man does not cut back in on the man who just cut in on him. Double cutting, in which one couple changes partners with another couple, is popular with some people, but definitely not with others. It's best done between four people who are friends so there's no chance of one person feeling he's being "dumped."

THE THANK-YOU LETTER

Even though you thank the debutante and her parents at the end of the party, take time to write a note of thanks to the parents who put so much time and effort into the event. It will please them enormously, not only to know you had a good time, but that you cared enough to write. If you know them particularly well, you might want to send flowers along with your note. It's also nice to telephone or write the debutante to say what a great party she had and how pretty she looked and to gossip a bit about what went on. She will have been busy and distracted so she'll love to hear whatever you have to say, no matter how trivial.

BIRTHDAYS

Birthdays are special occasions that give you the opportunity to show people how much they mean to you. And it's a rare person indeed who doesn't expect, and rightly so, to be remembered by those closest to him on that day. Of course we all know someone who goes out of his way to say he wants his birthday to be ignored—that it's only a reminder of advancing age, etc. But such protests must not be taken altogether seriously. Probably a birthday card or telephone call would please him enormously.

The best way to remember birthdays is to write the names of the people to whom you give presents or send cards in your yearly calendar or engagement book. When it's time to get a new calendar or engagement book, copy the birthdays from the past year into the new one. If you are very organized, you may want to buy a so-called Birthday Book which you can find in bookstores or stationery stores. In it, you can keep a written record of what you give each person as a birthday present and how much it cost. That way, you won't duplicate a present and you'll also have an idea of how much you usually spend.

Although children want and should have a celebration every year, most adults have special parties only on milestone birthdays. The twenty-first is definitely special and so is each decade thereafter. Anything is appropriate from a seated dinner party to a big cookout, an outing at the ball park, or a theater party. Whatever pleases the birthday person is right.

Depending on the formality of the occasion, invite guests by fill-in invitation, a letter on your personal stationery, or by telephone. If you use a fill-in invitation, you may write either "To celebrate Bob's 50th birthday," at the top or in the body of the invitation, wherever it fits in best. Often the person being honored would prefer not to have guests obligated to bring presents (and he may not want to accumulate more possessions). In that case, add "No presents please," or, less formally, "Your presence is your present," on the lower right-hand corner of the invitation. A few very close friends might decide to ignore the request. Those who do should drop their presents off at the birthday person's house before the event rather than bring it with them. If any presents are brought to the party, they should be opened after the guests have gone home. Thank-you notes should be written as soon as possible for all birthday presents received.

What you choose for a present, of course, depends on your relationship to the person having the birthday and how much money you want to spend. If you're not going to go overboard, there are plenty of thoughtful and imaginative ways to honor someone on his birthday: by taking him to lunch, by sending a basket of flowers or a plant, by telephoning to say, "Happy birthday," by sending a birthday card or even baking a cake. A really good idea for a birthday present is an "I.O.U." written on a birthday card. What you do is pledge to the birthday celebrant a service of some kind. You might promise to cook a meal on a given date, to arrange a picnic in the park, to help plant a garden, to have lunch at a museum, or to give a free car wash.

Less imaginative or creative are the regular birthday standbys: the singing birthday telegram or the messenger in the gorilla suit who delivers a cluster of balloons along with a birthday greeting. These emissaries are fine to send to someone at home but it's just not appropriate to send them to a restaurant or public place. It's discourteous as well as distracting to other patrons. As for the singing telegram that features a male or female stripper, it's boorish and unattractive and an embarrassment to anyone who has to watch.

Stationery shops and card shops are all stocked with various types of birthday cards. Most are intended to be humorous and make jokes about age. As an example, there's the card that has a picture on the outside of what appears to be a group of military strategists sitting around a conference table working out a plan. Inside the card is a birthday cake with lots of candles and directly below is written, "We've finally figured out how to get all the candles on your cake." A card like this is fine to send to someone who you know is young and healthy, but to send it to someone who you know is sensitive about his age, or is elderly, is inappropriate, regardless of how great a sense of humor he has. Give some thought to the card you choose. A birthday card is supposed to be a source of pleasure. You don't want the message the card conveys to ruffle the recipient's feathers or hurt his feelings.

And don't forget that you're entitled to celebrate your own birthday—buy yourself something frivolous you see or have always wanted. If no one else offers, take yourself out to a sumptuous meal and enjoy your birthday that way. Do something pleasurable for yourself—it might be an opera or theater ticket, or a day off work for a hike in the woods, a ball game, anything that would please you and make you feel your birthday really had been celebrated.

BIRTHSTONES

January	Garnet
February	Amethyst
March	Aquamarine
	Bloodstone
April	Diamond
May	Emerald
June	Pearl
	Moonstone
	Alexandrite
July	Ruby
August	Peridot
	Sardonyx
September	Sapphire
October	Opal[a]
	Tourmaline
November	Topaz
	Citrine
December	Turquoise
	Zircon

[a] The opal is said to bring good luck to those born in October; bad luck to those born in other months of the year.

WEDDING ANNIVERSARIES

Most couples tend to celebrate wedding anniversaries in a fairly quiet way. What they're likely to do is have dinner at a favorite restaurant, perhaps taking in a movie or a show of some sort afterward. Or, for sentiment's sake, they may go back to where they honeymooned, or spend a weekend at a comfortable country inn. When couples go all out to celebrate a particular anniversary, it's usually the first, fifth, tenth, twenty-fifth, fiftieth, or, if they're lucky, the seventy-fifth. Essentially, the numerical year you choose to celebrate is unimportant; if you're in the mood to give a bang-up party after seven years of marriage, by all means do so.

While wedding anniversaries are celebrated only when both spouses are alive, it's nice to remember an anniversary even if one of the couple has died. If, say, the husband of a friend of yours dies, and you know the date of her wedding anniversary, she'll certainly be touched and pleased if you remember, particularly on her first anniversary alone. While an anniversary card would only be a painful reminder of her husband's death, there are other ways you can show you care. For instance, you can send her flowers or a plant with a note saying something like, "I can't let this day go by without you knowing I'm thinking of you. Love, Susannah." You don't have to mention her husband's death; it goes without saying that she'll know why you thought of her. Or, if your friend lives close by, you might invite her over for dinner or take her out to lunch with another close friend. As is often true, what you do is not what's important. It's the gesture of love and friendship that means so much to someone who has suffered a loss.

An anniversary party is usually given by the couple themselves, or one of their parents, or later their children may honor them with some type of festivity. A surprise party is always well intended, but don't attempt one unless you are certain the honorees appreciate surprises.

An anniversary does not always have to be celebrated on the actual date that the wedding took place. Should it fall on a Sunday, for instance, chances are you'd rather advance the party a day and celebrate Saturday night. How you extend the invitation to an anniversary party depends on the formality of the event being planned. A formal twenty-fifth anniversary invitation might be engraved or printed in silver, a fiftieth in gold. If expense is no object, a photograph of the bride and groom, taken on their wedding day, may appear as a part of the invitation, centered at the top. A less formal invitation may be extended by a personal note or over the telephone. Some couples, not wanting a fuss made over their anniversary, simply send out invitations saying, "Audrey and Bob Southwood request the pleasure of your company at dinner," or if it's in letter form, "Hope you and Jack can come for dinner, etc." Naturally, you may use fill-in invitations if you like.

A formal invitation to a wedding anniversary party might look like this:

Mr. and Mrs. Robert Southwood

request the pleasure of your company

at a dinner to celebrate

the fiftieth anniversary of their marriage

on Saturday, the sixth of June

at eight o'clock

876 Ocean Drive

Palm Beach

R.s.v.p.   Black tie

When an anniversary party is to be small, guests bring a present for the couple. However, if you know a large number of guests have been invited, it's not necessary to bring a present unless you want to. Actually, many couples celebrating an anniversary try to discourage guests from bringing presents to the party for the usual reasons: either they have everything they need or they don't want guests to feel obligated. To get this message across, you may write on an informal invitation, "No presents, please," or "Your presence is your present." You would not, however, engrave or print such a message. What you could do is insert with each invitation a printed piece of paper that says, "It's requested that no presents be brought to the party."

Planning a major anniversary celebration is no different from planning any party as far as food, music, and decorations are concerned. There are, however, certain sentimental touches you can give to an anniversary party. You might begin by inviting the original bridal party. For decorations, blown-up pictures from the wedding bring a touch of nostalgia to the event and are fun to look at as well. They can be placed on easels and positioned around the room. If you can somehow get your hands on the bride's wedding scrapbook without her knowledge, you can take the newspaper announcement of the wedding with her picture and have it blown up to place near the front door. An anniversary party is the type of occasion at which you will want to have a photographer. It's particularly nice to have a photograph taken of the couple with members of their immediate family who are present at the party. The picture can be saved for future generations and should be documented on the back with the date and information identifying each member of the group. Another picture to have taken is one of the couple with the original bridal party. Copies can be made, inexpensively framed, and sent to everyone in the photograph.

An anniversary party is certainly a time when champagne is in order, and toasts are an important part of the festivities. If children are giving the party for their parents, one of them gives the first toast: "We're so happy to have all of you here with us tonight to celebrate this memorable occasion. Sally, Amy, and I feel enormously lucky and proud to have Mom and Dad as parents. Their love and support over the years means more than we can ever say. And their devotion for each other is an inspiration to all of us. I hope you will stand and raise your glasses in a toast to Mom and Dad on their fortieth anniversary." If the couple are giving the party for themselves and have tried to keep the anniversary a secret, the husband may announce the occasion with a toast to his wife at dinner, saying, "I'd like you all to know that this is a very special day for Audrey and me as it's our fortieth wedding anniversary. I hope you'll join me in drinking a toast to Audrey, who has brought me much joy and happiness all these years."

At an anniversary party there should be some kind of cake, preferably with a white icing, reminiscent of the original wedding cake. There is no set procedure as to whether or not to have a receiving line. It all depends on how formal the affair is and the couple's wishes. If a couple is giving their own party, the wife stands first in line with her husband next to her. Often children of the couple also stand in line, taking their places after their father. When there are a number of children present, it's a good idea for them to take turns standing in the line; otherwise they hold up the flow of traffic. If the party is being given for the couple, the host and hostess come first in the receiving line, followed by the couple, wife first, husband next to her. If the couple is elderly, and it would be too tiring for them to stand in a receiving line, they may sit somewhere close to the entrance of the room so guests can stop and say hello as they arrive.

If presents are welcome and the party's not too large, the couple may open them in front of their guests. If there are too many presents to open all at once, however, or if the majority of the guests failed to bring presents, any gifts that were brought should be opened by the couple after the party, and the givers thanked by letter or by a telephone call.

A lovely anniversary present children can give their parents is a framed family tree. You can either get an artist to do a painting of a tree, or it's not too difficult for an amateur to draw one. Once the tree has been drawn, photographs of various family members can be pasted onto the appropriate branches with each person's name and date of birth written under his picture. The tree can then be framed and given to the couple at the party. Another nice present is a leather-bound scrapbook filled with anniversary cards and messages. While soliciting family members and friends to write, collecting the messages, and pasting them into the scrapbook is a time-consuming project, such a personal present always means a great deal to any couple.

There is a longstanding tradition associated with the giving of wedding anniversary presents, especially the major anniversaries, though, of course, it need not be followed. If the couple have received few sterling silver, crystal, glass, or linen wedding presents, the first few anniversaries are excellent occasions for friends and relatives to help fill in.

The following is a list of the traditional wedding anniversary present categories, plus a newer, revised list.

ANNIVERSARY	TRADITIONAL LIST	REVISED LIST
First	Paper	Clocks
Second	Cotton	China
Third	Leather	Crystal, glass
Fourth	Books	Electrical appliances
Fifth	Wood, clocks	Silverware

ANNIVERSARY	TRADITIONAL LIST	REVISED LIST
Sixth	Candy, iron	Wood
Seventh	Copper, bronze, brass	Desk sets, pen and pencil sets
Eighth	Electrical appliances	Linen, lace
Ninth	Pottery	Leather
Tenth	Tin, aluminum	Diamond jewelry
Eleventh	Steel	Fashion jewelry and accessories
Twelfth	Silk, linen	Pearls, colored gems
Thirteenth	Lace	Textiles, fur
Fourteenth	Ivory	Gold jewelry
Fifteenth	Crystal	Watches
Sixteenth		Silver hollow ware
Seventeenth		Furniture
Eighteenth		Porcelain
Nineteenth		Bronze
Twentieth	China	Platinum
Twenty-fifth	Silver	Sterling silver
Thirtieth	Pearl	Diamond
Thirty-fifth	Coral, jade	Jade
Fortieth	Ruby	Ruby
Forty-fifth	Sapphire	Sapphire
Fiftieth	Gold	Golden jubilee
Fifty-fifth	Emerald	
Sixtieth	Diamond	Diamond jubilee
Seventieth	Diamond	

FUNERALS

When a close relative or friend dies, we feel not only great sadness and a sense of loss but also an abrupt awareness of the brevity of life and of our own mortality. Perhaps that is why at this time even those who have never considered themselves religious find comfort in the traditional funeral service. The rituals of a funeral and the protocol surrounding burial provide a framework that is not only comforting but also assures that the last rites are carried out with dignity and appropriateness, giving much-needed consolation to the bereaved. The funeral is a way of reminding all of us of the continuum of life and death, of the importance of individual lives.

For all of us the funeral service and burial give a measure of finality or closure to death so we may continue with our lives. They are particularly important for a young child. It is valuable for him to see what happens when a grandparent or other close relative dies: that he or she didn't simply disappear. Shutting even a small child out of a ceremony at this time can be more harmful than letting him experience the grief. But parents of a small child must try to explain what is going on and reassure him that his life will most likely be a very long and happy one.

INSTRUCTIONS FOR NEXT OF KIN

While thinking of one's own death is seldom easy, everyone should have a file to be opened upon his or her death that includes instructions to help the survivors handle the funeral and estate matters. One person, preferably two, must know where the file is kept so it can be found easily. In the file, make it known whether you want to be cremated, whether you want a memorial service and, if so, what hymns and psalms you'd like. Some people even leave instructions to spend a certain amount of money on a remembrance party after their death.

Although each person's situation is unique, these are among the subjects that should be covered in the file marked: "To Be Opened Upon My Death." It would include:

- Location of will.
- Name/address/telephone number of attorney.
- Name/address/telephone number of accountant.
- Name/address/telephone number of bank and name of representative to call.
- Name/address/telephone number of clergyperson.
- Name/address/telephone number of funeral home.
- Note stating whether vital organs are to be donated.
- Note stating whether cremation is preferred and, if so, what to do with ashes.
- Place where funeral or memorial service is to take place and any instructions regarding the service (special prayers, psalms, or hymns)
- Location of burial plot.
- List of honorary pallbearers.
- List of ushers.
- If, in lieu of flowers at the funeral, donations to a specific organization or institution would be appreciated, note to this effect.
- Social security number.
- Medical insurance cards.
- List of bank accounts, savings accounts, money market funds.

- List of all securities owned, and where located.
- Where bank statements and checkbooks are located.
- Where tax information is located.
- Where credit cards can be found.
- Where safe deposit box and key are located.
- Where insurance policies are located.
- Where jewelry is located.
- Where silver is located.
- List of items designated for specific people (note: must also be in your will to be binding; otherwise your wishes may or may not be followed).
- List of organizations, agencies, schools, etc., to be notified.

WHEN DEATH OCCURS

When a person dies at home his physician is contacted. If the death was anticipated, the physician may need only call the funeral home and ask that they come for the body, telling them that he will deliver the signed death certificate to them. If death is sudden or due to an accident and the deceased had no personal physician, a funeral home director will be able to give advice as to what steps should be taken. If necessary, he may call in the county medical examiner or coroner for permission to release the body and to sign the death certificate. These formalities differ according to the particular town or city where the deceased resided.

If the deceased asked that his vital organs be donated under the Uniform Anatomical Gift Act, it is extremely important that his request be honored and that the physician know his wishes as far in advance of death as possible. This is an urgent matter, as donor organs must be removed from the body within hours of death in order to be of value to someone else. The body is delivered to a hospital for the organs to be taken; it is then sent to a funeral home. If the deceased's family does not know the name of a funeral home, the attending physician or the hospital can recommend one.

THE FUNERAL DIRECTOR

If you are the family member responsible for the funeral arrangements, remember that the wishes of the deceased must be respected, no matter what the personal feelings of the family may be or what the funeral home or friends suggest.

When you are dealing with a funeral home, you must realize that you are entering into a business contract. Be frank with the funeral director and tell him exactly what your financial situation is. Take care not to overextend yourself; it is sometimes months before funds can be released from an estate for payment of bills having to do with the funeral. In complicated cases it may even be necessary to get court permission to have them paid. The Federal Trade Commission's "Funeral Rule," adopted in 1984, requires that funeral directors give a written estimate of services and their costs.

One of the first things to decide is what type of casket you'd like the deceased to be buried in. If you ask for a simple casket, don't allow yourself to be talked into a more elaborate one—which all too often happens under the emotional strain of the situation. No one but the funeral director really knows or cares about the fine details of the casket.

At some point you will have to advise the director as to what clothes the deceased is to be buried in and when they will be delivered to the funeral home. Some people are buried in a nightgown or pajamas and bathrobe; others are buried in a favorite dress or suit. Young children may be buried in their nightclothes or favorite clothes. Of course, the matter of dress depends, in part, on whether the casket is to be open or closed. Wedding rings are often left on, although Jews do not follow this custom. Orthodox and Conservative Jews bury their dead in shrouds.

If you would like the funeral home to send a death notice to the newspapers, tell the funeral director. He can show you sample death notices or you may write your own to give to him. If he prepares the notice, make sure he shows it to you for your approval before sending it to the newspapers.

Most funeral homes provide limousines for the day of the service to take people to and from the cemetery, an option you may want to consider. Many will also provide you with acknowledgment cards for replying to condolence letters. Try to resist taking advantage of these. No card can take the place of a personal, handwritten letter on your own stationery. (If you do send out cards, make certain the message is simple and in good taste and that there is ample space for you to add a handwritten message.)

THE ATTORNEY

Soon after a death occurs, you'll need to be in touch with the attorney who drew up the deceased's will. If he is out of town or otherwise unavailable, an attorney from the same office will be able to help you with the legal matters.

SETTING A DATE FOR THE FUNERAL

Since a funeral is held within a few days after death, the clergyperson who is to perform the service must be called to set up the date and time. If it's to be held at the funeral home, then the funeral director is contacted. Once you have established the date and time, you'll want to go see the clergyperson or director to discuss the details of the service.

Family members must be contacted about the funeral arrangements as soon as possible so they can make their plans. Aside from family, you will want to call the deceased's closest friends and his place of work, to inform them of his death. The deceased's address book and Rolodex can be helpful in locating his friends and business associates.

A funeral most often involves two ceremonies: the service, which takes place in the church, synagogue, or funeral home, and the interment or committal of the body at the cemetery. The body is always present at the funeral and interment, but at a memorial service, which takes place after or instead of a funeral and after burial or cremation, there is no body.

ASKING SOMEONE TO HELP WITH ARRANGEMENTS

Because there are so many decisions to be made during this extremely emotional time, a widow or widower may want to call on someone to help shoulder some of the responsibilities. Most often this is a relative, in-law, or a close friend of the family. For instance, if the deceased had young children, the person helping out may be asked to pick them up at school and take them to a friend's house, or to see that their time is occupied in some other way. In addition the helper may take on any of the following assignments:

- Calling relatives and friends to tell them the date and time of the funeral.
- Answering the telephone.
- Keeping a list of people sending flowers to the house (a description of the flowers should be written on each card).
- On the day of funeral, keeping a list of flowers sent to the church (if the funeral is held at a funeral home, they'll handle this for you).
- Making hotel reservations for people arriving for the funeral from out of town.
- Meeting out-of-towners at the airport or train station.
- Marketing for food.
- Preparing meals.
- Feeding animals.
- Finding someone to stay in the house during the funeral. (Yes! There *are* people who read the obituary columns hoping they'll find a house to rob as the funeral is taking place.)

NOTIFYING THE NEWSPAPERS

Once the funeral date has been set, the newspapers must be notified immediately. That way people will know about the service at the earliest opportunity so they can arrange to be there. If there will be a memorial service at a later date, the urgency of reaching the papers is not so great.

There are two kinds of obituary notices that appear in newspapers. One is a biographical sketch of the deceased, which in the case of someone who was well known either locally or nationally is prepared by the newspaper from material in its files and with the help of the deceased's family. If the deceased was not prominent in the community, but you would like to see a profile of him appear in your newspaper, call the person in charge of the obituary page and ask what the possibility is of their running one. If he gives you the go-ahead and the paper's requirements, which may include sending a photograph of the deceased, you'll have to write up a biographical sketch for their consideration (if death is anticipated, it will be a lot less stressful to prepare the obituary in advance rather than waiting until death occurs, when there are a myriad of other details to take care of). Whether the obituary is printed is up to the newspaper and, if it is, it may be in a shortened version.

Biographical information should include the following:

- Name of deceased.
- Town or city where he lived.
- Date and place of death (name of hospital or "at home").
- Cause of death.
- Place of birth.
- Education, including honorary degrees.
- Military service.
- Corporate directorships.
- Membership in social clubs and professional associations.
- Awards received.
- What he or she contributed to society, to whom, what, where, etc.
- Names of survivors and their relationship.

The other kind of death notice is the paid obituary ad, which is placed in large city newspapers, either by the family or by the funeral home. If the funeral home is in charge of placing the ad, it should be checked for factual accuracy as well as the style of wording (many people like to keep it simple without adornments such as "beloved" wife or "devoted" son). When the ad is sent in by the family, the name, address, and telephone number of the funeral home must be given to the newspaper so it can verify the death.

The paid ad includes the name of the deceased; the date of death; the place of death; names of the immediate family (grandchildren may be included); calling hours, if applicable; date, time, and place of funeral; information on the burial, and often a request that in lieu of flowers contributions be given to an organization or institution. Giving the age of the deceased is optional. The ad can run for as many days as you like, two being the average. Most newspapers must have the notice by 4 P.M. in order to run it the following day. While a notice can be as long as you like and as verbose as you want it to be, you pay for each word, so you may want to avoid superfluous text.

Here is an example of a paid death notice:

Tomaston, Harold Gineen, died March 23 at Twin Oaks, Nebraska, in his 82nd year. Husband of Clarissa Bard Tomaston; father of Walter Tomaston of Chicago, Andrew W. Tomaston of Twin Oaks, and Betty T. Julliard of Grand Rapids. He is also survived by his sister, Florence Tomaston Jones, 8 grandchildren and 2 great-grandchildren. Calling hours at John McGrath Funeral Home, 23 Fulton Street, Twin Oaks, Wednesday, March 26, from 2 to 4 P.M. and 7 to 9 P.M. Funeral service Thursday, March 27, 11 A.M., Trinity Church, 43 Main Street, Twin Oaks. Burial private. In lieu of flowers, contributions to The Boys' Club of Twin Oaks, 11 Adams Street, Twin Oaks, NE [ZIP code], or a charity of your choice would be appreciated [or, "In lieu of flowers, the family requests donations in Mr. Tomaston's memory be sent to . . .].

When preparing the paid death notice, it's helpful to know that:

- For local papers, the state is not included.
- It is not necessary to give the person's age, although it often is if the deceased was very young.
- A paid notice usually does not include the cause of death, but it may.
- If death is due to an accident, the notice may read, "died suddenly March 23."
- A woman's death notice may or may not include her maiden name.
- A man's death notice may include his wife's maiden name and the maiden name of a married daughter or married sister. In the above example, Mrs. Tomaston's maiden name, Bard, is given to further identify her to friends she may not have seen in years but who read the notice.
- Children's names may be listed according to age, oldest first, or sons first or daughters first.

- If parents or siblings of the deceased are still alive, their names are listed, usually after the names of any children.
- If there will be calling hours at the funeral home before the funeral itself, this is stated in the notice.
- If the family wants either the funeral or the burial to be private, the notice says just that: "Funeral [or "Burial"] private." In such cases, only very close friends and family members are notified and no one else attends or asks to attend.
- When giving the name of the church or synagogue where the funeral will be held, be sure to include the street address.
- Often the deceased has requested that, instead of flowers, contributions be sent to a specific organization or institution. If he has not, the family may select a charity or other organization with special meaning to the deceased and include it in the notice, or else they can say, "a charity of your choice." The full address of the organization to which donations are to be sent must be given. If people have to look in the telephone book for the address, they may not bother to do so.

OTHER FUNERAL MATTERS

THE HONORARY PALLBEARERS While pallbearers are traditionally men, there's no reason why they shouldn't be women, and perhaps they will one day, particularly since it has become mostly honorary and the casket is almost never carried by the pallbearers anymore. In a Christian church, pallbearers are associated with a man's funeral, seldom with a woman's, whereas at Conservative and Reform Jewish funerals both men and women have pallbearers; and men and women also serve as pallbearers. Because it's an honor to be asked to be a pallbearer, a man chosen must accept unless there is some valid reason such as illness for refusing.

If no specific instructions were left by the deceased as to whom he'd like for pallbearers, a family member may ask from four to ten men who were close to the deceased to be honorary pallbearers at the service. When someone has been prominent in public life, professional associates as well as personal friends may be asked. The role of the pallbearers has changed over time. Originally they physically carried the casket into and out of the church. Today the casket is generally in place before the service begins but, if not, it's wheeled up the aisle by the honorary pallbearers. If men from the funeral home wheel the casket, the pallbearers precede it. Each church has its own system for this and will explain it to the pallbearers before the service.

If the casket is in place before the service, the pallbearers walk into the church, two by two, and take their places in the front pews to the left of the center aisle. At the end of the service, after the family has retired to the vestry, the pallbearers, walking two by two, leave the church. If the casket is rolled out, they precede it.

THE USHERS Although the funeral director can supply ushers for the service, or in a large church there may be a staff for this purpose, it is more personal and meaningful to ask relatives, godchildren, and close friends of the deceased to serve. If for no other reason, they will recognize many of the people arriving for the funeral and be able to give them an affectionate greeting. The ushers help seat those attending the service. Unlike ushers at a wedding, however, they do not take the guest's arm unless it is someone very old or infirm. They do not seat people in the front pews on the right of the center aisle, because that is where the family will sit, or in those on the left, which is where the pallbearers will sit. If there are no honorary pallbearers, the ushers precede the casket and sit in the front pews on the left and after the service walk two by two slowly in front of the coffin. If there are pallbearers, the ushers sit just behind them.

THE EX-SPOUSE One circumstance requiring special consideration is that of an ex-spouse of the deceased. Each family situation, of course, is different but in general a divorced spouse may certainly go to the funeral if he or she chooses to, and if there are children involved, they may wish the parent to be present, even if the divorce was acrimonious. The ex-spouse does not sit with the family unless asked to, but takes his or her place elsewhere in the church.

THE CHURCH OR SYNAGOGUE FEES Although the clergy does not ask a fee for conducting the service, the family nevertheless is expected to make a contribution. The check may be given to the clergyperson before or after the funeral or it may be mailed before or directly after the service. A personal letter should be enclosed, thanking the clergyperson for all he has done. The amount varies widely depending upon where you live and the size and formality of the funeral—from fifty dollars for a small funeral or memorial service to one hundred dollars or more for a larger one. The church or synagogue will specify to whom the check should be made out. In many cases, the sexton who opens the church, the organist, and any vocalist who is participating also receive a fee. It's best to consult with the clergyperson regarding the appropriate amount.

FLOWERS AT THE CHURCH OR SYNAGOGUE Some churches are explicit about how and where flowers are placed, others leave it up to the family. At a Protestant funeral a member of the family or close friend may ask the minister if he or she may go to the church before the service to help arrange the flowers and collect the cards that come with them. This person makes sure that flowers sent by the deceased's spouse or children are placed where they can be easily seen and admired, usually close to the casket, if there is one. If the family is not allowed to be involved, then a church official will arrange the flowers. At a Catholic funeral, the family's flower arrangement and possibly one other for the altar may be all that's permitted. Orthodox and Conservative Jews do not have flowers at their funerals. Instead, they indicate a worthy cause, often a favorite charity of the deceased, that could be supported. Some Reform congregations allow flowers at the funeral. When in doubt, check with the funeral home or house of worship where the service is to be held.

MUSIC Aside from the organist, there may be a choir at the funeral, or a soloist who sings with or without a choir.

LIMOUSINES While it's not necessary for all family members to be transported to and from the funeral by limousine, it's a convenience for the immediate family. The person making the funeral arrangements should alert family members who are being assigned limousines. Later they should be given the number of their limousine so they'll know which is theirs when they leave the church or synagogue.

INVITING FRIENDS TO A LUNCH AFTER THE FUNERAL OR MEMO-RIAL SERVICE The family of the deceased often invite other family members and close friends they know will be attending the service back to their house—or it may be their club or a hotel—after the service for coffee and sandwiches or a buffet lunch. This is done by telephone or with a note. If everyone is welcome, the clergyman may announce this at the end of the service. When a memorial booklet or leaflet is distributed at the service, after the order of the service it may say, "Following the service, the family invite you to join them for lunch at 216 Roland Street." Sometimes a member of the family stands in the vestibule of the church, after the service, greeting guests and in a quiet voice asking special friends back to the house.

GUEST BOOK Frequently at a funeral or memorial service there is a leather-bound book for guests to sign. It is placed on a pedestal table which the church provides in the vestibule. If it's anticipated that many people will attend the service, there should be two tables and two books for guests to sign.

MEMORIAL BOOKLET Often a memorial booklet is given to each person as he arrives at the church for the funeral or memorial service. The booklet is printed in black ink on white or cream-colored paper. On the front may be written:

In memory of
Harold Gineen Tomaston
July 8, 1912–March 23, 1995

If the family wishes, an informal snapshot of the deceased on the front page may be included. Inside the booklet is the order of service and the names of those who will be presenting eulogies, if applicable. There's no reason for the family not to include as well the deceased's favorite poem or some other tribute of a personal nature, as well as the words of any hymns to be sung.

THE CHRISTIAN FUNERAL

At most Protestant funerals the casket is in position on a stand at the foot of the altar or chancel well before the service begins. It may be covered with a blanket of flowers, a simple spray, or a pall (heavy cloth that's draped over the casket). If the deceased was a member of the armed forces, the casket may be draped with the flag.

At a Catholic funeral there is usually a procession; if the deceased was prominent, or if the family wishes, there may be a procession at a Protestant service also, but it is not something you see often. A procession forms in the vestibule of the church. The clergyperson and the choir (in the Catholic service the choir is not part of the procession) walk up the aisle first, followed by the honorary pallbearers walking two by two and then by the coffin. The family follows the coffin, walking in pairs, generally with the chief mourner first. At the chancel, the choir takes its usual position, the clergyperson stands at the foot of the steps, and the honorary pallbearers take their places in the left front pews. If the casket is not wheeled up the aisle, it is placed before the altar by the time the service begins. The family take their places in the front pews to the right of the center aisle (while they usually sit in pews on the right side of the aisle, it depends on how the church is laid out; if the rooms where the family wait for the service to begin are on the left, then they sit in the left pews and the pallbearers sit on the right).

At some funerals, but by no means at all, there is a eulogy (a spoken memorial in praise of a person's life and character). Unless the clergyperson knew the deceased well, so that he can speak about him from the heart, he does not deliver the eulogy. Instead, the family asks someone in the immediate family or a close friend of the deceased to say a few words. If several people will speak, each must be told how long to speak and in what order they go to the pulpit or wherever they will stand to address the congregation.

When the service is over, the procession, if there was one, leaves in the same order it came in, with one exception—the choir remains in place.

The casket is rolled back down the aisle and placed in the hearse (the flowers in the church may or may not be placed in the hearse to be taken to the cemetery). The family either file out through the door to the room where they waited to enter the church proper before the service or they follow the casket down the aisle, walking in pairs or in any configuration they choose. When they do follow the casket, the deceased's spouse/and or son or daughter may stand in the back of the church or just outside the church to greet and say a few words to guests as they leave. This gives the family a chance to say hello to out-of-towners they otherwise might not see. Conversation should be kept to a minimum so as not to delay the people trying to leave the church. All that's necessary to say is, "Thank you for coming. It means so much to have you here." Greeting those who came to the funeral is a thoughtful gesture, but it is not necessary by any means and no family should feel obligated to do so if they feel it will be too much of an emotional strain.

CREMATION Many people prefer cremation to interment. If the cremation has been preceded by a funeral service in a church or funeral home, the funeral director takes the body to the crematorium after the service. If there has been no funeral service beforehand, then there may be a short service at the crematorium. Many have small chapels just for this purpose and usually only family members attend. Later on a memorial service may be held.

The ashes are given to the family either at the crematorium or some time later. If the deceased left directions in a will or letter of instruction about what he wanted done with his ashes, the family should honor those wishes. If no such directions were given, the ashes may be left in a container or urn and placed in a section set aside for this purpose at either the crematorium or the cemetery. Most families choose to bury ashes in the family plot.

THE MEMORIAL SERVICE If the deceased is cremated directly after death, there is no casket, so the service that follows is a memorial service rather than a funeral. The service may take place a few days after the death occurs or as much as a month or more later, depending on the family's wishes. There are no pallbearers at a memorial service because there is no casket, but there may be ushers. The memorial service is similar to the funeral service in that there may be prayers, hymns, and often eulogies.

There's a second kind of memorial service which may take place a number of weeks after the funeral or the original memorial service. It's usually held in another city or town, perhaps where the deceased once worked and lived for many years or where he spent summers. This type of memorial service is most often held in a church with a service similar to the original one. If it is not held in a church, it may take place at a club or organization the deceased was identified with, in a garden or some other appropriate setting. Sometimes, instead of a clergyperson a lay person conducts the program; a few prayers are usually said and a number of friends and members of the deceased's family stand up and speak about the deceased, much as they would if they were giving a eulogy.

Notice of the memorial service is placed in the paid death notice column of the newspaper. If it is a large city paper, memorial notices appear at the very end of the death notices in a separate category and therefore are often overlooked by readers. To avoid this, it's best to send the ad marked as a death notice rather than a memorial service notice.

The funeral home service Funerals are sometimes held at the funeral home or in a nonsectarian chapel at a funeral home. The family may receive their friends in a reception room located to the side of the chapel.

The funeral held at home Sometimes, but not often, a funeral is held at home. The service is generally conducted in the living room with the coffin placed in front of the fireplace or in some other suitable location. The funeral director will provide folding chairs for the guests. The service is exactly the same as one held in a church. As with a church service, relatives are seated nearest to the casket.

The interment When the burial is in the churchyard or very near the church, family members simply walk to the gravesite (if the interment is private, those who attend the funeral do not accompany them). Otherwise, family members are driven to the cemetery in assigned limousines. At the cemetery, the casket is placed beside the grave. Flowers may or may not be brought from the church and placed beside it. Sometimes the casket is lowered into the grave before the clergyperson says the prayers, but most often it is left until the mourners depart. As the assembled mourners leave the burial site, they may toss flowers brought from the church onto the casket.

THE JEWISH FUNERAL

Although Orthodox, Reform, and Conservative Jews have their own funeral traditions, they all hold the funeral as soon after the death as possible, although if family members must travel a great distance or if the death took place far from the deceased's home, the funeral may be delayed for two to three days. Cremation is not permitted in Orthodox or Conservative Jewish congregations.

The Jewish service in most cases takes place in the chapel of a funeral home, rarely in a synagogue unless the deceased person was well known for his or her good deeds or community leadership. Among Conservative and Reform Jews both men and women serve as honorary pallbearers.

The Orthodox casket is of plain, unvarnished pine. No flowers are placed on it or in the chapel. Friends and relatives instead make donations to charity in the name of the deceased. Conservative Jews tend to follow the same traditions. Reform Jews allow more elaborate caskets and some congregations allow flowers. The coffin at Orthodox and Conservative services is closed; some Reform Jews allow it to be open.

The service is generally short and includes specific readings by the rabbi from the prayer book as well as one or two of the psalms. He will also speak briefly about the deceased. At Reform services, a number of eulogies may be given, and sometimes the rabbi asks if anyone present wishes to say something. The Jewish service ends with a prayer called *el male rahamin*. Afterward family members leave the chapel first, following the casket directly to the hearse.

At the gravesite the prayer or kaddish is recited by the rabbi and all who know the words. Male mourners, beginning with those closest to the deceased, toss handfuls of dirt into the grave. The mourners stay until the coffin is covered. In a synagogue with many rabbis, one may conduct the service and another the gravesite service.

There is a seven-day period of mourning following the burial known as "sitting *shivah*" (*shivah* is the Hebrew word for "seven"). It begins when the family returns from the cemetery. During this week, condolence calls are made to the home of those in mourning, who customarily offer food to callers, especially at the time of morning or evening prayers. The first three days are traditionally reserved for close relatives. Then, starting on the fourth day, friends come to pay their respects, although this schedule is not rigidly adhered to. Devout Jews do not conduct business during this period nor do they participate in social events.

In Orthodox and Conservative Jewish funerals, special attention is paid to the meal for the immediate family of the deceased following the interment. Providing this meal for the family is considered a *mitzvah* or good deed. The meal, which is kept simple, almost always includes eggs in some form.

THE ROLE OF THE MOURNER

THE CONDOLENCE LETTER When someone close to a relative or good friend of yours dies, the first thing you should do is sit down and write a condolence letter to your relative or friend. If you do not hear about the death until many weeks later, you still should write. This is a time of great sadness for your friend and it is never too late to offer sympathy, love, and support. Write a condolence letter on your personal stationery in black or blue ink. While there are plenty of commercial condolence cards designed to speak for you, they are no substitute for expressing your own thoughts and feelings about the person who died. The purpose of such a communication is to give comfort to the bereaved, and your own words will be far more effective than any printed sentiment.

SENDING FLOWERS For a Protestant funeral, unless there is a notice in the paper requesting no flowers, you may send flowers to either the church or the funeral home. If the service is being held at home, flowers may, of course, be sent there as well. The envelope of the card accompanying the flowers is addressed to "The Funeral of Harold Gineen Tomaston [address]." The card itself is handwritten and says something like "With our deepest sympathy, Alexis and Gene." If there's any question in your mind that the family won't know who "Alexis and Gene" are, then you should include your last name. At a Catholic or Reform Jewish funeral, the customs of the local congregation determine whether or not flowers will be allowed at the service. If the family are Orthodox or Conservative Jews, do not send flowers to the funeral.

If you are very close to the family of the deceased, you may want to send flowers to them at home instead of the funeral. In that case, you'll want to write a personal message on your informal or on a card provided by the florist.

SENDING A CONTRIBUTION TO A CHARITY IN LIEU OF FLOWERS When a death notice in the newspapers includes the phrase, "in lieu of flowers, contributions to [name of charity, institution, or organization] would be appreciated," or "charity of one's choice," it really means the family does *not* want flowers. Giving to a charity in the name of the deceased provides comfort to the family and helps them feel something positive will result from their loss. You send a check to the organization along with a note: "Enclosed is my check for twenty-five dollars as a contribution in memory of Harold Gineen Tomaston." Include your address so the organization can send you an acknowledgment (which you can claim as a tax deduction). The charity will send a notice of your contribution to the deceased's family without mentioning the amount. The guideline as to what amount to send is that it should not be less than what you would have spent on flowers.

SENDING A MASS CARD Because flowers are not always accepted in a Catholic church, friends may wish to send a "spiritual bouquet," that is, have a Mass said for the soul of the deceased. The parish priest will make arrangements for the Mass and will provide the donor with a printed Mass card to send to the family. Mass cards may be sent by Catholics and non-Catholics alike. The person who orders the Mass makes an offering or contribution to the church, usually from about ten to twenty dollars.

VISITING THE FUNERAL HOME In most cases the deceased's body stays at the funeral home until the day of the funeral. Members of the family sometimes receive close friends there at specified times, rather than at home. This is often called a viewing or a wake. The times that the family will be at the funeral home are given in the newspaper notice. Most often it includes an hour or two in the late afternoon or early evening so people can stop by after work. The family may stand in an informal receiving line if a large number of people are expected, otherwise they circulate around the room. A wake may also be held at the house of the deceased's family. This custom, which was once very popular, is now less commonly observed.

Even the most eloquent individuals are often at a loss for words when called upon to express their sympathy to the family of someone who has just died. It is difficult, but what you should say to the bereaved is what you feel: "I've been thinking of you so much these past days," or "How I'll miss all the fun I had with Harold," or "Everyone at work loved Harold." Later, if you have the chance to talk to the bereaved for a few minutes alone, tell her any personal memories you have of the deceased; if they're humorous, that's fine too. In general avoid asking specifics about the deceased's illness or death. And, above all, do not say to the bereaved that you know what she is going through. You can't; only she knows the extent of her loss.

The matter of whether the casket is open or closed is up to the family, unless there is a religious stipulation. For example, Orthodox and Conservative Jews do not have an open casket. If the casket is open, visitors are expected to walk by and pay their respects, but if you find this difficult, you need not do so. In some cases, a bench for kneeling is placed before the casket for those who wish to say a silent prayer. Catholics usually have a crucifix above the casket. If you are not a Catholic you do not have to cross yourself. Merely stand and bow your head for a moment to show respect. If you like, you may of course kneel and say a silent prayer.

Your call to the funeral home need not last more than ten or fifteen minutes. After expressing your sympathy to each member of the family present and talking with any friends who may be there, you may leave. To remain too long is inappropriate and may give the impression that you consider the occasion a social one.

If you cannot pay a visit to the funeral home during the calling hours when the family is present, you may stop in at some other time to pay your respects. Be certain to sign the guest book so the family will know you have been there. You sign your names "Alexis and Gene Haskell," or if you do not know the deceased's family that well, you can put "Mr. and Mrs. Gene Haskell." Either you or your husband may sign the book. Handwriting must be legible so the family can read names without difficulty.

If your children knew the deceased, they too may go to the funeral home if you feel they are old enough. The age at which a child attends his first funeral depends upon his emotional maturity. Many parents believe it's best that his first funeral be that of someone older to whom he was not very close.

GIVING A EULOGY If you are asked to give a eulogy at a funeral or memorial service, you should spend some time thinking about what you want to say. Find out who else will be speaking and discuss what you will say with that person so there's no chance of duplicating remarks. Brief details about the person's life and accomplishments are in order but need be given by only one speaker. There may be some warm personal story about the deceased you will want to tell or you may want your tone to be reflective. Humor can be helpful in the face of grief and is perfectly appropriate. What you don't want to do is be maudlin or overly sentimental or to talk longer than you are supposed to. The person who asks you to speak will give you a time limit. Abide by it.

When you begin your eulogy, if there's no program saying who you are and the clergyperson does not introduce you, tell the congregation your name and briefly your relationship to the deceased or how you came to know him.

It is possible that just as you are about to begin your eulogy you may become extremely emotional. If this should happen and you feel you cannot make your speech, ask the clergyperson to read it for you. If you are in the middle of giving the eulogy and your voice begins to quaver say, "I'm sorry." Wait a few seconds, and continue when you've gained your composure. Everyone will understand.

DRESSING FOR THE FUNERAL It is no longer necessary to wear black to a Christian funeral, although ushers and pallbearers wear dark suits, white shirts, dark ties, and black shoes and socks. Other people attending wear conservative clothes in somber colors—women preferably solid colors or a very muted print; men dark suits.

The dress for mourners in the Jewish faith is simple and conservative. Men wear yarmulkes at Orthodox and Conservative funerals (they are provided for those who arrive at the service without one); sometimes women wear black lace caps. Women also wear long sleeves so their arms are covered.

SOME DO'S AND DON'TS FOR MOURNERS It may be helpful to have read the following when someone you know dies.

- Whether or not you attend a funeral is a decision only you can make, depending on your relationship to the deceased. Never criticize someone for not attending a funeral.
- When talking about death, stay clear of euphemisms like "he passed away," or "she's found her resting place." Death is what it is. Pretending otherwise is unrealistic.

- Unless you are an intimate friend of the deceased's family, don't drop by their house to offer your condolences. Call first. When you do call, ask if there is anything you can do to be of help to the family. Or make your offer very specific, such as putting up relatives or friends from out of town.

- If you cannot go to the funeral home during calling hours, you can stop in at another time. Be sure to sign the guest book, so the family knows you were there (even though you sign your name in the guest book, you should still write a condolence letter).

- If the obituary notice states that the funeral is private, do not ask to attend.

- If you attend a funeral and the interment is private, do not go to the interment unless specifically asked to.

- When you arrive at the church or funeral home, you will be shown to your seat by an usher. A woman does not take the usher's arm at a funeral, unless she is frail or unsteady on her feet.

- If the clergyperson announces at the end of the funeral that you are invited to the deceased's family's house for lunch and you already have a lunch date, drop by anyway for a few minutes. The family will be grateful you did.

- When a Jewish family is sitting *shivah*, it means they are available for condolence calls, especially during morning or evening prayers. It's best not to call at mealtimes, and calls are never made on the Sabbath—from Friday sundown to Saturday sundown. If you are uncertain about when to make a visit, you may call the family and ask.

- Try to remember a friend who has had a recent death in the family when Christmas or some other holiday comes around. This is a time when she will most need your love and support. Instead of a Christmas card, write a note saying, "I know this Christmas will be a sad one for you, but I cannot let it go by without your knowing you are in my thoughts and that I send you a great deal of love." You can be certain this thoughtful gesture will be important to your friend.

- Mark the date of the deceased's death on your calendar so you can write a note to your friend, the survivor, on the anniversary. Just a short note saying you're thinking of her will be a source of comfort. Flowers are also appropriate at this time.

AFTER THE FUNERAL

After the funeral is over and when the members of the deceased's family feel up to the task, they will have to start writing personal thank-you letters. The person closest to the deceased must write the clergyperson who handled the service (also, if possible, the pallbearers, the ushers, and those who gave eulogies), any friend who helped with the funeral plans, those who were attentive to the deceased during his illness, and those who sent flowers, Mass cards, and condolence letters (letters are written later on to people who gave a charitable contribution in memory of the deceased). Letters do not have to be written to people who sent sympathy cards.

While every situation is different, and it depends on the number of letters to be written, a reasonable amount of time for completing the task of answering condolence letters is six to eight weeks. The letters are written on your personal stationery in black or blue ink. They may be short and say something like "It means so much to know I've been in your thoughts," or "It was so thoughtful of you to send me the beautiful basket of spring flowers." Printed acknowledgment cards, which are for sale at stationery stores and which most funeral homes will also supply, are cold and impersonal and should not be used. If someone took the time and trouble to reach out to you in your bereavement, you owe him a hand-written letter to express your appreciation. If the deceased was a public figure, however, or very prominent in the community, so that hundreds of letters were received, the family is justified in sending out an engraved or printed white or ecru card, with or without a black border. The message on the card may read:

> The family of
> Harold Gineen Tomaston
> wishes to thank you for
> your kind expression of sympathy

A short message should be handwritten on each card or, at the very least, on cards sent to family and close friends. All that has to be said is, "Your letter was a great comfort," or "Hearing from you meant so much."

THE GRAVESTONE

The most permanent public memorial to a loved one is the gravestone. This is ordered by the family from a monument maker. The price of gravestones varies widely and depends on the material and the ornamentation. If the family decides not to have a gravestone or monument, the funeral director can make arrangements to have a simple bronze plaque placed on the grave bearing the essential data. Such plaques cost considerably less than a gravestone. The inscription should be simple and dignified: the name of the deceased, the dates of his birth and death, and, frequently, his family relationship: "[beloved] father of," "[beloved] son of." Titles are not used except for members of the clergy or those who were active in the military service. Sometimes an epitaph appears below the name and dates.

Most cemeteries have perpetual care plans so that the gravestone and plantings surrounding it are automatically tended, but families usually visit and take care of their own plots from time to time, especially on the anniversary of the deceased's death and on religious holidays. Any fresh flowers or green plants, however simple, or even a single flower, is preferable to plastic or imitation flowers or plants.

The practice of erecting a gravestone goes back to early times in the Jewish tradition. In most Jewish communities the gravestone is "dedicated" or "unveiled" about a year after the death, but this can be done any time after *shiva*. There is no set ritual for the dedication service, although it usually includes a reading of Psalm 1, 15, 16, 23, or 121 and perhaps Proverbs 31 if the deceased was a woman. A brief and personal talk by a rabbi or friend of the family is given. The talk discusses the Jewish attitude toward life, death, and immortality and reminds mourners how the deceased will be remembered. Then the gravestone is uncovered or unveiled and a memorial prayer is said.

MEMORIALS

There are, of course, many concrete ways to honor and remember those we love. A family might arrange for a memorial in keeping with some aspect of the deceased's life. It may take the form of donations to a hospital for a specific purpose (a new piece of equipment, the renovation of a particular room), to a hospice, to a library or university for books, or to a cathedral or church for prayer benches or new hymnals, or even building stones (this can be done at the Cathedral of St. John the Divine in New York City). If donations are made to a music organization or park, the name of the deceased may then be attached to a seat in a concert hall or to a bench in a beautiful park. A lovely memorial was set up by a widow who had lived all her married life in a small village on the Atlantic Ocean. She arranged for a mile-long row of trees to be planted along both sides of the street leading to the local train station. A plaque near one of the trees reminds everyone who walks down this winding road of the love her husband had for nature and for his town. Another personal memorial was a small garden with pleasant seating for readers, designed for a small library in Wyoming. This was dedicated to the memory of a woman who had worked tirelessly for the town and its library. Jewish mourners may wish to have a tree planted in Israel in the name of the deceased. This can be arranged through a local synagogue. Donors are usually told approximately where the tree will be planted. Another valuable and appropriate memorial might be to endow a school that meant something to the deceased with a scholarship, a graduate award, or an achievement prize.

DISPOSING OF POSSESSIONS

We all have possessions we will leave behind when we die. Even someone who doesn't have a large estate might own a car, books, silver, china, or other cherished items that have been collected over the years. Major property such as real estate, a boat, fine art, or a business should be part of an overall estate plan. Not to take time to write a careful will can only cause problems for your family.

Obviously, it would be impossible to list in a will or letter of instruction all the things one owns and add the names of those to whom they are to go. Nor can one anticipate which child or relative will either want or need individual pieces of furniture, clothing, jewelry, or anything else. But a parent, in particular, as a guideline for survivors, should write a letter outlining how he would like his possessions dispersed. Such a letter is not, however, legally binding, so to make absolutely certain that individual items go to the designated person it must be so stated in your will.

If there is no letter of instruction or notation in the will, or if there are many items not specifically earmarked for one person but designated to go to "the children," for example, these possessions should be divided fairly and evenly so that each child receives an equal portion of the estate. There are a number of ways in which this can be done, but the fairest is to write down the various categories of items to be distributed on separate slips of paper—rugs, lamps, tables, chairs, ornaments, pictures, costume jewelry, etc. Place the category slips in a bowl and draw straws to see who goes first, second, etc. The person who goes first takes a slip of paper from the bowl and has first choice of any item in the category listed on the paper. The person who came in second on the draw is next to choose what he would like in the same category. In rotating fashion, this continues until all items in that category have been spoken for. Next, the person who was second on the draw becomes number one and pulls the second category from the bowl and receives first choice. The system continues until the last category has been disposed of. This method virtually assures each child of an equal number of choices in a specific category and an equal share of the estate. Of course, afterward, children may trade or exchange items, if they want to.

THE MOURNING PERIOD

Some people take much longer than others to recover from the death of a loved one. The healing time should never be rushed; in fact, expressing grief is an important part of the recovery process. There is no longer such a thing as a prescribed mourning period for those close to the deceased. In the past, a widow or widower was expected to mourn (and wear black) for a year or, in some religions, for the rest of his or her life. Fortunately this has changed. Sensible people would want their surviving loved ones to continue on with life.

Today, as soon as one feels up to it, social and business activities may be resumed. Well-meaning friends should be sensitive and not push social engagements on someone who has lost a spouse until that person indicates interest. On the other hand, one would obviously not give or attend wild parties or go dancing immediately after the funeral of a loved one.

In general, if you are the bereaved, try to assume a positive attitude about life. Enjoy your family and friends without resisting or denying your quite understandable feelings of sadness. You will find that time doesn't completely erase the pain of being left, of the loss of someone dear, but it does dull it. Unless you wish to, events that have already been scheduled, such as a trip abroad, a wedding, or a graduation party, need not be changed. Those who can should celebrate these and the other joyous events of life as they come along.

Judaism provides for a thirty-day mourning period. Orthodox Jews extend this to one year. During the month, the mourner is not permitted to attend festive occasions, travel on business, or marry. On the thirty-first day mourning officially ends and a routine life is resumed.

CHAPTER 5
YOUR PROFESSIONAL LIFE

INTRODUCTION

You may associate manners with social events—weddings, dining out, cocktail parties—yet manners are the basis for getting along in all aspects of our lives. Nowhere are they are more important than in the business world where so many of us spend so much of our time. Here, the way we behave, along with how well we do our job, determines what others think of us. Whether business is being conducted over the telephone, on a corporate jet, or in another country, good manners smooth the way and, along with intelligence and hard work, are the key to success in the working world.

A recent survey on manners in the workplace found that across the nation there were common concerns. Some of these seemed to be based on an assumption that we are all free to "do our own thing," and that business relationships are not the same as other human relationships.

Nothing could be further from the truth; people with jobs often spend more time with colleagues than with family and friends. The office is a community and, like all other communities; it functions best when people are polite and kind to one another. This means being polite to people at every level of the office hierarchy, not just those who are higher up.

But sometimes common courtesy isn't enough. There are a number of situations in the business world that require exact knowledge of what to say, how to act, what to wear, what to write. People who are successful in their work succeed partly because they know how to behave in almost any situation. Their knowledge may be instinctive, it may be the result of good training by their parents, or it may be learned—by watching others and reading about correct behavior. If you are new to the business world you need not be intimidated. With practice, manners can easily become a part of your everyday life at work.

Good manners also make good business sense. We all prefer to work with those who are polite, tactful, and even compassionate. Conversely, if you use poor judgment about the clothing you wear, if you speak crudely, make serious grammatical errors, turn in sloppy work, or are awkward and tongue-tied in meetings or business-related social gatherings, you are less likely to be promoted than the self-assured man or woman whose behavior and work reflect well on the company.

Good manners will be noticed and approved of, just as poor manners will work against one. At a corporate dinner dance given by a Wall Street brokerage firm, a woman who has her own legal practice was seated to the left of one of the brokerage firm's rising young vice-presidents. After she introduced herself, he turned his back on her and spent the entire evening gazing into the eyes of the much younger woman on his right. This left the lawyer with only the man on her left to talk to, from soup to dessert. Fortunately he was aware of the awkward situation and included her in his conversation with the woman on his left. Shortly after this, the courteous man was named president of the Wall Street firm. When it came time to select a number two person from among the vice-presidents, he picked someone other than the young man who had been so inconsiderate of his dinner companion. The new president had made careful note of the young man's behavior that evening.

In short, in the business world as elsewhere, good manners and consideration for others are timeless and those who recognize that will find themselves not only sought after and promoted but, more importantly, at ease in any business situation.

GETTING A JOB

You may find looking for a job exciting, a journey of discovery, but for most of us it's more like a visit to the dentist—it causes considerable anxiety. The most difficult aspect, and what produces the anxiety, whether you have lost your job, are just out of school, or are looking for a new challenge, is that it means you will be judged and evaluated, possibly found wanting. Yet much of that anxiety can be diminished if you take a rational, carefully planned approach to job hunting.

From the outset, remember that your greatest asset is self-knowledge. Know what your special abilities and skills are, what you like to do, what your true interests and passions are, and of course what you do best. Make a list of these assets and then search for a job in which you can use them. Far too many people wind up doing work that makes them unhappy because they never considered what it is they *like* to do. It's a great mistake to force yourself to become a lawyer because your father is, or a hotel manager simply because the position was offered to you.

As you look for work, bear in mind that the process means you will be in direct competition with others. Not everyone enjoys or responds well to competition and even the most self-confident person can grow discouraged when the search seems to take too long. Yet, if you are well organized, informed, and view looking for a job as simply one part of your life to take care of, you can minimize your concerns about competition and, at the same time, maximize your chances of landing the right position.

Some people think the business world is a jungle and that you have to be tough to claw your way to the top. Nice people, they believe, those who are gracious and compassionate, don't stand a chance. In fact, people who are congenial, sociable, sensitive to others' feelings shine in an interview and on the job. Employees who are principled, motivated, and hard-working are the ones most likely to succeed.

So view your job search not as a battle campaign but as a systematic way to find the job best suited to your skills and experience. Armed with good research, a good résumé, and a positive outlook, you will impress any interviewer.

WRITING A RÉSUMÉ

A good résumé, or summary of your work experience, is essential when selling yourself to a potential employer. In the process of writing it you'll learn to focus on your strengths, your interests, and your qualifications. There are many helpful books on preparing a résumé, but what follows are some of the key points to bear in mind should you write or update your own.

Begin by thinking about who you are, your experience and education, and what type of job you would like. Review the aspects of your previous job that you most and least enjoyed. What skills and knowledge did you acquire? Think about what would be your ideal job. Would you like a large corporation or a smaller, more intimate firm? Take the time to focus on your career goals. What would you like to do most? Where do you want to be one, three, or five years from now?

The résumé is divided into several parts: personal information, employment and experience, and education. It is essentially a succinct synopsis of your adult, professional life.

PERSONAL INFORMATION Include your full name, home address, and telephone number. Even if your present employer knows you are looking for a job, it is still better to give your home rather than your work number. If you do not have an answering machine at home, invest in one to take messages from potential employers.

Do not include a photograph or any physical characteristics such as age, height, or weight. These facts are not pertinent; neither is your marital status. At one time, married men commonly included their marital status and children in order to make them appear more responsible. Married women included this information for similar reasons, or didn't include it because they were afraid it would be a disadvantage. If raising a family helps explain a gap or gaps in your résumé, then you might choose to put this information in your cover letter but omit it from your résumé.

EMPLOYMENT AND EXPERIENCE List employment in chronological order; beginning with the most recent; Include the company name, address, your title, and dates of employment. Summarize your responsibilities and achievements. Volunteer work or other experience that is applicable should also be mentioned. Include skills, such as foreign languages, computer knowledge, or operation of business machinery, that might aid you in the performance of a job. Although word processing and the ability to use a computer are assets to even the most senior executive, list these skills only if they are directly applicable to the job. If the position you are applying for is nonclerical, it is not necessary to list "secretarial" skills such as typing.

Americans have traditionally used job-hopping as a way to advance their careers. However, too many job changes could be perceived as a sign of instability or the inability to make a commitment. If your résumé shows an unusual number of jobs, you should be prepared to explain. (Employers are particularly anxious about the employee who leaves whenever he is offered more money elsewhere.) Be sure to make it clear that your moves have been for career or personal advancement, not just for financial advancement.

EDUCATION If high school is your highest level of education, list the name and location of that school. Otherwise omit high school and begin with your undergraduate education and include graduate work. You may also list any applicable continuing education courses and degrees. You may or may not want to include dates. Some older people feel dates will emphasize their age and be detrimental to getting an interview.

If you are directly out of school you will want to expand on your educational background: mention your grade average (if it is above 3.0), major or curriculum, any awards or honors, and extracurricular activities. A recent graduate with only one or two jobs lists his education before employment.

CAREER GOALS If you have a specific career goal, include one or two sentences describing it at the start of your résumé. It is perfectly acceptable, however, not to list a career goal as it can be limiting. Above all, never include a goal that is too vague to be of value, such as "to utilize my management skills" or "to pursue my interest in XXX." With a computer, it is easy to change parts of the résumé so it is targeted to the special type of job you are applying for.

REFERENCES The giving of references has now become a complicated legal issue. Because any employee who has been given a damaging reference might take his or her employer to court, some companies now prohibit management from providing references to departing employees and will only verify dates of employment and title or position. If your employer is willing to give you a written reference, by all means accept it. Otherwise, you might supply personal references from people who know you well, such as your attorney or a former teacher or business colleague.

RÉSUMÉ TIPS

- Keep your résumé up to date.
- *Triple*-check for spelling errors.
- Type, do not handwrite. If you do not have access to a typewriter or computer, hire someone who does. (There are many services that prepare professional-looking résumés.)
- Use good-quality, heavy stock white or ecru paper.
- Keep it to one page, single spaced.
- Be truthful. Exaggerations and lies will catch up with you.
- List references as "Available upon request," and prepare a separate sheet with the names, addresses, and phone numbers of those who will provide references. Hand this list to the employer at the interview.
- Never use someone's name as a reference without having asked permission to do so.
- Do not list salary requirements.
- Ask several professional associates to review and criticize your résumé.

GETTING AN INTERVIEW

PERSONAL CONTACTS Although want ads and employment agencies are key sources of information on job openings, keep in mind the advice of job-hunting expert Richard Bolles, author of *What Color Is Your Parachute?*, that simply sending out résumés rarely gets you an interview, let alone a job. Well over half of all professional jobs available are filled through networking and personal contacts. You don't need to know captains of industry in order to hear about an available job, but you do need to tell everyone you know that you're looking. Make a list of friends and acquaintances in various fields that interest you. Then write and ask each one if he can give you a few minutes of his time. Explain that you don't expect him to offer you a job but you are interested in the type of work he does and would like to find out exactly what it involves. You'll find that most people are quite willing, even flattered, to be asked to talk ·about their work.

When you contact people about your job hunt, listen to how they respond. If they seem harried, busy, or hostile, do not pursue the issue. Instead, just ask them to keep you in mind if they hear of something.

If someone agrees to talk to you about his work, be prepared to ask specific questions. How did he happen to get into his field of work? What kind of experience or education did it call for? What is it he most enjoys about it?

While close friends and family on hearing you're job hunting will spread the word, don't forget to inform acquaintances and others you meet, too. Since word of mouth is generally the best way to find a job, TELL EVERYONE.

Professionals who work with a number of other people—attorneys, architects, teachers, clergy, financial advisers, journalists, public relations people, and the like—are in excellent positions to know about a variety of job openings. When you talk to these people, never be embarrassed to let them know you're looking for a job.

When someone expresses an interest in your job search, send him a letter describing your goals and a copy of your résumé. If he provides you with a lead, follow up on it right away. Be sure to tell him you have done so, either by letter or telephone, and thank him for his efforts on your behalf.

It's a good idea to keep a list of the people you speak to about helping you find a job. Then, when you accept a job offer, you can thank each one for his interest.

WANT ADS Thousands of people find jobs through want ads placed in the classified or business sections of newspapers by employers. Don't overlook trade magazines, such as *Publishers Weekly, Advertising Age, Variety*, as well as professional journals which also carry want ads. To locate the trade publications in your field, consult the *IMS Directory of Publications* and the *Magazine Industry Marketplace*. Respond to a want ad with your résumé and a covering letter. If only a phone number is given, call and ask to whom you may direct your résumé. Avoid being interviewed over the phone; the object is to set up a meeting in person. If you do not hear from a company within seven to ten days after sending your résumé, call about an interview. If the ad states "No Calls," then don't call; employers are not likely to hire someone who disregards their first request.

EMPLOYMENT AGENCIES Employment agencies typically do volume business, so their service may not be very personalized. Yet a well-run agency can be enormously helpful and ones that specialize even more so. For instance, some agencies handle only certain professions or skills, such as publishing, librarianship, word processing, paralegal, or secretarial placements. Choose an agency that does not require you to pay the job-finding fee; this should be paid by the employer.

An interview at an employment agency is like any other interview; you should dress appropriately, have copies of your résumé with you, and be enthusiastic and energetic. You want to make as fine an impression as possible, just as though you were being interviewed by the head of a Fortune 500 company. The more impressed the agency interviewer is with you, the greater effort he will make to put you in contact with the right employer.

EXECUTIVE SEARCH FIRMS Executive search firms (also known as executive recruiters) are hired by a company to find candidates for top-level positions. They rarely respond to résumés from people they do not know. In fact, job candidates usually come from the recruiter's own extensive network of contacts. However, if you do send an unsolicited résumé to a recruiting firm, be certain to call ahead and get the name of a specific person to write to. In your letter, briefly state your career goal as well as your present compensation level.

OUTPLACEMENT AGENCIES Many larger firms hire outplacement agencies to help personnel who have been laid off find new jobs. If your company offers such assistance, you certainly should accept it. An outplacement agency provides career counseling and job search assistance. It is not an employment agency, but it will help you write your résumé, prepare for interviews, and devise strategies for approaching suitable companies. In addition, it will help you target the work you're best suited to. Agencies provide office space, telephones, and secretaries for your use while you're conducting your search. Outplacement agencies are usually hired by corporations, but some offer a service to individuals. Since the typical agency fee is fifteen percent of your first year's salary, it's a costly way of finding a job, although it may eventually be well worth it.

OTHER PLACES TO LOOK You'll find, by using your imagination, that there are many other places to look for jobs. A good possibility is your college or university placement office. Even if you graduated decades ago, it may still provide help, so do not hesitate to call and find out what services are available. If you are a college student, begin working with the placement office early in your senior year. It will set up interviews with corporate recruiters who come to the campus as well as give you all kinds of useful advice.

If you are in your forties or older, find out if your town has a 40 Plus Club. These are self-help groups for unemployed professionals over the age of forty. Your Y.M.C.A. or Y.W.C.A., church, or synagogue may have similar programs to assist those looking for work.

Should you have a friend who works for an organization that publishes a house organ or newsletter, ask for a copy. Many list job openings.

If you are interested and have the time to do volunteer work while you're job hunting, the contacts you make there may prove helpful in finding permanent work. One woman, when her children were young, volunteered several days a month for her town's Heart Association. She had been an English major in college and helped edit the group's newsletter. She found that she loved the newsletter business so much that she eventually started her own and turned it into a successful, profitable business.

CONTACTING A POTENTIAL EMPLOYER   If you learn of a job possibility through one of your contacts, always ask that person if you may use his or her name when calling about the opening. Should he ask you not to mention his name—he may not know the interviewer well or he may not want to make a specific recommendation—you must honor his wishes. But on the other hand he might volunteer to set up an interview for you or make the initial contact.

Before writing a letter regarding a particular position, call the firm to get the name of a specific person to address your letter to. In the letter you can say that you will be calling in a few days to make an appointment. Or you may call without writing. However, if the job has not been advertised, and you can't get past a secretary to speak to the person you have been advised to contact, you have no alternative but to write a letter.

A letter accompanying your résumé is essentially an interview request. A good cover letter will distinguish your application from others and will help convince the person reading it that you have abilities and attributes that make you right for the job. But don't try to say too much. It is enough to: (1) identify yourself and your interest in the company and the position; (2) move on to a succinct summary of your skills and experience and how they might benefit the company; (3) request an interview; (4) close by saying you will call within a week.

When you do call, simply say: "Good morning, Mr. Donaldson. This is Susan Smith calling. I want to follow up on my letter regarding the opening in your art department."

Even if you are not granted an interview, it's a good idea to write a letter reiterating your interest in the company and asking that you be kept in mind for any future job openings. Attach another copy of your résumé.

Do not apply for a job by sending a letter or your résumé by fax. Since a fax machine is almost always located in a public place within an office, if the employer is replacing someone who has not been informed of this fact, your fax may be a source of embarrassment to him. However, if you talk to the interviewer on the telephone at 11 A.M. and he says he would like to meet with you after lunch but needs your résumé, ask if you should send it by fax.

PREPARING FOR AN INTERVIEW

At any interview, even for an entry-level position, you should have background knowledge of the company and its policies. To prepare, read the company brochures or company fact book, which should be available from the public affairs or public relations office of the firm. Also ask for a copy of the company's annual report in order to study its financial condition, its products, services, and the direction it is taking.

One of the details your research should focus on is what areas of expansion or problems the company or industry is facing. Try to find out if there are any impending mergers or takeovers. You should be aware of the company's most successful products or services and those of its competitors. You can learn much of this information by reading the business sections of newspapers and magazines. An understanding of the company hierarchy or the structure of the department you're interested in joining will also be useful.

There are many books that are good sources of information on numerous companies: *Everybody's Business* or *The 100 Best Companies to Work for in America*, both by Robert Levering and Milton Moskowitz (with Michael Katz also as joint author of *Everybody's Business*), offer statistics and insights about places of employment throughout the United States.

Information can also be found in the *Readers Guide to Periodical Literature*, the *Business Periodicals Index*, the *Funk & Scott Index*, and *Findex: The Directory of Market Research Reports, Studies and Surveys*. These reference indexes, which can be found in any public library, list articles that have appeared in business magazines and elsewhere. *Business Newsbank* (News Bank Inc.), a reference service that provides business articles selected from periodicals in over four hundred U.S. cities, and the publications of the U.S. Department of Labor are also excellent sources of information on individual companies. Magazines such as *Fortune, Forbes, Financial World*, and *Business Week* feature articles on the country's fastest-growing companies and industries, as well as information on their CEOs. Knowing the names of top management people and something about them can also be helpful. You may find their biographies listed in Who's Who in America or Who's Who in Business.

Your research needn't stop with the printed word. Talk to people who work in the industry you're interested in; if you are lucky enough to have a friend in the company where you'd like to have an interview, he can give you an overall picture of the firm and what it's like to work there. He may even be willing to arrange an interview for you.

When the time comes for an interview, the more you know about the company the more impressed the interviewer will be, the more interesting and successful the interview is likely to be, and the greater your chances of being offered a job. Preparing answers to predictable questions will assist you in reviewing your strengths, qualifications, and experience. The interviewer will be trying to gauge the personal and professional qualities most employers seek: motivation, responsibility, and enthusiasm. You may have done your homework exceedingly well and the interviewer may be impressed with your knowledge of the company, but he will also be looking for more intangible qualities: optimism, seriousness, willingness to work hard.

FREQUENTLY ASKED QUESTIONS Although every job is different and each employer has his own personal style, interview questions are remarkably uniform.

(1) "Tell me about yourself" or "How would you describe yourself?" Remember, the employer is not interested in whether you consider yourself a cheerful person or that you like sports (unless the job is related to sports). What he wants to know is whether you are a good candidate for the job he has in mind. Take this opportunity to summarize your abilities and past job experiences.

(2) "What are your faults? Weaknesses?" Take a slightly lighthearted approach to this one, perhaps pointing out a past weakness that has been overcome, such as "I used to have some difficulty negotiating contracts, but since I've been raising money for various groups, I now find it's fun to get into the negotiation process, trying to think of ways to reach mutually satisfactory agreements."

(3) "Why are you applying for this job?" The interviewer wants to know if you are motivated and whether you will be an asset to the firm. This is where your research is useful. Make your interest in the position as specific as possible. State your qualifications in a way directly related to the particular company and the particular job. Obviously you should not answer that you are interested because the job pays well or that they should hire you because you are cheap. Instead, mention what you've heard or read about the company that impresses you: its track record, the working environment, the leadership qualities of the staff, its employment practices, its innovative products or style.

(4) "Why should I hire you?" Employers often ask this question to see how adept you are at expressing yourself. Try to present your qualifications in a confident manner. Self-deprecation is out of place here but so is unnecessary self-aggrandizement. Say that you are known to be a reliable worker, that your sales record is excellent, or that your ability to give directions has often been praised by others. This is also the time to include any useful background information that is not in your résumé.

(5) "Why did you [or do you want to] leave your job?" or "Why were you fired?" Tell the truth and do not criticize your past or present employer. If you were fired, do not attempt to justify yourself. If you are still at a job at this point, you may tell the interviewer that your present boss or employer does not know you are job hunting and you would appreciate it if he would not contact your company until you have told them.

If you were fired because of economic conditions, mention who else was laid off and why, if it works to your advantage. For instance, some companies pursue the last-hired, first-fired strategy or they decide to eliminate a particular position altogether because of budget cuts.

(6) "How much are/were you making?" Answer honestly. If you are due for a raise, say so.

(7) "What are your salary requirements?" It is always best to postpone discussions over salary until a job offer has been made. Then a good response to this query is, "Can you give me an idea of what salary range you have in mind?" When you are given the salary range, request the high end. If forced to answer the question blindly, respond with your own salary suggestion: "I believe, with my experience and the responsibilities the job entails, I should receive a salary in the range of fifty to sixty thousand dollars."

ILLEGAL QUESTIONS It is illegal for a potential employer to ask your age, religion, national origin, or whether you plan to have children. In some states, it is also illegal to inquire about your sexual preference or orientation. If you *are* asked an illegal question, say, "I don't think that is relevant to my ability to perform the job we're discussing." If you feel the question has no significance with respect to getting the job, there's no reason not to answer it. For example, "Yes, I have two children, twelve and fourteen. The eldest is away at boarding school and my mother, who lives close by, takes care of my twelve-year-old daughter after school."

BEFORE TALKING TO THE INTERVIEWER In addition to doing research on the company or industry in which you're interested and preparing answers to the most common interview questions, there are several other steps you can take before a job interview that will help boost your confidence.

The interview outfit: In order to feel at ease during your interview, wear an outfit you're comfortable in. If necessary, have it cleaned or pressed. Usually, the most appropriate outfit for an interview is the one you would wear the first day on the job. You want to look your best and you want to fit in. If you know someone who works at the company where the interview is to take place, ask him for guidelines. If not, it is always best to err on the conservative side. If you follow the general rules of neat and clean, classic, modest, and low-key, you will be correct in any office environment. Women should wear a skirt or dress, only a small amount of perfume, and forgo flashy jewelry. Men should wear a jacket and tie and make sure their shoes are polished.

Carry a briefcase, attaché case, or a portfolio with copies of your résumé, references, and other pertinent papers.

The mock interview: When you are well prepared for your interview, ask a friend to conduct a mock interview with you. At that time, wear your interview clothes, carry your briefcase, walk into the room, sit down, and go through the entire interview procedure. Ask your friend to critique your appearance, your posture, tone of voice, handshake, and eye contact. If possible, audio or videotape the interview; that way, you can study yourself in depth. You will be able to note whether you appeared nervous, stumbled over answers, or said the wrong thing.

Job applications: At the interview you may be asked to fill out a job application form, so go prepared with a pen, a list of dates, names, addresses, and telephone numbers in order to answer questions about schooling, previous jobs, and references. Do not put "See résumé" after any questions; address each one. You may respond to the question on salary as "negotiable." Write legibly.

Pre-interview checklist
- Are your fingernails and hair clean?
- Are there any snags or stains on your clothing?
- Are your shoes polished?
- Have you reviewed your research?
- Have you recently rehearsed your answers?
- Do you have several copies of your résumé and references to take with you? A pen?
- Do you need to check the interview time?
- Do you know the company's exact address and floor number and how long it will take to get there?
- Are you sure of the interviewer's name and position?

The interview
It goes without saying that you *must* be on time for any job interview. Judge how long it will take to get to your appointment and then add on a good fifteen minutes for any unexpected delays, such as a traffic jam. The interview really starts the moment you arrive on the threshold of the interviewer's office although, if it's to take place in a large office building, be on your best behavior when you enter the elevator—the person riding up with you could be the interviewer.

Interview tips
- When the interviewer greets you, give him a firm handshake and say something like, "I'm so glad to meet you," or "Thank you for taking the time to see me."
- Remain standing until you're asked to sit down. When you are seated, sit up straight in your chair, but not so straight that you appear unrelaxed.
- Let the interviewer take the lead with a conversational ice breaker.

In all probability, he'll do his best to try to make you feel at ease. Once you have the opportunity to comment on a question of his, or to initiate a question of your own, you'll start to unwind and feel less nervous.

- After the initial pleasantries are over and the interview begins, you'll have a chance to tell the interviewer something about yourself and why you feel you are qualified for the job.

- When you speak, look directly at the interviewer. Try to appear poised and do not speak too slowly or too fast. In addition, do your best to restrain any nervous habits, such as fussing with your hair.

- An interview is a dialogue, not a monologue, and the best interview is one in which the interviewer and interviewee spend an equal amount of time talking and listening. But if the interviewer becomes long-winded, no matter what, don't interrupt him.

- Listen carefully. If you've reviewed the responses to the common interview questions you may be asked and studied the company's brochure or annual report, you'll be better able to focus on the interviewer. Pay close attention to his questions. It's easy to forget what's being said when you're nervous or apprehensive. Remember that the interviewer's tone and the nuances of his words can influence your responses.

- When the subject of your present or past job comes up, whatever the circumstances may be, make no derogatory remarks about your former employer or the company.

- During the interview, it's to your advantage not to ask any self-serving questions, such as whether you would ever have to work overtime or how many vacation days you get the first year. Once you have a firm job offer, you can bring up such questions.

- Don't smoke. On the off chance you are offered a cigarette, politely refuse even if the interviewer smokes.

- When the interview is over, don't linger, but leave promptly. The interviewer will give you a clue as to when it's time to leave. He'll thank you for coming and probably say how much he enjoyed meeting you. Or he may look at his watch or simply stand up. He will probably tell you, "I'll be in touch in a week or so," or "Please give me a call next week." If he doesn't say either, you are free to ask, "May I call you in a week or so to see if you've come to a decision?"

As you leave the interview, look the interviewer in the eyes, shake hands with him, and thank him for having seen you.

AFTER THE INTERVIEW Take note: people have sometimes been offered jobs because they were the only applicant to write a thank-you letter to the person who conducted the interview. This simple, courteous gesture demonstrates these three valuable qualities mentioned before: motivation, enthusiasm, and responsibility.

Your letter should be written the same day as the interview. Refer to some topic discussed during the interview to show you concentrated on what was being said. You may want to reinforce a specific point or add something you forgot to mention at the time of the interview. Close by thanking the interviewer for his time. The letter can be brief; only four or five sentences are necessary.

Even if you decide you don't want the job, you should write and thank the interviewer. Not only is it the polite thing to do, but you may want to call on that person at some future time for advice or help.

THE ROLE OF THE INTERVIEWER Employers too need to prepare for interviews. Always read the résumé of the applicant before the interview and treat him with the same attention and courtesy you would an important client. At the time of the interview, do not take any telephone calls. It's unnerving for an applicant to have to wait, perhaps losing his train of thought, while you talk on the telephone.

As an employer, make every effort to respond to all job requests, even if you have to use a preprinted postcard. As soon as a position for which you have been interviewing has been filled, contact each unsuccessful applicant and inform him of this and wish him luck in finding the right job.

Many employers are as afraid of rejecting a person as an applicant is of being rejected. It's easier to turn someone down in writing than in person, but if you told the applicant he may call you and he does, then take his call and explain that someone else has been hired (never ask your assistant or secretary to give out the news).

REENTERING THE WORKING WORLD

If you are applying for a job after having been absent from the work force for any length of time you must be prepared for questions. If your absence was because you have been raising a family, simply explain this in your cover letter. Very few employers will look upon such a hiatus unfavorably if you are otherwise qualified.

If during your absence from the work force, you acquired new vocational skills, from learning a foreign language to taking continuing education classes, be sure to mention them in your résumé or accompanying letter. Free-lance assignments, work with the P.T.A., and volunteer positions can all be important assets and you should consider them as such.

THE OLDER APPLICANT The number of people over fifty pounding the pavement in search of a job has risen dramatically in the last few years. Whatever the reason—whether it's to come out of early retirement, change careers, move on to greener pastures, enter the job market for the first time, or relocate because of a spouse's job transfer—the older job applicant is no longer an anomaly.

Given the three qualities most employers say they seek—responsibility, motivation, and enthusiasm—the older applicant has a built-in edge. Older workers are generally thought to be more reliable, loyal, and stable than younger employees; responsibility is deemed a natural outcome of age; and a lifetime's worth of experience is a definite asset.

Nevertheless, be aware of the generalizations about the older worker, such as that he is stubborn, unwilling to change his approach, or unable to learn or uninterested in learning new technology. As an older applicant, you can counteract these perceptions by keeping abreast of current business trends and during the interview stressing your openness to change and to technology. In other words, show that you are flexible, adaptable, and willing to learn.

WOMEN RETURNING TO WORK If you are an older woman entering or reentering the job market, you may find the idea daunting—women today in work settings may appear younger, more stylish, more sophisticated than you. However, demographics are in your favor. Population trends indicate that the pool of young workers entering the job market up to the year 2000 is declining. This means employers will be more likely to need you, especially to fill entry- and near-entry-level jobs.

If you are a woman hoping to land a job after several years at home, remember that, unlike the worker in her twenties, most older women have a lot of applicable experience and many learned skills. Negotiating with tradesmen and landlords, running a household, raising children—all of these involve skills essential in the workplace. Have you done volunteer work such as participating in a political campaign or grassroots movement, or leading a scout troop? Have you organized a benefit, worked with the aged, served on a board, supervised other volunteers, written brochures, publicity releases, or reviews? Are you an expert gardener or cook, or a skilled do-it-yourselfer? All of these involve organizational and managerial skills and thus are excellent preparation for employment.

A smaller workplace is typically best if you are an older entry-level employee because you have a better chance of being noticed and promoted.

It's fine to explain a gap in your résumé by saying you took time off to raise your children. But leave it at that. It may seem natural to talk about your children, but don't. Certainly don't volunteer that they went to expensive private schools, that your husband holds down an important position, or that you know a lot of famous people. Instead, review the list of most frequently asked interview questions and prepare answers; write them out if it helps you feel more confident.

GETTING UP TO DATE If it's been some time since you were a part of the working world, you may need to give some thought to your appearance. Begin by taking a hard look at yourself in the mirror. Be candid about your weight, hair color and style, and your posture. If you are not entirely happy with what you see, you can improve certain features. A day with a good hair stylist, consultation with a makeup person, and the purchase of one or two "interview" outfits may be all that's necessary.

Many department stores have personal shopper services, and will be happy to help you put together a suit or dress and jacket that you can wear to interviews. You might also get help from a fashion-conscious friend, or, if you're one of those lucky people who has a daughter with a flair for dressing well, consult her. She'll be delighted you asked.

If middle-age spread has caught up with you, go on a sensible diet and schedule regular exercise. You'll not only look better but you'll feel better if you're trim and in good physical shape. You don't need to be Ms. America to go on a job search, but the happier you are with your appearance the more self-confident you'll feel.

LEAVING A JOB

BEING FIRED

One of the greatest shocks that can happen to any of us is losing a job. "You're fired" are probably the two most dreaded words in the working world. And they are being heard more and more in recent years because many American corporations have eliminated thousands of jobs in an effort to cut costs and improve profits. No companies, not even the top blue chip firms, are immune to cutbacks.

If you are fired it is important to keep your wits about you. It's only natural to feel upset, but if you panic or react in anger it won't help the situation. You need to behave in a way that will increase the likelihood of finding a new position as quickly as possible. Keep in mind, too, that being fired may be the first step toward a better career, a more fulfilling life.

To increase your chances of finding new work, don't unleash any resentment you may feel toward your employer or boss. It will only jeopardize the possibility of getting a letter of recommendation. Accept the news with dignity. You certainly may ask why you are being let go. It may be because of staff cutbacks or because you are not meeting specific goals. As painful as it is to hear criticism, it is important to know why you were fired so you can learn from the experience and do better in your next position.

After you have received the news that you've been fired, you may decide to tell one or two close colleagues, but do not talk or gossip about it with a great number of people. You will probably be told how much time you have to gather personal belongings together and leave. It may be one or two days or perhaps longer. In most cases it's best to pack up as quickly as possible—ideally within a day or two.

Increasingly, middle and/or top managers negotiate the terms of their termination. If you think you have *good* reasons to defend your performance in the face of being fired (you have increased productivity, landed important jobs, or clients, devised inventive methods and solutions to problems, saved the company money, etc.) you might be justified in hiring legal assistance to have the reason for your leaving changed from dismissal to resignation. You might also be able to negotiate for severance pay, continued health and pension benefits, the termination date, and even secretarial help and office space with a telephone while looking for a new job.

If the company offers to help you find a new job, never be too proud to accept the offer. An outplacement agency can provide you with career counseling as well as job search assistance. While it is not an employment agency, it will help you draft a new résumé, prepare for interviews, and devise a list of appropriate companies to approach. You might also want to read *The Outplacement Solution: Getting the Right Job After Mergers, Takeovers, Layoffs and Other Corporate Chaos* by Karen S. Wolfer and Richard G. Wong. It's full of useful information.

There are other ways to help bolster your spirits during the traumatic period between being dismissed and finding new work. For example, you may have friends who are also out of work and with whom you can form a support group to take early morning walks. This encourages you to get up and get dressed in the morning. You might go as a group to collect unemployment checks, meet for breakfast, visit the library, or share information.

IF YOU KNOW SOMEONE WHO HAS BEEN FIRED When a friend or colleague tells you he has been fired, the natural response is to say how sorry you are to hear the news. But also try to make a constructive remark, such as: "You know you're one of the most knowledgeable/talented people in your field. Other companies will recognize that fact." If you know the person was fired for good reason, then suggest that he take a course to improve his business skills or that he make an appointment with a career counselor who will be able to give him good sound advice. You'll be doing him a favor by tactfully acknowledging the reason why he was let go. You may also be in a position to offer to write a letter of recommendation or give specific suggestions about where to look for new work. Right after you hear a friend's been fired, give him a call. If he'd rather not talk about the firing, respect his wishes and wait a few days before calling back to see how he is doing and to give his morale a boost. The same attitudes apply to someone in your family who loses his job. Acknowledge that the situation is indeed difficult and make it very clear that you care and want to do what you can to help.

TELLING YOUR CHILDREN If you have children, you need not explain every detail of being fired to them, but neither should you hide the fact that you are out of work. Give them the simple facts and explain how you are going about looking for new work. Reassure them that life will go on, although there may be some changes. The more concrete you can be in your discussion, the more secure children will feel about the future.

RESIGNING FROM A JOB

If you decide to leave a job, give ample notice. The human resources department can advise you as to how much notice is legally required. When you leave, don't criticize your employer to anyone. In the future you may need a letter of recommendation or other favor from him. If you are resigning to go to another job, say so and tell your current employer and colleagues how much you enjoyed working with them. If your employer gives you a farewell party, be sure to write him a letter of thanks. And if coworkers contribute toward a going-away present, you should thank each one personally.

ISSUES FOR THE EMPLOYER TO CONSIDER

FIRING

One of the more unpleasant tasks any boss has is telling an employee that he is fired. If you can, tell your employee the news at the beginning of the week (being fired on a Friday means a weekend of brooding). As soon as he's gathered his thoughts, he can make telephone calls and begin looking for a new job. Be sure to discuss with the employee how he would like his coworkers to be informed of his leaving—if it's by memo, you may want to consult him on its wording.

Always deliver the news in private—either in your office or in the employee's. The latter may be the more appropriate as, when you leave, the employee is free to shut the door, cry, get angry, or call his spouse. Regardless of where the firing is done, it should be behind closed doors.

The conversation should take no more than ten to fifteen minutes. Beyond that it becomes repetitive. Be sympathetic but firm. Be sure to emphasize whatever strengths you honestly feel the person has. Give the reason or reasons for your decision: "You haven't been meeting our stated goals," or "Your behavior is causing problems." Employees have a legal right to know why they are being fired. Explain carefully about severance pay, how medical and retirement benefits will be handled, and what you are prepared to do to help the employee find a new job.

Under some circumstances you can make things a little easier by letting the employee make some choices about the terms of his dismissal—letting him resign, for instance, rather than being fired. For some, giving up unemployment benefits is preferable to the humiliation of having been fired.

HIRING RELATIVES

If you own your own business, the question of hiring relatives often arises. You have every right to hire whom you wish, but if you bring your son or daughter in, or take on a nephew or cousin, make it clear that he or she must work the same hours as the other employees and that no special favors will be granted because of the relationship.

REFERENCES

Employers should be well acquainted with their firm's policy regarding writing references for former employees. Many companies will not provide negative references for ex-employees because such statements recently have led to lawsuits. Consequently they will only verify a former employee's date of employment and position.

VOLUNTEERISM

One of the greatest gifts one can make to society is to be a volunteer. Many men and women work long and hard hours without pay for institutions and organizations—putting forth as much effort as their conventionally employed counterparts. Like a traditionally paid job, volunteerism frequently involves being trained for a specific assignment, such as reading to the blind or tutoring students, and then being regularly evaluated.

If you are in a position to work hard for a cause, to help those who are less fortunate, or to improve the quality of your neighborhood, museum, church, synagogue, or school, you will find much personal satisfaction.

Remember, too, that giving of yourself is a great antidote to loneliness, depression, or isolation. It's also a wonderful way to meet other involved, committed men and women.

Before taking on a volunteer job, carefully assess your time, your abilities, and your other commitments. Get involved only in some area of work that truly appeals to you, something that captures your imagination. For example, if you love flowers, you can put your talents toward beautification of your town's parks and gardens. If you enjoy teaching, you can help adults learn to read or speak English, or tutor schoolchildren who are having trouble in a particular subject. If you are a retired executive, you can advise other business people. If fund-raising is something you do well, become involved in your favorite charity's annual auction, dance, or night at the theater. If you are an ardent art lover, see if your museum needs docents to take visitors through the collections. Secretarial and accounting skills are welcomed at any organization.

Bear in mind that serving on boards of local or national organizations can be demanding. Make certain you have the time to devote to this type of work. Then think of it as just that—work—and when people ask what you do, say proudly, "I'm a volunteer with the public library," and never, ever apologetically say, "I'm just a volunteer." There is no such thing as "just" a volunteer. A dedicated volunteer exercises executive skills, fulfills complicated tasks, takes initiative, and works as hard as many corporate executives.

LIFE IN THE OFFICE

Manners are just as important in the business world as they are in our social life. Acceptable work behavior facilitates the smooth operation of any organization regardless of its size or purpose, whether a household, a small office, or a multinational corporation. Like traffic signals and road maps, office protocol keeps us from crashing into one another, from hurting colleagues' feelings, or from damaging a firm's reputation.

Although courteous behavior, such as saying "thank you" and "please" is universal, in the world of business the nuances of what is "right" are also formed by the style and traditions of individual companies. What may be considered correct attire at an advertising agency may not be acceptable in a bank or law firm. In some offices, first names are always used; in others, superiors are addressed as Mr., Mrs., or Ms. If you are lucky enough to work for a company which has written material on office protocol, finding out what is acceptable is easy. Otherwise, observe others, use common sense, and follow the general guidelines outlined in this chapter.

INTEGRITY AND ETHICS AT WORK

Integrity—the character, decency, and honesty—of people, is the true infrastructure supporting businesses. In the 1970s, Peter F. Drucker's books on management explored, among other issues, the need for changing attitudes between management and staff. In the preface to *Management*, Drucker stated, "Without integrity, one can not inspire the confidence of others; and no man, no matter how brilliant, is able to perform his job without the support of others. The conductor can only conduct if there's an orchestra willing to respond."

Integrity is important at all levels in a company. Honesty and respect must flow both ways, between employer and employee. Regardless of your position in the company hierarchy and regardless of whether others around you are honest, preserve your integrity by following these basic guidelines:

- Work a full day.
- Call in sick only when you *are* sick.

- Use company perks only as intended to be used.
- Tell coworkers you cannot lie for them or back up their lie.
- Use the company letterhead only for business matters.
- Use office supplies only for office purposes.
- Be honest about your expense account.
- Make as few personal calls as possible.
- Use the fax machine only for business purposes.

EVERYDAY MANNERS IN THE OFFICE

Office etiquette is based on the concern and consideration you show for your coworkers. Just one person can make an office a nicer place in which to work.

Some points to keep in mind are:

- Be punctual. Don't keep others waiting. If you are habitually late to work, to appointments, to interoffice meetings, or if you frequently miss deadlines, you will soon be seen as unreliable.

- Set reasonable deadlines for others. Except in emergencies, your staff or assistant should not be expected to meet unrealistic deadlines.

- Always praise someone who handles an assignment well or makes an effort to improve.

- Give credit where credit is due. Don't even dream of accepting praise for someone else's work.

- If you are in a supervisory role, you must give criticism if it's justified and necessary. People cannot learn if you don't point out their mistakes. But if you must correct or reprimand someone, do it in private. There's no need to embarrass someone in front of coworkers. And avoid criticizing or blaming people behind their backs.

- Avoid shouting for people to come to you.

- Be neat. Clean up after using communal spaces such as a kitchen or conference room. If you pour the last cup of coffee, make a fresh pot. Make an effort to keep the bathrooms neat, wiping the sink clean with a paper towel and depositing towels in the appropriate receptacle.

- Refrain from primping at your desk and never file or paint your nails at the office.

- Return anything you borrow from a coworker such as a pen, book, or umbrella. And don't fall into the habit of borrowing money for lunch, bus fare, or incidentals. It's easy to forget to pay back small amounts of money, yet the person who makes the loan rarely forgets that you owe him a dollar or two.

- Respect others' privacy. Never go through someone else's desk or read material that's not yours.
- If someone you work with looks ill, has lost weight, or seems despondent, unless you know him well, wait for him to bring up the subject of his health. If you do know him well, you can simply say, "Are you feeling all right?"
- Don't be a pest. People who habitually drop by other people's offices to chat, repeatedly interrupting them, are a dedicated worker's biggest annoyance.
- Obey rules on smoking. In most large companies, unless you have a private office, you must go outside to smoke. Whatever the policy is at your company, don't cheat.
- Keep your voice down. Particularly in partitioned offices where the walls do not go to the ceiling, it's essential to respect your neighbor's need to concentrate.
- Offer support to colleagues who need it. If you know someone is having a personal crisis or a difficult time at work, lend him a sympathetic ear. You might bring him flowers or a fresh Danish with the message that you hope this will brighten his day.
- If someone does something nice for you, respond with a note of thanks.
- Be sympathetic and attentive to a colleague who has been fired. Try to help him find a new job, offer to proofread his résumé, or simply call him occasionally to bolster his spirits.

OFFICE GOSSIP

> "What some invent and the rest enlarge . . ."
> *Jonathan Swift*

Every company seems to have at least one person who likes to spread gossip. Even if you don't spread it yourself but only listen to it, you may be categorized as a gossiper. So steer clear of the rumor mill. If someone comes to you with a piece of gossip, excuse yourself diplomatically. If the gossipmonger persists, you may have to be more forthright: "I really don't like talking about other people," or, "I've learned over the years [or with experience] to be wary of secondhand information."

You should be equally circumspect if you are told something in confidence by either management or a coworker. Do not repeat it. Office gossip often centers around "management's plans," and if rumors of this sort are affecting employee morale, you may want to point this out to management, without asking for confirmation or denial: "I thought you should be aware that there's a rumor going around that there are going to be some layoffs in the marketing department. Whether or not this is true, I felt you should know about it."

GENDER AND SENIORITY COURTESIES Several years ago, as women came to assume more authority in the world of business, old-fashioned courtesies such as opening a door for a woman or letting her into or out of an elevator first came to be seen by many as unnecessary. Some women even took offense at such gender-based courtesies. Things have settled down a bit since then and today, fortunately, men and women now open doors for each other. If you are ever in doubt as to what to do, simply use common sense, regardless of sex.

Courtesies based on seniority are still found in the more formal office setting. A young executive (man or woman) rises when a senior executive comes into his office; the senior executive goes through the door or onto the elevator first.

THE OPEN-DOOR POLICY

The open-door policy is wisely cultivated by many managers. This is to encourage employees to speak up on matters of concern. However, just because you have access to your boss you don't want to become a nuisance. If you typically have several quick questions each day for your supervisor or boss, let them accumulate so they can be discussed all at once. What you don't want to do, is grab your boss in the hall, lunchroom, or elevator to ask a question. If you are the boss and someone interrupts you while you are in the midst of working on a project, you are *not* obliged to drop everything unless it's an emergency. Explain that you are on a deadline and say when you expect to be free.

NAMES, TITLES, AND INTRODUCTIONS

When you're new to a job, one of the first questions you face is how to address your colleagues. Each office has its own protocol, but generally employees of equal rank call one another by their first names while a subordinate speaking to a supervisor or higher-ranking executive calls that person by his or her surname *unless* invited by that person to use the first name.

When in doubt, err on the side of formality. It's far better to have a senior executive say, "Please, call me Ralph," than to have him say, "I prefer to be addressed as Mr. Jenkins," or, "It's Mr. Jenkins."

When you refer to a company executive in conversation, use his full name. For example, "Michael Harris, our CEO, suggested I call you."

Mrs. and Miss have been replaced in business by Ms., which happily requires no knowledge of marital status. However, it's a matter of preference; if you want to be called Mrs. or Miss, just let people know.

It has become common for a woman who marries after she has established a career to keep her maiden name professionally. If you wish to take your married name, you will need to let your associates know.

Send a memo stating your new name to the staff, including those who answer the telephones, and to any clients you work with. The same applies if, after a divorce, you want to return to your maiden name.

Sooner or later you will need to introduce yourself as well as coworkers to business associates. Be sure always to use full names when making an introduction. For example, "John, I'd like to introduce you to my colleague Mary Harris. Mary, this is John Smith, director of human resources at XYZ, Inc." Or: "Hello, Mr. Campbell. I'm Louise Jones from the research library." It's helpful if you can give more than just a name and title. For example, "John, I'd like to introduce you to Rob Whittaker. Rob's a sales manager at XYZ Corporation and he's also their Salesman of the Year." This will give the two people a conversation starter.

Many people have difficulty remembering names, even of someone they've just met. Or they have a memory block when they have to make an introduction. This happens especially if the person is nervous or tired. Here are a few tips to make such common lapses a little less awkward.

- If you forget the name of someone you have met only once or twice, don't feel bad. It happens to almost everyone. It's for this very reason many people routinely reintroduce themselves: "Hi, I'm John Billings. We met at the spring sales conference."

- Sometimes you may be greeted by someone whose name you have forgotten and have to introduce him to a third person. It's tempting to avoid or postpone the introduction while you feverishly search your mind for the name. Instead, simply say, "I'm sorry, but your name suddenly escapes me." As you make the introduction, if you can, include something specific about the person whose name you had forgotten: "Ms. Williams is vice-president of Lansing, Inc. She's responsible for their most successful fabric line." This shows Ms. Williams that, although you may have temporarily forgotten her name, you do indeed remember her.

WORKING WITH OTHERS

Two people crucial in any office are the receptionist and the switchboard operator. It goes without saying that they must be preternaturally polite to everyone, even to those who are rude or abrupt. They are usually the first contacts anyone has with the company and it is important they make a good impression. They should be trained to answer questions and calls without sounding rushed. It's also helpful if they are prepared to give visitors precise directions about how to reach the office. The receptionist should keep on hand such items as the company's annual report, its catalog if there is one, a copy of the morning newspaper, current magazines, a spare umbrella and shopping bag, subway and bus maps, even extra tissues. And, depending upon how the office is set up, the receptionist may offer visitors coffee or a soft drink while they are waiting.

Of equal importance to an office is the assistant. The assistant who pays careful attention to detail is a treasure. Beyond accuracy at the word processor and excellent telephone manners, the topnotch assistant knows how to set priorities, is honest and expresses opinions tactfully. In addition, an assistant lets her boss know when a coworker or customer is ill so he can send a note or flowers and reminds him of staff and client birthdays or other significant occasions. The best assistant is also loyal, never making critical remarks about her boss to others in the office. She also gets coffee and orders lunch, if asked to do so, understanding that getting coffee does not a servant make. (A considerate boss will periodically offer to do the same for his assistant.)

On the other hand, the boss or executive must also be loyal, gracious, organized, resourceful, considerate, respectful, and responsible. For instance, a secretary or assistant should never be asked to do personal errands for her boss, such as picking up laundry or buying personal presents, *unless* this was agreed upon as part of the job description. Leaders must not only set an example in all areas of business; they must set the *best* example.

It is important to praise people who work for you or with whom you work. Remember how thrilled you were when your teacher complimented you on your term paper or your ability to do fractions in your head? As adults, we have not outgrown the need for praise, nor should we be expected to. When we do well and that fact is recognized by our colleagues—whether they are our peers, seniors, or staff—our confidence is bolstered. It's particularly important not to forget congratulations when someone masters a task he was previously unable to comprehend.

Praise need not come only from above. Junior staff members can also praise their supervisor or even the president of the firm. A group of colleagues in a San Francisco law firm sent this mailgram to the firm's top negotiating attorney:

Congratulations on winning the Simpson case. We are very proud to be on your team.

It is equally important, of course, to criticize people when necessary and to accept criticism. For some people, it is as difficult to offer it as to be criticized—maybe more difficult. If you are a supervisor, helping your staff improve their work habits is part of your job. When you need to criticize someone, be polite yet direct, discuss the problem calmly, and end on a positive note:

"Michael, I've noticed that you're still making some careless errors in your reports. I suggest you either double proofread them or get someone else to go over the material. Maybe you need to build more time into your schedule so you're not rushing at the last minute. You and your work represent the company and we cannot afford to turn out inaccurate reports. Jim and I feel you're excellent at handling clients in meetings—you were particularly good with George Simpson, who's not easy to impress. I'm sure with a little added effort you can get your written material up to the same level."

No one likes to be criticized, but one of the best ways to learn is from your mistakes. When someone criticizes your work, be professional about it. Do not react emotionally, as though you are being personally attacked.

In business, confrontations are inevitable. They are generally best settled face to face, not in writing. If the confrontation is with a subordinate, don't take unfair advantage of your seniority. And, of course, apologize if you turn out to be wrong.

OFFICE APPOINTMENTS

When *you* arrive for an appointment, give your name to the receptionist or secretary along with the name of the person you are to see. If your last name is complicated, show your business card to the receptionist. If you arrive ten or more minutes ahead of time, say to the receptionist: "I'm early. Please tell Mr. Roberts I'm ahead of schedule and in no rush."

When a *visitor* arrives for an appointment at your office, you or your assistant should greet him in the reception area and show him to your office. If the visitor is early or you are running late, tell the receptionist to let the visitor know how long you will be and to offer him coffee or a soft drink along with something to read.

Some executives like to play the "I'm-busier-and-more-important-than-you-are" game by keeping people waiting. Don't fall into this category.

When a visitor enters your office, stand up to greet him regardless of his sex or age—or yours. Step forward and shake hands. If your office is equipped with a sofa and/or a chair or two, sit in one of these places. It's less formal than if you sit behind a large, intimidating desk. Have your telephone calls held during your appointment unless you're expecting one that you simply must take. If it comes through, tell your visitor, "I'm sorry. I must take this call. Please stay right where you are; I'll only be a minute or two." Or, if you know the call is confidential, explain this to your visitor and ask him if he'd mind stepping out of your office for a minute, or ask the switchboard operator to transfer the call to a place where you can speak in private.

If you set up the appointment, then it's up to you to initiate the subjects for discussion. If the meeting drags on and it seems your visitor will never leave, look at your watch and say, "I have another appointment in five minutes. I'm sorry but we'll have to wind up now." Or have your assistant knock on the door or ring you at a specified time to remind you that you have another appointment.

Your visitor should be escorted from your office to the reception area by either you or your assistant.

OFFICE FRIENDSHIPS

It's quite natural for people who work together to become friends. But a word of caution: you want to avoid forming friendships only with those above you in the office hierarchy—such friendships can make you appear opportunistic. Also, too close a friendship between a boss and an employee (or sometimes between colleagues) can make others feel threatened or jealous or left out. In a small office, people of different ages and levels usually get to know one another well. If you work in a small office and several of you are going out together after work, include other employees as often as possible. They may not accept your invitation, but at least they won't feel excluded. And remember, even the boss doesn't want to feel left out.

INAPPROPRIATE TERMINOLOGY Sometimes people forget or even are unaware that they are using certain locutions that are inappropriate in an office setting. Women should never be called "honey," "dear," "sweetie," or any other term of endearment. Even if it is not offensive to the person involved—although it usually is—it colors the perceptions of anyone who overhears them.

Never refer to your assistant as "my girl" or "my boy," as in "Get your girl to call my girl for an appointment."

THE OFFICE ROMANCE The last decade has seen an alteration in feelings about romance in the office. It is no longer the absolutely outrageous offense it once was considered, and in many offices is now quite accepted. It's not clear how much of this acceptance is based on approval or a change in attitude and how much on a grudging sense that there's little an employer can do about it. Yet, because people working together share a natural bond and common interests, inevitably some of them will become romantically involved. Despite the more relaxed standards, office romance can still be problematic and can pose complicated questions of propriety.

Romances between employees at different levels create problems—usually because of what others suspect to be both parties' motives. If you and your boss fall in love, be smart and start looking for another job. In the meantime, make every effort to keep your romance a secret. If you are the boss and you fall in love with an assistant or secretary, all you need are one or two suspicious employees to create a raft of office gossip you will then have to contend with. Sincere as you both may be, an affair between the boss and an assistant is too hot a topic for even the most laid-back office to take in its stride.

Even between peers, a departmental romance can become complicated. If the relationship you're involved in ends and you still have to continue to work with that person on a daily basis, it could be extremely awkward for you both. You might feel you can handle it well, but can you be certain about the other person? If on the other hand the romance leads to marriage, one employee may be asked to leave—usually the employee in the lower position or with less seniority.

An affair in the office or otherwise with a married man or woman is a definite no-no. Enough said.

YOUR FAMILY AND YOUR OFFICE

For most of us, office life is not entirely separate from our social life. If a colleague's spouse or parent is in the hospital, for instance, office friends may wish to send a card or flowers. It is quite natural from time to time to discuss our families, to share our joys and sorrows with special coworkers. You must take care not to bring too much of your home life into your work life, however. And there are three times when it's particularly tempting to do so: when you marry, when you have a child, or when you get divorced.

GETTING MARRIED It's important when you become engaged to be sensitive to the feelings of those with whom you work. You're excited and busy, and it's bound to impinge on your work time. Tell your employer about your engagement first so he won't hear it through the office grapevine. Limit the amount of work time devoted to wedding-related calls and errands. And, above all, keep wedding talk to a minimum during office hours, especially if you're not inviting all of your colleagues. Remember, the celebration of your wedding vows may be the most important event in your social life, but it's not the most important event in your business life. Your wedding should not interfere significantly with your day-to-day business activities.

If you are an executive, you may receive wedding invitations from employees. If neither the bride nor the groom is on your personal staff or is a close friend, it is perfectly acceptable to decline. You should, however, send a note of congratulations. If the colleague is one with whom you work closely on a day-to-day basis and you have been invited to the wedding, you should send a wedding present. In addition, it's nice to have a bottle of wine or champagne waiting on his desk when he returns from his wedding trip.

THE EXPECTANT MOTHER If you are expecting a baby, tell your boss and colleagues as soon as it is noticeable in a low-key way so the announcement is not turned into a major office event. Colleagues should refrain from asking too many personal questions. You may volunteer information but should steer clear of issuing bulletins on your physical condition. During your pregnancy you should take every care to handle your responsibilities as fully as possible for as long as you come to work.

You must discuss with your immediate supervisor or employer how long you plan to take off from work and whether or not you plan to return after the baby is born. Federal law requires employers with more than fifty employees to provide men and women with twelve weeks' unpaid leave upon the birth or adoption of a child.

Expectant parents, especially if it is their first child, may appreciate a baby shower. However, this should be organized quietly and held after work and away from the office. When the colleague has had the baby, the office may wish to send her a small present or a congratulatory card with everyone's signatures.

After the baby is born and you return to work, refrain from spending too much time talking about your child or showing endless pictures. If you bring your baby into the office to show him off to friends, keep the visit short so as not to interfere with the office routine.

There are times, of course, when a woman who has been pregnant loses the baby, either during pregnancy or at birth. Although such matters cannot be totally ignored by colleagues, fellow workers should not be too solicitous. A colleague may say something like, "I've missed you and I hope you're feeling all right," or, "I'd like to take you out for lunch one day next week."

DIVORCE Going through a divorce can make even the most organized, stable person feel depressed, unenthusiastic, and like a failure. His work often suffers. If someone in your office is getting divorced, remember that emotional support at this time is often called for. Avoid prying questions, but by all means ask if there is some way you can be of help.

If you are the one getting a divorce, try not to let your work suffer, although it is inevitable that at times you will find it hard to concentrate. Let your employer and close associates at work know your situation. It will help to eliminate needless gossip. Try not to talk too much about the divorce, and refrain from disclosing personal details. It's not only poor taste to do so, but will embarrass those you tell. And never ask colleagues (or anyone) to introduce you to new people or find dates for you until the divorce is final.

DEATH IN A COLLEAGUE'S FAMILY When a colleague suffers a tragedy in his life, it's important to show kindness and concern. You can do this by writing a warm note, sending flowers, or even giving him a special book, perhaps of poems. Although it's often difficult to know what to do or say, to ignore the situation is uncaring and thoughtless.

When someone close to a colleague dies, it is natural to be supportive at the time of the funeral. But the most difficult period is often several weeks or months later. This is the time to invite the bereaved to dinner, to the theater, or on a picnic with your family and friends.

SEXUAL HARASSMENT

Although a closet issue for decades, women—and men—are now stepping forward and taking action to stop this particularly loathsome form of power abuse.

What is sexual harassment? The rule could be, if you feel you are being harassed you probably are. "A good general definition [of sexual harassment] is unwelcome sexual advances in the context of employment, and those advances can be verbal or physical, . . ." says Claudia Withers, deputy director of employment programs at the Women's Legal Defense Fund in Washington, D.C. "It can lead to a 'put out or get out' situation or require the person to work in a hostile environment." Public attention has forced employers to confront the problem. If you're the victim of sexual harassment, by an opposite-sex or gay or lesbian coworker, don't feel shamed or embarrassed—the abuser should feel that way.

You can help avoid being harassed sexually by making it clear you are not interested. Never respond in any way to sexual innuendoes or jokes—don't even smile slightly. Don't allow coworkers to talk about their sexual problems or interests with you or to refer to their spouses or lovers in a sexual way.

Be prudent when complimenting a fellow worker. It's not wrong to tell a man or woman that they "look nice today," or to say, "That's a great color on you," or, "I like your new haircut." But it's an entirely different matter to say, "Wow, that dress fits you really well," or, "That's certainly a sexy outfit." Finally, never kiss or hug colleagues. To avoid any sign of encouragement, stick to handshakes.

If an unwelcome advance is forced on you, you can either ignore the pass, excusing yourself and walking away, or confront the harasser directly (this is more likely to prevent its happening again). If the latter, be direct: "John, we are colleagues and I'm not interested in a more personal relationship. Your behavior is making me feel very uncomfortable. Please stop." If he doesn't stop, or if he approaches you at another time, be even more direct: "Your behavior is unprofessional and offensive. If you don't stop, I will report you to human resources."

If the person continues to harass you, back up your threat with a written memo. Keep a log and write down all conversations and actions with dates and times. If anyone else is a witness to the harassment, ask for corroboration in case you need it.

If your supervisor is the one harassing you, go above him to *his* supervisor or to the appropriate executive—for instance, the company attorney, the head of human resources, or employee relations. Many large corporations have formal harassment policies and grievance procedures; if you work for such a company, use them. Many companies, because of the successful lawsuits brought by women and men, have been forced to pay attention to these all too frequent occurrences, so they are less likely to ignore your complaints these days.

Employees are often reluctant to report harassment because they fear it will place their jobs in jeopardy. This could happen. On the other hand, do you want to work in an environment where you're subject to harassment?

If all else fails, consult your union, a lawyer who specializes in such cases, or the Women's Legal Defense Fund, 2000 P Street NW, Suite 400, Washington, DC 20036; 202-887-0364.

DRESSING FOR WORK

Elton John and Madonna may be able to get away with eccentric wardrobes; Albert Einstein was simply too busy to think about clothes; but unless you're a superstar or a genius, you need to pay attention to what you wear to work. Not only will you *feel* more confident if you look your best, but your good looks will reflect well on your company. There's also a pragmatic reason: if you are not attractively and appropriately attired, you may be passed over for a promotion in favor of someone who is. This is particularly true among professionals and executives; an investment banker or lawyer who dresses carelessly may give the impression that he's poorly organized in his job as well.

Different industries and businesses have different dress styles, and in each region of the country the degree of formality or casualness differs. New York, Boston, Washington, and Chicago, for instance, are more formal than San Antonio, San Diego, and Orlando. String ties and cowboy boots may be fine in Boise but not on Wall Street where the rule is dark suits and neckties. On the other hand, a pin-striped suit might seem pretentious in most of Montana.

KNOWING WHAT'S RIGHT

How do you know what clothes to choose for work? How offbeat can you be? It all depends on where you work. If it's for a conservative law firm, for example, the latest fashion fads won't fit in. Look about you to help decide what clothes are appropriate. The firm's top executive and the person in a position above you who is admired and successful are usually good models.

Keep in mind the advice of the *Wall Street Journal*: "always consider the source." The *Journal*, reporting on a survey which stated that "American executives, by an eight-to-one margin, are adopting more casual dress," pointedly noted that the study was conducted by an athletic shoe manufacturer. And, when fashion magazines proclaim to women readers: "Pants Go Professional" or to men: "Power's Behind the No-Tie Suit," they are promoting the latest look, which may be fine if you work in the fashion industry or for a small family-run business. For most of us, however, it's better to stay with a classic, conservative style.

If you are a new employee, you may have had an opportunity to observe how people in the office dressed when you were being interviewed. As with virtually all things in business, it's best to err on the conservative side. If you did not see women wearing slacks, don't you wear them. If all the men you saw were wearing ties, then wear one. If you are still uncertain, it never hurts to ask. Once you have accepted a job, your new employer or the human resources director will probably take time to fill you in on company policies such as office hours, vacations, sick leave, medical benefits, etc. This is the perfect time to ask about dress. Don't be embarrassed; you will be seen as conscientious, someone with the foresight to prepare yourself for a new situation.

No two companies are exactly alike. Some—notably those in the entertainment industry, advertising, and the fashion industry—encourage flair and innovation. There, hair is grown longer or shaved, hemlines rise and fall, ties are discarded and rediscovered, and people tend to adopt the look of the moment. In other fields, such as law and banking, everyone dresses conservatively and looking too trendy is frowned upon.

Styles not only vary from company to company, but there are often different looks within the company: one for executives, another for the creative departments, and another for the sales reps. For example, in some companies, jeans may be considered perfectly suitable for an art director, while an account executive is expected to wear a jacket and tie. And an account supervisor who regularly meets with clients is expected to conform to his client's standards no matter how casually he may dress at work.

But whatever the specific codes of any organization, there are two standards that cross all company and industry lines: one is good grooming and the other is modest, not provocative, dress. A polished, clean look is as important for the mail-room employee as for the president.

Regardless of whether you wear a three-piece suit or jeans to work, you should have a well-groomed appearance, meaning:

- Clean, tidy hair
- Neatly trimmed beard or mustache
- Clean teeth and fresh breath
- Clean fingernails (for women, no chipped nail polish)
- Clean, pressed clothes with no spots, stains, tears, or missing buttons
- Polished shoes

If you wear sneakers or running shoes to get to your office, change them once you arrive. They are not appropriate during the workday, and that includes business lunches, dinners, or cocktail parties. If you bike or rollerblade to work, keep a clean shirt or blouse and deodorant at work.

Under no circumstances should you wear provocative clothes. This, of course, is more of an issue for women than for men. Your ideas, skills, and talents are what are important at work, and women who want their opinions to be taken seriously should dress seriously. Save plunging necklines and see-through fabrics for your private life.

CONSERVATIVE, STANDARD, OR CASUAL OFFICE ATTIRE

Most workplaces fall into one of three broad categories: the conservative or corporate look, the standard business look, or the casual (sometimes, the anything goes) look.

THE CONSERVATIVE OR CORPORATE LOOK In the world of banking, investment, insurance, and law, clothing is always conservative. For men that means dark suits with white or pale blue shirts with straight collars and buttoned or French cuffs, laced oxford shoes, dark socks, and conservative ties. For women, suits or conservative dresses (never sleeveless) and classic, closed-toe pumps with medium or low heels. Hemlines are worn at the lowest current acceptable length.

THE STANDARD BUSINESS LOOK In less conservative fields, professional men, including business executives, teachers, publishers, architects, consultants, engineers, etc., typically wear either suits, dark blue blazers, or tweed sports jackets with ties. In some offices, ties are not regarded as necessary. Male doctors wear a white coat over a dress shirt with a tie and trousers. Female doctors wear a white coat over a dress or blouse and skirt, or slacks.

Men vary their wardrobes with colored or striped shirts. Button-down collars are acceptable but only on broadcloth shirts. In addition to oxfords, plain or tasseled loafers may be worn.

Women wear skirts and sometimes slacks in addition to suits and dresses. Sleeveless dresses and blouses are not considered professional unless they're worn under a jacket.

THE CASUAL LOOK In artistic fields—photography, design, communication, fashion, journalism, advertising, filmmaking, and the art world—as well as in many smaller companies, individual style is just fine, even encouraged. That may mean that jeans are allowed, but worn with a crisp shirt or a turtleneck, an attractive leather belt, and a classic blazer. Whether you're a man or woman, be very realistic about how you look in jeans. They definitely are not flattering on everyone.

Anything that is in good taste—i.e., not immodest—is generally allowed in these businesses, but do not mistake the anything-goes policy for license to wear any old thing you feel like. The standard is usually set by the head executive or the owner of the company.

No matter where you work, these fashion tips will help you.

DAY TO EVENING

You may find yourself going straight to a cocktail party or dinner at the end of the workday. Instead of carrying a complete change of clothes, convert a good business suit or dress into an evening outfit by changing your blouse or adding jewelry. If you do change, leave whatever you took off at the office rather than taking it to the party.

A WORD ABOUT FURS

These days you wear a fur coat at your own risk. There are many animal lovers who find it offensive and others who find it ostentatious. And some of these people feel so righteous about their position that they'll tell you about it. Also, if you work in an office where most of the women earn less than you do, you may want to think twice before wearing your fur coat to work. You can always save it for evenings and weekends.

WHEN DOING BUSINESS IN FOREIGN COUNTRIES

The rule of thumb for traveling abroad is that business people elsewhere dress more formally than we do. Jackets and ties for men and dresses or suits for women are standard, with a few exceptions. In Israel, for instance, men rarely wear ties and often go without jackets. Before taking a business trip to a country you have never been to before, find out about the specific dress code. For example, in Arab countries, women should not wear pants, short skirts, or bare their arms. In China, white is the color for mourning. And if you are an executive, be prepared for black-tie dinners, which are much more common in Europe than in America.

FASHION TIPS FOR MEN

- The most formal daytime suit is a dark blue pinstripe; almost as formal are plain dark blue and dark gray.
- Brown suits are generally not considered professional, although the tan summer suit is.
- Shirt sleeves should extend a half inch beyond jacket sleeves.
- Bow ties are acceptable in all but the most conservative offices.
- Colored dress shirts with white collars and cuffs have become acceptable in all but the most conservative offices.
- If you are an executive and you take your jacket off in the office, never wear short-sleeved shirts; instead roll up long sleeves.
- Suspenders should not be worn if trousers have belt loops.
- White socks are not worn with dress shoes.
- Socks should be high enough so even when legs are crossed no bare leg shows between the top of the sock and the hem of the trouser.

FASHION TIPS FOR WOMEN

Coco Chanel, one of the most fashionable women of the twentieth century, advised: "Elegance does not consist in putting on a new dress."

- Buy well-made timeless clothes and update them with accessories: scarves, belts, etc., instead of replacing your wardrobe every two years.
- Clothes should fit well—be neither too tight nor baggy. Have them altered if they don't. Clothes that fit well not only look more expensive but are more flattering.
- Always wear pantyhose, even in the summer, unless you have fabulously attractive and tanned legs. Never walk around the office in your stocking feet.
- Keep extra pantyhose at work in case you get a run.
- Always keep your shoes and handbags polished and in good condition.
- Navy blue is becoming to almost every woman; it is professional, classic, and seasonless.
- Synthetic fabrics have improved dramatically in recent years and have been adopted by designers for everything from sportswear to haute couture. They wrinkle less and are easier to clean, so don't bypass a label that includes synthetics.
- Wear pants only if you have a trim figure.
- Too much jewelry or jewelry that jangles when you move is distracting; people will look at your jewelry instead of listening to you.
- Long, drop earrings are inappropriate for office wear; save them for the evening. The same is true for rhinestones.
- Long hair has a more professional look when it's pulled back.
- Some fabrics are totally inappropriate for work: satin, velvet, brocade, and anything with sequins or sparkles.
- Sheer blouses, even when worn with camisoles, are not appropriate for the office.
- Never let your underwear straps show.
- Unless you live in a warm-weather resort area, white shoes and handbags should be avoided between Labor Day and Memorial Day.
- Makeup should be subdued. Heavy makeup, if worn at all, is for evening.

ORAL COMMUNICATION IN BUSINESS

Over three quarters of our workday is spent engaged in oral communication, either face to face or over the telephone, so the ability to use the spoken word skillfully in a variety of situations is essential in the business world.

You may be brilliant and have wonderful ideas, but if you make grammatical errors, swallow your words, have a phony accent or a harsh or unappealing voice, you will have difficulty persuading others to accept those ideas or buy your products. You may even be passed over for promotions and raises.

All aspects of language are important. If you are in a managerial position, your style of communication will set the tone in your department. If you speak cheerfully and respectfully to others, people will want to work for you and will work harder, whereas if you are negative, complain, or whine, chances are your employees will too.

Generally, we are most comfortable speaking to people face to face because our facial expressions, our gestures, even our posture, help us substantiate what we have to say. If you are interested in your nonverbal signals—how they affect others—you can ask colleagues or friends or, better yet, videotape yourself talking to others. Are your gestures effective yet restrained; do you maintain eye contact? How do you appear when you're listening to others? Does your expression convey interest? Do you fidget, move your body too much, fuss with your hair, jingle the change in your pocket?

Ever since the publication of *Body Language* by Julius Fast in 1970, lay people have been interpreting the nonverbal communications of others. But as with all amateur endeavors, layman psychology can mislead. Crossing one's arms is not necessarily evidence of defensiveness; leaning forward may not indicate aggression; yet we all trust such clues to some extent. Someone who habitually frowns does give the impression of having a dour or unpleasant disposition. Someone who does not look at the person speaking certainly appears inattentive. Pay attention to what your body is communicating: stand tall and don't slump in your chair. Shake hands firmly. Smile. Have a pleasant expression and always look people in the eye. Do not let your head hang down.

YOUR VOCABULARY

A good vocabulary and carefully chosen words are effective ways of getting your message across. But using words you do not understand or that you *think* sound right will probably have the opposite effect although you may never know it. If you have any doubt as to the exact meaning of a word (or its pronunciation), don't use it. Play it safe and stick with a more familiar one. However, be careful of overusing rhetorically empty words such as "interesting," "nice," "great," "neat," "gross," "fantastic." We tend to be lazy and resort to them too frequently. "That was an interesting point." "That was an interesting report." "We had an interesting conversation."

Phrases to avoid are: "know what I mean," "like," "you know," "I mean," "Have a nice day," and "I'm into . . ." Slang—"classy" or "awesome" for "elegant," "pad" instead of "home," "bucks" instead of "money"—is not acceptable in a professional situation. And don't be fooled into thinking that dropping swear words here and there will impress colleagues; it's simply not true.

Some basic points to keep in mind about using oral communication skills in the workplace:

- Follow through on what you say—broken promises are unforgivable in business. If you are speaking for your company, make certain that the company is going to back your word.

- Generally it's better to say too little than too much. The person who rambles on or monopolizes the conversation not only loses the interest of the person he's talking to but prevents that person from contributing to the discussion. Conversation must go both ways.

- Just as talking too much is a detriment in the work setting, silence is too if it is used to force the other person to talk or to make him feel uncomfortable. None of us enjoys doing business with those who make us feel ill at ease.

- Don't be afraid to admit you don't understand what's being told to you. It's better to say you missed the point than to bluff your way through a conversation only to make a fool of yourself.

- Avoid prophesying. Your predictions may not come true and your words will come back to haunt you.

- Awkward silences are, of course, from time to time inevitable. In a business setting it's not difficult to break the silence: simply mention that there are only twenty minutes left and "we should move on to the next point." Or, if the silence is the result of a stalemate, try, "I don't know how to resolve this issue, but do you think we could take it up another time?"

TELEPHONE MANNERS

Children like to play with phones, teenagers love to talk on them, and everyone in business relies on them. In fact, a business is often judged by how its employees use the telephone. Sometimes the only contact the public ever has with a company is a telephone call, so anyone answering the phone or placing a call contributes to that company's image.

Time, opportunity, and money can be lost through careless telephone manners.

Although voice mail, automatic redial, conference calls, and speed dialing are all well and good, in the end, the true power of the phone lies in its ability to transmit our ideas.

One advantage the telephone has over either the letter or fax is that you can hear or at least get a sense of the other person's response to your message. You can then adjust your tone and words accordingly.

When you speak on the telephone, you are judged by your diction, your ability to articulate thoughts, and whether or not you listen and treat others courteously. A good telephone voice is cheerful, clear, and warm. You may want to listen to your own voice to see how you sound to others. Is your voice too low? Too high? Do you speak too rapidly? Do you mumble? Say "yeah" or "un-huh"?

ANSWERING OTHER PEOPLE'S TELEPHONES Office policy should include specific instructions on how employees are to answer the company's telephones or an executive's line. Should they answer with the executive's name, their own name, the name of the department or company, or some combination of these? Such things are a matter of preference but all employees should take time to speak distinctly, sound friendly and be willing to help the caller. No employee should be allowed to answer with a mere "hello."

If the company has a large number of employees, telephone policy should be written out, complete with examples of how employees should answer the telephone, put people on hold, and so forth. Keep in mind, too, that the switchboard operator is often the first contact others have with the company. She should be told precisely how to answer the telephone, for instance, "Good morning, the ABC Corporation. May I help you?" An executive and her assistant should also work out their own telephone policy. But among the givens should be:

When your assistant answers your calls: She should say in a clear voice, "Good morning, Ms. Howard's office." Simply "hello" lacks professionalism.

When you answer your own telephone: Some executives prefer to answer their own telephone. This gives the impression of accessibility, a refreshing attribute in today's business world. The proper greeting for an executive is, "Hello, this is Mary Anderson," or, "Good morning, Mary Anderson," or simply "Mary Anderson," never just "Hello."

Answering your own calls when time permits, eliminates the need to return calls. A drawback, however, is that you run the risk of having to deal with nuisance calls—someone looking for a job for his third cousin or complaining about your product or service. If you want to cut such a caller off, say in an apologetic tone, "I'm sorry I can't talk now. My assistant is waiting to go into a meeting with me." Or, "I'm involved in something right now. Could you please put your ideas in writing and send them to me."

Some people, of course, never seem to want to get off the telephone. You can take charge of this situation by pleading an urgent incoming call, a meeting, or a deadline. If you remember to thank someone for calling he is less likely to feel rejected.

When your assistant places your calls: Be ready to speak as soon as your secretary says the person you are calling is on the line. Making the person wait a few seconds is a senseless form of one-upmanship.

HANDLING INTERRUPTIONS There are times when you may need to be interrupted during a meeting. When this is the case, give your assistant the name of the person whose call you want put through.

When a visitor you have an appointment with is in your office, it's poor manners to take any telephone calls. Tell the switchboard operator or your secretary to take messages or forward your calls to someone else.

In the case of a call of great importance, if the subject matter to be discussed is of a confidential or delicate nature, explain this to your visitor and ask him if he'd mind stepping out of your office for a minute, or ask the switchboard operator to transfer the call to a more private extension and take it there. If you do take an important call, make it brief.

If you have a visitor and no one to field your calls, simply say, "This is Bruce Ryan. I'm in a meeting now but if you'll leave your name and number I'll call back when I'm free." On the other hand, if someone comes into your office without a prior appointment, you are free to take calls.

THE LENGTHY BUSINESS CALL Frequently it is necessary to do business over the telephone. This being the case, it is essential to take notes so you can summarize the key points in a follow-up letter that will document what's been said. If there's a difference of opinion later, you can always say, "According to the notes I made during our conversation on May 12 . . ."

USING THE SPEAKERPHONE A speakerphone is appropriate on two occasions—when several people in an office need to hear what the caller has to say and when you have to take notes during the conversation and need your hands free. Keep in mind that many callers are uncomfortable about having their voices broadcast into a room, so use the speakerphone with discretion. It's best to ask permission of the caller first and explain why you need to use the speakerphone.

WHEN YOU ARE NOT THERE TO ANSWER When you are out of the office or otherwise occupied, instruct your staff or assistant to say, "She's not available now. May I take a message?" (You may or may not wish her to say when you will be back.) Some executives instruct their assistants to ask who is calling before advising the caller, "She's away from her desk." This is actually impolite to the person calling because it implies that if the caller were more important the call would probably be put through.

TAKING MESSAGES When taking telephone messages, get *all* the facts and leave a legibly written message, including the caller's name, company, and telephone number, the message, the date, time, and your name. Do not write the information on the back of an envelope or a tiny scrap of paper that may easily be overlooked or pushed aside. Be sure to include your name in case the person receiving the message needs to verify a telephone number or other information. Leave the message where it will easily be seen by the recipient.

SCREENING CALLS Ideally, someone calling you identifies himself to your assistant: "This is Raymond Spencer from the ABC Company." If the caller does not identify himself, your assistant should say, "May I tell Ms. Jones who is calling?" (not "Who is this?"). She may also say, "May I ask what this is in reference to?" This information prepares you for the call and allows you time to grab a file or collect any pertinent material. If the caller is annoyed by this question, your assistant can say, "Ms. Jones has asked me to always inquire what the call is about." If the caller's response is "It's a personal matter," your assistant should not press further.

PUTTING SOMEONE ON HOLD When a company telephone operator receives two calls simultaneously, she should say to the first caller, "I'm sorry but I must put you on hold for a minute to answer another call." She then answers the second call, puts that person on hold or takes his number, and then returns to the first caller to handle his request.

RECORDED MUSIC AND NEWS REPORTS Some companies play recorded music or give recorded news reports while callers are placed on hold. People seem to disagree violently over whether this soothes the nerves or irritates the waiting caller. Pure silence at least enables callers to read the newspaper or write a memo while holding.

TRANSFERRING CALLS It's very annoying—and sometimes time-consuming—to be transferred from one person to another within a business organization. Each time you speak to someone new you have to ask the same questions or explain your situation again. If a caller becomes sufficiently frustrated he may just hang up and the company may have lost a client or a sale. Train your staff to handle as many types of calls as possible in order to avoid transferring calls unless absolutely necessary. If a call must be transferred, the caller should be told why, the name of the person to whom he is being transferred, and that person's extension—in case he is cut off. If it's not possible to transfer the call, the employee should ask for the caller's name and telephone number so he can be called back.

If a caller starts to explain the purpose of his call and the employee knows he's the wrong person to talk to, he should interrupt and say, "Forgive me for interrupting, but that request/complaint is handled by Ms. Seymour in customer relations. Her extension is 410. I'll transfer you now."

WRONG NUMBERS All too often on discovering he's dialed the wrong number the caller will simply hang up instead of saying, "I'm sorry. I must have dialed the wrong number." Make it a point to apologize for having dialed the wrong number. On the other hand, when you are on the receiving end, ask, "What number are you calling?" That way, the caller will know whether he misdialed or wrote down the wrong number.

PERSONAL CALLS AT WORK Everyone has a life beyond the office. Some personal calls at work are inevitable. Many companies enforce stringent policies about personal calls during the business day. Policy or not, it's never wise to spend an excessive amount of time on the phone with friends or family. Your boss may come to the conclusion either that you do not have enough to do or that you are ignoring your work in favor of a social life. Keep personal calls short, ideally to two minutes or less. And, if someone else, especially a senior employee, enters your office while you are discussing a personal matter on the phone, quickly and discreetly conclude the conversation.

Working parents often check in with children or babysitters during the course of the day; this is best done at lunchtime or on breaks. If your child is away at boarding school or college, or traveling, and for some reason must call you collect at work, make certain you reimburse the company for the call. Personal long-distance calls should be charged to your credit card.

LONG-DISTANCE CALLS OUTSIDE THE OFFICE When you have a business appointment at someone else's office and need to make a long-distance call, always use a telephone credit card. If you offer cash, in all likelihood it will be refused.

SOME TELEPHONE DO'S AND DON'TS
- Give the caller your full attention: don't rustle papers or sound distracted.
- Do not chew gum, eat, or drink while on the telephone.
- If you get disconnected, it is the caller's responsibility to redial.

• If a coworker is on the telephone when you go to his office, stay outside the office unless he beckons you in. Better still, leave and go back later.

ANSWERING MACHINES AND VOICE MAIL

Any outgoing message on a business answering machine should be concise and clear. Let the caller know that you will return the call as soon as possible, or that the office is closed and will reopen at such and such a time and date. After recording your message, play it back to hear how it sounds. A business answering machine message should be authoritative, not silly. People are now familiar with these machines, so it's no longer necessary to instruct them to speak slowly and clearly, although it is wise to tell them to wait for the beep or series of beeps if that is the case. Resist background music or jokes—even if you are a musician or professional comedian. Design your message to capture business, not send it away. For example: "Hello. This is the Sunshine Company. Our hours are 9 A.M. to 5 P.M. Central Time, Monday through Friday. Please call back at that time," or add, "Please leave your name and number after the beep and we will return your call during business hours."

Or: "You have reached Communications House. For a trial copy of our newsletter, please leave your name and address after the beep. Be certain to include your ZIP code. If you need to speak to someone, leave your telephone number and we will return your call as soon as possible. Thank you."

Many larger offices have elaborate phone systems that include voice mail. This allows the caller to bypass the switchboard or central operator so that, if no one picks up after a number of rings, voice mail connects the caller to an answering machine on which he can leave a message. Voice mail annoys some callers, but the shrinking number of support staff able to take other people's messages is making it an accepted form of communication within the business community.

If your company uses a voice mail system, you will soothe irritated or frustrated callers by checking it frequently and returning all calls promptly.

CELLULAR TELEPHONES AND PAGERS

Telephone technology is progressing with dizzying speed. In many cities now, seeing people talking on their telephones as they walk down the street has become common. It has a deliciously pretentious look, but there isn't anything truly unmannerly about it. There are some public places, however, where the buzz of a cellular telephone calls forth righteous indignation. Phones (and beepers) must be turned off in church, at the movies, theater, concert, and opera. Nor should they be used in museums or libraries. A good rule of thumb is to turn off phones and beepers in any place where by custom the atmosphere is quiet.

It goes without saying that no executive should ever leave his phone on during a meeting in someone else's business office.

Restaurants are for dining and conversation and should not be treated as telephone booths. Turn off the sound of your beeper so it does not disturb the other diners. You can periodically check the window slot where the caller's telephone number appears to see if you have had a call.

A NOTE OF CAUTION: Cellular and cordless phones transmit by radio signals which can be picked up by anyone. Recently, politicians and other public figures have been embarrassed by tapes of their conversations being released to the public. A portable or cellular phone is not a wise choice when discussing sensitive information.

FAXES

Today almost every office has at least one fax machine. It should, of course, only be used for business purposes. When you send a fax, be certain your name, fax number, telephone number, address, and date are on your transmission. If you share the fax with your colleagues, take care not to read their incoming faxes. And, of course, don't fax anything confidential unless you know the recipient has his own private fax. Also avoid sending unnecessarily long or irrelevant documents which use up the recipient's paper and time.

PUBLIC SPEAKING

George Jessel once said, "The human brain is a wonderful thing. It starts working the moment you are born, and never stops until you stand up to speak in public." Most people—even those who do it for a living—are nervous when faced with an audience. Yet executives, business owners, lawyers, and others in the business world are often called upon to speak in front of groups, to make presentations, to introduce others, to give or accept awards. If you find yourself in such a position and are paralyzed with dread at the thought, it may help to take lessons with a public speaking consultant to gain confidence and learn the basic techniques.

For more on this subject, see "Public Speaking" in Chapter 8.

BUSINESS STATIONERY, CARDS, INVITATIONS

You will find most of what you need to know about stationery, envelopes, invitations, and how to address them (as well as details about engraving and printing) well covered in Chapter 8, "The Art of Communicating." Some stationery details are specific to the business world and therefore are discussed here.

STATIONERY

The standard business letterhead is 8½″ × 11″. It is placed in its matching envelope, folded twice, bottom edge first. Honorifics are not used on business stationery unless you have a professional title such as Doctor or Reverend. If you are a doctor, your name is written Harold Nicholas, M.D. (Your social stationery reads Dr. Harold Nicholas.) If you have a name like Lesley, which could be male or female, you may wish to put Mr. or Ms. in front of your name. Some companies include an executive's name on the company letterhead with his title in smaller lettering under it. Many executives supplement the company letterhead with personal business stationery. The correspondence card used for writing thank-you notes and other short messages has become increasingly popular.

BUSINESS CARDS

Business cards are given out to people to help remind them of who you are and where you can be reached. They can also be clipped to an enclosure in an envelope—perhaps a report, newspaper clipping, or photograph—or used as an enclosure card when sending a business present, but not for a personal gift.

Many companies have two conventional business cards: the general employee card and the executive card. Layouts vary widely according to company preference but the traditional style for the general employee card has the name and address of the company printed in the center, with the person's name in the lower left-hand corner. An executive's card has the person's name in the center with the title (vice-president, chairman, etc.) directly below it, and the company name and address in the lower left-hand corner. Company telephone and fax numbers appear in the lower right-hand corner.

Although imaginative business cards with unusual shapes are interesting and attention-getting, they can look cheap and are difficult to file or keep in a card case. If you wish to have an anomalous card, it should be professionally designed by a graphic artist and look sophisticated rather than merely unusual. The color of the card as well as the color of the ink should, of course, be coordinated with the company's stationery.

Depending on your work and how many cards you use for what purpose, it may be practical to have both engraved and printed cards.

Here are a few tips having to do with business cards:

- Use only clean and up-to-date cards.
- Always wait for a senior executive to offer his card first; then give him yours.
- With someone you've met casually, on a plane for example, wait until you part company before presenting your card in order not to appear pushy.
- When cards are exchanged in a group, give your card to everyone present so as not to slight someone.
- Be circumspect about presenting your card (or talking about busi-

ness) when having cocktails or dinner at someone's home or at a restaurant when the evening is a social one. You should never appear to be making a social event a business one, but, of course, if someone asks for your card, give it inconspicuously.

There are times when you may want to write a short message at the top of your business card, for instance when attaching it to a report or other material you are sending to a customer. To personalize the card, put a diagonal slash through your (engraved or printed) name and write something personal in ink above it.

INVITATIONS

There are occasions that call for a company party. It may be to honor a board member or a civic leader, to introduce a company president to the community, or to present a new merchandise line. When you give a business party, you want to be sure the style of the invitation reflects the company's image and is in keeping with the formality of the event. If you are uncertain about the design and layout of the invitation, stationers and printers can show you samples. Because of the cost, engraved invitations are limited to very special celebrations, perhaps a company's hundredth anniversary. Usually business invitations are printed on quality paper stock often with the company logo placed at the top. The company name and address appear on the upper left-hand corner of the envelope.

Avoid issuing an invitation in the name of the company—"The Sunshine Company requests the pleasure, etc." It is cold and impersonal. It's far better to issue the invitation in the name of a company official—"Seth Lee Hawkins, President, The Sunshine Company, requests the pleasure, etc."

If the invitation is sent with an enclosed R.s.v.p. card and envelope and cost is not a major consideration, have the return envelopes stamped. Even if an R.s.v.p. card is enclosed, it's a good idea to put an R.s.v.p. on the invitation as well. Then, if the recipient mislays the card, he has a name and telephone number to call.

BUSINESS ANNOUNCEMENTS

Sometimes you may want to communicate business news by sending out an announcement—when for example there is a company merger, a change of address or company name, when someone joins the firm or is promoted, or when a new company is formed. When sending an announcement to close friends or associates, you may personalize it by writing a short note on the card.

Announcements may be sent on cards (usually white or ecru) with or without the company logo engraved or embossed on them. Depending on the firm's budget, cards may be engraved, thermofaxed, or printed. The envelopes are either typed or handwritten. Preprinted labels are not appropriate in this case.

If you are the recipient of a business announcement, and the person sending it is a friend, it's nice to write or call in response to the news. The announcement of a new company would read:

Seth Lee Hawkins
Louise Lauren Smith
announce the formation of
Hawkins & Smith Publishers, Inc.

1033 West Lincoln Road
Des Moines, IA [ZIP code]
[telephone number]
[fax number]

An announcement sent to tell the business community that the firm has promoted an employee to be a new officer might read:

The Sunshine Company
is pleased to announce that
Martha S. O'Brien
has been named Executive Vice-President
October first

800 Lake Shore Drive
Chicago, IL [ZIP code]
[telephone number]
[fax number]

WRITTEN COMMUNICATION IN BUSINESS

Since the moment when Alexander Graham Bell invented the telephone, the well-written letter has become increasingly rare. In fact, many corporations lament the large number of young people entering the workplace incapable even of distinguishing between complete and incomplete sentences. Some of us write easily and well, but just as many of us find it an arduous and time-consuming task. If you do not have confidence in your writing skills it is in your best interest to educate yourself. Begin by reading *Elements of Style* by Strunk and White (Macmillan), a classic guide to good writing.

WHAT TO WRITE

Words committed to paper can have a powerful and lasting effect. And, unlike what we say to one another, we read and often reread business letters and memos. Therefore:

- Don't put anything in writing that you would be embarrassed to have read out loud.

- Take care not to write something you might want to change later. In the middle of negotiations or conflict, anger sometimes outweighs good sense.

- Put praise in writing; reserve a reprimand for face-to-face discussion.

- Follow up an important phone call with a letter that restates the key points.

- Keep file memos—written accounts of important actions or conversations you have had with others.

- Think carefully before you promise anything in writing.

- Write and send all forms of business communication promptly; meet your deadlines.

WHAT NOT TO WRITE

Much of yesterday's slang or jargon becomes, through widespread usage, tomorrow's accepted language. But wait until "tomorrow" before using it in a formal letter. Younger people should also be aware that men and women who grew up in a more formal era are far less accepting of slang.

- Although swear words have gained a degree of acceptability in recent years, they should *never* be used in a business letter—or any letter for that matter. They appear harsher on paper than when used in passing conversation, and it's foolish to risk a possible negative reaction to your letter by the reader.

- Rote phrases or words that are currently popular business jargon become tiresome when used too often. Take care to avoid overusing them.

- "Thanking you in advance," implies a presumption that the correspondent will *do* the favor. Instead say, "Your help will be appreciated," or even better, "Any help that you give me will be appreciated."

- "In fact." This phrase is often unnecessary and should be used sparingly to contradict a previous assertion: "Chris Jennings is, in fact, a man," is a reasonable response to the statement that Chris Jennings is a woman. Or it can also be used to emphasize a point, in this case the role he played at the conference: "Chris went to the sales conference. In fact, he was the key speaker."

THE LENGTH OF WHAT YOU WRITE

"Excuse the length of this letter. I had no time to write a short one."
Blaise Pascal

Cultivate the art of writing short business letters and memos. One way is to stick to the point. No one wants to be burdened by reading material that is wordy or repetitious or to have to struggle to understand (or find) the message. If your letters tend to run more than one and a half pages long, study them and begin taking out unnecessary phrases or words. If your sentences are long and complex, make them short and simple. Other points to keep in mind when writing business letters:

- The first paragraph should convey the point or objective of the letter or memo.
- A positive tone, even in a letter of rejection, is best.
- Avoid overused clichés or hackneyed phrases such as "in the fire," "state of the art," "net-net," "done deal," "coals to Newcastle," and "on the ball."
- Finally, check for grammar and spelling. Perhaps Montaigne overstated the case when he said, "Most of the grounds of the world's troubles are matters of grammar," but it's not overstating it to say that improper grammar and spelling errors imply that the writer is uneducated or careless. You certainly don't want either characterization. A business letter should convey that you know what to say and how to say it.

IMPROVING YOUR WRITING STYLE

You can develop a good business writing style by saving and reviewing any well-written letters you receive or by reading sample letters in letter-writing books. Or see the sample letters that follow. In addition, use these guidelines:

- Make a list of the points you want to cover in your letter before you start to write.
- Use descriptive phrases and an animated tone. A thesaurus will help you find descriptive words to enliven your prose.
- It's fine to add a little humor to your letters. Of course, the better you know the addressee, the easier it is to judge how much humor will be appreciated.
- Praise those who deserve praise. Everyone, including heads of state, welcomes a pat on the back.

THE FORMAT OF THE BUSINESS LETTER

Business letters, it goes without saying, should be neatly typed, properly spaced, and contain no spelling or grammatical errors.

THE SALUTATION In the past, before women held as many executive positions as they do today, the general salutation for a business letter if you didn't know whom to address it to was, "Dear Sir" or "Gentlemen." Today, however, you would address such a letter, "To Whom It May Concern." Of course, it's always more effective if you can find out the name of a specific individual to whom you can address the salutation.

The salutation in a formal business letter is followed by a colon, not a comma. The form of the salutation depends on how formal a person you are and how well you know the person you are writing to. Of course, if you are replying to a letter someone wrote to you, you can be guided by that person's salutation, unless the letter came from someone considerably older than you or someone who calls you by your first name whereas you address him by his title.

Here are the three salutations to consider:

- "Dear Mr. Thomas:" This salutation is used if you have not met the person, or you may have met but are not on a first-name basis. In the case of a woman, the customary salutation is "Dear Ms. Jordan," although "Mrs." or "Miss" is never incorrect.
- "Dear Michael Thomas:" A useful salutation if you have met the person and he is a peer but you do not know him well. It is less formal than using a title.
- "Dear Mike:" The salutation you use for friends and colleagues you are on a first-name basis with.

THE CLOSING The two most common closings to a business letter are "Sincerely" and "Sincerely yours." Naturally, if you are writing to a close business associate or a friend, you would use a less formal closing such as, "All the best" or "Best wishes."

Your name is typed four spaces below the closing. If your company title does not appear with your name on the letterhead, it is typed one space below your name.

You sign your name "Sally" or "Sally Jordan," depending on your relationship to the person you are writing.

THE BLOCK FORMAT The most formal style for a business letter is the block format, whereby the body of the letter is aligned to the left margin (paragraphs are not indented).

The spacing of a block letter is easy to follow: The recipient's name and address appear six spaces below the date; the salutation two spaces below the last line of the recipient's name and address; the body of the letter two spaces below the salutation; the closing two spaces below the body of the letter; and the letter writer's name four spaces below the closing.

[LETTERHEAD]

December 20, 1995

Mr. Michael Thomas
General Manager
XYZ Corporation
555 Lakeview Drive
Orange, NY 55555

Dear Mr. Thomas:

It was a pleasure to meet you on Tuesday. Your presentation was most impressive, and I look forward to continuing our discussion of the marketing plan on January 12th.

I am enclosing the materials we discussed.

Sincerely,

Sally Jordan
Vice-President

SJ/erg
Enclosure (1)
cc: Thomas C. Farkas

THE INDENTED FORMAT The indented format is less formal but the spacing is the same.

[LETTERHEAD]

Mr. Michael Thomas
General Manager
XYZ Corporation
555 Lakeview Drive
Orange, NY 55555

December 20, 1995

Dear Mr. Thomas:

    It was a pleasure to meet you on Tuesday. Your presentation was most impressive, and I look forward to continuing our discussion of the marketing plan on January 12th.

    I am enclosing the materials we discussed.

Sincerely,

Sally Jordan
Vice-President

SJ/erg
Enclosure (1)
cc: Thomas C. Farkas

OTHER BUSINESS LETTER CONVENTIONS

When a letter is typed by someone other than the sender, two lines below the typed name of the sender and flush with the left margin the sender's initials, upper case, should be typed, followed by the typist's initials, lowercase. The initials of the sender and the typist are separated by either a colon or a slash.

The word "enclosure" is used to indicate that something, such as a brochure, is being sent with the letter. "Enclosure" is typed on the line directly beneath the initials of the sender and typist. If there is more than one enclosure, the number is given in parentheses.

It is customary to send copies (they are not signed by the sender) of a business letter to whoever is mentioned in the letter or to someone who will be interested in its contents. True carbon copies are a thing of the past, so instead of the old abbreviation "cc," which stood for "carbon copy," a new abbreviation has gained favor and is used to indicate those to whom copies are being sent. It is the single letter "c," standing for "copied," short for "photocopied"; "c" or "cc" is typed directly below the initials of the sender and typist and is followed by the name or names of those to whom copies are being sent. Always place a check mark next to the name of the person to whom that particular copy is being sent. If you want a copy to go to someone, but don't want the recipient of the letter to know that person is being "copied," "bcc" for "blank carbon copy" appears on that particular copy.

TYPES OF BUSINESS LETTERS

In the course of doing business, or volunteer work, you will no doubt write and receive **thank-you letters**—for a job well done, for a lunch or presentation, for a company perk, gift, or party, or for a favor. Here are some sample sentences which you may incorporate into your own letters:

The beautiful silver bowl, engraved with my dates of service at the ABC Corporation, will always remind me of the many wonderful years we worked together. It has a place of honor on my mantel. I hope sometime soon you will come by to see it.

I heard today that you defended my position on the Abbott report at yesterday's board meeting. It is difficult to express my appreciation adequately in words, but I do want you to know that I hope sometime to be able to return your act of friendship.

Our annual picnic would never have been the great success it was without your hard work and creative talents. You and your staff pulled off a miracle—one we all appreciate.

The story you wrote for the *Chronicle* on our new product line was well done and accurate. Thank you for taking the time to interview me and for letting me tell you about our firm. I look forward to reading other pieces you plan to write on our local businesses.

The benefit, to which you gave us tickets, was great fun. Mike Thomas from advertising and his wife, my husband Ralph, and I will long remember the excellent dinner and the amusing speech the mayor made. We had a wonderful time and were pleased to represent the company at an event for such a worthy cause.

Thank you for lunch yesterday. I was delighted to meet you and to learn about your current project. It sounds like an exciting new venture—and I wish you great success. As we discussed, I'll contact you in October to continue our conversation about ways the XYZ Corporation might assist you in the future.

Thanks for lunch yesterday—and particularly for urging me to try the crème brûlée. You were right; you shouldn't count calories at restaurants with such splendid desserts! It was great to see you again. Your plans for expanding XYZ's business are exciting—and I hope we will be able to help. I'll call you next week with the information we discussed.

You will also find you are sending and receiving **letters of congratulation**—about a new job or a promotion, a merger, a speech, a marriage, or an adoption.

Congratulations! Your promotion is well deserved. I know the marketing department will benefit from your fresh ideas and great organizational skills. We will miss you in research. Much luck in your new position.

I slipped into the back of the auditorium today just as you were beginning your speech. Your delivery was excellent—both informative and entertaining. Everyone paid close attention. Many colleagues even took notes. Bravo for a job well done.

It's always thoughtful to write a **letter of encouragement** to a colleague or employee who is coping with a stressful situation or working on a difficult or complex task. Offer help if you can, or the very least, a reassuring word of support.

I just heard the news that you were let go from Parsons & Reid. Although it must have come as a shock, never forget how talented you are. You will undoubtedly find a new position where you will be greatly appreciated, so I hope you regard this only as a temporary setback. I'll call you soon to see if we can get together for lunch or dinner.

When someone at work suffers the loss of a family member or a close friend, take time to write a brief **condolence note.** Even if you are a junior employee, do not hesitate to write to a senior executive or the head of the company.

I just heard the news of your father's death and want you to know you are in my thoughts. In fact, all your friends in the East Coast division are thinking of you, wishing we could do something to be of help. Please do call on us if we can.

Whether you are resigning by choice or by request, your **letter of resignation** will remain in the company's files and may very well be read by someone with whom you will be doing business in the future. Therefore, keep your letter as positive as possible even if you are leaving the company in a rage. Be certain to indicate your appreciation of the opportunities you've been given and experiences you've gained at the company and express your regret at leaving. Give a specific reason for your resignation—but one that is either positive or neutral, such as that you are leaving to make a career change, to learn new skills, to relocate, not that you were unjustly treated or overlooked for promotion. Avoid saying that you are leaving for "personal reasons" as this could be interpreted as meaning you have emotional or family problems. And, if that were the case, it might be difficult for you to get an enthusiastic recommendation.

An exception would be if you are leaving to care for someone who is very ill.

It is with deep regret that I must submit my resignation to Larchmont Inc. as of January 1st. I am leaving to make a career change that I feel is timely. I have truly enjoyed my four years at the firm and have appreciated the opportunity to work with such a professional and dedicated group of people.

Thank you for your help and support over the years. I wish you and the other employees at Larchmont much success and I hope our paths cross again.

No matter how long you have been in business, **rejection letters** are never easy. Even the highest-level executives put them at the bottom of their to-do piles. Yet it is less kind to keep someone waiting to hear whether or not he has gotten a job or assignment than to say no right away. You can soften the blow by leaving the possibility of future collaboration open-ended, and try to praise whatever skills or work you admire. You may also explain why someone else was offered the position. The optimal rejection letter ends on an upbeat or positive note. Here are some sample rejection letters:

• *Most positive:*

It is with regret that I must inform you we have selected MWP as the advertising agency best suited for the toy campaign. We were truly impressed by your presentation, but in the end we felt it was more prudent to select a company with direct experience in that particular market.

I will certainly recommend your agency to others and perhaps sometime in the future we will have a chance to work together. Thank you for all of your efforts. I wish you much success.

• *Positive:*

Your presentation yesterday was commendable. However, at this time we are not prepared to commit the necessary funds to a venture with such a high risk factor.

We will keep you in mind for future consideration. I wish you the best of luck in your search for investors.

• *Least positive:*

It was a pleasure to meet you when you applied for the position of marketing director. However we have selected another candidate who has had more specific training in this particular area.

I hope very much you'll find a job to your liking soon.

Follow-up letters are warranted on a number of occasions: to summarize a discussion, to take negotiations a step further, to remind someone that you are waiting for information or an answer, or simply to keep in touch.

Thanks for taking the time to meet with me on October 19th. Although our product does not meet your specific needs at this time, I found our discussion to be fruitful, and I hope we will be able to assist you some time in the future.

I'm enclosing a report produced by ABC. *Textbooks for the '90s* examines the issues facing textbook publishers and the necessity of producing books that meet the changing needs of school districts across the United States. I hope you'll find it interesting and useful.

Just a brief note to remind you that I'm waiting for your background information on the Rosen Company. This looks like a terrific opportunity. We should get back to them within the next two weeks.

IF A LETTER IS WRITTEN IN YOUR ABSENCE

If you are away from your office, you may want your secretary to answer certain letters explaining that you will respond more fully when you return. For example:

I am acknowledging on Mr. Thomas's behalf your letter to him of January 11th. He is out of the office for several days and will be in touch with you when he returns.

or, if you are ill:

I know Mr. Thomas will appreciate having heard from you. He will answer your letter next week when he is back in the office.

If a letter from you is signed in your absence, the initials of the person who has signed your name go after the signature. The phrase: "(signed in his/her absence)" may be added in parentheses, but it is not necessary.

INTEROFFICE MEMOS

Memos—short business notes—enable you to summarize a meeting, a report, an event, an idea. They are also a useful way to communicate with employees, to give praise, or to respond to inquiries. In a well-written memo, the topic is immediately obvious to the reader and indicates what response, if any, is expected.

Each office has its own preprinted memo paper. Interoffice memos include the date, the name of the recipient or recipients, and the sender. Salutations are never used in the memo format. Copies are sent to everyone mentioned in the memo or whose responsibilities will be affected by its content. Like good letters, memos should be brief and to the point.

Memos may be sent to an individual or to an entire staff. Among the topics that might be in a staff memo format are: a new no-smoking policy, the holiday and vacation schedule for the year, the news that the company has posted a profit, a thank you to the staff for the successful launching of a new product.

The typical memo looks something like this:

MEMO FOR: Department heads

RE: Fire Drill

DATE: October 17, 1995

> There will be three unannounced fire drills between now and December 31. Please appoint a fire warden and one substitute for your division and have both report to my office for a brief meeting at 11 A.M., October 25. In the meantime, send my secretary, Alice, the names of your two wardens and their extensions.

Your name

Title

BUSINESS ENTERTAINING

Before reading the following entry, you may want to refer to Chapter 2, which gives specific information on planning a buffet dinner, reception, cocktail party, etc.

Blending business with pleasure creates a relaxed way to get to know colleagues, to create good will, and, most important, to cement professional relationships. This can happen at a cocktail or dinner party, a baseball game, or a summer picnic, and has become very much a part of today's working world. Regardless of the reason, whether you are celebrating the opening of a new branch office or achieving a sales goal or hosting a large party or fund-raiser to help make a favorable impression in the community, when you entertain for business you want to do it right.

Depending upon your company's budget (or, if it's your own firm, *your* budget), you can entertain simply and economically with a breakfast or lunch in your company or executive dining room, at a modest restaurant, or with a drink after work. In some cities, tea at a hotel or club has become popular. If you wish to impress an important prospective client, you can invite him to lunch at a really fine restaurant or at your club. If you can afford to tip the scales, consider buying tickets to a popular sports event, such as the World Series or the Super Bowl, or to a Broadway play or the opera, preceded or followed by dinner. Another suggestion, but not quite as exciting, is dinner at your home.

Here are descriptions of the most popular forms of business entertaining:

THE BUSINESS LUNCH

THE ROLE OF THE HOST Remember that the business lunch, although social, is a business occasion as well and anything you do or say reflects not only upon you but also upon your company or firm.

When you invite someone to a business lunch, offer several choices of restaurants—you want to make it geographically convenient—and one or two possible dates. If you know your guest likes Japanese food, consider including a Japanese restaurant among the choices. But suggest only restaurants you know are good (or, better yet, where you are known) so you won't be in for any unexpected surprises. A Chicago insurance man had a surprise when he invited a prospective client to an Italian restaurant near Lake Shore Drive that had received rave reviews. When they arrived, the executive discovered, much to his horror, that it was a "family style" restaurant with everyone sitting at long tables, a dozen or so diners at each, and no elbow room or privacy. The food was excellent, but it wasn't the right atmosphere in which to discuss business. When it comes to deciding on a restaurant, choose one that you know is quiet so you can talk without having to shout. And you don't want to sit too close to another table, especially if you have something confidential to discuss.

If you are entertaining a younger client (or anyone with a healthy appetite) avoid restaurants specializing in nouvelle cuisine where three asparagus spears tied together with a scallion stem constitute a salad. On the other hand, older people and those on diets may be put off by a heavy lunch. Also keep physical constraints in mind. If you know your guest has difficulty walking, stay clear of restaurants with split-level dining rooms. And take only the agile to a Japanese restaurant where diners may have to either kneel or sit on the floor.

If your client smokes and you do not, either tell him that you never sit in the smoking areas of restaurants—in which case he will not be able to smoke during lunch—or, if you are not bothered by smoke, you may offer to sit in the smoking section. Conversely, if you are the smoker and your client is not, the polite thing to do is to make the reservation in nonsmoking and leave your cigarettes behind. These days, because many people feel inhaling smoke is almost as harmful as smoking itself, smokers are apt to have to do the compromising.

The morning of the lunch, you or your assistant should reconfirm the date with both your client and the restaurant.

At the lunch: Since all aspects of restaurant etiquette, including the role of the host and guest, and ordering wine, are covered in Chapter 1 (see "Restaurant" under "Behavior in Public Places"), they will not be repeated here. What follows are the specific areas of restaurant etiquette that have to do with business entertaining.

As the host, arrive first. If your client has not arrived within twenty minutes of the appointed time, call his office. If a half hour or so passes and he has still not arrived, either order lunch for yourself or, if you prefer, leave. Explain the situation to the waiter, asking him to keep an eye out for your client in case he arrives after you depart. You should give the waiter a tip for tying up the table. An appropriate amount would be five dollars in a modest restaurant, ten to fifteen dollars in an expensive one.

While you are waiting for your client, you may want to have a drink at the bar or at your table. When your client does arrive, offer him a drink. If he declines, you can say, "I'm planning on having a wine spritzer. Are you sure you wouldn't like something?" In today's health- and weight-conscious world, alcoholic drinks at lunchtime are usually limited to one, particularly at a business lunch.

While there's no protocol that says when you start talking business, it's usually social conversation until the main course is on the table, and after that business takes over.

When you leave the restaurant, as the host, it's your responsibility to pay the coatroom attendant tip for you and your client.

THE ROLE OF THE CLIENT If you are the person who has been invited to a business lunch, respond promptly. *Never* suggest bringing someone along to a business lunch unless there's a particular reason why you feel that person could make a valuable contribution to the discussion.

The morning of the lunch, if you do not hear from your host, you or your assistant should call to reconfirm.

Sometimes it is necessary to cancel a lunch date at the last minute. As soon as you know you cannot make it, call and give the exact reason. Apologize and suggest rescheduling. A trustee of an Ohio college who had to cancel a lunch date with the provost at the last minute sent a club sandwich and flowers to the provost's office with a note that read, "I thought these flowers and the sandwich from my favorite deli might make the fact you had to stay in for lunch a bit more pleasant. Thanks for being so understanding." This thoughtful touch made up for any annoyance the provost might have felt.

At the lunch: If you arrive at the restaurant before your host, the maître d' will show you to the table. Officially, you wait for your host before ordering a drink or eating a roll, but if your host is a longtime friend, there's no reason why you shouldn't have a drink. Again, if you order a drink, best to keep it to one.

When it's time to leave the restaurant, your host should tip the coatroom attendant for both your coats. If he fails to do so, you will have to ante up.

LUNCH AT THE OFFICE When a business lunch is held in the office, you can assume it will be a genuine working lunch, consisting of sandwiches and salad. Of course, if you'd rather, and time allows, you can always order from a takeout restaurant. Keep a menu or two in your office just for that purpose. If you entertain frequently in your office, have a supply of china plates, cups and saucers, and large paper napkins on hand.

THE BUSINESS BREAKFAST

There are many advantages to the business breakfast, the first and foremost being that it is quicker than lunch or dinner, and, second, it's less expensive. Be certain, however, that whomever you are planning to invite is an early morning person. Some people much prefer lunch to breakfast.

AFTERNOON TEA

Afternoon tea, particularly for female executives in urban areas, has become increasingly popular. It takes place sometime between three-thirty and five-thirty, so it, too, imposes a welcome time constraint and, except for perhaps a small glass of sherry, doesn't involve alcohol. You can certainly invite a man to tea, but it's probably best if such invitations are issued only to a man you know well enough to gauge how comfortable he will feel in this setting.

THE BUSINESS DINNER

A business dinner is usually more of a social occasion than breakfast or lunch and the setting is more formal. There are two types of business dinners: ones with spouses and ones without. If spouses are not specifically included in the invitation, don't ask if you can bring yours along.

If you are new to the company or a younger executive, it's best not to invite your boss and his or her spouse to dinner unless you also know one another socially. In all circumstances, you must use good judgment in determining whether it is appropriate to invite your boss or other senior executives for a meal. It depends upon your position in the company. In general, if you are an executive and have been with the company for some time, it is acceptable to invite your boss and spouse to a cocktail party. However, if you are uncertain, don't.

PAYING THE BILL

The person who initiates the invitation to a business meal pays the bill. If a male guest being entertained by a woman tries to pay (which he should not), the woman should say, "Thanks for your offer but this is on the company."

When two colleagues dine together, the senior one usually pays, unless it was agreed upon ahead of time that they would share the bill.

THE BUSINESS RECEPTION

Often a company or an organization holds a large reception. If the purpose of the reception is to introduce a new president or CEO, you'll have to decide whether or not to have a receiving line. There is no need to have one if there are fewer than fifty guests. If there is no line, several people from the company should be assigned to introduce all guests to the new president. These staff people should also introduce guests to one another.

If there are more than fifty guests, a receiving line is practical as it means everyone has a chance to meet the guests of honor and vice versa. The line can be located wherever seems most convenient as long as it does not block the flow of traffic.

Be selective as to who will stand in the line and keep it as short as possible. Obviously the person being introduced, the host (sometimes there will be more than one host), along with other top management, such as the chairman of the board, will be in the line. More difficult is the question of whether or not to include spouses. The top executive's spouse certainly may be included, and in the case of a reception to introduce a new president, for example, that person's spouse would also stand in the line, although including spouses indicates a social rather than a strictly business decision.

If you are in the receiving line, do not hold a drink. Nor should guests have drinks in hand when they go through the line.

POINTS TO KEEP IN MIND WHEN YOU RECEIVE A BUSINESS INVITATION

- Respond to all invitations immediately. It is rude not to respond at all or to wait until the last minute.
- The invitation is only for the person to whom it is addressed. Don't ask if you can bring your spouse or a friend.
- If the invitation says "not transferable," do not hand it over to someone else.
- If the invitation reads "and guest" you may bring someone; if it's a dinner invitation, call whoever is handling the acceptances, and give the name of your guest.
- If your spouse has also been invited but cannot attend, respond by saying, "I'm delighted to accept; however my husband/wife will be out of town that evening."

A WORD ABOUT OFFICE PARTIES

In recent years, company Christmas or holiday parties have become more restrained than formerly. Less liquor is served, hours are shorter, and there are fewer embarrassing moments, fewer people staggering home. Regardless of the size, type, or length of an office party:

- Remember that, whether you are host or guest, your manners are on public view.
- Never drink too much.
- Don't consider the occasion as an opportunity to kiss everyone, and certainly not on the lips.
- Don't dress outrageously.
- Do talk with people from other departments, not just with your own group of friends.
- Do remember to thank the CEO, or whoever hosted the event when you leave. While not obligatory, if you follow up with a brief note of thanks, it will certainly be appreciated.

Some offices celebrate each employee's birthday. Care should be taken that these celebrations do not get out of hand or take up too much time. A small firm may want to serve a birthday cake and coffee after lunch, for example, and perhaps give the employee a card signed by everyone. In larger organizations, the event should be celebrated only by close friends, who, for instance, might decide to take the birthday person out for lunch.

Sometimes coworkers join together to purchase a present for a colleague—for an expectant mother, for example, or for someone who has earned a degree or reached a special birthday. Only close friends of the honoree should be approached for money and then it should be for a manageable amount. Whoever is collecting the money should make the request in a tactful way by asking for "a few dollars," or saying, "People are giving anywhere from five to fifteen dollars." If you are asked to give money toward an office present and you don't know the person well or feel it's beyond your budget, you should decline by saying, "Thanks but I just can't afford to right now," or, "I don't really know Sally very well so I'll pass this time."

MEETINGS AND CONVENTIONS

England may be known as a nation of shopkeepers; Americans are certainly a nation of meeters and conventioneers. It's an old tradition with us that may have begun with the New England town meeting. Naturally, some meetings are a waste of time while others are extremely productive. The ones that work have a purpose, are tightly run, and both the leaders and participants are polite, come prepared, and know and abide by the rules. The bible of meeting protocol is a small book entitled *Robert's Rules of Order*, which carefully spells out the guidelines for how a meeting is run as well as how participants should behave.

THE PURPOSE OF THE MEETING

A meeting should have a goal. It may be to communicate information, to instruct or train personnel, to set policy, to come up with (brainstorm) an idea or plan, to coordinate a plan or effort, to review progress, to solve a problem or reconcile a conflict. Most meetings combine two or more of these goals.

THE ROLE OF THE MEETING CHAIRMAN

The chairman is the person who is most responsible for determining the success or failure of a meeting. Not only does he run the meeting, he also draws up the agenda and largely decides who is invited, and he or his assistant sees to it that the meeting is scheduled at a convenient time. The chairman also introduces the participants to one another, makes certain that the meeting moves along at a steady pace, and sees that everyone has a chance to speak. If the meeting is a long one, he calls for a break every two hours so participants can take a breather, move about, use the rest rooms, make telephone calls, get fresh cups of coffee.

The chairman also sees to it that people speak in turn and that disagreements do not turn into screaming matches—in other words, that courtesy and professional behavior prevail. And he is responsible at the end of the meeting for summarizing what has taken place and, shortly thereafter, for distributing a written summary to all who attended. The summary should mention by name those who offered ideas, proposed solutions, or helped organize the gathering. It should also indicate what follow-up action will be taken.

Another hat the chairman must wear is that of a diplomat. He has to smooth ruffled egos and be sensitive to feelings and aware of the pecking order. For instance, if someone in a position of authority is completely wrong about a specific point, the chairman should discuss this with the individual after the meeting, rather than undermining his authority in front of others. If anyone presents an idea and it's obvious he has insufficient knowledge of the subject or is laboring under false assumptions, the chairman can say, "If I understand you correctly, I'm not sure you have all the background information necessary here. To keep on schedule, I'd like to get back to this point at the end of the meeting if we have time or we can talk about it after the meeting."

It's an unfortunate fact that people with potentially good ideas often don't speak up at meetings and instead approach the chairman *afterward*. Behind such reticence is often a fear that they will be publicly embarrassed or criticized. It may mean that the employee lacks confidence, but it may also mean that the chairman has not created an atmosphere that encourages participation and is conducive to free and open discussion.

A skilled chairman can diminish this "fear factor" by always acknowledging everyone's ideas positively and by being sure never to ridicule participants or allow others to do so. He must always encourage individuals to speak up, especially those who are shy. He can do this by saying something like, "Sam, you're probably our most informed person on the cash flow situation. Could you tell the others where we stand this month?" Or, "Ellen, I know you've only been with the company a short time, but perhaps you could give us your ideas on the proposed marketing plan."

The chairman should also be alert to head off those other people who are so sure of themselves that they will monopolize a meeting while expounding on a bad idea. If someone really goes off on a tangent, the chairman should say, "That's quite interesting, although there are a couple of reasons why it might not work. But by all means let's discuss it after this session."

The chairman also decides how to deal with latecomers. The toughest, most experienced leaders begin meetings exactly on time or at most five minutes late. If a latecomer's contribution is absolutely crucial and must be made at the beginning of the meeting, then the chairman will decide to wait for him. If someone is habitually late to meetings (or seminars), the wise chairman will discuss this matter with the laggard in private.

THE AGENDA Once it is determined that there is a need for a meeting, the chairman draws up an agenda. It is basically a list of the topics to be covered. In the following example the meeting is to evaluate current sales, analyze why sales have increased, and set new sales goals. It might look like this:

MEETING: Sales staff and marketing directors
TIME: 8:30–10:00 A.M., Tuesday, September 1st
PLACE: Conference room; 4th floor
(Juice, coffee, and Danish will be served)

AGENDA

   A. Review third-quarter sales.   (20 minutes)
       • Presentation by director of sales regarding overall data and trends.
       • Report by direct marketing personnel on increase in response ratio.
   B. Open discussion on third-quarter sales data, and how it's best interpreted.   (10 minutes)
   C. Set goals for coming fiscal year.   (15 minutes)

- Report by director of marketing on future issues that could affect sales.
  D. Open discussion.   (25 minutes)
  E. Summary and follow-up assignments.   (20 minutes)

Agenda topics are arranged in order of priority. Then, if for some reason the meeting runs longer than expected, those topics that must be postponed will be the least important ones. Each topic is also allotted a specific amount of time to avoid unnecessary discussion. The agenda, along with any necessary background information, is distributed to participants well in advance of the meeting so they can do their homework.

DECIDING WHOM TO INVITE The size of a meeting is largely determined by its purpose. For instance, a meeting that reviews progress requires that all those who hold positions of responsibility and are involved in that progress attend, whether that means three people or fifteen. Clearly, a meeting with too many or too few people may be less effective. It's up to the chairman to determine the suitable size, and experience generally proves to be the best guide.

Although there are no hard and fast rules, generating an attendance list using a two-step process works well. First, put down the names of those whose jobs or responsibilities could be affected by the meeting as well as those who will make important contributions. Then review the list to see if any of these people can be eliminated. When making up the list, consider how individuals work together. For instance, if you've invited half a dozen people to brainstorm an idea and you know two of them are adversaries, their conflict might dominate the meeting. Evaluate whether department subordinates or assistants should be informed of the content of the meeting from their department heads. Finally, be sensitive to hierarchy. If you invite subordinates you must invite the head of the department, or if you invite most of the key management you must invite all. If you cannot invite everyone from a certain level or department, then rotate invitations so that eventually everyone will attend a meeting.

SEATING At many board meetings, seats are assigned and name cards are placed on the table before the meeting begins. Smaller and less formal meetings usually do not have assigned seats and, if this is the case, participants stand and wait for the chairman to indicate where they should be seated. If the chairman simply sits down with no comment, then everyone else does the same. Unless you are a high-ranking member of the group, do not take a place next to the chairman—these are considered the two best seats. This custom evolved over centuries when the king's worst enemy was seated on his left and his closest ally on the right. This assured that the king had control of his enemy's sword hand, the right, while the king's ally had control of the king's sword hand. This is the genesis of the phrase "right-hand man."

THE ROLE OF THE PARTICIPANT

PRESENTING YOUR IDEAS A meeting offers participants a chance to shine, often in the presence of people with whom they do not work on an everyday basis. Once you receive an agenda, it's your responsibility to review it and consider what contribution you can make to the meeting. If you have some ideas, make a list and take time to prepare your thoughts thoroughly beforehand.

There are times, however, when it's best to be silent. If you are new to an organization or in a fairly subordinate position, don't be the first to speak up. Instead, listen to what other, more experienced people have to say, then if you do want to make a point take care not to talk too long. If you are unfamiliar with the topic under discussion, it is better not to speak than to show that you are uninformed.

Tact when proposing a new solution or idea is essential, but don't undermine your idea by introducing it with a negative, such as "This might not be right," or, "I'm not sure if this is the solution, but . . ." Instead, be positive: "I've given this some thought, and I believe . . ." or, "According to my research, I consider . . ." To soften suggestions even further, you can use the editorial "we" instead of "I." But don't overdo this locution; it can sound pretentious.

DISAGREEING WITH OTHERS Typically, the more seniority you have, the more you can say, "I disagree." However, meetings are convened for the purpose of gathering viewpoints and assembling the knowledge of a number of people. If everyone at the meeting agreed on every point there wouldn't be much purpose to the meeting.

If someone's opinion is dominating the meeting and you know that there is a sound basis for disagreement, it's your obligation to raise the alternative view. You can exercise diplomacy in presenting the other side by introducing your statement with a tactful qualifier, such as "I believe we should also consider . . ." or "We may have overlooked . . ." or "Perhaps we could view this from another angle." Again, if you use the "we" rather than the "I" you may generate a cooperative spirit.

HOW TO SHINE AT A MEETING

- Prepare thoroughly.
- Be on time.
- Stand until asked to sit.
- If you're not introduced to others by the chairman or other executives, introduce yourself.

- If you are a junior or a new employee, listen to others before speaking.
- Volunteer when you have a contribution to make.
- Couch your ideas as recommendations, not orders.
- If you must disagree, do so diplomatically.
- Don't be afraid to be wrong. No one's right all the time.
- Work with the group toward a consensus.
- Look at others when they are speaking, not down at the table.
- Never let boredom show. Take care not to fidget, slump in your chair, drum your fingers on the table, or play with your hair or glasses.
- If the host does not offer refreshments, don't ask for them.
- Place your dirty coffee cup, napkin, or glass on a side table, if there is one, rather than leave them on the meeting table.
- If soft drinks are served in a can, pour the soda into a glass or paper cup; do not drink from the can.
- If it was a helpful meeting, let the chairman know. Say something specific, such as that it cleared up a given matter, set the record straight, or produced some effective ideas.

CHECKLIST FOR A MEETING

If you are in charge of setting up a meeting, look at the room or rooms where it will be held several days in advance. If this isn't possible because the meeting is at an out-of-town location, try to get as much physical information as possible about the rooms from the convention coordinator. Check the size of the table or tables, the number of chairs, the lighting and ventilation. If the meeting is in a difficult-to-locate section of a building, you may want to include directions for finding it when you send around the agenda. If building security requires a list of those attending, make certain this is taken care of well in advance. If name cards or badges are being used, these too must be made out ahead of time.

Among the items you should check to see if you will need at your meeting are:

- Badges or name tags. Although you do not write Mr. or Ms. on a name tag, if someone is a doctor or dignitary (mayor, senator, etc.) you should include such titles. If there are people from several different companies attending the meeting, write the company name under the person's name.
- Copies of the agenda
- Writing pads
- Sharp pencils

- Pencil sharpener
- Paper clips, stapler, rubber bands, cellophane tape, scissors, small sticker pads
- Glasses and pitchers of water
- Lectern
- Microphone
- Blackboard, chalk, pointer
- Audiovisual material, such as a video projector
- Typewriter or word processor and paper, printer, photocopier
- Expense voucher forms
- Flowers for speaker's table
- Cloth for speaker's table
- Cups, saucers, teaspoons, coffee and tea (regular and decaffeinated), milk, sugar, lemon
- Juice, soft drinks, including diet drinks
- Finger pastries, Danish, muffins
- Napkins

CONVENTIONS

If you've ever attended a convention, more than likely you have seen some rather embarrassing behavior from the person who drinks too much, the flirt, the executive who berates the waiter, or the goof-off who spends more time socializing than paying attention to business. It's easy to let go at a convention, especially one that is held out of town. But bear in mind that whatever you do will be observed by others and may be reported to the company management. Unscheduled convention time is not personal or private time. Even when you're lounging beside the pool, joining someone for a drink, or teeing up on the golf course, remember that, although you may be in a relaxed atmosphere, you're still in a business setting. America's cowboy wit and philosopher, Will Rogers, said it best: "There is no better place in the world to find out the shortcomings of each other than a conference."

To avoid revealing your shortcomings, here are some points to keep in mind when you attend a convention:

- You may wear more casual dress during nonmeeting time, but it should always be neat and appropriate. Don't suddenly reveal a whole new side of your personality or a whole lot more of your body. Leave the skimpy bikini at home. Both men and women should bring conservative "convention" bathing suits and cover-up tops to wear over them.

The convention agenda usually spells out whether events require formal attire or casual clothing. If you are unsure, you may call the person in charge and inquire about appropriate attire so you can pack accordingly.

- Drink moderately and don't smoke where smoking isn't welcome. Never use drugs.

- Avoid being too aggressive when participating in any sport or recreational activity. You don't have to win every set or round to prove you're a great employee.

- Treat everyone—regardless of his or her position—with respect and courtesy. If the hotel lost your reservation or the airline misplaced your luggage, deal with the situation calmly. A temper tantrum directed at the desk clerk makes a poor impression on others who are in the lobby or arriving at the same time.

- Don't be a sponge. When it's called for, pick up the tab for your own drinks or meals.

- Participate in all sessions except those you can honestly justify not attending. Conventions are a huge company expense and yours deserves its money's worth.

- If spouses are not attending, don't bring along a companion.

- Finally, remember that a convention is not a vacation; it's business.

RECORDING THE EVENT Take notes to use in preparing a memo for your immediate supervisor to convey the highlights of the convention and the information you have acquired.

CONVENTION EXPENSE ACCOUNT ETIQUETTE Before you attend a convention, you and your supervisor should agree upon a clearly defined budget. Some companies give their employees a per diem dollar amount while others will trust them to spend wisely. If no one offers guidelines, you might say, "Naturally, I'll try to keep expenses within reason, but can you give me an idea of what you consider reasonable?" Find out whether you are expected to frequent expensive restaurants, to entertain clients or customers, or to take a five-dollar bus rather than a thirty-dollar cab from the airport to the convention site. Whom are you supposed to treat and how much should you spend?

The question of who is picking up the tab can be unclear at a convention. If you've been invited to join someone for dinner, is that person acting as host or is he simply being friendly and trying to include you in the group? If it is a large group and several people have been responsible for its ultimate formation, who should pay? It's not always clear. You may have to learn from experience. Generally, if someone has personally invited everyone at the table, taken charge of ordering the meal and overseeing the evening, then he can be expected to pay the bill.

If the meal has no clear host, the most senior executive present offers to pay.

Sometimes members of a group decide beforehand to split the check. When just a small group of peers are dining together, play it safe and offer to pay or at least split the bill. Regardless of the size of the group, if you've been invited as someone's guest and have asked and received permission to bring along one of your colleagues, you should offer to pick up your guest's portion of the bill.

Inevitably, from time to time you will get stuck paying for a large group of people. If this happens, you may feel uneasy when it comes time to turn in your expense account. If so, attach a brief note of explanation. Most companies would rather have their employees appear gracious than cheap.

Be certain to keep a careful record of all your expenses. And it shouldn't be but is necessary to add: don't cheat on or pad your expenses at a convention or anywhere else. Never inflate your written account of cash expenses such as tips, taxis, etc. And by all means, never use receipts that aren't yours or include your spouse's expenses if you're expected to pay for them yourself.

WHEN SPOUSES OR FRIENDS ATTEND Participants in some conventions are encouraged to bring their spouses. Often a program will be set up to keep them entertained: tours of historic sites or other points of interest, exercise classes, lessons, special demonstrations, exhibits, or lectures. They may even be invited to sit in on some of the business sessions. And then, of course, they attend all the social functions. They should plan to participate as much as possible in the activities.

Spouses attending a convention must realize that the impression they make can be very important to a husband's or wife's career. They should make it a point to know something about the company and its business and to be able to speak intelligently about topics of general concern. And, of course, they should always be friendly with the employees and other spouses. Any spouse whose aim is to pull his or her husband or wife away from the meetings to play tennis or go nightclubbing or who doesn't want to socialize with the other spouses should stay home.

An unmarried couple attending a convention will have to use their judgment about sharing a room. If they sense disapproval or know that the company is very conservative, they should check into two separate rooms and pay for one of them themselves.

BUSINESS TRAVEL

Someone once said that travel is something you enjoy three weeks after unpacking. Not if you know how to do it well. In fact, business travel can be tremendously exciting. It provides an opportunity to learn, to meet new people, to see new places, to expand the possibilities for the ways you do business. When you are asked to travel for your company you become an instant ambassador, representing the firm and its employees. And when you go abroad, you also represent the United States to foreign businessmen and women.

TAXIS, LIMOUSINES, AND CARS

Everybody winds up in a taxi at one time or another. Keep these simple rules in mind when you travel in one for business. Give the best seat to the senior employee or the client. That is the seat nearest the door you enter. The worst seat is in the middle if there are three passengers. In a limousine, the junior employee rides in the jump seat. The senior employee pays the fare. If your company has a car service, use it only if you are authorized to do so. In urban areas, for example, employees who work late at night are often entitled to use a car service to take them home safely.

Whenever you travel in someone else's car, treat it as you would their home. That means don't prop your feet on the dashboard, drop food on the seat or floor, leave papers about, or slam the doors.

AIRLINE TRAVEL

It seems as though airports and airplanes bring out the worst in people, and when there's no escape an annoying individual quickly becomes obnoxious. When you have to spend several hours in a closed compartment with a hundred or so people, courtesy is essential. To make your flight and that of your fellow passengers as pleasant as possible:

- Take care not to spill over into your neighbor's seat. You have one seat assignment, so keep your arms, legs, and belongings within it— unless you're lucky enough to have an empty seat next to you. Don't ask to store your carry-on luggage under your neighbor's seat back if he isn't using it. It's his space for his legs.

- Carry your garment bag with care so you don't knock into others ahead of or behind you.

- If you wear a stereo headphone set, make sure its sound isn't leaking. This is extremely annoying to the person next to you. Take it off, turn it down, or buy better equipment for your next trip.

- Don't use the fact that there's no escape on a plane to pester someone sitting next to you, to flirt, to carry on in any way if your neighbor is clearly not interested.

- If someone is reading, working, or has his eyes closed, he doesn't want to talk. Don't try to engage him in conversation. This is probably the number one faux pas of airline passengers.

- If you're one of the last to board, ask the stewardess to help you find a free compartment instead of jamming your belongings into an already full overhead storage area.

- Wipe the rest-room sink clean.
- Return used coffee cups and other utensils to the stewardess. Don't leave them on the floor or in the seat pocket.

Many people are frightened of flying yet must use the friendly skies for business. If you are one of these, take a training session on airline safety. These are offered from time to time by some of the airlines and travel agents for their clients. By knowing what to do in case of trouble you may find flying less frightening. Among the things you can do are request an aisle seat or one close to an emergency exit, pay attention to the instructions given by the flight attendants in case of an emergency, and listen to them when they are pointing out safety rules and exit doors.

If you travel a great deal on business you've undoubtedly accumulated frequent flyer points. Check with your company's travel coordinator or your boss to see if you may use these for personal trips or if they must go toward future business flights.

Since deregulation and increased security measures, airplanes rarely arrive on time. Consequently, schedule your appointments on the assumption that the plane will be an hour late. If you have an early morning meeting out of town, it's usually best to arrive the night before. Not only will you feel more refreshed, but you're more likely to be at the meeting when it begins.

To save time, get your boarding pass and seat assignment from your travel agent before you leave for the airport. Keep all reservation confirmation numbers—for flight, hotel, and car rental—handy.

Always wear business attire on the plane and, if possible, bring only carry-on luggage. Lost luggage is a significant problem for the business traveler. If you wear jeans or sporty clothes and arrive in New York to find your luggage went to Detroit, you will have to move fast and spend a great deal of money to arrive at your meeting properly dressed. Even if you carry your luggage with you, dress professionally: the CEO of your competitor might be in the next seat.

It's a good idea to join an airline's club so you can use its lounge while waiting to board or during stopovers. These lounges are far more comfortable than the airport's public facilities and they have many services: telephones, fax and copying machines, free coffee, drinks, and snacks; some even have showers.

Don't forget to pack: an umbrella, an extra pair of glasses, an alarm clock, an address book, your business cards, stationery, and stamps.

CONDUCTING BUSINESS Laptop computers and phones aboard airplanes have made it easier to work while you're traveling. Both the short commute and the cross-country trip offer many executives a chance to catch up with work or prepare for the next meeting. However, you should never procrastinate and count on the two or three hours it will take you to get there for your preparation time. You might be seated next to a screaming child, or turbulence could keep you buckled into your seat with trays up.

A plane is not an office. If you're traveling with a business associate, it's not fair to use the flight to bring up an unpleasant subject or to berate or criticize your companion, who will have no privacy in which to regain his or her composure.

Someday it might happen: you will find yourself sitting next to a business V.I.P. you've always wanted to meet. Respect his or her privacy. If you buttonhole a business person with an unwelcome sales pitch for you or your firm, you're more likely to make an unfavorable impression than a pleasing one. Don't begin the conversation by presenting your business card. If the V.I.P. acknowledges your pleasantries, you may introduce yourself and your company, but after that try to respond only to his questions or interest and don't force information on him.

FOUR TIPS FOR ARRIVING REFRESHED

1. To prevent dehydration, avoid caffeine and alcohol, and drink plenty of water.
2. Adjust your watch to the time at your destination when you board the plane and try to regulate your sleeping and eating accordingly.
3. Don't wear restrictive clothing or uncomfortable shoes. It's hard enough to be comfortable on an airplane.
4. Stretch your legs by walking about the plane every hour or two.

HOTELS

The majority of hotels cater to *business* travelers, offering value for money and the combined conveniences of a home with those of an office. Yet many travelers are unaware of or don't take advantage of all these services. The concierge is there to help you make local travel arrangements and find activities—such as great restaurants or tickets to the symphony—for your leisure hours. Simply by picking up the phone in your room, you may have access to laundering and tailoring, manicures and shoeshines. Secretarial services, computers, faxes, photocopying, messenger services, office stationery and supplies, and small conference rooms are just a few of the services the business traveler can find in a good hotel.

If you need to hold meetings at your hotel, book a suite or select a hotel with small conference rooms that can be reserved. Avoid holding a meeting in your hotel bedroom if possible. Not only can it make members of the opposite sex feel uncomfortable, it gives the impression that the company is stingy. If you must hold a meeting in your room, make sure it is neat, with all clothing put away and the bathroom door closed.

If you frequently travel to the same destinations, try to find a hotel you like and return there on subsequent visits. Once you're known, the service will only get better.

WOMEN TRAVELING ON BUSINESS

Women traveling alone still face a few obstacles, one of which may be getting good service. When you register at a hotel, include your title and business address and don't be afraid to speak up. If you're given an undesirable room or receive poor service, talk to the manager. Present your business card and explain the problem. Hotels can't afford to turn away business clientele and should accommodate you. You might also tell the manager that you plan to return to the city often and you would like to be able to stay at his hotel next time.

You should certainly be cautious in an unfamiliar city, but you needn't be a prisoner of your room. Enjoy the hotel bar or restaurant—simply carry your briefcase or work along to signal that you're a business traveler. If a man approaches you and you don't want to speak to him, explain to him that you're working. In a restaurant, if someone is bothering you and won't leave, signal the maître d' or a waiter. All you have to say is, "Perhaps you could find a table for this gentleman."

Obnoxious men are not the rule, of course. You might meet someone interesting or pleasant. If a man joins you, you can let him pay for one drink if you wish. If a second round is ordered and he has paid for the first, insist that the second be put on your tab. If you're invited to dinner, your good judgment is all you need to decide whether to accept. Remember, you can always excuse yourself at any time with the pretext that you have work to do.

Single diners—and particularly women—are not always provided with the best table or service in a restaurant. Men are accustomed to asking for good service, but sometimes women who are alone feel conspicuous and are reluctant to speak up. If you're led to a poorly located table, simply say, "I'd much prefer the table over there," before you're seated. If you wish to dine outside your hotel, make a reservation or ask the concierge to make it for you; a single reservation made ahead is more likely to be accepted.

MEN AND WOMEN TRAVELING TOGETHER

No one should assume that if a man and woman travel together it means they're on intimate terms. If that presumption is made incorrectly, it's up to both parties to clarify the situation.

Men and women don't share suites for the same reason they avoid hugs and kisses in the workplace. And to avoid any embarrassment or crossed signals with an opposite-sex traveler:

• If you share a drink, have it in the hotel bar, not in either bedroom.

• Say good night at the door.

When traveling together, men and women should share the responsibilities for cars, reservations, entertaining, etc. A man may offer to carry a woman's luggage and a woman may accept, but the wise woman travels with no more than she can comfortably handle on her own.

THE OUT-OF-TOWN CLIENT

If an out-of-town client travels from another city to meet with you, it's thoughtful to assist him before he arrives by asking whether he needs a recommendation of a good hotel, restaurants, a car service, or directions to your company.

If you want to impress an out-of-town client, arrange for a basket of fruit or flowers to be placed in his room when he arrives, and send a car to bring him to your office. Such personal attention makes a lasting impression.

If you've made an appointment with someone flying in to see you, be prepared to keep that appointment. There's nothing worse than what happened to two executives who flew from Atlanta to Chicago only to find that the man they were to meet was ill at home. Not only had they purchased airline tickets and rented a car, but they had spent hours getting there and back. Be there, or have someone knowledgeable and of equal status to take your place.

BUSINESS GIFT GIVING

IN THE OFFICE

There are a number of occasions on which you might wish to give a present to someone with whom you work: to say thank you to a colleague who did you a favor, to wish someone well in a new position, to congratulate an office mate for winning an award or having a baby, or to remember someone who is in the hospital or recovering from illness at home.

There are no hard and fast rules governing the giving of gifts in an office but you must use good judgment. Presents that are inappropriate or given improperly will create problems. Here are some basic guidelines to bear in mind:

• Give a present when there is a good reason to do so but, as with any gift, give it promptly. A present sent six months after a colleague has retired or had a baby has far less meaning.

• Take care not to send the same gift to everyone, without regard to the recipient's taste or the occasion. In other words, a bottle of wine is not appropriate for those who do not drink.

• A humorous gift is fine for someone you know well, but make certain it's not offensive: a diet book for an overweight colleague is not funny.

- If you are new in the company or within a department, do not give your boss a present. It will be seen as apple polishing.
- Avoid giving clothing, especially articles that come with sizes, unless you know the recipient's exact size.
- Cash gifts are generally not appropriate for colleagues.
- Flowers are always suitable. If you are sending them to an office, however, it's better to select either an arrangement or a plant rather than cut flowers because not everyone has a vase available. When you send flowers to a hospital, select a variety that will stand up to heat—hospital rooms are often very warm. Best choices: chrysanthemums, daisies, orchids.
- If you need some gift suggestions, consult with the person's assistant, close colleague, or spouse, if you know him or her.

If it's at all possible, your present should be given in person rather than sent, unless of course the person is ill and not receiving visitors. It should always be beautifully wrapped. Write a thoughtful note on an enclosure card or on your personal notepaper. Take care with the wording: "Thanks for the lovely dinner" is not as meaningful as "Our dinner at the Four Seasons was one I'll never forget. Thanks so much for thinking of me."

Presents, of course, need not always be things. When someone is promoted or lands a new account, a manager may wish to show his appreciation by taking the employee out to lunch or to a baseball game or concert.

HOLIDAY TIME Many companies regularly give each employee a present at this time of year. (A bonus is money that has been earned and is not a true present.) Company practices on handling holiday gifts vary widely. Some have a policy of no gifts at all, some even prohibit gifts. Others give employees turkeys, food packages, or fruit. Some give employees catalogs from which they can order an item of their choice. Many organizations consider the company Christmas lunch or party as the holiday gift. And a few give gifts to the needy instead of to employees. If you receive a company present, be certain to write a thank-you note to the person whose name is on the card or, if it just says "From the AGC Company," to the president.

Regardless of the company's policy, you may wish to give holiday presents on your own—perhaps to express your appreciation to your assistant for his hard work all year. Such gifts should not be too personal; for example, a male executive should not give his female assistant stockings or lingerie. Instead, six all-purpose wineglasses, a beautiful book, a gift certificate, a scarf, or tickets to a play are appropriate.

While an employee is not expected to give a holiday present to someone in a senior position, taking the time to bake a batch of cookies, needlepoint a pillow, or make a drawing of his house or boat (and having it framed) will certainly be appreciated. Your boss might also like a bottle of fine brandy or a box of good chocolates. An expensive gift for one's boss, however, is inappropriate.

WEDDING PRESENTS Many company presidents and other high-level executives receive wedding invitations from employees in their firms. In order to avoid hurt feelings, because no executive can attend the wedding of every employee, especially in a large organization, many executives have a firm policy of simply regretting all wedding invitations except from those on their personal staffs or those to whom they are especially close. A company executive need not send a wedding present when he regrets an invitation, although he will almost certainly want to, if the invitation is from someone on his personal staff. In other cases, he should write a note to the employee, wishing him much happiness.

An employee does not give her boss a wedding present unless she has been invited to the wedding. She may, however, wish to volunteer her time to help address envelopes or be of assistance in some other way.

UPON RETIREMENT When someone in the company retires the occasion should be marked with a thoughtful gift. The type of gift is determined somewhat by the length of the person's service and position within the firm. Some companies have standard gifts, often a gold watch or silver bowl inscribed with the dates of the person's service.

Other ideas:

- A hobby gift: golf clubs, fishing or tennis equipment
- Tickets for the retiree and spouse for a cruise or trip to Europe
- A photograph of the retiree with his colleagues framed with a brass plaque giving the employee's dates of service
- Commission an artist to paint the retiree's portrait

GIFT GIVING TO CLIENTS AND CUSTOMERS

CORPORATE GIFTS Many companies give presents to clients, customers, and other important people, such as the firm's banker, lawyer, accountant, public relations person. Such gifts should be kept inexpensive enough so they are not seen as bribes. A nice touch is to have the corporate logo or trademark inconspicuously printed or engraved on the present. Among suitable items would be napkins, coasters, glasses, paperweights, letter openers, notepads.

Food and wine also make wonderful business gifts. Within the inexpensive gift category are gourmet jams and jellies, pure maple syrup,
cheese baskets, baked goods, and candy. More expensive items include
smoked salmon, smoked turkey or ham, pâtés, frozen steaks and lobsters
flown in from the Midwest or Maine.

Small promotional items bearing the company logo may be given by
salesmen to customers or potential customers or others when appropriate.
These items, known as giveaways, are usually under twenty-five dollars
and often cost only a dollar or two.

Many companies have policies which spell out to whom client and
customer presents may be given, in what price range, or even what items
are appropriate and never give the appearance of a bribe.

A number of large stores have corporate gift departments which can be
very helpful, especially in selecting the right presents to take to a foreign
country. In most cases, corporate gift accounts receive a discount from the
store.

SOME SUGGESTIONS FOR ITEMS WITH THE CORPORATE LOGO

- Pen and pencil sets
- Mugs
- Scarves
- Key chains
- Credit card cases
- Neckties
- Flashlights
- Umbrellas
- Thermos bottles
- Tie clips
- Balloons
- Measuring tapes
- Calendars
- Diaries
- Posters
- T-shirts

Some general suggestions:

- Crate of Florida or California oranges and grapefruit
- Champagne
- Crystal paperweight
- Silver letter opener

- Gold-tooled leather desk set
- Brass carriage clock
- Fully equipped picnic basket
- Framed antique map or print

HANDLING INAPPROPRIATE PRESENTS

Some companies do not permit employees to accept presents from anyone associated with their business for fear of making the employee feel in some way obligated to the donor. If the firm has such a policy, a notice of this fact should be sent to all employees at least once a year, around holiday time.

Sometimes you may receive a present that is too expensive or too personal, such as an expensive piece of jewelry or something in poor taste, such as a gift with sexual overtones. Sometimes presents are simply "wrong": a bottle of wine for someone who doesn't drink or a car accessory for someone who doesn't have a car.

If you receive a present that smacks of sexual innuendo or bribery, return it immediately. Don't even keep it for a day—that will make it appear to the donor that you have accepted it. Send a note saying, "This is not an appropriate present so I am returning it to you." Keep a copy of your note. As usual, etiquette in such situations is just a combination of sensitivity to others and common sense.

INTERNATIONAL BUSINESS ETIQUETTE

In our global marketplace, to learn the customs and business manners of foreign countries is crucial. Other cultures' approaches to decision making, to oral agreements and contracts, to business entertaining, and even to gift giving can be quite different from those Americans are used to. And the protocol for greeting people, presenting business cards, punctuality, dress, and even humor changes quite dramatically when you cross borders. In addition to local mores, foreign firms often have distinct national ways of approaching business. For instance, in the East you will quickly grow to understand the Chinese proverb, "Nothing is so full of victory as patience." In Switzerland you must be not only extremely well prepared but also ready to live up to any sales pitch you deliver, since anything you say can be evaluated under their more stringent contract law.

GENERAL GUIDELINES

Some general rules to follow when doing business abroad are:

- Be informed about the country's current social, economic, and political climate, but stay away from discussing political stands, strong opinions, or controversial topics.

- The custom of using first names in business is American. West or East, don't use someone's first name until you have been invited to.

- Most countries conduct business more formally than in America. Always err on the side of dignity and conservatism.

- If you travel frequently in non-English-speaking countries, your business cards should be printed on the reverse side in the appropriate foreign language. The concierge at a major hotel can usually direct you to a place that can perform this service, but it will take from two days to a week. If possible, have your business cards printed before you leave the United States.

- If you are not sure your foreign contact speaks English, you will need a reliable translator. Never assume that "someone" in a company will know English.

- Learn a few phrases—such as "Please," "Thank you," "Good morning"—in the local language.

- Don't be what sadly is known as an Ugly American: loud, rude, and ignorant of local custom.

- Do be an ambassador—express appreciation for a country's culture, art, architecture, climate, cuisine, beauty, or whatever else merits praise.

SPECIFIC COUNTRY GUIDELINES

You'll be at ease and feel self-confident if you know just a few of a country's basic cultural idiosyncrasies. It's also easy to make inadvertent faux pas when abroad—in fact you may never realize you have done so. So bear these few guidelines in mind not only when doing business abroad but also when hosting foreign businessmen and women in this country and you'll be much more likely to forge a successful foreign business relationship.

- In **Arab countries** you should not point or beckon to a native; these gestures are reserved for dogs. And under no circumstances use expletives or the word "God." Muslems do not eat pork, and most do not drink alcohol. Although they exchange handshakes, in their homes you are likely to be greeted with a kiss on both cheeks and you should return the gesture in kind and without hesitation. Women should not wear slacks or body-hugging clothing and their arms must be covered from shoulder to wrist.

- In **Australia** it is considered rude to pick up the drinks tab out of turn or to neglect to pay for your round when the time comes.

- **Austrians** should be addressed by their business titles as they appear on their cards. Handshaking is done in descending order—in other words, shake hands with the company's president first, then the second-ranking person, and so on.

- In **Central and South America,** people stand closer to each other when talking (four to eight inches) than they do in the United States, so restrain yourself from backing away when someone is speaking to you. And be prepared for the fact that business proceeds at a slower pace than in the United States and your host is apt to be at least thirty minutes late. (Caveat: Brazilians insist on punctuality, and in Venezuela *you* must be punctual, although *they* may be late.) Incidentally, do not refer to Brazilians as Latin Americans; Brazilians speak Portuguese and do not consider themselves part of Latin America.

- Patience is the key to doing business in **China.** Decisions are made by committee and take months or even years. Keep in mind that an appointment is required for all business dealings. A man should dress conservatively in a dark suit. White shirts are acceptable but white dresses and suits are not because white is the color for mourning. Bow your head slightly when you are introduced and don't hug or kiss a Chinese; they do not like to be touched by strangers. Remember to speak quietly—the Chinese find loud behavior very offensive. The family name in China is given first; thus Lee Wang is addressed as Mr. or Madam Lee.

  Your Chinese host will probably give you a banquet. He will be in complete control of the event and may even take food from the serving dishes, explain what it is, and place it on your plate. Make every effort to eat some of each dish served, using chopsticks if you can manage them. (At some banquets Western flatware is not available, so you may want to practice using chopsticks before traveling to China.) Follow your host's lead at all times. That means, don't eat or drink until he does and never leave until he indicates the meal is over. When a Chinese makes a toast (and they make many during the course of a banquet), he empties his glass each time. You are expected to do the same, but be forewarned—their alcoholic drink is very powerful.

- The **French** traditionally prefer lunch to dinner for business and almost never hold breakfast meetings, so don't suggest one. Even if you are hosting the meal, let your French counterpart select the wines—the French regard themselves as far better at this than Americans—and they usually are.

- **Germans** are very reserved and formal and don't like to waste time, so punctuality is extremely important. Anything spur-of-the-moment is put down as lack of planning. Jokes and humor are out of place at a business meeting. Germans are addressed by their positions or titles—Herr Direktor, for example—rather than by their names. This is also true for **Italians**—when in doubt address your contact as "Dottore," or the feminine form, "Dottoressa," which is the title for anyone with a college degree.

- We may share a common language (almost), but the **British** are more reserved than Americans. A common faux pas is to refer to them as English. Whether they're from Ireland, Scotland, or England, they prefer to be called British, not English. Avoid talking about money (Americans often seem very materialistic to the British). Also avoid wearing a striped tie; these are often versions or copies of a regimental or school tie and in Britain you never wear such a tie unless you have served in the regiment or attended the school.

  When the British workday is over, usually by five-thirty, even if you're being entertained, business is rarely discussed again. Wait for your host to bring up any business matters and if he doesn't neither should you.

  Business is frequently conducted over afternoon tea (don't mistakenly call it "high tea," a term that once referred to a working-man's supper). Regular afternoon tea consists of freshly made tea with finger sandwiches, scones, pound cake, tiny fruit tartlets, and other sweets. The tea is made from loose tea leaves, not tea bags. Your host will ask you if you like your tea weak or strong and whether you want milk (never cream) or lemon or sugar (in this case lump sugar) in it. When it comes time to pour the tea, he will rest a strainer on your cup to collect any loose tea leaves, after which he will place the strainer on a small bowl. He then puts whatever ingredients you asked for in your cup. If the tea is too strong, he will add water from the hot-water pitcher.

  Tea sandwiches are not devoured in one hungry bite, and the scone, eaten after the sandwiches, is cut in half and then spread bite by bite with butter, jam, and/or clotted cream just as you eat it, bite by bite. The butter, jam, and clotted or Devonshire cream are served in attractive dishes for the whole table. Place a small amount of each on your side plate and return the service spoons and knife so others can help themselves.

  If you're taken to the theater—a favorite way of entertaining in Britain—you will be charged for your program. Have several small coins ready so the usher will not have to make change.

- The **Greeks** love to do business over coffee and ouzo, the national liqueur. And although it's a relaxed country where punctuality is not terribly important, there are several things you should not do. Making the U.S. sign for okay with the thumb and finger joined to form a circle is an obscene gesture in Greece (and in Japan too). Another gesture to avoid is signaling the number five by holding up five fingers. This is the Greek symbol for the evil eye. And, although you've seen it in movies, breaking glasses at a wild Greek dance or party should be left to the Greeks.

- In **India** it's customary to wash your hands and rinse your mouth before dining. Always use your right hand when passing food (even if you're left-handed). There are many dietary restrictions which vary among Hindus, Muslims, and other religious groups. Most Hindus are vegetarians and you should try to avoid eating meat in front of them.

- **Israelis** are known for being casual except when it comes to certain religious regulations: you should not smoke on the Sabbath, which goes from sundown on Friday to sundown on Saturday, nor should you ask for butter or milk in a kosher restaurant or kosher home. Steer clear of discussing the amount of foreign aid the country has received.

- Even though the **Japanese** and Americans do a great deal of business with one another, many Americans still make a key mistake by pushing to get down to the task at hand too quickly. The Japanese not only approach issues circuitously, but they want to know you and the firm you represent before they do business. They dislike overfamiliarity, being kissed or touched by strangers, or loud behavior. The exchange of business cards is done very exactly: when you meet someone of a higher status, offer him your card with both hands; if the person is of a lower status, present your card with one hand. If you are in doubt, present your card with both hands. Men wear conservative business suits, always with a white shirt. When entering a Japanese home and many restaurants, you must first remove your shoes. Greet your host and hostess not with a handshake but with a long, low bow. If you have not been invited for a meal, stay no more than forty-five minutes, though you will be urged to stay longer. Foreign guests are honored. You will be shown many courtesies and expected to precede even a more senior-ranking or older Japanese into a room. You may be entertained to the point of exhaustion, even into the small hours of the morning. It is important to the Japanese businessman to see how you handle yourself in extreme social situations.

- In **Switzerland, the Netherlands, Norway, Sweden,** and **Finland** it's important that you don't touch your drink until your host has proposed a toast. Then you should, in turn, toast your host. Privacy and punctuality are respected in these business communities.

- When in **Spain** and **Portugal** be prepared for the fact that the business day is set to a different clock, beginning at 10 A.M. or later, with lunch seldom before two. Many establishments are closed for two hours in the afternoon. Dinner doesn't begin until 10 or 11 P.M.

INTERNATIONAL GIFT GIVING

Gift-giving customs also vary widely from country to country. It's not only polite, but it makes good business sense as well to know a society's customs. Make it a point to know what sort of gift is appropriate, the time it should be given, and the way it should be presented in countries you visit. You can begin gathering this information by speaking to a native of the country, to a colleague who has conducted business there, or with an official of the country's consulate. It's a good idea also to read a book that discusses the country's history, government, culture, and customs. Two helpful general books are *Do's and Taboos Around the World* compiled by the Parker Pen Company and published by the Benjamin Company, Inc., and *The International Herald Tribune Guide to Business Travel in Europe* published by Passport Books.

The actual presentation of gifts is much more important in other countries than it is in the United States, so make certain yours is nicely wrapped. If it has your company's logo on it, the logo should be small, discreet in size so it doesn't look like blatant advertising. Gifts should not be brought to the first meeting or given to people you do not know well.

Bear in mind that a gift purchased in the United States is more prized than something bought in the country you are visiting. American books, tapes, food packed in tins, attractive T-shirts or caps of famous American sports teams, museum and concert posters are always popular. Foreigners also enjoy receiving small items from well-known American stores. It's best, however, to refrain from giving too generous or too large a gift that will seem ostentatious, materialistic, or even possibly misconstrued as a bribe.

If you are a guest at the home of a foreign colleague, you may bring gifts for the children, provided your colleague has mentioned them to you or you have met them previously. American-made toys and games as well as books by American authors are fine choices.

Women doing business abroad, especially in countries where there are few women executives, need to be more cautious when giving gifts. Wait until you know your foreign colleague quite well or until you receive a gift from him before giving yours. Gifts given to men should be impersonal, such as a book, pen, letter opener, or paperweight.

Each country has its own custom regarding flowers as gifts. In general, gladiolus and chrysanthemums symbolize mourning while in many countries, such as France and Germany, red roses are given only to lovers. In the Far East, white flowers are for those in mourning. Take care to give an uneven number of flowers, except for the number 13. In Japan, flowers are generally restricted to courtship, illness, and death; in Germany, they are always presented unwrapped. When giving flowers to a dinner hostess, it is more thoughtful to have them delivered before the dinner so she can arrange them in advance.

SPECIFIC COUNTRY GUIDELINES There are some other customs to observe in international gift giving. For instance, you should never give a Chinese a clock, as the sound of the word in Chinese has a morbid implication. And gifts are given only in private and only after all business has been completed.

You should wait for the Arab businessman to give you a gift first, then you must reciprocate in kind. You should present the gift in front of others to avoid any suggestion of a bribe. Be careful about praising any object in an Arab's possession. No matter what its value, he will immediately insist that you keep it. Then you will have to give him something of equal value. And always use your right hand when presenting your gift (or business card) as Arabs use the left hand for toilet paper.

The cow is sacred in India; therefore do not give a gift made of cowhide.

In Russia gifts are often exchanged during toasts at dinner, so you should be prepared with yours.

In most countries a gift is given upon arrival, but in Japan you should not give a gift first because it will cause the Japanese to lose face; let the Japanese host be the first to give a gift and then reciprocate. In China and Japan, do not give gifts in front of other people.

CHAPTER 6
TRAVEL

INTRODUCTION

Because of today's technology more people than ever before are able to travel both here at home and abroad. Packaged tours, charter groups, and specialized associations for students, the elderly, and others have made travel accessible and affordable to huge numbers of people. Whether in Paris or Rome, Chicago or L.A., Hong Kong or Sydney, the airports and terminals are bustling with people from every part of the world.

For anyone who loves to see new places, eat different foods, sample new cultures and languages, and for whom travel is an exhilarating adventure, the rewards far outweigh any inconveniences that may turn up from time to time.

It is always important to be well informed before you take off on a trip. Do some advance research on your destination by reading books and travel brochures. Talk to friends about their travel experiences and study the customs of the places you plan to visit. As this is not a travel book, complete travel information is not provided. Many fine travel books exist for almost every region of the world, and in this country there are government-supported tourist bureaus in major cities that can supply you with good information. Also, keep an eye on the travel sections of your newspaper and make use of all the informative travel magazines available. Decorum and behavior differ widely from place to place, and while you can't expect to know everything about where you are going, be sensitive to the local customs and norms of conduct. Observe how the natives behave, and don't leave your high standards of politeness at home. They are as essential as a good pair of comfortable shoes.

Speaking of which, as you study the customs of the country you're visiting, pay attention to appropriate attire, which can vary from country to country. Dressing appropriately is also a mark of respect and should not be overlooked. In most parts of the world dress and manners are more formal than they are in North America. Throughout Europe, for example, it is customary to dress for dinner or an evening cultural event (jacket and tie for men, a neat dress or pantsuit for women). In some Catholic and especially Muslim countries tourists are expected to dress in ways that may seem strange to us, but an effort should be made to conform. Long sleeves and a headscarf for women (sometimes required) show respect in churches and cathedrals. In mosques, shoes are left at the door. Neat, appropriate dress in public is as admirable as good taste and tactfulness. T-shirts and sweatsuits are not suitable for many occasions. Nor is a baseball cap worn indoors by men. Men should always remove their hats when inside. (But that should be the case in any country.)

Take along a phrase book or a small dictionary—especially one that translates menu items. You can probably manage in most of the world speaking only English, but if you know even a few phrases of the language of the country you are traveling in it will make life easier for you and more fun.

PLANNING YOUR TRIP

USING A TRAVEL AGENT

A good travel agent is worth her weight in any precious metal you can imagine. She can save you a great deal of time and effort in all aspects of planning your trip, providing you with everything from passport and visa forms to information about the climate. Best of all, perhaps, a good agent can often save you money. Remember, you don't pay the agent for her services. She is paid a commission of about eight to twelve percent by the airline, hotel, or other travel services. (You will, however, probably have to pay for faxes or telephone calls the agent makes for you abroad.)

A particular advantage to working with a travel agent is that she can often get you a seat on a plane or a room in a hotel when you might not be able to get it for yourself. A knowledgeable agent will also know about special package deals and travel restrictions and have fare-comparison computer programs that allow her to find the best rates and schedules within minutes.

The best way to find a travel agent is the same way you find any service professional: ask for recommendations from family or friends who travel a great deal. (Make sure you get the name of the individual agent, not just the name of the agency.) Try to make sure that you and the agent are on the same wave length. That way you will be assured of someone who will carry out your wishes and hold to your budget. If you trust your agent and think she knows your tastes well, accept her recommendations and don't try to second-guess her. But don't expect the impossible from her, particularly at the height of the season when reservations can be tight.

As soon as you are sure about the dates you want to travel, tell your agent—but not until then. Be certain. Tell her as much as you can about where you'd like to go, when and how you prefer to travel, and what your budget is. If you absolutely have to have quiet to sleep, tell her; if you and your husband are more interested in local color and don't care for the ultrachic, let her know that too. An agent can set up a deluxe, independent tour with chauffeurs and guides, first-class or five-star accommodations, but can also, and with the same dedication, arrange for more modest but excellent group tours, by bus or train.

Pay your agent's bill promptly. Travel agents cannot extend credit, because they have to pay the airline, hotel, or cruise company when they issue the tickets.

A final word: even though several million Americans today may have personal computer systems with access to airline guides and data bases with fares and schedules, these services are expensive and difficult to use, so if you can find an agent who suits your needs and with whom you are compatible, it will be worth your while to work with her.

GETTING READY TO GO

To enter most countries and return to this one you must have a valid passport. It's a good idea to keep it up to date at all times. Larger cities have passport offices where you can apply in person, and in smaller cities or towns application forms can be obtained at the county courthouse. Allow about six weeks after you apply for the passport for it to arrive— more if you apply by mail, still longer during the heavy season. To obtain a passport you need proof of citizenship, such as your birth certificate, baptismal record, or an old passport. You must also provide two identical, recent passport photos, as specified on the application. Each member of the family must have a passport. There is a fee.

Most countries do not require visas (a permit to travel or live within their borders for a limited amount of time). But if you plan to work, study, or live abroad for an extended period, you will need a visa for that purpose. Apply for your visa at the consulate of the country you plan to visit, and take your valid passport with you. You will need it to obtain the visa. Your travel agent can advise you about which countries require visas, what the costs are, and in many instances can get the visa for you.

Label all luggage with your name and address, and be sure to put a label inside your suitcase with this information too.

HEALTH REQUIREMENTS

Most tourist areas in the world require no special health certificates or precautions these days. Check with your travel agent, or with the tourist office or consulate of the countries you will be visiting to confirm this. A few places in the world may present particular health hazards, so it is wise to get the latest information from your travel agent or local board of health.

If you are concerned about other kinds of danger in the area you plan to visit, call the Citizens Emergency Center at the State Department in Washington, D.C. (202-647-5225). They will tell you about any State Department travel advisories issued on areas of unrest.

INTERNATIONAL DRIVER'S LICENSE

An international driver's license is still required in a few countries, but usually your valid U.S. driver's license and proof of insurance will be enough. Ask your travel agent or contact a local office of the American (or Canadian) Automobile Association to see if the country you are visiting has any restrictions if you are not sure. Some of the major car rental agencies can supply you with a list of their offices abroad as well as the license and insurance requirements in different countries.

TRAVELING WITH MONEY

Traveler's checks are still the most convenient way to carry your money for a trip. They can be bought for a percentage fee at your bank in various denominations. (You can also get traveler's checks in foreign currencies but may have to order them in advance.) If you have credit cards, ask your bank whether they give you access to automated teller machines abroad: you may save some money by using an ATM, because there is a fee for cashing a traveler's check. It is useful to take a small amount (about fifty dollars) in foreign currency with you so that you will have money for tipping, taxis, and other small expenses on arrival and in case money exchange booths at the airports are not open. Be sure to tuck some American money in a safe place to pay for taxis, etc., when you get home.

TRAVEL INSURANCE

It might be advisable to invest in trip cancellation insurance that will get you a partial or full refund if you have to cancel the trip for medical reasons or on account of a death in the family, particularly if you have taken advantage of restricted economy fares or booked an expensive tour or cruise far in advance. Many credit cards automatically provide insurance for luggage and personal effects or you may find that you are protected by your homeowner's policy. An excellent idea is to keep a list of what is in your suitcases so that you can itemize any claims. Keep the list separate from your luggage.

PREDEPARTURE CHECKLIST

Before leaving on a trip, you will want to take into account the following:

- Give your house key to a good friend, or to your superintendent (if you live in an apartment) and ask that the house or apartment be checked periodically while you are away.
- Make suitable arrangements for your pets well in advance of depar-

ture. This is especially important at holiday time when pet care centers may be booked up.

- Arrange to have newspaper and mail deliveries held during your absence.

- Leave a copy of your itinerary and a list of service people (electrician, plumber, heating company) with a friend, relative, or house sitter.

- If you have an alarm system, make sure it is in working order. You may also want to install automatic timers so lights in your house go on and off during the day. Advise the local police that you will be away too—especially if the trip is a long one and no one is going to house-sit. If you live in a small town, don't tell too many people you will be gone, and don't tell the local newspaper about your trip.

- Test the smoke alarm batteries.

- Put your jewelry or other valuables in the safe deposit vault of your bank.

- If you don't have a house sitter, make sure someone will come in to water your plants and tend your garden (a neglected lawn is a clear signal that no one's at home). You'll want to bring back a present for the person who takes on this responsibility.

- Take photographs of the contents of various rooms so you can substantiate your household inventory in case you have to file an insurance claim.

LEAVING CHILDREN AT HOME

If you have a trustworthy sitter (or a relative) who will stay with your children, ask her to come a day or so before you leave so she can get accustomed to their everyday routines: the rules for bedtime, meals, TV watching, and anything else. Show her where the fuse boxes, water main switch, furnace reset button, and fire extinguishers are located. Leave a list of the names and numbers of the following:

- A reliable friend or neighbor to call in an emergency. (You must first ask this favor of your friend.)
- Doctors, pediatricians, dentists, police, fire department.
- Drugstore.
- Service people: electrician, plumber, heating service.

Also leave:

- A letter authorizing medical treatment in an emergency (the pediatrician should have this too).
- Your itinerary with phone numbers of the hotels where you will be staying.

WHAT THE WELL-PACKED TRAVELER CARRIES

- An extra pair of prescription glasses and/or contact lenses.
- Sunglasses.
- Shampoo and soap, although most good hotels supply small samples.
- Along with your cosmetics or toilet kit, a small medical kit with Band-Aids, aspirin, digestive aids, diarrhea medication, and any special medicines you take. (If you carry liquids in plastic bottles, keep them less than full so they don't burst on an airplane.)
- A medical information card showing your blood type, allergies, chronic ailments, or anything pertinent to your medical history.
- Hair dryer and electrical converter, although, again, many hotels have these in bathrooms.
- Needle and thread (black and white); safety pins, neutral shoe polish and buffer.
- Raincoat, folding umbrella, rubber boots or galoshes.
- Traveling alarm clock.
- Foldup tote bag for purchases.
- Camera and film (very expensive abroad).
- Names and addresses of family and friends to send postcards to.
- Extra batteries for electronic devices, including hearing aids, cameras, clocks, etc.

TRAVELING ALONE OR WITH OTHERS

TRAVELING ALONE

If you are not an experienced, independent traveler, you might first try a group tour. These are advertised everywhere, or your travel agent can recommend one. The organizing principles vary, and you can take your pick among such sponsoring groups as college alumni associations, museums, and cultural or scientific groups (the Smithsonian Institution, the Audubon Society, the Sierra Club, etc.). You can also find group tours for opera lovers, hikers, bikers, food and wine buffs, snorkelers, and even for a "working group" such as those that go on archaeological digs in Greece, Turkey, New Mexico, Latin America, or elsewhere.

Cruises are also fun for the single person and a good way to meet others, as are dude ranches and tennis or golf schools. Also many resort hotels have special social programs created for singles.

The Elderhostel organization offers opportunities for educational courses, biking and hiking tours, attending music festivals and the like at reasonable rates all over the United States, Canada, and many places abroad. People over sixty are eligible and participants' spouses of any age are welcome. Companions of age-eligible participants, however, must be at least fifty. Elderhostel receives rave notices from those who have gone with them and may be contacted at 75 Federal Street, Boston, MA 02110. (617) 426-8056.

Traveling alone need not be intimidating. A day or even a whole trip on your own gives you the luxury of doing whatever you want to when you want to. With some imagination and daring, you can go almost everywhere solo, no matter what your budget. Once you have traveled alone for the first time, chances are you will be well primed and eager to go it alone again.

When you travel by yourself, it is up to you to reach out to others. Waiting for someone else to make the first move doesn't necessarily work. As an icebreaker, a friend of ours often carries odd things with her such as an enormous umbrella (on a sunny day) or a huge atlas—anything unusual enough to attract an amused comment, thereby starting a conversation.

WOMEN TRAVELING ALONE Today women are more confident and independent and are traveling more on their own. They're going to golfing schools, taking windjammer sailing cruises, hiking in the Rockies, joining horseback treks, or going white water rafting. There is a lot of information aimed specifically at the single female traveler, including books for women traveling alone which are helpful in suggesting places to go and things to do.

Some women are uncomfortable eating alone, especially in the evening, but room service is not the only option. A woman should feel at ease eating by herself in the restaurant of her hotel. For that matter, the hotel bar is a perfectly suitable place to have a drink alone. If sitting in a bar alone makes you feel self-conscious, you can take a book, a newspaper, or postcards with you. That way, if an unwelcome overture is made, you can politely say that you want to finish the book you're reading or the postcards you're writing. On the other hand, if the person who speaks to you appears to be pleasant, and you are in the mood, then by all means accept a drink if offered. If he extends the invitation for another drink or for dinner at the hotel, you may accept, but tell him you would like to buy the next round of drinks and pay for your own dinner.

If you want to eat dinner out, the concierge of your hotel will be able to suggest an appropriate restaurant within your budget: one with good food and where you will feel comfortable. (It's a sad fact that in many establishments, even some of the more expensive ones, women alone are not always treated as well as single men.) What you can always do is eat on the early side, because restaurants are often more accommodating when they are not too busy. And if you find a restaurant you like, by all means keep going back to it.

A cultural event—theater, a concert, or the ballet—is perfectly fine to attend alone. In some parts of the world a movie house may be uncomfortable for the single woman, but sitting on the aisle makes it possible for you to move if someone bothers you.

How adventurous you want to be on your own depends as much on local customs as it does on your personality. In some cities and countries the single woman must be particularly prudent. But in all instances, if someone tries to engage you in conversation on the street in a foreign city, it is best not to get involved.

TRAVELING WITH FRIENDS

Travel is a way of life we do not all handle in the same way. If you are planning a trip with one or more companions, keep in mind that you may have expectations which do not necessarily dovetail with those of your friends. Traveling together is an amazingly intimate kind of experience and even people who know each other well may run into difficulties. What stands everyone in good stead is a willingness to compromise, an agreement to separate occasionally, to laugh at mishaps, to be patient and understanding, and, above all, to keep a sense of humor. Most likely the shared memories and experiences will forever be a bond between you and your traveling companion.

Temperamental differences between friends can be overlooked at home, but when traveling together these same differences may become acute. One way to avoid problems before traveling with a friend is to discuss what interests you have in common. If you don't like spending time in museums or churches, say so and volunteer to be on your own while your friend visits them. Traveling companions (either individuals or couples) can decide before they go whether they will have lunch and/or dinner together every day or whether they will take afternoons "off" from each other. You might even decide to split up every four or five days, then meet up again.

Discuss your budget. Be as specific as possible. If you want to stay in first-class or deluxe hotels but your friend is thinking of bed and breakfasts, it is important to know this before you go. If you require privacy and don't want to share a room, you have to make this clear too. And remember, your companion's preferences are as important to her as yours are to you. For instance, if your friend doesn't like to drive in strange towns or countries, you will have to do most of the driving. Travel is rigorous enough. Try to solve as many potential problems as possible before you embark.

Money can often be a source of friction. A good way to handle common expenditures such as gas, tolls, picnic fare, etc., is to set up a trip kitty. Each person or couple puts the same amount of money into the kitty at the beginning of the trip and adds to it equally as necessary. It makes good sense to designate one person "Chancellor of the Exchequer" to keep track of expenses and to ask for donations to the kitty. Generally, meals are best handled separately, as are wines or liquors.

An unmarried man and woman traveling together as a couple will usually have no difficulty checking in or sharing a room except possibly in a few parts of Eastern Europe, Africa, and very rural areas in Latin America or (rarely) in Western Europe. If a problem should arise, it's best to solve it by taking separate rooms, rather than getting upset or angry about what is, after all, a cultural difference. It might be helpful to get advice beforehand from your travel agent or friends on this.

A couple do not have to be romantically involved to enjoy traveling together. A woman friend who went to study folk music at a college in Texas met a very compatible single man there. Several months later he called her from Dallas and asked if she would like to go to a folk music festival in another city with him. He tactfully explained that he fully expected to have his own room. They have since gone on a number of enjoyable trips together.

LOOKING UP FRIENDS OF FRIENDS

If a friend gives you the name of local residents to look up in the city or town you plan to visit, take advantage of the opportunity. One of the highlights of traveling is getting to know the natives. Your friend should send a letter of introduction to her friends, at the same time telling them when you will be in their vicinity, and that you might give them a call. You are not obligated to see them, but if your friend has gone to the trouble of writing, you should at least call to say hello. If time permits, you may want to invite them for a drink, tea, or lunch at your hotel, or at a café or restaurant you know. If you are a single woman and are afraid they will not let you pay for the lunch or dinner, you can ask the hotel concierge to write out a card (if you don't know the language) to give the captain or waiter, asking that you be given the bill. If instead they insist on entertaining you in their home and you accept, be sure to write and thank them afterward, or send flowers or a small present along with a card. Guidebooks often give suggestions on appropriate gifts for various countries you may be visiting.

TRAVELING WITH CHILDREN

Nothing is more fun or instructive for the experienced, well-traveled adult than to see the world through the fresh eyes of children. But you need to be sensible about where you plan to take children and what their capabilities and limits are. Four- or five-year-olds are probably too young to go too far afield, unless it's a trip especially geared to their tastes, such as a children's museum or zoo.

Here are some things to remember when traveling with children:

- Your child should always carry identification. An I.D. bracelet or dog tag serves this purpose well.

- Take along games, cards, stuffed animals, crayons or pencils, and paper to while away hours of waiting and being cooped up in a plane, train, or bus.

- Take snacks for unexpected delays that leave you with hungry or thirsty children.

- Pace the day, making allowances for short attention spans and fatigue; break the day up into part sightseeing and part recreational activities.

- Let your children make some decisions about where to go—zoos, parks, beaches, aquariums, etc.—to give them a personal input in the trip.

- If you are visiting a foreign country, it can be fun for your child to learn a few useful phrases. Young children easily mimic the sounds of foreign languages and are often not the least self-conscious about using foreign words and phrases.

- If your child is old enough, take library books and a map to trace the route you plan to follow.

- You may want to give your child a travel diary. He will have fun reading it years later, as will you. A scrapbook in which to keep photos and mementos such as postcards, ticket stubs, and foreign coins is also a good idea and helps pass the time.

- Giving your child responsibility for his own tote bag is another way of encouraging his participation in the trip. Or you might ask him to be the one to count the pieces of luggage each time you get ready to move on.

- Pay your child his customary allowance in the currency of the country you are in—it's diverting and can be educational.

- If your child is to have his own room at a hotel or motel, ask for adjoining rooms, preferably with a connecting door.

- Encourage your child to try foods he is not familiar with, but don't expect miracles!

Most hotels and motels have special rates for families with young children, and some even offer free lodging for the very young. For a modest fee, a cot can be set up in your room. If you want to go out at night without the children, good hotels can suggest a babysitter. Ask the concierge.

If there are gym or pool facilities in the hotel or at the motel, your children should always be under your personal supervision. Instruct them not to run through the corridors or ride the elevators up and down. Don't allow them to make a lot of noise at the pool. Being away from home is not a reason to forgo good manners; in fact, it is an excellent opportunity to learn to consider the comfort of other travelers.

BY AIR

The numbers of people who travel by air for business or pleasure have reached staggering proportions. Airports are crowded with travelers making their way from continent to continent, or city to city within those continents. The result is that air travel, while the only way to go if you must travel great distances in reasonable time, presents particular challenges. Depending on the class you can afford to fly, the conditions of comfort vary, but the reality is that accommodations on the average flight cannot be described as luxurious. One or two airlines manage not to make a passenger feel cramped (and perhaps your travel agent can advise you which ones), which is especially important on transoceanic flights. But as the airline's purpose is to get as many seats as possible onto the aircraft, space for each passenger is necessarily restricted.

Other problems with air travel are the frequent delays. The worst are generally caused by heavy traffic at holiday times but weather is responsible for a great number of holdups and delays too. And some delays are caused by trouble with the "equipment" (the aircraft). The seasoned traveler must learn to cope with these frustrations and accept any inconveniences with patience. Remember how miraculous it really is to be able to hop from hemisphere to hemisphere with such speed.

There is little we can do to avoid the aggravations that go along with air travel, but we can try to maintain good manners in the face of annoyance. Such potential for frustration makes it imperative that we be sure to show special consideration for our fellow travelers. We should also not forget to treat those who serve us on the ground as well as those in the air with courtesy and respect. You would be surprised how much better it can make an unhappy situation seem.

At this writing, the top of the line in terms of service and speed is the supersonic Concorde, which flies from New York, Miami, and Washington to London or Paris in about three and a quarter to four hours. The Concorde is also tops in terms of cost, well over eight thousand dollars for a round trip between North America and Europe. The Concorde flies at approximately 1,350 miles per hour, or MACH 2 (twice the speed of sound), generally at an altitude of fifty to sixty thousand feet. Some people find the Concorde cabin a bit cramped, but the service is so special both on the ground and in the air, the food and wine so delicious, and the flying itself so free from the normal bumps and sounds experienced at subsonic speed, that it is a wonderful experience for the one hundred or so passengers it carries. An awe-inspiring bonus is the view it affords of the curvature of the earth.

There is only one class on the Concorde. A choice among four main entrees is offered (one is a "light" meal). Any dietary restrictions you observe can be accommodated. Everything, including all drinks, is served without charge, in the air as well as in the comfortable Concorde departure lounge. Two flights every day both ways between New York and London and three flights a week from Washington or Miami are available.

On subsonic flights there are normally three classes of travel: first, business, and coach or economy class. What distinguishes the different classes from one another are space, quality of service, food, and, naturally, the cost. The first-class cabin is small and accommodates only about twenty passengers. The seats are wider than in coach, the food is somewhat better, all drinks including alcoholic ones are free, and the flight attendants can be more attentive to individual passengers, because there are so few of them. Video machines at every seat are now a feature in many first-class sections, as are "sleeper seats" with reclining backs and footrests. Individual phones are often provided, and in time faxes and computer modems may well be available. If you fly first class you may depart on any scheduled flight; there are no maximum or minimum stay requirements, no cancellation penalties, and you may take advantage of free stopover privileges when traveling abroad.

Business class is available on international flights and increasingly on domestic flights. It is considerably more expensive than coach class but somewhat less expensive than first. There are fewer passengers in business class than in coach, and the seats are more comfortable. The airlines offer many amenities to frequent business travelers. For instance, most business-class sections have phones and individual videos (with tapes of various films) available. The seats feature deeply reclining backs and footrests. No discounted business-class tickets are offered, although you can possibly upgrade a coach ticket if you accumulate enough mileage.

Give your travel agent the dates you want to leave and return once you are absolutely sure of them. Let her know if you have a seat preference (aisle or window) and if you want to order a special meal. The airlines provide meals for every diet including kosher, vegetarian, low sodium, low calorie, high protein, diabetic, bland, etc. (Some seasoned travelers request a special meal as a matter of course. These meals are produced in smaller numbers and are therefore slightly better than the regular meals.) Also, tell your agent if you will need any special help, such as a wheelchair, so she can ask for this when she books the reservation. If you have very long legs, ask for an aisle seat, especially when traveling coach.

Smoking is no longer allowed on domestic flights or on most international ones. Smoking in the aisles or in the lavatories is a punishable federal offense.

For domestic trips, you should get to the airport at least an hour before flight time. Remember that the airline has the option of rescinding your advance seat assignment thirty minutes before departure time if you have not checked in. And if you turn up less than ten minutes before departure, your seat may have been resold. It is always better to allow too much rather than too little time. If you have to purchase your ticket or have it rewritten, you must allow time for that. If you are late getting to the airport it is very bad form to go directly to the ticket agent behind the check-in counter, ignoring other people standing in line. If you are in danger of missing your flight, find an airline agent to help you. These agents usually station themselves around the area in front of the ticket counter for just such problems.

On international flights, because of the size of the planes, the number of passengers, and because of the extra security or passport controls you may have to go through, get to the airport at least two hours before flight time. It is still strongly recommended by most agents and experienced travelers that you reconfirm your return flight, especially on international trips or if you've had to change your reservations.

For those who travel a great deal and can afford it, the major airlines have set up "clubs" with names like "Admiral's Club" at the larger airports. For an annual fee of about two hundred dollars, members are entitled to wait for their flights in private lounges. The clubs also offer various services and amenities such as free drinks and snacks (you may buy liquor or wine), magazines, newspapers, TV, check cashing, credit card phones, and facilities for getting boarding passes and seat assignments for connecting flights. Some of the lounges also provide business facilities such as fax machines, copiers, and computers. As most users of these special lounges are traveling for business or professional reasons, dress should be appropriately conservative.

If you decide to fly on the spur of the moment and space on a flight is sold out, you can sometimes get a seat at the last minute on standby. But you must be at the gate and ready to go with all your luggage whenever you are called.

The airlines have resorted to overbooking their flights to allow for "no shows"—people who do not cancel reservations they don't use. It's fine to book several reservations if you are not sure of your exact departure date, but never fail to cancel the ones you won't need. If you have canceled a ticket, don't throw it away, as you will need it to get a refund. When a plane is overbooked, the agent at the gate will call for volunteers to give up their seats in return for some compensation, such as a bonus flight or even a cash inducement. If you are bumped, it's natural enough to blame the agent at the gate, but remember, the agent did not do the booking. Getting angry will not get you a seat. It is far better to remain calm and show you understand the system. You may win the agent's good will, which could be useful if he or she has any say about filling one last seat. If you feel your treatment has been unfair, your recourse is to write a complaint to the airline's director of customer relations.

If you are bumped, ask the agent to make sure that any reservations on continuing flights are not canceled, so you don't lose those seats. Also, ask to see a copy of the airline's rules for bumped passengers. If you are bumped because a flight was overbooked, it is some consolation to know that most airlines guarantee to get you off to your destination within two hours or pay you for the inconvenience. If a travel voucher is offered as compensation for being bumped, ask about any possible restrictions such as limited advance booking. You can give yourself some protection against being bumped from a flight by asking your travel agent to send your boarding card and seat assignment with your ticket. Still better, get to the airport early.

TRAVEL LIGHT!

Strong, flexible, lightweight, woven polyester bags are what seasoned travelers prefer. Expensive leather bags can easily be damaged by rough baggage handling and can be an enticement for thieves. Sidewalk check-in for your luggage is a great convenience, but you must have your ticket in hand in order to avail yourself of this service. Make sure you have identification on your suitcases, and don't forget to get the baggage checks from the porter. Tip him about one dollar per bag. If you check your bags in at the ticket counter, you may be able to use one of the baggage carts to get your bags there from the curb, but a useful rule is: if you can't carry it yourself, don't take it.

On domestic flights there are no weight restrictions. You may carry on two bags, so long as one of them fits beneath the seat and the other will fit in the overhead compartment (a briefcase counts as one carry-on bag). Wardrobe bags count as one of the two carry-ons, but don't overpack them to the bursting point. It is inconsiderate to assume you can take up all the space in the wardrobe closet (airline personnel call such overstuffed bags "mobile homes"). You also should not expect help in shoving an oversized bag into the overhead compartment—if it doesn't fit comfortably, it should not be there. You may carry on a reasonable amount of reading material, a camera, etc. Golf bags must be checked. Ideally, you should have a rigid, heavy-duty traveling bag for golf clubs. Skis must be checked, but you may carry your tennis racket with you on the plane. All of this and further information is spelled out in the small print on the back of your ticket.

If you are carrying only two suitcases, it's doubtful you'll encounter any size or weight restrictions at airports in this country. But within Europe you are charged if your baggage exceeds whatever the size and weight regulations may be. Your travel agent will be able to advise you in this matter. Worth noting is that many airlines, both domestic and foreign, do charge extra for golf bags.

In North America, almost all flights now go through "hub" cities which utilize the most sophisticated baggage-handling apparatus. Therefore the chances of your bags being lost have decreased. But if it should happen, the airlines will do everything possible to retrieve your bags within twenty-four hours and will deliver them to your home or other destination. The airline's liability for lost luggage is limited, but you may declare excess valuation at the check-in counter to cover any items of value that you absolutely must travel with. It is always a good idea to have an itemized list of your belongings for verification and claims. If your baggage doesn't show up, report it as soon as all the baggage has appeared on the carousel with the luggage from your flight. Remember to label all bags, and carry medicines, your toilet kit, and a change of clothes or nightwear as well as any cash or jewelry in your carry-on bag. (Check your ticket envelope for a list of articles such as lighter fluid, poisons, explosives, etc., that are not allowed on the plane either in the cabin or the cargo hold.)

If all metal objects were packed in suitcases to be carried in the cargo hold, the passenger security check lines would move quite a bit faster. The metal detectors are very sensitive and the agents are paid to be careful, so you will hold up everyone in line if you have any metal object in your carry-on bags. But if you must carry such an item, pack it on top for easy retrieval and inspection. On your own person, keys, money clips, and metal hearing aids can trigger the alarms, so drop them into the cup at the screening machine, and you'll probably sail through. No computers larger than a briefcase are allowed on board.

Never leave a bag or a package unattended in an airline terminal. Be particularly careful about this when you are abroad; your belongings might be stolen or, because of the fear of terrorism at many major airports, security patrols may seize the bag, take it away, and destroy it, with no questions asked.

When boarding begins, passengers who need help for whatever reason—including small children, unaccompanied minors, or the elderly—will be called to board first. Remaining passengers will be boarded by seat rows, starting at the back. When your row number is called, move to your seat quickly. Don't hold up those behind you by walking up and down the aisle looking for overhead space for your luggage, or checking for extra pillows or blankets. It is a kind and gracious act to lend a helping hand to an overburdened mother or an elderly person having trouble stowing his gear. Flight attendants agree that most people try to be cooperative and considerate; don't prove the exception.

Most of the flight attendant's training is aimed at passenger safety, not passenger comfort. When you are asked to pay attention to the in-flight safety instructions, do so. It's vitally important that you know where the nearest exit is, how to get into your life jacket, or how to use the oxygen mask. If you find yourself sitting next to an emergency door, you will be asked if you would mind helping with the evacuation of passengers should the need arise. If you would rather not, you can ask to be moved to another seat. When the plane takes off and lands or when there is turbulence in the air, remain in your seat with your seat belt fastened. On arrival, do not get up from your seat until the aircraft is docked at the gate. It is against federal regulations to be out of your seat before then.

Be reasonable about the blankets, pillows, and magazines provided. Don't hog. If you are sitting on the aisle, be prepared to let your seatmates in and out. Try to time a trip to the lavatory when the attendants are not serving drinks or food. A personal toilette should never be made in your seat, and, since there are more passengers than lavatories, it is common courtesy not to occupy one for too long a time. Women should not attempt complete makeup jobs, for example, and men should not spend excessive time shaving. Above all, leave the lavatory neat. Use a paper towel to wipe the sink, throw away used towels, and flush the toilet.

Don't monopolize the flight attendants; there are many people to be served and only so much time. If you want to stretch your legs in the aisle, do so when nothing much is going on. If you feel like chatting with your seatmate, that is fine, but if your seatmate is reading or working, it may be that she would prefer not to talk, except possibly when the meal is served. If someone insists on talking to you when you would rather not, you can always say quite pleasantly that you need this time to do some reading or writing, or maybe even some thinking or meditating. Casual conversations on airplanes can be fun and interesting, but be sensitive to the needs and preferences of those traveling with you.

Now that telephones have become available on flights, there's another reason for good manners. Being forced to listen to a loud or penetrating voice discussing business, love affairs, or whatever can be tiresome at best. If someone is annoying you and other passengers by talking loudly on the telephone, you should feel no compunction about asking him to lower his voice, just as nonsmokers used to request that someone not smoke. You might say you are trying to sleep or to concentrate on the book you are reading. In the same way, you should remember that others may overhear your conversation, so keep your voice well modulated when using the telephone.

Being mindful of the comfort and needs of others is the precious gift of courtesy. When in-flight movies are shown on long flights, it is thoughtful to lower your window shade to keep the light out. However, as many people travel for business reasons, it may be that they have to work or read and need the light. Be careful about dropping your seat abruptly into the reclining position. It could cause a major disaster if the person behind you has a tray in front of her. Should someone do this to you, ask him to raise his seat slightly while you finish your meal. And be careful too about slamming your tray into its upright position, which may disturb whoever is sitting in front of you (who might be sleeping). There's an old saying, "Evil is wrought by want of thought as well as by want of heart." So, even if your intentions are not malicious, think before you act.

FOR YOUR COMFORT

Some medical sources report that the body loses valuable amounts of vitamin C on long trips and recommend taking supplemental pills before, during, and after a long-distance flight. (Check with your doctor.) Because the humidity level in the cabin air is very low, the body can be significantly dehydrated, causing fatigue, general malaise, and severe drying of respiratory passages. Be sure to drink plenty of fluids—juices and water, not alcohol or caffeine drinks, which aggravate the dehydration and energy depletion. Some authorities suggest drinking eight ounces of water for each hour of flight time, and recommend taking along bottled water, especially on international flights. Eye drops are an excellent idea for contact lens wearers, as is moisturizing lotion for the skin. If your ears tend to become blocked during the plane's descent, chewing gum is useful, or close your mouth, pinch your nose, and push air up into your ears to help equalize the air pressure. Take along a sweater or a light shawl or scarf to ward off chills from the air conditioning.

How you dress in public is important. Slacks can look as neat as any other attire and are a comfortable way for women to be dressed on an airplane. For men, slacks and sport coats or neat, good-looking sweaters are quite acceptable. While it is hard to avoid some rumpling, try to choose fabrics that can withstand long periods of sitting. Many flight attendants complain about the low standards of dress. A dirty, unkempt appearance is offputting. And you are apt to get better service from agents and flight attendants if you are neatly groomed and dressed. The wearing of sweatsuits, shorts, and sporting garb of almost any kind has become all too common these days, and looks sloppy.

Some travelers equip themselves with eyeshades and earplugs to shut out noise and light, while others seem to be able to fall asleep like babies the minute they are airborne. If someone in the seat beside you is snoring heavily, you'll just have to bear it, but if two people are involved in a loud conversation, you are within your rights to ask that they lower their voices.

A word about alcohol: FAA regulations prohibit allowing anyone who is intoxicated to board an aircraft. If an attendant feels a passenger is close to intoxication, she can deny him further drinks. You are not allowed to bring liquor into the cabin. Most airlines limit you to two drinks. If you want to have a cocktail and wine with your meal, ask for both drinks at the same time. You may have to pay for alcoholic drinks (except in first and business class) and so it helps to have the correct change available. If someone beside you is intoxicated, ask an attendant to handle the situation. If there is an empty seat, the offender can be moved, or you can move.

Should you be in your third trimester of pregnancy, your doctor may suggest that you not fly. If you look extremely large, it may be a good idea to have a letter from your obstetrician, certifying that you are fit to travel.

Each airline has its own regulations and fees for pets. Certain airlines allow one dog or cat in the cabin and all require dog kennels or cat carriers.

According to many flight attendants, the most annoying aspect of airline passengers is the astonishing amount of trash they leave behind, all of which the attendants have to clean up if it is a continuing flight. Dispose of your refuse in the large garbage bags attendants bring by at the end of the flight, and stack newspapers neatly on your seat.

As you leave the plane, say a few words of thanks to the flight attendants standing near the exit door. If the captain is in the vicinity, thank him also. A compliment on the landing, if it was smooth, is always appreciated.

CHILDREN ON THE PLANE

At the time you make your airline reservations, tell your travel agent or the airline if you will be traveling with a baby (a child travels free until age two). An airline has the option of refusing passage to an infant younger than seven days. When traveling with a baby, request a bulkhead seat, which allows you more space. Most airlines can supply a bassinet on overseas flights. If you have an *approved* child restraint seat, you may bring it (it must have been manufactured after February 1985), but tell the airline agent in advance. You must bring any supplies you will need for your baby: food, formula, diapers, wipes. The logistics of changing your baby in the lavatory may not be that easy, but it must be done there, not on your seat in front of seatmates. Put the used diaper in an airtight airsickness bag and dispose of it in the wastebin in the lavatory. The flight attendants will be happy to heat up your baby's bottle and will probably be gracious about helping with the baby, although this is not part of their duties. They should not be thought of as babysitters or mother's aides.

Special children's meals (hamburgers or hot dogs) must be ordered in advance. Bring snacks for your child, who may get hungry before the in-flight meal is served. Infants and toddlers are often sensitive to the cabin pressure changes when the plane takes off and lands. However, if you pop a pacifier or bottle into a baby's mouth just before take-off and landing, it will help clear his ears. For older children, chewing gum or hard candy to suck will do the same thing.

At the age of two, a child is required to have his own seat (a toddler seat fits into the regular seat). The percentage of the fare he pays is based on the fare structure of the ticket of the accompanying adult. At age twelve, full fare is required.

Before you take your child on his first flight, talk to him about what it will be like. Make sure he understands that he must remain in his seat, except for a trip to the lavatory or for an occasional, accompanied stroll. Some parents may think it cute for little kids to romp in the aisles (and of course the sight of a happy, well-mannered child is very engaging) but it can be dangerous for the child as well as for others if there is a sudden bump of turbulence. Just as with the younger child, don't forget to bring a number of favorite toys or games, some crayons and coloring paper, a book, and maybe a special new toy to help fill the time.

On most airlines, children starting at the age of five are allowed to travel unaccompanied. Until they are eight, they may fly alone only on a direct or nonstop flight. Children twelve and over are considered "young adults." A child traveling alone is given an "Unaccompanied Minor Pouch" to hold all documents she will need: ticket, boarding pass, Unaccompanied Minor Form, passport (if overseas). Take your child to the gate agent, who will pre-board the child and introduce her to the head flight attendant, who will assign a particular flight attendant to her. If you alert the gate agent in advance and it is convenient you may be allowed to see your child onto the plane. Don't linger on the plane, however, because it will only upset your child and will delay boarding the other passengers.

If a child eight or older has to make a connection, a flight attendant should escort the child to the gate agent. The flight attendant will make sure the child is wearing the Unaccompanied Minor Pouch and check that all his in-flight belongings are with him, and the gate agent will see that he makes the connecting flight. At the destination city, the flight attendant there will hand the child over to the person designated on the Unaccompanied Minor Form (whose identity must be verified) to meet him, or to the gate agent if no one is allowed to meet deplaning passengers at the arrival gate. Airlines usually charge a fee of about twenty-five dollars for such escort services.

An unaccompanied child should always have identification on him, some cash for emergencies, and clear instructions about how to call the person meeting him or, in case there's a problem, a relative or friend. Warn your child not to go anywhere with strangers and to obey airline personnel. If your child appears apprehensive about traveling alone, identify and discuss his fears beforehand. You might give him a brief rundown of what happens on planes, including the in-flight instructions, meal service, staying seated with seat belt buckled. (There are picture books and story books for young children describing traveling alone on a plane.) Make an airplane trip seem special to your child and be sure to allow plenty of time to get to the airport to avoid rushed goodbyes.

BY SHIP

Twenty-five or thirty years ago there were many transatlantic passenger steamships sailing back and forth across the Atlantic to Europe. "Getting There Is Half the Fun" was a familiar advertising slogan and it was if the weather cooperated. Today, only one great passenger ship—the *Queen Elizabeth II*—has a regular, nonstop transatlantic route, but only during the summer months. Most ocean travel today is on cruise ships. The largest carry as many as 2,400 passengers, the smallest about 200, and they sail virtually all the seas of the world. There are cruises on steel hull sailing clippers, or on windjammer ships with full sails, or on huge yachts. You can travel on the rivers of China, Egypt, Africa, France, England, the United States, or South America. In one recent year, 4 million passengers from the United States and Canada chose to cruise somewhere in the world, and in the early nineties, eighteen new cruise ships were licensed, as the boom in marine travel escalated.

Cruises are some people's idea of heaven: a calm, leisurely way to get away and visit interesting ports of call, in which two of the most difficult travel decisions—where to stay and where to eat—are taken care of. All-inclusive prices also make things easier.

If you enjoy the pleasures offered by a well-run ship and the smells and sights of the ocean, the allure of foreign or domestic port cities, the charm of unexpectedly interesting and amusing people, and the holiday atmosphere which shipboard cruises encourage, then cruising is for you. But whereas long, lazy hours at sea with books, card games, deck sports, lectures, or just watching the horizon can be highly relaxing and enjoyable, some people may find the confinement and the enforced socializing with strangers not their cup of tea. So it's important to think carefully about your preferences before signing up for a cruise.

You can, of course, book a cruise directly with the steamship company, but a good travel agent is of enormous value as he will be able to tell you what cruises are available at the time you want to travel, which ones might appeal to you, the various levels of accommodations available and their costs, the schedule of payments necessary, and many other logistical details.

Generally, a cruise line asks for a deposit representing about ten percent of the total fare when the booking is made, with final payment due about six weeks before departure. If you cancel after the deadline, you will probably have to pay a percentage of the fare as a penalty. If, because of illness or a death in the family, you must cancel your trip, the amount of the refund you receive depends on how far in advance you cancel and whether the cabin can be resold. Cancellation insurance is recommended if you make your plans very far in advance.

The price of your ticket includes accommodations, all meals, entertainment on board, and the use of pools and sports and spa facilities on board. You must pay extra for shore excursions, port taxes, any wines or liquors (except at ship-sponsored cocktail parties), dry cleaning, laundry, personal services such as a massage or haircut, and tips. Tipping can be a significant expense on cruises, so be sure to include it in your budget.

The more expensive your cabin, the larger and higher up on the ship it is likely to be. Outside cabins with portholes are more desirable than inside cabins and therefore more expensive, and forward in the ship is preferable to aft because of the engine noise in the stern. Your travel agent will be able to show you a plan of the ship and recommend the most desirable cabins in your price range.

Most ships nowadays have smoking and nonsmoking sections clearly indicated. It's never safe to smoke in your berth. And never flip your cigarette or cigar or pipe ashes overboard. The wind could blow the cigarette or a spark back onto the ship or into someone's eye.

On the larger ships there are usually two dinner seatings, one at 6:30 P.M. and the other (considered more fashionable) at 8 P.M. At the time you make your reservations you should put in a request for the dinner seating you prefer. (When traveling with young children, the early sitting is probably the better choice.) On smaller ships, there may be only one sitting. While you can indicate how large a table you'd prefer, since there are few tables for two, they must be booked early. When you travel alone, ask to be put at a large table with other single travelers, not exclusively with couples. Once aboard, if for some reason you aren't happy with the table you have been assigned, ask the dining-room steward or the purser if you can be moved.

If you are going to be traveling with children, find out before you book a cruise what facilities are available for them. On the larger ships, for instance, there is often a Teen Room for games, sodas, and general hanging out. On just about any cruise, babysitting can be arranged for a fee, and often child care with supervised playrooms, toys, games, and activities for younger children is available during the day.

It is recommended that you make appointments for facials or to have your hair done before you sail. The most popular times (the day of a gala, for instance) are booked well ahead of time. If you want a deck chair in a specific location, book that early also. Reconfirm all appointments and dinner and deck chair assignments soon after your ship leaves port.

When you receive the cruise line packet with your tickets and boarding instructions (boarding is usually two hours before departure time), you will also receive baggage tags (each piece of luggage must have a properly filled-out tag attached, as well as your own personal identification tag), perhaps your dining-room reservation card, and perhaps a pamphlet describing life on board the ship. Also included will be information about the ports of call, money exchange, postal information, and an itinerary with mailing addresses to give to your family and friends. All ships now have radiophone or satellite equipment for ship-to-shore communications. Telexes and faxes may be sent and received on board as well.

One thing you will be required to do is participate in the fire and lifeboat drills. Pay close attention and follow instructions carefully, even though the chances are that no such emergencies will arise.

When you board the ship, porters will take your bags directly to your cabin. It is thoughtful to tip them, even if stated cruise line policy is otherwise. While unlikely, in some ports there may be people milling about offering to take your luggage on board. Hand your luggage over only to identified personnel, who must wear badges showing their photograph and ship's company number.

If you are planning a cruise on the *QE II* your dining room is determined by the category of cabin you are in. Those with the more expensive cabins who eat in the smaller dining rooms dress formally every night for dinner, the men in dinner jackets and the women in dinner dresses, dressy pantsuits, or cocktail dresses. In the other dining rooms there are usually only one or two nights when formal wear is requested, but not required, although many couples enjoy the chance to dress formally. Traditionally, the first and last nights out no one dresses for dinner. On a cruise, formal dinner dress is probably needed only for the captain's dinner, but jackets and ties for men and cocktail-style dresses for the women are the preferred choices for the other nights. The information you receive from the cruise line will include guides for proper dress. But remember, closet space on board ship is limited except, possibly, in the most luxurious cabins. And although there are usually no restrictions on luggage, it is not sensible to overpack, especially if you are sharing a small cabin or returning by air.

During the day dress is quite casual. Sports clothes such as shorts, slacks, and jogging suits are fine for breakfast and lunch (bathing suits may not be worn in the dining room, unless you have a cover-up). The evening meal is a little dressier. Light jackets for men and shawls or sweaters for women are good to have along. Nights at sea, even in the tropics, can sometimes be quite cool.

If a friend of yours is taking a cruise, and you want to give him a present before he departs, books, a travel diary, or some small traveling game set (backgammon, cribbage, or chess) are good ideas. Otherwise, an arrangement can be made with the steamship company to deliver champagne or a bottle of wine, a basket of fruit, or flowers to his cabin.

If you want to entertain in your cabin, or give a small party in one of the ship's lounges, you will be charged for the food and liquor if the party is held before the ship sails; just for the liquor during the cruise. Most ships, because of security concerns, do not allow visitors to come aboard before sailing, so for the most part "Bon Voyage" parties are a thing of the past.

If you decide to have a cocktail party in your cabin or in a ship's lounge, speak to the purser or to the cruise director and he will make the necessary arrangements. You'll probably want to invite the people you sit with in the dining room and others you have met around the swimming pool or elsewhere. Should you be sitting at the table of one of the ship's officers, there's no reason not to invite him to the party if you want to.

It's shipboard etiquette to know that the captain of the ship is addressed as "Captain," and the other officers as "Mr.," "Mrs.," or "Ms." The ship's doctor, however, is called "Dr." It is considered an honor to be invited to eat at the captain's table during the cruise. If you are so honored, be on time for meals and don't order until he arrives. Introduce yourself to everyone at the table and make an effort to keep the conversation lively. Usually the captain will give a cocktail party sometime during the cruise in order to greet the various passengers. When it's your turn, shake his hand and say, "Hello, Captain," or "Hello, Captain Smith," followed by a brief comment about the trip. Don't detain him as there will be others anxious to meet him. Usually the ship's photographer is at the party to take a picture of each passenger as he greets the captain. The photos are later tacked onto a bulletin board for everyone to look at and order as a souvenir of the trip.

Wherever you cruise there is the possibility of rough seas. If you are prone to motion or seasickness, before leaving on the trip ask your doctor what medicine he recommends. Ginger is a good stomach settler, as is fresh air, unless the weather is so foul and the deck is rolling so badly it would be foolhardy to venture out. If you feel real discomfort you can, of course, visit the ship's doctor.

On certain cruises the boat may dock for a night or two, allowing passengers to take day trips ashore. You will be given explicit information about the ship's departure time, so it's your responsibility to be back on board at the specified time.

Ship's news is distributed in daily handouts slipped under your cabin door early in the morning. The availability of sports and library facilities will be announced, as will various activities, such as bridge and Ping-Pong tournaments, costume parties, children's entertainment, movies, lectures, and concerts. The cruise or social director is on hand most of the day, eager to make sure everyone enjoys the voyage as fully as possible. If you're traveling alone and you'd like to play bridge, or be introduced to people, mention this to the cruise director.

At the end of the cruise, thank crew members and officers who were particularly helpful. The social director will also be pleased if you tell her you enjoyed the activities she organized. The list of those to be tipped is a long one and includes your cabin steward, the dining steward (possibly the maître d' in the dining room), the wine steward if used, and the deck steward. The cruise line often provides tipping information in its brochure sent to you with your tickets; if not, you can call to ask for advice on the subject of tipping.

BY CAR

Traveling by car is second nature to millions of North Americans. But driving a car is a serious responsibility. If you are at the controls of a two-thousand-pound piece of moving machinery, your paramount concern should be for the safety of yourself, your passengers, and everyone around you, whether they are driving, cycling, or walking on the road. Good driving is synonymous with good manners, and courtesy and safety go hand in hand on the road.

As a driver, your first obligation is to know how to operate a car properly. It is also important to have the car you drive serviced frequently to ensure that it is operating safely. If, while you are driving, your car should suddenly experience any mechanical difficulties, turn on the hazard signal to show other drivers that you may have to stop suddenly or cannot maintain normal speed.

It is the law that you and all passengers in your car buckle up your seat belts. You, the driver, are responsible morally as well as legally for the safety of your passengers, so see that everyone uses his or her belt. Children moving around in a car are a safety hazard. The very young should ride in special safety seats (mandated in many states) and when older always strapped in with seat belts whether in the front or back seat. Pets should be carried in a pet carrier. If necessary, there are special barriers available to set up between the backseat and the rear of the car to keep pets in a specified area.

If you've ever driven with a well-trained, disciplined driver, you will appreciate the calm, in-control, intelligent way she handles the car. She never takes chances when entering traffic, or darts out in front of an oncoming car, or tries to edge another driver out of a parking space, or passes in a no-passing zone or when road conditions are hazardous. She dims her headlights at night when an oncoming car draws near and, if the other car does not lower its headlights, she blinks hers as a reminder. A careful driver never tailgates; does not exceed posted speed limits or drive too slowly given road, weather, or traffic conditions. To drive carefully you have to be alert at all times. Drinking or eating while driving is dangerous, and eyes should be kept on the road while operating the tape deck or cellular phone. Driving demands your complete concentration. Never drive when sleepy; find a safe spot to pull over to take a break or nap. And don't carry more passengers than the car calls for; not only is it illegal, it also makes it difficult to drive.

If you are setting off on a long trip with one or more people, it's a good idea to alternate drivers every hundred miles or so. Take along a thermos with cold water or tea or coffee, whatever will help you stay awake. It's also a good idea to take exercise breaks to stretch your legs.

If you have an accident with another vehicle, exchange names and addresses and insurance information with the driver of the other car(s) involved and report the accident to the police and your insurance company. Insurance coverage is mandatory in all states.

If you have a breakdown on a major turnpike or interstate highway, pull your car as far off the road as possible. Tie a white handkerchief to the aerial or door and raise the hood of the car to indicate you need assistance. Avoid walking on a high-speed artery to get help. It can be dangerous, especially at night. In fact, on some major highways it is advised that you not leave your car, but remain in it with the doors locked, until a police car comes by.

The pressures of our daily lives sometimes make us forget good manners, especially when in a car. But a friendly greeting to a toll taker or giving way to a car trying to make a turn is not too much to ask of anyone. Don't litter the roadside with trash or anything else. Several states have laws on the books to punish such offenders.

SOME DO'S AND DON'TS

- Obey all posted speed limits.
- Leave the parking spaces designated for handicapped drivers for their use (it's illegal not to do so).
- Be aware of other cars, and check the rear-view and side mirrors frequently.
- Be ready to respond to trouble or to make a sudden stop if necessary.
- Always keep your emotions in check, no matter how trying the situation.
- Keep a small first-aid kit in the car, along with a flashlight and emergency lights or a reflecting triangle to set up on the road to signal that your car is disabled. (Use the flashing lights while driving if your car is disabled.)
- If you travel during the winter in Northern areas, keep a car blanket, boots, collapsible shovel, and ice scraper in the trunk.
- Join a national automobile association that provides emergency help on the road.
- If you frequently travel alone at night in places where there are few gas stations, you might want to carry a can of gas and invest in a cellular car phone.
- If you're stopped by a state trooper for speeding or other infraction, don't try to talk your way out of it if you are clearly in the wrong. It will do you no good. Be polite in accepting the ticket or warning.
- Don't litter the roadside.
- Don't use your horn except when necessary.

SOME SAFETY TIPS

- Park in well-lighted lots and always lock your car.
- When you return to a parking lot to get your car, have your key in your hand ready to open the door.
- Check the backseat of your car before you get in.

- If another driver tries to get you to pull over on the pretext that there is something wrong with your car, don't stop, but head for the nearest gas station to have your car checked.

- Don't stop for flashing white lights; lights on emergency vehicles are red or red and blue.

- Don't pick up hitchhikers.

- If you must leave your car on the street overnight, get an anti-theft locking device to put on the steering wheel.

- If your car is stolen, or if you have an accident, report it to the police immediately. If it's a rented car, report it to the rental company by telephone. They will shunt your call to their nearest agency office and will send someone to pick you up and provide a replacement.

TRAVELING BY CAR WITH CHILDREN

If you plan to travel any distance by car with children, some special thought is called for. For instance, you will need to stop frequently because children get restless when they are cooped up. Think up some simple but fun games to play with crayons and paper, or take along small toys or hand-held electronic games. Road games, such as counting the number of birds on telephone wires, or noting the different car licenses, can be played by everyone and can help relieve the tedium of long days of driving. Talking about the surrounding countryside or your destination helps pass the time and educates as well. There are books on traveling with children that suggest clever game ideas that don't require much equipment. Don't forget to bring a child's favorite stuffed animals, dolls, or blankets. Car doors should always be locked for safety, and be sure to secure the rear door of a station wagon.

A favorite aunt of ours used to send us off on long car trips with a box of wonderful surprises, including coloring books, small dolls, and trinkets as well as chicken sandwiches, fruits, sour balls, and chocolate, which made our trips exciting adventures. You can do the same for your child by packing a box of small toys, books, simple puzzles, word games, and snacks, each one wrapped separately in colored tissue paper to be opened at determined intervals. If the trip is for several days, be sure to take along any medications the children might need, for diarrhea, for pain relief, cortisone creams for skin rash, adhesive bandages of several sizes, packets of moistened towelettes, and ginger capsules for motion sickness.

Children understandably don't like being confined for long periods of time, but they need to be taught that poor behavior is not permissible on the road. If squabbling breaks out, some parents take fairly extreme measures such as pulling off the road and declaring that, until the fighting ends, the car will not move. If this works for you, fine, but naturally it will not work for everyone.

DRIVING ABROAD

Rules of the road vary in different countries, so it's important to consult the consulate or tourist bureau of the country or countries you will be driving in or ask your regional American or Canadian Automobile Association to provide you with specific information about speed limits, road signs, the use of directional signals, headlights, and other driving courtesies which may be the law of that particular country. In many European cities, for instance, honking the horn is against the law; instead you must flash your headlights. And anywhere you see striped pedestrian "zebra" marks, it means you must give the pedestrian the right of way. It is a good idea to familiarize yourself with international road signs before going abroad.

Driving in Great Britain or Japan is on the left side of the road, which may be confusing at first, although not that hard to get used to if you rent a left-hand-drive car. If you think shifting with your left hand will be problematical, rent an automatic shift car (not many companies abroad have automatic shifts, so reserve early).

A cautionary note: in some European cities you may see a "Control Zone Parking" sign in municipal parking lots. These are zones that are checked by security police from time to time throughout the day. If you leave your car unattended in one of these zones for more than the time you have paid for, the security people may become suspicious. They might haul it away or put a "boot" or clamp on the wheel, requiring you to pay a fine at police headquarters before you can drive the car away.

CAR RENTAL

It is common sense to make a reservation for a rental car well in advance on particularly busy weekends and holidays. If you are flying into a city where you will need to rent a car, ask your travel agent or the airline to arrange this for you. There are several national chains of car rental agencies, but don't overlook the local agencies, which sometimes cost less than the national organizations.

You must be at least twenty-five years old to rent a car and have a valid driver's license. Some car rental agencies will waive the age minimum for an extra premium. You may pay for the rental with a credit card or by check (most agencies prefer credit cards). You will need to make your reservation twenty-four hours in advance if you want to pay by check, to allow the company time to run a cash qualification on you. If you pay by check, you may be asked to show a credit card anyway.

The contract you sign with the rental firm will spell out the basics: mileage charge, daily rental fee, time of pickup and drop-off, the mileage as shown on the car's odometer, and also the insurance options you select, if any. The agencies will often try to sell you extra protection, but check the coverage you have from your credit card or your personal insurance.

Recently, some national car rental chains have instituted a screening check of drivers' records to see if they have a history of violations. At this writing, only a few companies and only a few states are set up for such screening, but it is possible it will become a national trend as the rental companies have suffered large liability charges.

Before you accept the rental car, check to make sure that it is in good condition with a usable spare tire and that everything is clean and in working order (lights, signals, brakes, horn). Make a note of the mileage when you pick up the car and when you drop it off. Drop-off options vary from company to company; be sure you are aware of the particular policy if you plan to leave your car somewhere other than where you pick it up. If another person will also be driving the car, the name of that person must be included on the rental contract. When you return the car, be sure to fill up the gas tank, or the rental company will do so at a very high per-gallon cost.

If you want to rent a car abroad, your travel agent can arrange this for you (probably the best idea, as she may be able to get you a particularly good rate). She will give you a voucher to present to the rental agency when you arrive. Specify exactly what kind of car you want (size and manual or automatic shift). Your agent can also advise you on whether you need extra insurance and/or an international driver's license (not necessary in most European countries anymore).

By Train

As the end of the twentieth century approaches, railroad buffs can take heart that the United States nationwide Amtrak train service, run by the public-private National Railroad Passenger Corporation, is alive and functioning well. The system links all major cities and covers the country from coast to coast, north and south. You may dial one toll-free number, 1-800-USA-RAIL, to plan your itinerary, receive schedule and fare information, or buy your tickets. You can pay for your ticket with a check or a credit card and it will be mailed to you if there is time, or you may pick it up at the terminal or at a local ticket office in the larger cities.

In Canada, Via Rail Canada operates throughout the nation, and its famous cross-country train runs three times a week from Toronto to Vancouver and return. If you leave Toronto on a Tuesday, you will reach Vancouver on Friday morning and along the way see some of the most spectacular scenery in North America. For information, call 1-800-561-3949.

In both the United States and Canada your travel agent will tell you about various discounts, tour packages, and the like and will make the necessary arrangements. Also, Amtrak publishes a national timetable twice a year and a Travel Planner information book, "Amtrak's America," which lists its services, baggage allowances, the cities served, information on connecting services, special bus-rail, air-rail packages, car-rail options, hotel packages, escorted tour vacations and destination vacations which include hotel and sightseeing possibilities. Discounted family fares are available at certain times of the year.

In general terms, there are two classes of train travel: first class and coach. First class includes club service, custom class (in a deluxe reserved-seat car), and sleeping-car accommodations which you must reserve and pay for over and above the cost of the rail ticket. Coach tickets (unreserved seats) are available on almost all trains, except on a few "All Reserved" trains. Accommodations differ. For example, in the West, the trains are all Superliners, bilevel trains with coaches, sightseer lounge cars, and full-service dining and sleeping cars. In the East, there are a variety of short-distance trains (Metroliner, Amfleet, and Horizon Fleet) and several long-distance trains, each of which includes choices of accommodations in first and coach classes.

First-class accommodations must always be reserved. They offer more room, more comfortable seats, and fewer passengers per car than coach, plus an attendant for each car and meal service, often served at your seat. While dress is not overly formal (especially on long, overnight trips) the attire of first-class passengers usually reflects this choice of travel class.

In overnight first-class sleeping cars, complimentary meals may be served in the dining car, where particular attention should be given to neatness of appearance and clothing. Linen, towels, soap are also complimentary and you can get your shoes shined, get a free newspaper and a wake-up call with your coffee and juice. In club service (generally only daytime service) beverages and complimentary meals are served at your seat. Complimentary coffee, or tea or juice and newspapers are available.

Metropolitan Lounges for first-class passengers have been set up in major stations such as Chicago, New York (Penn Station), Washington, Philadelphia (30th Street Station), and Los Angeles. In these waiting rooms, located for easy access to trains, various amenities such as complimentary beverages, conference rooms, TV, phones, fax machines, even working fireplaces are available. Staff are on hand to offer information and help, should it be needed. These lounges are intended to be places of relaxation, so you should not compromise the comforts of other passengers by being noisy or impolite. Respect your fellow passengers here as well as on board the trains.

Because coach class (both daytime and overnight) is cheaper than first class and is the more common way to travel by train, the atmosphere tends to be informal. Seating is unreserved, so if you travel on busy weekends or during the holidays be prepared for crowded conditions, possibly standing room only. In coach, sandwiches, snacks, and beverages are sold in the café or lounge cars, and you can either eat there or take your food back to your seat. Dispose of your trash in the receptacles at the end of the cars.

Don't leave orange peels, sandwich wrappings, or soda cans on or under your seat.

Smoking is allowed only in sleeping cars, designated sections of the lounge or club car, or in designated coaches. Smoking is not permitted in dining cars. If you want to listen to a radio or tape player, you must use earphones. Even if you have earphones, however, you should keep the volume down so as not to disturb fellow passengers. Always be considerate of others and refrain from loud conversations late at night. People may be trying to sleep. If you use on-board telephones, keep your voice low. If you are traveling with children, do not let them play in the aisles.

Trains offer a variety of sleeping accommodations: roomettes, family bedrooms, slumber coaches, and special roomettes for the disabled. Some of the sleeping-car accommodations have toilet facilities in the room; a few even include a shower. If your room does not have its own toilet, it's acceptable to wear a dressing gown or bathrobe in the corridor to and from the rest rooms. But keep your visit to the public rest room as brief as possible and leave it as clean as you would hope to find it.

Some long-distance trains feature Sightseer and See-Level Lounges from which to enjoy spectacular views of the countryside. In some lounges, video, movies (cartoons for the kids), a piano, and late night snacks are available. Pillows are provided for overnight trips in coach and souvenir Amtrak blankets can be purchased, or you can bring along your own. Cafés and lounges are for socializing and, if you are in the mood, a conversation with an interesting stranger can be a wonderful way to pass the time. At your seat, however, if the person next to you seems unwilling to chat, don't persist. If you are the one trying to read or get some work done, or just want to watch the passing scene, politely tell your seatmate that you need the time to do some thinking, to doze, or offer some other excuse.

If you are sitting by the window, before you pull down the shade by your seat, it is considerate to ask if your seatmate would mind. If you are sitting on the aisle, get up graciously to let your seatmate in or out of her seat. If someone needs help in stowing luggage in the overhead rack, it is basic courtesy to offer a helping hand. If you are not reading at night, turn off your reading light so it doesn't bother others, and don't feel shy about politely asking someone to turn off hers if the hour is late. An eyeshade and/or earplugs can be helpful when trying to sleep at night in coach.

Children under eight traveling by train must be accompanied by an adult. Children between eight and eleven may travel alone under certain conditions, which you should ask the ticket agent about. Unaccompanied children are charged full fare, but often special discounts, such as free travel, are available for accompanied children from two to fifteen.

Redcap service for luggage is provided at the major train terminals, but Amtrak cautions travelers to use only properly identified handlers. Redcaps should be tipped about one dollar per bag, more if the bags are heavy or unwieldy. All passengers may check up to three bags per ticket, so long as no one bag weighs more than 75 pounds and the total per ticketed passenger is no more than 150 pounds. Unless you will have a sleeping compartment, it's sensible to check your large bags and keep only a small overnight bag with you for things you will need en route.

COMMUTER TRAIN TRAVEL

Those who commute to work every day by train experience an entirely different sort of train travel, one that is a culture in and of itself. It is characterized by informal but carefully observed rules, which are easy to get the hang of and probably vary from region to region. Still, a few common themes of "proper" behavior are evident on most commuter trains.

One of the most noticeable things about commuters is their relative lack of sociability. Usually the earlier the hour the less conversation there is. A pleasant "Good morning" is never out of place, however, for friends and acquaintances. Most people in the earliest hours of the morning value their privacy. They like to read the morning newspaper, study business papers, or catch a little extra sleep. The atmosphere on a commuter car in the morning is generally quiet and calm.

The novice commuter should be alert to the territoriality some commuters feel about their seating. Technically no seats are reserved on commuter trains, and at times the battle for seating can be intense. Window and aisle seats are preferred, but if you are obliged to sit between two people accept it with good grace. It is selfish and discourteous to put a briefcase, suitcase, or raincoat on the seat next to you in an effort to keep the seat for your own use. If you see a seat with someone's belongings on it, you should not be timid about asking the person to remove them so you may sit there.

Smoking is not allowed on commuter cars or in many stations. If you take a cup of coffee, a drink, or a snack with you on the train and there are no trash receptacles available, you're responsible for disposing of the trash after you leave the train. Some stations have large recycling bins on the platforms into which you can toss your newspaper.

If two people are traveling together on the train and are looking for adjoining seats, offer your seat if there is an empty one next to it and provided there are other single seats available. It is a particularly nice gesture to offer to move for a mother and child traveling together. It is still customary to give up your seat to a man or woman of a certain age, or to anyone you think might need it more than you do: the elderly, and most certainly a pregnant woman or someone who is disabled. If they refuse, fine. If you see someone struggling to hoist a large bag up onto the baggage rack, offer a hand.

If you must use your portable telephone on a commuter train, keep your voice down. And beware: it can be dangerous to use a cellular phone or any phone in public. There is a current scam whereby thieves operate scanners to pick up the number you charge your calls to, then use that number (or sell it) to run up telephone bills which you may be responsible for.

Again, if you use a personal headset radio or tape player, use the headphones and keep the volume down.

It is thoughtful to say good morning to the conductor you see every day and to have your ticket ready when he or she comes to punch or collect it. Conductors work hard to keep the train on schedule and to look out for your safety. They much appreciate your good manners and civility.

BY BUS

During the eighties, more than 20 million people annually traveled by bus in the United States and Canada. As bus travel is generally cheaper than travel by plane or train, most of these travelers tend to be under thirty-four years of age. If you look at the route map of Greyhound, the major national bus company in the United States, its routes cover virtually every bit of the country. The company fields about three thousand buses which serve three thousand plus destinations, covering nearly 300 million miles per year. In Canada, Canadian Greyhound (a separate company) criss-crosses Canada, connecting at several points with United States bus lines. Buses are equipped with reclining seats, air conditioning, and toilets, and feature huge, tinted windows from which the view of the country is even better than from a train. As the slogan says, "Go by bus and leave the driving to us!" For a close-up view of the countryside with none of the responsibilities entailed in driving your own car, nothing can beat it.

Schedules are usually changed three times a year. There is an increase in service during the summer months and holiday times when travel is heaviest. Special discounts are given on fares bought seven, fourteen, or thirty days in advance of the trip. Special long-distance "Ameripasses" allow unlimited travel throughout the system.

Tickets may be purchased directly from the bus company at their terminals. Local telephone directories list the numbers for schedule and fare information in the yellow or business pages under "Bus." (Travel agents do not generally book this type of travel, because the amount of money involved makes their commissions too low to be worth their while.) Every passenger is allowed to check two pieces of luggage on a bus and to carry on two small pieces that fit in the overhead bins or in front of (or under) his feet. The maximum size and weight allowed for a bag varies according to the line you are traveling with. The company will insure up to four bags on one ticket for a maximum of two hundred and fifty dollars.

The atmosphere of bus travel is informal and casual dress is the norm.

Loose-fitting shirts, sweaters, and slacks for both men and women are ideal. A pair of socks or slippers are useful on long trips. Layering clothes makes sense in case the bus is too hot or cold. Although blue jeans are universally popular, they are not that comfortable if you have to sit for a long time in a confined space. It is not easy to move around on a bus. Walking in the aisle is not encouraged because there's always the possibility that the bus will swerve or make a sudden stop. When it comes to sleeping, bring along an eyeshade and earplugs. Scarves come in handy for covering your eyes, or keeping your neck warm, or even, in an emergency, for mopping up spills. Bring along a small bag with a few cosmetic items, such as soap, toothpaste, and moistened towelettes, with which to refresh yourself from time to time. If reading on a bus makes you carsick, you will have to entertain yourself some other way.

The driver pulls into a rest stop approximately every two hours, to allow passengers to buy snacks or use the rest rooms. The average stay is thirty minutes. Take advantage of these rest stops by having a quick walk to get the kinks out of your joints and to breathe some fresh air. Although long-distance buses have toilet facilities, many passengers prefer to wait to use the toilets at the rest stops. In urban areas, the bus terminals are usually located somewhere near the center of town, while out in the country a "terminal" may be an all-night truck stop, a restaurant, or a gas station.

In the close and casual atmosphere of a bus, chatting with your seatmate is a good way to pass the time, but the usual common-sense rules apply. If you don't want to talk, bring a book or magazine, or politely demur when your seat companion strikes up a conversation. And if your attempts at friendly conversation are not met with enthusiasm, don't persist. Let your seatmate sleep or read or enjoy his privacy. And if you do find a compatible soul, speak quietly. Especially at night.

Smoking is not allowed on buses, but many of the bus terminals have designated smoking areas. On most long-distance trips, to pass the time, movies are shown. Radios and cassette players may be used on the bus, but only if equipped with individual headphones. Even with headphones, the volume of the music should not be so loud that it disturbs anyone. No pets are allowed, although Seeing Eye and hearing-ear dogs may travel with their owners. No alcohol is permitted on buses, but you are free to bring along snacks, as long as they are not messy to eat. Bottled water or soda is fine provided you can recap the container. Keep your trash in a plastic bag and toss it into the garbage at the rest stop. Never leave any litter, including newspapers and magazines, on or under your seat when you reach your final destination and leave the bus.

While seats are not reserved on buses, passengers customarily stay in the same seat for the length of a trip. Leave a book or raincoat on your seat when you get out at a rest stop. For some reason, the back of the bus seems to be the area where the chattiest people sit, so if you're looking for companionship, that's where to find it. The midsection is the smoothest ride (the roughest is over the wheels). The very front seats of the bus have the widest views of the road ahead. Among the rules posted in all buses is one forbidding engaging the driver in conversation—it could distract him and therefore be dangerous.

CHILDREN ON A BUS

On a bus children under eight must be accompanied by someone twelve or older. Children alone must travel during the daytime, be on the bus for no more than five hours, and arrive at a time when the destination terminal is open. A parent or guardian must complete and sign an "Unaccompanied Child Form." The parent should give the child careful instructions not to leave the bus, except at the authorized rest stops. A child should always have identification on him as well as the telephone number of the parent or person who will be meeting him at the terminal. If the person meeting him is late and if he has to wait at the terminal for any length of time, he should be advised not to speak to strangers and to stay near the ticket counter or wherever the bus official tells him to wait.

Children traveling alone pay the full adult fare. But if an adult is with them, one child under two may travel free and one child aged two through four may travel at ten percent of the adult fare. And any number of children aged five through eleven can travel for half price with an accompanying adult.

If you are traveling with young children, explain to them that it is not safe to walk up and down the aisle as the bus may make a sudden stop. When the bus stops for food and for rest-room use, see that your children walk (or trot) around to work off some of their pent-up energy. To keep your children entertained on the bus, take along coloring books, small toys, and some books to read quietly to them. Electronic games can be entertaining for bus trips, although the electronic beeps, clicks, and zaps they emit might annoy some passengers. Young children sometimes get carsick on buses, so bring along several sturdy plastic bags for an emergency. Disposable wipes are good to have for cleaning hands and faces. Don't forget to carry whatever you might need for a baby, including diapers, bottles, snacks, plus a blanket and a pillow, for naps.

Don't pile packages, knapsacks, coats, etc., on the seat beside you in hopes of discouraging a seatmate. It won't work on crowded trips and can cause confusion and delays.

A disabled person traveling alone, or using a battery-operated wheelchair, must give the bus line forty-eight hours' notice so that special assistance can be set up along the route. At rest stops, the driver or other bus personnel will assist the disabled person on and off the bus and with stowing and retrieving a wheelchair or any other equipment he brings along.

Bus drivers on commercial buses are not tipped, unless you are on a chartered bus tour and the driver acts as guide as well as driver.

GROUP TRAVEL BY BUS

Chartered bus tours are convenient ways to see a lot in a short amount of time and are an extremely popular way to travel. While bus tours are an inexpensive way to sightsee, the trade-off is some compromise in comfort and independence. The bus company or the booking agent hires the bus driver and tour guide and takes care of the logistical details, such as checking in at hotels. Traveling this way with a large number of people has many rewards, principally the convenience of having the itinerary already determined, the hotels and some meals paid for, and visits to the most important tourist sights scheduled.

If you are on a bus tour, you must be sensitive to and tolerant of the group as a whole. When the bus stops at a tourist attraction or for a meal, stay with the group. Don't wander off on your own. If you are asked to have your luggage outside your hotel room at a certain hour for pickup, see that it is there on schedule.

On bus tours, it is customary for tour members to pass the hat around to collect a tip for the bus driver, although not necessarily for the tour guide, unless it's an overnight trip or the group has been particularly pleased with his services.

HOTELS AND MOTELS

HOTELS

Hotels are ranked in various categories ranging from quite simple to premier class or deluxe, depending upon the quality of accommodation, the extent of personal services, the location, and the cost. An experienced travel agent or a recommendation from a friend is the best way to find a good hotel. Some hotel restaurants are renowned for their chef's talents, or feature famous entertainers (pianists or cabaret singers) in their bars or lounges, and also have gift shops, florists, jewelers, and elegant clothing boutiques. Large, well-organized hotels will handle messages for you (motels do not generally have twenty-four-hour desk coverage), give you a wake-up call for early rising, and the best hotels pride themselves on their ability to extend a number of special personal services—with a smile. Little can compare, in fact, to the wonderfully cosseted feeling you get at a well-managed deluxe hotel.

Many luxury hotels offer enticing extras, such as terry-cloth robes, hair dryers, and an assortment of cosmetics in the bathroom. Mini-bars in the bedroom are stocked with all types of snacks, liquor, beer, and soft drinks that are as tempting and convenient as they are expensive. On request a key to the mini-bar is given to the guest along with his room key. The mini-bar (actually a small refrigerator) is checked each day and the cost of any item removed is added to the guest's bill. Stationery, postcards, and information regarding the hotel's services, are placed in each room. If a terry-cloth robe is provided, and you want to take it with you, tell the clerk at the front desk and he will charge it to your account. Towels, ashtrays, soap dishes, etc., are the property of the hotel, not souvenirs of your stay.

Luxury hotels are normally booked far in advance, so ask your travel agent to reserve space for you, or phone or fax the hotel yourself, well ahead of time. The room will be held for your arrival if you give your credit card number or send a deposit. A deposit check must arrive far enough in advance so there is time for it to clear before your arrival.

The wonderful European tradition of the concierge has become quite widespread in the finer hotels of North America. The concierge's desk is usually located somewhere near the registration desk in the hotel lobby. An experienced concierge can be helpful to hotel guests in a dozen ways. He can get tickets for the theater or other cultural or sporting events, make restaurant reservations, hire cars, book a sightseeing tour, help find a babysitter—in short, satisfy any individual needs or wishes you might have. A really well-trained concierge adds a separate dimension of service to the luxury hotel.

When you arrive at your hotel, the doorman will greet you and call for a porter to take charge of your luggage. If the doorman does little more than that, you need not tip him, but if he carries your bags into the lobby or takes care of garaging your car, tip him two dollars. Later, if he calls a cab for you, tip him about a dollar, unless it's pelting rain or snow—then give him slightly more.

You first check in at the registration desk. If you have a confirmation slip for your reservation, give it to the desk clerk. If you are married and arrive before your spouse, register for both of you as "Mr. and Mrs. Paul Robinson." If you are traveling alone, sign your name without a title (i.e., Paul Robinson). A married woman on a business trip who uses her maiden name professionally may want to give her husband's last name as well, so that she can be reached quickly in an emergency. If you are traveling with children, you can sign the register, "Mr. and Mrs. Peter Betts and family," or "Mr. Peter Betts and Emily Betts." When an unmarried couple register, both of them sign the register.

After you have registered, the desk clerk will give your key to the porter who will show you to your room. Even if you have only one bag, it's given to the porter. If there's no porter available once you've registered, you may be told to go directly to your room and that the porter will follow with your bags.

When you arrive at the door of your room the porter will open the door, turn on the lights, put your bags on the luggage stands, open the curtains, turn on the air conditioning, and give you instructions about the operation of the mini-bar, TV, or whatever else you want or need to know. Depending on the number of bags you have, you should tip him at least a dollar or two per bag. If you are not happy with your room, call the front desk to see if you can be assigned another room. Make your request in a calm, reasonable manner and explain why you wish to move. Most hotels will be happy to comply if they can.

As a guest in a hotel, you should familiarize yourself with the location of emergency exits and read any instructions about evacuation in case of fire. Take note of the exact location of the fire exit in relation to your room, knowledge that could save your life in a smoke-filled corridor. In case of a fire, always use the stairs, never the elevator.

Call housekeeping if you need extra blankets, pillows, towels, or clothes hangers. A hotelier friend reports that the ideal hotel room (like a guest room) should have two pillows for each occupant, excellent lighting, a desk with a chair, at least one comfortable armchair, and plenty of hangers, including skirt or trouser hangers. Many experienced travelers take earplugs and a 100-watt bulb with them in case the hotel is noisy or the room poorly lighted.

The "commercial" hotel, patronized largely by business travelers, is in a separate category. These hotels are as efficient and comfortable as others but perhaps somewhat less disposed to extra niceties of décor and service. However, they include conference rooms, a few large dining rooms and banquet halls for conventions, as well as whatever equipment, such as fax machines, copiers, or computers, may be needed for conducting business. They can also provide secretarial services.

One test of a truly fine hotel is its room service. Nearly all deluxe or first-class hotels offer room service at any hour of the day or night. It is also a good way to gauge how hard both employees and management work. It is amazing how swift and courteous this service can be. Breakfast service usually begins at 7 A.M. As many people will be ordering their breakfasts at about the same time, it's advisable to pre-order breakfast by marking the menu card in your room with what you want and when you want it. Hang the card on the outside knob of your door the night before. Even in the most efficient hotels, breakfast room service may be delayed, a point to keep in mind if you have an early appointment. The coffee shop might be a better idea if your appointment is crucial, or perhaps you can put in a special request for earlier service.

Deluxe hotels pride themselves on their room service and lay out fine china, crisp linens, shining cutlery, sparkling crystal glassware, and flowers for decoration. A local newspaper is included with breakfast. Greet the waiter (you don't need to worry about being completely dressed, a robe will do), and sign the bill. Ask if the service charge has been added; most hotels include a fifteen or twenty percent service charge and perhaps a surcharge for room service. If it hasn't been added in, give the waiter a fifteen or twenty percent tip. If you order a meal in your room, a special table with an insulated cabinet beneath it for hot foods will be wheeled in by the waiter. He will set up the table where you want it, remove food from the insulated cabinet, set it at your place, and remove any covers. When you've finished, call room service and ask to have the table or tray removed. As a courtesy to other guests on the floor, do not put the table outside your door. Leftover food is not attractive to look at.

Afternoon tea is a pleasant, relaxing interlude in the day's bustle. It may be served informally in your room or grandly in a lounge near the hotel lobby. A harpist or pianist (or a string quartet) may play music in the background. The custom of taking tea is a highly civilized one and civilized attire should go along with it. If you opt for the public version of this lovely afternoon ritual, dress appropriately. Blue jeans, sneakers, sweatsuits, and similar athletic wear are not suitable. Nor is teatime an occasion for agitated business negotiations or noisy celebrations which quickly dissipate the serenity of others.

Security is a growing problem these days in many cities both here and abroad. There are several things you can do to protect yourself and your belongings in a hotel. Leave any cash, jewelry, or other valuables in the safe at the front desk. Never open your door to a knock unless you are expecting someone (hotel employees always identify themselves). Always double-lock the door when you are in your room and use the chain provided. Although the conservation of energy should be in all our minds, some people advise leaving a lamp lighted or the radio or TV playing (softly) when you are not in your room to discourage robberies. If you return to the hotel late at night, be aware of the people around you on the streets in front of the hotel. Tourists who are out late are too frequently assaulted within the vicinity of their hotels.

WOMEN ALONE IN A HOTEL A single woman should feel completely at ease about eating dinner in the hotel dining room alone or having a drink alone at the bar. Some women like to take along a book, a newspaper, or postcards so they do not have to stare blankly into space or, worse, find themselves staring at the other diners. If you are at a resort hotel that gives a welcoming cocktail party for guests once or twice a week, don't be shy about going. It can often be a great deal of fun, but if you find you aren't having a good time, you can always slip out.

LEAVING THE HOTEL The day before your departure, confirm the checkout time—usually around the middle of the day—to ensure you will not be charged for an extra night. You may be able to make use of express checkout, whereby you sign your bill when you arrive, let the management post the charges as you incur them, then leave without having to check out. Sometimes the bill is slipped under your door the night before you leave for you to sign. If you have only one small bag, you can carry it down with you. Otherwise, call the front desk and ask for a porter. He will take your bags down to the cashier's desk where you settle your bill. If you will be checking out but not leaving the city until later in the day, the concierge will hold your luggage for you. Tip him a couple of dollars, depending on the number of bags.

MOTELS

Typically located along the highways, motels (the word is derived from a contraction of "motor" and "hotel") provide easy access for drivers. They feature quick check-in and checkout, and you can park your car right outside the door of your room. Motels are also more casual and straightforward than hotels but, given the amenities they now offer, a deluxe motel can rival a good hotel. (The prices often reflect this upgrading.) Some motels have health clubs or gym facilities; most have restaurants; city motels often have porters and room service. Almost all are equipped with swimming pools, depending of course on their location. There are still, however, some budget chains with acceptable if not top-of-the-line décor and accommodations. Many of the chains extend special discounts for senior citizens and for children under a certain age (free lodging, in some cases) and many will accept pets. Also, if you are traveling with a group or on business, you may be allowed a discounted group rate. Always inquire.

If you need a room during busy travel times, it's wise to reserve one well in advance. You can use the toll-free 800 numbers all the chains maintain. If you give your credit card number, the room will be held for you no matter how late you arrive, unless you are told the front desk closes at a particular time. Once you arrive, the desk will be happy to book your next night elsewhere with another motel in their chain.

When you arrive at the motel, park your car in front near the registration office (there are usually reserved spaces for this purpose) and then check in. You will be asked to fill out a registration card with your name, address, and business association, if pertinent. Some motels also ask for the license number and make of your car. A married woman who uses her maiden name professionally should register using both names so that she can be reached quickly by family or business colleagues in an emergency. Even if you plan to pay with cash, you may be asked to show a credit card. If you made your reservation by credit card, you probably will have been assigned a room, speeding up the check-in process. You may want to choose automatic checkout and pay your bill the night before, unless you want a receipt. Look for instructions at the desk or in your room. Also, note the checkout time, which is posted on the door to your room. If you opt for automatic checkout, remember to leave the key in your room. Once you've checked in, you will be given a key or electronic card for your room. You then drive to the parking space nearest your room. As motels do not usually have porters (except in urban settings) you carry your own luggage into your room. If you arrive late at night, be considerate of those who may already be sleeping: don't slam the door to your car or your room, and keep your voice down.

Just about all motels supply conveniently located ice, soda, and snack machines. Newspapers, toothpaste, razors, combs, condoms, and other items can often be obtained from special dispensing machines.

If you use the swimming pool, either indoors or out, wear a beach cover-up or a robe over your bathing suit and shoes or slippers to and from the pool. You may be required to wear a bathing cap, so take one along. Towel off well before returning to your room, so you don't leave puddles on the carpet behind you.

At the pool, observe the rules posted. As the majority of motel pools do not have lifeguards, it is essential that children be accompanied by a responsible adult. Remind your children that they are in a public place and have to be respectful of other guests. They mustn't shout, run through the corridors, or play with the ice machine or the elevator buttons. In motels as in hotels, or anywhere for that matter, your children should not take the elevator alone.

If there is a hot tub at the motel, observe the same decorum. No alcoholic beverages are allowed at the hot tub (no glass either), and don't monopolize it. It's not healthy for one thing, but also there may be others who would like a turn at the tub. Never let your children use the hot tubs unless you are with them, and observe the posted precautions.

Dress for motels tends to be quite informal, but if you eat in the motel restaurant you should shower and change into fresh clothes or do a good, general neatening up after a long day's drive.

Even though motels are informal, observe all the other usual norms of common sense and polite behavior. Keep the TV or radio modulated and don't entertain with loud, late evening parties. Sometimes on popular football weekends large groups of people party far into the night before or after the "Big Game." This is inconsiderate, as other guests may be trying to get a night's sleep. If a late night party disturbs your rest, call the front desk, explain your problem to the clerk, and let him handle the situation.

If you have to make an early departure, be thoughtful. Don't yell out to your companions, rev your engine, slam the car doors or your room door. Don't leave the engine running while you run back to search for something in the room. Others may be trying to sleep.

While it's not obligatory to tip the maid, it is a kind gesture to leave her two or three dollars, and it will certainly be appreciated.

COUNTRY INNS, MOST PARTICULARLY
BED AND BREAKFASTS

In the thirties and forties, residential sections of towns across the country had rooming houses and small, family-run inns with names like "Dew

Drop Inn." During the fifties, however, the national interstate highway system was completed and as the traffic sped past towns and villages the national motel chains became the choice of most travelers. Fortunately, the 1970s saw a rebirth and proliferation of what we now loosely refer to as bed and breakfasts, or B&Bs.

Several types of accommodations can be classified as bed and breakfasts, including historic homes and estates, quiet country inns, or owner-operated houses or apartments in a city both "hosted" or "unhosted." The most classic B&B is a Victorian or colonial house, with three or more guest rooms, that has been converted into a gracious, comfortably furnished place to stay. Some B&Bs are more formal than others, to the point of being quite elegant and expensive. What these lodgings have in common is that breakfast is served and included in the price. Breakfast may feature fresh fruit, breads, or regional specialties, plus coffee and tea. They may be buffet style or brought to the guests, but the point is that there is a place to sit and eat at your leisure.

The owner probably (but not always) lives in quarters discreetly separated from the guest areas. Guests are usually allowed to use the sitting rooms and lounges. Complimentary wine or sherry may be served in the early evening, and tea may be offered in the late afternoon. Fresh fruit may be left in a basket in your room. What appeals to many travelers about B&Bs is the feeling of being a guest in a home. The quiet atmosphere of a B&B is more relaxing than the typical motel can ever be, and of course you have the use of much of the house in addition to your own room. Some bedrooms have a private bath, but usually you must share a bathroom with other guests. This being a possibility, bring a bathrobe with you. In metropolitan areas, if you are staying in the extra bedroom of the owner's own apartment, there is very little chance of a private bath. You will be given a key to your room and one to the front door so you can come and go as you please.

There are many guidebooks for B&Bs in the United States and Canada organized by region, such as Northern California, the Middle Atlantic States, the Southwest, New England, the South, etc. There are national and regional referral services that can give you the names of recommended B&Bs and handle reservations for you. Bed & Breakfast, The National Network, is an association of regional B&B reservation services covering both the United States and Canada. You can write for a brochure listing regional reservation services (Box 4616, Springfield, MA 01101). These reservation services regularly inspect B&Bs they recommend and also screen people seeking accommodations. Screening of potential guests is informal and usually done over the telephone. An experienced agency prides itself on being able to recognize guests who would be better suited to a hotel setting. If you book through a reservation agency (some are listed in the telephone book under "Bed & Breakfast") all taxes, the agency's fee, as well as breakfast are included in the nightly charge.

In an urban B&B you may be required to stay for at least two nights. Those in rural areas are not usually so demanding, except in popular tourist spots and during high season. When you make the booking, you will be asked to send a deposit for one night's stay or to give a credit card number to secure the room. It is a good idea to tell the B&B roughly what time you expect to arrive, especially if it will be late in the day.

Another category of B&Bs are small (or large) "unhosted" apartments. They may be rented for periods of more than two nights—up to a couple of weeks. Such accommodations are convenient for extended stays, as you have use of a kitchen for preparing your own meals. In some instances breakfast supplies are included. Prices vary, but in urban areas a couple can expect to spend an average of 60 to 100 dollars a night in a "hosted" B&B and from 120 to 160 dollars a night for an "unhosted" city apartment.

If you are traveling in the country and do not want to make advance bookings, you can often find listings of B&Bs at the state tourist offices that are located on interstate highways as you cross the border into a state. Prices vary widely throughout the country, but an average price for two should be somewhere around 60 to 80 dollars a night.

Because you will be sharing the premises with the owner and other guests, your comfort level will depend on the conduct of those around you and vice versa. Loud talk or a radio or TV at high volume will be irritating to anyone trying to rest. Shared bathrooms demand the ultimate in neatness and consideration. Don't slosh water on the bathroom floor, give the tub a good cleaning after you've bathed, and take your towels with you back to your room. Don't luxuriate in a hot tub when others might be waiting and be careful not to use up all the hot water. In short, act like any considerate, well-behaved guest in a private home.

The host-owner will likely be more than happy to chat with you when you arrive, and will certainly offer information about the local sights and recommend restaurants in the area. Most owners of bed and breakfasts are cordial, affable people who are genuinely interested in other people, and enjoy having them stay in their homes. But don't expect them to spend a good deal of time entertaining you. You are renting space from them, not friendship.

If your B&B has a public sitting room, you may borrow the books or magazines to read in your room, but be sure to return them before you leave. Private areas of the house will be indicated. Respect the owners' boundaries and invade them only in the case of a true emergency. For instance, if there is no public telephone, don't use the owner's private phone without asking first.

In the morning when you enter the dining area, a nod and a smile and a pleasant "Good morning" directed at the other guests are always appreciated. Introduce yourself if you wish. Some people are unnerved by too much chatter in the morning, so be sensitive to the prevailing mood and don't disturb those who may want to read their newspapers and drink their coffee in peace.

You never tip the owners of a B&B, but if a maid serves you in the dining room or cleans your room you should leave her a few dollars in an envelope. Observe the checkout times as you would in a hotel. If you want to sightsee in the area after checkout time, you can ask the owner if he will keep your bags for a few extra hours.

TIPPING

There are no hard and fast rules about tipping. What follows are just guidelines.

ON PLANES

There is no tipping on airplanes, although the skycap (luggage porter) at the airport is given one or two dollars per bag.

ON SHIPBOARD

Each steamship company has its own gratuity system and most provide their passengers with a printed list of recommended tips. You can check with your travel agent as to tipping suggestions or use the general ones given here. (It's a good idea to find out about tipping ahead of time so you'll know how much money to take along for that purpose.) Figure that your total amount of tips will equal fifteen percent of your cabin fare.

When you arrive at the ship's pier, a porter will put your baggage on an escalator or elevator to take it to the boarding level or he will take it directly to your cabin. Porters are tipped a minimum of two dollars per bag and more if trunks are involved.

Many veteran cruisegoers give a small tip of ten or fifteen dollars to their cabin and dining-room stewards at the beginning of the trip. They feel this makes a difference in the service they receive on board. If you are on a long cruise, it's nice to tip the key people—they include the chief dining-room steward, your dining-room steward, and your cabin steward—once a week, usually on Friday evenings. In all cases, tip slightly more if you are traveling as a family.

Your cabin steward and your dining-room steward should receive a minimum of three dollars a day. If you have a suite, the cabin steward gets slightly more. The bar and lounge stewards receive fifteen or twenty percent of each bill paid as they serve you. The wine steward is given fifteen percent of the bill. If you use the ship's hairdresser, barber, masseur, or other service person, tip the same amount as if you were on land—fifteen to twenty percent of the total bill each time. The ship's officers and the cruise director are never tipped.

On the last day of your cruise, put your tips in envelopes and enclose a note of appreciation with each one. "You did so much to make our trip a success," or "We'll certainly miss you every night at dinner. Thanks so much for everything." If possible, tips should be handed out personally; if that isn't possible, envelopes should be addressed to the various individuals and given to the purser, who will distribute them for you.

TIPPING ON THE *QUEEN ELIZABETH II* Passengers aboard the *QEII* can get a copy of this guide at the purser's office or it can be sent with your tickets.

A GUIDE TO GRATUITIES

On the QE2, normally passengers would offer gratuities as follows, based on their accommodations and dining rooms.

Passengers in the Queens/Princess Grill accommodations would normally give $5 for each person in a cabin per day to both the cabin staff and the restaurant staff. If you have more than one waiter or steward/stewardess, this amount will be shared.

Passengers in the Columbia accommodations would normally give $4 for each person in a cabin per day to both the cabin staff and the restaurant staff. If you have more than one waiter or steward/stewardess, this amount will be shared.

Passengers in the Mauretania accommodations would normally give $3 for each person in a cabin per day to both the cabin staff and the restaurant staff. If you have more than one waiter or steward/stewardess, this amount will be shared.

If you wish, you may reward, at your discretion, other staff, such as assistant restaurant managers, who offer extra attention and enhance your dining experience, and night stewards, if used.

In public rooms and bars with wine service in restaurants, there is a fixed ten percent gratuity included on your account. If any particular public room steward/stewardess or wine steward particularly pleases you, a further gesture would be at your discretion.

Courtesy of the QE2

ON RAILROADS

Railroad travel requires some tipping. The amount depends upon the length of the trip, the type of ticket you have, and the amount of service you require. If you travel first class you may be served a meal or a snack as part of the price of the train ticket. Service is also included in that ticket price. However, if it's a long trip and your waiter has been particularly responsive, it's appropriate to tip him five or ten dollars when you detrain. If the train ticket does not include the price of meals, then tip the waiter in the dining car fifteen to twenty percent of your bill, just as you would in a restaurant.

On an overnight train the sleeping porter receives several dollars per day if he makes up your berth, gets you up in the morning, brings you coffee and the paper, or performs some other helpful service. Whether you travel first class or coach, if the redcap (luggage porter) helps you with your bag, he receives one or two dollars per bag. In large cities the rates are usually posted by the checkroom or at the porter's stand.

On buses or by private car

You are not expected to tip commercial bus drivers—those who work for Greyhound or Trailways, for instance. But drivers of special charter or sightseeing buses may be tipped one to three dollars for the day if they were particularly helpful. Guides on sightseeing buses or day tours may be tipped anywhere from one to five dollars per day depending on their expertise, although it's not mandatory. If they are with you overnight, however, the guide is always tipped and often the driver as well. Someone in the tour group usually takes charge of collecting contributions for both guide and driver. Although the collector may suggest donating a specific amount, you should feel free to give more or less but you should give something—three or four dollars per day for the guide and two to three dollars for the driver is average, slightly more if the guide and driver share the tips. If you and your tour companions are uncertain about what to tip, check with the tour representative. If you prefer to have the amount you give remain private, put the cash in a sealed envelope.

If you have rented a private car and driver to take you sightseeing his tip should be ten to fifteen percent of the bill.

In hotels

If you are a permanent or long-term resident in a hotel, you tip on a monthly basis to avoid having to keep change available at all times. For stays of less than a month, use these guidelines:

In a first-class hotel

- One dollar to the doorman if he gets you a taxi; two dollars if it's raining and he has had to go out of his way to find a cab.
- A minimum of one dollar per bag to the porter when you are checking in or leaving; more if the bags are heavy. If you're part of a large group, then fifty cents per bag is usual.
- If someone from the manager's office shows you to your room, no tip is given.
- A minimum of two dollars to the room service waiter each time he brings you something. You can either write the tip on the bill or give it in cash (most hotels add a room service charge to the bill, but that does not take the place of a tip to the room service waiter).
- Two dollars per night to the maid; three dollars if two people are

sharing the room. Put it in an envelope with the maid's name on it, if you know it or write "Chambermaid" on the envelope. Hand it to her personally or give it to the desk clerk and ask him to deliver it for you. Many people make the mistake of leaving the tip on a desk or bureau in the room; there is no guarantee, if you do that, that the maid will receive it—someone else may enter the room before she does and unfortunately, in some instances, take the envelope.

- Two dollars when the porter or someone else brings something to your room, such as a newspaper; five dollars if he had to leave the hotel to purchase something for you, say from a drugstore.
- One to two dollars for the doorman or parking valet for bringing your car around.
- Three dollars or more for the concierge who does something extra, such as getting you airline tickets or seats to the opera. If the service performed took some doing, such as securing tickets to the hottest play in town, the tip may be ten percent of the cost of the tickets.

In some luxury hotels and resorts, all service is included, from the towel boy to the waiters and maids. However, if you stay in such a hotel several nights and have received excellent attention from the maître'd in the dining room, when you leave tip him fifteen or twenty dollars for the weekend, more if you stay longer.

In a less expensive hotel you can tip about twenty-five percent below these suggested amounts.

IN EUROPEAN HOTELS AND RESTAURANTS Abroad, the practice of tipping varies widely from country to country. You'll find that in most European restaurants and hotels a service charge is added to the bill—sometimes as much as fifteen percent. This charge is then distributed among the employees. If the service was exceptionally good, you may want to leave an additional small tip, say five percent of the total bill. Because Americans are uncertain about tipping customs in foreign countries, they tend to overtip. So, before going abroad, consult one of the reliable guidebooks and read the tipping section. If you know someone who lives in a country you are planning to visit, ask him for specific suggestions. Experienced travel agents are also good sources of information. They might tell you, for instance, that theater ushers are tipped about fifty cents in France but not in England, although in England there is a small charge for the program. And tipping is customary at stand-up coffee or espresso bars in Italy and France. You need leave only a small amount, but something is expected.

In European hotels the concierge provides a number of services. He can arrange for sightseeing, theater tickets, restaurant reservations, even babysitters. He will present his own bill at the end of your stay. However, he should also be tipped the equivalent of a dollar for each service he provides. If you stay long enough or use the concierge frequently enough that he knows you by name, tip him several dollars when you leave.

IN MOTELS

One of the great advantages to a motel is that there is no need to tip. Some of the larger motels do have parking attendants and porters and, if they help you with your car or luggage, you should tip them. When you stay in a motel, the chambermaid, room service waiter, and others who offer their services should be tipped just as they would be in a hotel.

IN BED AND BREAKFASTS

You do not tip the owner of a B&B, even if he brings you breakfast. However, if an employee serves your breakfast, tip the usual fifteen percent. The chambermaid is tipped the same as in a hotel (two to three dollars a day). Many B&Bs have a card in the guest room stating that tips will go to the staff, not the owner. However, if you stay more than a night or two and get to know the owner, or if the owner provides some special service, you may want to send him a small present with a note of thanks when you return home.

CHAPTER 7
SPORTS AND EXERCISE

INTRODUCTION

The ultimate aim of any kind of sport should be the enjoyment of a physical challenge performed in the best possible way. Noncompetitive sports such as fishing, hiking, and camping differ from competitive sports, however. In competitive sports, single individuals or teams struggle against each other to win a match, contest, or race. A competitive spirit is a necessity in tennis and other racket games, in team sports such as baseball, football, and basketball, in sailing, and in track. But competitiveness should never take the place of good sportsmanship. Naturally, we are not all equal in athletic ability, but we can all observe the proper forms of sports behavior.

For instance, with the current burgeoning interest in physical fitness, in the outdoors, and in sports in general on the part of most Americans, it is necessary to remember to take proper care of the environment. No one wants to restrict the outdoors experience, but campers, hikers, boaters, hunters, fishermen—all of us—have a serious obligation not to damage or despoil the forests, lakes, rivers, mountain trails, deserts, and beaches. Children should be taught to respect the land and its inhabitants, their fellow human beings, and themselves, in sports as in any other endeavor.

CHILDREN AND SPORTSMANSHIP

No matter whether it is softball, tennis, rollerblading, or hockey, children should be instructed early in the need for sportsmanship, fairness, and honesty. They should be encouraged to play as hard as they can, but always to be concerned as well about their teammates and their opponents, and to be sure to congratulate them when they do well. Cheating should never be tolerated. Cheating at sports is really stealing. Winning is important and should be commended, but children should know that good winners don't brag about a win. The self-congratulatory displays among professional football, basketball, and tennis players that we routinely see on television are unseemly and unbecoming and our children should be told so. It is just as important to be a good loser. Temper tantrums, excuses, and whining about bad luck or unfair actions by opponents are all to be discouraged. Children should be brought up knowing how to win or lose graciously, how to accept compliments modestly, and how to offer congratulations to a winning individual or team enthusiastically.

GOLF

Golf is a special game because of the honor system factor. In this personally regulated sport the player himself must referee his own playing and often penalize himself. Only he, for example, may see that his ball is out of bounds or that he illegally grounded his club in a sand trap. In the same way, on the green, if a player marks his ball before putting, he must replace it exactly where it was, and not an inch closer to the hole. Most important, a golfer is responsible for keeping his own score, so without honesty the game becomes a sham. Golf is perhaps unique among sports for the element of personal integrity that is essential to it.

The rules of the game of golf are devised, revised, and written down by the Royal and Ancient Golf Club of St. Andrews, Scotland, and the United States Golf Association every year. Anyone aspiring to learn the game should be equipped with this booklet. But there is also a code of behavior which should be learned by any golfer at the same time he is figuring out the difference between a hook and a draw, a slice and a fade, a bogey and a birdie. There is nothing arbitrary about this code but, with the great popularity of golf in the United States today, there has been some lessening of such courtesies. Nevertheless, no golfer should be afraid to speak to the golf professional at a club, or to the ranger or the management of a public course, to call attention to rudeness, lack of consideration, or boorishness on the course.

Standards of dress vary from place to place, but too much exposed flesh, whether male or female, is not desirable on the course. For one thing, it is unsightly and, in addition, we now know how dangerous the sun is. For women, slacks, long shorts, or golf skirts with long- or short-sleeved polo shirts are the recommended wear. Slacks or knee-length shorts with polo shirts are suitable for men. Blue jeans, either full length or cut off, are frowned on (they are actually too hot for playing golf) in most places. Most golfers will wear cleated golf shoes and a thin leather golf glove, as well as a cap or straw hat. It is useful to keep raingear in your golf bag.

The ability to concentrate intensely on each shot is essential to playing golf successfully. Therefore it is crucial that players never talk, move around, or stand too close to the ball when another player is about to take his stroke. Nor should they stand directly behind another player, whether on the green, the fairway, or the tee. A player on the tee should be given the whole tee to himself. One of golf's pleasures is its sociability, but not when someone is about to hit the ball. There is a contemplative appeal to golf and the occasional silences are very much a part of its allure. Players can enjoy the sounds of the outdoors at the same time they are enjoying the game.

In golf, good-natured ribbing is tolerated, especially between friends, as is commiserating over a poor shot as long as you are sincere. But in any kind of match play or with people you do not know well, always preserve a strict decorum in your remarks.

The order of play can be determined in several ways. The player with the lowest handicap often leads off. Or if a player is hosting a round, he may, as a courtesy, let the others hit first. Alternatively, the host may go first, to show his guests the best direction for the shot. Or a tee can be flipped into the air and the first player selected by the direction in which the tee lands. As the round continues, the "honor" of leading off goes to the player or team with the lowest score on the preceding hole. Technically, if a player must hit a "provisional" drive (if his first one goes out of bounds), he should step aside and let the others hit before he shoots again.

The handicapping system is one of golf's distinctive features, as it allows two players of varying skill to compete and gives the poorer player a chance against the superior one. Handicapping, however, works only if all golfers post all their scores honestly with the handicapping committee. "Sandbagging" (when a player only posts his worst scores to keep his handicap high) is scorned by honest golfers and regulated, if possible, by the Golf Committee. Because one of the first rules of golf is to credit your opponent with the same honesty you exercise, when you keep the scores for your twosome or foursome, you should never question their accounting, unless it is wildly wrong.

Except at a very few private golf clubs, caddies have gone the way of the dinosaur. This has influenced the construction of new courses that are not designed for walking but have rather unattractive asphalt cart paths. There are many rules of safety and courtesy to be aware of when using a golf cart, most of them based on plain common sense. Never drive recklessly or too fast. Don't dangle your legs or arms out of the cart, and don't allow more than two riders in a cart, or two bags per cart. The driver's bag should be on the side where he is sitting. Never allow children to drive the cart. And be sure to follow the signs on the course that indicate where the carts may not be driven and the direction of the next tee.

On the fairway keep the cart out of the sightlines of your playing partners while they are hitting. To keep the game moving, it makes sense to drive to the shorter hit, drop off the player with his club, and go directly to the longer hit, unless it means the cart will be a great distance ahead of the first player. In that case, stop the cart even with the ball and wait until the player has hit his ball. Don't drive too close to sand traps or greens, or between the two. And never park the cart in front of the green, but leave it by the side of the green nearest the next tee. If the ground is wet or marshy, avoid the wettest spots and take great care driving up or down hills. Always be sure to set the brake when you get out of the cart.

Be very careful when you take a practice swing, so that you don't hit anyone with your backswing, and never swing in anyone's direction, lest your club fly out of your hands or you spray your playing partners with pebbles or dirt. It is also extremely important that you never "hit into" the players in front of you. Always allow them to move out of range down the fairway before you tee off or hit subsequent shots. If you cannot see them because of the rise of a hill, walk up to see if the course is clear. Hitting into other golfers is very dangerous and a serious infraction of the rules of courtesy. If a shot of yours inadvertently heads in the direction of anyone on the course, yell, "Fore!" as loudly as you can. This will signal them that they should try to shield themselves from the ball, which will be traveling very fast and could cause serious injury. Never walk out ahead of a player; it is rude and could also be dangerous.

The pace of a golf game is another important component. Being ready to hit your ball when it is your turn keeps the game going. Taking too much time to line up a putt or searching too long for a lost ball (the Rules of Golf allow a five-minute search, an eon when you're playing) should be avoided. Also according to the Rules of Golf, too slow play is grounds for disqualification from a match. A foursome should be able to play eighteen holes in no more than three and a half to four hours; a twosome should take less. Always try to be aware of the position of the players in front of and behind you. If you realize that those behind you are having to wait because you are playing too slowly, you should wave them through if the hole ahead is open, standing to the side of the fairway or a safe distance from the green to give them a clear path. (It's always friendly if you tell them not to rush to get through, which is the normal tendency and can be ruinous to their game.) If the group in front of you is playing much more slowly than your group, and if you find you have caught up to them at a tee where they are about to tee off, it is permissible to ask if you may play through. Thank them for the courtesy.

Neophyte golfers tend to play more slowly than experienced golfers and should be sensitive to the holdups they may unwittingly be responsible for. If you want to teach your children, or anyone, to play golf, be sure you start them out on the practice tee and that you choose a time of day to play when the course is not crowded.

Twosomes always have precedence on a course, unless local rules state otherwise. A full-round (eighteen holes) match takes precedence over a shorter match. A single player on the course has no standing and should not play through, unless the group ahead of him invites him to.

On the green (as on the fairway), the player whose ball is "away" (farthest from the hole) goes first. When you have finished playing a hole, leave the green promptly. Don't stop to mark your scorecard until you have reached the next tee. Always be ready for your turn. As you approach your ball, be thinking about what club you will need, what sort of shot you will play, and how to hit it. After hitting the shot, do not stand looking after it admiringly or despairingly but move promptly on. Slow play today is an increasing blight on the game. Perhaps it comes from watching the professionals play on television, as they painstakingly scrutinize their putts from every angle and putt everything out. In ordinary play, it is silly to take so much time on the green. If you or your partner have already won the hole, don't putt out, but pick up your ball. Careless play, too, makes for delays. Always be sure you know what kind of ball you are using and announce it before teeing off on the first tee, so that your partners may use a different make or number. Keep your eye on your ball after you have hit it, carefully marking its direction so that you know exactly where it has gone. If your playing partner or opponent loses a ball, the sporting golfer helps look for it. Always carry a second ball in your pocket in case you cannot find your original one.

Technically, you are not allowed even to touch the clubs of an opponent; each player must play out of his own bag. In this context the reason two players should never share a bag is because of the delay it inevitably causes. When you are on the green, leave your bag to the side nearest the next tee, not in front of the green. On the green, do not step on the line between another player's ball and the hole. When you are closest to the hole, remove the flagstick for the person putting.

Golf courses are often extraordinarily beautiful, whether they are courses built beside the sea or inland courses with towering trees and undulating greenswards. It is the responsibility of every golfer to play the course with concern for its care and the players still to come. Whether the club attached to the course is a well-endowed one with deep resources for maintenance or is a much-played public course, the true lover of golf will always repair any inadvertent damage he may do. If your ball lands in a sand trap, be sure to rake the surface of the sand after you have blasted out. Whenever you leave a divot (a gouge in the ground) after your hit, retrieve the clod, replace it, and step on it to press it down. Some tee boxes are equipped with trowels and seeded sand which can be used to reseed a divot on the tee. On the green, repair any ball mark with a tee or with the small tool made for this. The Rules of Golf prohibit the repair of cleat marks on the green, so don't run, jump, or pivot in anger or jubilation on the green. Pick up your feet and don't drag them.

Americans have a reputation for being careless of the appearance of public places. On the golf course, take care to keep your litter in the cart or in your pocket or put it in the nearest trash bin. These days, when it seems people eat and drink everywhere, many resorts sell snacks, food, and drink, including beer, on the golf course itself. Although the custom of the "nineteenth hole" is acceptable when not overdone, drinking or eating on the golf course itself is inappropriate.

If you are invited to play golf at a friend's club, you should always offer to pay your greens fee and cart or caddy fee, but if your host really intends for you to be his guest, you should be gracious and accept. Repay his generosity in some way later. When you play a friendly match with a little friendly betting, pay up as soon as the match is over, and never forget to shake hands and congratulate the winner. Don't be a sore loser, blaming the wind, the rain, your headache, or anything else. As Jack Nicklaus puts it, "No one ever said golf is fair."

TENNIS

The popularity of tennis, like racquetball, squash, badminton, paddle tennis, and other racket sports, has increased enormously in the last few decades. Each of these sports has its similarities and idiosyncrasies, although the elements of sportsmanship do not vary. While sportsmanship is equally important in tennis and golf, the two sports differ in the following way. In a game like golf you play against yourself and the golf course, rather than directly opposing another player, and your will to win must be carefully contained, and your emotions kept strictly under control. In tennis you are directly affected by the abilities and strategies of your opponent. It is, therefore, important in a tennis game to psych yourself up with intensity and the will to win. Good tennis players are extremely competitive, but the code of sportsmanship forbids outward displays of fury, condescension, or gloating. There was a time when decorum was strictly observed by both players and spectators. Today, the clenching of fists, the bawling, yelling, and cursing of some of our most successful professional players have infected amateur players' behavior. The booing and general nastiness of tennis spectators are equally deplorable.

Nor should the self-congratulatory behavior which has afflicted (especially) the male side of professional tennis be admired or copied. It is puerile and unattractive to leap into the air, thrust your fists above your head in a victory salute to yourself, or collapse on your knees in grateful joy. And it has nothing to do with good sportsmanship, any more than shouting obscenities does. Americans recently have seemed to confuse winning with moral superiority, a childish delusion. Chris Evert, Martina Navratilova, the late Arthur Ashe, some of the Swedish players, and one or two others are models of dignity and graciousness in both winning and losing.

The well-mannered player is the one whom we are concerned with here. He neither under- nor overestimates his abilities. If a less skillful player asks him for a game, he will accept, knowing that his better game can help improve the other player's game (unless, of course, the difference in skill is so great that it might be humiliating). If the poorer player is completely outclassed, the better player will ease up a little and keep the ball in play. As the less proficient player, you should feel free to ask a better player to "hit" with you, but perhaps it would be wiser not to play a formal match. Do not apologize for your game; it only embarrasses everyone. If you are not a bad player, it also will seem disingenuous on your part.

You should make a point of learning and understanding the rules of the game quite soon after you first take it up. Rule books from various sources, including the United States Lawn Tennis Association, are available at most tennis facilities, private or public. It is the server's responsibility to announce the score before every point and it is assumed that every tennis player knows how and will keep it honestly.

It is also crucial to make correct calls and to make them distinctly. The rule is, if you cannot call, or "see," that a ball is definitely out, then it is good. The player closest to the line should make the call. If you are playing doubles and your partner calls a ball good that you thought was out, accept his call. Never ask anyone watching to make a call; it is your game and your call. Also, make your calls instantly. You should not return a serve that is not good, but block it back into the net or let it bounce past you. Check to make sure that the ball hasn't stopped somewhere where you could trip over it.

Do not indulge in social chitchat or loud cries of instruction to your partner when you are playing doubles. It's perfectly fine to call "Switch!" or "I've got it," to indicate coverage of the court, but anything more goes into the category of distraction. Even shouts of admiration for a good shot (by partner or opponent alike) should be kept to a minimum. They can be upsetting to players on nearby courts. (To express admiration you can raise your racket and silently tap it with your free hand.) Never, ever show you are upset by your partner's play, and never blame him for your losses. Close family members, such as husbands and wives or sons and fathers, should be sure they can play together without throwing fits of temper. And in spite of what you see on television, don't throw your racket or smash it against the fence, and above all don't hit the ball in disgust or anger *anywhere*. (Don't make excuses about the wind, the sun, a blister, or whatever, for playing poorly.) There is a custom of saying "Sorry" to your partner for a poor shot or to your opponent for returning a ball that he has to retrieve before he serves. This is not to be discouraged, but don't overdo it.

Some do's and don'ts

- Follow all posted instructions regarding sign-up for courts, length of time you may keep the court (different for singles and doubles games), and dress code.

- Do be on time for a scheduled game, or telephone to say you'll be late.

- Always wear tennis shoes; no spikes, cleated shoes, or bare feet.

- Bring a new can of balls.

- Don't hog the court when others are waiting to play. By the same token, don't rush others off; let them finish out their game.

- Don't walk directly behind a court if others are playing. Wait quietly off the courts until there is a pause in the game, then walk behind the baseline to your court, saying, "Excuse us, please."

- Return balls from other courts carefully to one of the players. Don't just bang it back in their general direction. Wait until the point they're playing is over.

- If a ball from another court bounces onto your court in the middle of a point, call a let.

- Don't dash onto another court to retrieve a ball. Wait until the point is finished, then call politely, "Thank you, Court Two. That Dunlop Five is ours."

- Ask your partner or opponent before starting whether he prefers two or three balls while serving.

- Return balls promptly when your opponent is serving and needs a ball.

- When you serve, wait until your opponent is ready to receive. As receiver, if you feel you are being rushed, hold your hand up to signal that you are not yet ready.

DOUBLES MATCHES

A few words on the etiquette of doubles, both mixed doubles in which a man and a woman play together, and same-sex doubles. Before any doubles game, you must decide which player will play which side of the court, which one will begin serving, and when and how to switch sides during a rally, as well as whether or not you will both try to take the net, and (perhaps) who should take the overheads. Some people feel that the stronger player should play the "ad court," but in social tennis it is perhaps better if you take turns playing the "ad" (left as you face the net) and "deuce" (right as you face the net) court, although if one player has a particularly strong backhand or forehand that should be considered. When you are playing a match, it's a good habit (if not a necessity) to call out "Yours!" or "Mine!" to take a shot when there is any question. (Some partners designate a "captain" to handle this.) The player with the stronger overhead should naturally take overheads in the middle, the other player getting out of the way. Whenever a player "poaches," that is, moves out of position across the court to take a net shot, he should call,

"Switch!" so that the player behind him knows to cover the other side of the court. In mixed doubles, it is usually assumed that the man will be the captain, that he probably has the stronger game, but this is not always true. Nevertheless, men are generally more aggressive players than women (or think they should be). But the male partner who hogs the court, dashing from side to side, taking everything, keeping his partner out of the game, is ludicrous and quite discourteous, as is the male or female player who constantly shouts instructions to a partner. A few husbands and wives have made very good mixed doubles teams, but you must decide for yourselves whether family harmony will survive a game of mixed doubles. Unless you are asked, do not offer advice to your partner, although words of encouragement and admiration are acceptable.

There are a few shots that are within the rules of the game but are not considered good form by many players in social tennis. For example, in mixed doubles it is fair to keep hitting the ball at the woman (or the weaker player, male or female). And it is permissible to hit the ball directly at an opposing player, although not very sporting if you are close to him. Obviously, you should never try to cause injury. If you happen to hit one of your opponents, always make sure he is not injured and apologize.

PRIVATE COURTS

As there are many private courts available today, a word on that. If you are asked to play on someone's court, arrive on time, equipped with a new can of balls. Don't just buzz in before the game, play, and then buzz off. It is nice occasionally to bring water and/or fruit juices, if your host is in the habit of offering them. If you have been invited to use the court in your host's absence and there is a sign-up system in place, observe it scrupulously, as you should any rules. If it's a clay court, don't play if it's soft from too much rain, and don't leave balls, cans, or litter scattered about; in short, don't leave any marks of your presence. If you are in a regular game that is played on a clay court, offer to help with maintenance and water the court, roll it, brush it, and sweep the lines. Occasionally reciprocate the generosity of your host in some way.

DRESS

Although all-white tennis outfits are not as religiously adhered to as once they were, a tennis player should dress neatly in clean, well-pressed shirts and shorts or skirts. Many facilities have by now resorted to posting instructions as to clothes. Men should never play without shirts and women should leave jewelry at home. Only shoes designed for use on the tennis courts are allowed; no basketball shoes or heavily cleated running shoes. Hats or visors are an excellent idea to keep the sun out of your eyes, but wear conventional ones, preferably white. If you wear eyeglasses, or if you have had any damage to your eyes, such as a detached retina, be sure to wear an eye guard shield.

In the name of commerce and marketing, manufacturers of clothes and equipment have created fashions in rackets, warmups, headbands, in fact in every kind of equipment. Some people (usually neophytes) seem excessively interested in the expense and quantity of their equipment, lugging huge, monogrammed leather racket bags to the court, with a handful of rackets which they break out as if they were on the tour. This is not wrong of course, but it's pretentious and ostentatious behavior and especially silly when done by a C-level player.

OTHER RACQUET SPORTS

Good tennis manners apply to all other racquet games. When you play in a relatively small area, as in squash and racquetball, there is the additional consideration that you must be very quick to get out of the way of your opponent, for the sake of safety as well as courtesy: to avoid obstructing his play. An eye guard is definitely indicated for these particular racquet games, most especially if you wear glasses or have any kind of eye problem.

SQUASH

Squash is one of the racquet games in which good manners and safety are closely related. In squash you are required to give your opponent a fair chance to see the ball and hit it, and you must make every effort to get out of the path of the ball's flight to give him that chance. That calls for a good deal of scrambling and is part of the challenge. Dress for squash varies from quite formal at old-line men's clubs to casual at public courts. But it should be simple, clean, and neat. White is the preferred color for official matches.

RACQUETBALL

Racquetball has recently become popular in various parts of the country and, while it is a far more casual game than tennis, it is still a courteous one. The rules for behavior are once again closely related to safety. Because it is played in the confines of a walled court, no wild swinging or flailing, no deliberate shoving or pushing is allowed, and you must never intentionally deny your opponent the chance to see and hit his return. There is a term—"an avoidable hinder"—for such obstructing which can be called and, if it is, gives the serve to the player interfered with. If the hinder is "unavoidable," a "let" is called and the point replayed. There is also a "safety hinder," which happens if a player checks his swing to avoid hitting his opponent. If called, the point is replayed.

PADDLE TENNIS

Paddle tennis (or platform tennis), which is played outside on a screened-in wooden platform during the winter, is a doubles game. The court is considerably smaller than a tennis court. A special feature of the game allows a player (if he must) to let the ball bounce once in the court, then carom off the back screen before returning it, adding a wonderfully perverse (and difficult) twist to the game. The secret to good paddle tennis is control and placement of the ball. Lobs, slices, chops, drop shots, play off the wires are usually the marks of winning play, not violent smashes. Dress is quite casual. Players usually start with several layers of clothing—mittens, hats, scarves, warmups—while warming up, then discard them in the course of play.

BADMINTON

The advantage of badminton is that it can be played with just a net, two racquets, and shuttlecock. Good manners are just as important in this ancient game as in any of the others.

BOATING

The popularity of boating has been increasing, with the numbers of those who own or rent boats, whether sailboats or powerboats, rising every year. Boating, dealing as it does with the uncontrollable elements of wind and wave, is already a hazardous pastime for boaters not experienced or trained in the ways of sailing. So if you are one of these boaters, whether as an owner or a guest aboard, safety must be foremost in your mind at all times. There are many books and magazines devoted to the proper rules and regulations for boating, and the United States Coast Guard is happy to supply information on safety (call its hotline: 1-800-368-5647). The BOAT/US Foundation in Alexandria, Virginia, is also a good resource (1-800-336-BOAT) for the novice. Classes in ship handling are available at almost any seaside (or lakeside) marina and are well worth the time and expense. For information about powerboats, check with the United States Power Squadrons National Headquarters, 50 Craig Road, P. O. Box 345, Montvale, NJ 07645.

There is a marvelous, specific language spoken by mariners, replete with terms that date back centuries. The neophyte sailor or guest cannot be expected to understand all of them, but he can equip himself with a few essential words before going down to the sea. Here is a short list:

Below—Anything below the main deck
Bow—Front of the boat
Bulkhead—Wall

Bunk—Bed

Chart—Map

Cleat—A wedge-shaped piece of wood or metal fixed to the deck
and used to secure a line

Deck—Floor

Dinghy—Small rowboat tied to boat by a painter (rope)

Galley—Kitchen

Halliard—A sheet (rope) used to raise or lower a sail

Head—Toilet

Heel—The movement of the boat when it tilts to one side in a
wind

Helm—The steering device, wheel, tiller

Jibe—Swinging a sail from one side to the other when the wind is
astern (from the rear)—a dangerous maneuver

Knot—A sea mile of 6076.115 feet, used as a measure of speed (as
in, "We sailed for an hour at three knots")

Ladder—Stairs

Lee—Side opposite to direction of wind

Mast—The upright wooden pole supporting the sails

Port side—Left, when facing forward

Porthole—Window

Sheet or line—Any rope used to work a sail

Shrouds or stays—Steel cables from mast to deck, supporting the
mast

Spinnaker—A large racing sail at the bow, used when running
before the wind (with the wind directly behind you)

Starboard—Right, when facing forward

Stern—Rear of the boat

Swab—To mop (as in, "Swab the deck")

Tack—Sailing a zigzag course into the wind, putting the wind
first on one side, then the other; on a starboard tack the
wind is from the right side, and on a port tack, from the
left side

Topside—The top portion of the outer surface of a ship on each
side above the waterline

Yar—Everything is fine and shipshape

Yaw—The ship's motion when it veers off course

Anyone who is not a strong swimmer should wear a life jacket while
on a boat. Information about the best sort of flotation devices can
be obtained from the Coast Guard or good boating equipment suppliers.
If you will be out on the ocean, everyone on board should know where
the life preservers are located in case of an emergency; the captain
must be sure to have a sufficient number available for all his crew and
guests.

THE ROLE OF THE CAPTAIN

A captain should always sail so as not to put either his boat or his passengers at risk. The Coast Guard has determined that most fatalities at sea are caused by alcohol consumption, so neither you nor your passengers should ever allow themselves to get drunk on board. Some states, among them Connecticut, New York, and New Jersey, have laws stipulating fines and even jail for persons found sailing while intoxicated. Learn how to handle possible emergencies at sea, including collisions, storms, fires, mechanical failures, capsizing, or men overboard. Your boat should be properly equipped with tools, charts, and safety devices and you should never sail beyond the limits of your expertise. Obey "No Wake" signs (not speeding so as to cause waves), never cruise too fast or speed too near fishing boats or a beach where swimmers may be. And simple good manners dictate that evening parties at moorings not go on too far into the night or reach a raucous level of noise.

No refuse should ever be tossed overboard. Stow it in bags to be disposed of correctly on shore.

DO'S AND DON'TS ABOARD YOUR BOAT

- Don't invite more guests than can be safely or comfortably accommodated.
- Brief your guests as to the accommodations on the boat, what clothing they should bring, and what responsibilities you may give them on board.
- Be patient with novice sailors.
- Think twice before taking anyone on board who is incapacitated and unable to move quickly if need be.
- Cordiality and courtesy toward other boatmen is expected and expressed by a wave of the hand and pleasant greetings in port or under way.
- Don't stare at others' boats, peering into portholes, or visit another boat unless given a clear invitation to come aboard.
- If you want to anchor at a private yacht club (usually not allowed unless you are a member of a yacht club), make sure you have permission and are informed about the rules regarding harbor taxis, the procedure for negotiating your anchorage, and the cost (if any) of these privileges.
- When in an unfamiliar port, be sure not to tie up at a private dock or private mooring; and never tie up at a navigational buoy except in an emergency.
- Never pass a vessel in distress. It is one of the oldest seagoing traditions that a sailor will always offer help to a boat in trouble.

And should you ever be in real difficulty, don't brave it out but signal for help.

- If you are invited to another boat for a friendly evening drink while anchored in port, don't overstay your welcome and reciprocate when you have an opportunity.

THE ROLE OF THE GUEST

If you are invited by friends for a day's sail or for a cruise of several days or weeks, it is crucial to understand that the captain, or skipper, is The Boss. His word is law, at least on board his ship. If he yells at you to duck or to get out of his way, don't take it personally, but obey as fast as you can. He is probably reacting to a sudden shift in wind direction, another boat's maneuvers, or a storm blowing up, and is concerned for the boat's safe passage. As a member of the crew, you must respect his decisions.

The best advice about what clothes you should take for a cruise is to pack simple, comfortable garments that can see you through several types of weather. These might include slacks or dungarees, shorts, several short-sleeved and one or two long-sleeved shirts; a warm turtleneck sweater and one or two other sweaters, underwear, nightgown or pajamas, several pairs of socks, a bathing suit and a cover-up, a windbreaker, and foul weather gear if you have it. If not ask your host if he has any gear you can borrow—it is a necessity no matter where you may be sailing. A bandana or several cotton scarves are very useful for women, and hats, whether knitted caps for cold weather or hats for protection against the sun, are essential. Shoes must be carefully chosen; leather-soled shoes should never be worn on a deck, and certainly not high heels. Sneakers are all right for fair weather, but nonskid Topsiders are the best, as the deck can get very slippery when it's wet. You might also ask if you should bring a towel and washcloth. If not, remember to use towels sparingly—doing laundry in port may not be that convenient. If it's a cruise that will take you to a yacht club for a weekend dinner and/or dance, ask your host and hostess what sort of clothes you will need. In most circumstances, a jacket and a pair of slacks are suitable for a male guest, with one tie and a dress shirt. For a woman, a silk dress or pantsuit, plus a shawl, is sufficient. Whatever you take should be packed in a duffel bag which can be stowed easily in the ship's cabin, never a suitcase.

As a guest, one of your primary responsibilities is to be cheerful and compatible, and to make an effort to get along with the other guests. Act as if you are having a good time regardless of whether you are. Take part in the sailing procedures if your captain wants you to; stay out of his way and that of the crew (if there is one) if he does not want your help. The best guest is one who contributes. You might ask the captain if there is a regular chore you can take charge of, such as polishing the brightwork, pumping out the bilges, or cleaning up the dishes after a meal. If you want to take a gift, bring something that can be shared or consumed, such as a book or a game, wine, beer, some special cheese, or even a cooked turkey or ham if you'll be on the boat for more than a day or two. And remember to be considerate of those you are sharing confined quarters with. Don't stay up late at night on deck or below talking or reading with the light on. If you still smoke, never smoke below deck or anywhere near the galley stove (which is probably run by alcohol, gas, or kerosene) and be careful not to toss a butt into the wind. Be as tidy as you can with your belongings. A good ship is a neat ship, with everything stowed in its proper place so that in an emergency you can instantly put your hands on whatever it is you need.

A cruising boat, of course, is equipped with a bathroom—on a boat called a head. There may be some printed instructions next to the toilet describing how it should be used. Follow these instructions to the letter as you certainly don't want to be responsible for clogging that most vital piece of equipment. Be courteous about not monopolizing the head, especially in the morning when everyone will be waiting to use it.

SOME DO'S AND DON'TS FOR GUESTS ON A BOAT

- Take seasickness medication with you, just in case. If you feel sick, stay on deck in the fresh air and don't be embarrassed; no one is totally immune if it gets rough enough.

- One of the most important rules is never to offer unsolicited advice or criticism of his sailing skills to your captain. If the way he sails makes you nervous, don't accept another invitation.

- Never jump off a moving boat, for it will soon be yards away. Swim only when the captain says you may.

- Be sparing in your use of fresh water. On board it is a scarce commodity. Bathe in the sea when possible, or wait until you're ashore to shower and wash your hair.

- Be as self-sufficient as you can.

SWIMMING

Swimming is without question the sport with the best all-round conditioning benefits and the least risk of physical injury. It is also one to which the greatest number of people have the easiest access. Swimming etiquette, as with most sports, is really consideration for the pleasure and safety of yourself and others.

If you don't know how to swim, or are not satisfied with your swimming ability, take lessons at your community pool, the local Y pool, or at a beach club by a lake. Never swim alone, even in a pool, and never let children, even very strong swimmers, swim alone.

Teach your child early to swim and to respect the water. Small children should always wear some kind of life preserver near any body of water.

As your child grows more confident in the water, you can reduce the size of the life preserver, but better to err on safety's side.

Always obey the lifeguard's instructions. But don't make the mistake of thinking she is there to supervise you or your child. You must always be on the alert and keep a constant eye on your child. Small children, especially, can slip noiselessly into a pool and be underwater before anyone can dive in after them.

At the pool or beach, don't let your child disturb others. This includes restraining him from screaming or running along the side of a pool (where it is very slippery) or too near people on a beach, spraying them with sand; an older child should be taught not to splash, dunk, jump, or dive on top of another swimmer.

If you must take music along, use your private Walkman with the earplugs.

AT THE BEACH

- Be aware of and always obey the system of signals (sometimes written on a chalk board, but usually indicated with colored flags) used by lifeguards to indicate rough seas, strong undertow, sharks, jellyfish, and other hazards.

- It is never a good idea to swim in the ocean if there are no lifeguards on duty. If a storm comes up, get out of the water immediately, as lightning is a hazard on the water.

- Don't overestimate your strength as a swimmer and don't swim alone in unfamiliar waters.

- Never leave litter on the beach. If you take a picnic, when you leave throw away whatever is left over in designated trash barrels. If you plan an evening cookout, check first to see if it is allowed. Take special care putting out the fire. Douse it first with water, then cover it with sand. If it is still hot, repeat the process until you are sure it is out.

- Sand dunes at the beach are fragile, so don't walk across or run or slide down them. (Also, there may be ticks in the dune grasses which can be harmful to you.)

A FEW ESSENTIALS FOR A DAY AT THE BEACH
- Sunblock, a hat, a long-sleeved shirt, sunglasses, a beach towel, and possibly a beach umbrella.
- Dark shirts with long sleeves or beach cover-ups if an all-day outing is planned.
- Very young children should be carefully protected against the sun, and monitored from time to time.
- Plenty of fresh, cool water.

- Simple sandwiches, fruit, soda, and/or fruit juices.
- Insect repellent and maybe a soothing lotion in case someone gets bitten.

PRIVATE BEACH CLUBS

One reason people join beach clubs is to ensure a modicum of privacy for themselves. Unless you are the guest of a member, it's best not to plant yourself on a club beach, since you will inevitably be asked to leave.

If you are invited to a friend's beach club you may or may not be able to pay for food and drinks, but if the club does accept cash, you can offer to pay for whatever charges you incur. If you have been invited for the day, you can probably assume your host intends to pay for your lunch. Each club will have its own rules about tipping of locker-room attendants or beach boys. In all aspects of club life, be guided by your host.

Take along a towel, sunblock, a pair of beach shoes or sandals, and a cover-up to wear if you are going to have lunch in the dining room or on the outdoor patio. A book or magazine (not a newspaper, which is hard to control in a wind) is a good diversion on the beach, but don't take along a radio unless it has headphones.

PUBLIC POOLS

Rules are posted, generally as follows:

- Shower before entering the pool.
- Wear a bathing cap.
- Do not swim if you have any discharge from a nasal or ear infection or with any open skin lacerations or wounds.
- Choose the lane that correctly reflects the speed you want to swim, i.e., fast, moderately fast, and slow. Then stay in your own lane.

PRIVATE POOLS

As the owner of a pool it's up to you to establish guidelines for its use by friends and neighbors. You might want to spell them out on a notice posted near the pool. For example: "To Our Friends and Guests, Please: No pets. No running around the pool. Watch your children and don't let them come alone. No radios." Additions might be "No glasses by the pool. No swimming near the diving board," or the like.

If you issue a blanket invitation to "Come any time," you may regret it. Tell your friends to feel free to call any time they feel like a swim and don't be afraid to say when it is inconvenient for you to have them.

As the considerate guest, observe all the host's rules, if any, and don't abuse your host's generosity. Even if your friend says come whenever you like, call first. It can be mighty embarrassing to arrive for a swim to find a party in progress, either at the pool or in the house. Don't take elaborate snacks or lunch to the pool and don't always accept the offer of a cool drink, unless you reciprocate with drinks of your own from time to time. Don't let your children invite their friends to someone else's pool, and don't take adult guests unless you ask first. Remember to bring your own towel and sun lotion and not to outstay your welcome—about two hours is a suitable amount of time. There are all sorts of ways to repay your host, from offering to clean the pool, skimming it for grass, debris, insects, picking up and straightening up the deck around the pool, to taking over homemade cakes and cookies, or giving your host some sort of pool equipment he might need.

WATER SKIING

Water skiing is another sport in which safety is a major concern. Flotation belts are required by law in many states and are an excellent precaution, even if you are a very experienced skier. Accidents can and do happen, and you may be injured and unable to swim—the belt could save your life.

Be careful, too, where you ski. Ski in deep water, a good distance from any swimmers; a lone swimmer on the surface is difficult to see, so the driver of the boat should be very watchful and make every effort not to endanger anyone's life or property. Stay off private beaches and away from buoy or tow ropes or fishermen's lines. The boat driver should never play games with the skier but adjust the boat's speed and maneuvers to the skier's skill. Ideally, in addition to the driver, someone should be along to keep an eye on the skier.

Before starting the boat, driver and skier should make sure they are clear about the various hand signals they will be using for "stop," "slow down," "speed up," "turn left" or "turn right," as well as for "help." If the skier falls, the driver should stop immediately and turn back in a wide circle while the skier recovers the line and his skis.

SKIING

Skiing, whether Alpine (downhill), with its speed and excitement, or Nordic (cross-country), which is more strenuous than Alpine skiing, is one of the most exhilarating of sports.

DOWNHILL SKIING

A beginner should certainly take lessons—quite a few—before tackling a downhill ski trail on her own. All ski resorts and centers offer instruction for every level of skier. If you can afford to join a small class or take one-on-one instruction, you will progress that much more rapidly. Ski areas all have equipment to rent. It's a good idea to start by renting if you're not sure you want to make the investment that ski equipment requires.

You need to be in excellent shape to ski and, unless you are generally quite active, you should do some serious, specific conditioning beforehand. There are many books and magazines to consult for exercises specifically directed at strengthening the legs and increasing flexibility in the upper body.

Skiing is easiest to learn when young. Children, with their flexibility, their low centers of gravity, and their eagerness to absorb information, make natural ski students. A comparison of photos of the racing form of world-class skiers with that of very young skiers (untrained in racing techniques) revealed that the young skiers remarkably and instinctively replicated the balance, rotation, and grace of the mature athletes. Still, it is never (well, almost never) too late to learn to ski as long as you get proper instruction.

The International Ski Federation publishes a Code of Conduct which is worth including here, although if you rely on your good common sense you won't go wrong.

> Always ski so as not to put anyone at risk of danger or injury.
>
> Choose the route down that does not endanger those in front. The slower skier in front of you *always has the right of way*. If you do wish to pass, do it so as not to interfere with his route.
>
> When you overtake another skier, call out your intention to pass. "Track left" or "Track right" tells the other skier you intend to pass on his left or his right.
>
> If you traverse (cross) the slope somewhere in mid-course, be very careful to check both uphill and downhill to be sure there isn't any "traffic" coming along.
>
> When climbing on skis or on foot, stay well over on the edge of the trail; the same thing if you decide to walk down. If visibility (snow, rain, fog) is poor, be extremely cautious, or simply forgo skiing that day.
>
> In the event of an accident, it is the skier's duty to stop to help, to make sure the ski patrol has been summoned. Keep the skier warm with your jacket. Take off his skis, but never the boots. If he is hurt, stay with him, marking the spot on his uphill side with crossed poles or skis stuck in the snow, until someone comes along, then go get the ski patrol. Be sure to mark the spot in your mind so you can indicate exactly where the injured skier is. Don't move him until the ski patrol arrives unless you must relieve serious pain. If you have to move him, the best way is for several people to lift him by grabbing his clothes, not his body.
>
> Always ski with identification on you and be ready to identify yourself, if you are the injured one, or a witness to an accident.

There are a couple of more recommendations in the case of an accident: if the skier is conscious, ask where he hurts; if he is bleeding, elevate the injured limb (if possible) and apply pressure on the wound with your hands or a scarf. Frostbite is fairly common, recognized by the intense whiteness of the skin and numbness of the area. Never rub the frostbitten area with snow, but as soon as possible put the affected area into luke-warm water and gradually add hot water to raise the temperature to about 120 degrees F. (fifty degrees C.).

OTHER SKI SAFETY RULES

- **Never ski alone.**

- In the line for the ski lift, hold your skis upright in front of you, not over your shoulders. Make sure you are ready to go when the tow line, chair lift, poma, or T-bar comes along. If you are alone, share the double T-bar and double chair lift with another single skier.

- Don't ski beyond your capabilities or attempt a trail that is too tough for you. Conversely, the expert skier should stay off the easier trails and not terrorize the less experienced by schussing past or around them.

- Learn the trail markers that indicate the difficulty of the trail: a green circle means Novice, a blue square Intermediate, and a black diamond is for Expert. Watch for signs posted along the trails which warn of narrow runs, tight turns, danger ⚠, and where lift lines may cross the slope. "Descent routes" may be off trail and are only for top skiers. Usually they are not groomed or pa-trolled.

- Don't show off on skis. Maintaining control is a mark of good skiing and "hot dogging" (taking unnecessary risks to look flashy) is foolish and dangerous to you and others.

- If you're tired, stop to rest or stop altogether. Most accidents happen on that "just one more" run when fatigue has set in.

- Never ski on a trail that has been closed—it has been closed for a good reason (ice on the track, or it's being reserved for a special event, etc.). Moreover, closed trails are not groomed, nor are they regularly attended by the ski patrol.

- Skiing with a few friends is lots of fun, but only if you all ski at about the same level of skill. The two best skiers should bracket the group, one leading the way down and the other bringing up the rear. The same order should be maintained all the way down the hill.

- Set a time and place to rendezvous with your friends to have lunch, to "check in" with each other, or to go home. Then keep to that schedule. Don't keep a group waiting at the end of the day while you squeeze in one more run.

- Put your skis on (and take them off) out of the way of others.

- Obey the instructions of the ski patrol.

SKI LIFTS

At most ski centers, lift tickets can be bought for the day, or a certain number of runs, or as a pass for the entire season. Weekday rates are less expensive than weekend ones as is "night skiing."

There are several things to know about getting on and off the various lifts. Consult a good skiing handbook for the details of each type. If you're not sure, ask the lift attendant to explain them to you and/or observe the other skiers. Always have your skis parallel when it's your turn to get into the chair lift. When the lift comes along, let the chair slip beneath your seat and sit as it begins to rise. Hold your poles in your outside hand, away from the lift, until you are well away. Usually, as you near the drop-off, a sign on a pylon will alert you. Be prepared well ahead of time. As you reach the top, (there will be a run-off ramp or a flat area) open the safety bar (which you have pulled down in front of you on the way up). Ease your weight forward in the chair, keeping the tips of your skis up. Slide off the seat just as you reach the lip of the slope and lean forward, placing your skis parallel on the slope of the ramp. The chair will swing up and away from you. If you need to, snowplow down the ramp. Be sure to get quickly out of the way of the skiers behind you.

For a poma lift, T-bar, etc., position yourself to maneuver against the bar (don't sit on it). With the T-bar, both skiers simply ski away from the lift, letting it swing past and above them. If it's a cable car, you either carry your skis or fasten them to the outside of the cable car or gondola.

EQUIPMENT

It would be impossible in this book to cover the enormous range of ski equipment available today, but the essential pieces are skis, poles, and boots. Proper fit is everything in skiing. Get advice from friends and consult books to learn as much as you can and don't be timid about asking the experts who sell the equipment for help; part of their job is to make sure a skier is correctly fitted. Perhaps the second most important fit (after the length and type of skis) is that of the boots. Take great care in selecting your boots and buy the best you can afford. They must be rigid horizontally and must hold the heel and ankle in place with no upward or lateral movement possible, yet allow the correct amount of forward flexion. The best material for the outer shell of the boot is polyurethane. The inner shell is generally made of leather, soft plastic, or foam; it can be adjusted somewhat to fit your feet if necessary. Boots are either front-entry or rear-entry. If the boot has three buckles, tap your heel firmly down into the boot, then fasten the middle buckle first. Next the top one, making it as tight as possible (you may have to adjust the middle buckle again). And finally the bottom buckle.

A few years ago the Graduated Length Method of ski instruction was very popular; it is less so today. The principle of that method was to start pupils out with short, wide skis that allowed the novice to learn to control the skis much faster than with the long, thin, faster skis. As the beginning skier progressed, she moved to a longer ski. Today the "compact" ski (somewhat shorter than the faster mid-length ski) is very popular among average skiers. You need to be fitted according to your ability and your height; any good store can handle this task easily.

CLOTHES

When spending a day exercising vigorously in the cold, the choice of clothing becomes crucial to enjoyment. You want to be as warm, dry, and comfortable as possible. To that end, your clothing should be water- and skid-resistant, windproof, well fitted, and allow a wide range of motion. Jeans, while popular among skilled skiers, especially on the sunny spring-time slopes of the Rockies, are a poor choice. If they get wet, they stay wet all day. Basically, what you need is the following:

- Ski pants, or high-waisted ski overalls with shoulder straps
- Ski jacket
- Thick sweater (wool)
- Turtleneck (cotton)
- Long underwear
- Hat or cap
- Goggles and/or sunglasses
- Sunblock cream
- Heavy socks and a pair of thin socks
- Fanny pack
- A pair of lightweight, waterproof après ski boots

Ski clothing has improved significantly with the perfection of thermally efficient, lightweight materials. As a safety feature choose brightly colored outer wear which will show up against the snow white background—reds, oranges, pinks, yellows are best. If possible, buy nonskid fabrics that will help to keep you from sliding if you fall.

Ideally you should wear three layers of clothing to handle moisture and to allow your skin to breathe. The first layer—long underwear—should be made of a natural fiber that will "wick" perspiration away from the body. The second layer—a turtleneck and/or sweater—should be able to absorb the moisture and the third layer—the jacket—should give you protection from the wind but let the perspiration evaporate outward. The jacket should cover the kidneys, have close-fitting collar and cuffs to keep out the snow, and have large, top-opening pockets. You should wear two pairs of socks, an inner, silk sock for warmth and comfort and an outer, thicker wool sock preferably lined with cotton. Ski pants should fit tightly at the ankle. Lightweight, quilted pants are less expensive than stretch pants (which are sporty and look best on the young but aren't quite so warm). If you choose a ski suit, it must be fitted exactly at the "maximum stretch" positions your body attains during skiing. Ski gloves with long, snug, woolen cuffs allow for better dexterity than mittens but are less warm. Some people wear silk inner gloves. As most of the body's heat is lost through the head, a hat is a necessity. It should be able to be pulled down to cover the ears and neck when wind and weather are severe. Children should wear helmets while learning and when they first start skiing at any speed.

Goggles are designed to protect from glare and to help you see on overcast days or in bad weather. Brown-gold or green tints are for general use; wear the darker shades for very bright light. The best goggles are ventilated with sealed double lenses, or have lenses which have been treated with antifog chemicals. A fanny pack is a good idea for items you don't want to carry in your pockets. Equip yourself with Band-Aids and a small knife (Swiss Army type) with a screwdriver attached to use for tightening bindings. A down vest is useful for warmer days when a full ski jacket isn't necessary.

APRÈS SKI WEAR If you are staying at a hotel or ski resort, part of the fun of a ski vacation takes place off the slopes, and a different wardrobe is required. How formal or elegant it is depends on the resort. If you stay at a fancy hotel in Sun Valley or a chic European resort, you will naturally have to provide yourself with suitably elegant après ski wear. But for most of us informal is all right so long as it is neat, comfortable, and clean, and it's better to be under- than overdressed in the mountains. For women, that means slacks and/or long woolen skirts with sweaters, and for men, relaxed, casual (never shabby or dirty) slacks and sweaters. T-shirts and blue jeans have become a tiresome blight recently; use a little imagination in selecting clothes for the cocktail and dinner hour. Too much expensive jewelry or "glitz" is not needed.

CROSS-COUNTRY SKIING

Nordic, or cross-country, skiing is older than Alpine skiing by many hundreds of years. A wooden ski found in Sweden several years ago, and known as the Hoting Ski, has been determined to be 4,500 years old. The earliest skiing was utilitarian: for transport, travel, hunting, and warfare. Today we think of it largely as a recreational sport.

The cross-country ski is long, thin, usually made of fiberglass, has no metal edges, and is designed for traversing flatlands as well as for negotiating moderate slopes. Cross-country skiing is much easier to learn than Alpine skiing and provides excellent aerobic exercise. You need to be in good physical shape but you can build up your stamina as you learn. The risk of injury is far less than in downhill skiing, and the entire family can ski together as a group. Wonderful excursions on cross-country skis are possible, many of them organized by inns, ski centers, and touring groups. The equipment is less complicated and somewhat less expensive than that for Alpine skiing.

Although there are a lot of clothes specifically designed for cross-country skiing and touring, you really don't need more than protection against wind and moisture to be comfortable. Tightly cuffed pants or knickers with long socks and a hat and gloves or mittens complete the necessities. As you ski, you will grow very warm, so dress in layers that can be shed. For instance, it may be necessary to remove your windbreaker, vest, even a sweater. The boots are of several types, but all are lightweight and attached to the ski with toepieces that are locked into the binding. You can buy a complete package of skis, boots, and poles, but rental equipment is generally widely available.

Lessons are a help for the beginner but are not really necessary, especially if a friend can give you a tip or two.

A FEW SAFETY POINTS
- **Never ski alone.**
- Keep the tracks free of litter.
- If you ski with a group, stay in line; keep an eye out for slower skiers behind you and wait for them if they get too far behind.
- When you want to overtake a skier, call "Track!" He should relinquish the track, stepping to the side, just as you must if someone wants to pass you.
- Don't overestimate your stamina and strength. Remember, you have to return to your starting point and you may find you are very tired on the long way home.

ICE SKATING

Skating, although strenuous exercise, is a good sport for people of all ages, provided they have well-fitted skates, strong ankles, and a willingness to get up and try again if they fall. On the ice good manners—i.e., consideration for everyone's enjoyment—are imperative. Here are a few tips for ice skaters:

- Teach children the importance of caution and courteous behavior on the ice.
- At a public rink, obey all posted rules. They are for your safety as well as everyone else's.
- Don't skate recklessly or erratically, and always be aware of other skaters, behind as well as ahead of you. Loss of control on the ice can

be perilous. Skate blades are potentially dangerous weapons that can cause an immense amount of damage.

- At an ice rink, beginners tend to cling to the walls for balance as they try to learn the basics of skating. Faster skaters should skate several feet in, away from and out of the way of beginning skaters. Figure skaters and teachers should work in the center of the rink.

- Everyone should skate in the same direction around a rink. This is also the case on a small pond, although if the skating area is larger— e.g., a lake or a river—you can be a bit freer. But wherever you are, if it is crowded, don't skate against the stream. At some rinks skating backward is prohibited. Even if it is not, be careful and don't skate backward if there is a crowd.

- Don't skate arm in arm more than two abreast. Most rinks prohibit this anyway and will break up longer lines.

- Eating while skating is not allowed, for good reason. Food or any litter dropped on the ice is a safety hazard. Pick up any debris you see.

- Hockey is allowed only at special times on public rinks. Outdoors on a lake or pond, hockey games should not be played if they might interfere with other skaters.

- Don't shove anyone even in fun—it's too dangerous. Apologize if you bump into anyone.

SAFETY ON NATURAL ICE

You should never skate alone on natural ice outdoors, no matter how solid you think it is. The local papers sometimes carry information on thickness of local ice, or the community sports commission may, or the owner of a pond who has made it available. Always be sure to check. Small bodies of water freeze faster than large ones and the ice is usually smoother and more consistent. Never skate near a pond's feeder source because the ice is apt to be thinner there, and do not skate out too far if there is any question of the ice's thickness.

DRESS

Your primary concern when dressing for ice skating is that you be as warm and comfortable as possible. Warm tights, pants, or woolen skirts are quite adequate, worn over long underwear when you're skating out of doors. Indoors, sweaters and/or light jackets or anoraks are ideal. When it's cold, you will need a hat and, of course, gloves inside or out. As in cross-country skiing, wear layers because you will get warm very quickly and want to shed some of your clothes.

JOGGING AND WALKING

On a Saturday or Sunday morning in many cities all over the country it appears the whole world is out for a run, in the parks, along the riverbanks, on the streets, the bridges, and even sidewalks. Photographs of the major marathons, such as the ones in New York City or Boston, show just how immense the numbers of people addicted to jogging and running are. And while there might not be quite so many, walking has its own passionate advocates. (A true walker is one who does five or more miles every day at a speed far above the normal walking gait.) Both are fabulous cardiovascular exercises, and a look at the dedicated, regular runner or walker quickly shows that fat doesn't cling to the bodies of these folk.

Before you set foot on pavement, read as much as you can about how to start on a running or walking program and remember, as a beginner, you must build up your endurance and stamina gradually. Above all, if you feel serious pain, stop your running program and find out what's causing it. Use moderation and good sense and don't push yourself too hard too soon. You are not being graded on your performance.

Walking—fast walking—is a recognized form of serious exercise, and the strain on hip, leg, knee, and foot is much less in walking than in jogging. Anyone, and that means anyone, no matter what shape he is in or what age, can begin a healthy walking program, even if that means walking at a somewhat brisk pace for only ten or fifteen minutes at first and building up gradually. Much research has shown how beneficial a good walking program can be, and advice from many sources is easy to find in books, magazines, and from doctors and friends.

Nothing special is really called for in the way of apparel, except excellent running shoes to protect your feet, knees, and body from the bruising impact of the roadway. Warmup suits, running shorts, sweatshirts, T-shirts, and jogging bras and supporters make up the average runner's wardrobe, whereas racers (and marathoners) are distinguished by the minimalism of their clothing. Some runners might want raingear and well-insulated and ventilated clothes for winter runs, plus a hat and gloves for cool weather. A fanny pack or a wrist strap to hold keys or a bit of money are helpful accessories.

National and local Road Runner Clubs offer a great deal of help and information about running. They organize safety programs in the cities, lobby for safeguards and running spaces, and sponsor major races. While some of the rules for safe running apply particularly to urban areas, most are sensible advice for anyone anywhere. (They should also be kept in mind by walkers.)

SAFETY POINTS

- Run with a group or a partner. If you don't know someone, join the local runners club. There is safety in numbers.

- Run against traffic on the road, and stay on designated running paths, if any. Stay as close to the shoulder of the road as practical.

- Obey traffic regulations. At intersections, look in all directions. Cross the road where you can be seen and cross directly, not diagonally.

- It is less risky to run during the daylight than at night. If you do have to run at night, wear a light-reflecting vest and light-colored clothing and be especially attentive.

- Be familiar with your exact route so that you look decisive. Note where there are police or fire stations, hospitals, twenty-four-hour businesses, and phones and call boxes. Don't run in deserted or badly lighted areas.

- Vary your routines. Don't always run the same route at the same time.

- Hone your instincts and pay attention to them. Be aware who is around you at all times. If you sense you're in danger, be prepared to deviate from your route. Ignore any verbal harassment.

- Carry a whistle or an air horn for emergencies, or scream or yell, "Fire!" if you think you are about to be attacked.

- Don't wear jewelry, even imitation: no chains, rings, bracelets, or expensive watches.

- Don't wear headphones—stay alert.

- Carry identification, including medic alert information, if applicable.

HIKING

Related to walking quite obviously, yet really an altogether different activity, is hiking and/or backpacking. There are of course hikes and hikes. A lot of stamina is required to hike with a backpack over rough terrain, so know your strength and the lay of the land before you go. Respect for and a clear sense of your own capabilities are crucial to your safety and enjoyment. The best advice is to start out with some good strength training. Then don't walk by yourself for any length of time until you have gained solid experience and know how to orient yourself. When you do embark on a solo walking venture, always leave word with family or friends about where you're going and how long you expect it will take.

The equipment you will need depends on the length and difficulty of the trail you've chosen. Excellent walking or hiking shoes with good support are a must. Wearing several layers of comfortable clothing, so you can add or subtract according to temperature and weather, is a priority too. Carry water in a plastic canteen bottle that can be strapped to your waist. Snacks such as dried or fresh fruit, trail mix, and chocolate ought to be included for a day trip, but serious food just adds weight to your backpack. And take along a compass, a knife, some Band-Aids, sunscreen, a scarf (always useful in various ways), a hat or cap, and—most of all—a good map showing the trail. Calculate your time carefully and be conscious of how much daylight is left. Getting caught in the dusk a long distance from your destination can be alarming.

Observe all trail markers and be careful not to wander off the trail. If you decide to do a lot of hiking, get a book on it and learn the various signals used by hikers and woodsmen (in the old sense of one familiar with life in the wilds). If you're camping, find out before you set out where you are allowed to camp, where you may light a campfire, and whether you need a permit.

Never leave litter behind you. A useful phrase to keep in mind is: "What goes in with you must come out with you." The environmentalists' phrase is "minimum-impact" camping and/or hiking, meaning that a good hiker leaves no trace of his passing. He has gained maximum pleasure from the unspoiled natural world but inflicted minimal hurt on the land and its flora and fauna. It's been repeated ad nauseam but is worth saying once again: be certain that your campfire is under control at all times. Don't set a fire at all if there is a fire alert posted by park or trail rangers. And when you put your fire out, take extreme measures to be sure it is really out, every bit of it. After dousing the fire with water or dirt, pull it apart, stamp on it, and finally sift the ashes by hand to check if any heat or spark of fire remains.

CYCLING

While cycling has long been a popular sport, both for competitive and recreational bikers in many European countries, in the United States its popularity has grown slowly. Cycling actually has a long history in this country attested to by the League of American Wheelmen, founded in 1880, now located in Baltimore (1-800-288-BIKE). The LAW lobbies for recognition of the rights of bikers, publishes a magazine, *Bicycle USA*, and can offer anyone who is interested a gold mine of information on safety as well as on biking certification, on touring, national and international bike rallies, or how to start a cycling group or lobby for programs for commuting by bicycle—in short, on all aspects of the sport. Or get a copy of a handy booklet published by the Rodale Press called "Street

Smarts: Bicycling's Traffic Survival Guide," which is packed with useful safety advice, including some valuable tips on how to brake properly, using front and back brakes independently to minimize skidding, and how to brake under poor conditions, i.e., on slippery surfaces and when turning.

As with many sports, safety is the major issue in cycling, what motivates the behavior of everyone involved. Before starting out, however, a biker should have the following safety precautions firmly in mind:

- Carry personal identification, which should include your name, address, medical information, and an emergency contact.

- Learn the hand signals and use them to indicate turns, slowing down, and stopping.

- Keep your bike in good condition; carry a tool kit with you and learn how to make basic repairs.

- Always wear an approved helmet and goggles to protect your eyes from flying stones, pebbles, dirt, etc.

- Obey all traffic signals and markers on the road.

- Ride with the traffic as close to the shoulder as is practical. In the 1970s the bicycle was granted status in all fifty states as a vehicle with the same rights and responsibilities as any other vehicle on the road.

- Don't ride in the dark. At dawn and dusk wear light-colored clothes and during the day wear bright colors. If you must bike after dark, wear a reflecting vest and make sure the bike is well equipped with reflectors.

- Keep your eyes focused on the road ahead to avoid dangerous spills. Loose dirt or sand, oil, water, and ice are menaces to the rider.

- On or off the road, a cyclist must give the right of way to walkers and horses. Pedestrians always have the right of way.

- Make eye contact with pedestrians and motorists at intersections to make sure they see you and to help you judge in which direction they might be heading.

- Always look in every direction before making a turn. Be aware not only of cars but also of pedestrians and other cyclists.

- When you pass another biker, always pass to his left and, when you come up, distinctly say, "On your left," to let him know your whereabouts.

- Always alert a walker on a walking/biking path when you are about to pass.

- When it rains, roads become slippery and hazardous. If you have a mountain bike, use it rather than a narrow-tired racing bike. Mountain bikes have more traction and are more stable. Also be aware that in the rain handbrakes don't always grip the tires as they should.

- If you are cycling in a group, point out upcoming dangers or obstructions to those behind you.
- Carry young children only in recommended child seats and make sure the children wear an approved, well-fitting helmet.

Most experts recommend that a beginning rider start with a mountain (all-terrain) bike with "knobby" tires. The hybrid bike, styled between the ultra-lightweight, road-racing bike and the mountain bike, is also a suitable choice for the beginner. Take your time, shop around, look for bargains at end-of-season sales, and try out various bikes until you've found the one that best suits your body, your objectives, and your budget. If you find a shop entirely devoted to bikes and cycling, you have almost certainly located a bicycle fanatic in the owner. Such an enthusiast is usually pleased to share lore and information. He will be able not only to counsel you if you need to buy a bicycle but also to guide you to local biking groups and point you to the trails and routes best suited to a neophyte.

The tight-fitting elastic skinsuits, leggings, and shorts are not designed solely for aerodynamic reasons or for looking sexy; the stretch materials, such as Spandex, give a bicyclist's leg muscles much-needed support on long trips. And because the wind drag caused by loose, flapping fabrics is fatiguing, the aerodynamic benefits of such clothes are also important. Most of the shorts, leggings, and suits come with padded buttocks—again, a real benefit. Biking is largely a spring-fall sport. There are lightweight, insulated suits in which to brave the cold, but for most of us anything under about fifty degrees is too painful. Proper cycling shoes are a must for a serious biker, as are gloves, to protect your hands from blisters as well as injury and to give you a firm grip. Fanny packs, water bottles, and repair kits for long rides are most important.

Biking requires a minimum fitness level, so work up to it gradually if the only exercise you've been doing regularly is a slow walk from couch to kitchen and back.

Learn to ride with the land by paying close attention to it and don't worry too much if you're "dusted" or "smoked" (passed) at first by the more proficient "roadies."

HORSEBACK RIDING AND FOX HUNTING

Riding is a sport for people of all ages, but an expensive one and therefore not feasible for many of us. The love of horses is powerful, and young girls in particular are often fascinated and enthralled with them. Riding can be a maturing experience for young children as it helps them learn to deal with and care for these large, beautiful creatures.

As with all sports, a primary concern for all riders should be safety. Not only is a horse big, and often moving fast, it also has a lot of hard parts which can be painful to come into contact with. A few tips to bear in mind are:

- Never be diffident about refusing to mount a horse you feel incapable of handling.

- Never mount a strange horse without first inquiring about its disposition and idiosyncrasies.

- When you ride in a group it's up to you to be careful if you are on a kicking or biting horse. Keep a safe distance from the other horses. If yours is a kicker, tie a red ribbon on his tail—a standard warning. But don't try to do it yourself.

- If someone dismounts momentarily, rein in until he has remounted.

- If you want to gallop when the others are walking, trotting, or cantering, explain this to the other riders and ride your horse at your pace far enough away from the group so that a sudden burst of speed will not disturb them.

- If you are riding fast on woodland trails, watch for low limbs, holes, or impediments on the path and warn those behind you.

- When you come upon another group, slow down until you are past and well beyond the other horses.

- Slow your horse to a walk when you approach roads.

- Always walk your horse back to the barn. This will not only keep him from bolting, it will also give him a chance to cool off and relax.

- Gates must be treated with respect and always securely closed behind you. The leader will open the gate, the group will walk their horses slowly through, one by one, keeping a safe distance between them. Then all riders wait for the leader to close the gate and resume his position as leader of the group.

- Only ride abreast with another horse if the trail is wide enough and you are walking.

- Keep up with the others. If you cannot stay up with a fast ride, tell the wrangler before starting out so he can put you with a slower group.

- Don't carry anything in your hands or strapped to your body or around your shoulders. Pack your camera, picnic lunch, blanket, sweater, or anything else securely in a saddlebag. Make sure your hat or scarf is well secured.

- If you have to put on raingear, do so on the ground, not while on your horse. Flapping material may spook the horse and also you should have both hands free at all times when mounted. Tell the rider in front, so he will know to slow down.

- Always wear a hard hat for jumping. (Many think a hard hat should always be worn when riding.)

- If you are inexperienced, do not go out on the trail until you are comfortable with your horse and sure of your abilities. Do your riding in a ring under supervision. Get to know your horse.

- Never ride under anything low or ride into a stall with a low ceiling.

HACKING

Hacking is informal (as opposed to show riding or hunting) riding in the country. Dress is very casual: blue jeans, sweater, flannel shirt—typical country clothes, worn preferably, of course, with boots that protect your feet in a way that sneakers, loafers, or bare feet do not.

Traditional hacking wear for both men and women consists of a single-breasted tweed coat with back vent; breeches in buff, canary, tan, or rust; a single-breasted waistcoat (in cold weather), either checked or plain; a tailored wool or cotton shirt, possibly button-down, worn either open or with a tie (which should be well secured). A turtleneck sweater may also be worn, in hunting yellow or any of the leafy muted colors. Traditional hacking boots are brown and may be laced field boots but should be as long and as narrow as the calf can accommodate. For safety's sake, particularly when riding alone, one is well advised to wear a hard hunting cap. Instead of breeches, jodhpurs may be worn for hacking. These fit the leg tightly with a flare to accommodate the low jodhpur boots worn with them. These boots, strapped or elastic-sided, have become informal wear with slacks or trousers for both men and women. Knit shirts, turtleneck sweaters, and tailored sports shirts are worn with jodhpurs usually (but this is not obligatory) with the formality of a tie in city park riding. Stocks are not worn for informal riding, but ascots, properly secured, may be worn with collarless shirts. Suitable gloves of leather, cotton, or string (or any combination thereof) are useful, particularly in wet weather when reins are slippery. When it is warm, a shirt with short or rolled sleeves and open collar is fine. A waistcoat alone is not worn.

The traditions governing hacking garb have been greatly relaxed. Now more attention is paid to wearing something bright red or blaze-orange while riding during hunting season as some measure of protection.

WESTERN RIDING

The major visible difference between Western and English riding is the saddle. In Western riding a stock or working saddle with a horn in front to which the lariat may be attached, is used. The stirrups of a Western saddle may also have covers (*tapaderas*) to protect the feet in brush country. The reins are held in one hand, leaving the other hand free to work with the rope. The differences for the rider are that when riding Western he does not post (rise to the trot) and guides his horse with a neck rein in his one hand.

Western gear for riding can be very elegant and is often terribly expensive, especially the hand-tooled, custom-made leather boots. These have a high heel and a pointed toe. However, jeans, a flannel or cotton work shirt, a bandana, and a broad-brimmed hat (felt or straw with a brim to shade the eyes) are all that are needed to complete the costume. Chaps may be worn as an extra protection against briars, inclement weather, and other dangers of the ranch or trail. In the mountains a full-length slicker or duster is sometimes added for protection against the elements.

The men who handle the horses are wranglers, not cowboys. When you are riding with a wrangler who is leading, never pass him. It is not only bad riding manners but unsafe.

FOX HUNTING

This is the most formal of all riding sports. Any infringement of the rules of fox-hunting etiquette is intolerable to those who take this very special sport seriously.

The etiquette of fox hunting, as for most sports, is based on a concept of sportsmanship combined with safety. But in addition fox hunting has conventions the reasons for which are not always explicable but should be followed nonetheless, out of respect for the sport's conventions as well as courtesy to the Master and the staff of the hunt.

The position of the Master of Foxhounds (M.F.H.) can be compared to that of the captain of a ship. He commands total respect and obedience. His orders cannot be questioned. Each member of the field should ride up to greet the Master at the meet before it begins. At the end of the hunt, the riders say good night and thank the Master for having provided them with the day's sport. The hunt staff consists of the huntsman (sometimes the Master), who hunts the hounds, assisted by the "whippers-in." Those riding to hounds behind the Master are referred to as "members of the field." The Master, or his deputy, the field master, directs the staff and is in charge of the field.

JOINING THE HUNT Different hunts have different rules about guests. In some, one must be an overnight guest of a member in order to be allowed to hunt, but in most hunts all that is necessary is for the person wishing to be a guest to write to the M.F.H. or the secretary for permission. One does not need sponsors. The "capping" fee or "cap" is a fee paid by the guest, or his host on his behalf, to hunt that particular day. The money should be sent or given to the hunt secretary *before* the meet. If you are an inexperienced rider and have never ridden cross country or jumped, do not accept a hunting invitation.

Some hunts require that those seeking to be regular members of the hunt be landowners who live in the area. With urban spread and consequent limitation of areas available for fox hunting, hunts have had to limit the number in their field. Other hunts have a rule that restricts a guest to three "caps" a year, and if he is not asked to join as a regular member at this point, he should not cap again until the next year.

HUNT COLORS Every hunt has its distinctive colors. Not all members wear them, however. Only those who have been regular members of the hunt and have proved to be knowledgeable fox hunters are invited by the M.F.H. to wear the hunt colors, a band sewn on the collar of the hunting coat. The honor extends to buttons, which are usually made of dark bone, silver, or brass, depending on the color of the coat. The hunt insignia is usually engraved on the buttons. If you do wear the colors of your hunt and will be joining another group, even for the day, you must ask the Master for permission to wear your own colors.

HUNTING ATTIRE If you plan to hunt more or less regularly, traditional hunting attire is called for. If either the rider or the horse is turned out improperly, it is a great insult to the Master. If the Master of Foxhounds is a stickler for form, he will not allow you to join the field if you are dressed too informally. If it is your first time with a hunt, ask your host what you should wear. "Ratcatcher" attire is permissible during the "cubbing period." This consists of a tweed jacket, well-fitting jodhpurs, shirt, stock with an appropriate plain gold safety pin worn horizontally, brown gloves, plus the black hunting derby. (Women should put long hair in a net.) The stock is said to have been designed to serve in an emergency as a sling or bandage and is truly functional. The plain safety pin can be used to secure the sling or bandage.

Formal hunting attire, whether worn by members of the field or by professional hunt staff, is rigidly prescribed. Although each hunt has its own colors and livery worn by the Master and staff, only those invited to wear the colors may do so. All others wear dark gray or dark blue coats, according to the tradition of that hunt, with breeches in white, canary, buff, or brick. Only black calf boots are correct. The "pink" coat, tailored like a frock coat, or a cutaway (shadbelly) worn by men is really a vivid scarlet and may be worn only by those who have received a special invitation to do so from the M.F.H. (Confusingly, the same frock coat, worn in the evening for the hunt ball, is now called "scarlet.") With the pink or the gray melton frock coat or shadbelly, black calf boots with tan tops are worn.

A high silk hat is always worn with a pink coat, a frock coat, or a cutaway. A guest should always wear a top hat and the gray melton frock coat. A black derby, never worn with a pink coat, is worn with every other outfit. The black velvet hunting cap is worn only by the M.F.H., by other masters or ex-masters, by the staff, or by juniors under the age of eighteen. (The Master will upon special request grant permission to others to wear the black velvet cap.) The waistcoat is usually a tattersall or canary wool flannel, but it may be of any distinctive color that has been adopted by the hunt.

THE SPECTATORS Following the hunt on foot is almost as exciting as riding to hounds, but foot-followers can cause havoc, especially if they travel from one jump to another by car. Anyone with a car should park well out of the way of the staff and field, avoid loud talking, laughing, or honking of horns, and keep the engine turned off. Followers must never in any way interfere with the hunt either at the meet or during the chase. Spectators should take care to avoid littering or damaging the fields and fences in any way.

GYMS AND HEALTH CLUBS

A health and fitness trend has taken over all across the country. It includes the national diet mania and workouts at a health club, spa, or gym. As with any exercise program, it's always a good idea to consult with a doctor before embarking on a course of strenuous exercise.

Getting some exercise used to be a pretty simple notion, but as we've learned more and more about the body's physical, psychological, chemical, and biological complexities, exercise has become increasingly better defined and targeted. Today you can take aerobics (high and low impact), "step" exercises, stretching, toning, body shaping or "body sculpting," yoga, and belly dancing. Cardiovascular or aerobic exercise, which increases the heart rate and raises and improves the efficiency of oxygen intake, is one kind the body needs. Another is "resistance" exercise for toning and strengthening the muscles. This usually involves working out on a weight machine to strengthen particular muscle groups. Many women are getting involved in weight training, even quite elderly women. The exercise seems to be beneficial in helping prevent osteoporosis, a serious problem for many women of a certain age. To prepare the muscles for all these exercises, stretching is also a necessary part of any program. Whew!

At most health clubs there is an initiation fee and/or annual membership dues, although some allow monthly memberships. Competition among health clubs can be intense in large cities, so you might be able to take advantage of seasonal specials whereby initiation fees are reduced or waived. Special classes, for instance in step exercise or aerobics or body shaping, may be included in the fee, or you may have to pay per class.

The fashion industry has seized on this national workout craze and created snazzy workout clothes and shoes that are worn on the street as well as in the gym. Attractive as the colorful, form-fitting Spandex and

Lycra tights, unitards, leotards, and capris are, running shorts or sweat-pants and a T-shirt will really do almost as well for a workout. There is some advantage to the specialized clothing, however. Shoes made for aerobics or "cross-training" shoes for walking are lightweight yet provide good cushioning against the impact of the hard floor or road. And elasticized fabrics such as Supplex and the ones named above also have some protective benefit. They can help support the muscles against pulls, strains, and other injuries.

Lockers are usually provided so you can take your workout clothes and change at the club. Almost all clubs have showers and hair dryers, scales, and other amenities such as towels, soap, shampoo, and skin moisturizers. In the locker rooms, leave the shower and facilities as neat as possible, depositing the towel in the bins provided. If there is only one hair dryer, don't monopolize it for too long.

A trained instructor is always on duty in the workout areas to answer questions or to give one-on-one instruction. He will also familiarize you with the machines (this is usually required). Pay very careful attention to what he says, as you must use the machines properly to get the full benefits of the exercise. Also it's possible to injure yourself if you use the machines incorrectly. You'll be told how much weight you should use and how many repetitions and sets to do. In addition to the machines, there are usually free weights to use. You need to be particularly well versed in how to use these safely.

WEIGHT MACHINE COURTESY

- Although it can be tempting, don't stare at fellow exercisers while they are working on the machines. It can make people very uncomfortable.
- While there's nothing wrong with polite, light chat with the person on the machine next to you, if he prefers not to talk, respect his wishes.
- In some gyms, televisions are left on all day. If they bother you, take a Walkman and listen to your own music.
- Shoes are always required for safety and health reasons.
- Bare torsos are not *comme il faut* ordinarily, and it is healthier to wear a shirt of some sort to absorb perspiration.
- Keep a hand towel or washcloth with you as you work out so that you can wipe the equipment off after you've used it. Some clubs post rules about this.
- If you are doing very vigorous workouts, your body is working hard and losing water, so a plastic bottle of water is handy to carry with you to sip as you exercise.
- There may be sign-up sheets for the step machines and treadmills

with time limits. When it's crowded the limit is generally twenty minutes.

- In many gyms there is a preferred order for the use of the machines and everyone is expected to conform. Don't jump in and out in front of people.

CROQUET

You are wrong about croquet if you think it is (a) a genteel Victorian sport for debonairly dressed gentlemen and ladies; (b) a children's game played with balls rolling all over the backyard, through the fence, across the driveway; or (c) a "polite form of war" in which everyone aches to slam the opponent's balls to kingdom come. The true six-wicket game of croquet bears little resemblance to "backyard croquet" with its nine wickets and freewheeling disregard for "heady" (subtle and clever) play.

Real croquet has been well organized for years, with precise rules of play and comportment, developed techniques, and extremely refined strategies. It is played in cities and suburbs on well-tended greenswards of regulated size. It used to be thought of as a game played only by rich "swells" like members of the fabled Algonquin Round Table and various New York socialites such as the Phippses, Harrimans, and Swopes, or by denizens of Hollywood and Palm Springs. Today, as its popularity has grown, it has lost most of that reputation. In the past fifteen years the number of croquet clubs in the United States has increased sevenfold. It is hard to know how many croquet clubs there are today, but joining one is generally easy. The United States Croquet Association was founded by Jack R. Osborn in 1979 and is headquartered in Palm Beach, Florida. It sponsors an active program of regional tournaments and an annual national championship tournament. It publishes a book (*Croquet, the Sport*) and various other handbooks for anyone interested in taking up the sport. The USCA has lists of affiliated clubs across the continent and conducts year-round instruction schools. It has also developed a system of national handicapping, which allows players to compete no matter what the level of their skill. As an individual you can become an "at large member" or you can start a club of your own. About forty-eight states in the United States have organized, affiliated croquet clubs. Canada and the Virgin Islands, as well as Bermuda and Central America, are also represented in the USCA lists.

Herbert Bayard Swope, Jr., called croquet a "form of chess played on your feet." Others have compared its competitive tactics to those of corporate business. Two essentials for good play are the ability to concentrate on mapping an overall game plan and the ability to see angles and to strike the ball the way a billiard player does. Mental agility is far more important than physical strength, which means that both sexes and almost all ages may play the game on an even basis. In 1903 in England, for example, willowy twenty-five-year-old Lily Gower beat England's best male players and took the gold medal in a national match.

Croquet does not demand a great deal of equipment, beyond the "real" (as opposed to backyard) croquet implements. Beautifully crafted hardwood mallets with a 36" long shaft and a head 9" long and 3" wide, balls, wickets, and two stakes are the essentials. These are usually made in England, but some are also made in Canada and this country by one or two specialty manufacturers. Depending on how serious you are about the game and how much you want to invest, you can choose round- or square-headed wood or plastic mallets, the United States Croquet Association wicket, which is 3¾" to 4" wide (just ⅛" to ¼" wider than the balls) or the Roehampton wicket or the "winter wicket," etc. (Caution: Never use a hammer to pound the wicket into the lawn, for you may damage the wicket, unless you use a wooden block to cushion the blow.) A croquet ball is solid wood, about the size of a softball, and has one colored stripe around the equator. The stripe identifies which player the ball belongs to—red mallet, red ball. A deadness board that shows which balls may not be hit without incurring a penalty and loss of turn is just about a necessity for a correctly played game. The only other essential item is a copy of the USCA Rule Book.

Accessories, such as clips, corner flags, ball markers (in the same blue, red, black, and yellow colors of the balls), and a wooden smasher for driving wickets into the ground are useful but not necessary. The best croquet sets can cost as much as 3,500 dollars, but you can get by with one for 300. (Backyard sets cost less, ranging from 40 to 250 dollars.) It might be wiser not to invest in the very best equipment at first unless you are really bitten by the bug. You will need a level grass playing area 84' × 105' (for the official USCA six-wicket court). This lawn should preferably be well groomed and of a rich green.

You may wear whatever you choose so long as all of it—slacks, skirts, shorts, sweaters, caps, and shoes—is white. Shoes should be flat-soled, comfortable, and afford good support and balance so you can set up properly and hit the ball squarely. Sneakers or walking shoes are good choices. A water-repellent jacket is useful and an umbrella is a must. (As in golf, when you hit the ball, you may not shelter under an umbrella held by anyone, so it's important to carry your own. Don't count on anyone lending you one.)

This book cannot give the reader even the most basic idea of the rules, techniques, or strategy of this most appealing, gentle (and ferocious) game. For such information, consult the several good books available or contact the USCA, 500 Avenue of Champions, Palm Beach Gardens, FL 33418 (407-627-3999). The object of the game is to beat your opponent through all the wickets and hit the finishing peg before he does (or they, if it's a doubles game). You earn one wicket point and one stake point each time you clear a wicket properly or hit the finishing stroke. Play is conducted in the descending sequence of the colors on the finishing stake (peg): i.e., blue first, then red, black, and yellow. Each player's turn ends if he fails to score a wicket point or hit another ball on the first stroke. But if he does either he earns a continuation stroke. The object is to make as many wicket points as possible (preferably all in one turn). Competitive croquet is played by two single players or two teams of two players and is usually timed (forty-five seconds per shot per player, an hour and a half for the match).

A few terms might convey a sense of the game's unique flavor:

Bisque—A handicap of an extra stroke for less skilled players, taken to replay a shot from its original position.
Croquet—The first of the two strokes you earn when you roquet; to "take croquet," place your ball against the roqueted ball and hit your ball, moving both balls with the one stroke.
Deadness—After you have hit (roqueted) another ball, you are "dead" on that ball until you have cleared the next wicket. If you hit the dead ball before clearing the next wicket, your turn is over and both balls are put back where they were.
Fault—An unacceptable stroke or one that results in a penalty.
Foot shot—A croquet shot taken with the striker's foot on his own ball. (Legal only in backyard croquet.)
Roquet—When you hit your ball so that it strikes another ball.
Rover—After a ball has scored all its wicket points, it is a rover and can then hit the finishing peg.
Striker—The player who is striking the ball with the mallet.

The etiquette of croquet is simple enough and quite like golf in that the rules of the game include proper behavior. As in golf, do not distract your opponent by standing in his line of sight; don't move around or talk while he is planning and/or executing his stroke. Speed of play is also important and the player whose turn is next should always be ready. Discussions between partners are subject to the forty-five-second rule. When time is running out, it is unsportsmanlike to delay play in order to eat up the clock and protect a lead.

On the court, a courteous manner must always be maintained; no displays of outright anger are acceptable. Above all, never hit your opponent with your mallet. According to one book, it's even worse to swing at a tree or other solid object, as you could seriously damage the mallet head. Croquet players like to joke that the only permissible place to throw a mallet is straight up in the air, but it's better to hang on to it at all times, even in moments of murderous rage.

The role of spectator is to observe, applaud politely, and sometimes to sip tea, but never to offer advice, comments, or point out a player's infraction. No player may offer or receive advice from anyone other than his partner. Good sportsmanship and courteous conduct are required by the rule book, which states:

"Players are under an obligation to avoid acts that may be considered detrimental to the game."

This means, the book goes on, that "profanity, swearing, insults or abusive or obscene" language should never be uttered audibly. Nor are obscene gestures tolerated (this is defined to include deliberate throwing or hitting the ball in the direction of an official, a player, or a spectator).

BOWLING

Our modern game of bowling in which a ball is rolled or "bowled" down an alley at pins is related to ancient games played in Egypt, Greece, and Roman territories. Stone balls and targets dating from 5200 B.C. have been found in a child's tomb in Egypt. In several of the ancient versions, however, the ball was thrown underhand through the air at a smaller ball. The object was to get your ball as close as possible to the smaller ball, or to knock your opponent's balls away from it. Today, these games are played in town squares, on hard dirt or sand "pitches," around the Mediterranean. It is called boccie in Italy and *jeu de boules* in France. In Britain, illuminated medieval manuscripts show examples of bowling games.

These somewhat ruminative games, which call for extremely dexterous play, plus a good head and eye for strategy in which little seems to happen, have never seemed to suit the impatient temperament of Americans. Our bowling more properly derives from the game brought to New York in the seventeenth century by the Dutch settlers. Bowling quickly became associated with gambling and with spirits, which led the Puritans to ban ninepins. The game played with ten pins was perhaps invented as a way around the prohibition. The small pins the game started with proved too difficult to knock down, so in the nineteenth century larger pins that could be knocked over more readily were developed. On the East Coast of the United States, ninepin bowling (the smaller pins) is still a sport, but its popularity is largely limited to the East.

The American Bowling Congress, 5301 South 76th Street, Greendale, WI 53129 (414-461-6400), is the coordinating organization for standards, rules, tournaments, etc., associated with the game. The Congress sanctions bowling leagues for players of all levels of play (from handicap to scratch players) throughout the country.

As in just about every human endeavor, consideration for the safety and well-being of yourself and others is the foundation of good manners and conduct. Common sense also helps determine proper behavior on the bowling lanes but a few guidelines can be indicated here:

• Always be on time for matches or league games. If you are late you will hold up not only your own companions but also the players who follow you.

- Be ready to take your turn, but if a bowler on either of the adjacent lanes is about to bowl, wait before going to your starting spot. If two bowlers approach the line simultaneously, some centers rule that the bowler on the right should go first.

- Think out your delivery but don't dawdle or stand too long at the approach. That can be distracting to other bowlers.

- Remain in your own approach area and back off after every delivery.

- Never use another player's bowling ball, resin, towel, or anything else without asking permission.

- Don't offer advice unless asked. Never mock another bowler's efforts.

- Keep your emotions—positive or negative—under control always.

- Wait for the pin-setting machine to finish its cycle completely before you roll the ball.

- Be careful not to toss or loft your ball into the air—it can damage the lane and could be dangerous to other bowlers.

- No refreshments are allowed on the approaches or the lanes.

- When a bowler (especially an opponent) is ready to bowl, keep silent and respect his right to concentrate on his delivery.

- If you win, celebrate with modesty and restraint. If you lose, be gracious and congratulate the winner(s).

A regulation bowling ball must not weigh more than sixteen pounds. But it may weigh less, and elder bowlers and some women who find that sixteen pounds is too heavy should feel free to use a somewhat lighter ball. It is important that the finger holes on the ball be correctly located for your grip, so take time to measure what will work best for you. It is also important to learn the correct way to pick up a ball from the rack to avoid injury. Take some lessons to learn the proper way to grip, to deliver the ball, to follow through, and the various ways you can bowl a ball (hook, straight, curve, or backup).

Besides a ball, shoes are about the only special equipment needed for bowling. All bowlers must wear the proper kind, which are soft-soled, give some support, allow a slide, and do not damage the delivery area. Clothes are quite informal, but naturally should be clean and neat. At some centers, the league teams may be required to wear league jackets or shirts.

CHAPTER 8
THE ART OF COMMUNICATING

INTRODUCTION

The single most important characteristic that separates man from beast is the gift of language. Whether talking to a friend, making a speech, writing a letter, talking on the telephone, being interviewed, or introducing people at a party, the effective use of language is central to easing one's way through life.

As with any art, becoming adept at communication takes dedication and practice. But one of the pleasures of learning to communicate well is that every single day you have new and interesting opportunities to study and strengthen your skills. And the more expert you become the more you will appreciate the benefits acquired from this skill.

This chapter will serve as a guide to communication in all its forms, from personal stationery and how to use it, to extending and responding to invitations, to the correct way to introduce government officials and other dignitaries. You will also find sample letters covering a variety of situations and occasions for you to model your own correspondence on. But remember, this is only a guide. Your own common sense and social antennae should be your final arbiters.

STATIONERY

When the first paper mill was built in this country in 1690, paper was made by hand from cotton. By the mid-nineteenth century a new technique was developed in which wood pulp was used instead of cotton to produce a lower-quality, less expensive paper. In time, however, it was discovered that this technique was not entirely satisfactory, because breaking wood into pulp requires acid and acid continues to work on paper, causing it eventually to decompose. Acid is not used to break down cotton fiber, so stationery made from one hundred percent cotton fiber is the best choice for letters, particularly those with sentimental value, as it allows them to be preserved for the longest possible time.

YOUR STATIONERY

Today, people are using imagination when it comes to their choice of stationery; the texture of the paper, its size, color, and imprint are all carefully thought out. And just as their clothes reflect their personal styles, their stationery "wardrobes" tell a great deal about them and their particular tastes.

What stationery is right for you and how much you need depends on the type of life you lead and how much you want to spend. If you lead a busy social and business life and are also active in community affairs, you may want to supplement your regular stationery with printed postcards and memo pads.

You can always buy boxes of plain notepaper at a stationery or department store, but you may want to invest some extra money and have your stationery engraved or printed. It's important to take time when choosing your stationery as making the wrong choice, whether in color or lettering, can be costly, particularly in the case of engraving.

ENGRAVING, THERMOGRAPHY (RAISED PRINTING), FLAT PRINTING

To personalize your notepaper you have a choice of engraving, thermography (raised printing), or flat printing. Of the three, engraving, which was introduced in the seventeenth century, is by far the most elegant and graceful. It has a three-dimensional quality which no other process can reproduce. The major single factor in the cost of engraving is the making of the die (die stamping is the process of transferring ink to paper from an engraved die). The die can be used over and over again, so it's the initial stationery order that's most costly. There are people who still do hand engraving, but a modern technique known as photoengraving is the more common procedure today.

Thermography, sometimes called raised printing, gives a raised impression but is not so refined as engraving, nor is it in any way a substitute. But since the thermography process is done without a die, it is considerably less expensive than engraving. You can tell the difference between the two processes in three ways: the inks used in thermography are shinier than those used for engraving; engraving creates an indentation in the back of the paper and causes a "bruise" on the front of the paper (the paper around the copy is slightly smoother than the rest of the card or sheet).

Printing, the third choice, is the most common process and the least expensive. All it requires is the setting of type. Printed stationery is acceptable for all types of correspondence except for extending and replying to a formal invitation or for a condolence letter. In these instances, if you can't afford engraved or thermographically printed paper, you may use a good-quality plain notepaper.

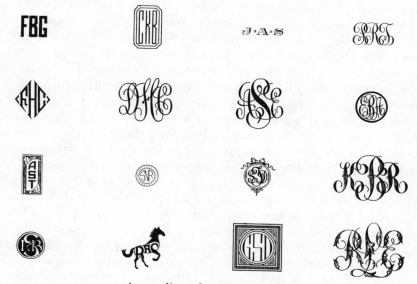

A sampling of monogram styles.

THE ENGRAVED MONOGRAM

Whether or not you have your stationery monogrammed is a matter of preference. If you decide on a monogram, it's best to use two or three of your initials; one alone has an unfinished look. If your three initials together spell a word like A.S.S., however, two are better than three. While you can design your own monogram, a standard stationer's monogram is considerably less expensive. The two most common monograms feature initials of the same size, placed in consecutive order, and the one in which the initial of the last name is set in the center and is larger than the other two initials, which are set on either side. A single or married woman who keeps her maiden name uses the initials of her first, middle, and last names, while a married woman who takes her husband's name uses the initials of her first, maiden, and husband's last names.

THE CREST

A full coat of arms—shield, crest, and motto—belongs to a man only, and therefore cannot be used by a woman. However, a woman with heraldic standing, whose father had a right to arms (or who had been granted arms himself), can use a crest on her stationery. Furthermore, under certain conditions, she can use a coat of arms in a diamond-shaped device known as a "lozenge." For a complete description of the subject of heraldry, see "Heraldic Devices (Crests)" later in this chapter.

STATIONERY FOR WOMEN

Most women find that they can get along well with two types of stationery, one for formal use, such as answering invitations, and the other for everyday use. While white or ecru (cream color) notepaper is still traditional for extending or replying to a formal invitation or for writing a condolence letter, a less formal color such as pale blue or gray is also acceptable. So long as the paper is conservative in style, it's fine to use for formal purposes. Your formal writing paper may be engraved with any of the following: your crest (if it applies), your monogram, your name only, your address only. If engraving is too expensive, you may use a plain paper of good-quality stock. (Don't compromise with thermography; it can't be put in the same category as engraving.) For your everyday stationery you can be as original as you like when it comes to color and printing. You'll want your name, address, and possibly your telephone number printed on the paper. If you are not listed in the telephone book, it's a good idea to have half your stationery printed with your number. There are times when you'll find it convenient for the person to whom you're writing to have it. In addition to these basic styles, you may find it useful to have informals and correspondence cards on hand. It all depends on your needs.

A married woman may use her full name on her stationery: Mrs. Arthur White, or, if she prefers, she may use Sally White. If she is a doctor and goes by her maiden name, her name appears as Doctor (or Dr.) Sally Richter (her professional stationery reads "Sally Richter, M.D."). If she goes by her husband's name she has the choice of Dr. Sally White, Doctor Sally Richter White, or Mrs. Arthur White. A widow does not change her name when her husband dies; she is still Mrs. Arthur White. If she lives in the same town as a son who drops Jr. from his name after his father dies, she will need to add Sr. to her name so as not to be confused with her daughter-in-law. If, when her husband was alive, she went by her professional name, Ms. Sally Richter, she would continue to do so. A divorced woman's own first name appears with the title Mrs. Sally White or Ms. Sally White or, if she prefers, no title. (The old-fashioned form of divorced women using their maiden names with the ex-husband's last name, as in Mrs. Richter White, is rarely if ever seen today.) A single woman's name is written on her stationery without a title, although Miss Sally Smith is not incorrect.

What follows here are descriptions of traditional stationery styles in descending order of formality. While not everyone today feels bound by tradition, this will give you a point of reference so you can make your own personal modifications.

LETTER SHEET (APPROXIMATELY 5¼″ WIDE × 7¼″ HIGH) The letter sheet (traditional name) is folded vertically with the fold on the left. It may be white or ecru. It is engraved with a crest (if applicable), monogram, name only, address only, or it may be plain. A letter sheet is used for writing a condolence letter or any other correspondence. It is also used for extending and replying to a formal invitation (traditionally it is not used for invitations when it is engraved less formally with an address).

INFORMAL (APPROXIMATELY 5" WIDE × 3½" HIGH) The informal is folded horizontally. It is either white or ecru. It may have a crest (if applicable), a woman's full name, or a couple's name engraved on the front. The informal is used for writing short notes or as a gift enclosure card. It is also used for extending and replying to informal invitations or for replying to a formal invitation.

MESSAGE CARD (APPROXIMATELY 5" WIDE × 3½" HIGH) The message card is a single white card with a satin finish, which is smoother than a kid finish. It may have a woman's full name or a couple's name engraved on the top in the center of the card. It may or may not have the street address on the upper right-hand corner. The message card is used for writing a thank-you or other personal note. It may be used for extending or replying to an informal invitation.

CORRESPONDENCE CARD (APPROXIMATELY 6¼" WIDE BY 4¼" HIGH) The correspondence card is a single heavyweight card, which may be any color and often has a colored border. It may be engraved with a crest (if applicable), monogram, name, or name and address. The correspondence card is used for writing short notes and for extending and replying to an informal invitation.

HALF SHEET (APPROXIMATELY 5¾" WIDE × 7¾" HIGH TO 6¼" WIDE × 8½" HIGH) Known as the half sheet, this is a single sheet that may be any color. As it is used for writing letters, blank second sheets are necessary. The first sheet is engraved with a crest (if applicable), monogram, or name and address. While the strict traditionalist stays with the letter sheet for formal use, the half sheet that's white, ecru, pale gray, or pale blue has grown in popularity as a substitute for the letter sheet. When writing a condolence letter or extending or replying to a formal invitation, only white or ecru is used.

FOLDED NOTES (APPROXIMATELY 5¼" WIDE × 3½" HIGH) While the folded note resembles the informal in size and shape, it differs in the following way: paper color may be pale blue, pale gray, or other soft color; the front page is blank or a monogram is placed in the upper left-hand corner or in the center. The folded note is used for general correspondence, in particular thank-you notes.

MONARCH SHEET (APPROXIMATELY 7¼″ WIDE × 10½″ HIGH) The monarch sheet, formerly used only by men, has become increasingly popular with women. It is similar to the half sheet but larger and is used for general correspondence and quasi-business letters.

AIR MAIL Air mail paper comes in a variety of sizes, in either single sheets or pads. A woman who corresponds frequently on air mail paper may have her crest or name and address engraved on the paper. Because of the texture of air mail paper, only one side can be written on. Therefore, if it is engraved, blank second sheets are necessary. Air mail envelopes are tissue-lined so they cannot be seen through.

POSTCARDS Personalized postcards come in various colors, often with a darker-colored border. They may be printed with your name and address or just your address. A postcard must be no larger than 6″ wide × 4¼″ high to be mailed at the postcard rate.

MEMO PADS Memo pads may be any size, shape, or color. It's a matter of preference as to how they are printed: with your initials, first name only, name and address—it depends on what they are to be used for.

ENVELOPES The envelopes that come with personal stationery may be either lined or unlined. If there's a lining, it usually matches the border of the writing paper, if there is one, or it is white tissue paper. The envelopes of formal stationery traditionally have the address only (with apartment number, if applicable) on the flap. In the most formal manner, a house or apartment number is spelled out only through the number 10, although all street numbers are spelled out (for example, Eight East Ninety-ninth Street or 20 East Ninety-ninth Street). Today, however, you'll find that the less formal style 8 East 99th Street is used even for the most formal wedding invitation. If the address is not engraved or printed on the envelope, it may be written in by hand, preferably on the upper left-hand corner of the front of the envelope.

THE POST OFFICE AND ENVELOPES The post office, for its convenience, requests that a return address appear on the upper left-hand corner of the front of the envelope, rather than on the back flap. This way, when a letter has to be redirected to the sender, it is only necessary to cross out the name of the addressee, stamp the envelope "Return to sender," and draw an arrow pointing to the sender's name and address. This request is seldom followed when it comes to traditional social stationery; tradition prevails, with the return address appearing on the flap of the envelope. Where the postal service has won out, however, is in the ruling that an envelope smaller than 5″ wide and 3½″ high will not be accepted in the mails.

STATIONERY FOR MEN

A man's stationery has traditionally been more conservative than a woman's but men today are showing more interest in their stationery and are buying it in a variety of sizes and colors. Correspondence cards are particularly popular with men for writing thank-you notes and short messages. On all stationery, a man's name is engraved without a title unless he happens to be a doctor, in which case he uses Dr. before his name (M.D. is only used professionally). If he is a member of the clergy or the military he also uses a title so people will know how to address him correctly. For engraving, Gothic and Roman are the most popular lettering styles.

For his personal use, a man's stationery may include the following:

MONARCH SHEET (APPROXIMATELY 7¼" WIDE × 10½" HIGH) The monarch sheet is a single sheet that is folded three times to fit into its envelope. Since it may be used for writing longer letters, blank second sheets are necessary. It is engraved with a coat of arms (if applicable), name only, address only, or name and address without a telephone number. The monarch sheet is used for general correspondence and for extending and replying to a formal or informal invitation.

CORRESPONDENCE CARD (APPROXIMATELY 6¼" WIDE × 4¼" HIGH) A correspondence card is a single heavyweight card, which may be any color and often has a contrasting border. It is engraved with a coat of arms (if applicable), name only, or name and address. It is used for thank-you notes and other brief correspondence.

HOUSE STATIONERY

House stationery may be used by all members of the family as well as by houseguests. It may be any standard size and is either a letter sheet (folded on the left side) or a single sheet. The color should be suitable for the general correspondence of all members of the family. It is not used for extending or replying to an invitation or for writing a sympathy letter. House stationery may be engraved with the address only or may include the telephone number, usually engraved on the upper right-hand side of the paper, often with a telephone number symbol directly above the number. Stationery for a country house is sometimes engraved with just the name of the house, "Manderley."

CHILDREN'S STATIONERY

When a child is old enough to write his name, he is ready to be taught the art of letter writing and the significance of a thank-you note. For the beginner, lined paper is the best choice. There is a wide variety of boxed notepaper available, many with colorful illustrations showing popular storybook characters, or possibly an airplane, a dog, or a doll. A child graduates to writing paper with his first name written in bold letters; then around the age of ten he may be given his first stationery with name and address. Not until he is of college age would his stationery be engraved.

STATIONERY WHEN YOU MOVE

If you are planning to move, you should order new stationery as soon as possible. You should also inform all your personal correspondents of your new address well in advance of the move, using cards with envelopes, or postcards, printed with your new address. These are known as "ppc" cards for the French *pour prendre congé* ("for the purpose of saying goodbye").

If you'd rather not go to the expense of printing, there are many original and entertaining fill-in change-of-address cards which you can buy in almost any stationery store.

It is more efficient and effective to inform stores, credit card companies, and others you do business with of your change of address by personal letter. This way you can give them your account numbers and other pertinent information that does not appear on a printed card.

After you move, you may use your old engraved or printed stationery for a reasonable period of time, say four to six months. Draw a line through your old address and simply write in the new one above it. If you are writing something formal, such as a condolence letter, use plain unmarked stationery.

CALLING CARDS

Until World War I, "calling" on friends and acquaintances at their residences was an important formal social custom. This duty fell to the woman of the household. If the person she was calling on was not home, she left her husband's calling card with her own on a sterling silver card tray set on a table in the front hall of every genteel home. Only on certain occasions, such as calls of condolence or congratulations, or calls on the sick, would a man make an appearance and leave his own card in person.

Also known as visiting cards, from the French *cartes de visite*, personal calling cards with matching envelopes have gone the way of many of life's formalities and are no longer thought of as a social necessity. For the most part they are used only by men and women who can afford the luxury of their distinctive look and by those in diplomatic and military circles.

There are several reasons why calling cards are no longer popular: by tradition they are engraved, an expense which is not within most people's budgets; they can no longer be used as invitations since their envelopes are smaller than the minimum post office requirements; we have become less rigid when it comes to conforming to stationery protocol and for the most part have replaced the calling card as a gift enclosure card with an informal—which allows for more writing space—or with a store's gift enclosure card. Even though calling cards may not be as popular as they once were, it's doubtful they will ever completely disappear. As an enclosure card with flowers or any kind of present, nothing can replace their quality and distinction.

Mrs Anton Farley Briggs

A woman's calling card.

Mr and Mrs Christopher W. Williams

A couple's calling card.

THE STYLE OF CARDS

In order to distinguish a calling card from a business card, which it resembles closely in size, it's frequently referred to as a social card. While white is the most popular color for a calling card, you may prefer cream color. Either is correct. Calling cards are always engraved in black ink. A script typeface is traditional and is therefore considered by some the correct lettering style for a calling card. Actually any simple face is correct; what you want to avoid are quaint or ornate letters not in keeping with the formality of the card.

It's up to you whether you have just your name on your calling card or your name and address. If you do include your address, it's engraved in small letters without abbreviations in the lower right-hand corner of your card. If there's any possibility of your moving from where you presently live, you certainly would not want to go to the expense of engraving your address. If you choose not to include your address, you can always handwrite it and/or your telephone number on the card.

WRITING A MESSAGE AND SIGNING YOUR NAME TO A CALLING CARD

While you don't have to write a message on your calling card, to do so is certainly more personal. If you are enclosing your card with flowers to the family of a friend who has died, all that's necessary is a brief message handwritten on the face of the card: "With deepest sympathy." The same thing applies when you enclose your card with a present: "With best wishes for your happiness always"; "Have a great graduation party." In the case of close friends, to personalize your card, put a fine diagonal line through your name and sign above it "Love, Helen" or "Jim" as the case may be. For those you don't know as well, you can put a line through your title and first name only and write "Helen" above. Write the recipient's name, or name and address, on the front of the envelope. This is important in case the store mislays the card. Unless the message is personal, the envelope is left unsealed.

CALLING CARD AS BIRTH ANNOUNCEMENT

A nice way to announce the birth of a baby is to attach a small, engraved calling card, bearing the baby's name, to the father and mother's card. Sometimes the baby's card is pink- or blue-bordered and attached to the larger card with a pink or blue ribbon.

SIZES OF CALLING CARDS

The sizes of calling cards for a man, a woman, a married couple, and a child vary slightly. For example, a woman's card is squarer than a man's, and a man's card is longer than a woman's. These are the accepted sizes for such cards:

- Man (single or married) 3⅜" x 1½" or 3½" x 2"
- Single woman 2⅞" x 2"
- Married woman 3⅛" x 2¼"
- Married couple 3⅜" x 2½"

CALLING CARDS FOR MEN

Traditionally, a man's name is written out in full on a calling card. Titles other than Mr. are also written out in full: Doctor, The Reverend, General. If a man's name is too long to fit properly on the card, he may drop his middle name or abbreviate his title by using Dr. or Rev. Generally speaking, people today are more relaxed in their responses to tradition and the man accustomed to using an initial in place of his middle name may feel free to do so on his calling card. If the man is a lawyer his card reads Mr. Scott Grunwald, or more formally Scott Grunwald, Esquire. A doctor's title is written out on his card: Doctor Arthur White. His professional card, however, reads Arthur White, M.D. A title may be followed by Jr., Sr., II, III, IV. If "junior" is written out (a more formal style), a lower-case *j* is used. While the suffixes Jr. and Sr. are preceded by a comma, there is no comma before a Roman numeral suffix (II, III, IV). The letters of degrees, such as Ph.D., no matter how important, are not used on social cards. The holder of a D.D. has the privilege of calling himself The Rev. Dr. Charles Forgan (spelling it out if there's room). If you have an honorary degree, it's in better taste to omit Dr. on your card. Even a professor uses Mr. on his calling card, not Professor or his academic degrees.

CALLING CARDS FOR WOMEN

MARRIED WOMAN A married woman's name appears on her calling card exactly as her husband's name appears on his, except of course with the title Mrs. If she wishes, her address is engraved on the lower right-hand corner of the card. The calling card of a woman doctor who goes by her maiden name is engraved Doctor Sally Richter (her professional card reads Sally Richter, M.D.). If she goes by her husband's name she has a choice of Doctor Sally White, Doctor Sally Richter White, or Mrs. Arthur White.

DIVORCED WOMAN Formerly, a divorced woman's calling card always appeared as Mrs. Richter [maiden name] White. While this form of address will always be correct, it's rarely used anymore. Today you see Mrs. Sally White, Mrs. Sally Richter White, or Sally Richter White. If a divorced woman has children, she keeps her ex-husband's name so her name is the same as her children's. If a woman has no children and wants to resume her maiden name, her calling card reads Sally Richter (she's no longer Mrs.; Miss is for a woman who's never been married, and Ms. is not used on a calling card).

WIDOW A widow may continue to use her calling card after her husband dies, just as she continues to use his name. She shouldn't call herself Mrs. Sally White, because that indicates she is divorced. If a man drops Jr. after the death of his father, and lives in the same town as his mother, his mother adds Sr. to her name so as not to be confused with her daughter-in-law.

SINGLE WOMAN A single woman may use the title Miss on her calling card or, if she prefers, just her full name without a title.

WHY MS. IS NOT USED ON A CALLING CARD The question of using Ms. on a calling card frequently comes up. Because this title has been incorporated into our forms of address only recently, you'll find that many stationers feel its style does not conform with the long-established tradition of the calling card. Instead of Ms. they suggest either Mrs. or Miss, or no title.

CALLING CARDS FOR COUPLES

A joint calling card for a couple often includes their home address. The card is written Mr. and Mrs. or The Reverend and Mrs. plus the husband's full name. If possible, titles should not be abbreviated and initials should not be used. But if the name is a particularly long one you have to abbreviate (i.e., Rev.) or use an initial or omit a middle name. If both husband and wife are doctors a card may read The Doctors White or Doctors Sally White and Arthur White (Doctors Sally and Arthur White is also correct) or, if the wife keeps her maiden name, it's Dr. Sally Richter and Dr. Arthur White (length here necessitates abbreviation of Doctor). If the husband only is a doctor the card reads Doctor and Mrs. Arthur White. If the wife only is a doctor it's Doctor Sally White [or Richter] and Mr. Arthur White. Or, if she prefers, she may use Mr. and Mrs. Arthur White. A lawyer does not use Esquire on a joint calling card. Since, as stated earlier, Ms. is not used on a calling card, the joint card of a couple when the woman uses her maiden name is written without titles (i.e., Sally Richter and Arthur White). For a retired military officer, because the word "Retired" must appear, the card reads:

Admiral Lande Crouse, Retired
Mrs. Crouse

INVITATIONS

Formal Invitations

EXTENDING A FORMAL INVITATION

The traditional formal invitation never varies. It should be engraved on a white or ecru card in black ink; English Script, Shaded Roman, and Shaded Antique Roman are the most popular lettering styles. Card sizes vary depending on the length of the text of the invitation.

A second category for the formal invitation is the engraved fill-in invitation or one that's issued on your personal stationery. This invitation is less formal in style than the traditional formal invitation and is frequently used to invite guests to a dinner party.

Formal invitations are sent out first class mail three weeks before the party's to take place; during the height of the holiday season, they should be mailed four weeks in advance so there's less chance of a conflict of dates with other party givers.

RULES FOR PREPARING A FORMAL INVITATION

- On an engraved fill-in invitation the hosts' name may be engraved at the top. It is most practical for those who give formal dinner parties fairly frequently.
- When a party is in honor of someone, the person's name should appear in the body of the engraved invitation. On a fill-in invitation, you write "In honour of" and the person's name on the top center of the invitation.
- On a formal invitation the words "honor" and "favor" are spelled in the British way: "honour" and "favour."
- In the past, a formal dinner invitation automatically meant a black-tie affair. It was not necessary, therefore, to write "Black tie" on the invitation. Today, with our less formal life style and manner of dress, the hostess of a black-tie dinner party may feel it is necessary to write "Black tie" on the lower right-hand corner of the invitation.
- The formal invitation includes titles. An exception is the wedding invitation.
- Tradition calls for a first or middle name to be written out in full on a formal invitation. Over the years there's been an easing of this custom, so that a person who always uses an initial in place of one of these names may feel free to do so on a formal invitation.
- The word "junior" is written with a small *j*. When it is abbreviated, which is usually the case, the *J* is capitalized: Jr.
- When a guest's name is handwritten on an invitation: ". . . requests the pleasure of *Miss* [*Ms.*] *Janet Agnew's*[a] company . . ." it's optional to omit the given name, in the more formal style: "*Miss Agnew's*[a] company . . .".
- The date is written formally on an invitation as "on Wednesday, the third of May." Less formally, but equally correct, is "on Wednesday, May third," or simply "Wednesday, May third." The use of the word "on" is optional.
- When guests are invited to a noon lunch, the time on the invitation is written "at twelve noon" or "at twelve o'clock."
- If guests are invited on the half hour, the invitation reads, "at half after eight o'clock," not "at half past." Less formally, it's "eight-thirty o'clock."
- When the town or city where the party's to be held is obvious to all invitees, it's not necessary to include it in the body of the invitation.

[a] *Italic* type indicates handwriting.

For example, "The Anglers' Club," with the street address beneath, is all that's needed.

- The name of a state is written out in full on a formal invitation.
- The ZIP code does not appear after the name of the state in the body of the invitation. It does, of course, appear with the address below the R.s.v.p. (The letters "R.s.v.p.," which can also be written R.S.V.P., are the first letters of each word of the French phrase, "*Répondez s'il vous plaît* (Please respond)."
- While it's not necessary to put the address under the R.s.v.p. if it appears on the back flap of the envelope, it's practical to do so, because many people throw the envelope away before answering the invitation.
- On the formal invitation the R.s.v.p. is to an address, never a telephone number. If a reply card is to be enclosed with the invitation, no address is written below the R.s.v.p.

TYPES OF FORMAL INVITATIONS

A FORMAL ENGRAVED FILL-IN INVITATION Here the hosts' names are engraved on the invitation.

Mr. and Mrs. Arthur Taylor White
request the pleasure of
Miss [Ms.] Eileen O'Sullivan's[a] company
at *Dinner*
on *Tuesday, the third of May*
at *eight* o'clock
430 Jefferson Street

R.s.v.p.
430 Jefferson Street
New Orleans, LA (ZIP code)

[a]*Italic* type indicates handwriting.

The second type of fill-in invitation does not have the hosts' names engraved on it. In answering the invitation below, you write to Mr. and Mrs. White but address the envelope to Marie Lindstrom, who is handling the responses.

Mr. and Mrs. Arthur Taylor White
request the pleasure of your company
at *Dinner*
on *Tuesday, the third of May*
at *eight* o'clock

The National Hunt Club
11 Greene Street

R.s.v.p.
Ms. Marie Lindstrom
11 Main Street
New Orleans, LA (ZIP code)

When a Guest May Bring an Escort

Mr. and Mrs. Arthur Taylor White
request the company of
Miss Ohrstrom and Escort
[or, in the case of a man, *Mr. Whipple and Guest*]
at a dinner dance
in honour of their granddaughter
Miss Amanda White
on Tuesday, the third of May
at half after seven o'clock

The Prescott Hotel
7 Sherman Street

R.s.v.p.
430 Jefferson Street
New Orleans, LA (ZIP code)

A HANDWRITTEN FORMAL INVITATION If the letterhead does not have the address at the top, the address appears in the body of the invitation.

Mr. and Mrs. Arthur Taylor White
request the pleasure of
Mr. and Mrs. Buxton's company
at dinner
on Tuesday, the third of May
at eight o'clock
430 Jefferson Street

R.s.v.p.
430 Jefferson Street
New Orleans, LA (ZIP code)

AN ENGRAVED INVITATION IN HONOR OF A SPECIAL GUEST

Mr. and Mrs. Arthur Taylor White
request the pleasure of your company
at dinner
to honour
Mr. and Mrs. Joseph Schwartzkoff
on Tuesday, the third of May
at eight o'clock
430 Jefferson Street

R.s.v.p.
430 Jefferson Street
New Orleans, LA (ZIP code)

AN ENGRAVED FILL-IN INVITATION IN HONOR OF A SPECIAL GUEST
With a fill-in invitation, the guest of honor's name is written in at the top of the invitation.

In honour of
Governor F. Vernon Osborne

Mr. and Mrs. Arthur Taylor White
request the pleasure of your company
at *dinner*
on *Tuesday, the third of May*
at *eight o'clock*
430 Jefferson Street

R.s.v.p.
430 Jefferson Street
New Orleans, LA (ZIP code)

AN ENGRAVED INVITATION TO AN OFFICIAL LUNCHEON

Mr. and Mrs. Arthur Taylor White
request the pleasure of your company
at a luncheon in honour of
His Excellency, the President of Chile
and
Señora de Martinez-Gracia
Sunday, the twenty-fourth of March
at one o'clock

aboard "The Mermaid"
Happy Crayfish Yacht Club

R.s.v.p.
430 Jefferson Street
New Orleans, LA (ZIP code)

WHEN SEVERAL COUPLES ISSUE AN INVITATION When several couples give a party that will be held at the house of one of them, the couple hosting the party is listed first on the invitation. It's also their address in the body of the invitation and under the R.s.v.p. In the example, the party will be at the Landbrookes', who live at 1022 Park Avenue. If the party will be held at a club or hotel, the hosts' names are listed alphabetically, or however the couples choose to be listed. The couples decide among themselves to whom the replies will be sent and that name and address are listed accordingly. Because it's obviously a black-tie affair, "Black tie" is not mentioned on the invitation.

Mr. and Mrs. Josiah Landbrooke II
Mr. and Mrs. Seymour Robert Ackerman
Mr. and Mrs. Arthur Taylor White
request the pleasure of your company
at a small dance
on Wednesday, the third of May
at ten o'clock

1022 Park Avenue

R.s.v.p.
1022 Park Avenue
New York, NY (ZIP code)

AN ENGRAVED INVITATION TO AN ANNIVERSARY PARTY

Mr. and Mrs. Reynolds White
Mr. and Mrs. William Kahn
Mr. Stephen White
request the pleasure of your company
at a dinner dance to celebrate
the fiftieth wedding anniversary of their parents
Mr. and Mrs. Arthur Taylor White
on Wednesday, the third of May
at eight o'clock

The National Hunt Club
10 Berkeley Square
New Orleans

R.s.v.p.
Mrs. Reynolds White
47 Lake Shore Drive
Chicago, IL (ZIP code)

AN ENGRAVED INVITATION TO A DEBUTANTE DANCE In this invitation the debutante is referred to as Miss since a woman uses this title until she is twenty-one; after that she may change to Ms. if she chooses. Black tie is included here, in case some men are not certain what the dress code is.

Mr. and Mrs. Macy Linde Turner
request the pleasure of your company
at a dance in honour of their granddaughter
Miss Charlotte Sue White
on Wednesday, the twenty-third of December
at ten o'clock

The Pendennis Club
43 Chamberlain Street
Louisville

R.s.v.p.   Black tie
1200 St. James Court
Louisville, KY (ZIP code)

If the parents give the debutante dance, the invitation follows the same form as the previous one, or their daughter's name may be listed under their name. Instead of the word "dance," "small dance" is often used, regardless of whether the party is a small or large one.

Mr. and Mrs. Arthur Taylor White
Miss Charlotte Sue White
request the pleasure of the company of
Mr. John Albright
at a small dance
on Wednesday, the twenty-third of December
at ten o'clock

430 Jefferson Street

R.s.v.p.   Black tie
430 Jefferson Street
New Orleans, LA (ZIP code)

AN "AT HOME" INVITATION An invitation to an "at Home" debutante party usually means a tea dance held in the afternoon, either at the
home of the person giving the party, or at a club or hotel. The time is
usually prescribed ("until" is a more formal usage than "to"), and the
invitation may be worded as follows:

Mr. and Mrs. Arthur Taylor White
Miss Charlotte Sue White
at Home
Saturday, the sixteenth of March
from five until seven o'clock

430 Jefferson Street

R.s.v.p.
430 Jefferson Street
New Orleans, LA (ZIP code)

THE REPLY CARD

The reply or "R.s.v.p." card, it seems, is here to stay. It entered our lives
when people no longer had the good manners to reply to an invitation.
Whether they weren't taught to or just couldn't be bothered to take the
time to answer is a matter of debate. When hostesses' frustration at not
receiving replies to their invitations got to a breaking point the reply card
was invented.

As the host or hostess, you have to decide whether to enclose a reply
card with your invitation. The advantage, of course, is that you are apt to
get more replies if you enclose a card rather than relying on the invitees to
answer in the proper written form. The reply card is made of the same
stock as the invitation and follows the same style. A common reply card is
given as example here.

The favor of a reply is requested

M_____

will_____attend

Saturday, February fifth

If the party is a private one, a dance or a wedding, for instance, the return envelope often has a stamp on it. This is not the case if the invitation is to a charity event where of necessity costs need to be controlled. An alternative to the reply card and envelope, much less formal, is the reply postcard.

MAP ENCLOSURE

If you live in an area that's difficult to find, you'll want to enclose with your invitation a detailed map and explicit directions to your house. The map must be easy to read and printed on paper that complements the invitation. Your address and telephone number should appear on the map.

ACCEPTING FORMAL INVITATIONS

When you respond to a formal invitation, you do so in the third person. Your reply is handwritten on your personal letter sheet or half sheet, your informal (if a couple, a "Mr. and Mrs." informal is used), or on plain, conservative notepaper. Address the envelope to both host and hostess. The reply follows the same general form whether it's for a dinner, a dance, or some other formal party. If several couples issued the invitation and you do not have space to list all the names in your reply, you need only use the first name listed. When answering an invitation from a couple whose name is followed by Jr., II, or III, if you omit the hosts' given name, you also omit the suffix (see the second invitation below). You never accept or regret an invitation "for" dinner. The correct form is "to" dinner (i.e., "to eat"). Also, when replying to an invitation to a "small dance," omit the word "small" in the reply. In your acceptance, repeat both the date given on the invitation and the time. It's optional as to whether you repeat "to dinner." If not, the following acceptance would read "for Saturday, the fifteenth of June."

Mr. and Mrs. Arthur Taylor White
accept with pleasure
the kind invitation of
Dr. and Mrs. Arthur Newman, Jr.
to dinner
on Saturday, the fifteenth of June
at eight o'clock

or

Mr. and Mrs. Arthur Taylor White
accept with pleasure
Dr. and Mrs. Newman's
kind invitation to dinner
on Saturday, June the fifteenth
at eight o'clock

ACCEPTING A FORMAL INVITATION ON AN INFORMAL While an informal is not used to extend a formal invitation, it may be used to reply to one. Since Mr. and Mrs. Arthur Taylor White's name is written on the front of the informal, the reply is written on the inside directly below the fold (page 3). Their name need not be repeated.

accept with pleasure
the kind invitation of
Dr. and Mrs. Arthur Newman, Jr.
to dinner
on Saturday, the fifteenth of June
at eight o'clock

WHEN ONLY ONE OF A COUPLE CAN ACCEPT When a husband and wife receive an invitation and only one can accept, the acceptance comes first and the regret follows.

Mrs. Arthur Taylor White
accepts with pleasure
the kind invitation of
Dr. and Mrs. Arthur Newman, Jr.
for Saturday, the fifteenth of June
at eight o'clock

Mr. Arthur Taylor White
regrets that he will be unable to accept
due to absence from the city

REGRETTING A FORMAL INVITATION
In regretting, as in accepting, a formal invitation, there's a standard form. A formal regret usually states briefly the reason for the refusal—"because of their [her] absence from town," "due to a previous engagement." Avoid giving illness as a reason since the host and hostess will feel obliged to respond in some way. If you are a very close friend of the hostess, it's proper to call or write her a note explaining why you cannot be there.

In regretting an invitation, give the date; it's not necessary to include the time. Follow the same form for regretting a formal invitation on an informal as the one shown for accepting a formal invitation.

Mr. and Mrs. Arthur Taylor White
regret that they are unable to accept
the kind invitation of
Dr. and Mrs. Arthur Newman, Jr.
to dinner
on Saturday, the fifteenth of June

or

Mr. and Mrs. Arthur Taylor White
regret exceedingly
that due to a previous engagement
they are unable to accept
Dr. and Mrs. Newman's
kind invitation to dinner
on Saturday, the fifteenth of June

or

Mr. and Mrs. Arthur Taylor White
regret that
owing to absence from the city
they are unable to accept
the kind invitation of
Dr. and Mrs. Arthur Newman, Jr.
for Saturday, the fifteenth of June

Informal Invitations

EXTENDING AN INFORMAL INVITATION

There's much greater flexibility and variation as to the style, paper color, and wording for informal invitations than there is for formal ones. You may have the invitation specially printed or use one of the fill-in types. In addition, you may extend the invitation on your personal writing paper or on an informal, message card, or correspondence card. Informal invitations are often issued in the third person but in a less prescribed way than the truly formal invitation.

TYPES OF INFORMAL INVITATIONS

AN INFORMAL FILL-IN INVITATION

Sally and Arthur White
invite you
to *cocktails*
on *Wednesday, May 3rd*
6–8 [or six to eight] o'clock
430 Jefferson Street

R.s.v.p.
879-6402

or

To meet Jill Gruson
please come for
cocktails
Sally and Arthur White
on *Wednesday, May 3rd*
6–8 [or six to eight] o'clock
430 Jefferson Street

R.s.v.p.
879-6402

AN INVITATION ISSUED ON AN INFORMAL

Cocktails
Mr. and Mrs. Arthur Taylor White
Wednesday, May 3rd
6–8 [or six to eight] o'clock
430 Jefferson Street

R.s.v.p.
879-6402

While the example above is correct, it quite obviously lacks a personal touch. If you prefer, you may write a short message such as "Hope you can come" somewhere on the informal, or substitute "Please join us for cocktails" for "Cocktails."

AN INVITATION ON A FOLDED NOTE WITH A MONOGRAM You may also issue an invitation by writing a short note on your folded note. Since the initials are customarily set on the center of the front page, you write your message on the inside directly below the fold (page 3). If the initials are placed on the upper left-hand corner, you would write on the front page.

JWR

Dear Ralph,
I hope you'll be able to come for dinner on
Tuesday, May 3rd at 7:30 before the Community
Theater play. You can call to let me know at
879-6042.

Best to you,
Sally

430 Jefferson Street

REPLYING TO AN INFORMAL INVITATION

Most R.s.v.p.'s on an informal invitation give a telephone number. If they do, you may reply by telephone. If there's an address, you reply on your personal writing paper, or if your stationery includes informals, message cards, or correspondence cards, you may use one of these.

"REGRETS ONLY" AND WHEN THERE'S NO R.S.V.P. Sometimes the R.s.v.p. to a cocktail party invitation says, "Regrets only," followed by a telephone number. This phrase evolved because so many people, lacking in good manners, were not responding to cocktail invitations. While you are under no obligation to reply to a "Regrets only" party if you're planning to attend, it's thoughtful to take the time to do so. Not only will the hostess be pleased to hear you're coming, but it will give her a better idea of how many people to expect.

It is not necessary to respond to an invitation if no R.s.v.p. is given.

USE OF NAMES AND TITLES

While you may not be a traditionalist as far as protocol is concerned, it's important to have a basic understanding of how names and titles work in English and to be able to use them accordingly. The following will give you the essentials on the use of names and titles as they apply today.

MARRIED WOMAN KEEPING MAIDEN NAME

A woman who keeps her maiden name is Ms. Sally Richter. If, however, Sally Richter only uses her maiden name professionally, then socially she is Mrs. Arthur White.

HYPHENATED NAMES

According to statistics, a man and woman joining their last names with a hyphen (it's customary for the woman's name to come first: Ms. Sally Richter-White) is not nearly so popular as it was in the 1970s. While the idea of combining names may have sentimental or political value, in practice it's a lot less confusing when children come along if they have only one last name to deal with. (Even more complicated is a woman choosing to use both last names without a hyphen: Sally Richter White. In this situation someone meeting her for the first time has no way of knowing whether Richter is her middle or maiden name.)

WIDOW

When a woman's husband dies, she does not change her name; she remains Mrs. Arthur White. (Mrs. Sally White would indicate that she's divorced.) If she lives in the same town as her son and he drops Jr. from his name when his father dies, she adds Sr. to her name in order not to be confused with her daughter-in-law.

DIVORCED WOMAN

It once was the custom, when a woman divorced, that she used her maiden name in place of her husband's first name. Therefore, Sally Richter, divorced from Arthur White, became Mrs. Richter White. To-day this custom, while still correct, is seldom encountered. Instead, a divorced woman is known as Mrs. Sally White. If a divorced woman remarries, she may continue to use her first husband's name if she is known professionally by it. A divorced woman who has taken back her maiden name drops the Mrs. and is known as Ms. Sally Richter (Miss belongs to a woman who has never been married). This only applies to a divorcée without children. If she has children, she continues to use her ex-husband's name, the same name as her children.

SEPARATED WOMAN

A woman who separates is legally Mrs. Arthur White until she's divorced. If, however, during the separation period she'd prefer to be known as Mrs. Sally White, she should be referred to that way.

SINGLE WOMAN WITH A CHILD

A woman who has a child but has never been married may use the title Miss or Ms. She does not use Mrs. since that form of address is reserved for a woman who is or has been married. In this case, it seems more practical to use Ms., a term that applies to a single or married woman.

A WOMAN WHO USES TWO FIRST NAMES

When a woman is known by two first names like Mary Louise (Blankarn) or Helen Ann (Blankarn), she may use her middle name in place of her maiden name when she marries. In other words, instead of becoming Mary Blankarn Husted, she can be Mary Louise Husted. Whatever combination of names she prefers is correct, including four names if that's what she likes best.

THE USE OF MS.

The use of the title Ms. has come a long way since the 1960s and the early days of the women's movement when it was first introduced. Having worked its way into the dictionary and overcome opposition from language purists, you can almost say the term received its ultimate acceptance in this country with its first use in the venerable *New York Times* on June 19, 1986.

Almost all single women today use the title Ms. instead of the more spinsterish Miss. One reason they choose it over Miss is because Ms. is a closer equivalent to Mr. in that neither reveals whether a person is married or single. For the same reason, Ms. is a convenient form of address when you are writing a woman whose marital status you don't know. Popular as Ms. may be, however, there are still women who prefer the more traditional Miss and, if they do, they should be addressed that way.

Ms. is the correct title for a married woman who keeps her maiden name. When Sally Richter marries Arthur White she is known as Ms. Sally Richter. If instead she goes by her husband's name, she is Mrs. Arthur White, never Ms. Sally White or Ms. Arthur White. Since Sally Richter is married she can't use the title Miss, and if she uses her maiden name she can't go by the title Mrs.

HOW JR., SR., 2ND, 3RD WORK

When a man is given the identical name as his father, he is junior (Jr.). When written out, junior has a small *j*. The wife of a man with a suffix also has a suffix after her name: Mrs. Arthur White, Jr. If a Jr. in turn gives his son the same name, the son is III or 3rd. (a comma precedes the suffixes Jr. and Sr.; there is none before a Roman or Arabic numeral suffix.)

After the death of his father, a man does not keep the Jr. unless the suffix is so closely identified with his name, as in William F. Buckley, Jr., that he feels it would confuse people to drop it. If his mother lives in the same city, she takes on the suffix Sr. so as not to be confused with her daughter-in-law.

A man named after a member of his family, such as an uncle or grandfather, is a II or 2nd. When the original holder of the name dies, the suffix II is dropped. A man with the suffix III or IV usually retains it until he dies, but he may drop it, if he chooses, when his predecessors with the name die. The only reason the suffix III or IV is kept is that it would be confusing to people who know you as IV to suddenly have to change to III.

Sometimes a father may feel he does not want to burden his son with the identical name of a long line of successful predecessors but instead gives him his first name with a different middle name.

CHANGING YOUR NAME LEGALLY

If you change your name with or without legal recourse, you may send out an announcement card to friends and business associates. If the change has gone through the courts, "changed his [or her] name legally" may be included in the announcement.

LISTING NAMES ON A COMMITTEE

In the past, a woman listing her name on a committee used her husband's name (Mrs. Arthur White). If you look at a benefit invitation or program today, you will see some names with titles and others without. Since any list looks better when the style is uniform, the organizer of a benefit may suggest that committee members all list their names in the same way. She should not make too big an issue of this, however, or she'll alienate committee members who want their names to appear as they like to see them, rather than how the organizer thinks they should be. As to whether names should be listed with or without titles, it depends on the degree of formality of the event and the custom of the area where you live. If the party's a fancy benefit ball, titles add style, formality, and cachet to the invitation. In the case of a less formal event, such as an outdoor barbecue, using first and last names only is more in keeping with the occasion.

NICKNAMES AND CONTRACTIONS OF NAMES

Many adults are known throughout their lives by the nicknames they acquired as children and by which family members and old friends still call them. Just because you hear someone called by a nickname doesn't mean you should do the same. Wait to be asked. Many people are offended by assumed familiarity being thrust upon them. Or it might be that they don't like the nickname and would prefer not to encourage its use. If someone starts calling you by your nickname and you'd prefer they didn't, don't be timid. Speak up and say so. You don't have to go into reasons—just let them know you prefer to be called by your given name.

If someone named Robert chooses to be called Robert, don't call him Bob thinking it sounds friendlier. It may only irritate him.

USE OF ESQUIRE

This title is rarely used today except in the case of lawyers. (See "Esquire" under "Addressing Envelopes" later in this chapter.)

USE OF "MA'AM" AND "SIR"

"Yes, ma'am" and "No, sir" are terms of respect still used in certain areas of the South, particularly by children when addressing adults—or by younger adults to their seniors. It's still common practice in many schools for students to address a male teacher as "Sir." It's a matter of personal choice—if you want your children to adopt this custom, you must instruct them.

USE OF "LADY" AND "GENTLEMAN" VERSUS "WOMAN" AND "MAN"

"Lady" and "gentleman" are basically old-fashioned words, once widely used when referring to upper-class men and women. Today, you may talk about a "ladies' " tea or bridge party, or refer to an elderly man as a "gentleman" but, generally speaking, these terms have been replaced by "woman" and "man." For example, you'd say, "I know the man who won the golf tournament" rather than "the gentleman who won the golf tournament." If you translate the usage to a female, you'll see that "woman" is applicable rather than "lady." "Lady" and "gentleman" are used in legislative bodies as forms of respect, as in "The gentleman from North Dakota."

USE OF "MISS"

Whenever possible the word "Miss" should be avoided when trying to catch someone's attention. If you're being served by a waitress in a restaurant and need to call her, "Waitress" is a better term than "Miss," or you can get her attention by looking at her and saying, "Excuse me, may I have a glass of water?" Well-trained salespeople use the word "Madam" instead of "Miss" unless they are talking to a very young girl. A customer wanting to get the attention of a salesperson may signal her by saying, "Excuse me."

SIGNING YOUR NAME

ILLEGIBLE SIGNATURE

People shouldn't have to struggle to decipher your signature on a letter. It's not only annoying but can cause confusion. If your signature is beyond reading, and won't be familiar to the recipient, use engraved or printed stationery with your name and address or type or print your name under your signature. In the case of personal checks, most banks require that your name appear on the face of the check.

SIGNING CHECKS, LEGAL PAPERS

A married woman normally signs a check or legal document with her given name plus her married name, i.e., Sally White. If both names are common ones, in order that she not be confused with another Sally White, it makes sense to include her maiden name in her signature: Sally Richter White. A single woman with a common name can use her middle initial to further identify herself.

A WOMAN SIGNING A LETTER

A woman signs a letter to someone she knows well just with her first name. If she is writing to someone she is not on a first-name basis with, she signs her first and last name. She never uses her title (Mrs. White) when signing a letter. If she is married or a widow and her full name is not engraved or printed on her stationery, she writes under her signature in parentheses (Mrs. Arthur White). If the letter is typewritten, she types Mrs. Arthur White under her signature; in this case parentheses are not necessary. A single or divorced woman writes in parentheses (Miss) or (Ms.) to the left of her name, i.e., (Miss) Charlotte Guggenheimer.

If a professional woman who uses her husband's name both socially and professionally wants to establish the fact that she is married, when signing a business letter, she puts Mrs. and her husband's first name to the left of her signature in parentheses. For social use, she writes her married name in parentheses under her signature as stated above.

WHEN YOU HAVE A COMMON FIRST NAME

If you have one of the more common first names like Joan, Mary, Bill, or John and are writing a letter or sending a postcard to someone who may not recognize your signature, you should include your last name. You can personalize it by writing your last name in parentheses either beside your first name or slightly below and to the right of it. Or it may be that the recipient knows you well enough that you need only sign your name Joan L. or Bill W.

NAMES THAT APPLY TO BOTH A MAN AND A WOMAN

Should your name be Marion, Lee, Beverly, or Leslie and you sign a letter to someone you don't know on unmarked stationery, the recipient won't have a clue as to whether you are a man or a woman. For your own sake as well as others', you should make an effort to have stationery that includes your title with your name. While it is true that in certain situations titles are never used when engraving or printing your name on stationery, for practical reasons an exception may be made in the case of names which could indicate either a man or woman. If you do not have engraved or printed stationery and are writing on plain notepaper, you can solve the problem by putting Mr., Mrs., Miss, or Ms. in parentheses to the left of your signature or by writing your full name, with title, and address at the top right-hand corner of the notepaper, or on the top left-hand corner of the envelope.

HUSBAND AND WIFE JOINT SIGNATURES

A husband or wife can always sign a mailgram, postcard, birthday card, or any card for that matter using both their names: i.e., Sally and Arthur, or Arthur and Sally White (the person signing puts his or her name last). When signing a guest book at a wedding, a funeral, or other such occasion, the last name should be included to identify the couple properly. In the case of a letter, since only one person is doing the actual writing, only one person signs it. If Arthur White is writing to a mutual friend of his and his wife's, he refers to her by mentioning at the end of the letter, "Sally joins me in wishing you all the best, As ever, Arthur."

ADDRESSING ENVELOPES

Addresses on social envelopes may be written by hand or typed. If a letter is handwritten, then the envelope is handwritten; if the letter is typewritten, there's no reason not to handwrite the envelope if you want to. On an envelope written by hand, the writing, of course, should be neat and legible. The address may be written with flush left margin or with each line indented slightly more than the previous one; city, state, and ZIP code appearing on one line. In the most formal style, as in the case of wedding invitations, a house or apartment number is traditionally written out through the number ten, while all street numbers are written out throughout. For example, Eight East Ninety-ninth Street or 20 East Ninety-ninth Street. Today, however, for the convenience of the post office, numbers are used throughout, even in the case of a wedding invitation. It used to be that convention decreed that a middle name was always written out on an envelope. This is no longer true. If Mr. Arthur Taylor White always uses his middle initial *T*, you address the envelope to him that way, even in the most formal circumstances such as a wedding invitation. The same applies to writing out the name of a state. It no longer has to be written in full; an abbreviation is equally correct in formal situations. If your return address is not engraved or printed on the flap of the envelope, you may write it there or on the upper left-hand corner of the front of the envelope, which is preferred by the post office. Addressing an envelope is somewhat more involved than in the past because many professional women have opted to keep their maiden names. No longer is it simply Mr. and Mrs., Mr. or Miss. Ms. has crept into our vocabulary and is commonly used by both single and married women. Included here are some of the more common title occurrences you may want to know about when addressing an envelope.

MARRIED WOMAN KEEPING MAIDEN NAME

When addressing an envelope to a couple when the wife has kept her maiden name, write Ms. Sally Richter and Mr. Arthur White on the same line. If a couple's combined names are too long to fit on one line, address the envelope this way:

Ms. Sally Richter
and Mr. Arthur White

(NOTE: The "and," which is slightly indented and written out, indicates that Ms. Richter and Mr. White are married.)

The only exception to this practice is when only the husband has a professional title; then his name comes first. For example: Reverend Arthur White and Ms. Sally Richter. If Sally Richter only uses her maiden name professionally (Ms. Sally Richter), you would, of course, address a social envelope to Mr. and Mrs. Arthur White.

WIDOW

A woman whose husband has died does not change her name; she remains Mrs. Arthur White. It's not correct to address an envelope to her as Mrs. Sally White as that indicates she's divorced, not a widow. If Mrs. Arthur White's son drops the Jr. after the death of his father, and lives in the same town as his mother, his mother adds Sr. to her name in order not to be confused with her daughter-in-law.

DIVORCED WOMAN

It once was the custom, when a woman divorced, that she used her maiden name in place of her husband's first name. Therefore, Sally Richter, divorced from Arthur White, became Mrs. Richter White. Today this custom, while still correct, is just about obsolete. Instead it's customary to address an envelope to a divorced woman as Mrs. Sally White. In the case of a divorcée who has taken back her maiden name, you write Ms. Sally Richter (Miss belongs to a woman who has never married and Mrs. is not compatible with a maiden name). This only applies to a divorcée without children. If she has children, she continues to use her ex-husband's name, just because it's less complicated if she has the same name as her children.

SEPARATED WOMAN

When Sally White, who goes by her husband's full name, separates from him, she is legally Mrs. Arthur White until she divorces. If, however, you know she prefers to be known as Mrs. Sally White during this period, then you address an envelope to her that way.

SINGLE WOMAN WITH CHILD

You address an envelope to a woman who has a child but has never been married as Ms. To use Mrs. would not be correct, since it is a title reserved for a woman who is or has been married. While you may use Miss, in the case of a woman with a child it seems more appropriate to use Ms., a term applied to both single and married women.

DOCTORS

In writing to a couple who are both medical doctors, you address the envelope The Doctors White or Doctor (Dr.) Sally White and Doctor

(Dr.) Arthur White. Doctors (Drs.) Sally and Arthur White is also correct. If the wife goes by her maiden name, the envelope is addressed to Dr. Sally Richter and Dr. Arthur White (length here necessitates abbreviating Doctor). If only the husband is a doctor, it's Doctor (Dr.) and Mrs. Arthur White, or Dr. Arthur White and Ms. Sally Richter. If only the wife is a doctor, the envelope is addressed to Dr. Sally White (or Richter) and Mr. Arthur White.

UNMARRIED OR GAY COUPLE

You address an envelope to a couple who are living together on separate lines, flush margin, without the word "and," either name first.

Stella Cusack
Harley Argyle

CHILDREN AND TEENAGERS

By tradition, a girl from birth is addressed in writing as Miss, although it is perfectly correct, and more usual, to write to a young girl as Sally Richter. Once she's a teenager, however, she's addressed as Miss, a title she keeps until she's twenty-one, at which time she may change to Ms. if she chooses. A letter to a boy may or may not be addressed as Master until about the age of eight, when he becomes Arthur White. At age eighteen, he takes on the title of Mr.

JR., SR., II, III, IV

When a suffix follows a name, the envelope is correctly addressed as Mr. Arthur White, Jr., or Mr. Arthur White II (a comma precedes the suffixes Jr. and Sr. but there is no comma before a Roman numeral suffix). If "junior" is written out (a more formal style), a small *j* is used. In the case of a doctor, the suffix and prefix match; "junior" requires "doctor" and "Jr." requires "Dr." Instead of Roman numerals, equally correct is 2nd, 3rd, or 4th.

THE USE OF MESSRS.

Messrs. is the abbreviated form of the French for Misters (Messieurs). It should be used only for letters addressed to brothers, never for father and son. It is always used instead of the English word. In sending a Christmas card or a wedding invitation to two young men in a family which includes several others to whom you do not wish to address the card or invitation, you write The Messrs. Guy and Donald Perkins. If there are just the two brothers in the family, you address them as The Messrs. Perkins or simply Messrs. Perkins.

THE USE OF MISSES

When addressing an envelope to two sisters, you use "The Misses" in the same way you do "The Messrs."

THE USE OF MESDAMES

You rarely see the French word "Mesdames" today. It's a term used in writing only, when addressing a group of women. For example:

> The Women's Christian Temperance Union
> Address
> Mesdames:

The title is not preceded by "Dear." The substitution of the word "Ladies" in this case seems awkward, which is why it is not recommended.

ESQUIRE

Esquire was originally a lesser English title. It indicated a knight's eldest son and the younger male members of a noble house whose hereditary title was borne only by the eldest male heir. While the word was once used widely in this country when addressing an envelope to a man of social or professional standing, it is seldom seen today and then only if the addressee, man or woman, is a lawyer. When Esquire is used, it follows the person's name and is usually abbreviated as Esq., although it may be written out in full. If Esq. is used when writing to a lawyer (Arthur White, Esq., or Sally White, Esq.), the name is not preceded by Mr., Mrs., Miss, or Ms. The salutation of a letter reads "Dear Mr./Mrs./Miss/Ms. White." When writing to a lawyer and his or her spouse the envelope is addressed to Mr. and Mrs. Arthur White, and no Esq. is used.

WRITING "PERSONAL," "PLEASE FORWARD," "OPENED BY MISTAKE" ON AN ENVELOPE

You may assume that a letter you send to someone's house will be opened only by the person you are writing to. It's therefore rude to other members of the family to mark such a letter "Personal." If, however, you are writing a purely social, and perhaps confidential, letter to someone at his or her office where the mail may be opened by an assistant, you may write "Personal" on the lower left-hand corner of the envelope.

If you want to write to someone and you only have an old address, not a current one, write "Please Forward" on the lower left-hand corner of the envelope. It makes more sense to try to find the new address, however, as a safer way to assure delivery of the letter.

If you live in a large apartment building, there is always the possibility that a letter addressed to someone else will find its way into your mailbox. If you inadvertently open a letter addressed to another person, reseal the envelope, mark it "Opened by Mistake," sign your name, and mail it for the post office to redeliver.

CHRISTMAS AND EASTER SEALS

Christmas and Easter seals or those of other charities are centered on the back of an envelope to cover the point of the flap and seal it.

RETURN ADDRESS LABELS

Because there is a commercial look about return address labels, it's best to use them only when sending or paying bills, writing to stores, or for other business-related matters. If you are writing a personal letter on stationery that is unmarked, write your name and address on the top left-hand corner of the envelope. The post office, if necessary, will then be able to return the letter to you.

MASS MAILING LABELS

The technical age has brought with it computer-generated labels, used for most large-scale mailings. It makes sense to use labels for ordinary bulk mailings as it saves time and manpower. But if you are sending out a special mailing, for instance asking people of importance to make a major contribution to a fund-raising drive, do not use a mailing label. Hand-write or type the envelope, just as you would when writing a personal letter of solicitation.

If you receive an envelope on which your name appears on a label, don't automatically toss it out unopened on the assumption that it's only an advertisement. Look at the envelope carefully. You may find it comes from your credit card company or your child's school.

LETTER WRITING

Sadly enough, in this era of instant communications, transmitting our deepest thoughts and emotions by means of a letter seems to be all but lost. It's unfortunate because the written word is always far more expressive in style and spirit than any telephone call or fax machine message. Saying you're sorry, offering congratulations, or declaring love have a great deal more meaning when put down on paper. What's so special about letters is that they can be read and reread, savored and saved; a perpetual reminder of past generations or relationships and life's significant moments.

No one is a born letter writer. It takes experience to become accomplished. The more letters you write the more adept you'll become at expressing yourself well. If you're writing a chatty, newsy letter to a friend, pretend he's in the room with you and you're talking face to face. Keep your language simple. Don't use obscure words just because you think they'll make the letter sound more interesting or impressive. Specific details, such as colors, sounds, quotes, are what give good letters their character and quality.

If your letter is quasi-formal—if, for instance, you are writing your first letter proposing someone for membership in a club—don't panic about what to say. Look in books such as this one for sample letters which will give you guidelines about what to include in the letter.

THE CORRECT FORM FOR SOCIAL LETTERS

If your address is not printed or engraved at the top of your stationery, write it on the upper right-hand corner of the paper, unless, of course, your address is well known to the recipient. Even if the envelope has a return address, it makes sense to write it again on the face of the letterhead because an envelope is often thrown away before the letter is answered.

> *320 Crescent Street*
> *Denver, CO ZIP code*
> *the date*

Dear Natalie,
> *The body of the letter starts here.*
> > *Love*
> > [Sincerely,
> > Affectionately,
> > or whatever closing
> > you choose to use],
> > *Signature*

(alternative placement of date)

THE BODY OF THE LETTER A personal letter should have adequate margins so it can be read easily. There should be ample space between lines and extra spacing between paragraphs. While exclamation marks, underlinings, and dashes give an informal, spontaneous tone to a letter, they can be distracting if overused. Have a dictionary on hand in case you need to look up the spelling of a particular word. A thesaurus is also helpful so you don't repeat the same adjectives or other words too often.

WRITING IN COLOR If you are writing a sympathy letter or extending or replying to a formal invitation, use dark blue or black ink. For other kinds of correspondence it's fun to experiment with different-colored inks. If you have stationery with a green border, for instance, you may use green ink. And it's festive to use red ink for Christmas cards.

THE DATE On a short note or casual letter, simply write "Monday" as the date. If your letter requires an answer or you think it has personal or historical significance, it's important to write the date in full (October 13, 1995). While dating a personal letter 10/13/95 is not incorrect, it's a style that's used more frequently for memos or business letters. In some foreign countries, this short form is written with the day first rather than the month (13/10/95).

THE SALUTATION "Dear" and the name of the person you're writing to is the customary salutation for any letter. "My dear," a formal salutation that brings to mind Edith Wharton or Henry James, now appears old-fashioned. Lovers may start a letter with "Dearest" or "Darling," and friends may sometimes start off with a casual "Hi there," but, generally speaking, if you stick with "Dear" you can't go wrong.

STARTING A LETTER Looking at a blank sheet of notepaper can be intimidating when you are trying to start a letter. Even well-known, professional writers confess to having trouble getting started at times. If starting a letter doesn't come easily to you, take a piece of scratch paper and jot down a few ideas for an opening sentence. That way, you won't have to worry about making a mistake on your finest stationery and having to start all over again. Once you've found a sentence or phrase you're satisfied with, transfer it to your notepaper. The best letters begin by projecting a positive attitude such as, "Your letter made my day," or "You can't imagine how much I've looked forward to writing you." Avoid negative or apologetic beginnings like, "I'm sorry I haven't gotten around to writing sooner." As you continue to write, imagine that you're talking directly to the recipient of the letter.

ENDING A LETTER While the first sentences of a letter are important to the tone, the closing ones make the final impression the reader is left with. It's always best to end a letter on a positive, uplifting note. You might want to say something like, "I always have the best time writing you my news," or "I can't wait to get back to Los Angeles for another visit." What you want to avoid are negative-sounding remarks like, "I hope you haven't found this letter too boring." It's not hard to end a letter when you've made the right beginning; your attitude will be carried throughout.

CLOSINGS There are many forms of closings for ending a letter. Your choice should be based on the formality of the letter, your sex and that of the recipient (a man, for instance, would probably not close a letter to another man with "Fondly"). In general you would close a letter to a family member or close friend with "Love," "Best love," "Fondly," "Affectionately." If you are writing to someone you know less intimately you might use "All the best," "As always," "As ever," "With love," or, depending on the relationship, "Affectionately." When writing to someone you don't know very well "Sincerely" is appropriate, or less formally, "Best wishes." "Sincerely" may also be used if you are writing to someone you've never met, for example, a teacher at your child's school or the manager of your club. "Sincerely yours," "Very sincerely," and "Very sincerely yours" are all variations of "Sincerely," although somewhat more formal in style. "Very truly yours" and "Yours truly" are less personal than "Sincerely" and are appropriate when writing to a store to place an order. "Cordially" and "Cordially yours" are rather old-fashioned terms, perfectly correct but not used as often as they once were. "Gratefully" is a closing you might use when thanking someone for doing you a favor and "Respectfully" or "Respectfully yours" is reserved for addressing religious personages.

SEQUENCE OF PAGES IN A LETTER SHEET When writing a letter on a letter sheet (notepaper folded vertically with the fold on the left), you start on page one; if the letter runs to a second page, finish on page three. If all four pages of a letter sheet are used, they may be written on in the usual sequence—one, two, three, four (less usual, but equally correct, is to write first on pages one and four and then open the stationery flat, but with the fold horizontal. Writing goes from top to bottom with the pages numbered. The sequence is really not that important, but keep in mind that air mail paper is impossible to read if both sides are written on.

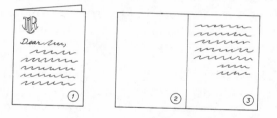

The sequence of pages for a letter sheet.

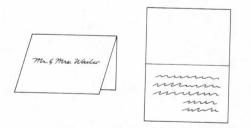

The sequence of pages for an informal.

SEQUENCE OF PAGES ON AN INFORMAL If an informal has a monogram or name on the center of the front page, nothing is written on that face and the note, if it is a short one, begins on the inside below the horizontal fold of the paper. If the note is to be long enough, the informal is opened out flat, with the fold horizontal, and the writing begins at the top of the page and may continue on to the bottom half of the back page. If a monogram or name is engraved on the center of the front page, because of the indentation caused by the engraving process, you cannot write on the reverse side.

INSERTING LETTER IN ENVELOPE It once was said that if you inserted into an envelope a letter folded once, folded side down, the person opening the letter risked a paper cut. On the other hand, if the open side was down, the letter could be slit in half by a letter opener. What this means is that either way is correct: folded side or open side down. Regardless of which side is up, a letter is always inserted into an envelope so that when it's removed and unfolded the writing is right side up, ready to be read. When inserting a letter that is folded twice, the bottom third is folded first, then the top third.

If you are writing a letter that will be hand-delivered, it is left unsealed unless the contents are of a private nature.

HANDWRITING VERSUS TYPING No matter how bad your handwriting is, condolence letters and replies to formal invitations are handwritten. Thank-you letters in general are warmer and more personal when handwritten. If your handwriting is hard to read, make a special effort to write legibly.

"DEAR MADAM" AND "DEAR SIRS" This form of address in writing to a store or catalog outfit is pretty much a thing of the past, mainly because of the gender problem. After all, you have no way of knowing the sex of the person who will be opening the "Dear Madam" letter. If you don't have the name of a person to direct your letter to, simply write in memo form.

Mail Order Department
Saxon Brothers
55 West Street
Clayton, MO (ZIP code)

To Whom It May Concern:

I would appreciate your sending me the woman's turtleneck sweater (#557K/$34.00) which appears on page 11 of your spring catalog. I would like it in size 10, cinnamon color.

Please send the sweater to the above address and charge to my (give credit card information).

Very truly yours,

Sally White
(Mrs. Arthur)

Sample Letters

When you thank a couple for a present they gave you, such as a graduation or wedding present, you write to the husband and wife. In the case of thanking a couple for a weekend visit or a dinner party, you can direct your letter to the couple or the wife only. If only to the wife, make mention of her husband, ie, "Many thanks to you and Ed . . ."

Everyone has to write letters in a style or manner characteristic of his or her personality. The sample letters that follow are not intended to tell you what you should say in a letter but to spark your imagination in a variety of situations when you sit down and take pen in hand.

THANK-YOU LETTERS

An early start in writing thank-you letters: Once a child knows the fundamentals of writing, about age six or seven, he's ready to write his own thank-you notes. As a starter, a parent may write a simple message which the child can copy. "Dear Aunt Nancy, Thank you for the magic set. It's the best present ever. Love, Oliver." Until a child's handwriting is fully developed so it can be read easily by the post office, the envelope should be addressed for him.

When a child is somewhat older, his letters tend to be more imaginative; more original. Here's one that was worth saving.

Dear Uncle Foxy,
    Thanks for the combination screwdriver and knife. A screwdriver is always handy to have and I've been trying to stab my little sister with the knife.
                Love,
                Matthew

Thank-you letter for a present: The best thank-you letter of all is the spontaneous one that comes from the heart and tells why the present means so much. Length is not important, only what you say and how you phrase it.

Dear Dick,
    The automobile emergency kit is a really neat present, particularly when you think of the age of our car. Now we're all prepared for the first major breakdown. I don't know who appreciates it more, Susie or I.
    Many thanks for remembering my birthday. I'll call you soon to make a lunch date.
                All the best to you,
                Sam

Thank you for money: When you receive a check as a present, it's poor taste to mention the amount in your thank-you letter—only because you should be less concerned with the amount than with the present itself. It will make the giver happy, however, if you mention how you plan to spend the money.

Dear Mr. and Mrs. Thornberg,

So many thanks for your generous birthday check (or present). Since I plan to put it toward the Snake River rafting trip I'm taking in August, it means you will have contributed to a very special and exciting event in my life. I hope it makes you happy to know how happy you have made me.

When I get back from the trip, I'd love to come by to show you some of the pictures I'll have taken. Have a great summer and thanks again.

With love,
Ginger

Thank you for dinner: While you thank your hostess as you are leaving a dinner party, it's polite to telephone her the next day or drop her a short note of thanks.

Dear Helen,

I can't remember when Rod and I have had a better time than at your house last night. You did a spectacular job with the barbecued lamb and we were delighted to see the Benjamins again. I only hope we didn't stay too long.

Many thanks to you and Joe for including us.

As ever,
Janice

Thank you for a wedding shower present: Even though you open a present at a shower and thank the giver at the time, it's thoughtful to follow up with a short note of thanks.

Dear Betty,

I have to tell you once again how much I love my striped sheets and pillowcases. I have very little in the linen department so you could not have chosen a more perfect present. I should add, too, that the colors are just right for our bedroom. A million thanks.

I'm so glad you could make the shower. It would not have been the same without your being there.

All the best,
Molly

Thank you for a wedding present: Every bride-to-be should do her best to keep current with her thank-you letters, time-consuming as it may be. While her fiancé can help by writing some of his friends, in the long run it's the bride's responsibility to see that everyone is thanked. A thank-you letter for a wedding present should be written two to three weeks after receiving the present, certainly no more than six to eight weeks after.

Dear Barbara and Jim,

You can't imagine how thrilled I was to open your present and find the set of folding tables. You obviously remembered my admiring yours! Frank and I will put them to good use the minute we move into our new condo, either for having breakfast on the deck or for guests to use when we have a buffet. I'm sure they will be brought out for a million other reasons as well, once we are settled. Aside from being practical, they are also extremely good-looking.

A million thanks to both of you. You are the best friends ever.

Love,
Molly

"Bread and butter" letters: If you're a guest of friends for a night or longer, unless you visit them on a regular basis, when a telephone call is all that's necessary, write them a letter of thanks, known as a "bread and butter" letter. Here are a few helpful points to remember when writing this kind of letter.

- Unless there's a good reason for not doing so, write your thank-you letter no more than three days after the visit.
- The letter may be directed to the wife of the couple or to both. If only to the wife, mention of her husband is made: "Do tell Jim I loved fishing with him," or "Many thanks to you and Jim."
- While only one person writes a bread and butter letter, that person thanks on behalf of his or her spouse and any other members of the family.
- Make a few significant remarks about the visit: the guest bedroom was so comfortable; how good the meals were; how much you enjoyed meeting a particular person; what fun a picnic was; or anything that was new or different.

Dear Rachel,

All the way back on the train, Joe and I did nothing but talk about the weekend and what fun we had. Staying in your cozy apartment is always a treat to say nothing of the gourmet meals you presented with seemingly little effort. Joe particularly enjoyed getting together with the Randolphs and having the chance to see the Matisse exhibition.

There's no couple we'd rather visit than you and Alex and we send our thanks to both of you for giving us such a wonderful time.

Love,
Marilyn

When you don't receive a thank-you letter: If after a month or so you have not received a thank-you letter for a present (other than a wedding present), write the person to whom you sent the present and ask if it was received. After all, if it was lost in the mail, or the store neglected to send it, you need to know. In the case of a wedding present, it's usual for the bride to be given a two-month grace period for writing her thank-you letters.

There's no reason to be the least bit apologetic about writing to ask if a present you sent someone was received. If it was received but the recipient happened to misaddress his thank-you letter to you, at least you'll have found out the two important factors: the present arrived and the recipient had the good manners to acknowledge it. On the other hand, if the present was received and the recipient couldn't be bothered to let you know—the thought, time, and money you expended apparently meaning little—you'd be smart to drop that person from your gift-giving list. There's no excuse to justify the rudeness of not thanking someone for a present.

Dear Arthur,

Having not heard from you, I am worried that you may not have received the wallet I sent you for your birthday. I'm concerned there may have been some slip up on the part of the store or the package was lost in the mail. I'd appreciate a note or a call from you.

As ever,
Uncle Bill

LETTER TO A FUTURE SON-IN-LAW

A letter that's bound to be appreciated is one the mother or father of the bride-to-be writes to their future son-in-law welcoming him into their family.

Dear Bob,

Jenny just called to tell us the happy news that you're going to be married. I hope you know without my saying that Mr. White and I are pleased beyond words. It's obvious how much Jenny loves you and we feel very fortunate to have you as a future son-in-law. When you and Jenny next come for the weekend, we'll break out a bottle of champagne and raise our glasses in a special toast to both of you.

Mr. White joins me in sending you our love.

Affectionately,
Sally White

CONDOLENCE LETTER

Of all letters, the most difficult one to write is certainly the condolence letter. Your aim is to say something special to the bereaved, to express the greatest degree of love, comfort, and sympathy, but it's not unusual when you sit down to write to find yourself at a loss for words. The more you think about the letter, or the longer you put off writing it, the more difficult it becomes. If you sit down and write as soon as you hear that a person has died, you'll find it a great deal easier to be spontaneous. Write as if you were talking to the mourner, putting down your feelings as they come to you. "I just heard the sad news that Sam died this morning." Don't use euphemisms like "you lost Sam," or "he passed away," or "he's gone." They only skirt reality. Death is death no matter how you choose to look at it. It always means a lot to the recipient if you include some personal memory you have of the person who has died—some incident or occasion you shared together. If it's amusing, that's fine too. It may bring a wistful smile to the reader. If death comes after a long illness, you can say, "At least Sam has been released from his suffering," but avoid saying, "It's all for the best," which has a preachy note. Besides, it's often hard for someone grieving to see how it could possibly be for the best. If you know the person you're writing to well, end the letter by saying you hope you'll be called upon if you can be of help in any way. In the case of a young person's death, direct the letter to both the mother and father.

Dear Mr. and Mrs. Warburg,

You have been in my thoughts all day. I only wish there were something I could say or do that would help ease the pain of your loss. Holly was special in so many ways. Her wry sense of humor and enthusiasm for life brought so much pleasure to others. I'll always remember and cherish the happy times we had together and be grateful to have had her as a friend.

I will call you after the funeral to see if I can come by to see you. In the meantime I send you my love and sympathy.

Affectionately,
Camilla

If a couple you know divorced but remained friends, and one dies, there is no reason not to write a condolence letter to the ex-spouse, if you feel it's appropriate. If a friend dies and you don't know any member of the family, get the name of the closest relative and write that person a letter. It will please him or her enormously to know you cared enough to write. Or, if the spouse or parent of a colleague dies without your having met that person, write to your friend. A letter can mean a great deal to the recipient.

Dear Harry,

There is nothing more difficult to accept than the death of a parent. Suddenly, someone who has been a part of your life always is no longer there and no one can possibly take his place. I only hope that the happy memories of times you spent with your father will soon replace the sadness you feel at this time.

I know how much you admired and respected your father and regret that I never had the chance to meet him.

With my deepest sympathy and love,
Affectionately,
Marcia

LETTER SUPPORTING A FRIEND

When you hear that a friend is having a difficult time, such as going through a divorce or illness, or has lost a job, a letter expressing your concern and offering your support can be a great comfort. Don't give advice in your letter; just let the person know you're there to call on if you can be of help.

Dear Charlie,

I just heard you were let go from Green Petroleum as a result of its economy cutback. I know what a blow this must be, but with your longstanding reputation in marketing, I can't believe you won't find a job to your liking as soon as the word gets around.

Sally plans to call you in the next day or so to see if you can come by and have a meal with us. Meanwhile, know that I'm thinking of you and that I'll be in touch if I hear of something that might appeal to you.

As ever,
Bill

Dear Helen,

Betsy just told me that you and Frank have separated. I know what a difficult time this is for you and the children and want you to know I've been thinking of you a great deal. I'll give you a call later this week to see if we can get together for lunch.

With love,
Elaine

THE UNEXPECTED LETTER

One of the most gratifying letters to receive is one that's written for no other purpose than to convey a happy message to a friend—or anyone you know for that matter. It's nice to think that there are lots of these letters in circulation as they're fun to write and fun to receive.

Dear Barbara,

I can't let another minute go by without writing you to say how much our entire family loved having Dan for the weekend. His sense of humor and love of life are what make him so very special.

I don't know if Dan told you but Saturday, at our neighborhood soccer game, he was the star player on his team, making both goals. I only wish you could have been there to watch him. He certainly has the qualities of a born athlete—perfect coordination, skill, and timing. And, of course, he has the added plus of knowing what good sportsmanship's about.

To add to all this, Dan was great around the house, making his own breakfast and helping us chop wood. He's a delight in more ways than I can say and we hope he'll come back soon again and often.

Sincerely,
Marjorie

LETTER WRITTEN IN ANGER

You should never write a letter in a fit of anger, but if you can't resist letting off steam by putting pen to paper, at least don't mail the letter until you've had time to sleep on it. When you reread an angry letter after you've simmered down, you'll probably think twice about it. Maybe you'll rewrite it, or want to toss it out and vent your irritation over the telephone. Talking directly to the person is usually the better way to settle a serious problem. But don't let it just fester. You don't want to lose a friend or neighbor forever over something you could clear up with a firm but courteous statement.

Dear Mr. Robbins,

When I came home from work this afternoon, I was most upset to hear that Billy was knocked off his tricycle and nipped by your dog. Fortunately, it was only a superficial wound but Billy was badly shaken by the experience—so much so that he may easily have a fear of dogs for some time to come.

While Billy may have provoked your dog in some way, at the same time dogs in the community are not permitted to roam around unleashed. Since your dog has run loose on our property twice before this month, I feel I must ask you and Mrs. Robbins to see that this doesn't happen again. I regret having to write this letter but trust you'll understand that I must do so for the safety of our son.

Sincerely yours,
William Grosjean

LETTER OF APOLOGY

Occasionally you may need to send a letter of apology. Perhaps you have had to back out of a dinner party at the last minute, or broken the lawn mower you borrowed from your neighbor, or lost an out-of-print book belonging to a friend. In any of these cases, a short note saying you're sorry can mean a great deal to the person who was inconvenienced. An apology of a more serious sort, when someone's feelings were hurt, are often difficult to put in writing and may be better explained in person.

Dear Angela,

Having heard that you and Jim have decided to get married, I am filled with remorse for having told you he was not the right person for you. It was an unjustified, insensitive remark to have made, and I am devastated by the hurt I have caused you.

While I can't expect you to forgive me, I do want you to know that my impulsive comment has taught me a lesson I'll never forget.

You must be very excited about the wedding and your new life and I wish you the greatest happiness ever.

With my love,
Andrew

LETTER OF CONGRATULATIONS

What can mean more to a friend than a letter acknowledging his good fortune?

Dear Walter,

I just heard the exciting news that you have been made President of Buchanan & Buchanan. What a tremendous honor and what a great challenge you have ahead of you! Barbara and the children must be so proud of your accomplishments, just as all your friends are.

The best of luck always.
Sincerely,
Arnold

A RETIREMENT LETTER

A retiree should write a note of thanks to each fellow employee or associate who contributed toward a retirement present. When a particularly large number of employees contributed, instead of individual letters, a single letter may be posted on the company bulletin board for all to read.

Dear Arnold,

Thanks more than I can say for the part you played in presenting me with the silver tray. Not only is the tray a particularly handsome one, but the facsimile signatures make it all the more special. It's now sitting on a table in our living room where it can be seen and admired by all.

I'm so glad I had the chance to work with you at Charter House and wish you all the best in the future.

Sincerely,
Carolyn

LETTER TO A PUBLIC OFFICIAL

You can and should express approval or disapproval about some action a public official has taken, even if you don't know that person or expect to meet him or her. Public officials welcome comments of this sort as an indication of how public opinion is running on various issues.

It's pointless to telephone a legislator because you'll never be able to talk to him or her directly, but you can send a letter voicing your support or dissent. Whether you approve or disapprove of legislative activities or of pending bills, write and tell your elected representative in the Congress. If you are adamantly opposed to something your representative has done, don't send an emotional letter venting your anger. Reason is far more effective than an emotional outburst. Try to be as objective as possible, bearing in mind the respect the office deserves. If you don't know the names of your representatives, you can always find out by calling your mayor's office, the local newspaper, or the library.

If you plan to write a letter to a head of state, it would be unrealistic to expect to have your letter read and answered personally. For instance, the White House receives about fifty thousand letters a week. All correspondence is read and answered by a staff member or with a form letter. Family members and close friends of the President or First Lady are given a special code word to put on the envelope of a letter so it can be delivered directly to the First Family.

The Honorable
Barbara L. Wadsworth
House Office Building
Washington, DC 20515

Dear Ms. Wadsworth:

I would like to add my protest to those you have received concerning your recent attack on the Moreland Bill (H.R.267). I believe the passage of this bill is essential to the proper maintenance of our local highway system and to the safety of the motorists in our district. I urge you to reconsider your stand in this important matter.

Sincerely,

Julia S. Di Palma
(Mrs. Paolo Di Palma)

PERSONAL LETTER OF INTRODUCTION

The traditional letter of introduction is no longer a part of our system of communication. It worked this way. If a close friend was going abroad, you would give him a letter which he would personally present with his calling card on making a formal call. Or if it was more convenient he would write the name of his hotel on his calling card and mail it with the letter of introduction. Today, introductions of this sort are made by telephone or with a letter written in advance of the friend's arrival.

Write a social letter of introduction only when you know the people involved well enough to be certain they will enjoy meeting each other. If you write a friend in another city asking if she'd look up Sally and Arthur White who have moved there, she's under no obligation to entertain the Whites, although as a friend of yours she'll probably want to do so when her schedule permits. Writing your out-of-town friend is the most sensitive, correct way to make this type of introduction. Reversing the situation and giving the Whites your friend's name and number is not as polite. If the Whites call your friend, she's put in the awkward situation of having to invite them to her house. In the event the Whites are given your friend's name, they should call and invite her to their house, not wait for her to extend an invitation.

When writing a letter of introduction, include a little information about the Whites and their family, why they have moved, and what some of their interests are. You can phrase the letter so that your friend does not feel trapped into inviting them for a meal if she's too busy.

Dear Celeste,

Very good friends of ours, Sally and Arthur White, are moving to Cedar Rapids next month. Arthur has been promoted to senior partner at Weinberg & Weinberg. Sally's main interest is the theater and she hopes to be able to give drama lessons once they are settled. Their two boys, aged eleven and fourteen, will be going to school next fall in Cedar Rapids.

While I don't want you to feel any obligation, it would be great if you and Andrew had a chance to meet the Whites sometime during the summer. I think you'd really enjoy each other a great deal. Their address will be 111 Baxter Street. I don't have their telephone number right now but will send it to you later.

We just came back from Charleston . . . [give your news].

Love,
Ellen

LETTER PROPOSING SOMEONE FOR MEMBERSHIP IN A CLUB

When a member of a club wants to put up a friend for membership, he writes a letter to the head of the membership or admissions committee.

Dear Morris,

I would like to propose Allen and Claire Nevius for membership in the Fairstone Beach Club. Allen, who is with the architectural firm of Bisbee & Bisbee in Clearwater, is a graduate of Boston University. His father, the late Peter Nevius, was a long-time member of the club. Claire Nevius is presently editorial director of Carter Publications; their children are Benjamin, age sixteen, and Nona, age twelve.

I have known the Neviuses ever since Allen and I were on the board of the Riverside School. Both he and Claire devote a good portion of their nonworking hours to community affairs, Allen most recently heading the Community Chest drive. From a personal point of view, I can recommend the Neviuses as prospective members of the club without qualification. They are an engaging, interesting couple whom I admire and respect as much as any two people I know. Aside from their personal attributes, their love of swimming and sailing make them ideal candidates. While I know you have a long list of applicants, I do hope that the Neviuses will be given every consideration as prospective members. If accepted, I am certain they will make a fine contribution to club life.

Sincerely,
George

LETTER RESIGNING FROM A CLUB

Sometimes it's necessary to resign from a club. It may be for lack of use, financial reasons, because you're moving away, or for some other reason. Whatever the motive is, a letter of resignation giving the reason must be sent to the appropriate person, usually the acting secretary of the board of directors of the club.

Dear Ms. Cranshaw,

It is with regret that I must submit my resignation as a member of the Fairstone Beach Club as of November first. My family and I are moving to the West Coast, which is the reason for this decision. We will miss the club greatly but hope that one day we will return to the area and, if so, that we may have the opportunity to rejoin the club.

Sincerely,
George Blackwell

LETTER ASKING FOR A DONATION

If you're asking for a donation, whether to your local community chest or the Red Cross, don't mention the amount you feel the person you're approaching should give. Instead emphasize the need of the organization or charity and how the money will be used. This kind of letter may be written by hand or typed and should not be too long. It always includes material on the institution, organization, or charity.

Dear Albert,

I'm writing you about the annual Southington Hospice Drive. Our goal this year is to raise fifty thousand dollars to renovate one of the rooms, making it into a patients' library. It may seem hard to believe but the patients in this facility have no access to books other than the ones brought to them by family and friends. Reading is one of the greatest therapies for the patients and it seems only right that they have books at their disposal.

I am enclosing material which describes Southington Hospice better than I ever can, as well as a contribution card. I will call you in a week or so with the hope that you'll be able to help with this important endeavor.

All the best,
Charlie

LETTER OF RECOMMENDATION FOR SOMEONE IN YOUR EMPLOY

When someone leaving your employ asks for a letter of recommendation, you can convey your feelings about the person by the mood of your letter.

A lukewarm letter:

To Whom It May Concern:

I am writing this letter of recommendation on behalf of Janet Rice, who has been in our employ for three years as a housekeeper. Janet is honest and willing and has done her best in all areas of her work. We wish her luck in the future.

If you would like further information, please call me at (telephone number).

Very truly yours,
Alice Slocum
(Mrs. Robert F. Slocum)

A more enthusiastic letter:

It is with the utmost pleasure that I write this letter of recommendation on behalf of Janet Rice. Janet has been our family housekeeper for the past three years and is leaving us now to pursue other work.

Janet has been the greatest joy to our family. She's bright, intelligent, hardworking, and has a delightful sense of humor. She's quick to take the initiative and always anxious and willing to please. We are sad to have her leave and will miss her a great deal.

If you have any questions about Janet, please don't hesitate to call me at (telephone number).

Sincerely,
Alice Slocum
(Mrs. Robert F. Slocum)

LETTER OF COMPLAINT TO A STORE

Browning & Company
55 Charlton Street
Englewood, NJ (ZIP code)

To Whom It May Concern:

On October 12, I ordered a parka costing $57.30 from your store, charging it to my account number 78 009 431. Two weeks later, I was informed by mail that the parka was no longer in stock and that the $57.30 charge would be deleted from my next bill. This has not been the case although I have made repeated telephone calls to the billing department asking them to rectify the error. Today, to add more fire to my irritation, I received a letter from the billing department referring to the balance due and asking that I settle my account in full.

While your store has always given superior service, I am at the point where my patience is being tried beyond all reasoning. I would appreciate your looking into this problem and contacting me by telephone (telephone number).

Sincerely,
Alice Weiss
(Mrs. James Weiss)

OTHER FORMS OF COMMUNICATION

THE ACKNOWLEDGMENT CARD

When a public official receives a great many messages of congratulations from his supporters, or when someone prominent in business dies and the family receives an overwhelming number of sympathy letters, it may not be possible to acknowledge each and every one with a handwritten note. What's practical in these instances is to have a card specially engraved or printed with a message of appreciation. In the case of a public figure who wants to thank his supporters, a printed card might read:

Your thoughtful message of congratulations is very much appreciated and I am deeply grateful for your support. I only regret that the number of letters received prevents me from sending you a personal reply.

(facsimile signature)

Any card of thanks can be personalized, and if possible should be, by a handwritten word or two at the top or bottom of the card: "Dear Flo, Thanks for your kind words. As ever, Karl." While a busy official rarely has the time to scribble a note on an acknowledgment card, if he can be selective, writing a few words to people he knows personally or who have been particularly helpful to him, it is a thoughtful gesture that can mean a lot to the recipient.

POSTCARDS

Postcards are handy to have around as an easy, convenient form of communication. Even if you have postcards printed with your name and address, it's useful to have a batch of museum or other picture postcards on hand for general use. You can use a postcard as a thank you for a cocktail party, a bridge party, or other informal occasion, or for other purposes such as sending out notifications of a committee meeting. Postcards are not appropriate to use as thank-you notes for being a guest at a dinner or lunch party or a houseguest, or for acknowledging a present. Many people like to write across the entire width of a postcard and then enclose it in an envelope for mailing. Naturally, if you're writing anything of a confidential nature, it's best to send a postcard in a sealed envelope. If you buy one of the oversized postcards you often see, don't forget that a postcard larger than 4¼" × 6" cannot be mailed at the official United States postcard rate.

A CASSETTE-RECORDED LETTER

While not everyone wants to take the time to listen to a letter on cassette, a taped letter can be great fun for the family to receive. A grandchild who hasn't the patience to sit down and write a letter may send a message to a grandparent, or a child away at school may find it quicker and more satisfactory to speak his news than to write it. The only drawback with communicating by tape rather than letter is that you will not have the written word to refer to and reread, a more personal form of communicating. Still, it's something to consider, particularly if you have little time and a great deal of news to tell.

COMMUNICATING BY FAX

It's not unusual today for people to have a fax machine at home. It's a fast and efficient way to communicate and just as effective as leaving a message on an answering machine. If you can't reach someone on the telephone to extend an invitation, you can always fax the message (mention in the fax that you had no luck telephoning). To reply to a faxed invitation, it's more polite to do so by telephone.

COMMERCIAL GREETING CARDS WITH A MESSAGE

Americans love commercial cards, also known as "greeting cards." You can find greeting cards for just about any occasion in drugstores, bookstores, and specialty or stationery stores. There are cards for Valentine's Day, Halloween, Passover, Thanksgiving, Easter, St. Patrick's Day as well as cards to mark almost every one of life's special happenings such as a birthday, a first communion, a graduation, or an anniversary. In addition to cards that mark an occasion, Hallmark has a series of "Just for Today" greeting cards with fifty-one inspirational messages to choose from— many of which express an apology on the part of the sender, who apparently is unable to do so on his own ("I'm a different person now. And I want to apologize for who I was and what I did . . .").

A popular specialty card is the "get well" card and one can mean a great deal to a person who is sick. There's something reassuring and comforting about being reminded that friends are thinking of you when you're not feeling up to scratch. However, you have to use discretion and tact when choosing a get well card; the sarcastic card you might send someone with a broken leg is highly inappropriate for the person suffering a terminal illness. In the latter case, you don't send a card that says, "Get well soon," but instead a card that says something like, "Sorry you're not feeling well." Or better still, you can send one of the so-called "friendship" cards with a handwritten message.

Some cards you see in stores are meant to be funny but actually are in poor taste. Before you buy a card that's suggestive or just plain lewd, think about the person you're sending it to. Does he or she share your sense of humor? Are the circumstances ones in which humor will be appreciated? Also ask yourself, "Would I be embarrassed to have people know I chose this card?"

Always write a few words or a short message on any greeting card you send. Just signing your name shows a lack of imagination and a "I can't be bothered" attitude. The message doesn't have to be long but it will personalize your card and show you care.

Greeting card companies probably invented the thank-you card for people who don't know how to say thank you or don't want to take the time to write a note. Whether or not that's the case, it's definitely a cop-out to send a thank-you card in place of a letter. It absolutely never replaces a personal, handwritten note of thanks. After all, if someone has taken the time to buy you a present, give a dinner party for you, or have you for the weekend, the least you can do to show your gratitude is handwrite a personal note.

Card stores and most stationery stores carry a wide variety of cards with envelopes; a picture or design of some kind is on the front of the card. It might be a pastoral or hunting scene, a vase with flowers, or a well-known painting. The inside of the card is blank, so these cards are perfect to use in place of greeting cards with messages already in them, or for the purpose of writing a short note.

CHRISTMAS CARDS

Christmas cards are the most popular of all greeting cards and the traditional way to share joy and happiness with friends at this time of the year. They are a wonderful way to keep in touch with old friends and family members whom you don't see during the rest of the year, and they provide a perfect opportunity for sharing a little of your news. It's also nice to send cards to friends you know well but with whom you do not exchange presents. If you do not have the time or inclination to send a handwritten Christmas card, then it's best not to send one at all. A card printed with your name but without a handwritten greeting is not a satisfactory substitute for a personal holiday message. A photograph of your family may be included or become part of the card itself. People enjoy seeing what their friends' children or grandchildren look like and how they've changed over the years (be sure to add names and ages). Some people like to send a picture of a new house they've moved into. This can be of interest to friends who live some distance away. However, a picture showing a large mansion with a long driveway leading up to it can seem pretentious. The best guideline is to use common sense and to choose a photograph that doesn't appear too boastful.

You can buy boxed or individual Christmas cards at any stationery or card store. Museum and UNICEF cards of course help support worthy causes. Many museum postcards, in particular ones with a religious theme, make attractive Christmas cards. You can mail them simply as postcards or put them into green or red envelopes. Or, if you have a creative flair, you can make your own cards. Children like to make their own Christmas cards and adults love to receive them.

ENGRAVED CHRISTMAS CARDS Very few people send personalized engraved Christmas cards unless they are public officials or are well known professionally. Large-size cards are used in this case, usually nonreligious ones that show a winter scene or some other picture appropriate to the occasion. The message inside the card may say, "Mr. and Mrs. Arthur Taylor send you best wishes for a Merry Christmas and a Happy New Year," or "Governor and Mrs. Arthur Taylor White wish you a Happy Holiday and a Peaceful New Year."

EMBOSSED CHRISTMAS CARDS Another type of Christmas card is the rather formal white or ecru card with a border in red or green and an embossed design in the center at the top—of a Christmas tree, a wreath, or a branch of holly, for example. It can be ordered from a good stationer and is either engraved with a Christmas greeting such as "The Arthur White Family sends you warm holiday greetings" or left blank so you can write a short note on each card.

WHEN NAMES ARE PRINTED   Over the years the custom of having the name or names of all the members of a family printed at the bottom of a Christmas card has developed. The seasonal spirit of love and giving is greatly diminished when the person sending the card does not bother to include a message. Somewhere on the card write a greeting such as "Merry Christmas," "Happy Holidays," "Here's to 1995," "We miss not seeing you," or "May your New Year be the best ever." If you are on a first-name basis with the person you are sending the card to, put a slash through your last name only.

SIGNING CHRISTMAS CARDS   Every Christmas card should bear a short message. Just signing your name alone appears quite cold. All you need to write is "Merry Christmas and Happy New Year," which personalizes the card and gives it far more meaning.

When a married couple sends Christmas cards, whichever one signs the card writes his or her name last as a courtesy. If the card is being sent to close friends, only first names are necessary. If the first names are common ones like John and Mary, the last name can be written in parentheses so there's no confusion on the part of the recipients of the card as to just who sent it.

When children's names are included the card may read, "Arthur and Sally White (or Sally and Arthur White) and Arthur, Jr." If there are several children, it can say, "The Whites—Arthur, Sally, Arthur, Jr., and Melissa." Equally correct is "From the Arthur Whites."

If a husband and wife have been married before and have children from previous marriages, they need not sign all their names if doing so appears complicated. Instead, the parents may sign their name—"Arthur and Sally"—and then add the words "and all the family" after their signatures.

If a widow or widower or a divorced parent and child are sending out cards together, the parent's name is written first, followed by the child's name: "Arthur White and Melissa."

ADDRESSING CHRISTMAS CARDS   A personal Christmas card is addressed to both husband and wife, even if you know only one of the couple. If you're sending a card to an entire family, you may address it to "Mr. and Mrs. Arthur White and Family."

THE CHRISTMAS NEWSLETTER   Christmas cards afford an excellent opportunity to share news of the year with friends you have not seen or spoken to recently. You may want to tell about the birth of a child or grandchild, or that you were divorced or married during the year and have a new address. Such news may be conveyed in a sentence or two, or a brief paragraph. Nonetheless some people insist on sending a typewritten letter, often single spaced and several pages long. These "newsletters," usually photocopied or mimeographed, typically contain minute details about the health of every member of the family, the grades the children received in school, specifics about the annual vacation, and the weather report for the area for the year. Very few people are really interested in this much information, even about their dearest friends. If you can't resist documenting the year's events in a newsletter, send it only to your very closest friends. But it really is preferable simply to add a handwritten note to your card, describing one or two highlights of the past year.

EXCHANGING HOLIDAY CARDS Both the Christian Christmas celebrating the birth of Christ and the Jewish Hanukkah celebrating a Jewish religious victory fall during the same season, so both faiths enjoy exchanging holiday cards. Cards to be sent to people of a different faith must be selected carefully. A nonreligious card with a picture of a winter scene, animals, or birds and a greeting such as "Happy Holidays" or "Season's Greetings" is appropriate to send to anyone. Christians should never send a religious card—one with a nativity scene or the star over Bethlehem—to Jews nor should Jews send a card that reads "Happy Hanukkah" to Christian friends.

A CHRISTMAS CARD TO SOMEONE IN MOURNING Christmas is a time when a friend in mourning most needs to be remembered. A humorous or jubilant Christmas card is not an appropriate choice, but a simple one wishing peace in the New Year would certainly be welcoming and comforting. You should add to the card something like, "Just to say you are in my thoughts." Or, instead of a Christmas card, you can always write a note on your stationery saying, "I know this will be a difficult Christmas for you but I didn't want to let it go by without saying I am thinking of you."

CUTTING YOUR CHRISTMAS CARD LIST At some point you may decide your Christmas card list is too long. It's a good idea to cull your list each year. Begin by eliminating those people whom you have not heard from in a year or two or those to whom you've been sending cards merely out of habit. You may also want to cross off some people you give presents to, particularly those you see frequently. Regular pruning of your Christmas card list means you'll be sending cards to friends you aren't in regular contact with but whom you truly care for.

INTRODUCTIONS

Knowing when and how to make introductions is very much a part of good manners. Being able to introduce friends, or yourself for that matter, gracefully makes any social situation easier and gives you a sense of confidence. While it's no longer a social disgrace to mispronounce a name or to introduce someone to the same person twice, it does help to know the basics of what it takes to make a proper introduction. For instance, an enthusiastic introduction followed by a few words about the person is a helpful conversation starter. "This is George Draper. He's city editor at the *Chronicle*," or "He just won first prize in the Sausalito amateur art show." Use discretion in deciding what to say, however, as you don't want to embarrass the person you're introducing or cause others to think you're bragging about knowing someone of importance.

There's no specific rule as to when to use a title and last name or just first and last names. The level of formality depends on who's being introduced to whom and under what circumstances, as well as the custom of the community. Certain areas of the country are by tradition more formal than others. If you're uncertain as to the correct form of address to use, you're less likely to offend if you take the more formal approach.

What you want to remember is that strict protocol, other than in diplomatic circles, is not nearly as important as warmth and spontaneity.

HOW TO MAKE INTRODUCTIONS

Common sense and a little knowledge are all that's needed to make a proper introduction. By tradition and out of respect, the younger or less important person is introduced *to* the older and more important one, regardless of sex. "Arthur, I'd like you to meet Mrs. Lincoln," or more formally, "Mrs. Lincoln, I'd like to present Arthur White." Common sense enters the picture in, for instance, the case of an elderly woman and a young senator being introduced to each other. While convention says the older woman is introduced *to* the senator, in deference to her age it's more courteous to introduce the young senator *to* the older woman. Similarly, it once was the custom for a man to be introduced *to* a woman. Today it can be done either way. If you trust to your intuition when making an introduction, chances are you'll have no problem.

What follows are guidelines for making everyday introductions:

- Always give a last name when introducing people to each other. Never say, "Sally, this is Bill. Bill, Sally." Those who say it's the person, not the name, that's important are wrong. Your full name is a distinguishing feature in the overall "you" as a person. It's what distinguishes one Mary from another Mary, one John from another John.

- While you may be introducing a group of people to one another using first and last names, in the case of a doctor or someone in the clergy or the military, it's usual to include a title in the introduction: "This is Dr. Jennifer Noyes" or "General John Frankfurt." Including the title will let people know the proper way to address the person.

- When introducing your husband to a friend, what you say is, "I'd like you to meet my husband Arthur [or Arthur White]." Never refer to him as "Mr. White" or "Dr. White." The same formula applies when your husband introduces you.

- If you're introducing a couple and the wife has kept her maiden name, say, "This is Sally Richter and her husband Arthur White."

- When a heterosexual or homosexual couple living together go out socially, they may want to get across the point that they are romantically involved and not available to others. The way they handle this is to say, "I'd like you to meet my companion, Bill Wooster." This is a term that corresponds to "This is my wife" or "This is my husband." The person who introduces an unmarried heterosexual couple living together may say, "I'd like you to meet Mary Rosewall and her companion Barry Brown."

- Since the term "Ms." has been thoroughly integrated into our language, a woman who chooses to use this title may be introduced as Ms. White.

- If you call your boss by his title, then you'd introduce your wife to him by saying, "Mr. Foster, I'd like to introduce my wife Sally to you. Sally, this is Mr. Foster, our president."

- A child always calls an adult by his or her title when introduced, unless of course the older person says otherwise.

- When introducing a young person to someone considerably older, it's polite to acknowledge the older of the two by using his or her title. "Ben, I'd like you to meet Mr. White." It's up to the older person to ask the younger one to call him by his first name. It would be presumptuous for the younger of the two to say, "May I call you Arthur?"

- If someone is introduced to you, do not repeat the person's name in your response. And do not say, "Charmed," "Delighted," or "Pleased to make your acquaintance." In fact, under ordinary circumstances either a casual hello or "I've heard a lot about you" is an acceptable response.

- Few things are more irritating than being introduced to someone for the umpteenth time only to have that person not remember you. If this happens, speak up. Say, "Yes, we met at the Barzuns'." If you're lucky, the next time she may remember you.

- If you know the housekeeper who answers the door when you and your husband go to a friend's house for dinner, greet her by saying, "Good evening, Peggy. This is my husband, Mr. White."

- If you have not been introduced to your dinner partner during the cocktail hour, once you're seated at the table, take the initiative and introduce yourself: "I'm Sally White. I'm staying with Peg and Frank." Either a man or woman may initiate the introduction.

- If you're walking down the street with a friend and someone you know stops to say hello, introduce the person you're with. It would be rude to ignore his presence. If the person does not stop, all you have to do is wave or say hello in passing.

- If you pass a table in a restaurant at which someone you know is seated, if at all possible just say a quick hello as you pass by. Stopping to chat interrupts the conversation of the people seated at the table, blocks the passageway for the waiters, and causes general confusion.

- When introducing a speaker at a banquet or some official function, you introduce the person by his full name. "It gives me great pleasure to present John Randolph Combs" or "Rabbi Benjamin Wise."

INTRODUCTIONS AT A PARTY At a small dinner party, as each guest arrives, introduce that person to the others. At a large dinner party or a cocktail party it's not possible to take a guest around the entire room and at the same time greet each new arrival. All you really must do is introduce each new arrival to four or five people standing close by who are talking to one another. In making the introduction you address the group: "I'd like you to meet Sally White. She's here on a business trip from Minneapolis. Sally, this is Gladys Gombrowski, Fred Whiteman, Arnold Jones, and Beth Greenman."

If you are a guest who suddenly finds himself in the awkward position of standing alone with no one to talk to, it's easier to approach a number of people talking together than two people engrossed in conversation. Putting self-consciousness aside for the moment, go over to the group and when there's a pause in the conversation or someone acknowledges your presence speak up, "Hello [or Hi], I'm Sally White. I was Martha's roommate at Carlton College." Admittedly, it takes a certain amount of courage to break into a group, particularly when everyone knows everyone else, but it's a lot less painful than standing alone with no one to talk to. Also, by handling the situation yourself, you're not burdening your host or hostess with further introductions.

If you take a houseguest to a party, it's up to you to introduce him to other people and to see that he's having a good time.

As you pass through a receiving line at a wedding or other formal occasion, don't linger in conversation or you'll hold up the line, which isn't fair to those waiting their turn. Introduce yourself to the person at the head of the line: "Hello, Mr. Kirby, I'm Arthur White, a colleague of Albert's." Giving your last name as well as your first makes it easy for Mr. Kirby to introduce you to the person standing beside him.

Similarly, if you're in a receiving line, don't hold everyone up by engaging in a conversation with one of the guests. All you need say is, "I'm so glad you could come," or "It's great to see you again," or "Let's get together once the receiving line is over." You then introduce the guest to the person standing beside you in the line: "This is Arthur White, who works with Albert at Harding Brothers."

Rising when introduced: The host and hostess at a party stand up to greet each guest who enters the room. At a small party, a man always rises when a woman enters the room; there's no reason for a woman not to rise also, if she chooses to. At a large party, however, no one is expected to jump up and down each time someone new arrives. Whether you rise or remain seated depends on how well you know the other person, when you last saw each other, and the formality of the occasion. It's customary for a man and woman to rise for a member of the clergy, a dignitary, a guest of honor, and in many instances for an elderly person. If you're sitting down and the hostess brings a guest over to meet you, stand up, shake hands, and say hello. But if you catch the eye of someone at the other end of the room, all that's necessary is an acknowledging nod or gesture. If a woman is seated and a guest comes over to speak to her, depending on how well she knows that person or whether it's someone a great deal older, she either stands up or extends a greeting while remaining seated. A man always rises when being introduced to a woman. At a party it is not necessary to shake hands with friends or other people you know and have seen recently, but when you are introduced to a stranger always shake hands.

In a restaurant, if a woman passes the table of a man she hasn't seen in quite some time, she may stop briefly to say hello. The man half rises from his seat as a form of acknowledgment and introduces the woman to the person he's eating with. He does the same half rise if she stops to introduce him to a friend of hers, unless there's sufficient space so he can stand up easily.

SHAKING HANDS AND THE SOCIAL KISS

The way you shake hands is considered to be an indication of your personality. The weak, insipid handshake translates into a wishy-washy person, while a firm handshake of substance spells out someone with character. Of course, you don't want to go overboard with a bone-crushing grip that brings forth a gasp from the recipient; a moderately firm clasp is best. When you shake hands, take the other person's hand for no more than two or three seconds, using one hand only, not both hands in a cupping fashion. Although tradition says a man must wait for a woman to extend her hand in greeting, there is no real purpose to this custom. It's a lot more spontaneous and friendly for whoever has the impulse to put forth his or her hand to do so.

Since the purpose of the handshake is to convey warmth and feeling between two people, always remove your glove before offering your hand. An exception is if a woman is wearing long, twenty-one-button white gloves.

If you are introduced to someone who has no right arm, take his left hand with your right hand. In most circumstances the amputee will take the initiative by extending his hand first.

Kissing as a greeting should be reserved for family members and really close friends. The reason is that many people resent being given a kiss that merely brushes the air with no particular meaning. They consider it a gesture of false intimacy. When you do kiss someone in greeting, go for the right side of the face and touch the cheek. Foreigners (Europeans mostly), who traditionally use the social kiss, start with the right cheek and then move on to the left one.

FORGETTING A NAME

It is always horribly embarrassing to forget someone's name. The only comfort comes from knowing that it happens to everyone. What can you do when you draw a blank just before an introduction? The best course is one used by people in public life all the time, extremely successfully; bluff your way through. For example, let's say you're at a museum with your wife when you run into a former colleague whose name escapes you. Respond to his greeting with, "How great to see you after all these years! This is my wife Sally. We were married after my days at Blakenworth, so you've not met her before. Are you still with the firm?" By the time the nameless colleague has answered your question and the conversation is rolling along, the fact that you never mentioned his name will not occur to him. If bluffing is not part of your nature, then just swallow your pride and confront the problem head on. "I'm sorry. I'm having a total memory lapse; your name has gone straight out of my head." Try not to act embarrassed or you'll make the person feel ill at ease.

One of the most tactless remarks you can make to someone you've met only occasionally and who may not remember your name is, "Do you remember me?" Instead, before the other person has a chance to speak, say, "Hi, I'm Arthur White. You may remember me from the Boston

Marathon." Whether you're remembered or not, the person can respond with, "Of course I remember you. Great to see you again."

BEING CALLED BY THE WRONG NAME

If someone mispronounces your name or calls you by the wrong name, don't take it as a slight and act irritated. Do, however, correct the error right away. "I'm sorry to interrupt you but my name is Geraldine, not Josephine."

ETIQUETTE IN CONVERSATION

Each of us spends a good portion of most days in conversation. Sometimes we're talking to family, friends, and colleagues, at other times it's people we know less well, such as a doctor's assistant, a child's teacher, an exercise instructor. And some of our conversations are with those we don't know at all: a taxi driver or a waiter in a restaurant. If you are talking with people you don't know well you need make only polite conversation, but with those closer to you, both socially and professionally, communication becomes more complicated, with attitudes and emotions playing a larger role. As the famous lexicographer and writer Samuel Johnson once said, "That is the happiest conversation, where there is no competition, no vanity, but a calm quiet interchange of sentiments."

BROADENING YOUR CONVERSATIONAL SKILLS

Here are some thoughts and suggestions that can help you out in social situations.

USING A FOREIGN PHRASE Foreign phrases such as *"C'est la vie"* or *"Comme il faut"* are fine to use occasionally provided you pronounce the words correctly and are talking to people who understand them. Using too many foreign phrases, however, is pretentious.

EXPRESSING YOUR OPINION ON CONTROVERSIAL SUBJECTS It is always potentially dangerous to express a strong opinion on controversial subjects such as religion, politics, or morality. Use tact or you may find yourself embroiled in a heated argument. If another person holds the opposing position, listen to her and then express your thoughts with diplomacy. Above all, don't give the impression that your belief is clearly the correct one; rather suggest that it's one you are entitled to.

INTERRUPTING A PERSON The chronic interrupter who compulsively interjects his own thoughts while another person is talking can be exasperating. While it may be tempting to break into a conversation, don't. It's rude to the person speaking. When someone interrupts you, listen for a few seconds and then, with conviction, return to the point at which you were interrupted.

BEING A GOOD LISTENER One of the nicest things that can be said about a person is, "She makes you feel you're the only person in the world." The good listener is telling the person talking, "I really care what you have to say." It's an art to concentrate and really *hear* what someone is saying. Books are written about it, and classes are given to teach it.

THE PERSON WHO TALKS TOO MUCH The opposite of the good listener is someone who talks too much. Tiresome as it may be, there's not much you as the listener can do about it. You can only hope the person will eventually discover that it's the exchange of ideas and thoughts that make for stimulating conversation.

DON'T TALK DOWN TO PEOPLE OR ABOVE THEIR HEADS Respect the level of the people you're talking to. If you're talking to people much younger than you are or with less education or experience, don't be condescending or patronizing. But neither should you talk over their heads so that they feel self-conscious or inadequate.

WHEN SOMEONE REPEATS A STORY It's fine to give someone the pleasure of repeating a favorite story but twice is enough. You can head off another repetition by saying, "Oh, I remember your telling me about the time you outwitted a shark. What an experience you went through!" Once you've said this, quickly introduce another topic of conversation.

PAYING A COMPLIMENT It is always a joy to feel appreciated. The secure person has no trouble paying a compliment. It's the insecure person who finds it difficult to praise others. Too often, we fail to express a happy thought about someone although it's really easy to see something in a person to comment favorably on.

ACKNOWLEDGING A COMPLIMENT Many of us, especially women, were taught not to preen. So we feel self-conscious and act disingenuous when paid a compliment. When you are complimented on a fine speech or a superb game of tennis, your response should not sound apologetic. React with enthusiasm: "It's so nice of you to tell me so," or "It was definitely one of my better days on the court." After all, that's exactly the reaction the giver of the compliment had hoped for.

PASSING ON A COMPLIMENT It is particularly satisfying to receive a secondhand compliment. "Cynthia told me your sales presentation was the best given" can mean much more than if you heard it directly from

Cynthia. Passing on a compliment is a mark of generosity that can't help but please.

RESPONDING TO A NONRESPONSE It's a compliment to admire something a friend is wearing but if you ask where it was bought and the answer is, "I can't remember," don't press the issue. Drop it. Ridiculous or not, many people resent the question.

ASKING HOW MUCH SOMETHING COST While you may exchange information on the cost of a new coat or car with a friend, generally speaking, it's poor manners to be asked how much you spent on a particular item. If someone does, best to say, "I really can't remember." It's a comment that conveys the message that you'd rather not say what you paid.

ASKING FOR A FAVORITE RECIPE Lots of people are reluctant to give out recipes, particularly to someone they view as a competitive cook. If you can't resist asking for a recipe, at least be aware of what the response may be. Say something like, "Someday I'd love to get your great lasagna recipe." If the person is evasive, don't push. It means she's not about to let you in on her culinary secrets.

ADMITTING YOU ARE WRONG If you know you're wrong, say so with good humor and sportsmanship. You'll be respected for it and perhaps save a friendship. You can say, "Nothing irritates me more than being wrong, but I have to admit I made a mistake in giving the advice I did at the P.T.A. meeting yesterday."

MAKING AN APOLOGY Saying, "I'm sorry," is not sufficient. An apology calls for an explanation. For instance, if you were as much as twenty minutes late for your lunch date, say to your friend, "I'm embarrassed thinking about how long I've kept you waiting. Being distracted at work is no excuse either. I should have had my eye on the clock. Next time lunch is on me."

OFFERING AND ACCEPTING AN APOLOGY It's not easy to apologize since it means admitting you said or did something wrong. Similarly, if someone hurts your feelings it may be hard to acknowledge the apology. For the sake of friendship, however, it's important to put self-interest aside and offer or accept an apology with grace. It clears the air and can save a friendship.

STANDING UP FOR A FRIEND There's no higher calling than being a loyal friend; nor is there a more valuable gem than a friend who stands up for you. Never let a friend be criticized unfairly, even though it may be to your advantage to take the opposition's side. Speak up on behalf of your friend, pointing out the positive side of her character. You can say, "Helen's a close and valued friend of mine. I'm sure she gave great thought to Karen's suitability as a candidate before expressing her opinion." Sometimes, for instance at a business meeting, it may not be appropriate to interrupt the person doing the criticizing. If that happens, take the person aside after the meeting and say a few words in defense of your friend.

DEFENDING YOUR RELIGIOUS OR POLITICAL VIEWS   In much the same way that standing up for a friend is a great virtue, so is championing your beliefs. If your religious, political, or moral convictions are impugned, stand up for them both firmly and without reservation. A word of advice, however: make your beliefs known without being argumentative; it gives you a stronger position.

SAYING, "LET'S GET TOGETHER" WITHOUT SUGGESTING A FIRM DATE   Sometimes you run into an old friend on the street, someone you're uninterested in, or who perhaps bores you. You may find yourself nervously saying, "Let's get together. Call me sometime." If you really want to get together, make a firm date. Don't ask the other person to assume the responsibility for contacting you. He'll see it for what it is: an excuse to avoid seeing him.

ASKING, "WHAT ARE YOU DOING NEXT THURSDAY?"   This is what's known as a "trapping" invitation. The person being asked the question has no idea whether he's going to be invited on an all-day hike, to a benefit fashion show, or a black-tie dinner party. He may love the idea of an all-day hike but would go to any length to get out of a black-tie affair. If you're ever asked, "What are you doing next Thursday?" the best response is, "Why are you asking?" Once you know what's involved, you have the option of accepting the invitation or making an excuse.

"WHAT ARE YOU DOING SATURDAY NIGHT?"   If Saturday night is date night where you live, don't ask someone conversationally what he's going to be doing that evening unless he's a close friend. The suggestion is you're asking him because you assume he will have a date, and if in fact he doesn't, it will make him feel his loneliness more acutely.

TELLING SOMEONE HE HAS AN IRRITATING HABIT   It's unsettling to have an irritating habit pointed out. A habit by definition is so ingrained in a person's nature that it's not easy to break; in fact, he or she may not even be aware of it. Except in the case of a family member or a very close friend, it's best to accept or overlook irritating habits in others.

SAYING, "UH-HUH" One day you may realize that you've been saying "Uh-huh" instead of "Yes" to indicate that you understand what's being said. Aside from not being a particularly attractive sound, "Uh-huh" sounds sloppy and lazy, as if you're unable to summon up the energy to say, "Yes."

POLITICAL CORRECTNESS It's the height of intolerance to use any derogatory terms when referring to people of another cultural background. If you do not know how a specific category of people want to be referred to, make an effort to find out. For instance, the term African-Americans has replaced "blacks"; Japanese and Chinese are referred to as Asiatics and Hispanics as Latinos. The point is, various cultural groups want to convey their own definitions rather than have them imposed.

TURNING DOWN A REQUEST TO BE ON A COMMITTEE It's wrong to accept a request to join a committee if you know you won't be able to fulfill the requirements that go with being a member. Be up front and say, "I feel sorry that I can't accept, but my time is limited because of other obligations."

WHEN YOU DON'T WANT TO SIGN A PETITION A member of your family or a good friend may ask you to sign a petition for some political awareness cause or community action. Don't be intimidated into signing; give careful thought to the issue. It's your obligation to form your own opinion before agreeing to sign anything. If you don't want to sign a petition, say, "I've spent a great deal of time investigating this subject and I'm afraid I can't give you my support. I do hope you understand."

BRAGGING At some point in life we all run into the person who thrives on describing his accomplishments, his child's achievements, how much property he owns, or how much money he has. Bragging is a form of insecurity and does nothing to enhance one's image. Don't give the bragger the satisfaction he's looking for—that of responding to his boasting. Acting uninterested is definitely the best way to curb a braggart's tongue.

NAME DROPPING Name dropping is another form of bragging. It's all right to mention the name of a prominent person you know in conversation occasionally, but when it becomes a habit it takes the form of name dropping. The name dropper most often suffers from insecurity. He thinks that if he's associated with someone with influence people will be impressed. Don't give him the satisfaction he's looking for by reacting to his stimulus.

TELLING AN OBSCENE JOKE It's best to confine the telling of lewd jokes to those you know will appreciate them. To tell an obscene joke merely to shock people is juvenile. If an obscene joke offends you, don't laugh just to satisfy the person telling it. Either don't respond at all or say, "I must have missed the point of the joke as I don't find it the least bit funny."

SWEARING　Everyone knows the same relatively few swear words, but not everyone uses them. If you listen to people you admire, you'll hear few swear words.

BEING TOLERANT OF REGIONAL ACCENTS　Around this country one hears many regional accents. To criticize or be openly amused by someone's pronunciation when it is the result of where he was brought up is both unkind and rude. You are, in effect, denying that person his heritage. Accents and regional expressions make people and our language different and colorful.

MAKING AN ETHNIC REMARK　It may seem unbelievable in today's world that some people still make ethnic remarks but, sadly, they do. The person who makes an ethnic joke can only be thought of as a bigot, intolerant of those who are not of his cultural or religious background. If someone drops an ethnic remark or makes a demeaning comment when talking to you, simply say, "I note your prejudice and I find it upsetting." Or, if the remark is made when others are present, just walk away without commenting.

WHEN REFERRING TO HOMOSEXUALS　Male homosexuals are known by the word "gay." No other reference is ever used in conversation. Women homosexuals prefer to be called lesbians to distinguish themselves from gay men.

THE GOSSIP　Beware of the gossip! He has a real problem keeping anything to himself. The temptation to be the first to pass on something scurrilous is overwhelming. And it doesn't work to confront a gossip. He'll always deny he's said anything indiscreet.

THE COMPLAINER　Some people appear to be born complainers. Nothing's right, nothing satisfies them. It can be a real downer to spend time with someone who sees only the negative side of life, so try not to be that way.

TALKING ABOUT YOUR HEALTH　Few subjects can be more tiresome to others than detailed descriptions of your health problems. When asked, "How are you?" it's best to say, "Fine," and leave it at that. While your health may be uppermost in your mind at times, resist the temptation to discuss it constantly, even with good friends. It is of course different if you have been ill and it's a genuine inquiry, for instance, "Are you finished with your radiation?"

SAYING TO SOMEONE, "YOU DON'T LOOK WELL." It's amazing how often you hear someone say, "Are you feeling all right? You don't look very well." Remarks of this sort are truly insensitive. If you're well, nothing can make you feel sick more quickly and if you are sick it only confirms that your poor health shows.

ASKING SOMEONE'S AGE There are some people who are perfectly willing to tell their age. They are perhaps the fortunate ones. But there are those who don't want to admit that time is marching on. If someone asks you how old you are and you don't want to say, you can laugh the question off with, "I'd rather be shot than tell my age," or "The last time I told my age was when I hit twenty-one." Oscar Wilde said, "A woman who will tell her age will tell anything."

ASKING SOMEONE IF HE OR SHE HAS HAD COSMETIC SURGERY People who have had cosmetic surgery have very different reactions about saying so. Some want the whole world to know, others prefer to be discreet about the subject. What anyone who's had a cosmetic lift loves to hear is: "You look terrific. Obviously, you've been on vacation."

ASKING "WHAT DO YOU DO?" Many people in a social setting, such as a dinner party, resent being asked by someone they've just been introduced to, "What do you do?" They feel it's nosy; that the asker is trying to ascertain whether they have a spellbinding job and that, if they don't, the person won't be interested in talking to them. Before asking someone what he does, give the conversation a chance to lean in that direction. Most often it does just that.

ASKING SOMEONE WHY HE OR SHE IS NOT MARRIED This is something that is strictly a personal matter, not anyone else's business. It's a question that should not be asked.

ASKING WHY A WOMAN OR A MAN DOESN'T HAVE CHILDREN They may not be able to have a child or they may have chosen not to have children. It may even be a painful subject. This also is not a question that should ever be asked.

GIVING UNSOLICITED ADVICE It is tricky to give advice unless you are asked; there's a strong possibility that the person you're advising will resent it. On the other hand, if you feel your advice could save a friend's job or marriage, then it's worth the risk involved. If you do offer unsolicited advice, it's important that it be with a supportive, nonjudgmental attitude, emphasizing that you are speaking only from your personal experience, hoping to be of some help.

DON'T TELL A FRIEND HIS OR HER SPOUSE IS HAVING AN AFFAIR There's no excuse for interfering in a friend's marital life. Why should you be the judge as to what's best for your friend to know? As far as you're concerned, the affair may have ended the day before you told your friend about it and you could have spared him or her the pain of knowing. Also, it's none of your business.

ENCOUNTERING SOMEONE WITH A PHYSICAL DEFECT It's highly insensitive to ask someone how he developed his limp or lost an arm. Let him bring up the subject. Nor should you embarrass someone by drawing attention to a flaw in his appearance. For instance, don't ask, "Why do you have that Band-Aid on your face?" It will only make him more self-conscious.

RESCUING SOMEONE FROM AN EMBARRASSING SITUATION It happens to all of us. You find yourself in a roomful of people talking to a man who forgot to zip up the fly of his trousers. While you may be tempted to pretend you haven't noticed, the kindest thing to do is bite the bullet and save him the embarrassment of finding out later on his own, wondering how many people observed his plight. If he's a friend of yours, tell him out of earshot of others "XYZ" ("Examine your zipper"). If you don't know him, find someone in the room who does and turn the task over to him. Another person you can rescue from an embarrassing situation is someone who has a piece of spinach stuck to his tooth while he's eating. Again, it's less embarrassing for him to be told on the spot rather than finding out when he looks in the mirror later on. You can quietly say to him, "You have spinach on your tooth" or give him the message by pointing to your own tooth with your finger.

MISUSE OF WORDS; WORDS AND PHRASES TO AVOID

Words should be used as exactly as possible. You don't need more than good, native intelligence and a lively curiosity to build an interesting vocabulary. An interest in the correct use of one's language is not unrelated to an interest in people and as we refine our vocabularies we also add to our self-esteem.

There are certain words that have crept into American usage—incorrectly—and become entrenched. There are plenty of euphemisms and trendy expressions that should be avoided, because they're either outdated or have been overused. What you will read here is a brief and thoroughly subjective collection of some commonly misused and not-to-be-used words and phrases.

"COMFORTABLE WITH" This is an overused, oversolicitous, and grammatically imprecise expression. People ask, "Are you comfortable with . . ." when they mean, "Do you like it?" or "Is it all right with you?"

"DRAPES" This is an advertising word for "draperies" or "curtains."

"HAVE A NICE DAY" This expression is unequaled in inanity; it is rarely heartfelt and is therefore an insincere way of saying, "Goodbye." Another silly parting comment is, "Enjoy."

HOUSE AND HOME Contrary to common usage, these are not wholly interchangeable words. A "house" is a building in which people make a "home." When referring to the style, structure, or position of a building, you would say "house"; you would not say, "Mine is the second home on the left." You may be "at home" or "going home," but you would have groceries delivered not "to my home" but rather "to my house."

HOSIERY "Hosiery" is an old trade word for "stockings." "Pantyhose" and "stockings" are the acceptable words.

"LITTLE GIRL'S" OR **"LITTLE BOY'S ROOM"** In someone's house you would say "bathroom." In a restaurant or other public place, you'd ask for the "ladies' " or "men's" room or rest room.

"PARDON" This is an order. It is wrong to use it in the same context as "Please excuse me," "Please forgive me," or "I beg your pardon."

PARTY The word "party" relates to a celebration, not a person. Leave expressions such as "parties of the first part" to the lawyers.

"PASSED AWAY" The euphemisms for "died" are many, and range from the coy to the ridiculous. We all die; death cannot be glossed over by inexact language.

"RICH" AND "WEALTHY" Supposedly, there are some class guidelines regarding these two terms. The common wisdom goes that the truly well to do use the word "rich" while the uninitiated say "wealthy." It seems ridiculous to worry about such things but, to avoid the issue, you might merely say, "They have lots of money."

"SHARE WITH" A peculiar 1980s expression that came out of California encounter-group talk, "I want to share something with you," has come to mean, "I want to tell you a story," or "pass on some information." It's overused and has an ingratiating tone. Better to say, "I want to tell you," or "Listen to this."

FOREIGN WORDS AND PHRASES

Although the time when all well-educated Americans spoke French is now part of history, it is still *de rigueur*, when using French terms, to pronounce them properly and to use them correctly. The following is a mélange of some of the French words and phrases that have been absorbed into our contemporary vocabulary and so might be encountered in everyday speech.

bon voyage (bohn vwoi-ahje)	pleasant voyage
bouquet (boo-kay)	flowers fastened together in a bunch
boutique (boo-teek)	small specialty shop
buffet (boo-fay)	a meal at which guests help themselves to food set out on a buffet table
chaise longue (shez long)	a chair with an elongated seat
chiffon (sheef-fone)	a sheer material
clique (kleek)	small, exclusive circle of people
coup de grâce (koo deh grahs)	the finishing stroke; the last straw
croissant (krwah-sant)	crescent-shaped bread roll
façade (fah-saad)	the front of a building, but it has also come to mean a fake favorable impression
faux pas (foe pah)	"false step," a social blunder, tactless act or remark
hors d'oeuvre (or durv)	appetizer
lingerie (lan-zher-ree)	women's underwear
parquet (pahr-kay)	inlaid wood in geometric or other patterns, generally used in flooring
pâté (pah-tay)	a meat paste
prix fixe (pree feeks)	a meal at a stipulated price

TELEPHONE MANNERS

In 1876, Alexander Graham Bell spoke his famous first words, "Come here, Mr. Watson," into the mouthpiece of his invention, the telephone. Today not only can you make and receive calls when you're on the go, your telephone call can be answered in an empty house; you can talk to two or more people in different places at the same time; you can direct-dial to practically any place in the world; and you can receive an incoming call while you're on another call. With the telephone playing such a vital role in human communications today, we need to use common sense and sensitivity when calling and speaking to friends and colleagues. Good telephone manners mean not calling a friend at 7 P.M. when you know that's his dinner hour or calling anyone before 9 A.M. or after 9 P.M. unless you've been told otherwise. It means calling a friend at work only when it's necessary, and then being brief.

ANSWERING YOUR TELEPHONE

The way you answer your telephone sets the tone for a conversation. A well-modulated, cheerful voice is best. A loud, harsh voice or a tiny, wispy voice that lacks enthusiasm does not project a favorable image to the caller.

Although Alexander Graham Bell proposed "Hoy, hoy" as the correct way to answer the telephone, he was, fortunately, overruled by Thomas Edison, who voted for a simple "Hello." That is still the best way to answer the telephone. "Yes" is too abrupt; and saying "Mrs. White speaking" is appropriate only for an office. If the call is for someone other than you, put your hand over the mouthpiece before raising your voice to summon the person. Don't put the receiver to your chest, which is where your voice resonates. If it will take more than a minute or so to find the person, take the caller's name and number and pass the message on.

ANSWERING SOMEONE ELSE'S TELEPHONE

Don't answer the telephone in someone else's house unless you're specifically asked to. And, if you do, don't ask who's calling. Answer the call by saying, "Hello." In response to the caller's request to speak to someone living in the house, you say, "I'm sorry, Mr. White isn't here. May I take a message?"

WHEN YOU MAKE THE CALL

Let the telephone ring at least six times to give the person on the other end plenty of time to answer. It's annoying to jump out of the bathtub only to have the caller hang up after three rings. In response to the "Hello" of the person answering, say, "May I please speak to Mrs. White?" Or "Is Mrs. White there? This is Mrs. Arnold calling." If you recognize the voice on the other end, exchange a few words before asking to speak to your friend. For example, "Hello, Arthur, this is Jane. How are you? I hear you had a great trip south." After Arthur's response, don't launch into another subject but ask, "Is Sally there?" If you're calling Sally purely to chat, ask her, "Is this a good time to catch up, or would you rather I called you tomorrow?"

THE HOUSEKEEPER AND THE TELEPHONE

Tell your housekeeper exactly how you want your telephone answered and how to take a proper message. A simple "Hello" is quite satisfactory. While there's nothing wrong with "Mrs. White's residence" or "The White residence," it's unnecessary. In addition, for security reasons, you may not want your name given out when the telephone is answered. When you make a call and a housekeeper you know answers, say, "Hello, Adelaide, this is Mrs. Arnold. May I please speak to Mrs. White?"

A YOUNG CHILD ANSWERING THE TELEPHONE

When you make a telephone call and get a three-year-old on the other end of the line it can be pretty exasperating. Many parents encourage their small children to answer the telephone, thinking it's cute, and because small children love to. To satisfy both child and caller, be close to the telephone when your child answers it. Let him say, "Hello," and then take the receiver away. When a child is older, and left at home for any period of time, he should be warned never to tell any stranger who calls that he is alone in the house.

BEING CUT OFF

If you've made a telephone call and are cut off in the middle of the conversation, it's your responsibility to initiate the return call. This is particularly true if it was a long-distance call.

ASKING SOMEONE TO HOLD ON

It's not polite to ask someone to hold on so you can speak to the mailman or check something on the stove. If you need to interrupt a telephone call, say, "I'm sorry, the back doorbell's ringing. I'll have to call you right back." And be sure you do.

ENDING A CALL

Some people love to talk on the telephone and have plenty of time to do so. If you're caught in a conversation that seems unending, you'll have to take the initiative. Wait until the person pauses for breath and say, "Oh, dear! I just noticed the time. I'm late for the dentist." You don't have to be rude, but you may have to be emphatic.

THE WRONG NUMBER

If you've called a wrong number, don't just hang up, say, "I'm sorry to have bothered you." Don't ask whose house you've reached, and don't answer this question if it is asked of you. When you're the one answering the telephone and it's the wrong number, you don't have to tell the person your number. "No, I am sorry there's no one here by that name. What number are you calling?" If the number the caller gives is not yours, say, "Sorry, you've dialed the wrong number." If the number is yours, say, "You have reached the wrong number. There's no one here by that name. You'd better recheck the number."

CALL WAITING

It's been called "call hating" and "call bothering." It's perhaps the most controversial of the recent advances in telephone technology. Anyone who receives a great many telephone calls, or lives in a house with lots of other people, particularly teenagers, might consider an alternative to call waiting: a telephone with a separate number and an answering machine connected to it.

Call waiting is something of a trade-off. If you are the caller, it means avoiding the irritation of a constant busy signal. If you are the person receiving the call-waiting signal, it means not missing an important call because you are talking to someone else. Still, to interrupt a friend in the middle of a sentence with "Hold on a minute, I have another call waiting for me" gives the impression that you are more concerned with knowing who is on call waiting than with listening to him. When you answer call waiting, be as quick as possible: "I'm on another call. I'll get back to you as soon as I can." What's best to do when someone calls you and you are expecting an important call is to say, "I'd love to talk to you now but Arthur may be calling me from Houston, and if he does I must take his call. But I'll call you right back." If you pick up on call waiting and it's someone telephoning long distance, ask him to hold on. Quickly return to your original call and say, "I'm so sorry. I have a long-distance call. I'll call you right back." Since that person will be waiting, call back right away with apologies. If someone who has left you to answer another call does not come back on the line after a few minutes, hang up and wait to be called back. The most important thing to remember about call waiting is that you don't have to answer it.

SOLICITATION CALLS

These calls invariably come in the evening when the person soliciting has a better chance of finding people at home. If you're not interested in whatever he or she is proposing, you can politely interrupt with "Thanks so much for calling but I have someone who handles my investments" or "We bought a set of the encyclopedia last year." Although solicitations can be annoying, particularly if they interrupt you, remember that the voice on the other end of the telephone is that of someone who is doing a job, trying to solicit your interest. In the case of a computer-generated solicitation, all you have to do is hang up.

OBSCENE TELEPHONE CALLS

If you receive an obscene telephone call, hang up immediately. Don't give the caller the satisfaction of showing irritation or fear. If he calls back, again hang up. If it happens a third time, take your telephone off the hook. If the caller continues, get in touch with the telephone company.

There's a device that can be attached to your telephone to trace the number of the caller.

ANSWERING MACHINES

More and more people have answering machines at home. Older machines required that the outgoing message be twenty or thirty seconds long, which spawned all sorts of gimmicks such as sound effects, music, or jokes. While such messages may be amusing the first time they're heard, they quickly become tiresome.

Most answering tapes are now voice-activated, which means you need record only a short, simple message. For example: "Hello, you have reached 555-1234. We are not here at the moment, but if you leave a message after the beep tone, we'll call you back as soon as possible." Should your machine be one whereby the caller can speak as long as he needs to, you may want to say so as part of the message. If you are going on vacation, for security reasons it's best not to announce it on your answering machine. When leaving a message on a machine, speak clearly and slowly. Many machines only record for two or three minutes, so you need to keep your message short: "This is Mary Flannery. It's Tuesday morning at ten o'clock. I'm calling to confirm lunch on Thursday. If you need to get back to me my number is 555-9823."

Answering machines are great inventions and can make life easier. They are no substitute, however, for a real telephone call. If you have something important or special to say to a friend, don't leave it on an answering machine. It's too impersonal and you never know who else will hear it.

AUTOMATED MESSAGE-TAKING SYSTEMS

An alternative to the answering machine, and one that offers more privacy, is the automated message-taking system. This works on the same principle as voice mail, a common message-taking procedure in large offices and other places. If no one answers the telephone at home, the system picks up and instructs the caller to press 1 for Mr. White, 2 for Mrs. White, 3 for Janie White. Each person has a code of his own, and unless he tells another member of the family what it is, no one can hear his messages. Like an answering machine, this system can also play or erase messages. Other advantages are that callers never get a busy signal and there are no machines to break or replace.

PERSONAL PORTABLE TELEPHONES

In every busy city we have become used to seeing people dodging traffic while talking on the telephone. The portable telephone may be a great invention for someone who feels he has to be in touch every minute of the day, but it can be an irritant to those who have to listen to the signal go off. If you carry a portable telephone around with you, turn it off when you're at the theater or walking through a museum or other such public place where people need to concentrate. When you go to a restaurant, you can always check the telephone with the coatroom attendant and have her come and get you if a call comes through while you're eating. You would, of course, give her a tip for this service.

EMERGENCY BREAK-INS

If you desperately need to get through to someone who does not have call waiting and there is a legitimate emergency reason to interrupt a telephone call, such as needing to notify him of an accident or other disaster, you can ask the operator to break into the call.

CREDIT CARD CALLS, PERSON-TO-PERSON, CALLING COLLECT

Never make a long-distance telephone call from someone else's house without paying for it. You can charge the call either to a telephone credit card or to your home telephone number. Or you can place the call through an operator and say you would like time and charges when the call is completed. You can then give the person the exact amount he will be billed in cash.

Person-to-person calls, like all operator-assisted calls, cost more than regular telephone calls, but you don't have to pay if the person is not home. Person-to-person is particularly useful if you are calling someone with an answering machine, because you are not charged if the machine picks up.

Collect calls are primarily for family use—when children call home from a friend's house, school, or college. You would not call collect to friends. And at some point children, ideally when they have graduated and are working, should give up calling collect.

HINDRANCES TO GOOD TELEPHONE HABITS

- Carrying on a conversation when you're entertaining guests. (Get the caller's number and say you'll have to call back.)
- Carrying on some nonverbal but noisy activity such as dishwashing while talking.
- Talking to someone in the room with you while the caller is speaking.
- Leaving the television or radio turned up too loudly.
- Eating while talking.
- Rattling your number off too quickly when you leave a message.
- Not returning calls promptly.
- Not listening attentively.
- Mumbling, or speaking too loudly.
- Sneezing, coughing, etc., directly into the receiver.

For business telephone manners, see under "Oral Communication in Business" in Chapter 5.

TOASTS

The word "toast" is derived from the custom of putting toasted, spiced bread in a cup to give the wine flavor. When you drank to someone's health, you had to drain the cup to get to the saturated toast, which sank to the bottom. In England today a bit of toast is still occasionally placed in a drink.

Toasting is still more usual in European countries than in the United States, although we have certainly taken to the practice wholeheartedly. On important occasions when people get together formally—engagement parties, dinner parties honoring a friend or colleague on his promotion or retirement, christenings, celebrations to acknowledge successful business deals—toasts are usually called for. The best are short but apt. Sincere, simple words of friendship are much more effective than any long-winded oratory. For example: "We are delighted to be here to wish our dear friends great success and happiness on the eve of their departure. Let's raise our glasses and drink a toast to Alice and Frank and to their years in London." If you are accustomed to speaking in public, you may want to give a more eloquent toast complete with personal anecdotes but, for those less comfortable speaking in public, brevity is the soul of wit.

A joke can enliven a toast, as long as it is appropriate to the occasion. There are lots of books of stories and jokes specifically for such occasions. Look through such a book to find something suitable. It will add a bit extra to your toast. For a retirement party, check the book's index for "retirement," "leisure," "age," or "work" and look for a saying that speaks to the event at hand. Don't force the issue—if you can't find a quote, use your own words. If they are heartfelt and well thought out, they will be perfect.

If you are called on to make a toast in a foreign country or you're giving a dinner party for a foreign visitor, it may not be possible to give a toast in the honoree's native language, but if you can say "To your good health," it will certainly impress and please him. What follows is a list of some foreign-language equivalents. Check your pronunciation with someone knowledgeable in the language you're using, as words are said differently from province to province.

Arabic:	Fi sihitaek (fee seh heh' tahk)
Armenian:	Genatz (geh nahtz')
Bulgarian:	Na zdrve (nahz drah' vee)
Chinese:	Gān-bēi (gahn beeh)
Danish:	Skaal (skawl)
Dutch:	Proost (proast)

Finnish:	Kippis (kip' piss) or salut (sa-lu)
French:	À votre santé (ah vo' tra san' tay)
German:	Prosit (pro' sit) or Zum Wohl (tsum voal)
Greek:	Steniyasas (steen ee yah' sahss)
Hebrew:	L'chayim (leh khy' yim)
Italian:	Salute (sah loo' tay) or chin chin
Japanese:	Kanpai (kahn pay)
Korean:	Kŏn-bae (kahn bay)
Norwegian:	Skål (skawl)
Polish:	Na zdrowie (nah zdro' vyeh)
Portuguese:	Sáude (ser oo' dher)
Russian:	Na zdorov'e (nah zdah ro' vyeh)
Serbo-Croatian:	Ziveli (zhee' vehlee)
Spanish:	A su salud (ah soo sah loodh')
Swedish:	Skål (skoal)
Turkish:	Şerefe (shereh feh')
Yiddish:	L'chayim (leh khy' yim)

For the etiquette of proposing a toast, see "Proposing a Toast" under both "The Role of the Hostess" and "The Role of the Guest" in the section called "The Formal Seated Dinner With a Staff" in Chapter 2, as well as "The Wedding Toasts" under "The Wedding Reception" in Chapter 3.

PUBLIC SPEAKING

Although there are those lucky few who are born orators, most people would rather die or be audited than stand in front of a crowded room and give a speech. In fact, the American Psychological Association found public speaking to be the number one dread of most Americans. Nevertheless, whether it's in the classroom or the local Y, at a P.T.A. or other community service meeting, the boardroom or a retirement party, chances are one day you'll be called on to stand up and say something in front of a group. Whether you're asked to introduce a speaker or be the speaker yourself, practice and preparation are the key factors of a successful performance. Once you've mastered the art of public speaking, you'll find that talking in front of an appreciative audience can actually be one of life's more satisfying experiences.

INTRODUCING A SPEAKER

If you're asked to introduce the speaker, the way in which you address the audience can help set the tone or mood for the occasion. Your introduction should be friendly and sincere and above all on the short side; not an occasion for a speech of your own. You'll want to give the audience a little background information on the speaker and how you happen to know her. If the speaker is well known, there's no need to list all her credentials or accomplishments. After all, people have come to hear her speak and will be anxious to have her get started. If you are making a simple introduction after a welcoming remark, you might say, "It gives me great pleasure to present to you Mary Dalton, whose twenty-five years in publishing give her a fund of information on the making of a best-seller, which she has agreed to share with us. Mary is also a valued member of the community, and I've had the pleasure of working with her on numerous neighborhood projects. Let's welcome Mary Dalton." Telling an amusing anecdote about the speaker, one that will make the audience and speaker smile, can help spark the audience's enthusiasm.

PREPARING TO GIVE A SPEECH

Although many people are blessed with pleasant voices that lend themselves naturally to speech making, others are not so fortunate. The ideal speaking voice is pitched low, is resonant, and has an even tempo. Your voice should also rise slightly at the end of a sentence—if it drops, you'll sound dispirited. A fine speaking voice requires good breathing and good posture. Fear, anxiety, and ill health can constrict the vocal cords and make your voice thin and tight. The voice of a relaxed speaker is likely to be full and pleasant.

Of course, it's not always easy to learn to relax or breathe correctly, or to achieve the proper posture for the ideal speaking voice. You may want to get some professional training. Speech lessons can strengthen a weak voice, modify a heavy accent, teach proper timing, and enable you to overcome the fear of speaking in front of strangers. The story about the Greek orator Demosthenes, who conquered a speech impediment by orating on the seashore over the roar of the waves, his mouth filled with pebbles, may or may not be true, but the moral of the story is: speech problems can be overcome.

Practice your speech in front of a mirror or ask a friend or family member to listen and comment on the way you sound. Or you might videotape your speech and then analyze it. Practice, polish, then practice and polish some more. No one ever made a mistake by being too well prepared.

Unless you're a virtuoso performer, you'll need some hard copy in front of you when you speak, just to keep you on track. Some people like a stack of 3 × 5 index cards containing key catchwords and phrases from the speech. Each card has a brief comment or observation that serves as a cue for your next remarks. For example, on the first card you might write: "Thank host and audience. 'I am delighted to be a part of this distinguished company and honored that I have been chosen to speak before you.' " In place of file cards, however, you may prefer to have a typed copy of your speech, with the main points highlighted; or you could use a formal outline of the speech written on a legal pad. The practiced speaker, however, never reads from a prepared text; he engages the audience in a one-sided conversation.

WHAT TO WEAR

Dress appropriately for the occasion at which you will be speaking: evening clothes for a formal banquet, business attire for a daytime event. To be on the safe side, check with whoever is in charge to find out what sort of dress is expected. If you're to be seated on a dais with dignitaries in black tie, you'll want to conform to their dress and not wear the less formal outfits of those in the audience. A man at a business function wears his best business suit with a conservative tie. A woman wears a conservative dress or suit. Bright patterns and unusual designs can be distracting to the audience, but wear a touch of color so you don't look drab or dreary. Dangling or overly large earrings are also distracting, as are bangle bracelets that may make a noise. Subtle makeup is advisable if you will be under bright lights. Apply light face powder to eliminate a shiny face, which might be mistaken for nervous perspiration. Comfortable shoes for both men and women are essential.

JUST BEFORE THE SPEECH

Arrive early so there will be time to relax as well as to do a last-minute check on the lighting, the microphone, and any props you may be using. Make sure you won't be standing in the glare of a spotlight; check that the lectern light is bright enough for you to read your notes with ease and yet not so bright as to distract the audience, if you will be showing slides. The microphone may have to be adjusted for your height and must be checked to ensure that people sitting in the back of the room will be able to hear you. If you're using props such as graphs, charts, or slides, make certain they are within easy reach. You do not want to have to step out of the range of the microphone in order to grab exhibit A or B.

Once you're assured that the mechanics of the speech are in order, take time to relax. If you feel nervous, try deep breathing, an ancient and effective method for soothing nerves. If you're tense, you may involuntarily hold your breath or take shallow breaths, depriving your system of oxygen and making it difficult for you to speak clearly. Find a quiet place to sit down. Close your eyes and breathe in through your nose as deeply as you can, filling your lungs, chest, and abdomen. Then breathe out slowly. The exhalation should take at least as long as the inhalation. Count each breath—in for two, hold for two, out for two, hold for two, and so on—until your heartbeat slows down and your mind calmly focuses only on your breath. Deep breathing must be done slowly and deliberately. If you feel lightheaded, return to normal breathing. Some people even find that a quick prayer works wonders to calm their nerves before they have to speak in public. You might also try smiling in the face of fear—it's harder to be tense when you have a smile on your face.

THE SPEECH

One rule of successful speech making is to ingratiate yourself with the audience. Start by greeting any dignitaries present, thanking the people who invited you to speak, and welcoming the members of the audience. For example, "Mr. Mayor, Judge Smith, and members of the assembly, I am grateful for the opportunity you have given me to speak before such a distinguished group today." You also want to acknowledge the person who introduced you. Humor is often used as an icebreaker, although starting with a joke can sometimes sound stagy or forced. Unless you're a natural at telling jokes, you're better off opening with simple and affable remarks and saving the jokes for appropriate times in the text of your speech. You're not expected to be a Winston Churchill when you speak. People will respond to the real you more than they will to any oratorical tricks or poses. Be likable. Be positive, pleasant, interesting, approachable, warm, expressive, and sincere.

Talk to your audience as you would to a friend. Address them warmly. Show your respect by getting right to the point, proving your point, and concluding your speech. Don't talk longer than you have been asked to. If you need to pause to think, remain silent rather than filling in the time with "uhms" or "let's see." Your audience will wait; and in fact a pause in your speech can be an effective way of creating suspense. Too many pauses, however, and you lose your audience.

Look at the audience, not at your notes. You will find some faces are friendlier than others; make eye contact with those faces. Don't get stuck looking at just one person; you will make him nervous and will seem to be excluding the rest of the audience. Give thought ahead of time to what you'll do with your hands; will them to rest quietly at your side or place them on the podium. If you must use reading glasses, keep them on during the entire speech rather than continually putting them on and removing them.

Keep your language as clear as possible of jargon or slang. Use short sentences. Remember, you are talking to a friend. Since that friend is spread out all over a large room, you need to use a little extra emphasis to get your ideas across. Speak more distinctly and slowly than you would in the course of normal conversation, and be sure to vary the tempo and pitch of your voice. Use a smile, a shrug, an upturned palm, raised eyebrows to your advantage.

If you need to cough or sneeze, go ahead. You can't stop a sneeze or a cough anyway without looking as though you might be having a seizure. Be sure you turn away from the microphone and the audience if you do sneeze or cough; there's no reason to comment or apologize, just go right back to your speech. If you have a cold, take some mild (nonalcoholic) cold medicine before speaking and keep tissues nearby. The water glass and pitcher are put there for your comfort; feel free to use them. A strategically timed sip of water can put the audience on the edge of their seats waiting for you to continue.

Your closing remarks are crucial to the success of your speech. It's important that you take pains to perfect them. Memorize them so they are delivered as skillfully as possible. Ideally, your final comments are the culmination—the very apex of the pyramid you've been building through the structure of your speech; they summarize and illuminate your entire talk. Many a speech loses its effectiveness if the closing is too drawn out or terminated too abruptly. Give some indication that you have said about all you are going to say on the subject a few minutes before you finish. Wit and wisdom are the guiding principles of closing remarks, followed by sincere thanks for the audience's attention.

Following the conclusion of the speech, the chairman or whoever made the introduction will rise and thank you. If you are not particularly well known, he should repeat your entire name for the benefit of anyone who arrived late or who might have forgotten it. It is not necessary for him to comment on the speech.

If a question and answer period has been planned, the chairman may ask a friend or two to be ready with questions in case no one else in the audience raises a hand. As the speaker, you should remember that a question is not an invitation to go on for another fifteen minutes or so. Give a short answer or say, "I'm sorry, but to answer that question properly, I'd need too much time. You can see me after we finish the question period, if you like." If you don't know the answer, admit it. If you don't understand the question, admit it. If the question is overtly hostile, don't rise to the bait. "I don't think this is the time or place for further discussion on this subject; let's talk later," is a reply that's neutral and polite. If a particularly long, involved question has been asked, you may repeat it for the benefit of the audience.

LISTENING TO A SPEECH

If you are a member of the audience, you should sit quietly during the speech and be attentive. You should never leave before the speech is finished, no matter how bored you may be. If you can't hear the speaker, try to find the chairman of the event or someone else in charge to tell about your problem. Don't shout out, "Louder." In a smaller group, you may gesture to the speaker. Point to your ear and shake your head. He will catch on to the fact that he can't be heard in the back of the room. When the question and answer period comes, don't raise your hand until you know exactly how to phrase your question. Speak distinctly. Questions are not a forum for the questioner. You should make your question short and to the point.

TELEVISION AND RADIO APPEARANCES

All the general principles of public speaking apply to television and radio but, in addition and most important, solicit and heed the advice of professionals in those fields.

It can be very exciting when you've done something important—written a book, formed an organization, been made director of a local business, or been asked to head a charitable group—and your achievements catch the attention of the media. But when the producer of a television or radio program calls and asks you to appear on his show, your next reaction might be fear and anxiety over what kind of a performance you'll give. That's normal but, if you've prepared well, you'll find that speaking to a television or radio audience is not nearly so intimidating as you might have imagined.

Once you've agreed to be on a program, familiarize yourself with the show's format by watching and listening to it a number of times. Note how the host conducts the program, in particular the types of questions he asks and how fast he keeps the pace going. When you know what to expect, you'll be better able to prepare yourself, and the more you prepare, the more spontaneous you will appear.

If you will be appearing on television, pay attention to how the host and guests on the show are dressed. Study what works and what doesn't: which colors show up well, which patterns are too busy and which ones add an element of interest to the person's appearance. Look at women's jewelry. Small pieces, no matter how beautiful, are generally lost on the television screen, whereas large chunky earrings, necklaces, and pins show up well. Body language is crucial (but not to the point of having a distracting effect); notice how important smiling and being animated are to getting the message across to the audience. Novices tend to sit too still and look stiff.

The talent coordinator of the show, or whoever your contact is at the studio, will discuss your segment with you. Ask how much time is allotted to you, when you should arrive at the studio, and if you are going to be on television, whether there's any particular way you should dress. If it's an interview-type program and you'd prefer not to be asked personal questions, or questions on a particular subject, say so. Whether the host will agree to such a request is another matter, especially if he prides himself on being feisty and controversial.

It's important to be properly made up. Under bright lights skin can take on a shiny look, dark circles show up under the eyes, lips can seem unusually large and eyes very small. Put yourself in the hands of the studio's makeup artist, who specializes in making people look attractive under the glare of bright lights needed for the camera.

There are a number of differences between making a speech and appearing on television or radio, the most important being the time factor. When you are giving a speech, you can run over your allotted time (although you really shouldn't). But television and radio are on split-second schedules and you must be aware of the clock. If only three minutes are left, for instance, you may have to shorten your response or wind up your remarks so the host will not have to break in and cut you off. But don't rush or babble.

Among other points to keep in mind if you are to appear on either television or radio:

- Don't interrupt the host, but if the host interrupts you, stop talking right away. Two people speaking at once is unprofessional.

- If there's a pause, long enough to constitute dead air, and the host doesn't jump in with a remark, make any appropriate comment you can think of to break the silence.

- Try to avoid saying "um," "ah," and "uh-uh."

- Answer the host's questions with more than just "yes" or "no." Instead say, "Yes, that's right," or "No, I don't agree."

- Mentioning the town or city where the show takes place draws in the audience and captures their attention. For example, "I always love being back in Charleston. It's one of my favorite places." Or, "Our charity has always had a great response from the people of Chicago."

SPECIAL POINTERS FOR BEING ON TELEVISION

- Find out if you'll be photographed only from the waist up; if your entire body will show, decide how best to place your legs.

- Try not to fidget by touching your face or adjusting your glasses, necktie, or hair. If you won't need your glasses, don't wear them.

- Although it may be tempting to look around the studio, don't. Focus on the interviewer unless you're told to do otherwise.

- If you're promoting a book or other product, take it with you; don't count on the host having it. And always mention the book by name, not by "the book." The same goes for any organization you are promoting.

A WORD ABOUT RADIO

One of the advantages of radio, of course, is that you needn't worry about how you look—but you will need to think about how you sound. Before going on the air, have a sip of water, sit straight up, and take three deep breaths. Clear your throat if necessary. If you tend to have a dry throat, take some lozenges with you. Your first sentence should be firm and clear. For instance, after the host welcomes you, say, "Thanks very much, Lenny. I'm delighted to be here." Or "I'm so pleased to be back on your show." By forcing yourself to say one or two full sentences you'll get used to the sound of your voice and become more confident and composed. If you need to cough, move out of range of the microphone, or use the cough button that shuts off the mike. If the program you're on is one that has listeners call in to ask questions, you will be given earphones through which you'll hear the callers' questions. Answer each one quickly. Keep the pace moving. If a caller wants to talk on, interrupt politely but firmly: "I'm afraid I've given all the time I can to your question" or "Thanks for calling. Now we'll hear from another listener." Keep in mind that no one caller should monopolize the show.

The seasoned television or radio personality comes to the program well prepared. He knows all he needs to about the subject being discussed. Be sure you, too, are well prepared so you can speak intelligently and with authority. The more you know about your subject, the more easily you'll be able to talk about it and the less you'll think about how you look or about your delivery. If you focus on the interviewer and your conversation with him, you won't think about the huge, unseen audience listening to or watching you at home. Whenever your nerves start working against your self-confidence, remind yourself that you've been invited to appear on the show because *you*, not the host, not the audience, are the expert.

HERALDIC DEVICES (CRESTS)

While the true traditionalist follows established customs of heraldry, in recent years heraldic practice has become somewhat more relaxed among Americans of armigerous standing. Full coats of arms are sometimes used on small pieces of silver, wedding announcements, and stationery; women use heraldic devices; arms are often seen on yachting flags; and women who are not heiresses use their family arms on lozenges after marriage.

THE ORIGIN AND CUSTOM OF HERALDRY

The subject of heraldry is very complicated. The usage described here covers Americans with arms derived from British forebears. For those who trace their heraldic status to continental Europe (France, Germany, Spain, Italy, etc.) the customs are somewhat different.

Heraldry originated in the twelfth century, when a warrior in armor, his visor down, preparing to engage, would have been indistinguishable by either friend or foe. To avoid the obvious problems this would have caused, each warrior took as his trademark a device that was emblazoned on his shield and embroidered on the sleeveless jacket he wore over the armor—hence "coat of arms." To further identify himself each warrior wore a crest—say a falcon or a dragon—forged to his metal head covering. And often the helmet had distinctive shapes and designs as well.

By the late fifteenth century many families other than those descended from crusaders and knights had assumed arms. It therefore became necessary for the Heralds' College, established by law in 1483, to make an official "visitation" of all noble families using arms in each of the shires of England and to record both arms and pedigrees. These pedigrees form the basis of the mass of records now collected in the College of Arms.

If your surname is English, Welsh, or Irish, for a fee the College will examine your claim to the right to use a coat of arms. If that right cannot be established, the College will, for another fee, grant you a new coat of arms. If you are of Irish descent, you may also apply to the Genealogical Office, Dublin Castle, Dublin, Ireland. If your family is of Scottish descent, the Lord Lyon King of Arms, Edinburgh, will verify your arms or make a new grant.

Although in the United States there is no legal or governmental authority to issue a coat of arms or rule upon your right to a heraldic device, the New England Historic Genealogical Society, 101 Newbury Street, Boston, MA 02116, has had a Committee of Heraldry since 1864. This committee does not grant a coat of arms or do any genealogical search—it merely authenticates claims. It will examine a claim to the right to bear arms and rule on its validity. If the claim is found to be authentic, the arms will be included in the committee's periodically published Roll.

To determine your family's right to a coat of arms, you will need to know not only the full name of your earliest patrilineal American ancestor but his connection with an armigerous (anyone who used arms) British—or continental—family and your exact line of descent from him.

The right to use a coat of arms was given in perpetuity to all agnates (male descendants) of the grantee. If your name is Clark, Smith, Carpenter (all occupational names), or even such an unusual name as Blenkenship, Hungerford, or Cobleigh, it isn't enough to ascertain that there were coats of arms for these families and proceed to appropriate them for your own use. It may be happenstance that your name is the same. One Miller family, say, may have the right to use the coat as listed in Burke's General Armoury; another, quite unrelated, cannot legally use the coat. Using a coat of arms not rightfully yours is like telling a genealogical lie. Some coats of arms actually are copyrighted in the United States using another registered trademark.

Because the elder sons inherited the titles and lands, it was the younger sons who were more likely to emigrate from Europe to our country when it was new. These younger sons sometimes came alone, sometimes with families, but most had limited funds and even more limited experience in the kind of work they were to do in a new, rough country. In a generation, two perhaps, former claims to gentility were abandoned as all struggled to build the new nation. But male heirs of the name, of direct descent from the original armigerous forebear, still had the right to the coat of arms, a right many families here today don't realize they have.

THE LOZENGE

If you are an heiress or coheiress (with sisters) of an armigerous family and have no surviving brothers, you have the right to use your father's coat of arms (as may your sisters) in a diamond-shaped "lozenge." If you marry you may "impale" your arms with those of your husband—the shield is divided in half vertically and his arms are blazoned on the left, yours on the right. Your children then "quarter" (that is, divide them in half again horizontally) their parents' arms. Technically, if you as an heiress marry a nonarmigerous husband you and your children lose their armigerous standing. If you are an heiress you may continue to use the lozenge yourself even though you marry a nonarmigerous husband. But if you are not an heiress you are not correct in using your family's arms on the lozenge after your marriage.

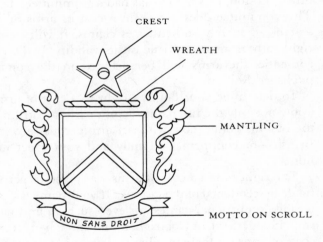

CREST

WREATH

MANTLING

MOTTO ON SCROLL

NON SANS DROIT

FULL COAT

A full coat of arms consists of the shield with the appropriate heraldic insignia, called the charge, on it; in this example the chevron is the charge, below a crest. The crest is simply the insignia (generally quite different from that on the shield) surmounting a wreath (taken from the medieval helmet). The crest may be used by itself on stationery or silver. The lozenge, the lady's equivalent of the shield, must be used with a crest.

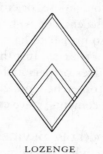

LOZENGE

If Mr. Jones marries Miss Brown (an heiress) their coats of arms are impaled thus:

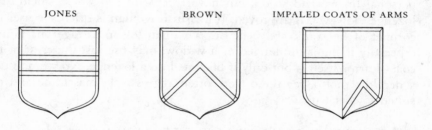

JONES   BROWN   IMPALED COATS OF ARMS

and they use this coat during their lifetimes. Their son and heir quarters the Jones and Brown arms, and he and his descendants continue to use the quartered arms.

QUARTERED ARMS

HOW HERALDIC DEVICES ARE USED

The most common uses of a coat of arms are on a bookplate or drawn or painted (blazoned is the technical term) and framed as a wall decoration. It may also be used on stationery if the paper is the best quality and the coat of arms engraved (in color, if you choose) or embossed. This should appear only on the first sheet, and the envelopes should be stamped in the same fashion as the paper. It is also proper to have the full coat engraved on a large piece of silver, such as a tea tray. Just the crest may be engraved on smaller pieces such as flat silver or personal articles such as a toilet set, cigarette case, or compact, or etched on glassware or reproduced on wedding invitations, announcements, place cards, and menus.

A WOMAN'S USE OF HERALDIC DEVICES The full coat of arms—shield, crest, and motto—or what is known as a "gentleman's heraldic bearings" is never properly used on personal belongings by a woman. Women in medieval days did not normally go forth in battle and therefore did not carry shields. It is proper form in England, to which we look for precedent since we have nothing resembling heraldic authority in our country, for a woman to use a crest on her stationery, her personal linens, and so on, but never a coat of arms or a shield. The lozenge, however, is approved. If a British woman is titled she uses the coronet of her rank above it. But a woman of an armigerous family, especially if she is unmarried or a widow, may use just the crest or the coat of arms itself—but only if blazoned on a lozenge. No woman uses a heraldic motto, for these were often aggressively masculine and not suited to social use.

A MARRIED WOMAN'S USE OF THE DEVICE A woman whose father has a coat of arms but whose husband does not shows better taste, actually, in saying goodbye to it and its feminine modifications once her family has used it on her wedding invitations and announcements and, if she wishes, on silver her family has given her. A painted coat could be displayed on the walls, not too conspicuously, but the device may not be adopted by either her husband or her children.

USE ON WEDDING INVITATIONS AND ANNOUNCEMENTS When the names of a girl's mother and father appear jointly on wedding invitations and announcements it is correct to use the father's coat of arms either in its complete form—shield, helmet, crest, and motto or, more commonly, the crest only—embossed without any color at the top of the invitation. If the bride's mother alone—or some woman sponsor alone—has her name on the invitation or announcement she should not use her husband's or father's coat of arms. She may, however, use her own crest or lozenge embossed without color.

SILVER MARKING AND THE COAT OF ARMS When the bride's family gives her silver they mark it with her father's crest and motto without the shield and helmet. Very large plain pieces such as soup tureens, punch bowls, and tea trays may carry a full marshaling—shield, helmet, crest, supporters, and mantling, with the motto on a "ribbon" beneath. If silver is given later to match the original set, it may be marked the same way. Silver given at any time by the groom's family may bear his crest. Additional silver purchased by husband and wife during the course of their marriage may, if they wish, have their respective arms "impaled" on it, but her family device should not be used, except possibly upon her personal silver or dressing table set. Even on strictly personal objects, however, it is better taste to use her husband's crest rather than her family's or, if he has none, to omit it altogether. As with any engraving of presents, no one should presume to engrave the family crest or coat of arms on any wedding silver unless the bride and groom have agreed.

CORRECT FORMS OF ADDRESS

At some time you may find it necessary to write a letter to your senator or representative, address an envelope to a couple of whom the wife is in the military, or introduce a friend to a member of the clergy. Such instances require special attention to the correct use of titles. Men and women who come by their titles either by presidential appointment, by election, by education, or through military service should as a gesture of respect be accorded the courtesy of being addressed properly, a form of protocol that should never be overlooked or ignored.

You are not expected to know or remember the formalities of address for every government official or religious personage, but if the occasion arises you should look in a reference book such as this one to find out how to write the Attorney General's name on a place card or what salutation to use for a bishop.

If you were to research the subject of addressing people in government positions, you would find variations in the usage of titles. For instance, the White House social office usage of a particular title may differ slightly from the United Nations' protocol division's practice, and the State Department in turn may differ from the Social List of Washington, D.C. (known as the Green Book). The Correct Forms of Address charts for government officials that follow are based primarily on what appears in the Social List of Washington, D.C.

UNITED STATES GOVERNMENT OFFICIALS AND INDIVIDUALS

In making formal presentations at banquets and so on, the form is always that of the full title: "Ladies and gentlemen, the President of the United States; the Vice President of the United States; the Honorable John J. Brown, Mayor of Trenton; Justice Coates of the Supreme Court . . ."

UNOFFICIAL RANKING OF GOVERNMENT OFFICIALS

The Table of Precedence that follows is titled "unofficial" because every administration can set up its own order of precedence for its members. The President, if he so chooses, can create new commissions and abolish others. He also has the right to raise in rank certain White House positions and to lower others. Traditionally, the order of government positions of cabinet rank and above has remained the same over the years. This list is carefully noted by the Green Book, but it is not officially published.

The President of the United States
The Vice President of the United States
The Speaker of the House of Representatives
The Chief Justice of the United States
Former Presidents of the United States
The Secretary of State
The Secretary General of the United Nations
Ambassadors of Foreign Powers
Widows of Former Presidents of the United States
Associate Justices of the Supreme Court of the United States
Retired Chief Justice of the Supreme Court of the United States
Retired Associate Justice of the Supreme Court of the United States
The Cabinet
    The Secretary of the Treasury
    The Secretary of Defense
    The Attorney General
    The Secretary of the Interior
    The Secretary of Agriculture
    The Secretary of Commerce
    The Secretary of Labor
    The Secretary of Health and Human Services
    The Secretary of Housing and Urban Development
    The Secretary of Transportation
    The Secretary of Energy
    The Secretary of Education
    The Secretary of Veterans Affairs
President pro Tempore of the Senate
The Senate
Governors of States
Former Vice Presidents of the United States
The House of Representatives
Assistants to the President
Chargés d'Affaires of Foreign Powers
The Under Secretaries and the Deputy Secretaries of the Executive
    Departments, when listed as the second person

Administrator, Agency for International Development
Director, United States Arms Control and Disarmament Agency
Director, United States Information Agency
United States Ambassador at Large
Secretaries of the Army, the Navy, and the Air Force
Chairman, Board of Governors of the Federal Reserve System
Chairman, Council on Environmental Quality
Chairman, Joint Chiefs of Staff
Chiefs of Staff of the Army, the Navy, the Air Force, Commandant of the Marine Corps (ranked according to date of appointment), and the Commandant of the Coast Guard
(5 Star) Generals of the Army and Fleet Admirals
The Secretary General, Organization of American States
Representatives to the Organization of American States
Director of Central Intelligence
Director, Office of Personnel Management
Administrator, National Aeronautics and Space Administration
Administrator, Federal Aviation Administration
Administrator, General Services Administration
Chairman, Merit Systems Protection Board
Administrator, Environmental Protection Agency
Deputy Assistants to the President
Deputy Under Secretaries of Executive Departments (See Cabinet for order)
Chief of Protocol
Assistant Secretaries of Executive Departments
Special Assistants to the President
Members of the Council of Economic Advisers
Active or Designate United States Ambassadors and Ministers (career rank, when in the United States)
The Mayor of the District of Columbia
Under Secretaries of the Army, the Navy, and the Air Force
(4 Star) Generals and Admirals
Assistant Secretaries of the Army, the Navy, and the Air Force
(3 Star) Lieutenant Generals and Vice Admirals
Former United States Ambassadors and Ministers to Foreign Countries
Ministers of Foreign Powers (serving in Embassies, not accredited)
Deputy Assistant Secretaries of the Executive Departments
Deputy Chief of Protocol
Counselors of Embassies or Legations of Foreign Powers
(2 Star) Major Generals and Rear Admirals
(1 Star) Brigadier Generals and Rear Admirals (Lower Half)
Assistant Chiefs of Protocol

United States Government Officials

PERSONAGE	OFFICIAL/BUSINESS ADDRESS	SOCIAL ADDRESS	SALUTATION
The President of the United States	The President[a] The White House 1600 Pennsylvania Avenue Washington, DC 20500	The President and Mrs. Adams[b] The White House 1600 Pennsylvania Avenue Washington, DC 20500	Dear Mr. President:
Former President	The Honorable William R. Watkins Office Address	The Honorable William R. Watkins and Mrs. Watkins[c] Home Address	Dear Mr. Watkins:[d]
The Vice President of the United States	The Vice President Old Executive Office Building Washington, DC 20501	The Vice President and Mrs. James[c] The Vice President's House Washington, DC 20501	Dear Mr. Vice President:
The Chief Justice	The Chief Justice The Supreme Court One First Street, N.E. Washington, DC 20543	The Chief Justice and Mrs. Meigs[c] Home Address	Dear Mr. Chief Justice:
Associate Justice[f] (man)	Justice Swenson The Supreme Court One First Street, N.E. Washington, DC 20543	Justice Swenson and Mrs. Swenson[c] Home Address	Dear Mr. Justice: or Dear Justice Swenson:
Associate Justice[f] (woman)	Justice Briggs The Supreme Court One First Street, N.E. Washington, DC 20543	Justice Briggs and Mr. John Briggs[h] Home Address	Dear Madam Justice: or Dear Justice Briggs:

[a] When writing or speaking to the President, his name is never used.
[b] When addressing a letter to the President's wife, only her last name is used: i.e., Mrs. Adams, The White House, Washington, DC 20500.
[c] In writing to the wife only, her husband's first name is included with his last name, i.e., Mrs. William R. Watkins.
[d] Out of respect and courtesy, it is common but not formally correct for former staff members and close friends to continue using the title Mr. President, or President Watkins.
[e] An alternative and more formal closing of a letter is "Very truly yours"; either is acceptable.
[f] A state Supreme Court justice would be addressed in the same manner, changing the address from Washington to the state capital.
[h] If the woman has the title, her husband's full name is included.

LETTER CLOSING	SPEAKING TO	INTRODUCING	PLACE CARDS
Most respectfully, or Very truly yours,	Mr. President or Sir	The President; The President of the United States	The President Mrs. Adams
Sincerely yours[e]	Mr. Watkins[d] or Sir	The Honorable William Watkins, former President of the United States; Former President Watkins	Mr. Watkins Mrs. Watkins
Sincerely yours,	Mr. Vice President or Sir	The Vice President; The Vice President of the United States	The Vice President Mrs. James
Sincerely yours,	Mr. Chief Justice; Mr. Justice Meigs or Sir	The Chief Justice	The Chief Justice Mrs. Meigs
Sincerely yours,	Justice Swenson; Mr. Justice or Sir	Justice Swenson	Justice Swenson Mrs. Swenson
Sincerely yours,	Justice Briggs; Madam Briggs or Ma'am	Justice Briggs	Justice Briggs Mr. Briggs

PERSONAGE	OFFICIAL/BUSINESS ADDRESS	SOCIAL ADDRESS	SALUTATION
Cabinet Member (man)	The Honorable[g] Joseph Suarez The Secretary of the Interior The Department of the Interior Washington, DC 20240	The Honorable The Secretary of the Interior and Mrs. Suarez[c] Home Address	Dear Mr. Secretary:
Cabinet Member (woman)	The Honorable[g] Katherine S. Rheinhold The Secretary of Commerce The Department of Commerce Washington, DC 20230	The Honorable The Secretary of Commerce and Mr. David G. Rheinhold[h] Home Address	Dear Madam Secretary:
The Attorney General (man)	The Honorable[g] Arthur Gosling The Attorney General of the United States The Department of Justice Washington, DC 20530	The Honorable The Attorney General and Mrs. Gosling[c] Home Address	Dear Mr. Attorney General:
The Attorney General: (woman)	The Honorable[g] Allison Anenberg The Attorney General of the United States The Department of Justice Washington, DC 20530	The Honorable The Attorney General and Mr. Frank Anenberg[h] Home Address	Dear Madam Attorney General:
Deputy Secretary of the Cabinet (man)	The Honorable[g] Frederick Greenberg Deputy Secretary of State Department of State Washington, DC 20520	The Honorable[i] Deputy Secretary of State and Mrs. Greenberg[c] Home Address	Dear Mr. Deputy Secretary:
Deputy Secretary of the Cabinet (woman)	The Honorable[g] Sarah Thorne Deputy Secretary of Transportation Washington, DC 20590	The Honorable[j] Deputy Secretary of Transportation and Mr. Wilson R. Thorne[h] Home Address	Dear Madam Deputy Secretary:

[g] This may more informally be abbreviated as "The Hon." or "Hon." In this case the title and name would all be on one line.

[i] A less formal but acceptable form is The Honorable and Mrs. (husband's first and last names). This alternative form of social address may be used for all government officials except cabinet officers. In the case of a senator, Senator and Mrs. Prentice Gates is acceptable. In the case of a judge, you may use Judge and Mrs. Arnold Warner, Jr.

[j] A less formal but acceptable form is The Honorable (wife's first and last names) and Mr. (first and last names).

LETTER CLOSING	SPEAKING TO	INTRODUCING	PLACE CARDS
Sincerely yours,	Mr. Secretary or Sir	The Secretary of the Interior, Joseph Suarez	The Secretary of the Interior Mrs. Suarez
Sincerely yours,	Madam Secretary or Ma'am	The Secretary of Commerce, Katherine Rheinhold	The Secretary of Commerce Mr. Rheinhold
Sincerely yours,	Mr. Attorney General or Sir	The Attorney General, Arthur Gosling	The Attorney General Mrs. Gosling
Sincerely yours,	Madam Attorney General or Ma'am	The Attorney General, Allison Anenberg	The Attorney General Mr. Anenberg
Sincerely yours,	Mr. Deputy Secretary or Sir	Deputy Secretary of State, Frederick Greenberg	Deputy Secretary of State Mrs. Greenberg
Sincerely yours,	Madam Deputy Secretary or Ma'am	Deputy Secretary of Transportation, Sarah Thorne	Deputy Secretary of Transportation Mr. Thorne

PERSONAGE	OFFICIAL/BUSINESS ADDRESS	SOCIAL ADDRESS	SALUTATION
Assistant Secretary of the Cabinet (man)	The Honorable[g] Robert G. Van Winkle Assistant Secretary of Defense The Pentagon Washington, DC 20301	The Honorable[i] Robert G. Van Winkle and Mrs. Van Winkle[c] Home Address	Dear Mr. Van Winkle:
Assistant Secretary of the Cabinet (woman)	The Honorable[g] Alice J. Proctor Assistant Secretary of Housing and Urban Development Washington, DC 20410	The Honorable Alice J. Proctor and Mr. Douglas Proctor[h] Home Address	Dear Ms. (or Mrs.) Proctor:
Speaker of the House of Representatives	The Honorable[g] Frank G. Conley The Speaker of the House of Representatives United States Capitol Washington, DC 20510	The Speaker of the[i] House of Representatives and Mrs. Conley[c] Home Address	Dear Mr. Speaker:
United States Senator (man)	The Honorable[g] Prentice Gates United States Senate Senate Office Building Washington, DC 20510	The Honorable[i] Prentice Gates and Mrs. Gates[c] Home Address	Dear Senator Gates:
United States Senator (woman)	The Honorable[g] Elizabeth King United States Senate Senate Office Building Washington, DC 20510	The Honorable Elizabeth King and Mr. George J. Miller[h] Home Address	Dear Senator King:
United States Representative[k] (man)	The Honorable[g] Richard Pelligrini House of Representatives House Office Building Washington, DC 20515	The Honorable[i] Richard Pelligrini and Mrs. Pelligrini[c] Home Address	Dear Mr. Pelligrini:
United States Representative[k] (woman)	The Honorable[g] Barbara L. Wadsworth House of Representatives House Office Building Washington, DC 20515	The Honorable Barbara L. Wadsworth and Mr. Gregory Wadsworth[h] Home Address	Dear Ms. (or Mrs.) Wadsworth:

[k] "Congressman" is never used. The word "Congressman" indicates either a senator or representative. "Representative" followed by last name is only used as an introduction.

LETTER CLOSING	SPEAKING TO	INTRODUCING	PLACE CARDS
Sincerely yours,	Mr. Van Winkle or Sir	Assistant Secretary of Defense, Robert Van Winkle	Mr. Van Winkle Mrs. Van Winkle
Sincerely yours,	Mrs. Proctor or Ma'am	Assistant Secretary of Housing and Urban Development, Alice Proctor	Mrs. Proctor Mr. Proctor
Sincerely yours,	Mr. Speaker or Sir	The Speaker of the House of Representatives, Frank Conley	The Speaker of the House of Representatives Mrs. Conley
Sincerely yours,	Senator Gates or Sir	Senator Prentice Gates from Idaho	Senator Gates Mrs. Gates
Sincerely yours,	Senator King or Ma'am	Senator Elizabeth King from Colorado	Senator King Mr. Miller
Sincerely yours,	Mr. Pelligrini or Sir	Representative Richard Pelligrini from New York	Mr. Pelligrini Mrs. Pelligrini
Sincerely yours,	Mrs. Wadsworth or Ma'am	Representative Barbara Wadsworth from Nevada	Mrs. Wadsworth Mr. Wadsworth

PERSONAGE	OFFICIAL/BUSINESS ADDRESS	SOCIAL ADDRESS	SALUTATION
United States Representative to the United Nations (man)	The Honorable[g] Roderick Horchow The United States Representative to the United Nations United Nations Plaza New York, NY 10017	The Honorable[i] The United Nations Representative to the United Nations and Mrs. Horchow[c] Home Address	Dear Mr. Ambassador:
United States Representative to the United Nations (woman)	The Honorable[g] Lydia Greeson The United States Representative to the United Nations United Nations Plaza New York, NY 10017	The Honorable[i] The United Nations Representative to the United Nations and Mr. Henry Greeson[h] Home Address	Dear Madam Ambassador:
American Ambassador[l] (man)	The Honorable[g] Norman J. Fenton The American Ambassador American Embassy 2, avenue Gabriel 75382 Paris, France	The Honorable[i] The Ambassador of the United States of America and Mrs. Fenton[c] American Embassy 2, avenue Gabriel 75382 Paris, France	Dear Mr. Ambassador:
American Ambassador[l] (woman)	The Honorable[g] Helen Povich The American Ambassador American Embassy Via Veneto 119 00187 Rome, Italy	The Honorable[i] The Ambassador of the United States of America and Mr. Albert G. Povich[h] American Embassy Via Veneto 119 00187 Rome, Italy	Dear Madam Ambassador:
American Chargé d'Affaires, Consul General (man)	The Honorable[g] Charles R. Edison American Chargé d'Affaires (or other of these titles) Office Address	The Honorable[i] Charles R. Edison and Mrs. Edison[c] Home Address	Dear Mr. Edison:
American Chargé d'Affaires, Consul General (woman)	The Honorable[g] Lisa Vincent American Consul General (or other of these titles) Office Address	The Honorable Lisa Vincent Home Address	Dear Ms. (or Miss) Vincent:

[l] In presenting American ambassadors in any Latin American country, always include the phrase "of the United States of America" after Embassy. Avoid the term "American Embassy" or "American Ambassador." For the latter say, "Ambassador of the United States." The reason for this is that Latin Americans consider the South and Central American states "America" too.

LETTER CLOSING	SPEAKING TO	INTRODUCING	PLACE CARDS
Sincerely yours,	Ambassador or Sir	The United States Representative to the United Nations, Roderick Horchow	Ambassador Horchow Mrs. Horchow
Sincerely yours,	Ambassador or Ma'am	The United States Representative to the United Nations, Lydia Greeson	Ambassador Greeson Mr. Greeson
Sincerely yours,	Mr. Ambassador or Sir	The American Ambassador, Norman Fenton	Ambassador Fenton Mrs. Fenton
Sincerely yours,	Madam Ambassador or Ma'am	The American Ambassador, Helen Povich	Ambassador Povich Mr. Povich
Sincerely yours,	Mr. Edison	Mr. Charles Edison	Mr. Edison Mrs. Edison
Sincerely yours,	Miss Vincent or Ms. Vincent	Miss Lisa Vincent or Ms. Vincent	Miss Vincent or Ms. Vincent

PERSONAGE	OFFICIAL/BUSINESS ADDRESS	SOCIAL ADDRESS	SALUTATION
Governor[m] (man)	The Honorable[g] John J. O'Connell The Governor of Connecticut State Capitol Hartford, CT 06115	The Honorable[i] The Governor of Connecticut and Mrs. O'Connell[c] Home Address	Dear Governor O'Connell:
Governor[m] (woman)	The Honorable[g] Louise Warburg The Governor of California State Capitol Sacramento, CA 95814	The Honorable[j] The Governor of California and Mr. Richard Warburg[h] Home Address	Dear Governor Warburg:
State Senator, Representative, Assemblyman (man)	The Honorable[g] Philip B. Hernandez Office Address	The Honorable[i] Philip B. Hernandez and Mrs. Hernandez[c] Home Address	Dear Mr. Hernandez:
State Senator, Representative, Assemblyman (woman)	The Honorable[g] Sylvia J. Wei Office Address	The Honorable Sylvia J. Wei and Mr. John Wei[h] Home Address	Dear Ms. (Mrs.) Wei:
Mayor (man)	The Honorable[g] Hugh O'Neill Mayor of Providence City Hall Providence, RI 02903	The Honorable[i] Hugh O'Neill and Mrs. O'Neill[c] Home Address	Dear Mayor O'Neill: or Dear Mr. Mayor:
Mayor (woman)	The Honorable[g] Susan Bartlett Mayor of Chicago Chicago, IL 60602	The Honorable Susan Bartlett and Mr. Francis G. Bartlett[h] Home Address	Dear Mayor Bartlett: or Dear Madam Mayor:
Judge (man)	The Honorable[g] Arnold Warner, Jr. Justice, Appellate Division Supreme Court of the State of New York Office Address	The Honorable[i] Arnold Warner, Jr. and Mrs. Warner[c] Home Address	Dear Mr. Justice: or Dear Justice Warner:
Judge (woman)	The Honorable[g] Barbara Cranston Family Court State of New York Office Address	The Honorable Barbara Cranston and Mr. Walter S. Cranston[h] Home Address	Dear Judge Cranston:

[m] The word "Excellency" may be used as a courtesy in any state: i.e., His Excellency, the Governor, State Capitol, Hartford, CT 06115; or Her Excellency, the Governor, State Capitol, Sacramento, CA 95814.

LETTER CLOSING	SPEAKING TO	INTRODUCING	PLACE CARDS
Sincerely yours,	Governor; Governor O'Connell or Sir	Governor John O'Connell of Connecticut	Governor O'Connell Mrs. O'Connell
Sincerely yours,	Governor; Governor Warburg or Ma'am	Governor Louise Warburg of California	Governor Warburg Mr. Warburg
Sincerely yours,	Mr. Hernandez	Mr. Philip Hernandez	Mr. Hernandez Mrs. Hernandez
Sincerely yours,	Mrs. Wei	Mrs. Sylvia Wei	Mrs. Wei Mr. Wei
Sincerely yours,	Mayor O'Neill; Mr. Mayor	Mayor Hugh O'Neill of Providence;	Mayor O'Neill Mrs. O'Neill
Sincerely yours,	Mayor Bartlett; Madam Mayor	Mayor Susan Bartlett of Illinois	Mayor Bartlett Mr. Bartlett
Sincerely yours,	Mr. Justice; Judge Warner	Justice Warner; Judge Arnold Warner	Mr. Justice Warner Mrs. Warner
Sincerely yours,	Judge Cranston	Judge Barbara Cranston	Judge Cranston Mr. Cranston

PERSONAGE	OFFICIAL/BUSINESS ADDRESS	SOCIAL ADDRESS	SALUTATION
Lawyer[n] (man)	Mr. Angus J. Gordon Office Address	Mr. and Mrs. Angus J. Gordon Home Address	Dear Mr. Gordon:
Lawyer[n] (woman)	Ms. Mary Leonard Office Address	Mr. and Mrs. Charles Leonard Home Address	Dear Ms. (or Mrs.) Leonard:
University President[o] (man)	Dr. Jonathan B. Horgan, President Brown University Address	Dr. and Mrs. Jonathan B. Horgan Home Address	Dear Dr. Horgan:
University President[o] (woman)	Dr. Constance West, President Carleton College Address	Dr. Constance West and Mr. Bernard West Home Address	Dear Dr. West:
Dean[p] (man)	Dr. Howard Williamson Dean of the School of Journalism Howard University Address	Dr. and Mrs. Howard Williamson Home Address	Dear Dr. Williamson:
Dean[p] (woman)	Dr. Joan Richter College of Business Administration Yale University Address	Dr. Joan Richter and Mr. David Fox Home Address	Dear Dr. Richter:
Professor[q] (man)	Professor George Bertolli Department of History Arizona State College Address	Professor and Mrs. George Bertolli Home Address	Dear Professor Bertolli:
Professor[q] (woman)	Professor Josephine G. Butler Department of Mathematics University of Colorado Address	Mr. and Mrs. Roger Butler Home Address	Dear Professor Butler:

[n] "Esquire" may be used after any lawyer's name: i.e., Angus J. Gordon, Esq. The practice is, however, not so widely used as formerly.
[o] Many prefer to use "President" instead of "Dr." in writing, speaking to, or introducing.
[p] If a dean does not hold a doctoral degree, "Dean" may replace "Dr." throughout.
[q] If a professor holds a doctoral degree, "Dr." may replace "Professor" throughout.

LETTER CLOSING	SPEAKING TO	INTRODUCING	PLACE CARDS
Sincerely yours,	Mr. Gordon	Mr. Angus Gordon	Mr. Gordon Mrs. Gordon
Sincerely yours,	Mrs. Leonard	Mrs. Mary Leonard	Mrs. Leonard Mr. Leonard
Sincerely yours,	Dr. Horgan	Dr. Jonathan Horgan	Dr. Horgan Mrs. Horgan
Sincerely yours,	Dr. West	Dr. Constance West	Dr. West Mr. West
Sincerely yours,	Dr. Williamson	Dr. Howard Williamson	Dr. Williamson Mrs. Williamson
Sincerely yours,	Dr. Richter	Dr. Joan Richter	Dr. Richter Mr. Fox
Sincerely yours,	Professor Bertolli	Professor George Bertolli	Professor Bertolli Mrs. Bertolli
Sincerely yours,	Professor Butler	Professor Josephine Butler	Professor Butler Mr. Butler

PERSONAGE	OFFICIAL/BUSINESS ADDRESS	SOCIAL ADDRESS	SALUTATION
United Nations Secretary General	His Excellency The Secretary General of the United Nations and Mrs. Meunier United Nations Plaza New York, NY 10017	His Excellency The Secretary General of the United Nations and Mrs. Meunier[c] Home Address	Dear Mr. Secretary General:
Foreign Ambassador (man)	His Excellency[r] Ricardo Correia The Ambassador of Brazil 3006 Massachusetts Avenue Washington, DC 20008	His Excellency The Ambassador of Brazil and Mrs.[s] Correia[c] Home Address	Excellency: or Dear Mr. Ambassador:
Foreign Ambassador (woman)	Her Excellency[r] Simone Audibert The Ambassador of France 4101 Reservoir Road, N.W. Washington, DC 20007	Her Excellency The Ambassador of France and Mr. Pierre Audibert[h] Home Address	Excellency; or Dear Madam Ambassador:

[r] Foreign ambassadors are referred to as "Ambassador," with the name of the country: i.e., Ambassador of Ireland; Ambassador of Peru, with the following exceptions: Ambassador of the Argentine Republic; British Ambassador; Chinese Ambassador; Ambassador of the Netherlands; Ambassador of the Union of South Africa. Ambassadors are addressed at the offices of their embassies: i.e., Ambassador of the Argentine Republic, Embassy of the Argentine Republic.

Foreign presidents, ambassadors, and cabinet ministers are referred to as His Excellency or Her Excellency; if they have royal titles or military rank, that title is included after "His Excellency" or "Her Excellency."

[s] In writing an envelope to a foreign ambassador's wife, address her as "Mrs." unless she has a royal or personal title, such as "Princess" or "Lady."

LETTER CLOSING	SPEAKING TO	INTRODUCING	PLACE CARDS
Sincerely yours,	Mr. Secretary General or Sir	The Secretary General of the United Nations, His Excellency, Pierre Meunier	The Secretary General Mrs. Meunier
Sincerely yours,	Mr. Ambassador; Excellency or Sir	The Ambassador of Brazil, Ricardo Correia	The Ambassador of Brazil Mrs. Correia
Sincerely yours,	Madam Ambassador; Excellency or Ma'am	The Ambassador of France, Simone Audibert	The Ambassador of France Mr. Audibert

United States military personnel

How to tell military rank Our armed forces, organized under the Department of Defense, consist of the Army, the Navy, and the Air Force. The Department of the Navy consists of two separate military services, the U.S. Navy and the U.S. Marine Corps. In time of war the Coast Guard is under the jurisdiction of the Navy but in time of peace operates under the Department of Transportation.

In the Army, devices signifying the corps in which soldiers serve—the caduceus of the doctor, the cross of the chaplain—are worn on the lapel. In the Navy these staff officer devices are worn on the sleeve above the stripes indicating rank.

The positions of General of the Army and Navy Fleet Admiral were created to give the highest-ranking American military leaders acting on international joint staffs during wartime a rank equivalent to the foreign position of field marshal. There are no longer the positions General of the Army and Navy Fleet Admiral.

The army
Cap device—eagle clutching two arrows

In order of rank the officer personnel of the Army are:

GENERAL—Four silver stars
LIEUTENANT GENERAL—Three silver stars
MAJOR GENERAL—Two silver stars
BRIGADIER GENERAL—One silver star
COLONEL—Silver eagle
LIEUTENANT COLONEL—Silver oak leaf
MAJOR—Gold oak leaf
CAPTAIN—Two silver bars
FIRST LIEUTENANT—One silver bar
SECOND LIEUTENANT—One gold bar
CHIEF WARRANT OFFICER—One silver bar with two, three, or four enamel squares (grades two, three, or four).
WARRANT OFFICER, JUNIOR GRADE—One silver bar with one enamel square.

The navy
Cap device—crossed anchors, shield, and eagle

On blue uniforms, rank is indicated by gold stripes on sleeves; on white uniforms, rank is indicated on detachable shoulder boards. On khaki and winter blue uniforms, rank is indicated by gold or silver collar devices.

In order of rank the officer personnel of the Navy are:

ADMIRAL—Four silver stars, one 2″ stripe, and three ½″ sleeve stripes, with star of line officer or corps device

VICE ADMIRAL—Three silver stars, one 2″ stripe, and two ½″ sleeve stripes, star of line officer or corps device

REAR ADMIRAL—Two silver stars, one 2″ stripe, and one ½″ sleeve stripe, star of line officer or corps device

COMMODORE—One silver star, one 2″ sleeve stripe, star of line officer or corps device

CAPTAIN—Silver spread eagle, four ½″ stripes, star of line officer or corps device

COMMANDER—Silver oak leaf, three ½″ stripes, star of line officer or corps device

LIEUTENANT COMMANDER—Gold oak leaf, two ½″ stripes with ¼″ one between, star of line officer or corps device

LIEUTENANT—Two silver bars, two ½″ stripes, star of line officer or corps device

LIEUTENANT, JUNIOR GRADE—One silver bar, one ½″ stripe with ¼″ one above, star of line officer or corps device

ENSIGN—One gold bar, one ½″ gold stripe, star of line officer or corps device

CHIEF WARRANT OFFICER—One ¼″ broken gold stripe and specialty device

WARRANT OFFICER—One ¼″ broken gold stripe and specialty device

THE MARINE CORPS
Cap device—eagle, globe, and anchor

The top rank in the Marine Corps is general. He wears the four stars and shoulder rank of the Army. Other insignia for officers in the Marine Corps are the same as those in the Army.

THE AIR FORCE
Cap device—wings flanking U.S. great seal

The top rank in the Air Force is general. All insignia in the Air Force are the same as those in the Army.

THE COAST GUARD
Cap distinguished by a single anchor, eagle, and shield

The top rank in the Coast Guard is admiral. All insignia are the same as those in the Navy.

MILITARY FORMS OF ADDRESS When two people in the service marry and the woman assumes her husband's last name, she naturally keeps her own rating or rank. If the wife outranks her husband, she comes first in formal address, in introductions, and in the way one addresses invitations to the couple: "Lt. Col. [Lengthy titles may be abbreviated] Marian Peabody, U.S. Air Force, and Captain John Peabody, U.S. Air Force, Andrews Air Force Base," etc.

Noncommissioned officers are addressed officially by title.

A naval officer while in command of a ship is always called "Captain" during the period of command regardless of his actual rank.

A medical officer is called "Doctor" except if he or she is the head of a base hospital, in which case the actual rank is used; and if a doctor becomes a general or an admiral, he is always addressed by his rank, even socially, as long as he or she remains in service.

Chaplains in all branches of the armed forces are called by their military rank, officially and socially. Informally they may be addressed as Chaplain, Father, or Rabbi.

National Guard and Reserve officers not on active duty do not use their titles socially or in business affairs unless their activities have some bearing on military matters.

In any service branch a warrant officer, both officially and socially, is called Mr., Mrs., Ms., or Miss except for formal or very official occasions.

After retirement a person retains his military title except in any instance where it might look as though his activity had the official sponsorship of the Defense Department or any section of it. When a retired officer travels abroad, he or she should not use an official service title while making a public appearance, unless the appropriate overseas commander gives his approval.

ABBREVIATIONS OF MILITARY RANK

	ARMY	AIR FORCE	MARINE CORPS
General	GEN	Gen	Gen
Lieutenant General	LTG	Lt Gen	LtGen
Major General	MG	Maj Gen	MajGen
Brigadier General	BG	Brig Gen	BGen
Colonel	COL	Col	Col
Lieutenant Colonel	LTC	Lt Col	LtCol
Major	MAJ	Maj	Maj
Captain	CPT	Capt	Capt
First Lieutenant	1LT	1st Lt	1stLt
Second Lieutenant	2LT	2nd Lt	2ndLt

	NAVY AND COAST GUARD
Admiral	ADM
Vice Admiral	VADM
Rear Admiral	RADM
Captain	CAPT
Commander	CDR

Lieutenant Commander	LCDR
Lieutenant	LT
Lieutenant, junior grade	LTJG
Ensign	ENS

Note: In official correspondences, rank and ratings are abbreviated and fully capitalized in the naval service, and are partially capitalized in the other services.

United States Military Personnel

PERSONAGE	OFFICIAL/BUSINESS ADDRESS	SOCIAL ADDRESS	SALUTATION
JOINT CHIEFS OF STAFF **Chairman**	General Jerauld L. Elwell The Chairman of the Joint Chiefs of Staff The Pentagon Washington, DC 20318	General and Mrs. Jerauld L. Elwell Home Address	Dear General Elwell:
Chief of Staff, U. S. Army	General Robert Telesco The Chief of Staff of the Army United States Army The Pentagon Washington, DC 20310	General and Mrs. Robert Telesco Home Address	Dear General Telesco:
Chief of Naval Operations	Admiral Gordon Bachman II Chief of Naval Operations Navy Department Washington, DC 20350	Admiral and Mrs. Gordon Bachman II Home Address	Dear Admiral Bachman:
Chief of Staff, U. S. Air Force	General Philip R. Wooster The Chief of Staff of the Air Force United States Air Force The Pentagon Washington, DC 20330	General and Mrs. Philip R. Wooster Home Address	Dear General Wooster:
Commandant of the Marine Corps	General Clark Walton The Commandant of the Marine Corps United States Marine Corps Headquarters United States Marine Corps Washington, DC 20380	General and Mrs. Clark Walton Home Address	Dear General Walton:

LETTER CLOSING	SPEAKING TO	INTRODUCING	PLACE CARDS
Sincerely yours,	General Elwell	General Elwell, Chairman of the Joint Chiefs of Staff	General Elwell Mrs. Elwell
Sincerely yours,	General Telesco	General Telesco, Chief of Staff of the Army	General Telesco Mrs. Telesco
Sincerely yours,	Admiral Bachman	Admiral Bachman, Chief of Naval Operations	Admiral Bachman Mrs. Bachman
Sincerely yours,	General Wooster	General Wooster, Chief of Staff of the Air Force	General Wooster Mrs. Wooster
Sincerely yours,	General Walton	General Walton, Commandant of the Marine Corps	General Walton Mrs. Walton

PERSONAGE	OFFICIAL/BUSINESS ADDRESS	SOCIAL ADDRESS	SALUTATION
THE ARMY, THE AIR FORCE, THE MARINE CORPS			
General	General Ann O'Hara, U. S. Marine Corps[a] Business or P.O. Address	General Ann O'Hara and Mr. James G. O'Hara Home Address	Dear General O'Hara:
Lieutenant General	Lieutenant General Ann O'Hara, U. S. Army Business or P.O. Address	Lieutenant General Ann O'Hara and Mr. James G. O'Hara Home Address	Dear General O'Hara:
Major General	Major General Ann O'Hara, U. S. Air Force Business or P.O. Address	Major General Ann O'Hara and Mr. James G. O'Hara Home Address	Dear General O'Hara:
Brigadier General	Brigadier General Ann O'Hara, U. S. Army Business or P.O. Address	Brigadier General Ann O'Hara and Mr. James G. O'Hara Home Address	Dear General O'Hara:
Colonel	Colonel Joseph Schmidt, U. S. Air Force Business or P.O. Address	Colonel and Mrs. Joseph Schmidt Home Address	Dear Colonel Schmidt:
Lieutenant Colonel	Lieutenant Colonel Joseph Schmidt, U. S. Army Business or P.O. Address	Lieutenant Colonel and Mrs. Joseph Schmidt[b] Home Address	Dear Colonel Schmidt:
Major	Major Albert S. Bowman, U. S. Marine Corps Business or P.O. Address	Major and Mrs. Albert S. Bowman Home Address	Dear Major Bowman:
Captain	Captain Patricia Van Westering, U. S. Army Business or P.O. Address	Captain Patricia Van Westering and Mr. Edward Van Westering Home Address	Dear Captain Van Westering:

[a] More informally, service designations may be abbreviated as follows: USA, USN, USAF, USMC, USCG. For Reserve personnel: USAR, USNR, USAFR, USMCR, USCGR.
[b] In formal social correspondence, military titles are not abbreviated, except in the case of lengthy titles, which may be abbreviated thus: Lt. Col., Lt. Cdr., 2nd Lt., etc.

LETTER CLOSING	SPEAKING TO	INTRODUCING	PLACE CARDS
Sincerely yours,	General O'Hara	General O'Hara	General O'Hara Mr. O'Hara
Sincerely yours,	General O'Hara	Lieutenant General O'Hara	General O'Hara Mr. O'Hara
Sincerely yours,	General O'Hara	Major General O'Hara	General O'Hara Mr. O'Hara
Sincerely yours,	General O'Hara	Brigadier General O'Hara	General O'Hara Mr. O'Hara
Sincerely yours,	Colonel Schmidt	Colonel Schmidt	Colonel Schmidt Mrs. Schmidt
Sincerely yours,	Colonel Schmidt	Lieutenant Colonel Schmidt	Colonel Schmidt Mrs. Schmidt
Sincerely yours,	Major Bowman	Major Bowman	Major Bowman Mrs. Bowman
Sincerely yours,	Captain Van Westering	Captain Van Westering	Captain Van Westering Mr. Van Westering

PERSONAGE	OFFICIAL/BUSINESS ADDRESS	SOCIAL ADDRESS	SALUTATION
First Lieutenant	First Lieutenant Gilbert Warren, U. S. Air Force Business or P.O. Address	First Lieutenant and Mrs. Gilbert Warren Home Address	Dear Lieutenant Warren:
Second Lieutenant	Second Lieutenant Gilbert Warren, U. S. Marine Corps Business or P.O. Address	Second Lieutenant and Mrs. Gilbert Warren Home Address	Dear Lieutenant Warren:
THE NAVY, THE COAST GUARD[c]			
Admiral	Admiral Russell B. Jordan, U. S. Navy[a] Business or P.O. Address	Admiral and Mrs. Russell B. Jordan Home Address	Dear Admiral Jordan:
Vice Admiral	Vice Admiral Russell B. Jordan, U. S. Navy Business or P.O. Address	Vice Admiral and Mrs. Russell B. Jordan Home Address	Dear Admiral Jordan:
Rear Admiral	Rear Admiral Russell B. Jordan, U. S. Navy Business or P.O. Address	Rear Admiral and Mrs. Russell B. Jordan Home Address	Dear Admiral Jordan:
Captain	Captain Alice Engle, U. S. Coast Guard Business or P.O. Address	Captain Alice Engle and Mr. John Engle Home Address	Dear Captain Engle:
Commander	Commander Rufus F. Williamson, U. S. Navy Business or P.O. Address	Commander and Mrs. Rufus F. Williamson Home Address	Dear Commander Williamson:
Lieutenant Commander	Lieutenant Commander Rufus F. Williamson, U. S. Navy Business or P.O. Address	Lieutenant Commander and Mrs. Rufus F. Williamson Home Address	Dear Mr. Williamson:
Lieutenant	Lieutenant Ann Schultz, U. S. Coast Guard Business or P.O. Address	Lieutenant Ann Schultz and Mr. John J. Schultz Home Address	Dear Mrs. Schultz:

[c] The rank of commodore is omitted here since it is used only during wartime and there are no commodores at present.

[d] When speaking to a lieutenant commander, it is proper to say "Mr.," "Mrs.," "Miss," or "Ms." However, current social usage allows the courtesy title of "Commander." The actual rank is indicated by the two and a half stripes on the uniform.

LETTER CLOSING	SPEAKING TO	INTRODUCING	PLACE CARDS
Sincerely yours,	Lieutenant Warren	First Lieutenant Warren	Lieutenant Warren Mrs. Warren
Sincerely yours,	Lieutenant Warren	Second Lieutenant Warren	Lieutenant Warren Mrs. Warren
Sincerely yours,	Admiral Jordan	Admiral Jordan	Admiral Jordan Mrs. Jordan
Sincerely yours,	Admiral Jordan	Vice Admiral Jordan	Admiral Jordan Mrs. Jordan
Sincerely yours,	Admiral Jordan	Rear Admiral Jordan	Admiral Jordan Mrs. Jordan
Sincerely yours,	Captain Engle	Captain Engle	Captain Engle Mr. Engle
Sincerely yours,	Commander Williamson	Commander Williamson	Commander Williamson Mrs. Williamson
Sincerely yours,	Mr. Williamson[d]	Lieutenant Commander Williamson	Mr. Williamson Mrs. Williamson
Sincerely yours,	Mrs. Schultz	Lieutenant Schultz	Mrs. Schultz Mr. Schultz

PERSONAGE	OFFICIAL/BUSINESS ADDRESS	SOCIAL ADDRESS	SALUTATION
Lieutenant, junior grade	Lieutenant, junior grade Ann Schultz, U. S. Coast Guard Business or P.O. Address	Lieutenant, junior grade Ann Schultz and Mr. John J. Schultz Home Address	Dear Mrs. Schultz:
Ensign	Ensign Alfred Grimes, U. S. Coast Guard Business or P.O. Address	Ensign and Mrs. Alfred Grimes Home Address	Dear Mr. Grimes:
UNITED STATES MILITARY ACADEMIES			
Cadet of the United States Military Academy	Cadet Florence Kruger Company D-2, USCC West Point, NY 10996		Dear Cadet Kruger:
Cadet of the United States Air Force Academy	Cadet Frank Rudolph United States Air Force Academy Colorado Springs, CO 80840		Dear Cadet Rudolph:
Midshipman of the United States Merchant Marine Academy	Midshipman Alice Telson United States Merchant Marine Academy Kings Point, NY 11024		Dear Midshipman Telson:
Midshipman of the United States Naval Academy	Midshipman John Barker United States Naval Academy Annapolis, MD 21402		Dear Midshipman Barker:
Cadet of the United States Coast Guard Academy	Cadet 2/c Gregory Cowles United States Coast Guard Academy New London, CT 06320		Dear Cadet Cowles:

LETTER CLOSING	SPEAKING TO	INTRODUCING	PLACE CARDS
Sincerely yours,	Mrs. Schultz	Lieutenant Schultz	Mrs. Schultz Mr. Schultz
Sincerely yours,	Mr. Grimes	Ensign Grimes	Mr. Grimes Mrs. Grimes
Sincerely yours,	Cadet Kruger; Miss Kruger	Cadet Kruger	Cadet Kruger
Sincerely yours,	Cadet Rudolph; Mr. Rudolph	Cadet Rudolph	Cadet Rudolph
Sincerely yours,	Midshipman Telson; Miss Telson	Midshipman Telson	Midshipman Telson
Sincerely yours,	Midshipman Barker; Mr. Barker	Midshipman Barker	Midshipman Barker
Sincerely yours,	Cadet Cowles; Mr. Cowles	Cadet Cowles	Cadet Cowles

The Clergy

PERSONAGE	OFFICIAL/BUSINESS ADDRESS	SOCIAL ADDRESS	SALUTATION
EASTERN ORTHODOX COMMUNION[a]			
Patriarch	His All Holiness, the Ecumenical Patriarch of Constantinople Istanbul, Turkey		Your All Holiness:
Archbishop[b]	The Most Reverend Michael Archbishop of Cincinnati Address		Your Eminence:
Bishop	The Right Reverend Basil Althos Bishop of Chicago Address		Your Grace: (preferred) Right Reverend Sir: (business) My dear Bishop: (social)
Archimandrite	The Very Reverend James Papas Address		Reverend Sir: (business) Your Reverence: (social) Dear Father Papas:
Priest[c]	Reverend Father Nicholas Kontos Address		Dear Father Kontos:

[a] Greek Orthodox clergymen choose before ordination whether or not they are to be celibate priests. All highest clergymen—patriarchs, archbishops, bishops, and archimandrites—are usually celibates. There are three other patriarchs in ancient sees, those of Jerusalem, Alexandria, and Antioch.

[b] Metropolitans, who supersede suffragan bishops in rank, are found in large cities, mainly among the Russian and Syrian Orthodox congregations, but in Greece they function, as well, for the Church of Greece. They are addressed as The Most Reverend Peter, Metropolitan of Boston, etc., and, like archbishops, are referred to as Your Eminence.

[c] In the case of a noncelibate priest the form including his wife would be The Reverend Nicholas Kontos and Mrs. Kontos in the United States, or, abroad, The Reverend Nicholas Kontos and Madame Kontos.

LETTER CLOSING	SPEAKING TO	INTRODUCING	PLACE CARDS
Respectfully yours,	Your All Holiness	His All Holiness	
Respectfully yours,	Your Eminence	His Eminence	His Eminence, Archbishop Michael
Respectfully yours,	Your Grace	His Grace	Bishop Althos
Respectfully yours,	Father James or Father Papas	Father James or Father Papas	The Very Reverend James Papas
Respectfully yours,	Father	Father Kontos	Father Kontos

PERSONAGE	OFFICIAL/BUSINESS ADDRESS	SOCIAL ADDRESS	SALUTATION
JEWISH			
Rabbi with scholastic degree[d] (man)	Rabbi Nathan Sachs, D.D., LL.D. Temple Emmanuel[e] Address	Rabbi (or Dr.) and Mrs. Nathan Sachs (some prefer Rabbi to Doctor) Home Address	Dear Rabbi (or Dr.) Sachs:
Rabbi with scholastic degree[f] (woman)	Rabbi Helen Kreisler, D.D., LL.D. Congregation Bnai Israel Address	Rabbi (or Dr.) Helen Kreisler Home Address	Dear Rabbi (or Dr.) Kreisler:
Rabbi without scholastic degree (man)	Rabbi Harold Schwartz Beth David Synagogue Address	Rabbi and Mrs. Harold Schwartz Home Address	Dear Rabbi Schwartz:
Rabbi without scholastic degree (woman)	Rabbi Joan Friedman Central Synagogue Address	Rabbi Joan Friedman and Mr. Arnold Friedman Home Address	Dear Rabbi Friedman:
Cantor (music minister of congregation; soloist at worship services) (man)	Cantor Chaim Levy Beth David Synagogue Address	Cantor and Mrs. Chaim Levy Home Address	Dear Cantor Levy:
Cantor (woman)	Cantor Marjorie Smith Central Synagogue Address	Cantor Marjorie Smith and Mr. Robert Smith Home Address	Dear Cantor Smith:
PROTESTANT			
Clergyman with doctoral degree	The Reverend Joseph E. Long, D.D. Address	The Reverend Dr. and Mrs. Joseph E. Long Home Address	Dear Dr. Long:
Clergywoman with doctoral degree	The Reverend Agnes Godfried, D.D. Address	The Reverend Dr. Agnes Godfried and Mr. James Godfried Home Address	Dear Dr. Godfried:

[d] Not all rabbis necessarily hold both degrees. In addressing a rabbi, give him whatever degree or degrees he possesses.

[e] The words "temple" and "synagogue" are interchangeable, but Orthodox and Conservative congregations tend to prefer "synagogue" while Reform congregations tend to use "temple." The word "church" is never used.

[f] At the present time, women rabbis do not serve in Orthodox congregations.

LETTER CLOSING	SPEAKING TO	INTRODUCING	PLACE CARDS
Sincerely yours,	Rabbi Sachs; Dr. Sachs; Rabbi	Rabbi Nathan Sachs; Dr. Nathan Sachs	Rabbi Sachs Mrs. Sachs
Sincerely yours,	Rabbi Kreisler, Dr. Kreisler; Rabbi	Rabbi Helen Kreisler; Dr. Helen Kreisler	Rabbi Kreisler
Sincerely yours,	Rabbi Schwartz; Rabbi	Rabbi Harold Schwartz	Rabbi Schwartz Mrs. Schwartz
Sincerely yours,	Rabbi Friedman; Rabbi	Rabbi Joan Friedman	Rabbi Friedman Mr. Friedman
Sincerely yours,	Cantor Levy	Cantor Chaim Levy	Cantor Levy Mrs. Levy
Sincerely yours,	Cantor Smith	Cantor Marjorie Smith	Cantor Smith Mr. Smith
Sincerely yours,	Dr. Long	The Reverend Dr. Joseph Long	Dr. Long Mrs. Long
Sincerely yours,	Dr. Godfried	The Reverend Dr. Agnes Godfried	Dr. Godfried Mr. Godfried

PERSONAGE	OFFICIAL/BUSINESS ADDRESS	SOCIAL ADDRESS	SALUTATION
Clergyman without doctoral degree[g]	The Reverend Frank K. Hanson Address	The Reverend and Mrs. Frank K. Hanson Home Address	Dear Mr. Hanson:
Clergywoman without doctoral degree	The Reverend Margaret Bruckman Address	The Reverend Margaret Bruckman Home Address	Dear Ms. Bruckman:
Presiding Bishop of the Episcopal Church in the United States[h]	The Most Reverend Peter Flagg, D.D., LL.D. Presiding Bishop Address	The Most Reverend Dr. and Mrs. Peter Flagg Home Address	Dear Bishop Flagg:
Bishop of the Episcopal Church (man)	The Right Reverend Gideon Carew, D.D. Bishop of Cincinnati Address	The Right Reverend Dr. and Mrs. Gideon Carew Home Address	Dear Bishop Carew:
Bishop of the Episcopal Church (woman)	The Right Reverend Caroline Keating, D.D. Bishop of South Dakota Address	The Right Reverend Caroline Keating and Mr. David Keating Home Address	Dear Bishop Keating:
Dean	The Very Reverend John Brown, D.D., Dean of St. Matthew's Cathedral Address	The Very Reverend and Mrs. John Brown Home address	Dear Dean Brown:
Archdeacon	The Venerable Charles G. Smith Archdeacon of Richmond Address	The Venerable and Mrs. Charles G. Smith Home Address	Dear Archdeacon Smith:

[g] The use of "Father," designating an Episcopal clergyman or a priest who is not a member of a religious order, is a matter of the clergyman's own preference. When "Father" is used in writing it is usually coupled with the surname of the clergyman—The Reverend Father Huntington, O.H.C., without the Christian name. In direct reference, it is Father Huntington. However, in the Episcopal order of Franciscans, where there is a name conferred by the order (as among Roman Catholic religious orders) it would be The Reverend Father Joseph, O.S.F., in writing, and Father or Father Joseph in direct reference. Lay brothers are addressed in writing as Brother Charles, O.H.C., and in direct reference as Brother or Brother Charles.

[h] All church dignitaries in any formal presentation before audiences of any kind are given their full titles—for example, The Most Reverend Peter Flagg, Presiding Bishop of the Episcopal Church, U.S.A.

LETTER CLOSING	SPEAKING TO	INTRODUCING	PLACE CARDS
Sincerely yours,	Mr. Hanson	The Reverend Frank Hanson	Mr. Hanson Mrs. Hanson
Sincerely yours,	Ms. Bruckman	The Reverend Margaret Bruckman	Ms. Bruckman
Sincerely yours,	Bishop Flagg	The Most Reverend Peter Flagg, the Presiding Bishop of the Episcopal Church	The Most Reverend Flagg Mrs. Flagg
Sincerely yours,	Bishop Carew	The Right Reverend Gideon Carew, the Bishop of Cincinnati	The Right Reverend Carew Mrs. Carew
Sincerely yours,	Bishop Keating	The Right Reverend Caroline Keating, the Bishop of South Dakota	The Right Reverend Keating Mr. Keating
Sincerely yours,	Dean Brown	The Very Reverend John Brown, Dean of St. Matthew's Cathedral	Dean Brown Mrs. Brown
Sincerely yours,	Archdeacon Smith	The Venerable Charles Smith, Archdeacon of Richmond	Archdeacon Smith Mrs. Smith

PERSONAGE	OFFICIAL/BUSINESS ADDRESS	SOCIAL ADDRESS	SALUTATION
Canon	The Reverend Canon Charles Pritchard Thomas, D.D., LL.D. Canon of St. Mary's Cathedral Address	The Reverand Canon and Mrs. Charles Pritchard Thomas Home Address	Dear Canon Thomas:
Bishop (Mormon)	Bishop John Richards[i] Church of Jesus Christ of Latter-day Saints Address	Bishop and Mrs. John Richards Home Address	Dear Bishop Richards:
THE ROMAN CATHOLIC HIERARCHY The Pope	His Holiness, the Pope or His Holiness Pope Benedict I Vatican City 00187 Rome, Italy		Your Holiness or Most Holy Father:
Cardinal	His Eminence, Patrick, Cardinal Kenin Archbishop of San Francisco Address		Your Eminence: Dear Cardinal Kenin:
Bishop and Archbishop	The Most Reverend Peter Judson, D.D. Bishop (Archbishop) of Dallas Address		Your Excellency: Dear Bishop (Archbishop) Judson:
Abbot	The Right Reverend Henry J. Loester[j] or Abbot Loester Address		Right Reverend Abbot: Dear Father:
Prothonotary Apostolic, Domestic Prelate, Vicar General, Papal Chamberlain	Reverend Monsignor Robert McDonald[k] Address		Reverend Monsignor: Dear Monsignor McDonald:
Priest	The Reverend Father James L. Cullen Address		Dear Father Cullen:

[i] In the Church of Jesus Christ of Latter-day Saints (Mormon), the title is used during the bishop's term of office (generally a five-year period); otherwise, "Mr." is used.
[j] After name add designated letters of the order; e.g., for members of the order of St. Benedict: The Right Reverend Dom Anselm McCarthy, O.S.B.
[k] If Prothonotary Apostolic, use initials P.A. after name; if Vicar General, use V.G.

LETTER CLOSING	SPEAKING TO	INTRODUCING	PLACE CARDS
Sincerely yours,	Canon Thomas	The Reverend Canon Charles Pritchard Thomas, Canon of St. Mary's	Canon Thomas Mrs. Thomas
Sincerely yours,	Bishop Richards	Bishop John Richards	Bishop Richards Mrs. Richards
Your Holiness' most humble servant; Respectfully yours	Your Holiness or Most Holy Father	His Holiness; the Holy Father; the Pope; the Pontiff	
Respectfully,	Your Eminence; Cardinal Kenin	His Eminence; Cardinal Kenin	His Eminence, Patrick, Cardinal Kenin
Respectfully,	Your Excellency; Bishop (Archbishop) Judson	His Excellency; Bishop (Archbishop) Judson	Bishop Judson
Respectfully,	Abbot Loester	The Right Reverend Henry Loester; Abbot Loester	The Right Reverend Loester
Respectfully,	Monsignor McDonald; Monsignor	Monsignor McDonald	Monsignor McDonald
Respectfully,	Father Cullen	Father Cullen	Father Cullen

PERSONAGE	OFFICIAL/BUSINESS ADDRESS	SOCIAL ADDRESS	SALUTATION
Brother	Brother William O'Hara[l] Address		Dear Brother William: Dear Brother:
Sister	Sister Joan Bannon[m] Address		Dear Sister Joan: Dear Sister:

[l] The use of the last name is a matter of choice; both Brother William and Brother William O'Hara are correct. However, since brothers in an order may have the same first names, it would be clearer to use the last name when addressing a letter.

[m] Older nuns may still use the religious names they took when taking their vows; most nuns, however, retain the first and last names they were born with.

LETTER CLOSING	SPEAKING TO	INTRODUCING	PLACE CARDS
Respectfully,	Brother William; Brother	Brother William	Brother William
Respectfully,	Sister Joan; Sister	Sister Joan; Sister	Sister Joan

INDEX

Accents, regional, 696
Acknowledgment cards, 440, 455, 680–81
Address, correct forms of, 719
  child addresses adults, 21–22
  clergy, 748–57
  government officials and individuals, 719–35
  military personnel, 736–47
Addressing envelopes, 660
  to children, 295, 662
  Christmas and Easter seals, 664
  Christmas cards, 684
  to divorced women, 661
  to doctors, 661–62
  Esquire, 663
  Jr., Sr., 2nd, and 3rd, 295, 662
  to married women keeping maiden name, 660–61
  mass mailing labels, 664
  Mesdames, use of, 663
  Messrs., use of, 662
  Misses, use of, 662
  return address, 636, 664
  to separated women, 661
  to single women with children, 661
  to teenagers, 662
  to unmarried or gay couples, 662
  wedding invitations, 294–95
  to widows, 661
  writing "Personal," "Please Forward," "Opened by Mistake" on an envelope, 663
Adoption, 19–20
  baby showers and, 417
  birth announcements and, 10
  engagement announcements for adopted children, 258–59
Advice, unsolicited, 697–98
Affair of friend's spouse, talking about, 698
Affairs with married persons, 486

Affection in public, displays of, 262
After-dinner coffee and liqueurs, 156, 163, 169–70
Agendas for business meetings, 521–22
Age of person, asking about, 697
Airline travel, 553
  aggravations of, 553
  alcohol use, 559
  attire, 559
  boarding the plane, 557
  "bumping" of passengers, 555–56
  business travel, 528–30
  checking in, 554–55
  children and, 560–61
  classes of travel, 554
  comfort concerns, 559–60
  Concorde supersonic flights, 553–54
  courteous behavior, 558
  fear of flying, 529
  frequent flyer points, 529
  luggage, 529, 556–57
  meals, 554
  overbooking by airlines, 555–56
  pregnancy and, 559
  safety precautions, 557–58
  security checks, 557
  smoking, 554
  standby flying, 555
  telephone manners and, 558
  tipping, 585
Alcohol, cooking with, 145
Alcohol use
  addiction to, 120–21
  airline travel and, 559
  boating and, 602
  business lunches, 516
  graduation parties, 425
  problem drinkers, 157, 209
  by teenagers, 49–50, 52–53, 54
  See also Liquor

Allergies, food, 159, 166
Allowances, 32–34
Alternative families, 21
Ambassadors, forms of address for
    American ambassadors, 728–29
    foreign ambassadors, 728, 734–35
American Bowling Congress, 629
American Psychological Association, 120
Amtrak train service, 570
Angry letters, 675
Anniversaries. *See* Wedding anniversaries
Answering machines
    at home, 704
    invitations and, 171
    at work, 500
Apartment personnel, tipping, 111–12
Apéritifs, 189
Apologies
    in conversation, 693
    letters of apology, 675
Appearance. *See* Personal appearance
Appetizer wines, 189
Appointments, 484
Après ski wear, 612
Arab countries, business etiquette in, 537,
    542
Arguments at formal dinners, dealing
    with, 154
Ascots, 77
Ashtrays, 180
Assemblies, 427–28
Association of Bridal Consultants, 319
"At Home" cards, 296–97
    second weddings and, 405
"At Home" invitations, 649
Attire
    airline travel, 559
    baby's christening clothes, 413
    boating, 603
    bus travel, 574–75
    children's clothing, 13–15
    conventions, 525–26
    croquet, 627
    debuts, 429
    fox hunting, 623–24
    funerals, 453
    golf, 591
    graduations, 424
    horseback riding, 621–22
    job hunting, 469, 474
    menswear, 77–79
    personal appearance and, 73, 75–79
    public speaking, 709
    restaurant dining, 85
    ship travel, 564
    skiing, 611–12

teenagers' clothing, 41–42
tennis, 598–99
travel in general, 543–44
women's clothing, 75–77
workout clothes, 624–25
See also Business attire; Wedding attire
Attorneys, death in the family and, 440
Auctions, 94–95
Australia, business etiquette in, 537
Austria, business etiquette in, 537
Automated teller machines (ATMs), 546

Baby equipment, 14
Baby showers, 416–17, 487
Babysitters, 16–17
Bachelor dinners, 368–69
Backpacking, 616–17
Badminton, 600
Balls and dances, 212
    car parkers, 216
    caterers, 214
    cocktails before, 209
    dancing at, 218, 219
    debuts, 426, 427–28
    dinner dances, 209, 212, 217–18
        service at, 219
    duration of, 218
    floor preparation, 215
    flowers, 216
    guest's role, 217–19
    hostess' role, 216–17
    indoor dances, 215
    invitations, 213
    liability coverage, 213
    locations for, 212–13
    orchestra or band, 214–15, 217
    party coordinators, 213–14
    photographers, 215
    receiving lines, 216–17
    supper dances, 213, 217, 218
        service at, 219
    teenage dances, 50–51
    in tents, 215–16
    thank-you notes, 218
Banquets in China, 538
Banquette seating, 81
Baptisms. *See* Christenings
Bar and *bat mitzvah* ceremonies, 419–21
Bartenders, 108, 206–7, 211
Bathrooms
    guest bathrooms, 240–41
    teenagers and, 40
Beach clubs, 606
Beach outings, 91–92, 605–6
Beaujolais, 190
Bed and breakfasts, 582–85, 589

Bed linen and towel sets, 318
Bedrooms
    of children, 12–13
    guest rooms, 239–40
    of teenagers, 39
Belated presents, 134
Bell, Alexander Graham, 700, 701
Benefits, 219–20
    advantages of, 224–25
    consultants for, 220
    invitations, 222, 223
    money matters, 223–24
    newspaper notices, 224
    planning of, 220–21
    ticket sales, 224
Beowulf, xi
Beringer, Guy, 200
Best man, 286, 360–61, 362, 380. *See also*
        Wedding attendants
Bicycling, 617–19
Birth announcements, 9–10, 640
Birthday cards, 432
Birthday celebrations
    adults, 431–33
    children, 26–27
    at work, 519
Birth defects, 11–12
Birthstone rings, 252
Birthstones, 254, 433
Black-tie outfits, 77, 78–79
Blended families, 18–19, 37
Blind persons, 98
Block letters, 507–8
Blue blazers, 78
Blue jeans, 75, 78
Boating
    alcohol use and, 602
    attire, 603
    captain's role, 602–3
    guest's role, 603–4
    information sources, 600
    safety concerns, 601
    seasickness, 604
    smoking, 604
    terminology, 600–1
BOAT/US Foundation, 600
Bolles, Richard, 463
"Boomerang" adult children, 55–56
Borrowing and lending
    money, 102–3
    personal possessions, 6
    at work, 479
Bouquets, 327–28
    bride's throwing of, 357, 397
Boutonnieres, 328
Bowling, 629–30

Bow ties, 77
Braces, orthodontic, 42
Bragging, 695
"Bread and butter" letters, 245, 671–72
Breakfasts
    business breakfasts, 517
    houseguests and, 241–42, 243
Breast feeding in public, 11
Bridal registries, 313
    bed linen and bath towel sets, selection
        of, 318
    china selection, 316–17
    consultants for, 314, 316–17
    flatware selection, 315–16
    glassware selection, 317–18
    informing wedding guests about, 314
    list of suggested presents, 314
    second weddings, 314–15
    where to register, 313–14
Bridal showers. *See* Wedding showers
Bride's attire. *See under* Wedding attire
Bridesmaids, 359. *See also* Wedding
        attendants
Bridesmaids' parties, 368
Bride's parties, 368
Bridge, 226–27
Bring-your-own parties, 235
Britain, business etiquette in, 539
Brith milah ceremony, 415
Brunches, 197, 200–1
    menu suggestions, 188
Buffet lunches and dinners, 174, 175, 195
    advantages of, 195–96
    arrangement of buffet table, 197–99
    classic buffet, 196, 198
    guest's role, 199–200
    hostess' role, 199
    invitations, 196
    with maid, 199
    menus, 187–88, 198–99
    number of guests, 195–96
    seated buffet, 197
    smorgasbords, 86–87
Bus boys, 81
Business announcements, 503–4
Business attire, 77, 489
    casual look, 491
    conservative or corporate look, 491
    day-to-evening situations, 492
    fashion tips for men, 492
    fashion tips for women, 493
    fur coats, 492
    grooming and, 490
    in international business, 492
    intracompany differences, 490
    knowing what's right, 489–91

Business attire (*continued*)
  provocative clothes, 491
  standard business look, 491
Business cards, 502–3
  in international business, 537, 540
Business communication, 494
  brevity in, 495
  faxes, 501
  following through on commitments, 495
  importance of, 494
  public speaking, 501
  silences, 495
  vocabulary, 494–95
  See also Business letters; Business
      telephone manners
Business entertaining, 514–15
  breakfasts, 517
  dinners, 517
  lunches, 515–17
  office parties, 519
  paying the bill, 517–18
  receptions, 518
  responding to business invitations, 518
  teas, 517
Business gift giving
  to clients and customers, 534–36
  holiday gifts, 533–34
  inappropriate presents, dealing with,
      536
  in international business, 540–42
  in office, 519, 532–34
  retirement gifts, 534
  wedding presents, 534
Business invitations, 503, 518
Business letters, 504
  block format, 507–8
  closings, 507
  condolence notes, 511
  congratulatory letters, 511
  copies, 509–10
  do's and don'ts, 504–5
  enclosures, 509
  encouragement, letters of, 511
  follow-up letters, 513
  formats, 506–9
  grammar and spelling, 506
  indented format, 509
  initials of sender and typist, 509
  interoffice memos, 513–14
  length, 505–6
  letters written in one's absence, 513
  rejection letters, 512
  resignation letters, 511–12
  salutations, 506–7
  thank-you letters, 510
  writing style, 504, 506

Business meetings, 519–20
  agendas, 521–22
  attendance list, 522
  chairman's role, 520–23
  checklist for, 524–25
  disagreeing with others, 523
  fear factor, 520–21
  goals of, 520
  interruptions, 497
  latecomers, 521
  participant's role, 523–24
  room preparation, 524
  seating, 522–23
  speaking up, 523
  See also Conventions
Business stationery, 501–2
Business suits, 77
Business telephone manners, 495–96
  answering machines, 500
  answering one's own telephone, 496–97
  answering other people's telephones, 496
  assistant-placed calls, 497
  cellular telephones, 500–1
  do's and don'ts, 499–500
  "hold" situations, 498
  interruptions, 497
  lengthy calls, 497
  long-distance calls outside the office,
      499
  pagers, 500–1
  personal calls at work, 499
  screening calls, 498
  speakerphones, 497
  taking messages, 498
  transferring calls, 498–99
  "unavailable" situations, 497–98
  voice concerns, 496
  voice mail, 500
  wrong numbers, 499
Business travel, 527–28
  airline travel, 528–30
  hotels, 530–31
  men and women traveling together,
      531–32
  out-of-town clients, 532
  taxis, limousines, and cars, 528
  tipping, 587
  women traveling alone, 531
Bus travel, 574
  attire, 574–75
  children and, 576
  courteous behavior, 575
  disabled persons and, 576
  group travel, 577
  luggage, 574
  rest stops, 575

schedules, 574
seating, 575–76
tipping, 577
Butlers, 144
Butter plates, 178–79
BYOB parties, 235

Cabinet officials, forms of address for, 724–25
Cafeterias, 88–89
Calling cards, 638
  as birth announcements, 640
  for couples, 642
  gift enclosure cards, 135–36
  loss of popularity, 638–39
  for men, 640–41
  sizes of, 640
  style of, 639–40
  for women, 640, 641–42
  writing a message and signing one's name, 640
"Calling" on friends, 638
Call waiting, 40, 703
Camping, 617
Candelabra, 178
Candles, 178
Captains (restaurant staff members), 81, 107
Car etiquette, 96–97
Car parkers, 216
Carpools, 29–30, 96–97
Car travel, 565–66
  accidents and breakdowns, 566–67
  business travel, 528
  children and, 568
  do's and don'ts, 567
  in foreign countries, 546, 569, 570
  private car and driver, 587
  renting a car, 569–70
  safety concerns, 566, 567–68
Car use by teenagers, 40–41
Casinos, 95
Caskets, 440
Cassette-recorded letters, 681
Catalogs, buying from, 132
Caterers, 144, 181–82
  for balls and dances, 214
  booking a caterer, 182
  contracts with, 183
  full-service caterers, 181–82
  initial visit of caterer, 182–83
  payment of, 183, 184
  services provided by, 183–84
  for wedding receptions, 321, 323
Catholicism
  christenings, 412

clergy, forms of address for, 754–57
  first communion, 417–18
  funerals, 446, 447, 451, 452
  interfaith marriages, 272
  naming a child, 8
  religious services, 90
  wedding ceremonies, 370, 382, 384
  wedding dates, 268
  wedding invitations, 292
Cellular telephones
  business use, 500–1
  personal use, 704–5
Centerpieces, 177–78
Central America, business etiquette in, 538
Ceremony cards, 296, 302–4, 305
Chablis, 189–90
Champagne, 190–91, 192, 193
Chanel, Coco, 493
Change of address, 638
Charades, 156, 163
Chargers, 178
Charitable giving
  by children, 13
  donation requests, 679
  gift donations, 130
  memorial contributions, 444, 451
Chartered bus tours, 577
Chemical dependency, 120–21
Child care
  babysitters, 16–17
  grandparents, 59
  nannies, 15–16
  nursery schools, 28
  parental travel and, 547
  teenage siblings, 41
Childlessness of another, asking about, 697
Childproof environments, 23–24
Children
  addressing envelopes to, 295, 662
  addressing of adults by, 21–22
  adopted children, 19–20
  airline travel and, 560–61
  allowances, 32–34
  baby equipment, 14
  bedrooms, 12–13
  bus travel, 576
  car travel, 568
  charitable giving by, 13
  clothing for, 13–15
  crush on a teacher, 29
  dancing classes, 32
  disciplining of, 24–25
  divorce and, 17–19
  extracurricular activities, 28–29, 31–32
  funerals and, 437–38, 452–53

Children (*continued*)
  gifts for, 136
  home's importance to, 12
  hotel accommodations, 552
  investing by, 34–35
  latchkey children, 30
  left at home while parents travel, 547
  manners, learning about, 24–25
  overscheduled child, 31–32
  parent's dating and, 22
  parent's loss of job and, 37, 476
  parent's second wedding and, 401–2
  parties for, 26–27
  peer pressure, 14–15
  religious services and, 90
  restaurant dining, 25–26
  routine, need for, 12
  savings accounts, 34
  self-sufficiency, learning about, 4
  ship travel, 563
  siblings of newborns, treatment of, 11
  of single-parent families, 21
  socializing by adults and, 5, 22–24, 25
  sportsmanship, 590–91
  stationery for, 637–38
  strangers, dealing with, 31
  telephone manners, 702
  television watching, 15
  thank-you notes by, 27, 669
  toddlers, 23–24
  train travel, 572
  travel, general guidelines on, 551–52
  at weddings, 351
  words, learning about, 25
  See also Family life; Newborns; School;
    Teenagers
Child support, 19, 36
China, business etiquette in, 538, 542
China selection for bridal registry, 316–
  17
Choking, Heimlich Maneuver for, 89,
  155, 166
Chopsticks, 86
Christenings, 411
  baby's clothes, 413
  ceremony, 413
  donation to clergyperson, 413–14
  gift giving, 414
  godparents, 411–12
  home christenings, 414
  invitations, 412–13
  siblings of baby and, 414
Christian Science wedding ceremony, 387
Christmas cards, 683
  addressing envelopes, 684
  cutting Christmas card list, 685–86

  embossed cards, 683–84
  engraved cards, 683
  exchanging holiday cards, 685
  to persons in mourning, 454, 685
  printed names, 684
  signing of cards, 684
Christmas Eve, 235
Christmas newsletters, 684–85
Christmas seals, 664
Church cards, 296
Cigarette smoking. *See* Smoking
Cigars, 156
Circumcision ceremony, 415
Civil weddings, 391
Claiborne, Craig, 188
Clergypersons
  christening fees, 413–14
  forms of address for, 746–53
  funeral fees, 445
  grace at meals, 6
  pre-wedding meetings, 271–73
Clothing. *See* Attire
Club life, 99
  behavior at a club, 102
  blackballing, 101
  fees and fee structures, 100–1
  guest privileges, 102
  joining a club, 99–101
  proposing a new member, 101, 678
  resigning from a club, 678–79
  tipping, 109
Coast Guard, 600
Coat of arms. *See* Heraldic devices
Coats of guests, care for, 151, 205–6
Cocktail hour
  dinner dance, 209
  formal seated dinner with a staff, 152–
    53, 159–60, 167
Cocktail parties, 204
  bar, location of, 206
  bartenders, 206–7, 209
  checklist for, 210–11
  coats of guests, care for, 205–6
  ending a party, 209–10
  food, 208
  glasses, 207
  guest's role, 210
  house preparation, 204
  invitations, 204
  liability coverage, 206
  liquor, 207–8
  number of guests, 206
  party hours, 205
  plastic glasses and paper napkins,
    208
  problem drinkers, 209

Coffee
  after-dinner coffee, 156, 163, 169–70
  houseguest situations, 243
  at teas, 202
Coffees, 233–34
Collect telephone calls, 705
College and university placement offices,
  465
College selection, 46–47
"Comfortable with" expression, 699
Coming out parties. *See* Debuts
Committees, listing names of persons on,
  657
Communication, 631
  acknowledgment cards, 680–81
  cassette-recorded letters, 681
  greeting cards, 682–83
  in married life, 64
  nonverbal communications, 494
  postcards, 636, 681
  with teenagers, 38–39
  See also Address, correct forms of;
      Addressing envelopes; Business
      communication; Calling cards;
      Christmas cards; Conversation;
      Faxes; Heraldic devices;
      Introductions; Invitations; Letters;
      Names and titles; Public
      speaking; Signatures; Stationery;
      Telephone manners; Toasts
Commuter train travel, 573–74
Companions, 687
Complaining
  in conversation, 696
  letters of complaint, 680
  about restaurant food or service, 83
Complimenting others, 692–93
Computerized travel information, 545
Concierges, 578, 588–89
Concorde supersonic flights, 553–54
Condiments, 165, 172
Condolence letters, 450–51
  to business associates, 511
  sample letters, 672–73
Confirmation ceremony, 418
Confrontations, 484
Congratulatory letters, 511, 676
Congressmen, forms of address for, 726–
  27
Consultants
  benefits, 221
  bridal registries, 314, 316–17
  wedding plans, 319–20
Contractions of names, 657
Controversial subjects, expressing
  opinions on, 691

Conventions, 525
  attire, 525–26
  do's and don'ts, 525
  expense account etiquette, 526–27
  reports on, 526
  spouses or friends, attendance by, 527
Conversation, 691
  advice, unsolicited, 697–98
  affair of friend's spouse, talking about,
      698
  age of person, asking about, 697
  apologies, 693
  bragging, 695
  childlessness of another, asking about,
      697
  complaining, 696
  complimenting others, 692–93
  controversial subjects, expressing
      opinions on, 691
  cosmetic surgery, asking about, 697
  defending a friend, 693–94
  encouragement of conversation at
      social events, 140, 154, 162
  errors, admitting to, 693
  ethnic remarks, 696
  foreign phrases, use of, 691, 700
  gossip, 696
  habits, talking to others about, 694
  health, talking about, 696–97
  homosexuals, referring to, 696
  interrupting a person, 691–92
  listening skills, 692
  misuse of words, 698–99
  name dropping, 695
  obscene jokes, 695–96
  occupation of another, asking about, 697
  physical defects, asking about, 698
  political correctness, 695
  prices, asking about, 693
  recipes, asking for, 693
  regional accents, 696
  religious or political views, 694
  repeating a story, 692
  rescuing someone from an
      embarrassing situation, 698
  responding to a nonresponse, 693
  saying "Let's get together" without
      suggesting a firm date, 694
  single status of another, asking about,
      697
  swearing, 696
  talking down to others, 692
  talking too much, 692
  "trapping" invitations, 694
  turning down requests, 695
  "Uh-huh," use of, 695

Cooking disasters, 155
Cookouts, 228–30
Cooks, hiring of, 145
Corkscrews, 193
Corporate gifts, 534–36
Correspondence cards, 635, 637
Corsages, 328
Cosmetic surgery, 74–75
    as topic of conversation, 697
Costume parties, 225–26
Cotillions, 427–28
Country inns, 582–85, 589
Coupe (champagne glass), 192
Couples
    calling cards, 642
    communication by, 64
    cultural issues, 65–66
    independent side of couple's life, 63
    money issues, 65
    religious issues, 65
    spouse's friends, 66
    two-career couples, 63–64
    working in different cities, 64–65
    See also Gay couples; Unmarried
        couples
Cousins, 56–57
Crashing a party, 429
Credit cards for teenagers, 35
Cremation, 448
Crests. *See* Heraldic devices
Criticism of others, 479, 483–84
Croquet, 626–29
    terminology, 628
Cruises. *See* Boating; Ship travel
Curfews, 49
Cycling, 617–19

Dances. *See* Balls and dances
Dancing
    balls and dances, 218, 219
    children's dancing classes, 32
    cutting in, 219, 430–31
    debuts, 430–31
    rehearsal dinners, 379
    wedding receptions, 274, 356, 395–96,
        398
Dating
    single parents, 22
    singles, 68–70
    teenagers, 44–46
Dating resources, 69–70
Death
    anniversaries of, 454
    attorneys, working with, 440
    Christmas cards to persons in
        mourning, 454, 685

in colleague's family, 487, 511
condolence letters, 450–51, 511, 672–
    73
disposing of possessions, 71, 456–57
engagement announcements for brides
    whose parents are deceased, 257
euphemisms for, 453, 699
in extended family, 62
memorials to deceased, 456
mourning periods, 71–72, 457–58
newborn's death, 12
obituary notices, 440, 442–44
occurrence of, 439
organ donation, 439
spouse's death, 70–71
terminally ill persons, visits with, 119
wedding postponement and, 348–49
See also Funerals
Debuts, 426
    assemblies and cotillions, 427–28
    attire, 429
    dances, 426
    dancing, 430–31
    debutante season, 426
    escort for debutante, 429–30
    flowers, 430
    invitations, 428–29, 648–49
    receiving lines, 430
    "reluctant debutante" situations, 426
    teas, 427
    thank-you notes, 431
Decorators, 116
Deep breathing, 709
Defending a friend in conversation, 693–
    94
Dessert forks and spoons, 179
Desserts, 165
Dessert wines, 190
Diamond rings, 252
Dinner dances, 212
    cocktail hour, 209
    guest's role, 217–18
    service at, 219
Dinner jackets, 78–79
Dinner plates, 178
Dinners
    business dinners, 517
    formal dinner table setting, 176–80
    informal dinner table setting, 181
    informal seated dinner with a maid,
        170–73, 186
    informal seated dinner without a
        maid, 173–75, 186
    menu suggestions, 185–86
    shipboard dinners, 563
    state dinners, 123–24

wine served at, 193–94
See also Buffet lunches and dinners;
    Formal seated dinner with a staff
Disabled persons
    assistance for, 98–99
    bus travel, 576
Disagreeing with others, 523
Discipline for children, 24–25
Divorce
    addressing envelopes to divorced
        women, 661
    birth announcements and, 10
    calling cards and, 641
    children and, 17–19
    engagement announcements for brides
        whose parents are divorced, 257–
        58
    engagement announcements for
        divorced women, 259
    engagement/wedding rings and, 402–3
    funeral of ex-spouse, 445
    grandparents and, 60
    money issues, 36
    office life and, 487
    repercussions of, 70
    wedding seating of divorced parents,
        373
    woman's surname following, 18, 70,
        482, 655
Doctor-patient relations, 116–18
Doctors, addressing envelopes to, 661–62
Doggy bags, 87
Donation requests, 679
Double weddings, 304, 374
    receptions, 398–99
"Drapes," use of word, 699
Drinks. *See* Alcohol use; Liquor
Driver's licenses, 546
Drucker, Peter F., 478
Drug use
    addiction to, 120–21
    by teenagers, 52–53

Eastern Orthodox churches
    forms of address for clergy, 748–49
    wedding ceremony, 388–89
Easter seals, 664
Edison, Thomas, 701
Elderhostel organization, 548–49
Elderly persons
    aging parent, caring for, 60–62
    older people living together, 72
    travel by, 548–49
Eliot, T. S., 7
Elopement, 274–75
Embarrassing situations, 698

Employers' concerns, 476–77
Employment agencies, 464–65
Encouragement, letters of, 511
Engagement, 246–47
    affection in public, displays of, 262
    announcements, 247, 254–56
        breaking an engagement, 263
        special announcements, 256–59
    breaking an engagement, 263
    disapproval of others, 248–49
    financial issues, 248
    in-laws, names used with, 250
    interfaith or interracial engagements,
        247–48
    length of engagement, 262
    letter from parents of bride-to-be to
        future son-in-law, 672
    office life and, 486
    parental disapproval, 248–49
    parents informed about, 247
    parents meet parents, 249–50
    party for engaged couple, 260–62
    prenuptial agreements, 248
    presents for bride and groom, 259, 262,
        263
    rings, 252–54, 260–61, 263
    second weddings and, 400–1
    single friends and, 263
    wedding attendants, invitations for,
        250–52, 358
Engraving, 632
Entertaining, 138–39
    brunches, 188, 197, 200–1
    coffees, 233–34
    cookouts, 228–30
    formal seated lunch with a staff, 175,
        186–87
    housewarmings, 236
    informal seated dinner with a maid,
        170–73, 186
    informal seated dinner without a
        maid, 173–75, 187
    informal seated lunch with or without
        a maid, 175, 187
    instruction groups, 228
    menus, 184–88
    open houses, 235–36
    picnics, 230–32
    potluck suppers, 234
    receptions, 211–12
    ship travel and, 564
    by singles, 67–68
    space concerns, 174
    See also Balls and dances; Benefits;
        Buffet lunches and dinners;
        Business entertaining; Caterers;

Entertaining (*continued*)
  Cocktail parties; Formal seated
    dinner with a staff; Houseguest
    situations; Parties; Table settings;
    Teas; Wines
Envelopes
  inserting letter in envelope, 668
  with stationery, 636
  for wedding invitations, 294–95
  See also Addressing envelopes
Errors, admitting to, 693
Esquire, 657, 663
Ethics in workplace, 478–79
Ethnic remarks, 696
Etiquette, xi–xii
Eulogies, 447, 453
Executive search firms, 465
Expense account etiquette, 526–27
Extended family, 2, 56
  aging parent, caring for, 60–62
  cousins, 56–57
  death in the family, 62
  grandparents, 59–60, 402
  in-laws, 57–58
  unmarried relationships, 58–59, 72

Family life
  alternative families, 21
  "boomerang" adult children, 55–56
  carpools, 29–30
  family therapy, 19
  harmonious living, 1–2
  meals, 4–6
  meetings together, 2
  neatness standards, 3
  neighbors, relations with, 6–7
  office life and, 486
  parental unity, 2
  rules to live by, 2
  sharing household duties, 3–4
  stepfamilies, 18–19, 37
  See also Children; Couples; Divorce;
    Extended family; Single parents;
    Teenagers
Family therapy, 19
Farewell parties, 236–37
Fast food, 88–89
Faxes, 681–82
  business communication, 501
  invitations and, 171, 682
  job hunting and, 466
Finger bowls, 165–66, 169
Fingernails, 73
Finland, business etiquette in, 540
Fired from a job, 474–75
  children told about, 37, 467

employer's role in firing, 476–77
friend's firing, 475, 480
job interviews and, 468–69
First communion, 417–18
First Lady. *See* President and First Lady
Flag protocol, 127–29
Flatware
  bridal registries and, 315–16
  in formal dinner table setting, 179
  at formal seated dinner, 144–45, 164
  heraldic devices and, 718–19
  monogramming of, 316
Floral designers, 325–26
Flower girls, 252, 281, 328
Flowers
  balls and dances, 218
  for business colleagues, 533
  debuts, 430
  formal seated dinner with a staff, 146,
    160
  funerals, 444, 445–46, 451
  as gifts, 131, 533
  international business etiquette and, 541
  weddings, 325–28
Follow-up letters, 513
Food allergies, 159, 166
Foot care, 73
Foreign phrases, use of, 691, 700
Forgetting a name, 482, 690–91
Forks, 164, 179
  methods of handling, 5
Formal dinner table setting, 176–80
Formal invitations. *See under* Invitations
Formal lunch table setting, 180–81
Formal seated dinner with a staff, 139
  after-dinner coffee and liqueurs, 156,
    163, 169–70
  arguments, dealing with, 154
  at the table, 153–56, 161–63, 164–67
  china, glasses, and flatwear, 144–45
  coats of guests, care for, 151
  cocktail hour, 152–53, 159–60, 167
  conclusion of, 156–57, 163–64
  conversation, encouragement of, 140,
    154, 162
  cook, hiring of, 145
  cooking disasters, 155
  dinner service, 168–70
  flowers, 146, 160
  furniture arrangement, 152
  game-playing, 156, 163
  going in to dinner, 153, 160–61
  guest list, 141–42
  guest of honor
    arriving and departing, 159, 163–64
    seating of, 147

toasting of, 155–56
guest's role, 157
 after coffee, 163–64
 at the table, 161–63, 164–67
 cocktail hour, 159–60
 going in to dinner, 160–61
 replying to an invitation, 157–59
 thank-you notes, 164
hostess' role, 139–40
 after coffee, 156–57
 at the table, 153–56
 cocktail hour, 152–53
 final preparations, 151–52
 first considerations, 140–42
 going in to dinner, 153
 invitations, 142–44
 just before the guests arrive, 152
 planning the dinner, 144–46
 seating a dinner, 146–51
"host for the evening," 141
invitations, 142–43
 guest's reply, 157–59
 reminder cards, 143–44
 telephone invitations, 141, 143
 when to invite, 143
late arrivals, 153, 154, 161
left-handed guests, 148
menu cards, 150–51
menus, 145
numbering of tables, 150
number of guests, determination of, 140–41
party book for future consultation, 140
place cards, 148
places of honor, 147
problems at the dinner table, 154–55, 166–67
rental equipment, 144
seating protocol, 146–48
single woman as hostess, 141
single women as guests, 142, 157
smoking, 167
staff
 hiring of, 140, 144
 paying of, 157
staff's role, 167
 after-dinner coffee and liqueurs, 169–70
 before the dinner begins, 167–68
 before the guests arrive, 167
 cocktail hour, 167
 departure, 170
 dinner service, 168–70
tablecloth and napkins, 145
table manners, 161, 164–66
table number cards, 148–49

thank-you notes, 164
toasts
 guest-initiated, 162–63
 host-initiated, 155–56
wines, liquor, liqueurs, and nonalcoholic drinks, 145–46
wine spills, 154, 166–67
Formal seated lunch with a staff, 175, 186–87
Formal wear, 77, 78–79
Fox hunting, 622–24
France, business etiquette in, 538
Frequent flyer points, 529
Friendships
 of teenagers, 48–49, 51
 at work, 485
Friends of friends, visits to, 551
Frostbite, 608–9
Fund-raisers. *See* Benefits
Funerals, 437
 acknowledgment cards for replying to condolence letters, 440, 455, 680–81
 assistance for making funeral arrangements, 441
 casket selection, 440
 children and, 437–38, 452–53
 Christian funeral, 447–49
 church services, 447–48
 clothes the deceased is to be buried in, 440
 cremation, 448
 date and time, decision on, 440–41
 death, occurrence of, 439
 eulogies, 447, 453
 ex-spouse of the deceased, 445
 family and friends, notification of, 441
 fees for clergyperson, 445
 flowers, 444, 445–46, 451
 funeral directors, working with, 439–40
 funeral home services, 449
 gravestone selection, 455–56
 guest books, 446, 452
 home services, 449
 instructions for next of kin, 438–39
 interment, 449
 Jewish funeral, 444, 446, 449–50, 451, 452, 453, 456
 limousines, 440, 446
 lunch following funeral, 446, 454
 memorial booklets, 446–47
 memorial services, 441, 448–49
 mourner's role
  attire, 453
  condolence letters, 450–51
  contribution to a charity in lieu of flowers, 444, 451

Funerals; mourner's role (*continued*)
    do's and don'ts, 453–54
    eulogizing the deceased, 453
    flowers, 451
    Mass cards, 451
    visiting the funeral home, 451–53
  music, 446
  newspaper notices, 440, 442–44
  open or closed casket viewings, 452
  pallbearers, 444–45
  thank-you notes, 454–55
  ushers, 445
Fur coats, 76, 87, 492

Gambling, 95–96, 227
Game parties, 226–28
Game-playing at formal seated dinners, 156, 163
Garage personnel, tipping, 112
Garter, throwing of, 397
Gay couples
  addressing envelopes to, 662
  alternative families, 21
  birth announcements, 10
  introductions, 687
"Gay" designation for homosexuals, 696
Gender-based courtesies, 481
"Gentleman" versus "man," 658
Germany, business etiquette in, 538
"Get well" cards, 682
Gift certificates, 130
Gift enclosure cards, 135–36
Gift giving
  anniversary parties, 435, 436–37
  asking what a person would like, 132–33
  bar and *bat mitzvah* ceremonies, 421
  belated presents, 134
  birthday gifts, 431–32
  catalogs, buying from, 132
  charitable donations as gifts, 130
  christenings, 414
  collecting presents throughout the year, 133
  eliminating someone from one's gift-giving list, 134
  engagement gifts, 259, 262, 263
  flowers or a plant, 131
  graduations, 425–26
  impulse presents, 134
  inappropriate presents, 134–35
  joint or group presents, 133
  keeping a list of annual presents, 133
  money, stocks, and gift certificates, 35–36, 130
  museum shop gifts, 131–32
  to new parents, 10–11
  "no presents, please" situations, 133
  philosophy of, 129–30
  to President and First Lady, 124–25
  recycling a present, 133–34
  returning or exchanging a present, 136
  sport- or hobby-related presents, 132
  suggested gifts, 136–37
  sweet sixteen parties, 422
  See also Bridal registries; Business gift giving; Wedding presents
Gift wrapping, 135
Glasses
  for cocktails, 207
  plastic glasses, 208
  wineglasses, 165, 179–80, 192
Glassware, bridal registries and, 317–18
Gloves, 75–76
  wedding attire, 283, 286
Godparents, 411–12
Golf, 591
  attire, 591
  behavior code, 591–92
  cart etiquette, 592–93
  damage to course, repairing of, 594
  eating and drinking, 594–95
  friend's club, playing at, 595
  handicapping system, 592
  hitting others, 593
  order of play, 592
  pace of a game, 593–94
  personal integrity and, 591
Gossip, 480, 696
Government officials
  forms of address for, 719–35
  letters to, 676–77
Governors, forms of address for, 730–31
Grace at meals, 6
Graduations, 423
  accommodations, 424
  announcements, 424
  attire, 424
  gift giving, 425–26
  parents' attendance, 423
  parties, 424–25
  pre-graduation events, 424
Grammar, 506
Grandparents, 59–60, 402
Gravestones, 455–56
Gravy, 165
Greece, business etiquette in, 539
Greeting cards, 682–83
Grooming, 72
  business attire and, 490
Groom's attire. *See under* Wedding attire

Groom's cake, 324
Guest books
  funerals, 446, 452
  wedding receptions, 276, 318–19, 356, 392
Guest of honor. *See under* Formal seated dinner with a staff
Guest privileges at a club, 102
Guest's role
  balls and dances, 217–19
  boating, 603–4
  buffet lunches and dinners, 199–200
  cocktail parties, 210
  houseguest situations, 242–45, 671
  housewarmings, 236
  informal seated dinner with a maid, 171–72
  restaurant dining, 85
  second weddings, 407
  teas, 204
  wedding showers, 367–68
  See also under Formal seated dinner with a staff; *under* Weddings
Gyms, 624–26

Habits, talking to others about, 694
Hacking, 621
Hairdressers, tipping, 110, 111
Hairstyles, 72
  of teenagers, 42–43
Handicapped persons. *See* Disabled persons
Hand-me-downs, 13–14
Hanukkah, 685
Hats, 77
  removal indoors, 544
"Have a nice day" expression, 699
Health, talking about, 696–97
Health clubs, 624–26
Health-related matters
  chemical dependency, 120–21
  doctor-patient relations, 116–18
  hospital patients, visits with, 119, 137
  hospital stays, 118
  psychological counseling, 120
  travel and, 545–46
Heimlich Maneuver for choking, 89, 155, 166
Heirloom rings, 253
Heraldic devices, 291, 714
  flatware and, 718–19
  full coat of arms, 716–17
  lozenges, 633, 716
  origin and custom of heraldry, 714–16
  stationery and, 633
  use of, 717–19

wedding invitations and, 718
  women's use of, 718
Highball glasses, 207
Hiking, 616–17
Hiring relatives, 477
Hobby-related presents, 132
"Hold" situations, 498, 702
Holiday gifts in business setting, 533–34
Holiday tipping, 110–13
Home christenings, 414
Home decoration, 116
Home funerals, 449
Home security, 547
Home weddings, 390–91
Homosexuals, 696. *See also* Gay couples
Honeymoons, 337–38
Hope chests, 313, 316
Hors d'oeuvres, 160, 208, 322
Horseback riding, 619–21
  fox hunting, 622–24
  hacking, 621
  western riding, 621–22
"Hosiery," use of word, 699
Hospital patients, visits with, 119, 137
Hospital stays, 118
Hostess' role
  balls and dances, 216–17
  buffet lunches and dinners, 199
  houseguest situations, 237–39
  informal seated dinner with a maid, 171
  informal seated dinner without a maid, 174
  restaurant dining, 81–84
  teas, 203–4
  wedding showers, 365–66
  See also under Formal seated dinner with a staff
Hotels, 577
  business travel, 530–31
  checking in, 578–79
  checking out, 580–81
  children, accommodations for, 552
  comfort concerns, 579
  "commercial" hotels, 579
  concierges, 578, 588–89
  mini-bars, 577–78
  reservations, 578
    for out-of-town guests, 336–37, 353
  room service, 579–80
  security concerns, 580
  teas, 580
  tipping, 578, 579, 587–89
  women alone, 580
"House" and "home," confusion of, 699
House buying and selling, 115–16

Houseguest situations, 237
  bathrooms, 240–41
  bedrooms, 239–40
  breakfasts, 241–42, 243
  guest's drawer, 241
  guest's role, 242–45, 671
  hostess' role, 237–39
  maids and, 244–45
  thank-you notes, 245, 671
Household duties, sharing of, 3–4
Housekeepers, 701–2
House sitters, 547
Housewarmings, 236
How to Enjoy Wine (Johnson), 189
Hygiene, 72
Hyphenated names, 655

Ice cream, 165
Ice skating, 613–14
India, business etiquette in, 540, 542
"In fact," use of phrase, 505
Informal dinner table setting, 181
Informal invitations, 652–54
Informal seated dinner with a maid, 170–
    73, 186
Informal seated dinner without a maid,
    173–75, 186
Informal seated lunch with or without a
    maid, 175, 187
In-laws, 57–58
  names used with, 250
Instruction groups, 228
Insurance
  balls and dances, 213
  cocktail parties, 206
  travel, 546
  wedding receptions, 325
Integrity and ethics in workplace, 478–79
Interfaith marriages, 272–73
Interior designers, 116
Interment, 449
International business etiquette, 536
  attire, 492
  general guidelines, 536–37
  gift giving, 540–42
  specific country guidelines, 537–40
  toasts, 706–7
Interoffice memos, 513–14
Interruptions
  of business meetings, 497
  of conversations, 691–92
Interviews
  for club membership, 100
  See also Job interviews
Introductions, 686
  forgetting a name, 482, 690–91

guidelines for making everyday
    introductions, 686–88
  kissing as a greeting, 690
  letters of introduction, 677–78
  at parties, 688–89
  rising when introduced, 689
  shaking hands, 689–90
  of speakers in public, 688, 707–8
  of unmarried couples, 687
  at work, 482
  wrong name used in, 691
Investing by children, 34–35
Invitations
  anniversary parties, 434, 648
  baby showers, 416
  balls and dances, 213
  bar and *bat mitzvah* ceremonies, 420
  benefits, 221, 222
  buffet lunches and dinners, 195–96
  business invitations, 503, 518
  christenings, 412–13
  cocktail parties, 205
  costume parties, 225
  debuts, 428–29, 648–49
  engagement parties, 260
  faxed invitations, 171, 682
  formal invitations
    accepting an invitation, 650–51
    to anniversary parties, 648
    "at Home" invitations, 649
    to debutante dances, 648–49
    extending a formal invitation, 642–43
    fill-in invitations, 644–45, 646
    for guest bringing escort, 645
    handwritten, 646
    in honor of a special guest, 646
    map enclosures, 650
    to official luncheons, 647
    regretting an invitation, 651–52
    reply cards, 649–50
    rules for preparing, 643–44
    from several couples, 647
  formal seated dinner with a staff, 142–
      44, 157–59
  informal invitations, 652–54
  informal seated dinner with a maid, 171
  rehearsal dinners, 377–78
  reminder cards, 143–44
  restaurant lunch or dinner, 81–82
  R.s.v.p. requests, 649–50, 654
  surprise parties, 225
  sweet sixteen parties, 422
  telephone invitations, 141, 143
  "trapping" invitations, 694
  wedding receptions, 300–1, 306
  See also Wedding invitations

Israel, business etiquette in, 540
Italy, business etiquette in, 538

Japan, business etiquette in, 539, 540,
    542
Jargon, 505
Jessel, George, 501
Jewelry
    for brides, 279
    business attire and, 493
    for men, 78
    for teenagers, 42
    for women, 76–77
Jewish faith
    bar and *bat mitzvah* ceremonies, 419–
        21
    brith milah ceremony, 415
    clergy, forms of address for, 750–51
    conversion to, 384
    funerals, 444, 446, 449–50, 451, 452,
        453, 456
    Hanukkah, 685
    interfaith marriages, 272–73
    kosher foods, 419
    mourning periods, 450, 454, 458
    naming a child, 8
    religious services, 90
    simhat habat ceremony, 415–16
    sitting *shivah,* 450, 454
    wedding ceremonies, 354, 370, 371,
        376, 384–87
    wedding dates, 268
Job applications, 470
Job-hopping, 462
Job hunting
    anxiety of, 460
    attire for, 469, 474
    college and university placement
        offices, 465
    competition aspect, 460–61
    contacting a potential employer, 466
    employment agencies, 464–65
    executive search firms, 465
    faxes and, 466
    getting up to date, 473–74
    interviews. *See* Job interviews
    networking and personal contacts,
        463–64
    older job hunters, 465, 472–73
    outplacement agencies, 465, 475
    reentering the working world, 472–
        74
    résumés, 461–63
    volunteerism and, 465–66
    want ads, 464
    women returning to work, 473

Job interviews
    attire, 469
    illegal questions, 469
    interviewer's role, 467–68, 472
    interview session, 470–71
    job applications, 470
    listening, importance of, 471
    mock interview with a friend, 469–70
    preparation for, 466–68, 469–70
    questions frequently asked, 468–69
    requests for interviews, 466
    thank-you notes, 471–72
Job loss. *See* Fired from a job
Jogging, 615–16
Johnson, Hugh, 188–89
Johnson, Lyndon, 229
Johnson, Samuel, 691
Jokes, obscene, 695
Judges, forms of address for, 730–31
Jr., Sr., 2nd, and 3rd, 656–57
    addressing envelopes and, 295, 662
Jury duty, 121–22

Kissing as a greeting, 690
Knives, 164, 179
    methods of handling, 5
Kosher foods, 419

"Lady" versus "woman," 658
Last names. *See* Surnames
Latchkey children, 30
Lawyers, forms of address for, 732, 733
League of American Wheelmen, 617
Left-handed guests, 148
Lesbians, 696. *See also* Gay couples
Letters, 664–65
    angry letters, 675
    of apology, 675
    body of the letter, 665
    "bread and butter" letters, 245, 671–72
    closings, 666–67
    club membership, proposal for, 678
    club resignation, 678–79
    of complaint, 680
    condolence letters, 450–51, 511, 672–
        73
    of congratulations, 676
    correct form for social letters, 665–68
    date, 665–66
    donation requests, 679
    ending a letter, 666
    handwriting versus typing, 668
    ink color, 665
    inserting letter in envelope, 668
    of introduction, 677–78
    to President and First Lady, 125

Letters (*continued*)
　to public officials, 676–77
　of recommendation, 679–80
　retirement letters, 676
　salutation, 666, 668
　sample letters, 669–80
　sequence of pages in a letter sheet, 667
　sequence of pages on an informal,
　　667–68
　starting a letter, 666
　of support, 674
　unexpected letters, 674
　wedding invitations, 310
　woman's signature, 659
　See also Business letters; Thank-you
　　notes
Limousines
　business travel, 528
　funerals, 440, 446
　tipping of drivers, 110
　weddings, 334–36
Liners, 178
Lipstick, 162
Liquor
　bottle sizes, 194
　brunches, 200
　cocktail parties, 207–8
　drinks per bottle, 195
　formal seated dinner with a staff, 145
　tipping with, 115
　wedding receptions, 324–25
　See also Alcohol use
Listening skills, 471, 692
Littering, 567, 617
"Little girl's" or "little boy's room," 699
Living wills, 60–61
Lozenges, 633, 716
Luggage
　airline travel, 529, 556–57
　bus travel, 574
　labeling of, 545
　ship travel, 563–64
　train travel, 572–73
Lunch counters, 89
Lunches
　business lunches, 515–17
　formal lunch table setting, 180–81
　formal seated lunch with a staff, 175,
　　186–87
　funeral lunches, 446, 454
　informal seated lunch with or without
　　a maid, 175, 187
　menu suggestions, 186–87, 188
　official luncheons, 647
　pre-wedding lunches, 369–70
　See also Buffet lunches and dinners

"Ma'am," use of, 657–58
Maiden name
　resumption of use following divorce,
　　18, 70, 482, 655
　retention following marriage, 347–48,
　　654, 660–61
Maids
　buffet lunches and dinners with, 199
　houseguest situations and, 244–45
　informal seated dinner with a maid,
　　170–73, 186
　informal seated lunch with a maid,
　　175, 187
Maids of honor, 359–60, 361. *See also*
　　Wedding attendants
Mailgrams, 349
Mail order companies, 132
Maître d', 81, 107
Makeup, 162, 493
Manners, 24–25
　common courtesies, 74
　for houseguests, 242–44
　swimming pool manners, 92, 233
　in workplace, 479–80
　See also Table manners
Man-woman interactions, 79–80
Marriage certificates, 376
Marriage licenses, 273–74
Marriage vows, reaffirmation of, 409–
　　10
Married couples. *See* Couples
Mass cards, 451
Mass mailing labels, 664
Mayors, forms of address for, 730–31
McCarthy, Daniel, 189, 194
Meals with family, 4–6
Meetings
　family meetings, 2
　See also Business meetings
Memo pads, 636
Memorial booklets, 446–47
Memorial contributions, 444, 451
Memorials, 456
Memorial services, 441, 448–49
Memory lapses, 482, 690–91
Memos, interoffice, 513–14
Menswear, 77–79
Menu cards, 178
　formal seated dinner with a staff, 150–
　　51
Menus, 145, 185–85, 198–99
　sample menus, 185–88
Mesdames, use of, 663
Message cards, 635
Message-taking for others, 498
Message-taking systems, automated, 704

Messrs., use of, 662
Military personnel, forms of address for, 736–47
Military ranks, 736–37, 738–39
Military weddings, 374–75
   invitations, 309–10
   uniforms worn at, 286
Miss, use of, 481, 658
Misses, use of, 662
Money
   being with those who have less money, 104
   being with those who have more money, 104
   benefits and, 222, 223–24
   borrowing and lending, 102–3, 479
   business meal bills, 517–18
   child care issues, 15–17
   children and, 32–37
   couples and, 65
   divorce and, 36
   doctor-patient relations and, 117
   engagement and, 248
   expense account etiquette, 526–27
   as gift, 35–36, 130
   restaurant bills, 69, 84, 105–6
   second weddings and, 400, 402
   talking about, 104–5
   teenagers and, 33, 34, 47–48
   thank-you notes for gifts of money, 669–70
   travel and, 546, 550–51
   wedding financial arrangements, 264–68
   as wedding present, 339, 345, 353
   See also Tipping
Monogramming, 314
   bed linen and towel sets, 318
   flatware, 316
   gift-giver's responsibility regarding, 352
   initials used for, 316
   stationery, 633
Moral convictions, defense of, 694
Mormon wedding ceremony, 390
Motels, 581–82, 589
Mourning periods, 71–72, 457–58
   in Jewish faith, 450, 454, 458
Movie-going, 94
Mrs., use of, 481
Ms., use of, 481, 656, 687
   calling cards and, 641–42
Museum-going, 94
Museum shop gifts, 131–32
Music
   funerals, 446

   second weddings, 408
   weddings, 329–30, 384, 386

Name dropping, 695
Names and titles, 654
   changing a name legally, 259, 657
   committees, listing names of persons on, 657
   contractions of names, 657
   Esquire, use of, 657
   forgetting a name, 482, 690–91
   "gentleman" versus "man," 658
   Jr., Sr., 2nd, and 3rd, 656–57
   "lady" versus "woman," 658
   "ma'am," use of, 657–58
   Miss, 481, 658
   Mrs., 481
   Ms., 481, 641–42, 656, 687
   nicknames, 657
   separated women, 655
   single woman with child, 655
   "sir," use of, 657–58
   wedding invitations and, 292
   women who use two first names, 655–56
   in workplace, 481–82
   See also Addressing envelopes; Surnames
Name tags, 524
Naming a child, 7–8, 9
   surname of child whose parents use different names, 9
Nannies, 15–16
Napkins, 145, 177
   folding of, 177
   paper, 208
   placement and handling of, 87
National anthem, 91, 128
National Flag Foundation, 128
Neatness standards, 3
Neighbors, relations with, 6–7
Nepotism, 477
Netherlands, business etiquette in, 540
Networking and personal contacts, 463–64
Newborns
   baby equipment, 14
   birth announcements, 9–10, 640
   with birth defects, 11–12
   breast feeding in public, 11
   death of, 12
   gifts for new parents, 10–11
   naming of, 7–8, 9
   visiting the new mother, 10
New England Historic Genealogical Society, 715

Newsletters, 684–85
Newspaper notices
  benefits, 224
  engagements, 254–59
  obituaries, 440, 442–44
  second weddings, 347, 405–6
  weddings, 346–47
New Year's Day, 235
New York Times Cookbook (Claiborne), 188
Nicklaus, Jack, 595
Nicknames, 657
Nonverbal communications, 494
Norway, business etiquette in, 540
Numbered cards for tables, 150
Nursery schools, 28
Nursing homes, 61, 62

Obituary notices, 440, 442–44
Obscene jokes, 695
Obscene telephone calls, 703–4
Occupation of another, asking about, 697
Office assistants, 483, 485
Office life, 478
  appointments, 484
  borrowing and lending, 479
  confrontations, 484
  criticism of others, 479, 483–84
  death in colleague's family, 487, 511
  divorce and, 487
  engagement and, 486
  family life and, 486
  friendships, 485
  gender and seniority courtesies, 481
  gossip, 480
  inappropriate terminology, 485
  integrity and ethics, 478–79
  interpersonal relations, 482–84
  introductions, 482
  manners, 479–80
  names and titles, 481–82
  open-door policy, 481
  praise for others, 483
  pregnancy and, 486–87
  romance in the office, 485–86
  sexual harassment, 488–89
  smoking, 480
Office parties, 519
Old-fashioned glasses, 207
Open-door policy, 481
Open houses, 235–36
Operagoing, 93–94
Orchestras
  balls and dances, 214–15, 217
  wedding receptions, 329–30
Organ donation, 439

Outplacement agencies, 465, 475
Overscheduled child, 31–32

Paddle tennis, 600
Pagers, 86, 500–1
Pallbearers, 444–45
"Pardon," use of, 699
Parties
  anniversary, 434–37, 648
  birthday, 26–27, 431–32
  bring-your-own, 235
  for children, 26–27
  coming out parties. *See* Debuts
  costume, 225–26
  crashing a party, 429
  engagement, 260–62
  farewell, 236–37
  game, 226–28
  graduation, 424–25
  introductions at, 688–89
  office, 519
  pool, 232–33
  surprise, 225
  sweet sixteen, 421–22
  for teenagers, 49–50
  See also Cocktail parties; Pre-wedding parties
"Party" as reference to a person, 699
Party books, 140
Party coordinators, 213–14
"Passed away" expression, 699
Passports, 545
Peer pressure, children and, 14–15
Personal appearance, 72–73
  attire, 73, 75–79
  cosmetic surgery, 74–75
  posture, 73–74
  public behavior, 74
Pets
  of houseguests, 238, 243
  traveling and, 546–47, 560, 566
Pew cards, 298
Photographers
  anniversary parties, 435
  balls and dances, 215
  engagement parties, 261
  rehearsal dinners, 378–79
  weddings, 330–34
Physical defects, asking about, 698
Pick the Right Wine (McCarthy), 189, 194
Picnics, 230–32
Pierced ears, 43
Place cards, 148, 178
  switching of, 200
Place plates, 178

Plan de table, 149, 160
Plane travel. *See* Airline travel
Plants as gifts, 131
Plates, 178–79
Pocket Encyclopedia of Wine (Johnson), 189
Poker, 226–27
Political correctness, 695
Politics as topic of conversation, 694
Pool etiquette, 92, 606–7
Pool parties, 232–33
Pope, audience with, 125–27
Port, 190
Portugal, business etiquette in, 540
Postcards, 636, 681
Posture, 73–74
Potluck suppers, 234
Praise for others, 483
Predictions, 495
Pregnancy
    airline travel and, 559
    brides and, 279–80
    bridesmaids and, 251–52, 358–59
    elopement and, 275
    experience of, 7
    office life and, 486–87
Premarital counseling, 272
Prenuptial agreements, 248, 399–400
Presents. *See* Gift giving; Wedding presents
President and First Lady
    forms of address for, 722–23
    gifts for, 124–25
    at White House social events, 124
    writing to, 125
Pre-wedding parties
    bachelor dinners, 368–69
    bridesmaids' parties, 368
    bride's parties, 368
    out-of-town guests and, 370
    pre-wedding lunches, 369–70
    second weddings and, 407
    ushers' dinners, 369
    See also Wedding showers
Prices as topic of conversation, 693
Printed stationery, 632–33
Prizes at game parties, 227
Problem drinkers, 157, 209
Professional life, 459–60
    business stationery, cards, and invitations, 501–4
    employers' concerns, 476–77
    job-hopping, 462
    leaving a job, 468–69, 474–76
    volunteerism, 465–66, 477–78
    See also Business attire; Business

communication; Business entertaining; Business gift giving; Business meetings; Business travel; International business etiquette; Job hunting; Office life
Professors, forms of address for, 732–33
Proms, 50–51
Protestant churches
    forms of address for clergy, 750–55
    wedding ceremonies, 382–83
Provocative clothes, 491
Psychological counseling, 120
Public officials. *See* Government officials
Public speaking, 501, 707
    attire, 709
    introducing a speaker, 688, 707–8
    last-minute concerns, 709
    listening to a speech, 711
    preparing to give a speech, 708–9
    successful speech making, 710–11
    television and radio appearances, 712–14
Punch, 325

Quaker wedding ceremony, 389–90
Queen Elizabeth II, 561–62, 586

Race, engagement and, 247–48
Racquetball, 599
Radio appearances, 712–14
Raised printing, 632
Reaffirmation of marriage vows, 409–10
Real estate brokers, 115–16
Receiving lines
    anniversary parties, 436
    balls and dances, 217–18
    business receptions, 518
    debuts, 430
    introductions and, 689
    official receptions, 212
    wedding receptions, 355–56, 392–94, 398
Receptionists, 482
Receptions
    business receptions, 518
    official receptions, 211–12
    See also Wedding receptions
Recipes, asking for, 693
Recommendation, letters of, 679–80
Rectory weddings, 391
Red wines, 190, 193
References
    employers' concerns, 477
    letters of recommendations, 679–80
    résumés and, 462–63

Regional accents, 696
Rehearsal dinners, 376–77
  concluding a dinner, 380
  dancing, 379
  food, 378
  guest list, 378
  invitations, 377–78
  photographing of, 378–79
  seating, 379
  toasts, 379–80
Rejection letters, 512
Relaxation techniques, 709
Religion
  couples and, 65
  engagement and, 247–48
  as topic of conversation, 694
  weddings and, 272–73
  See also specific religions
Religious services, 90
Remarriage. *See* Second weddings
Reminder cards, 143–44
Removing inedible food from mouth, 166
Rental equipment for formal seated
      dinner, 144
Renting a car, 569–70
Repeating a story, 692
Reply cards, 297, 649–50
Requests, turning down, 695
Resigning from a job, 476
  letters of resignation, 511–12
Restaurant dining, 80–81
  attire, 85
  brief hello to acquaintance at another
      table, 688, 689
  business telephone manners, 501
  cafeterias and fast food establishments,
      88–89
  with children, 25–26
  coat check, 85, 87
  complaints about food or service, 83
  doggy bags, 87
  do's and don'ts, 87–88
  guest's role, 85
  Heimlich Maneuver for choking, 89
  host's role, 81–84
  inviting a friend to lunch or dinner,
      81–82
  lunch counters, 89
  miscellaneous pointers, 86–87
  napkins, 87
  ordering the meal, 82–83
  ordering the wine, 83–84
  paying the bill, 69, 84, 105–6
  reservations, 82
  seating, 81
  staff of restaurant, 81

  table hopping, 86
  tasting from others' plates, 87
  tipping, 84, 107–9
  women dining alone, 531, 549
Résumés, 461
  career goals, 462
  education information, 462
  employment and experience
      information, 462
  personal information, 461–62
  tips on, 463
Retirement gifts, 534
Retirement letters, 676
Rice throwing, 328
"Rich" and "wealthy," confusion of, 699
Ring bearers, 252, 281, 363
Rings
  birthstone rings, 252
  divorced or widowed woman and,
      402–3
  engagement rings, 252–54, 260–61,
      263
  heirloom rings, 253
  second weddings and, 403
  wedding rings, 253–54, 382–83, 387
Rogers, Will, 525
Roman Catholicism. *See* Catholicism
Romance in the office, 485–86
Rose-petal throwing, 328–29
Rosé wine, 190, 193
Russia, business etiquette in, 542

Safe sex, 45
Salts and peppers, 165, 180
Sandwiches, 231
Savings accounts for children, 34
School
  first day of school, 27–28
  money for grades, 34
  money needs of children, 35
  nursery schools, 28
  parent-teacher partnership, 29
  working parents and, 28–29
School-related activities, 28–29, 31–32
  carpooling for, 29–30
Screening telephone calls, 498
Seasickness, 565, 604
Seating protocol, 146–48
Second weddings, 399
  announcements, 259, 347, 405–6
  attendants, 406
  attire, 406
  bridal registries, 314–15
  ceremony, 408
  children of previous marriage and,
      401–2

financial considerations, 400, 402
financial responsibility for, 400
guest list, 403
guest's role, 407
informing family and friends of engagement, 400–1
invitations, 310–11, 403–4
music, 408
prenuptial agreements, 399–400
presents, 314–15, 406–7
pre-wedding parties, 407
reaffirmation of marriage vows, 409–10
receptions, 408–9
remarrying ex-spouse, 409
rings and, 402–3
of widows, 401
Self-defense, 66–67
Senators, forms of address for, 726–27
Seniority courtesies, 481
Separated women
addressing envelopes to, 661
names used, 655
Service plates, 178
Sexual concerns, teenagers and, 44–46
Sexual harassment, 488–89
Shaking hands, 689–90
"Share with" expression, 699
Shaving, 73
Ship travel, 561–62
activities, 565
attire, 564
cabins, 562–63
cancellation of reservations, 562
captain's table, invitation to, 564–65
children and, 563
day trips ashore, 565
dinner seatings, 563
entertaining and, 564
fire and lifeboat drills, 563
luggage, 563–64
packet with tickets and information, 563
seasickness, 565
smoking, 563
tipping, 565, 585–86
Shirts, 77–78
Showers, baby, 416–17, 487
Showers, wedding. *See* Wedding showers
Signatures
on checks and legal papers, 658
common first names and, 659
husband and wife joint signatures, 659–60
illegible signatures, 658

names that apply to both a man and a woman, 659
woman's signature on a letter, 659
Silences, 495
Silverware. *See* Flatware
Simhat habat ceremony, 415–16
Single life
dating, 68–70
divorce and, 70
entertaining, 67–68
living alone, 66–67
older people living together, 72
self-defense and, 66–67
spouse's death, 70–72
Single parents, 20–21
birth announcements and, 10
child support, 19, 36
dating, 22
title used by single mother, 655, 661
Single status of another, asking about, 697
"Sir," use of, 657–58
Sitting posture, 73–74
Sitting *shivah,* 450, 454
Skiing, 607
accidents, 608–9
attire, 611–12
behavior code, 608
cross-country, 612–13
downhill, 607–9
equipment, 610–11
lifts, 609, 610
safety rules, 609, 613
trail markers, 609
Slang, 505
Smoking
airline travel, 554
boating, 604
business lunches, 515
formal seated dinners, 167
restaurant dining, 86
ship travel, 563
by teenagers, 53–54
train travel, 572, 573
workplace, 480
Smorgasbords, 86–87
Social cards. *See* Calling cards
Sofa beds, 243
Solicitation calls, 703
Sommeliers, 81, 107
Soup plates and spoons, 164–65
South America, business etiquette in, 538
Spain, business etiquette in, 540
Sparkling wines, 190–91
Speakerphones, 497

Special needs, persons with. *See* Disabled
    persons
Spelling, 506
Spills, wine and food, 154, 166–67
Spoons, 164–65, 179
Sporting events, behavior at, 91
Sport-related presents, 132
Sports and exercise, 590
    children and, 590–91
    sportsmanship, 227–28, 590–91
    See also specific sports and activities
Sports jackets, 78
Squash, 599
State Department travel advisories,
    546
State dinners, 123–24
State legislators, forms of address for,
    730–31
Stationers, 291–92
Stationery
    air mail paper, 636
    business stationery, 501–2
    change of address and, 638
    children's stationery, 637–38
    choosing right stationery, 632
    correspondence cards, 635, 637
    envelopes, 636
    folded notes, 635
    half sheets, 635
    house stationery, 637
    informals, 635
    letter sheets, 634–35
    memo pads, 636
    for men, 637
    message cards, 635
    monarch sheets, 636, 637
    personalization of, 632–33
    postcards, 636
    preservation concerns, 631–32
    for women, 634–36
Stemware, 317–18
Stepfamilies, 18–19, 37
Streisand, Barbra, 91
Substance abuse, 52–54
Supper dances, 214, 217, 218
    service at, 219
Support groups for unemployed persons,
    475
Supportive letters, 674
Supreme Court justices, forms of address
    for, 722–23
Surnames
    of children whose parents use different
        names, 9
    hyphenated names, 655
    of widows, 655

of women following divorce, 18, 70,
    482, 655
of women following marriage, 347–48,
    481–82, 654, 660–61
Swearing, 505, 696
Sweden, business etiquette in, 540
Sweet sixteen parties, 421–22
Swimming, 604
    beach outings, 605–6
    at motels, 582
    pools, 92, 232–33, 606–7
    safety concerns, 604–5
Switchboard operators, 482
Switzerland, business etiquette in, 540
Swope, Herbert Bayard, Jr., 626
Synthetic fabrics, 493

Tablecloths, 145, 177
Table hopping, 86
Table manners, 4–5, 24, 25
    formal seated dinner with a staff, 161,
        164–66
Table number cards, 148–49
Table settings
    formal dinner table setting, 176–80
    formal lunch table setting, 180–81
    informal dinner table setting, 181
Tailgate picnics, 231
Talking down to others, 692
Tattoos, 43
Taxis
    business travel, 528
    etiquette for, 97
    tipping drivers, 97, 109
Teacher-parent partnership, 29
Teas, 201
    arrangement of tea table, 201–3
    in Britain, 539
    business teas, 517
    debutante teas, 427
    food for, 202–3
    guest's role, 204
    hostess' role, 203–4
    in hotels, 580
    making of good tea, 203
    pourers, 204
    tea tray, 201–2, 203
Teenagers
    addressing envelopes to, 662
    "adopting" of another family, 48–49
    bathrooms and, 40
    bedrooms, 39
    clothing, 41–42
    college selection, 46–47
    communication at home, 38–39
    credit cards for, 35

curfews, 49
dating, 44–46
driving, 40–41
drug and alcohol use, 49–50, 52–54
fads and, 42–43
friendships, 48–49, 51
gifts for, 137
hairstyles, 42–43
jewelry, 42
letting go of one's teenager, 54–55
money and, 33, 34, 47–48
paid work, 47–48
parties, 49–50
physical changes, 44
privacy needs, 39
proms, 50–51
sexual concerns, 44–46
siblings, helping with, 41
smoking, 53–54
social life, 48–51
telephone use, 40
tensions of teenage years, 37–38
visiting a friend, 51
Telephone invitations, 141, 143
Telephone manners, 700–1
airline travel and, 558
answering machines, 704
answering one's own telephone, 701
answering someone else's telephone, 701
automated message-taking systems, 704
call waiting, 40, 703
cellular telephones, 704–5
children and, 702
collect calls, 705
credit card calls, 705
"cut off" situations, 702
emergency break-ins, 705
ending a call, 702
hindrances to good telephone habits, 705
"hold" situations, 702
for houseguests, 244
housekeepers and, 701–2
making a call, 701
obscene telephone calls, 703–4
personal portable telephones, 704–5
person-to-person calls, 705
solicitation calls, 703
wrong numbers, 702
See also Business telephone manners
Telephone use by teenagers, 40
Television appearances, 712–13, 714
Television watching by children, 15
Tennis
attire, 598–99

do's and don'ts, 596–97
doubles matches, 596, 597–98
private courts, 598
rules, 596
sportsmanship, 595–96
Tents, balls and dances in, 215–16
Terminally ill persons, visits with, 119
Thanksgiving, 234
Thank-you cards, 682
Thank-you notes
balls and dances, 218
in business, 510
debuts, 431
engagement gifts, 262
engraved or printed cards as, 344
failure to receive a note, 671–72
formal seated dinners, 164
funerals, 454–55
gifts to children, 27, 669
graduation presents, 425–26
houseguest situations, 245, 671
job interviews, 471–72
money gifts, 669–70
sample notes, 669–71
state dinners, 124
wedding presents, 343–46, 407, 670–71
wedding shower gifts, 670
Theatergoing, 92–93
in Britain, 539
Thermography, 632
Ties, 77
Tipping
apartment house personnel, 111–12
club personnel, 109
garage personnel, 112
general rules, 106
hairdressers, 110, 111
holiday tipping, 110–13
hotel personnel, 578, 579, 587–89
by houseguests, 245
limousine drivers, 110
liquor used for, 115
restaurant personnel, 84, 107–9
special situations, 114–15
taxi drivers, 97, 109
tip/not tip list, 113–14
travel situations, 565, 577, 585–89
Toasts, 706
anniversary parties, 435
engagement parties, 261
in foreign countries, 706–7
formal seated dinners
guest-initiated, 162–63
host-initiated, 155–56
rehearsal dinners, 379–80
wedding receptions, 396–97

Tobacco use. *See* Smoking
Toddlers, 23–24
Toenails, 73
Train travel
  Amtrak train service, 570
  children and, 572
  classes of train travel, 571
  commuter train travel, 573–74
  courteous behavior, 572
  information sources, 570–71
  lounges in stations, 571
  luggage, 572–73
  sleeping accommodations, 571, 572
  smoking, 572, 573
  tipping, 586–87
  Via Rail Canada, 570
Transferring telephone calls, 498–99
"Trapping" invitations, 694
Travel, 543
  attire, 543–44
  bed and breakfasts, 582–85, 589
  with children, 551–52
  children left at home, 547
  computerized travel information,
    545
  country inns, 582–85, 589
  driver's licenses, 546
  Elderhostel organization, 548
  with friends, 550–51
  friends of friends, visits to, 551
  health concerns, 545–46
  honeymoons, 337–38
  information sources, 543
  insurance, 546
  language concerns, 544, 552
  luggage, 545
  money concerns, 546, 550–51
  motels, 581–82, 589
  necessities for, 548
  passports, 545
  planning the trip, 544–48
  predeparture checklist, 546–47
  solo travel, 548–50
  tipping, 565, 577, 585–89
  visas, 545
  women traveling alone, 549–50
  See also Airline travel; Business
    travel; Bus travel; Car travel;
    Hotels; Ship travel; Train
    travel
Travel agents, 337, 544–45, 562
Traveler's checks, 546
Trousseaus, 313
Truman, Harry and Bess, 249
Tuxedos, 78–79
Two-career couples, 63–64

"Uh-huh," use of, 695
United Nations Secretary General, forms
  of address for, 734–35
United States Croquet Association, 626,
  627
United States Power Squadrons National
  Headquarters, 600
University officials, forms of address for,
  732–33
Unmarried couples
  addressing envelopes to, 662
  at conventions, 527
  introductions, 687
  older people living together, 72
  visits to parents, 58–59
  wedding invitations to, 290
Ushers, funeral, 445
Ushers, wedding, 251, 252, 360, 362–63.
  See also Wedding attendants
Ushers' dinners, 369

Vanderbilt, Amy, xii
Via Rail Canada, 570
Vice President of the United States,
  forms of address for, 722–23
Videotaping of weddings, 331, 333
V.I.P.'s, chance meetings with, 530
Visas, 545
Vocabulary, 494–95
Voice concerns when using telephone,
  496
Voice mail, 500
Volunteerism, 465–66, 477–78

Waiters, 81, 107
Walking for exercise, 615–16
Wall Street Journal, 489
Want ads, 464
Water skiing, 607
Wedding anniversaries, 433
  parties, 434–37, 648
  widows/widowers and, 433–34
Wedding announcements, 296, 298, 346
  second weddings, 259, 347, 405–6
Wedding attendants, 357
  attire for female attendants, 280–81
  attire for male attendants, 281, 285–86
  best man, 284, 360–61, 362, 380
  bridesmaids, 251–52, 358–59
  bridesmaids' parties, 368
  double weddings, 374
  dropping out by, 358, 363–64
  expenses of, 251, 280, 358
  flower girls, 252, 281, 328
  flowers for, 327–28
  friends, relatives as, 250–52, 358

junior bridesmaids, 252
junior ushers, 252
maid and/or matron of honor, 359–60,
   361
military weddings, 374–75
number of, 251
out-of-town attendants,
   accommodations for, 337
presents for, 342, 343
punctuality, importance of, 359
rehearsal dinners and, 379, 380
rehearsals and, 375–76
ring bearers, 252, 281, 363
second weddings, 406
substitute attendants, 358
ushers, 251, 252, 360, 362–63
ushers' dinners, 369
wedding receptions and, 392–93, 394,
   396
See also under Wedding ceremonies
Wedding attire
bride's attendants' dresses, 280–81
bride's wedding dress, 276–78
   accessories, 278–79
   nontraditional dresses, 280
   pregnant bride-to-be, 279–80
   renting a dress, 278
   type/time of wedding and, 282–83
gloves worn by men, 283–86
groom's attire, 283–85
   military uniform, 286
   nontraditional attire, 286
   type/time of wedding and, 284–85
guests' attire, 354
male attendants, 281, 285–86
military weddings, 286–87
mothers and stepmothers of bride and
   groom, 282–83
second weddings, 406
"something old, something new,
   something borrowed, something
   blue," 279
type/time of wedding and, 282–83,
   284–86
Wedding cakes, 323–24, 357, 397, 399
Wedding ceremonies, 380
attendants' duties and positions, 361–
   63, 371, 373
   Christian ceremonies, 380–83
   Jewish ceremonies, 384–87
bride's walk up the aisle, 370–71, 382
Catholic ceremonies, 370, 382, 384
Christian ceremonies, common
   elements of, 380–84
Christian Science ceremony, 387–88
civil ceremony, 391

divorced parents, seating of, 373
double weddings, 374
Eastern Orthodox ceremony, 388–89
families' sides of aisle, 371
flowers, 325–26, 327–28
giving the bride away, 370, 382
guest's role, 354–55, 362–63
home ceremony, 390–91
Jewish ceremonies, 354, 370, 371, 376,
   384–87
military weddings, 374–75
Mormon ceremony, 390
mothers of bride and groom, escorts
   for, 373, 374
music, 329, 384, 386
photographing of, 330–34
   formal bridal picture, 332
Protestant ceremonies, 382–83
Quaker ceremony, 389–90
rectory ceremony, 391
rehearsals, 371–74, 375–76
   dinner following, 376–80
reserved pews, 372
ring ceremony
   Christian weddings, 382–83
   Jewish weddings, 387
seating of family members, 372–73
seating of guests, 354–55, 362–63
second weddings, 408
transportation arrangements, 335
two main aisles and, 372
videotaping of, 331, 333
white canvas runner, unrolling of, 373
white satin ribbons on pews, 373
Wedding dresses. *See under* Wedding
   attire
Wedding invitations
accepting an invitation, 311–12, 350–
   51
addressing envelopes, 294–95
alternate plans, specification of, 293–
   94
"at Home" cards, 296–97
Catholic weddings, 292
ceremony cards, 296, 302–4, 305
ceremony/reception issue, 287
church cards, 296
date and time, specification of, 293
differences of opinion over whom to
   invite, 288
dinner at reception, specification of,
   293
double weddings, 304
enclosures, 295–98
envelopes, 294–95
foreign wedding invitations, 310

Wedding invitations (*continued*)
  guest list, 287–90
  heraldic devices and, 718
  inserting invitation in envelope, 298, 299
  location, specification of, 293
  mailing of, 298
  map to church or reception, 298
  military weddings, 309–10
  to mourning persons, 290
  nontraditional invitations, 308–9
  number of guests, 288
  to out-of-towners, 287, 288, 298
  as paybacks, 290
  personal letters, 310
  pew cards, 297–98
  reception cards, 300–1
  regretting an invitation, 312–13, 351
  reply cards, 297
  reserve list of names, 289
  return address, 294
  R.s.v.p. request, 293
  second weddings, 310–11, 403–4
  self-designed invitations, 308
  special situations, 305–9
  stationers for, 291–92
  tips on, 292–94
  titles used in, 292
  traditional invitations, 290–91
  transportation and accommodation information, 298
  to unmarried couples, 290
  wordings used for formal invitations, 300–4
Wedding plans, 264
  books on planning, 318
  bouquets, 327–28
  budgeting, 266–68
  clergyperson, meeting with, 271–73
  consultants for, 319–20
  dancing practice, 274
  date of wedding, 268–71
  financial arrangements, 264–68
  flowers, 325–28
  hotel/motel reservations for out-of-town guests, 336–37, 353
  location of ceremony, 269
  marriage license, 273–74
  miscellaneous details, 275–76
  mother of bride, role of, 265
  photograph arrangements, 330–34
  reception planning, 269–71, 320–26
  reserving the church or synagogue, 271–73
  time of day to be married, 269
  time of year to be married, 269

  transportation arrangements, 334–36
Wedding presents
  attendants, presents for, 342, 343
  bride's and groom's presents to one another, 341–42
  brief marriages and, 341
  for business colleagues, 534
  canceled weddings and, 341
  display of, 340
  exchanging and returning presents, 340–41
  family presents, 342
  guests' gift-giving protocol, 351–53
  keeping a record of presents received, 318, 338–39
  money, 339, 345, 353
  reception, receiving presents at, 339–40
  safeguarding of, 340
  second weddings, 314–15, 406–7
  shower presents, 365
  suggested presents, 342–43
  thank-you notes, 343–46, 407, 670–71
  See also Bridal registries
Wedding receptions, 211, 392
  beginning of, 392
  bouquet, throwing of, 357, 397
  bride's table, 394, 398
  cake-cutting ceremony, 357, 397
  catered receptions, 321, 323
  concluding a reception, 398
  dancing, 274, 356, 395–96, 398–99
  "dinner not served" situations, 398
  double receptions, 398–99
  flowers, 326–27
  food, 322
  garter, throwing of, 397
  guest book, 276, 318–19, 356, 392
  guest's role, 355–57
  hotel/club managers, working with, 320–21
  invitations, 300–1, 306
  liability coverage, 325
  liquor and wine, 324–25
  locations for, 270–71
  music, 329–30
  "no reception" situations, 399
  parents' table, 395
  photographing of, 330–34
  planning for, 269–71, 320–26
  presents received at, 339–40
  receiving line, 355–56, 392–94, 398
  rice throwing, 328
  rose-petal throwing, 328–29
  second or delayed receptions, 271, 303–4
  second weddings, 408–9

time of day, 269–70
toasts, 396–97
transportation arrangements, 335
wedding attendants and, 392–93, 394,
   396
Wedding rings, 253–54
   ring ceremony, 382–83, 387
Weddings, 246
   announcements, 296, 298, 346
   canceling a wedding, 341, 349–50
   children at, 351
   of co-workers, 486
   double weddings, 304, 374, 398–99
   elopement, 274–75
   in foreign countries, 274, 310
   guest's role
      attire, 354
      gift-giving protocol, 351–53
      hotel/motel reservations, 353
      invitation, response to, 311–13, 350–
         51
      letter acknowledging hosts'
         hospitality, 357
      wedding ceremonies, 354–55, 362–
         63
      wedding receptions, 355–57
   honeymoons, 337–38
   interfaith marriages, 272–73
   marriage certificates, 376
   military weddings, 285, 309–10, 374–
      75
   newspaper notices, 346–47
   postponing a wedding, 348–49
   pregnancy of bride and, 279–80
   premarital counseling, 272
   woman's surname, issue of, 347–48,
      481–82, 660–61
   See also Engagement; Pre-wedding
      parties; Rehearsal dinners; Second
      weddings; Wedding attendants;
      Wedding attire; Wedding
      ceremonies; Wedding invitations;
      Wedding plans; Wedding
      presents
Wedding showers, 364–65
   bride's role, 366–67
   guest's role, 367–68
   hostess' role, 365–66
   presents, 365
   thank-you notes for gifts, 670
   "wishing well" gimmick, 365
Weight machine courtesy, 625–26
Wheelchair-bound persons, 98–99
White House social events, 122–24
White-tie outfits, 79
White wines, 189–90, 191–92

Widowers
   getting on with life, 70–72
   wedding anniversaries and, 433–34
Widows
   addressing envelopes to, 661
   calling cards and, 641
   engagement announcements by, 259
   engagement/wedding rings and, 402–3
   getting on with life, 70–72
   second weddings, 401
   surname used, 655
   wedding anniversaries and, 433–34
Wilde, Oscar, 139, 697
Wills, 61, 438, 440, 457
*Windows on the World Complete Wine
   Course* (Zraly), 189
Wine baskets, 194
Wine cellars, 189
Wineglasses, 165, 179–80, 192
Wines, 188–89
   amount of wine needed, determination
      of, 194–95
   appetizer wines (apéritifs), 189
   bottle sizes, 194
   dessert wines, 190
   at dinner, 193
   drinks per bottle, 195
   food and wine, 191–92
   formal seated dinner with a staff, 145
   informal seated dinner with a maid,
      172, 173
   opening a bottle, 191, 193
   red wines, 190, 192–93
   restaurant dining, 83–84
   sparkling wines, 190–91
   storing and serving, 192–93
   wedding receptions, 324–25
   white wines, 189–90, 193
Wine spills, 154, 166–67
"Wishing well" gimmick, 365
Withers, Claudia, 488
Women
   attire, 75–77
   calling cards, 640, 641–42
   dining alone, 531, 549
   heraldic devices, use of, 718
   man-woman interactions, 79–80
   middle name following marriage, 655–
      56
   separated woman, name used by, 655,
      661
   signature on a letter, 659
   single mothers, title used by, 655, 661
   stationery for, 634–36
   surname of woman
      divorce and, 18, 70, 482, 655

Women; divorce and (*continued*)
    hyphenated names, 655
    marriage and, 347–48, 481–82, 660–
      61
    traveling alone, 549–50, 580
    two first names, use of, 655–56
    in workplace
      business travel, 531–32
      gender courtesies, 481
      names and titles, 481–82
      returning to work, 473
    sexual harassment, 488–89
    See also Widows
Women's Legal Defense Fund, 488, 489
Words, learning about, 25
Words and phrases to avoid, 698–99
Workout clothes, 624–25
Wrapping paper, 135
Writing style, 504, 506
Wrong numbers, 499, 702

Zraly, Kevin, 189